About Island Press

Island Press is the only nonprofit organization in the United States whose principal purpose is the publication of books on environmental issues and natural resource management. We provide solutions-oriented information to professionals, public officials, business and community leaders, and concerned citizens who are shaping responses to environmental problems.

Since 1984, Island Press has been the leading provider of timely and practical books that take a multidisciplinary approach to critical environmental concerns. Our growing list of titles reflects our commitment to bringing the best of an expanding body of literature to the environmental community throughout North America and the world.

Support for Island Press is provided by the Agua Fund, The Geraldine R. Dodge Foundation, Doris Duke Charitable Foundation, The Ford Foundation, The William and Flora Hewlett Foundation, The Joyce Foundation, Kendeda Sustainability Fund of the Tides Foundation, The Forrest & Frances Lattner Foundation, The Henry Luce Foundation, The John D. and Catherine T. MacArthur Foundation, The Marisla Foundation, The Andrew W. Mellon Foundation, Gordon and Betty Moore Foundation, The Curtis and Edith Munson Foundation, Oak Foundation, The Overbrook Foundation, The David and Lucile Packard Foundation, Wallace Global Fund, The Winslow Foundation, and other generous donors.

The opinions expressed in this book are those of the author(s) and do not necessarily reflect the views of these foundations.

Sustainable Landscape Construction
A Guide to Green Building Outdoors

Second Edition

(*Project:* Robert Murase. *Photo:* Tom Liptan.)

Sustainable Landscape Construction

A Guide to Green Building Outdoors

Second Edition

William Thompson and Kim Sorvig

with drawings by Craig D. Farnsworth, ASLA

ISLANDPRESS

Washington • Covelo • London

Library of Congress Cataloging-in-Publication Data

Thompson, J. William.
  Sustainable landscape construction : a guide to green building outdoors / William Thompson and Kim Sorvig ; with drawings by Craig D. Farnsworth. — 2nd ed.
        p. cm.
  Includes bibliographical references and index.
  ISBN 978-1-59726-142-5 (hardcover : alk. paper) — ISBN 978-1-59726-143-2 (pbk. : alk. paper)
 1. Landscape construction. 2. Landscape protection. 3. Green products. 4. Ecological landscape design.
I. Sorvig, Kim. II. Title.
  TH380.T46 2008
  712.01—dc22   2007026192

Manufactured in the United States of America
10 9 8 7 6 5

The Fine Print

This book reports information from designers, contractors, manufacturers, academic researchers, and many others. The authors have attempted to ensure that all the information herein is credible but have performed no independent testing of these reports. Reporting such information does not constitute endorsement of any product or method. Exclusion of products or methods does not imply a negative evaluation; please see the authors' request for updates, below. All trademarks remain property of their respective owners. The authors and publishers specifically disclaim any and all liability purported to result from inclusion or exclusion of a product or method in this book.

Variations among regions and sites result in very different performance from the same products and methods, and no assurance can be given that any information reported herein is suitable for any given site. The information reported herein may contain errors and omissions, and even where complete and accurate it is not a substitute for local expertise and professional judgment. Illustrations are not intended as ready-to-build, step-by-step instructions, but rather to depict concepts and processes. The authors and publishers specifically disclaim any and all liability for any situation resulting from use or attempted use of this information.

Contents

Principle 3: Favor Living, Flexible Materials   113

Principle 4: Respect the Waters of Life   152

Principle 5: Pave Less   198

Principle 6: Consider Origin and Fate of Materials   224

Principle 7: Know the Costs of Energy over Time   262

Principle 8: Celebrate Light, Respect Darkness   293

Principle 9: Quietly Defend Silence   312

Principle 10: Maintain to Sustain   322

List of Figures

List of Tables

Preface

The Why, What, and How of the Second Edition

The first edition of *Sustainable Landscape Construction* was released halfway between Y2K, the great nonevent, and 9-11, an event that appeared to change everything.

Since August 2000 much has changed and much has stayed the same about sustainability, and the field of green building specifically. That month, as SLC's first edition launched, hybrid cars were barely experimental, GPS a novelty, iPods not yet invented. Al Gore hadn't made a film, let alone won an Oscar.

When we first decided to write this book treating landscape construction as a value-driven activity, we weren't quite crying in the rapidly shrinking wilderness. Neither were the streets overrun with like-minded professionals. We were able to find some hundred firms whose mission and focus revolved around sustainable design and construction.

Today there are too many sustainability-driven planning, design, construction, maintenance, and even engineering firms to count accurately. In general we welcome this. The bandwagon has room to carry widely varied degrees of commitment. That, too, makes it difficult to count who's involved.

For better and for worse, sustainability has become mainstream in the past half decade. The broad trends supporting this, as well as new research and products, are the primary reasons for revising this book.

Why a New Edition?

By themselves, neither social acceptance nor technical advances would have warranted updating this book. Together, however, they indicate significant change and intensifying professional evolution.

Social trends reshaping sustainability itself include:

- The concept of living within our environmental means is far more widespread, though no better defined.

- Federal inaction has spurred surprisingly proactive local initiatives.
- Active support for sustainability has spread to new groups, even industrialists and conservatives.
- Green Business has become a recognized model for profitable enterprises.
- Coverage of green topics has spread to mainstream media.
- Major national and local conventions on green building are held annually.
- Research centers and school curricula are reflecting sustainability.

New landscape-specific developments include:

- Changes in land use and vegetative cover have been shown to play a major role in climate change, compelling landscape professionals to act.
- Efficiency has improved in landscape irrigation and lighting as those industries accepted "green" goals.
- Soil analysis and soil amendment have become more sophisticated, benefiting landscape restoration, maintenance, and integrated pest management.
- New official highway standards recognize "context sensitivity," traffic calming, and improved stormwater management, decreasing damage done by overpaving.
- Landscape publications are devoting several times as much space to sustainability issues as in 2000; even the *Wall Street Journal* has covered sustainable landscaping.

What's New in This Edition?

This section discusses *criteria* used in updating this edition and lists major subject-matter revisions for the convenience of practitioners, educators, and students who have been using the first edition.

One of our first challenges was keeping additions to this book manageable when the field has expanded so much. Although "what's new?" is the focus of much design writing, this book is explicitly driven by principles, and in the field of sustainability, newness is not the dominant virtue.

Thus, if an existing project example (or product or resource) still illustrates an important idea, we have not replaced it simply for the sake of novelty. Pioneering examples from the first edition are still included unless truly out of date; new examples were added if they clearly show new approaches or significantly improved results. The projects chosen for this edition are ones that, in our opinion, took a number of the right environmental steps and produced beautiful, intriguing results. Neither we nor the creators of these places would claim that these projects are perfectly sustainable. They exemplify attempts to reduce construction impacts, while increasing livability. Our reasons for considering them successful are detailed in their descriptions. Even more than in the first edition, the list is selective—including every worthy project would now require an encyclopedia.

In tracking this expanding field, we ask your help. Please send us news of exemplary work at www .SustainableLandscapeOnline.com. We also welcome lessons learned from failure, methods that could have been improved, and materials that gave unexpected results. (See "Contacting the Authors" in the acknowledgments.)

An Evolving Effort

Like the trend it represents, this book is an evolving effort, now in a second edition. We might have liked to produce a sort of best practices manual for sustainable landscapes, but sustainability is far from standardization. Any formulaic instructions for sustainability outdoors must always be adjusted for regional reasons, if no other. Detailed how-to information has seemed appropriate for only a few materials and techniques; more often, it seemed more honest to give a description, some principles, and references for following tomorrow's evolution. Sus-tainable landscape practices have grown, but not truly normalized.

For standard information, this book will not replace basic texts filled with details of retaining walls and decks or formulas for grading and drainage. An understanding of these conventional construction skills will be required as long as landscapes are built. This book offers tools and ideas for *adapting* these conventions to new conditions, new materials, new regulations, and new client demands, all driven by environmental concerns.

Future landscape construction will need to be more sophisticated, not only in technique, but in careful consideration of *why* build and *what* is appropriate. We expect this sophistication to grow from a combination of innovation, convention, and rediscovered tradition, not from new technologies alone.

Our original edition took an unusual tack: we treated landscape construction not as a functional, value-free topic, but as a step toward *applying* environmental ethics. That approach, which felt right to us as authors, clearly resonated with readers and reviewers. The second edition continues that approach.

Overview of Updates, by Chapter

This edition covers previous topics (sometimes more succinctly), *with the following updates and changes*:

- The Table of Contents now shows *only* the major subheads for each chapter; the first edition's list provided more depth, but was hard to read.
- The chapters called *Introduction* and *Successes and Challenge* in the first edition have been reorganized as an Introduction with three parts. *What is Sustainability* now covers definitions and controversies about concepts of sustainability and green building; how attitudes toward work support or hinder sustainable practice; and broad-scale social, demographic, and economic pressures. *Landscapes Against Climate Change* briefly covers this critical issue and what landscape professionals can and must do. *Sustainability, Substance and Style* now addresses paradoxes of ecological function and designed form: new and critical evidence that landscapes can indeed damage the environment; increased temptation to greenwash, now that sustainability is more widely accepted; and in-

creasingly complex relationships between appearing green and functioning as such.

- Principle 1 updates primarily involve developments in GPS tools and site-visualization software.
- Principle 2 updates landfill restoration and soil testing, looks at compost tea, and contrasts fire "prevention" fallacies versus forest restoration.
- Principle 3 reviews greenroofs in America (finally) and pros and cons of artificial turf.
- Principle 4 reflects major advances in irrigation, increased acceptance of graywater, and in-pipe engineering products to purify stormwater.
- Principle 5 notes a major initiative toward "context sensitive" highways and adds "green streets."
- Principle 6 updates recycling trends, sustainable certification of wood, and controversies about polyvinyl chloride (PVC), wood preservatives, and shady waste-to-fertilizer schemes.
- Principle 7 notes a few changes in tools and alternative energy generation (consolidating treatment of photovoltaics). It is strongly affected by what we've called the virtual appendectomy (below).
- Principle 8 notes new research in light pollution, the major impact of light-emitting-diode (LED) lighting and other less-dramatic changes. It now contains a lighting glossary.
- Principle 9 has also added definitions of key terms, plus information about noise-absorbing barriers and quiet-tool initiatives.
- Principle 10 adds bio-based lubricants and related products, organic maintenance for public landscapes, and alternatives to mowing.
- The conclusions reflect our current thoughts on landscape sustainability.

Visit and Contribute to the Web Site

One major change is what we have called the virtual appendectomy: the first edition's extensive Appendices about materials toxicity and energy are now online at www.SustainableLandscapeOnline.com; other basic information will be added over time. Posting the tables online allowed the print edition to expand its coverage without expanding its waistline, thus keeping both resource costs and price down.

Who Should Use This Book?

Sustainable Landscape Construction is intended for three main audiences:

- professionals in private- and public-sector landscape architecture, construction, and maintenance, and their suppliers. We have also heard from architects, planners, engineers, and developers that they have found the book useful.
- students in landscape construction and design courses, as well as some who study architecture, planning, project management, and engineering.
- landowners and others concerned with the health of specific sites, ranging from individuals and businesses to neighborhood associations or conservation groups.

We hope this book will be accessible to people with various levels of experience. Professionals will please excuse us for including basic definitions to help students and other readers. We also hope to offer some common ground between environmentalists and builders. This is a tall order, and we welcome suggestions via the Web site.

How to Use This Book

Use this book to develop or improve your ability to conceptualize sustainable materials or methods. Then adapt these concepts to site-specific conditions, referring to local consultants and the resources listed for further expertise and detail.

The chapters of this book can be read in almost any order. Each focuses on a central issue, such as sustainable use of water, and on construction related to that issue.

The Introduction considers larger, contextual questions. We urge you consider these political, social, and ethical issues, along with the technical ones.

A critically important addition is short sections that link landscape architectural practice to such global matters as fires, drought, floods, extreme storms, and climate change. Discussion of these connections has become a necessity for putting site-scale sustainability into context.

Principle-focused Organization

This book is organized by *principle* rather than by technique or material. Principles are *values that people act on.* Sustainability itself is a principle. Each chapter focuses on one overarching idea that *can and should* be implemented in the sustainable landscape. These principles, in various forms, have guided the landscape professionals whose work is reported here and should guide anyone who makes, modifies, or manages a landscape. Subsections of each chapter offer specific methods to accomplish the principle.

Many of these methods can be used in concert with each other. It is not unusual, however, to find two methods of achieving the same goal, which, if used simultaneously, would cancel each other. A commonly encountered example is that both porous paving and water harvesting are techniques for sustainably managing stormwater, but porous paving may reduce water available for harvesting, while harvesting water decreases the need for porous pavement. Some methods or materials also work best, or only, in certain climates. We suggest reading each chapter as a whole, then choosing from the range of techniques based on local experience.

The "principled" approach gives a clear picture of interrelationships in living landscapes. Where principles overlap or complement each other (which is frequent because the landscape is a web of interacting influences), cross-references are provided for easy access to techniques or materials covered in other sections.

Abbreviations

In general, we explain any abbreviated term when it is first used. However, a few agencies and publications crop up so often that defining them every time is truly tedious. These are:

- DOT for department of transportation, often combined with the abbreviation for a state (MNDOT for Minnesota DOT). FHWA is the US DOT.
- Caltrans for California's DOT.
- AASHTO for American Association of State Highway and Transportation Engineers.
- DER or DEP for Department of Environmental Resources/Protection.

- EPA for Environmental Protection Agency; unless specified, this is federal.
- ADA for Americans with Disabilities Act, which increasingly affects sustainable design by demanding excess paving, reconstruction of buildings, and even avoidance of planting.
- EBN for *Environmental Building News*, the incomparably useful newsletter from Building Green.
- LAM for *Landscape Architecture* magazine.
- ASLA for American Society of Landscape Architects and ALCA for Associated Landscape Contractors of America. Both have regional chapters.

Finally, US states are abbreviated when part of a city name, using the standard two-letter postal abbreviations. Anyone unfamiliar with these abbreviations (including our foreign readers, of whom we are proud to have many) can find a list at www.stateabbrevitions .us/ and a map on that site's sub-page, /states.htm. Canadian provinces are spelled out to avoid confusion.

Resource Lists for Further Information

The symbol ⊃ is found throughout this book. It points you to resources: organizations, suppliers, experts, Web sites, and publications. Each chapter has a resource section. The lists have been carefully rechecked and expanded for the second edition. We would appreciate updates and corrections, as well as additions, for these lists, via our Web site.

In many cases, resources provide real-time updates on recent developments. Others provide specialized detail about techniques and materials, which this book describes more broadly. Be sure to check closely related chapters for resources *indirectly* related to your topic.

Since the first edition, broader acceptance of sustainable practices has made information on the field far more widespread. There are many new publications about green building, as our resource lists reflect. Our criterion for updating the lists has been information quality and relevance—somewhat subjective and definitely selective.

In addition, the revised resource lists now include a selection of keywords or search terms that we have found helpful in locating current information. (See

"Finding Landscapes Along the Information Highway," below.) The explosion of green building publications, and especially Web sites, means that no printed book can catalog them comprehensively.

Periodicals that represent the landscape professions have greatly increased their coverage of and seriousness about sustainable practices. We are happy to take some of the credit (and blame) for this. This change, however, has been occurring throughout the design world, and credit for that goes to the professions themselves. As a result, our resource lists show more titles of periodicals and somewhat fewer specific article citations because there are now so many of them.

The *most general* resources, such as organizations, consultants, and suppliers, are listed *first* under each resource topic. Following them are books, periodicals, and Web sites. If your questions are broad or a bit fuzzy, human resources are generally best. If your question is fairly specific, there may be published information or a Web site that exactly meets your needs.

Manufacturers and suppliers of specific products have kindly provided information on many topics. We cannot possibly list all of them as resources, nor do we endorse individual products. Specific products are named as part of some projects. Because we cannot be all-inclusive, we have tried to be fair, using supplier information to promote broader awareness of sustainable construction, rather than to advertise particular wares.

For these reasons, suppliers are listed in resources if 1) we have found them to be a helpful source of *general* information, *and* 2) their product is either typical or not yet well-known. Where a dozen manufacturers of roughly the same product exist, they are not all listed; more likely, a magazine that regularly carries ads from most of them would be a resource on that topic. Associations are similarly general resources and can often help in locating consultants or manufacturers.

The endnotes also serve as information sources. They are usually much more narrowly specific than resources. They may, however, contain exactly the needed specifics to answer particular questions.

INDIVIDUALS AND FIRMS MENTIONED IN THIS BOOK

We have tried to introduce each person quoted *only* the first time they are mentioned (some are mentioned in several chapters). If information comes from a person's published work, an endnote cites this. People quoted *without* footnotes gave information in interviews. Job titles and locations are those *current at the time* of the interview or of the project described. Names of individuals and firms are in **boldface** in the index.

EXEMPLARY LANDSCAPES

This book would not exist if many people had not put sustainable principles into landscape practice already. Although a few of the ideas we discuss are still just that—ideas—we have been able to illustrate most concepts with one or more completed landscape projects. Projects and place-names are *italicized* in the index. Like names of individuals and firms, general project information like location is given only when first mentioned. Firm names are usually the one(s) most closely connected with *landscape* aspects of the project. Inevitably, some names have been omitted, especially on larger projects where the roster of names would be a chapter in itself. In a few cases, we were unable to determine who did the project. Please contact the authors to correct any factual errors in this list.

We hope this second edition of *Sustainable Landscape Construction* will help the landscape professions to mature, to prosper in what will almost certainly be difficult times ahead, and to keep fighting for a livable and beautiful environment.

Finding Landscapes Along the Information Highway

Because "landscape" is both a broad subject and a term often misappropriated, searching for landscape information can be awkward. It is often the only way, however, to find comprehensive, up-to-the-minute detail and *locally* adapted products or expertise.

Thus, you, gentle reader, *must* develop the skill of searching for landscape information. We can offer a few suggestions.

Finding Landscapes Along the Information Highway *(continued)*

Use the search terms that we have provided in this book's resource lists. These are keywords, combined in the strange and often unlovely grammar of search engines like Google, that will unearth a *reasonably* high percentage of relevant hits. They are the same terms we used to track down much of the information in this book, and have been further tested by our diligent graduate assistant, Allison Wait. Search engines are literal-minded things. In its advanced search section, Google (and some others) allows you to enter words in four boxes labeled With All the Words, With the Exact Phrase, With At Least One of the Words, and Without the Words. For the search terms, we use the following print conventions: All-the-words: no punctuation; "Exact Phrase": in quotes; At-Least-One: OR between terms; Without: dash before term (-Word). Therefore, Geology Topography (erosion OR river OR glacier) –wind –"glacial deposition" could be a search for landforms caused only by water or ice erosion.

Know the most specific name(s) for your topic. Search for "landscape" or "environment" and you will get "Political Landscape," "Landscape of Ideas," and "Environment (computer systems)," to name only a few. Try more-specific terms from geology, soil science, horticulture, or architecture. When in doubt, ask an expert, teacher, or research librarian what the accepted term(s) would be. For products, local suppliers may help you identify the generic name for That Widget That Goes Between the Whosit and the Whatsit.

One source of semi-standardized search terms is the Library of Congress Subject Headings (LCSH). www.loc.gov/catdir/cpso/lcco/ gives a list of major topics, from which you can download detailed subheading lists. For example, you would click on Fine Arts to download the subject heading list that includes architecture. LCSH are also published in book form, available in most libraries. Many databases and university or local libraries follow LCSH definitions. Because landscape spans many disciplines, however, even these terms make a long list.

The Gale Encyclopedia of Associations lists groups for every imaginable subject, by name or topic. Most libraries have these directories.

Search engines return mixed information, opinion, and irrelevancies. Always compare different sources. Ask yourself, "Who is this source" and "What is their motive for publishing this?" Google's linkage-rating system helps screen out irrelevant hits; Yahoo! is sometimes better for suppliers and products. Google's option to display what it considers to be "similar sites" is occasionally very useful.

Web sites disappear without warning. If information is valuable, save the html file for offline viewing or cut and paste text into a word-processor file. Copy the Web address and insert the date for a permanent record if the site crashes or gets pulled.

Governmental agencies like the Natural Resource Conservation Service (formerly Soil Conservation Service) or National Oceanic and Atmospheric Administration—NRCS and NOAA, respectively—maintain Web sites that bring together a wealth of disparate information related to central concepts like soils or climate. Sites specific to green building have proliferated. We've listed some, but be on the lookout for other good ones (and send us the links, please!).

Remember that some government sites, like the infamous caribou map, suffer from political editing. There are also many sites and organizations whose names look environmental, but on closer inspection turn out to be property-rights groups whose true agenda is eliminating all environmental regulation, under the guise of cost-effectiveness or "wise use." Searching for an organization's name plus the word "controversy" can often reveal their politics and funding.

Google Earth, though still in its infancy, is bidding to become a central repository for site-specific information, or at least links to that information. See p. 41.

Acknowledgments

A first-edition grant from the Graham Foundation for the Advanced Studies in the Fine Arts, Chicago, and general support for the Center for Resource Economics / Island Press, are gratefully acknowledged.

Books, like ecosystems, evolve through a web of interactions. Thanks to everyone who responded generously to our many requests, including those whose projects, pictures, or words *aren't* included for lack of space, time, or computer compatibility.

Specific second-edition thanks to:

Meg Calkins for her many contributions to the understanding of sustainable landscape issues. Alex Wilson for access to *Evironmental Building News,* and for all-around moral support. Allison Wait for painstaking Resourse List revisions and other research assistance cheerfully and carefully rendered; and Alf Simon of UNM for making assistance available.

Special thanks to Heather Boyer for editorial insight and patience on *both* editions. It's rare to find a good editor, let alone to get to work together a second time.

The first edition would never have happened without John Lyle and Ian McHarg for inspiration, J. B. Jackson for computer help, and The Nine Readers of the Manuscript.

For sustaining us, very literally, throught this book on sustainability, we thank our wives, Anne Herzog and Mary Sorvig, who have continually supported us as well as becoming friends with each other.

A toast to the now-twice-tried authors from each other—for surviving this *second* epic with friendsip, and at least *some* sanity, intact.

Contacting the Authors

Please use www.sustainableLandscapeOnline.com, which we hope will be up and running when the second edition is released, or shortly thereafter. The site is intended to collect information on projects, products, or methods that fit the general theme of sustainable landscape construction. Feel free to tell us about your own work or that of others. Unexpected results and problems with specific techniques are also of interest. We hope to hear from contractors, designers, planners, land-owners, and others.

Please help us keep this manageable:

- There will be a method of posting questions, probably a bulletin board. We cannot guarantee personal responses, nor referrals to firms or products.
- The website will have input forms to help catalog information you send about new or interesting techniques, projects, firms, and products, publications and other information listings. Please use the forms. (If your input really won't fit any existing category, post it on the bulletin board.)
- To correct, update, or comment on existing information (either in the book or from the website), you will be able to flag or cross-reference your input. Criticism of products or projects (including our book) is welcome as long as it is thoughtful, factual, and civil.
- Indicate if you have related images, but don't send them unles requested.
- Until the website is up, or if it isn't responding, try ksorvig@unm.edu.

Thank you!

Introduction:
"Sustainability" in Context

If we put our minds to it, can we gardeners, with our centuries of practical experience, help rescue species from the brink of extinction?
—Janet Marinelli, Stalking the Wild Amaranth: Gardening in the Age of Extinction, 1998

Concern for the health of outdoor places is a central theme in landscape architecture and landscape contracting. "Stewardship" is almost the mantra of the American Society of Landscape Architecture. It is a concern shared by many members of related disciplines like architecture, planning, public-lands administration, and horticulture, as well as by private gardeners. Yet in translating this concern to the materials and methods of *making* landscapes, there frequently seems to be a disconnect between ethical intentions and practical actions.

Several landscape theorists have suggested that landscape architecture and construction (as opposed to land-use planning at the larger scale) have nothing to contribute to a sustainable future.[1] Many practitioners feel that landscapes are (or even should be) merely decorative. Others have simply declared landscape architecture dead.[2] More proactive writers have identified ways to improve environmental practice and education.[3] (See p. 343.)

Those who believe that sustainability is essential in the landscape, and vice versa, must address these concerns. One way to start is looking at the context in which the landscape professions exist and operate—the definitions and conventions, policies and politics that surround sustainable practice.

Designers are used to focusing within their project boundaries. Thinking outside this box, more and more landscape professionals approach each project as part of a regional system of natural and cultural elements. Although this way of thinking has ancient roots, it began to acquire momentum in the 1960s and 70s, with books like *Silent Spring*, *The Limits to Growth*, and *Design with Nature*. The questions raised by those books are still new, the answers still evolving. What are the relationships between human technology and nature? What concepts can best guide people to live within our ecological means?

For landscape professionals, the central question is: how can people make environmentally responsible choices in the process of conceiving and constructing landscapes? In a book of technical strategies, such questions are of real importance. Without considering the big picture, it is nearly impossible to make good decisions on a project-by-project, site-by-site scale.

At the national scale, urban and suburban development reshapes millions of acres of previously undeveloped land each year—in Colorado alone, ten acres *per hour* by one estimate.[4] Worries about development usually focus on structures—tract homes, commercial strips, and industrial buildings—but the constructed *landscapes* that accompany these buildings also contribute to widespread environmental change, and sometimes damage. When self-sustaining ecosystems are converted to built landscapes, the hidden costs may include soil loss, degradation of water, toxic and nonrenewable materials, and unsustainable energy use. This does not need to be—in fact, it needs *not* to be.

Compare an ordinary quarter-acre landscaped lot with a two-thousand-square-foot house, each a mainstay of the American Dream. The landscape directly affects an area of environment five and a half times as large as the house. More important, if the landscape introduces toxic materials and invasive plants or diseases, they are free to spread; inside the house,

Figure 0.1 John Lyle's Center for Regenerative Studies sets a high standard for sustainable place making. Many of the materials are recycled; the beautiful landscape functionally supports and renews the center. (*Project:* J. Lyle. *Photo:* Tom Lamb.)

such problems might be contained or controlled by walls, filters, or mechanical systems. In addition, many landscape practices are "non-point" sources of pollution, crossing ownership and jurisdictional lines.

Historically, some of the green of the garden has been lost in the broader battle to "control" nature. Social expectations of appearance, style, and conformity bring heavy doses of industrial-strength technology into the landscape. To pretend the technology is not there, or to assume that all landscape technology is equally acceptable, is to continue the myth that gardens are 100 percent natural. This myth, ironically, plays into the hands of those who would happily let constructed environments replace natural ones everywhere.

If a new generation of designers and a new era in design is to contribute meaningfully to sustainability,

it is critical to think carefully about context, values, and goals. Sustainability is a framework, a systematic way of linking ourselves with the natural systems that support us. Without it, individual green buildings and restored landscapes will not *add up* to what is really wanted: a worldwide network of healthy places that sustain people and sustain themselves.

The first contextual issue that requires clear thinking is the idea of sustainability itself.

What Is Sustainability: Politics, Ethics, and Semantics

Despite its widespread popularity, "sustainability" is far from having a clear and agreed definition. Although the core vision seems simple—a lasting and nondestructive way to live on this Earth—the ques-

tions are many. It is important for those of us concerned with landscape construction to think clearly about the local good or damage that we do and about opportunities and limits that link our site-by-site actions to a global picture.

Probably the simplest, widely used definition of sustainability is *meeting the needs of today's population without diminishing the ability of future populations to meet their needs.*[5] The concept of a sustainable *landscape* also has a significant history. The Council of Educators in Landscape Architecture (CELA) published a definition in 1988, most of which remains valid today: sustainable landscapes "contribute to human well-being and at the same time are in harmony with the natural environment. They do not deplete or damage other ecosystems. While human activity will have altered native patterns, a sustainable landscape will work with native conditions in its structure and functions. Valuable resources—water, nutrients, soil, et

cetera—and energy will be conserved, diversity of species will be maintained or increased."[6]

In this book, where we say that a particular approach can contribute to sustainability, we mean primarily that the method or material appears to minimize waste, pollution, and degradation of the environment. For true sustainability, it is not enough, however, just to acquire and build with the greatest efficiency. "Do I need it?" choices about the scale and appropriateness of proposed landscapes must also play a role. At times, humans must make sacrifices in favor of maintaining habitat and biodiversity. In these choices, landscape professionals can (sometimes) guide their clients and their communities.

To some degree, sustainability has become a buzzword, and fuzzy. The term is bandied about in support of widely different causes[7] and to sell products (including landscape products) only vaguely related to ecology. Some writers have proposed different terms for the concept. "Alternative" is one of these; popular in the 1960s, it implies second-rate status, and we have chosen not to use it. "Appropriate Technology" is also widely used. To us, appropriate technology is an important part of sustainability. We prefer the latter word because it emphasizes *long-term* appropriateness.

In the 1990s the late John Lyle suggested that sustainability was not enough and that optimal design should be "regenerative"—capable of *renewing* the energy and materials of degraded ecosystems. By contrast, at least one group, the Bay Area Stormwater Management Agencies Association (BASMAA), talks about "less-toxic gardens" and "less-toxic methods" of maintaining them.[8] BASMAA, not without cause, implies that human activity will *always* have some negative impact on nature, particularly when concentrated in large urban areas.

The roots of sustainable design are in "ecological design," a term that raises still other misgivings. "Ecology," especially as a popular movement influencing attitudes toward the land, strikes quite a few authors as rigidly rational, bent on saving the world whether the world likes it or not. Some such accusations are so overstated that it is easy to dismiss them, but enough thoughtful concerns have been raised that they must be considered.[9]

"Environmentally responsible" is another frequently used term. Although it is a mouthful, it may yet be the best term: one can take responsibility for attempting something even when the outcome is uncertain, and one can take responsibility for mistakes. "Sustainable," "regenerative," "ecological," and "appropriate" all tend to assume that we can predict the outcome.

Although we have chosen to keep the term "sustainability" for this book, the points raised by these alternative terms bear keeping in mind.

The limits of what we as landscape-makers can hope to contribute must also be acknowledged. The "present/future needs" definition of sustainability can be criticized for oversimplifying several key questions: Which population's needs are to be met? How large a human population can be sustained? Where to draw the line between "needs" and desires? It would be naive to ignore the criticisms that have been leveled at the very idea of sustainability. Questions

about sustainability have pragmatic and political effects on the construction of landscapes, as they do on almost every human endeavor in the twenty-first century.

The following questions illustrate some of the doubts about sustainability, in terms specific to built landscapes. Operating locally and in isolation, landscape design and construction are unlikely to resolve these questions. With coordinated effort, however, the landscape professions can and must be part of the resolution.

- If nonpolluting, low-maintenance constructed landscapes covered the globe, at the expense of wild species and places, would that be a sustainable world?
- Is there any way to avoid impoverishing the natural world without drastic regulatory limits on human population, land use, and resource consumption?
- For a majority of the world's population, "landscape" means crops, firewood, and survival. In such economies, public parks and private gardens are fantasies far beyond reach, glimpsed on TV or through closed gates. Does this mean that all landscape construction should be sacrificed to achieve subsistence-level sustainability?
- Is stewardship of the Earth as a whole system possible without dramatic changes in jurisdictional divisions of land?

For some, the answer to these questions is that sustainability is an admirable idea but can never be achieved. The authors respect the belief that sustainability may be impossible, or that the idea merely disguises the seriousness of environmental degradation. Yet with due respect, we do not feel that defeatism is warranted.[10] The critics rightly remind us that there are limits to what sustainability can or even should be; that within those limits, small efforts can yield important results; and that local results in turn can contribute to cumulative global change.

A dramatic decrease in materialism seems necessary for the Earth to sustain us in the long term. Will landscape construction be among the sacrificial luxuries? Since our first edition, drought has brought this question into stark reality in many communities, where water conservation has been implemented by banning landscape plantings. We hope that the functional and psychological value of built landscape makes it more than a luxury. The tradition of gardening for pleasure has deep roots and has survived many a drought. Realistically, though, reducing the environmental costs of construction offers an alternative to no construction at all, a way of balancing a site budget that today is often overspent. The landscape professions have a special stake, and a special responsibility, in seeking a healthy environment.

We do not want to mislead anyone into thinking that changes in landscape construction can *single-handedly* reverse environmental degradation. We do feel strongly, however, that the only possibility of a sustainable future lies in initiatives from all sides, in contributions, large and small, from great numbers of individuals and groups. The landscape professions historically have made stewardship of the environment a goal, imperfectly achieved but deeply desired. To abandon this goal because our scope of influence is limited would be irresponsible; to be smug in our greenness, equally so.

Sustainability: Convention, Tradition, and Innovation

In discussing design and construction in this book, we distinguish between sustainable practices and two other approaches: "conventional" and "traditional." It is worth defining these explicitly, because they contrast with sustainability in different ways. It is also important to think clearly about sustainability's relationship to innovation and "progress."

Conventional practices are modern approaches, standard in much of the construction industry. Some of these practices are quite acceptable in terms of environmental impact, or can be with minor modification. The authors expect many conventional practices to be part of a sustainable future. Conventional construction, however, often relies on massive energy inputs, extensive transportation, toxic materials, and removal of many if not all existing site features. There may be rare occasions when high energy use and toxic materials serve some sustainable purpose. However, changing times and conditions (for example, rising

fuel prices) make it inevitable that conventional practices will change, even if environmental issues are ignored. The uncritical assumption that conventional practices are universally acceptable is the main thing that makes them destructive.

Traditional practices, as we use the term in this book, are those surviving from premodern times, and in some cases learned from preindustrial cultures. Most rely on non-mechanized tools. Not *all* traditional land-use practices are sustainable. When applied in different climates or to different population densities than those of their origins, they can even be environmentally destructive. Many traditional practices, however, are extremely well adapted to their home regions. The modern focus on convenience and mechanization has displaced far too many traditions, some irreparably lost. Of those that remain, many traditional practices are worth reconsideration in the search for sustainability.

A number of the techniques and materials in this book can truly be referred to as "*innovative*"—manufactured soil or solar irrigation controllers are examples. Many "conventional" practices, however, are or were recently innovations. As many authors have pointed out, modern American culture loves newness and invention—often uncritically. Sustainability asks for deeper thought about values and choices. Neither innovation, nor convention or tradition, is of unquestioned value for its own sake. Sustainability, if it can ever be achieved, will have to draw on the whole range of possible practices, judging whether each one contributes to a world fit for our great-great-grandchildren.

We have tried to evaluate specific practices and materials, old and new, as fairly as possible.[11] Conventional practices are not always the Bad Guys, and both traditional and supposedly sustainable innovations have their share of failures. Our critiques are intended to *reaffirm* something that is close to the heart of almost everyone who makes the landscape his or her profession: *a desire to create beautiful and healthy places.* That desire can go tragically awry when old habits outweigh the new and important knowledge available today about the larger environment. This book presents some of that knowledge and criticizes some of those habits in the confident hope of change.

We offer criticisms of some things for which we have no solutions. This is not to show that we are "greener" or more knowledgeable than everyone else—in fact, just the opposite. We hope and assume that somebody out there knows more than we do about many of the specific problems we raise. The only way solutions will be found is by many people thinking and experimenting, often about issues someone else saw but couldn't fix. We also hope that those who have solutions or suggestions will pass them on to us; see "Contacting the Authors," p. xxvii.

Green Building: Definitions and Initiatives

Moving from sustainability in general to "green construction" in specific requires careful thought. Many "simple things to do to save the planet" require only substituting "bad" products for "good" ones. Architectural and landscape construction, however, literally changes the face of the Earth. There are many situations where building *anything* is a poor choice. Yet shelter is a genuine necessity for humans, and a healthy landscape is equally essential to human existence. It is not surprising that the growing number of associations that promote "green building" have struggled to define just what that means.

When the first edition of this book appeared, many people thought of the green building movement as a fringe activity. Even then, this was hardly true, and today it is far less so. Certainly there is a vanguard of activists, but mainstream initiatives are now widespread and well established, though still with room for growth and improvement.

The number of green building associations, initiatives, and codes began increasing dramatically at about the same time this book was first published. At that time voluntary green building associations existed in some cities, working alongside or ahead of government environmental regulatory agencies. Associations in Austin TX, Boulder CO, and Portland OR were notable for having both government and industry backing. The positive aspects of these associations have only increased since this book's first edition. By 2002, the influential *Environmental Building News* listed thirty-two state and local jurisdictions that had publicly available, detailed standards for

green building. Today there are certainly more, and increasingly they involve realtors, appraisers, and lenders specializing in the market for greener design.

The most common initial goal of such groups is to provide a green "seal of approval" that builders can achieve by meeting energy efficiency and recycling goals, among others.[12] This strictly market-driven approach has both benefits and problems, exemplified by the controversies surrounding the nationwide voluntary initiative LEED (see next section) and its competitor Green Globes.

National programs aimed at greener buildings are numerous, with widely differing goals. Some, like EnergyStar, are governmental; others start from trade, industry, or research roots. Many focus exclusively on energy performance (of appliances, buildings, etc). Others incorporate "constructability," which emphasizes mechanical design and durability.[13] Though many are great information sources, none (including LEED) focuses deeply on landscapes.

Probably the most important current initiative at the national level is Architecture 2030, which aims to use green building methods to reduce fossil-fuel use and reverse global warming. (See Landscapes Against Climate Change, p. 14.)

LEED, Its Critics, and Competitors
LEED (Leadership in Energy and Environmental Design) is a voluntary point-based certification system developed by the US Green Building Council (USGBC). Its major public release[14] occurred just five months before the first edition of this book. Since then it has become a de facto US national standard for green architecture and development, indirectly but powerfully affecting landscape work as well.

By meeting LEED criteria, a building (or, more recently, a complex) can earn sixty-nine possible points, called "credits."[15] These credits are grouped into five "impact areas," Site, Water, Materials, Energy, and Indoor Environmental Quality. Wherever possible, criteria for each credit are based on existing standards; for example, energy credits follow ASHRAE 90.1.[16]

With enough credits, buildings can be certified—and marketed—as LEED Silver, Gold, or Platinum. Designers can also become LEED Certified Professionals. Some twenty thousand have done so.[17] Since

LEED 2.0 was released, many government agencies and private clients have made it part of contracting or regulatory processes. Competing for contracts now often requires LEED certification for design team members; cities, counties, and federal agencies require LEED-compliant buildings. A few cities, such as Portland OR, have modified LEED to fit local conditions.

LEED is credited by many people with almost single-handedly catapulting green building into the mainstream. It has certainly attracted many builders, designers, and clients. Credits set concrete standards for claiming that a building is green and are, in theory at least, straightforward to achieve.

From the start, however, there have been concerns about the LEED point system and the lack of regional adaptability. In 2005 a competitor to LEED was introduced, called Green Globes (GG).[18] Using a 1,000-point, seven-category system, initially for self-assessment, it recently began offering certification. Points may be eliminated as not applicable to a project; this avoids penalties for failing to achieve the impossible, but may reward opting out of hard points. Even its author admits that GG's detailed point criteria are "kind of a black box," unavailable for public review. Fees for GG are more than for LEED, although GG does not require LEED's extensive documentation.

Primary support and funding for the GG system has come from timber and homebuilding trade associations, through an organization confusingly named the Green Building Initiative. (USGBC offers no membership options for trade associations, which apparently caused animosity.) The timber industry prefers GG because it accepts any "certified wood" program, while LEED accepts only stringent Forest Stewardship Council certification.

We consider LEED, and even potentially Green Globes if it can overcome its tendency to put industry before environment, to be valuable tools, their flaws representative of broader green building issues.

LEAVING THE LANDSCAPE OUT

To be truly effective, green building programs must go beyond approving architectural products; they must also include landscape-related goals.

Site-intensive and site-only projects—that is, landscapes—cannot achieve LEED certification because it emphasizes structure-specific goals. A fair number of landscape professionals use LEED standards as guidelines for projects, without bothering about certification. Landscape architects form a very small fraction of USGBC membership or LEED Certified Professionals.

Of LEED's available point total, 22 percent are site credits, with another 18 percent under site-related water and materials categories. A project that achieves perfect site credits has 75 percent of the credits needed for basic certification.[19] While this appears to be strong representation for landscape matters, there have been concerns that the site credits are easily achieved substitutes for harder credits.

The credit-by-credit system is not as well suited to addressing the whole-system web that produces healthy landscapes, as to evaluating components of buildings. Philadelphia landscape architect Carol Franklin criticizes "earning some points and not others, and not thinking holistically about how the land works on each individual site."

Perhaps the most significant problem is LEED's low prioritization of landscape issues, mirrored by many other green building programs. In LEED 2.0, a ban on smoking is mandatory for certification, but site protection remains optional. LEED is structurally incapable of addressing siting on inappropriate land, because of its voluntary, commercial stance. Few commercial developers would voluntarily give up developing a site they already own.[20]

No building can be LEED certified unless it meets minimum energy performance and indoor air quality, and collects recyclables. Yet the same building can be built on a site, perhaps in Malibu, where wildfire, earthquakes, and landslides are known hazards, and still be LEED certified. The only mandatory site credit is for erosion control, something already mandated by the EPA. The question remains whether any voluntary program can change inappropriate siting practices, or whether land-use regulations are the only available tool for doing so.

Including site and ecosystem protection in green building is essential, but even today input from landscape professionals is too often overlooked or added as an afterthought. A perfectly resource-green house that replaces a healthy ecosystem is a poor substitute. Badly sited, such a building destroys the site and, with it, environmental services provided to "green" functioning of the building.

Regional siting also plays a large and often unconsidered role. For example, although the very green headquarters of Patagonia makes excellent use of a degraded site and is highly resource efficient, it is located outside the Reno NV public transportation network and leaves employees little option but to drive long distances to work. Balancing these factors is difficult—and current green building definitions that exclude site issues can disguise that difficulty rather than help solve it.

Including site protection in green building often highlights the fact that structures and construction are in some senses *inherently* damaging to the larger environment. The two factors that virtually *all* construction projects share are land clearance and creation of impervious surfaces—both detrimental to ecosystem function unless carefully mitigated. In an ideal world, green building should limit development to appropriate sites. Clearly, this conflicts head-on with land-use and land-ownership conventions. Green siting makes green building paradoxical, and to some, unpalatable—so site issues are left out.

Without site protection as a goal, green building can become a little like fat-free cookies—an excuse to consume more because it's better than other brands. Although the design and construction industries are understandably reluctant to be put on a diet, one important part of green building is *building less*. Meeting this challenge in a way that keeps the industry *and* the environment healthy is the great challenge.

In the growing number of green building books for architecture and engineering, landscape is usually accorded only an introductory mention. Too frequently, architectural writers assume that landscape is a minor subset of their profession, and that environmental evaluation of architectural materials can simply be transferred to landscape work. In researching this book, we have repeatedly found this to be far from true. Information for architects is increasingly focused on "building systems" and on component performance for *operating* the structure. This focus has

clear value, but requires translation to have meaning in the landscape, where construction is done with simpler materials and operating energy is usually low. The very favorable reception that this book's initial edition received from landscape professionals indicates that the architectural perspective on green building is not easily applicable outdoors.

Given these differences, the landscape professions may need to develop an independent set of standards or certification for sustainable landscapes. In the long term, standards should guide planners, site and building designers, and construction and maintenance professionals in an integrated, "cradle-to-grave" effort. In the short term, separate landscape standards may be necessary.

In fact, market incentive systems like LEED are inherently temporary. As green building becomes more widespread, the marketing value of a Gold or Platinum seal decreases. Eventually what is now cutting-edge will become baseline, expected by every client. Like a great many valuable tools, LEED must ultimately succeed by making itself unnecessary.

The Landscape Professions: NOT Construction "Versus" Design

Another contextual issue affecting sustainable work is the white collar versus blue collar split. Replacing that dichotomy with broader teamwork is a hallmark of many of the projects mentioned in this book.

Most landscape "construction" books have, in the past, been written for designers by designers. In these books (and the courses where they serve as texts), physical labor, machinery, and tools might as well not exist. The focus of these books, despite their titles, is primarily on detail and structure in *design*, not on how to *build* the design at the site. There is a legitimate need for detailed design information, and the fact that "construction" books are widely read by designers shows how much the contractor and designer rely on one another in their duties. We are convinced, however, that ignoring the contractor's actual work is a shortcoming in these books, perhaps reflective of a shortcoming in professional attitudes.

At the other end of the spectrum, there are many fine books on larger-scale design and planning issues.

It has now been more than thirty-five years since landscape architect Ian McHarg published his epochal book, *Design with Nature*. Since that time many books have dealt with ecological assessment, planning, and design. But even if these planning and design principles are sensitively followed, inappropriate *construction* methods and materials can still lead to unnecessary environmental destruction. Where those books start from the broad scale (design or planning), this book has its foundation at the site-specific scale of actually constructing landscapes.

Prior to this book's first release, information on better landscape *construction* alternatives was very scattered and poorly documented. Much of this information was available only in home-owner format, focused on maintenance issues such as reduction of pesticide use or the value of composting. This excluded many issues of importance to professionals in landscape construction and design. The situation has improved a great deal, but homeowner/professional, designer/contractor, and other dichotomies remain barriers to deeper sustainability.

Some information in this book is of interest primarily to one-half of the landscape profession, either to contractors or designers. Design and construction cannot truly be separated, though, and most issues affect both groups. Changes in construction materials and methods affect what designers can specify. New ideas in design affect what contractors can and are expected to build. We hope to accomplish two goals: to call attention to the environmental effects and potentials of physical landscape construction, and to state the case, repeatedly, for better *integration* of design and construction as an essential step towards sustainable land use.

Throughout this book, we refer to "landscape professionals" and the "landscape professions." By this we mean to include landscape architects, landscape contractors, and many others who support their work: horticulturists, arborists, nurseries, materials suppliers, grounds maintenance workers. Permaculturists, Xeriscape experts, and others are (to us, at least) part of the mix.[21] Some engineers, architects, and general contractors also deserve at least honorary membership. We have received some criticism for not directing this book exclusively at landscape architects,

but we feel our purpose goes beyond current professional definitions. Thinking of ourselves as members of a larger community of *professionals whose livelihood is the landscape* has great power and value, in our opinion.

Breaking down barriers to cooperation is especially important for those whose goal is sustainability. The old barriers serve no good purpose in the attempt to care holistically for the built environment. We have been happy to see more and more collaborative project approaches being adopted by sustainability-driven firms.

Get an Attitude

Besides appropriate techniques and materials, site protection relies on positive attitudes toward the landscape. Many "conventional" professionals share these attitudes, which are not the exclusive wisdom of environmental designers or specialists. It is too easy to assume that "They" (builders, engineers, contractors, conventional designers . . .) are insensitive to landscape preservation. There certainly are such cases, but throughout the design and construction industries are people who know and love the outdoors, and chose their profession accordingly: civil engineers who restore wetlands, or highway contractors who can quote dozens of literary naturalists.

Fundamental to protecting healthy sites is the recognition that each site is alive, unique, and connected to a web of off-site influences. By contrast, the common attitude that sites are just "unimproved land," blank-slate building locations, virtually guarantees site damage. Conventional concerns like practicality and keeping down costs must be balanced with respect for site health. A balanced attitude, whether among team members or in an individual conscience, is a major part of any attempt to build sustainably.

Designers and construction workers alike get great satisfaction from their power to change and rearrange the site. This power, and skill in exercising it, is well deserving of pride but can also become a "power trip." Designers can fall into the trap of arrogantly remaking the site on a whim. Cynicism and even despair are also occupational hazards, born of seeing too many good places deformed by carelessness, too many good designs denied by regulation or cost. Similarly, some construction workers begin to view site and materials as adversaries to be overcome, and use anger to crank up the energy needed to do the job. This combative attitude is expressed when existing trees are hacked unnecessarily, or equipment is driven carelessly, or construction scrap is thrown around the site. There are strong reasons, both conventional and sustainable, to avoid any of these attitudes, which poison both professional and personal relations with the land.

Successful design firms create a "corporate culture" in which creativity steers clear of arrogance. The best contractors discourage the site-as-adversary attitude; they make pride a constructive rather than destructive force. In design and construction firms, and between them, teamwork lightens the sometimes thankless task of pushing sustainability through a legal and social obstacle course. Professionals of all types work to make their *practices* sustainable. To paraphrase the basic definition, a sustainable business attitude aims for "meeting the goals of our office without diminishing the ability of other professionals to meet their goals."

The technical solutions found in this book can support, but cannot replace, an attitude that balances ecological health with human desires. This attitude, and the creative application of sustainable knowledge, thrives best in an atmosphere of collaboration.

BUILD A SITE-FOCUSED TEAM

Many of the world's greatest and best-loved landscapes were built and nurtured by many hands over decades or even centuries. Part of their appeal lies in the traces of so much attention from so many people. It is certainly possible for one person to build an entire landscape beautifully, if the site is small enough and the time for building quite long. For larger landscapes, for those that are ecologically complex, or for those that must be built in a hurry, teamwork is inevitable—and can work for sustainability or against it.

The minimum team for a high-quality, sustainably built landscape consists of four roles: the client, the designer, the builder, and the maintenance person. Sometimes several roles are played by one person: the client may act as designer or do maintenance; a design-build firm may do post-occupancy maintenance. Conventional wisdom favors narrow specialization, but overlapping arrangements have great value in creating healthy places.

Nearly as often, each role may involve several people. The client may be one or more organizations. Some sites are owned by one entity but *used* by other people; users of a public landscape may have more say than the agency that "owns" it. Building codes and regulations are often an invisible "team member" (usually uncooperative) for both the designer and the contractor. Consultants and subcontractors play many roles. Lending and insuring agencies are still notorious for refusing to fund "alternative" work—but can sometimes be instrumental in getting such methods approved.

What brings all this complexity together is a shared vision, a set of clearly stated goals that the whole team understands and supports. The vision may come from a single strong personality or from long debate leading to consensus. Unless the vision is *clear, doable, and communicated to every person involved* in the construction process, it has little hope of being realized. If the vision is some form of sustainability, clear communication is even more critical, given how wooly a word "sustainable" can be.

The architectural firm HOK recommends a *new design process* for sustainable results. The process has six phases. The last four are quite familiar: design, specification, construction, and operation/maintenance. But the first two—where the opportunities for change and cost savings are greatest—are team formation and education/goal setting.[22]

Conventional practice tends to work against team formation and education, by insisting that each expert has a narrowly defined niche, competitively kept near secret from all the other players. Although teamwork among designers is reasonably common, including a contractor *at the design phase* is not. Yet nearly all designers, if asked for their most-satisfying projects, would name jobs where the contractor was a trusted collaborator. By contrast, the most frustrating projects are those that run under low-bid rules and treat collaboration as conflict of interest.

HOK minces no words in saying that overspecialization cannot achieve the quality and insight re-

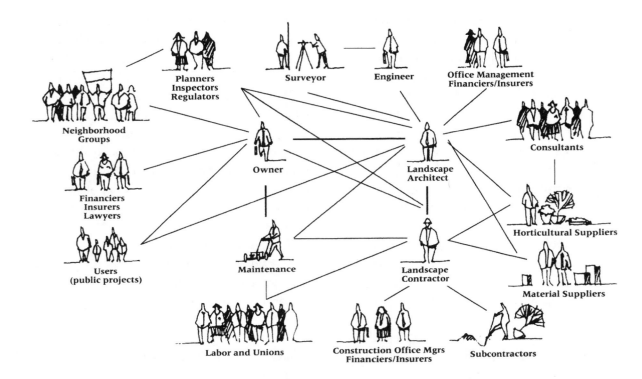

Figure 0.2 Constructing healthy and sustainable landscapes requires coordination of many specialists into a complex team. (*Illust.:* Craig Farnsworth.)

quired for sustainable work. The designer cannot afford to hand near-finished designs to a technical consultant. "Engineers need to be involved in the design process from the very beginning—so too must the construction professionals, including the major subcontractors, those ultimately responsible for operations, the various consultants, and in some cases key suppliers."[23] Although written with structural design in mind, this statement applies equally, if not more so, to landscapes that attempt ecological functions.

Many large design firms have revised their work processes in pursuit of sustainability.[24] Even governmental agencies have recognized the value of teaming with contractors and suppliers. Instead of a strict low-bid process, many agencies require prequalification for all bidders. Contractors and suppliers must demonstrate a track record, including quality work and ability to control costs, before they qualify to bid. Environmental knowledge and care may also be criteria. A graduated series of steps, from prequalification for small projects to inclusion on the large-project list, opens this process to new firms and keeps

it fair to all. At the same time, the client agency can have confidence that the low bidder for a project knows what is expected and has the skills to do the work. In this sense, the contractors become part of the team even within the limits of public-sector work.

The whole team needs to educate itself about environmental issues that will affect the project. On an effective team, among themselves the members already know most of the issues or how to find information quickly. Equally important, they have a well-defined way of sharing their knowledge. Once basic issues are defined and understood, project goals are set. These should be specific, and it should be possible to evaluate whether they were met. For example, a goal of "saving water" is too vague. "Reduce irrigation use of tap-water to 40 percent of the average for nearby landscapes" is a specific goal. Not all testable goals include numbers, but quantifiable goals are most easily tested.

For public lands, and for many private large projects, neighborhood input is today a legal requirement. This is changing the way that land-use decisions are made, and some conventional developers, designers, and contractors resent the change. Most landscapes, however, affect the neighbors, and public opposition that is ignored often translates to neglect, misuse, and even vandalism. Building a landscape only to have it destroyed by its users or neighbors is clearly not sustainable. We urge landscape professionals to look again at public input and see it as an opportunity. "Community-based planning" and "participatory design"⊃ are two approaches that are gaining more practitioners. The results can be quite remarkable. New York City Housing Authority landscape architect Leonard Hopper points to dramatic successes in making livable communities out of crime-ridden ones through redesign *by and for* the residents. It takes commitment and hard work: Philadelphia landscape firm Synterra attended over 200 community meetings in one year for a single large public-works project.

Collaborative effort may seem like a social issue, unrelated either to construction or to sustainability. In the conventional, compartmentalized mode, this is true. But that view contributes to direct and indirect waste of resources, the very opposite of sustainability. Poor coordination results in wasted site visits, consuming fuel. Incorrect drawings and specs waste paper (if they are caught and corrected) and waste materials if they get built. Failing to plan for standard available sizes of materials also leads to waste. Worst of all, a built landscape that fails to meet its goals is soon an unhealthy landscape and may take neighboring landscapes with it in decline.

ENVIRONMENTAL JUSTICE AND THE CULTURAL CONTEXT FOR SUSTAINABILITY

Sustainable design is a cultural activity and occurs in cultural contexts, an aspect of which is "environmental justice." Whether it appears by name in project discussions or not, "EJ" can have a pronounced impact on project success.

Emerging as a movement in the 1980s, the concept of environmental justice is simple and disturbing: ethnic minorities and low-income people are significantly more likely to live or work in places affected by environmental hazards. Polluting facilities are more likely to be located in or near such communities. Members of these communities are less likely

to be informed or consulted during planning decisions, and violations of existing environmental regulations are less likely to be enforced on behalf of such communities.[25]

We do not pretend to be experts on environmental justice, and this book is not the place to examine its root causes. Evidence suggests that race, rather than economic class, better predicts whether an individual or community will face unusual environmental risks. As such, the term "environmental racism" is frequently used, with environmental justice as the hoped-for solution.

Setting aside the ethical aspects of this issue as too large to address adequately here, this issue is important for purely pragmatic reasons to landscape professionals working toward sustainability.

- Affected communities often are potent allies in pushing sustainable design past convention-bound authorities.[26] Never assume that such alliances can be easily forged, nor that community goals will align readily with design-school priorities. Extensive community involvement is required, often across cultural divides that few landscape architects can navigate without help.
- Conversely, affected communities can be formidable opponents, often rejecting projects intended to be sustainable. The environmental justice movement typically views the "classic" environmental movement as concerned only with preserving nature for the elite. What a landscape professional might consider a model sustainability project, the community may perceive as irrelevant to more pressing problems such as pollution-induced illnesses. This is especially true of projects, however well-intentioned, presented to the public as complete plans without serious local input.
- The federal government created an Office of Environmental Justice in 1992, and two years later required *all* federal agencies to address the issue. Federal EJ efforts are governed by the Title VI Civil Rights Act and use federal definitions of minority or low-income status. This can cut both ways, easing environmental quality into some projects, and in others, snarling all hope of improvements in us-versus-them politics. The difference is

very often the design team's initial attitude toward cooperation with the community.

Landscape professionals can find good guidance about this thorny subject in the work of California landscape architect Randolph Hester. Hester, often working with Joe Edmiston, the visionary founder of the Santa Monica Mountain Conservancy in Los Angeles, has incorporated cross-cultural, community-based methods in all his work. While conventional wisdom has held that low-income nonwhites have no interest in nature parks and only want active sport facilities, Hester has acted on research showing the opposite to be true: poor neighborhoods vote in favor of bonds to fund nature conservation at strikingly higher percentages than adjacent wealthy neighborhoods.[27] Hester's recent book *Design for Ecological Democracy* takes the interesting position that "democracy bestows freedom; ecology creates responsible freedom [through] interconnectedness with all species. [Ecology] forges the basis for civil society to address a shared public good."[28]

In addition to avoiding unfair exposure to hazards, environmental justice also aims for equitable distribution of resources. Natural resources are distributed very unequally in the world's geographic regions, something that has strongly affected cultural and technological development, and thus differences in environmental destruction and pollution. It is well worth any landscape professional's time to read Jared Diamond's Pulitzer Prize–winning book on this subject, *Guns, Germs, and Steel*,[29] not only for background on environmental justice among cultures, but also as a forceful reminder of how interdependence with ecology and place has shaped human history.

EXPECT DEMOGRAPHICS AND ECONOMICS TO CHANGE
SUSTAINABILITY ITSELF

It seems obvious that economic channels create changing currents in which sustainable designers must swim. In fact, almost every junior designer hears "idealistic notions" like sustainability crushed by some crusty senior partner because they are not in line with The Economy.

Nonetheless, economic, political, and demographic trends *are* changing what sustainable practice means today. Anyone involved in construction has noted drastic increases in building material prices. Several factors are involved. China, whose rate of new building starts is nearly ten times that of the United States, is in effect outbidding American purchasers. Transportation costs (especially for heavy items such as building materials) have risen steeply with oil prices.[30] The severe storms that appear to be part of global warming have created shortages of *re*construction materials, most evident in the United States after Katrina.

None of these factors seem likely to go away, and the smart money says they will get worse. For sustainable design, this is bad news and good news. Some building materials have doubled in price in a matter of months, affecting both conventional and sustainable projects. Sustainable methods, however, which explicitly aim to save materials and use local and recycled products, actually gain attractiveness in this kind of economic climate.

The political climate since 2000 has repeatedly been described as the worst ever for the environment. Yet the Bush administration's antienvironmental posture[31] may have unintended consequences. Groups like the Environmental Council of the States and the US Conference of Mayors have become increasingly proactive on matters from the Kyoto accords to pollution standards, partly in protest against federal gutlessness. Green building has actually flourished during the same period.

The National Association of Home Builders and construction researchers at McGraw-Hill predict that 10 percent of US homes will be green by 2010; only 2 percent of new construction today is green building.[32] Large "spec" builders are the slowest to adopt green techniques: their focus is on lowering upfront costs, which they do by sacrificing the operational savings obtained by investing in green construction. The increase in initial costs due to building green is generally reported as from less than 1 percent to about 7 percent. Benefits (considering only actual financial savings) over twenty years amount to ten times the initial investment.[33]

The marketability of sustainable design is linked to how people value the environment, and that, too, is changing as the United States undergoes demographic shifts. Hispanics, expected to make up nearly a quarter of the US population by 2050,[34] have become increasingly active in environmental issues, more likely to support pollution abatement and urban parks than roadless areas or endangered species.[35] Aging boomers are an increasing demographic; some will quit using outdoor facilities, while demand for handicapped access will continue to grow. What a new generation of adults will do outdoors (if anything, given the fascination of electronics) remains to be seen. As one National Park Service official put it, "Are we ready for Extreme Sports in the Parks? Because they're coming."[36]

Neither we nor anyone else can truly predict such trends. It is clear, however, that America's dedication to the great outdoors is changing. With it, but not necessarily in any clear parallel, attitudes toward sustainable development will change.

How people define what they value in the environment is the context within which sustainable design flourishes or dwindles. At present, opportunities for green building are growing fast, driven by otherwise negative trends such as high materials costs or the threat of climate change. Sustainability has not only become mainstream, but in a sense has gone beyond being optional. Landscape professionals who invest in sustainable practice must continue to assess their surroundings and adapt accordingly.

Landscapes Against Climate Change

It is difficult today to talk seriously about sustainability without considering global warming, more accurately called global climate change. Without addressing climate change, many "sustainable" activities are almost irrelevant. Yet efforts like recycling, energy conservation, or site restoration *are* important, because they *add up* to affect global climate.

Understandably, many people feel helpless in the face of what could be a worldwide catastrophe, yet the situation is not one of unmitigated gloom and doom. In fact, recent initiatives have thrust architects into the spotlight as a professional group with real potential to reverse climate change using realistic and proven methods. Similarly, recent research that con-

nects land-use practices to weather extremes indicates that landscape professionals have a role to play as well.

Architecture 2030 and the Global Climate Initiative

Architects, according to Ed Mazria, "hold the key to the global thermostat." Mazria, a Santa Fe NM architect known for pioneering work on solar buildings, is the founder of Architecture 2030. This initiative could literally make architects the heroes that save the planet from climate catastrophe.

Perhaps that sounds like overstatement, but it is not. Mazria bases his proposal on a sophisticated re-analysis of US energy-use statistics. His work shows that when materials, construction, operation, and decommissioning are taken into account, the building industry uses *nearly half of all energy* consumed each year.[37] Energy use equates roughly to greenhouse gases and climate change. Thus, changes in energy use by buildings stand to have a major impact on the problem.

How major? The most catastrophic effects of climate change can be averted by cutting fossil fuel use for buildings by 50 percent immediately, and by an additional 10 percent every five years until 2030, according to Mazria. These goals, moreover, can be accomplished using well-known and tested methods familiar to green builders.[38] What is necessary is to make these universal, and to do it consistently *and soon*.

Late in 2006, Architecture 2030's goals were officially adopted by the American Institute of Architects (AIA), the US Green Building Council (USGBC, originators of the LEED program), the American Society of Heating, Refrigerating, and Air-conditioning Engineers (ASHRAE), and some twenty other building-related industry associations, plus the US Council of Mayors. That adoption may prove to be a watershed event; it thrusts designers to the fore in the fight against climate change.

Landscapes, as this book emphasizes, use relatively little energy and fuel compared to buildings. Does that mean that landscape professionals can sit complacently on the sidelines while architects ride out in shining armor? Definitely not.

Land and Climate

The first edition of this book noted a single piece of research about climatology and landscapes—an early indicator of what has become a much broader issue. In 1998, researchers Jonathan Foley and Roger Pielke demonstrated that land development had altered Florida's climate enough to affect its agricultural industry significantly. Clearing land, draining swamps, rerouting rivers, and urbanization had resulted in measurably hotter and drier summers, and in winters that damaged citrus crops farther south than anyone had ever seen before.[39]

Since that time, there has been growing consensus that clearing land—for agriculture or for structures and development—plays a role in global warming that must be considered alongside the better-publicized CO_2 emissions caused by fuel combustion. Pielke and others have stated that land clearance results in as much greenhouse gas as produced by fuel burning. Other sources, especially official bodies, tend to put the number lower, with land clearance and related changes causing about 20 to 25 percent of the total.[40] Scientific consensus is emerging, however, that the removal of vegetation and alteration of soil conditions is implicated in *between one-quarter and one-half* of these threatening atmospheric changes.

A great deal of conventional landscape construction contributes directly to these problems, bulldozing whatever vegetation existed on-site and replacing it with limited species or monocultures. Most techniques advocated for sustainability potentially affect climate for the better. Protecting healthy sites, restoring denuded ones, planting appropriate vegetation, managing stormwater for infiltration, and reducing impervious paving—in addition to localized benefits, all these techniques have significant global implications.

Landscape professionals, even those who focus on sustainability, still tend to concentrate on local benefits of healthy sites. The evidence has become overwhelming, however, that the landscape professions must also pay attention to the *global* effects of converting land from vegetated to paved, or from dense native plant communities to sparsely ornamental hor-

ticulture. This is imperative because sustainable practices work to slow global warming, while many conventional methods hasten it.

To make a difference, individual sustainable practices need to be understood in a larger context. Thus, although this book generally focuses on practical, close-to-home matters, this section gives a brief overview of documented links between land use and climate change. We know that some designers and contractors will be tempted to skip this section. We urge you strongly—if you read nothing else, read this.

Get the Facts

First, if you still harbor doubt that global warming isn't real or that humans bear little responsibility for it, please consult one of the following. Not only will they give you straight, clear facts, they will inspire you to leave doom and gloom behind and take positive action.

- *The Weather Makers: How Man Is Changing the Climate and What It Means for Life on Earth,* (Atlantic Monthly Press, 2005): an excellent, readable book by Tim Flannery, a respected Australian scientist, author, and commentator for the BBC, ABC, and NPR.
- *An Inconvenient Truth,* a documentary that provides a clear summary of climate issues, easy to follow, thought provoking, moving, and positive. (Now available on DVD from www.climatecrisis.org.)
- www.architecture2030.org, a concise graphic Web site that has united architects and other design professionals toward realistic climate-focused goals.

Whether you choose the book, the video, or the Web site, these sources offer clear and factual background on the issue. You may also want to download the Union of Concerned Scientists' January 2007 report, documenting ExxonMobil's $16 million campaign of disinformation, deliberately creating false uncertainty and controversy over climate change.[41]

Landscape-specific Changes That Affect Climate

The crucial link is carbon, in the form of carbon dioxide (CO_2). All plants and animals are carbon-based life-forms. Plants absorb carbon from air and bond it with hydrogen to store energy (photosynthesis). Ultimately, this is the world's only source of either food or fuel. Oxygen breaks these bonds and releases energy (combustion and respiration), which emits CO_2 into the atmosphere.

Carbon dioxide acts like glass in a passive solar design: light passes inward through the atmosphere, but CO_2 prevents heat-producing ultraviolet rays from escaping. The more CO_2 in the atmosphere, the more Earth's average temperature rises. There are other "greenhouse gases," some actually more potent than CO_2, but CO_2 appears to trigger the others.

Burning fossil fuels—which consist of carbon stored by ancient plants—has released large amounts of CO_2 into the atmosphere and raised the average global temperature.

That much is basic chemistry. Where does landscape change fit in?[42]

Of the many planetary reservoirs of CO_2, plants and soils are the most *active* in exchanging CO_2 with the atmosphere.[43] Plants take CO_2 out of the atmosphere and hold it in sugars and woody tissues. Soil is also a major reservoir of stored carbon.

When plant cover is removed, or its density is reduced, several things occur, all trending toward warming.

- No longer shaded by vegetation, soil bakes in direct sun, holding enough extra heat to raise local temperatures.
- Heated soils kill carbon-storing microorganisms and speed decomposition of organic matter, releasing CO_2.
- With less vegetation to protect it from rain, runoff, and wind, exposed soil erodes; this further releases organic matter and emits CO_2.
- Heating and erosion of soil kills more plants, leading to more heating and erosion in a vicious cycle.
- If removed plants are burned or eaten, CO_2 stored in them is released.

Loss of soil and vegetative cover is well known to historians under a different name: deforestation. Many of the world's deserts are the direct result of human deforestation practices.[44] Land clearance, for

whatever purpose, almost always tends to increase hot-season temperatures, drought, and wildfire.

What is less commonly understood is that landscapes with sparse vegetation and dead or dying soils are also typically colder and windier in winter, less capable of infiltrating precipitation and more prone to intense runoff and flooding.

In short, removal of any significant percentage of vegetative cover[45] from a large area, *or from many small areas cumulatively*, contributes to the extremes of heat and cold, drought, and flooding that are part of global climate change.

Is Construction to Blame?

Construction almost always involves some land clearance. This is nearly unavoidable. In some regions, cleared areas regrow rapidly if left alone. Most projects, however, create impervious surfaces, from which vegetation and soil are permanently excluded.

Even when a cleared landscape is replanted, this usually reduces the density and biodiversity of vegetative cover. As the Intergovernmental Panel on Climate Change states, "Conversion of natural ecosystems to croplands and pastures has resulted in . . . agro-ecosystems [that] continue to take up carbon, but at levels generally inferior to the previously forested ecosystems."[46] Ornamental landscapes are clearly agro-ecosystems in this sense and do not replace the CO_2-uptake of established regional vegetation. Most plantings also provide less shade, soil stabilization, and runoff prevention than mature forest cover.

Agriculture has been the main reason for land clearance historically, and remains so in developing countries today. In the tropics, 500,000 trees are cut *every hour*, primarily for forestry and new agriculture.[47] In industrialized countries like the United States and Europe, however, clearance for buildings, infrastructure, and landscapes may be outpacing new agricultural clearance. The cumulative effect of clearing 1.39 *million* sites (a low estimate of annual new US housing starts)[48] is directly linked to global problems.[49] This puts landscape professionals and land-use planners in a position of serious influence and responsibility.

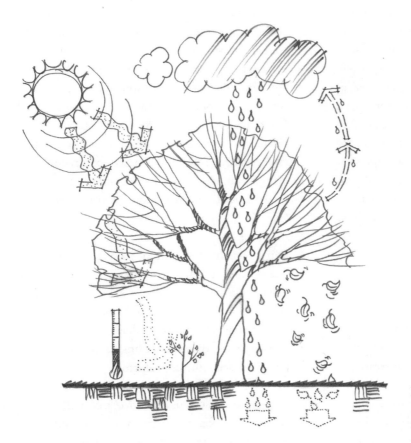

Figure 0.3 Vegetation cover protects soil, improves infiltration, and moderates climate. (*Illust.:* Craig Farnsworth.)

Figure 0.4 Vegetation clearance depletes and bakes soil, increases runoff, and warms climate, locally and cumulatively. (*Illust.:* Craig Farnsworth.)

Estimating the extent of US land clearance is not easy. Something like 500,000 to 1.5 million acres are probably cleared per year; 3 million acres are "lost to agriculture" annually.[50] The *smallest* Figure equals an area half the size of Rhode Island. A great deal of this cleared land remains as "landscape" of some sort; many architectural or engineering structures are surrounded by landscapes covering three to five times the area of the facility itself. Thus, what landscape professionals do about clearance, revegetation, soil protection, paving, and water management cumulatively influences huge areas. Areas, in fact, that are more than large enough to affect climate.

What the Landscape Professions Can Do

This is good news and bad news. The bad news is that landscape business-as-usual contributes significantly to what many believe is humanity's single greatest challenge. The good news is that the strategies advocated in this book offer practical contributions toward reversing climate change *if we act now*.

One hundred trees can remove five tons of CO_2 and half a ton of other pollutants from the air each year. The same hundred trees will also capture 250,000 gallons (or $6\frac{1}{4}$ acre-feet) of stormwater per year in temperate climates. Those one hundred trees, carefully located for shade, would cut air-conditioning usage in half for thirty-three houses (three trees per house). These effects have direct impact on climate locally and globally.[51]

Among the things landscape professionals can do:

- Collaborate with architects to achieve Architecture 2030's fossil-fuel-reduction goals for buildings; many landscape measures contribute directly.
- Avoid unnecessary vegetation clearing (using methods discussed in Principle 1)
- Lobby against "preclearing" of real estate prior to sale. (See p. 39.)
- Aim for canopy cover and density similar to regional plant communities, both in "restoration" projects and in planting design. (See Principles 2 and 3.)
- Find better methods of wildfire protection; especially, resist land clearance wrongly promoted as fire prevention. (See p. 106.)

- Use greenwalls and greenroofs to reinstate partial vegetative cover on structures. (See p. 118 and 125.)
- Manage stormwater with vegetation, infiltrating it to benefit soils and plants. (See Principle 4.)
- Minimize paving to avoid soil and vegetation loss through erosion. (See Principle 5.)
- Cut down fossil-fuel use for transportation of materials and workers and for construction machinery. (See Principle 7.) Bio-based fuels reduce (but do not eliminate) CO_2 from combustion.
- Learn about "carbon sequestration," by which CO_2 is locked up in trees, wood, and other materials.
- Don't buy the desperate or silly "solutions" proposed by industrial eccentrics. These have included giant mirrors in space, aerial spreading of tinfoil confetti, and even deliberately increasing opaque air pollutants, all to cut sunlight. The unintended consequences of such actions would almost certainly worsen climate problems.

Sequestration (discussed above) may well become the main economic reason for protecting and planting trees, surpassing even timber production and providing unheard-of funding for planted landscapes. Sequestration also gives wood construction a new justification: keeping carbon out of circulation until the wood rots or burns.

A Forest Service research center specializing in urban trees is testing which species sequester CO_2 most effectively. Regional variation and age of trees are critical, but the following trees were found highly effective in a 2002 study: horse chestnut, black walnut, sweet gum, bald cypress, Douglas fir, and London plane; scarlet, red, and Virginia live oaks; and ponderosa, red, Hispaniola, and white pines.[52]

Carbon sequestration is also the basis for "carbon trading" schemes, such as the Chicago Climate Exchange. In theory, polluters in rich countries fund sustainable developments in poor countries through these trades. There is considerable controversy over this concept, with charges of conflict of interest, falsified reports, and lack of oversight.[53] Other "mitigation banking" schemes—for example, wetlands banking—have had poor results. Pollution and cleanup affect specific places—can they be made portable? Under carbon-trading procedures, a Texas coal-fired plant whose pollutant output was obscuring the Grand Canyon could buy carbon credits from a forest in India. Although this would positively affect global carbon levels, it simply excuses rather than helping the pollution problem at the Grand Canyon.

Until recently, only large brokerages and corporations could trade carbon futures. Individuals and small firms, however, now use a growing number of trading services. These allow a person or firm to buy enough carbon credits to offset their car or truck's annual output (about 5.5 metric tons worth) for around $50, or a house's worth (23 metric tons) for $99.[54] Many committed environmentalists do so. We question whether this is merely paying for convenient absolution. Surely fixing the car or house, or one's own behavior, to generate less actual pollutants is more important than shuffling paper credits for them.

What the Landscape Professions Stand to Lose

Although every human being has a stake in reducing the greenhouse effect, landscape professionals stand to lose more and sooner because our livelihood *is* the environment. Warmer and drier local climates and shifted seasons are likely to snarl landscape work long before the world reaches true catastrophe. Drought has already ruined many landscape businesses, with planting or irrigation banned in many areas. Increased CO_2 is causing weeds to produce ten times more pollen, to the despair of both allergy sufferers and horticulturists.[55] Even slight climate changes will make the well-known Plant Hardiness Zones unreliable and could require major changes in building codes.

The question of how built landscapes damage the environment has become considerably more central to sustainability than anyone realized a decade ago. The stakes have dramatically increased in the debate over whether nature-like landscape forms matter, and why human landscape making so often oversimplifies those forms. "Greenwash," once merely misleading, is now nearly criminal.

The climate crisis powerfully increases the value of any activity that protects or restores vegetation and soils. Almost all the techniques of sustainable landscape making do so. They are detailed in the following chapters. The responsibility to use them has never been more important.

Sustainability, Substance, and Style

Success is always interwoven with challenges, and never more so than in the movement for sustainability. The more the public and the profession accept green building and sustainable landscapes, and the more such places are built, the more critical it becomes to distinguish between landscapes that contribute functionally to the health of the environment, and ones that do not.

Such distinctions require critical thinking, documentation of landscape performance, and the ability to see past superficial claims. None of those skills are simple, in part because of the many uncertainties about sustainability itself. It is challenging to understand how landscapes created to fit accepted, even beloved, social conventions can damage the environment. Since we raised this issue in our first edition, it has grown from a mainly site-specific question to one that influences global as well as local action. Especially as linked to global warming (see above), the pressure is on for claims of sustainability to have real substance.

Conversely, the danger of greenwash and misappropriation of sustainability as a marketing tool has clearly increased, paralleling the success and growth of genuinely sustainable practice. This amplifies the importance of ongoing discussions about what works, what is a good-faith experiment, and what is self-deluding or outright deceptive.

To have those discussions requires as much clarity as possible about the differences between built and natural form, and relating both to ecological function. It requires that designers train themselves to look beyond appearances, while still creating stylish and beautiful places that sustain people psychologically. The challenge for serious practitioners—including the authors—is to make an honest attempt at sustainable landscapes without becoming smug about successes achieved thus far.

But How Can Landscapes Damage the Environment?

For those of us who love landscapes, it is troubling and confusing to think that our creations damage the environment. How can a green growing place hurt the Earth? The question can be answered both in a technical way, and in terms of attitudes and cultural trends.

TECHNICAL ISSUES: RESOURCES AND BIODIVERSITY

Along with a generally positive report, this book also discusses materials and processes of landscape construction that contribute to ecological problems. Some are very specific, such as resource depletion when redwood or tropical hardwoods are used in quantity for consumer landscapes. Toxic materials are used in gardens both intentionally (pesticides, for example) and unintentionally (excess fertilizer which pollutes waterways, or materials like PVC, which are highly valued while in use but cause serious disposal problems). Land itself is "consumed" and "wasted" by some types of conventional construction. These are the *technical* answers to the question of ecological damage from landscapes; they are detailed throughout the book.

Landscapes and gardens, as constructed today, also have an effect on biodiversity, which can be quite negative. It may seem that gardens, especially those of enthusiastic horticulturists, are highly diverse, and in a sense this is true. Most built landscapes, however, are planted with only a dozen or so species; in many schools of landscape design, this is actually taught as a way to avoid a "busy" or "cluttered" design. Furthermore, the main commercially available plant species have become increasingly standardized by mass marketing, so that diversity is reduced *among regions* as well as at the site-specific scale. Dead plants, which in self-sustaining communities form important habitat, are usually removed from gardens, further diminishing diversity.

Real biodiversity is not merely about the *numbers* of species, however. It is about richness of interconnections *among* species. These interconnections take ages of coevolution to develop and cannot be recreated instantly in a garden. Plants brought together from different regions in a garden add visual diversity and may give great pleasure but remain akin to a diverse collection of animals in a zoo, separate and unable to interact. They do not support the great web of pollinators, predators, browsers, and symbionts

Figure 0.5   Is this a warning sign? (*Photo:* Kim Sorvig.)

that revolves around plants in their native habitats. When even a diverse *collection* replaces a biodiverse *community*, there is real ecological loss. Local richness and regional identity are diminished. There is increasing evidence that these localized losses add up to something global, especially where the loss involves vegetative cover on a cumulatively enormous scale. (See p. 99)

Natural "Look" and Ecological Function: A Paradox?

At the heart of landscape design are some expectations that are remarkably resistant to change: our expectations about the *appearance* of landscapes. Conventionally, aesthetic choices about the *style* of landscape are seen as unrelated to resource costs or environmental impact. But some styles require much higher investments in control than others. As sustainability focuses concern on the environmental costs of constructing landscapes, controversy over the appro-

Figure 0.6 Conventional and cheap attitudes toward landscaping abound—and often consume or destroy natural ecosystems. (*Photo:* Kim Sorvig.)

priate appearance of sustainable landscapes has flared. Should a sustainable landscape look untouched by human hands—a difficult task for the contractor? Should it, at the other extreme, look like an "ecology machine," the way some sustainable houses sprout high-tech engineered appendages?

A number of studies have shown that humans seem to prefer a fairly specific type of landscape form: large, well-spaced trees over grass or low ground cover, without much shrub layer or understory: the type of wooded environment commonly called "parklike."[56] Many landscape design traditions, notably the Olmstedian one, reproduce this type of vegetation, for which there are several natural prototypes. One natural parklike landscape is the African savannah, and perhaps the most influential theory uses that fact to explain why human landscape preferences seem almost fixated on parklands. Biophilia, biologist E. O. Wilson's concept of an innate attraction to

and interest in other living things,[57] says that humans evolved in the savannah and have been trying to re-find or re-create it ever since. (The fact that significant percentages of humanity love and choose to live in forests, deserts, mountains, or on seacoasts suggests that the truth isn't quite so simple, but the effect is certainly powerful.) Alex Wilson has summarized ways of incorporating biophilia and biomimicry into architectural, interior, and landscape design in an excellent EBN article.[58]

The intensely personal feelings involved in this controversy are strong evidence for the depth of human attachment to specific landscapes. Almost everyone who cares about landscapes, whether as professional, client, or amateur, has preconceptions about what sustainable landscapes ought to look like. These biases—and unresolved differences among them—strongly affect the work of the landscape professional: how we work, and whether we get work. This controversy is worth exploring briefly here.

THE HAND OF THE DESIGNER

A common definition of "natural" is "untouched by human hands." Where landscapes serve natural or ecological purposes, should the hand of a designer (or builder) be evident? Storm-water ponds, for instance, are sometimes designed to look like natural ponds with undulating edges planted with native wetland species. One example is the storm-water wetland at Fort Devens Federal Medical Center in central Massachusetts. The work of Carol R. Johnson Associates of Boston, this carefully engineered series of ponds looks as if it had always been there.

Landscape theorists like Rob Thayer, author of *Grey World, Green Heart,* have questioned whether concealing the designer makes sense. For example, applying a wild riverbank plant association verbatim to an urban drainage swale ignores its human origins, according to Thayer. Making such a constructed ecosystem look "natural" does not necessarily improve its sustainability. In fact, Thayer suggests that "sustainability requires neither the disguise nor the elimination of human influence."

On the contrary, says Thayer, because sustainable landscapes represent a higher level of complexity than "cosmetic" landscapes and incorporate ecological relationships that may be hard to observe, they demand "conspicuous expression and visible interpretation, and that is where the creative and artistic skills of the landscape architect are most critically needed."[59] Thayer refers to cosmetic attempts to make engineering look less engineered as "greenwash." Like many others, he sees the desire to hide the mechanical systems that support modern life as unreasoning, a NIMBY ("Not in My Backyard") attitude that wants the benefits of development but none of the costs.

One thoughtful theory about whether human design and management should be visible in the landscape is Joan Nassauer's "cues to care."[60] She argues that completely unmanaged ecosystems appear messy —to modern human eyes at least—and uncared for. Rather than tidy up whole parklands, Nassauer suggests designing and maintaining border transition areas that show that people care for the place. In some cases, making the human hand visible, even as simply as a mowed threshold between developed areas and protected ones, enhances visitors' respect for the wilder landscape.

Other landscape thinkers agree that the mechanics or infrastructure of built landscapes should not be hidden—in fact, should be revealed. William MacElroy and Daniel Winterbottom, faculty members in the Department of Landscape Architecture at the University of Washington, have coined the phrase "infra-garden" to describe a landscape that supports ecological and social values while incorporating landscape art.[61] As an example they cite Waterworks Gardens in Renton WA, by environmental artist Lorna Jordan.[62] Here, fanciful grottoes and basalt slabs adorn a stormwater wetland that treats runoff from several parking lots. But Richard Hansen, a Colorado-based sculptor and landscape architect, sees Waterworks Garden as "a shotgun wedding of environmental engineering overlaid by grottoes and other large decorative elements." Hansen argues for "a better interweave—a sculptural presence integrated with an ecological process."

Another ecologically functional landscape with a sculptural form is the stormwater garden at the Water Pollution Control Laboratory in Portland OR, designed by landscape architect Robert Murase,

Figure 0.7   Renton WA "infra-garden" makes storm water visible, overlaid with garden art. Surroundings worked against naturalistic design. (*Project:* Lorna Jordan. *Photo:* Daniel Winterbottom.)

working as part of a team of hydrologists and engineers. Runoff from a fifty-acre neighborhood uphill of the site flows to a retention/settling pond, eventually soaking into the soil or emptying into the Willamette River.

This utilitarian aim is expressed as sculptural form. The one-acre pond's upper and lower cells form converging circles. A stone-lined, curving concrete flume—an abstraction of a glacial moraine or the curve of a river—juts into the upper cell. When stormwater pours into the flume, the stones dissipate the energy in the water and allow solids to settle out; the water then seeps through weep holes in the side of the flume. Stones from the flume "spill out" and form a semicircular basalt wall that defines the second, lower pond. Although the landscape fulfills important ecological functions, Murase's design conceals neither the designer's hand nor his intent to create sculptural form on the land.

"Eco-revelatory Design"

If hiding the designer's influence is one side of a coin, making ecological processes visible is the other. Many highly engineered landscapes (as well as quite a number of naturalistic gardens) *hide* the ecological processes that go on around us. Stormwater (which, after all, is just rainwater running downhill) is one of those ecological processes. Before Murase's stormwater garden was built, neighborhood stormwater ran in a sewer and emptied directly into the river—out of

Figure 0.8 This Portland storm-water garden uses artistic form to reveal paths of runoff through the urban environment. (*Project:* Robert Murase. *Photo:* Scott Murase.)

sight, out of mind. The stormwater flume and pond, in essence, takes stormwater out of the murky underground realm of drains and pipes and "daylights" it, revealing it in the landscape.

"Eco-revelatory design" is a label that has been applied to such landscapes by the University of Illinois Landscape Architecture Department.[63] The department conceived a traveling exhibit of projects, design approaches, and elements that "reveal and interpret ecological phenomena, processes and relationships."⊃ Human influence is also revealed and interpreted as one part (not necessarily harmonious) of the ecosystem, in contrast with the desire to hide all trace of human work. The concept has been contentious; conventional naturalistic designers dislike the look, while some landscape architects view "eco-revelatory" as another word for making business as usual pretty.

Although he did not use the term, the spirit of eco-revelatory design was simply and eloquently expressed by John Lyle. In 1994 a visitor to Lyle's newly completed Institute for Regenerative Studies noticed a compost pile in plain view and asked why he had not bothered to screen it. "We don't want to screen things," said Lyle. "We want to *see* things. A lot of ecological problems come from hiding the way things really work."

That spirit is behind the Portland stormwater garden. By making stormwater visible, it teaches visitors about water's place in urban ecosystems. Threaded through this book are many other built landscapes that are equally honest about what they are and what they do.

The Portland and Renton examples each contrast with naturalistic landscapes, raising some important questions. The Portland garden's form and appearance are directly linked to the physical dynamics that govern water; it reveals these dynamics in a clearly constructed context, not a simulated stream. The Renton landscape allows environmental engineering to be seen (although it relies, not on gravity, but a 2,000 gpm pump), decorating it with garden-esque structures and forms. In neither case will vegetation be allowed to overgrow the site, nor will water be allowed to carve its own channels. In fact, as with most built landscapes, considerable effort and expense will be spent in *preventing* these ecological processes from changing the form of the landscape. The Renton infra-garden puts an artistic veneer over both the stormwater "problem" and its engineering "solution." The Portland garden relates engineering control to natural process, although at a level considerably simplified from actual ecosystem processes.

If "ecology" is taken in the scientific sense of large-scale complex processes, these projects, like Lyle's compost heap, are less about revealing ecology than about refusing to hide human influence. By strict definition, "eco-revelatory" would apply best to nature trails, where an educational path points out elements of an existing ecosystem and, among other things, human effects on it. Does this mean that sustainable design should always look like a nature trail? Since its earliest days, ecological design has been accused of being all ecology and no design. The authors do not believe this is so. What is critical is to be clear about what is actually being revealed, and why.

The hand of the designer can be as heavy on the land as a highway interchange or strip mine. It can also be a delicate interfingering of influence, as in a Japanese garden, where the artist's touch is visible but only to thoughtful observation. (The difference, frequently, is in the contractor's level of skill, so often overlooked.) To argue that human influence should *never* be hidden, without also asking whether that influence is destructive or sustainable, is to trivialize the complexity of relations between humans and the rest of the world.

Form Follows Function in Nature, Too

There is at least one strong reason to argue *against* artificially maintained naturalism as the only "look" for sustainable landscapes. The "natural" appearance of an Olmsted park or a Japanese garden is maintained by considerable inputs of energy and materials. Especially where this maintenance is mechanized, those resource inputs are sustainability concerns. If not hiding human influence reduces these inputs, it contributes to a sustainable landscape. However, there is strong evidence that some human landscapes do exactly the opposite: their form actually increases the costs of maintaining them and, in some cases, even prevents them from serving ecological functions.

The pipes and pumps of a stormwater system are a useful example. At some level, they substitute for the streams and wetlands of a watershed, fulfilling some functions (water transport) and failing others (aquatic habitat diversity, soil infiltration). The simplified forms of environmental engineering structures reveal, more than anything else, that ecological systems are far more multidimensional and complex than human engineering. Detailed study over the past two or three decades is showing more and more clearly that the complex *forms* of natural systems are essential to their functioning.

The attempt to straighten rivers and give them regular cross-sections is perhaps the most disastrous example of this form-and-function relationship. The natural river has a very irregular form: it meanders, spills across floodplains, and leaks into wetlands, giving it an ever-changing and incredibly complex shoreline. These irregularities allow the river to accommodate variations in water level and speed. Pushing the river into tidy geometry destroys functional capacity and results in disasters like the Mississippi floods of 1927 and 1993 and, more recently, the unnatural disaster of Hurricane Katrina. (A $50 billion plan to "let the river loose" in Louisiana recognizes that the "controlled" Mississippi is washing away twenty-four square miles of that state annually.[64]) Reducing irregularities of shape also decreases the variety of habitats available and cuts down on diversity of life in the river. Putting a stream into a pipe has an even more drastic simplifying effect, at the expense of multidimensional function.

In this book, we document the fact that, when grading slopes, the stiff geometry that humans favor actually *increases* soil erosion and slope failure. We note that natural wetlands have quite specific forms and locations and that created wetlands do not function properly unless these forms are approximated. We point out that the branching form of wild plants optimizes their ability to compete for sunlight and soil resources, plus their ability to clean pollutants from air and water. Where "the hand of the designer" goes too far in altering these forms, ecological function is affected, most often negatively.

Since the 1970s, the forms that make ecosystem function possible have been recognized as a specific mathematical type, called "fractals."[65] The branching patterns of trees are one example of fractal shapes. The name comes from the fact that these forms usually consist of endlessly repeated *fractions* of the whole, which create the overall form by growth over time. In the case of a tree, this basic element would be a single branch *and* its branching angle, proportionally repeated at many scales. River systems, landform surfaces, clouds, and whole plant communities follow fractal geometries because their function demands it. Human blood vessels and bronchial tubes have fractal patterns, too, which maximize delivery of blood or air; disruption of these patterns is diagnostic of serious illnesses, such as cancer.[66] Similarly, straightening a river or turning an undulating hillside into a constant 3 percent slope undermines ecological *function* because it changes environmental *form.*

The forms of natural systems also have documented effects on human beings. Studies in hospitals have shown that a view of trees or other natural features improves patient recovery time and overall health when released; views of structures and machinery have no such effect. Views of natural surroundings lower blood pressure, decrease the patient's need for painkillers, and lessen the mental confusion that often goes with injury or serious illness. These benefits come from merely *seeing* the scenery, not going out into it. In fact, a photo or realistic painting of a landscape provides similar benefits, so the effect is clearly a visual one.[67] This strongly suggests that Olmsted was right: naturalistic scenes have social benefits and are worth including in cities and preserving in undeveloped areas. If hard-nosed hospital administrators are increasingly paying to design buildings that give each patient a landscape view, shouldn't landscape professionals heed this research as well?

Thus the forms that "naturalism" tries to preserve or simulate are intimately linked to the ecological functioning of landscapes, as well as to human health and social benefits. Because the discovery of fractal mathematics is so recent, design theorists may be forgiven for continuing to treat natural form as random or irrelevant. In labeling as romanticism and nostalgia any attempt to mimic natural form, however, they reveal their ignorance of current science. For those concerned with sustainability, the relationship between natural form and ecological function needs to be revisited. Although real understanding of this relationship is still developing, it is quite clear that it is far more than a backward-looking aesthetic.

The Appearance of Sustainability

So what *does* the sustainable landscape look like?

Our most honest answer is that neither we nor anyone else really knows. We can offer the following suggestions:

- The sustainable landscape does not *exclude* human presence or even human engineering. It does not, however, blindly *glorify* human intervention, nor equate gentle human influence with massive human domination.

- The sustainable landscape does not waste energy or resources on trying to *disguise* human influence. Rather, it *eliminates* (functionally, not just visually) those influences that are in fact destructive or disruptive. Other influences it reveals and even celebrates. In revelation and celebration, it becomes an artistic expression.

- The sustainable landscape follows natural and regional form whenever this can improve the ecological functioning of a built or restored landscape. It builds nature-mimicking forms primarily because these harbor rich diversity of life and ecological function, and secondarily because many people prefer the visual effect.

- The sustainable landscape integrates and balances human geometries with natural ones. It is not enough to allow natural form to take the leftover spaces; spatial and visual integration between nature's fractal forms and humanity's Euclidean ones is essential. The means to this integration are those of the arts as well as of the sciences.

- The sustainable landscape is unlikely to be dominated by the visually simple and near-sterile extremes of urban or engineered space. It is likely to incorporate elements of urban space as people transform cities and industries to a more sustainable model.

- The appearance of a naturalistic landscape often contributes to ecological function, but does not guarantee it. For this reason, neither naturalistic nor sustainable constructed landscapes should ever be viewed as substitutes for wild places,[68] which will remain critically important no matter how "ecological" built landscapes become—or appear.

What does this mean for the practicing landscape professional? First and foremost, that the sustainable landscape will have room for creativity and diversity, perhaps even more so than the conventional styles that dominate our work today. It means, as great landscape design always has, an integration of the whole person—the supposedly opposite technical and artistic sides—in the work process. It means there will be less of a premium on clever ability to cover up compost bins or valve boxes, and more demand for people who can visualize and build integrally with the site. It means that fewer forms in the landscape will be oversimplified mechanical surfaces, and more will be interfingered in three dimensions, difficult to build well except by hand. It means that the appearance of the landscape will be influenced very directly by careful thought about resources and methods used to build it. It means, we hope, a wave of creativity rising to meet one of humanity's most important challenges.

Greenwash and Related Deceptions

Growing public concern about planetary life-support systems has prompted some designers, developers, and public agencies to do something about it—while others think it enough to *appear* to be doing something. The latter is "greenwash," which should not be confused with landscapes, natural or constructed, that perform genuine ecological functions. Greenwash is for designers who want on the "eco" bandwagon without the headstrong unpredictability of the horse that pulls that wagon—ecosystem dynamics.

Examples of landscape greenwash abound. They include "boutique wetlands," carefully positioned, *très chic* installations that look like functioning wetlands but depend entirely on artificial support systems.

Tanner Springs Park, a new park in downtown Portland OR, is an example. Built in memory of a stream now entombed in an underground culvert, the park collects the stormwater to maintain what looks like a small wetland. Storing what it collects in an underground cistern, it requires little or no city water. That's good. Recirculating stormwater through cleansing sand and wetland plants, it demonstrates how water is filtered in nature. That's good, too. But the park is not connected to any watershed, nor does it empty (except when extreme storms cause the cistern to overflow) into the Willamette River.[69] The park is only *stylistically* a wetland. That's deceptive.

Memories of vanished pastoral scenes underlie many greenwash landscapes. Extensive technology mimics the look without the function. In St. Louis, historic Forest Park boasts a man-made river. One of the most technically ambitious hydraulic engineering projects in any park in the world creates something called, with no apparent irony, River Returns, which looks as though it has always been there. The 2.5-mile constructed waterway roughly follows the historic course of the River des Peres, which since the 1930s has been buried in a huge concrete culvert. A team of engineers, hydrologists, and landscape architects constructed a convincing replica of the now-invisible des Peres, planting the banks with native wildflowers to complete the illusion.

Does it really make sense in the twenty-first century to create an imitation of a vanished river? This is something quite different from "daylighting" and restoring streams in cities—for example, restoring the natural meanders and floodplain of Buffalo Bayou in Houston. Forest Park is not a restored stream; it's a facsimile—and a profligate one at that. It takes *1.5 million gallons* of city tap water daily to keep the illusion convincing. Given the resource costs of building a 2.5-mile water feature today, why not give it a contemporary design that celebrates its ingenious technology?

Greenwashing may make some citizens feel that they are doing something to help restore local environmental systems. But boutique systems don't really restore much—they just look as if they do. They spread *ecological disinformation*: by lulling the public into thinking something substantive has been done, they dissipate the energy needed to undertake real ecological restoration.

Successful ecological design focuses on deciding what functions a given built landscape should perform and designing for those, not by setting out to achieve a certain look. Although the fractal forms of nature clearly have functional powers, natural functions can often fit into geometric shapes. The *illusion* of natural, long-established landscape can be costly and unnecessary.

A more subtle form of greenwash occurs when isolated buildings or sites are described as "green." Although energy efficient and built with minimum site disruption, these projects are undermined by their very isolation. Distance from mass transit or any

Figure 0.9 Tanner Springs Park in Portland OR, a "boutique wetland." Though totally artificial, it is designed to simulate a functioning wetland. (*Project:* Atelier Dreseitl. *Photo:* George Hazelrigg.)

Figure 0.10 The River Returns (St. Louis): rather than "daylighting" the actual river, culverted below Forest Park, this facsimile was built, an example of "greenwash." (*Project:* St. Louis Development Corporation. *Photo:* Scott Avetta.)

other low-impact form of transportation ensures high resource costs, no matter how efficient their internal workings. When the building materials for a 15,000-square-foot mansion are trucked miles up logging roads, and the owner arrives by helicopter, the result is far from green. Custom suburban homes suffer, to a lesser extent, the same distance-based problem.[70]

A related issue is the attempt to portray modular and prefabricated buildings as "green." To be sure, there are real efficiencies when buildings are produced in a factory-like setting. Efficient construction tools can be used, scrap can easily be recycled, and workers may not need to drive to work. However, trucking the structure cross-country to the site, and placing it once there, requires heavy energy inputs. The need for a straight line of unimpeded movement for something as large as a house usually means significant extra land clearance. (Structures built as small assemblies, moved onto the site for final setup, are quite different.) Standardizing structures necessarily reduces the ability to make sensitive adjustments to fit building to site. Although probably not utter greenwash, the greenness of such systems appears overrated.

Another problematic claim is exemplified by *Big and Green: Toward Sustainable Architecture in the 21st Century*, a 2003 exhibition in Washington DC.[71] While many of the fifty or more skyscraper projects featured in the exhibit had innovative features for ventilation, cooling, water management, and so on, calling their *overall* performance "green" seems highly debatable. Plants under glass were supposed to serve ecological functions such as water purification. It was evident from the drawings that the soil volumes allowed by the architects were woefully inadequate even to support the trees shown, let alone to produce a functioning ecosystem.

Besides unworkable details, there were two issues of scale. First, natural systems, such as wetlands, take a specific amount of space to process a given volume of water; compressing such systems into small spaces, as high-rise real estate demands, is dubious. Second, most of today's large buildings, whether skyscraper or big-box retail warehouse, function as unitary objects that are entirely the wrong scale to work with nature. Shadowing and wind-tunnel effects of tall buildings almost always decrease ecological functionality of large areas nearby, as do the monolithically impervious footprints of horizontal big-box structures. None of these giant buildings could survive without importing resources—food, water, energy—from a large supporting landscape.

Although it is unclear whether natural systems *require* specific natural or fractal forms, it is unquestionable that they are scale dependent. Green solutions cannot simply be scaled up until they are Big. Concentrating population in urban areas without productive landscapes already disrupts environmental resilience. The demand for "big, tall, and all under one roof" is a symptom of that overconcentration. The intellectual temptation to think giant buildings can be "greened" needs a reality check.

"Greenwash" is not a term to be used lightly. For one thing, it implies a deliberate attempt to mislead. Far more of the kind of problems discussed in this section result, we suspect, from incompletely thinking through basic assumptions, the kinds that should be questioned before design begins. Is this project really needed? Is this really an appropriate place for such land use? Is this the deepest cut in resource consumption that is possible, or merely whittling off enough to give bragging rights?

No project is perfectly sustainable, and no one should cast stones without thinking carefully. A final example serves to underline this point.

A number of recent articles have tried to make sustainability sexier: green *and* gorgeous, as one was titled.[72] Some manufacturers fear that calling their product "green" will associate it with aging hippies, ugly homemade shanties, and tofu-only diets—a kind of reverse greenwashing. But the attempt to "help environmentalism go upscale" is paradoxical. At one level, if sustainability doesn't shed its back-to-basics image and get some glamour, how will it ever catch on in consumer society? Excessive consumerism and its massive distribution systems, however, are clearly unsustainable. The all-luxury-all-the-time expectations of "upscale" markets amplify that problem. Green and glamorous is a difficult balance.

Until life-cycle performance analysis of sustainable projects becomes common, "greenwash" may remain one of those things that "I can't define, but I know it when I see it." Meanwhile, it is important not to rack up a few "better-than-usual" features and contentedly proclaim the whole project Sustainable with a capital S.

Rethinking Special Landscape Types for Sustainability

Almost any landscape's environmental performance can be improved, but several specific landscape types have recently attracted extra efforts. These land uses may have special "fit" with sustainable techniques, may cause extra problems if designed conventionally, or may typically be owned by environmentally attuned people.

UNIVERSITY CAMPUSES

College faculty have long been "talking the talk" of environmental responsibility. Academia's physical landscapes, by and large, have not kept pace. The traditional campus—trees amid vast manicured lawns and annual beds—is resource consumptive and habitat poor. The "weedy, wooly look" of a naturalized campus is at odds with the traditional groves of academe and requires reeducation to be accepted.[73]

Some campuses have created prototypes worth following. The Center for Regenerative Studies at Cal Poly Pomona (Figure 0.1) is a model sustainable campus. University administration initially misjudged its value, but today its future looks brighter. The School of Architecture and Landscape Architecture at Penn State University installed an extensive system of parking-lot bioswales, native plantings, and a green classroom and studio building.[74] Sustainability commitments are also reflected in the Center for Watershed Stewardship, a collaboration of foresters and landscape architects.

At Shenyang Architectural University in northern China, seven acres of working rice paddies challenge the artificial separation between designed landscapes and food production, between campus and countryside. This working landscape (by Turenscape, Beijing) includes strikingly patterned pedestrian paths and a student park among the paddies. Students participate in local herbicide- and pesticide-free farming methods, producing rice and vegetables consumed in the college cafeteria. Frogs and loach, a fish that eats

mosquito larvae, inhabit the fields during the wet cycle.[75]

Historically, food-producing campuses (especially at agricultural colleges) were common, but Shenyang is unusual among modern universities. Growing food on campus, with few chemicals, reduces its embodied energy and follows an international trend toward locally grown food. Campuses like Shenyang's could become links in what European designers call CPULs: Continuous Productive Urban Landscapes.[76]

Campus landscapes form venues for environmental learning. Some landscape architecture and architecture departments involve their students in tangible "greening" projects. Temple University Ambler campus and the University of Oregon contain fine examples of design-build projects accomplished by the students.

Landscape architect Meg Calkins suggests several green campus guidelines:

- Redefine public ideals of campus beauty.
- Limit lawn to culturally significant areas; promote native plantings.
- Use the campus to teach environmental literacy.
- Coordinate with facilities operations and maintenance.
- Cultivate support at the highest levels of administration.[77]

The movement toward green campuses goes well beyond the landscape, of course. As Peggy Bartlett, editor of *Sustainability on Campus*, points out, "Campuses across the United States alone represent an enormous investment in buildings and land, and therefore how [universities] maintain and build physical plant, engage in buying practices, dispose of waste, and consume energy is critically important to the environmental health of the broader society."[78]

"GREEN BURIAL" TO PRESERVE AND RESTORE LAND

Conventional cemeteries are extensive landscapes and, by and large, are among the most sterile landscapes imaginable: flat planes of grass with graves in industrial rows, often 1,000 per acre. Adorning the graves with plastic flowers is eerily appropriate, for these are truly deathly places. What a difference from the great

Figure 0.11 Shenyang University, China: sustainable rice paddies dissolve the separation between ornamental campus and food-producing landscape. (*Project:* Turenscape. *Photo:* Turenscape.)

nineteenth-century landscape cemeteries like Mt. Auburn in Boston, with its rolling topography and lush forest canopies!

Making cemeteries sustainable requires changing cultural attitudes, a potentially uncomfortable discussion. Conventional burial bears a disquieting resemblance to toxic waste disposal.[79] The body is pumped full of toxic embalming fluids to guard against natural processes of decay, then hermetically sealed in a coffin to prevent contact with soil, water, or microorganisms: it is to be utterly removed from the cycle of life. Cremation might seem more "ecological," but it requires large inputs of fossil fuels and releases air pollutants.

Frightening as bodily decay is to many people, we are part of that cycle. Some individuals and cultures have celebrated this: the painter Edvard Munch wrote,

"From my rotting body, flowers shall grow and I am in them and that is eternity."[80] Green cemeteries return to simple, un-embalmed burial in wood caskets or even shrouds.

Greener treatment of the body and of the landscape are parallel issues. Green cemeteries address both issues by burial in landscapes that are then reforested. The Natural Death Centre, a British nonprofit, began with a single cemetery in 1993. Today there are ninety.

Only one such cemetery presently operates in North America, although others are planned. At Ramsey Creek, near Westminster SC in the Appalachian foothills, graves are scattered throughout an existing forest, which, aside from walking paths, is under conservation easement. Gravestones are simple rocks from the immediate watershed. All plantings

Figure 0.12 Shenyang students experience direct connection with their landscape and their food source. (*Project:* Turenscape. *Photo:* Turenscape.)

must be native to the region. As the cemetery's Web site explains: "The use of the woodland as an environmentally conscious graveyard will help preserve the ecosystem intact—[preservationists can] tap into the $20 billion per year funeral industry to provide funds [for] endowments that save and restore beautiful land that might otherwise be lost to development."[81]

Joe Seehy, founder of the Green Burial Council, points out how graveyards and nature sanctuaries overlap: their intent to preserve land in perpetuity. Many states require that cemeteries be managed under long-term trusts. Land trusts have closely parallel organization and almost always need sources of funding. People routinely pay large amounts of money for tiny plots in sterile conventional cemeteries. The same money can fund protection for landscapes disturbed only by the occasional, carefully managed burial and a few visitors.[82]

Figure 0.13 At Ramsey Creek cemetery in the Appalachian Mountains, the deceased decompose naturally in the soil of a trust-protected woodland. (*Project:* Memorial Ecosystems. *Photo:* Sam Wang.)

Seehy notes that although he expected people to be squeamish about discussing this concept, his experience has actually been just the opposite. "People find it liberating," he says. "They are looking for meaningful alternatives to the conventional funeral industry." Green cemeteries offer such an alternative.

SKI AREAS

Downhill skiing requires clear slopes, often carved out of some of the nation's wilder landscapes. Their impact on wildlife, erosion, and visual quality can be significant. In addition, a large ski area like Aspen uses 45 million gallons of water each season for snowmaking and other purposes.[83]

Global warming seriously threatens the ski industry; US areas have declined in number from 727 in 1984 to 478 today, often due to waning snow pack. The National Ski Area Association (NSAA) introduced an environmental charter in 2000, updated in 2005. Aspen Skiing Company produced one of the first LEED-certified buildings; in 2006, 22 ski areas were 100 percent wind or solar powered.

The voluntary NSAA charter lists techniques to decrease the environmental impact of skiing. Water used in snow making can be recaptured, not only for ski area reuse but for summer uses, such as maintaining stream flow; grading soil moguls requires less snow cover (and less water use); ski-trail signage and snack-bar cups can educate the public. Forest clearing remains an issue unless everyone turns to cross-country, but short of such drastic measures, ski companies are reducing their environmental footprint.

One aspect of NSAA's approach is worth copying: their online database of case studies, keyed to each technique in the charter, promotes sustainable design to members and to broader audiences.

ECO-RESORTS, PARKS

In many national parks, such as Zion and Yosemite, pressures from increasing numbers of visitors has forced reassessment of transportation and facilities. A natural-gas shuttle system, for example, has replaced almost all private-car access to Zion, dramatically improving visitor experience and reducing impacts on the park.[84] Public-sector landscapes, of-

ten overlooked in glamour-focused professional publicity, are often sustainability models.

These changes are not without critics. At Yosemite, a $440 million project balances resource protection with public access, but has been assailed as for-profit development excluding all but the rich.[85] Less camping and more hotel rooms will be provided—but where 80 percent of 1970s visitors stayed overnight, today 80 percent are day-trippers. The plan includes a shuttle, removing a dam to let the Merced River flow through the park, and installing raised boardwalks to protect the floodplain while accommodating visitors.

Even with sustainable facilities, tourism's sheer numbers have real impacts on some of the world's best-loved landscapes. This issue sparked a national debate in 2000 when the Sierra Club sued to require the Hawaii Tourism Authority to perform an environmental impact assessment before spending public funds to attract more tourists.[86] Although the case was dismissed in 2002, the question remains: do heavily visited landscapes have a carrying capacity, and if so, what roles do design, planning, and policy play in making them sustainable?

AMENITY MIGRATION

Exceptional wild landscapes were once strictly visit-and-leave destinations. Today, however, people increasingly live in these landscapes, empowered by communication and transportation technology. These are "amenity migrants."

Laurence Moss, who coined the term "amenity migration," describes it this way: as the biosphere becomes degraded by unsustainable development, "a very influential but growing minority of humankind is seeking what remains, especially the best of it. Owning high-amenity landscapes or proximate property now constitutes a global driving force."[87]

Amenity migration is two-edged. Those communities that have protected their amenity landscapes, and that mandate sustainable development, are seeing economic booms. But in many desirable places, existing communities are overwhelmed by new people and money. Similar conflicts occur in the so-called Urban Wildland Interface where wildfires and residences collide (see p. 106).

Many amenity communities are leading markets for sustainable design. Yet privatization and intense development (green or otherwise) in fragile ecosystems give this trend a dark side. For both reasons, resort communities are a landscape type that bears watching.

Walkable Communities

The goals of sustainable design include human health, not just landscape preservation. Increasingly, sprawl landscapes are blamed for the US obesity epidemic. Of average Americans' daily trips, fewer than 6 percent are made on foot, according to the Federal Highway Authority. Reshaping the urban landscape toward walkability has become a focus for several research groups.[88]

Any planning initiative against sprawl will have major impacts on design work. Public spaces that encourage regular walking, but avoid overpaving, will require sustainable design and construction expertise.

Sustainable redesign of campuses, cemeteries, resorts, parks, and even The Suburbs is encouraging: the concept is maturing. Sustainable practices can be applied to a very wide range of landscape types, some of which offer more immediate incentive than others for this effort. The results can make a substantive change and be very stylish—or they can be all style and no substance. The ability to judge the difference, and to recognize the tradeoffs, is what makes the practical techniques of sustainability mean something in practice.

Resources

"Sustainability" in Context

General

Search Terms: sustainability OR environment OR ecology

Worldwatch Institute 800-555-2028, www.worldwatch.org/: Annual State of the World statistics.

Real Goods 800-762-7325, www.gaiam.com/realgoods/: On-site energy systems suppliers, consultants, training, books, including *Solar Sourcebook*.

Permaculture: A Designers' Manual Bill Mollison, 1988 Tagari Publications, Australia: Widely available at US booksellers; systematic, eccentric agriculture-focused techniques.

Alternatives Journal 866-437-2587, www.alternativesjournal.ca/: Canadian journal of environmental practice and theory.

E magazine 815-734-1242, www.emagazine.com/: General environmental magazine; covers restoration, materials, and maintenance.

Green Disk 1-888-GRN-DISK, http://gort.ucsd.edu/newjour/g/msg02279.html: Paperless environmental journal on disk; indexes to seventy related journals.

Cyberplaces/Architects First Source www.cyberplaces.com/: Links to anything about places—design, mapping, construction, etc.

Environmental Management Tools on the Internet Michael Katz and Dorothy Thornton, 1997 St. Lucie Press, Delray Beach FL

Geonetwork www.geonetwork.org/: Bookstore and information source.

Iris Communications 800-346-0104, www.oikos.com/: Bookstore and information source.

Island Press 800-828-1302, www.islandpress.org/, Washington DC: Not listed just because they're our publisher—wide-ranging list of books on applied and theoretical environmental issues.

Ethics and the Built Environment W. Fox, 2000 Routledge, New York

EnviroLink: The Online Environmental Community www.envirolink.org/: Access to thousands of environmental resources, news.

Ecology and Design: Frameworks for Learning B. Johnson and K. Hill, 2002 Island Press, Washington DC: Integrating ecological principles and design practices into teaching.

ecoDesign: The Sourcebook A. Fuad-Luke, 2002 Chronicle Books, San Francisco: Wide-ranging photo catalog; only three pages on "gardening" including solar-robotic mower and pedal riding mower!

Structure and Meaning in Human Settlements T. Atkin and J. Rykwert (eds.), 2005 University of Pennsylvania Museum, Philadelphia: Illustrates built environments across time and culture.

Landscape Architectural Graphic Standards L. Hopper (ed.), 2007 Wiley, New York: Extensive, highly condensed; some sustainability.

Landscape and Sustainability J. Benson and M. Roe, 2000 Spon Press, UK: Landscape as a *basis* for policy, science, and design.

The Cultural Creatives: How 50 Million People Are Changing the World P. Ray and S. Anderson, 2000 Three Rivers, New York: Study of demographic group most supportive of sustainable change.

Blessed Unrest: How the Largest Movement in the World Came into Being and Why No One Saw It Coming Paul Hawken, 2007 Viking, New York

The Environmental Impacts of Road Vehicles in Use: Air Quality, Climate Change, and Noise Pollution 1999 UK Department of the Environment, Transport, and the Regions, London

Ecology

Search Terms: ecology || forest ecology || aquatic ecology || desert ecology || soil ecology || activism AND ecology OR environment || environment publishers || deep ecology

Landscape Ecology Principles in Landscape Architecture Wenche Dramstad, James T. Olson, and Richard Forman, 1996 Island Press, Washington DC

Stalking the Wild Amaranth: Gardening in the Age of Extinction Janet Marinelli, 1998 Henry Holt, New York: Clear account, by garden lover, of damage and good that gardens do.

Restoration and Reclamation Review http://horticulture.coafes.umn.edu/vd/h5015/rrr.htm: University of Michigan Horticulture Science Department student online journal.

Foundation for Deep Ecology www.deepecology.org/: Important concepts, policies, publications.

Forging a West That Works: An Invitation to the Radical Center Quivira Coalition, Santa Fe NM, www.quiviracoalition.org/: Leading advocates of common cause between commercial land users and environmentalists.

Ecology.com: An Ecological Source of Information www .ecology.com/: General ecology information, science news, publications, and links.

Climate change

Search Terms: "LUCC" || climate change || global warming || land use + climate

Climate Science Research http://climatesci.colorado.edu/: Links to international research on landscape clearance and global warming.

Pielke Research Group http://cires.colorado.edu/science/group /pielke/: Active research on land use and climate change.

Human Impacts on Weather and Climate W. R. Cotton and R. A. Pielke, 2006, 2nd ed., Cambridge University Press, Cambridge

Vegetation, Water, Humans and the Climate: A New Perspective on an Interactive System P. Kabat et al. (eds.), 2004 Springer, Berlin

US Global Change Research Information Office www.gcrio.org/

Land Use and Global Climate Change: Forests, Land Management, and the Kyoto Protocol www.pewclimate.org/global -warming-in-depth/all_reports/land_use_and_climate _change/index.cfm: Prepared for Pew Center on Global Climate Change, June 2000.

Architecture 2030 www.architecture2030.org/, http://www.2010imperative.org/: Designers taking lead against global warming; 2010 is a curriculum-change program.

Adapting Buildings and Cities for Climate Change: A 21st Century Survival Guide S Roaf et al., 2005 Architectural Press, Oxford: Assumes global warming will happen and structures must change.

Green building

Search Terms: green building || green construction || sustainable building || LEED

Rocky Mountain Institute 970-927-3851, www.rmi.org/: Nonprofit research and education organization, especially strong on energy.

US Green Building Council 202-8287422, www.usgbc.org/: Promotes green building; publications; LEED.

GreenBuilding.com, www.greenbuilding.com/: Green building history, facts, resources, and links.

US EPA Green Building Web Site www.epa.gov/greenbuilding/: Wealth of green building information; resources for funding; national programs.

The HOK Guidebook to Sustainable Design Sandra F. Mendler, William Odell, and Mary Ann Lazarus, 2005, 2nd ed., Wiley, New York

Land and Natural Development (LAND) Code: Guidelines for Sustainable Land Development Diana Balmori and Gaboury Benoit, 2007 Wiley, New York

A Building Revolution: How Ecology and Health Concerns Are Transforming Construction D. M. Roodman and N. Lenssen, 1995 Worldwatch Institute, Washington DC

A Primer on Sustainable Building Dianna L. Barnett and Wm. D. Browning, 1995 Rocky Mountain Institute, Snowmass CO, 970-927-3851, www.rmi.org/

European Directory of Sustainable and Energy Efficient Building James and James Ltd: Annual directory.

Sustainable Building Technical Manual D. Gottfried and A. Osso, 1996:

Purchase loose-leaf from US Green Building Council; full text available at http://freshstart.ncat.org/articles/ ptipub.htm.

Building the National Parks: Historic Landscape Design and Construction Linda Flint McClelland, 1998 Johns Hopkins University Press, Baltimore

Green Building Materials: A Guide to Product Selection and Specification R. Spiegel and D. Meadows, 2006 Wiley, New York

Journal of Green Building http://www.collegepublishing.us/journal.htm

Building for a Future www.buildingforafuture.co.uk/

Environmental Building News **(EBN)** Brattleboro VT, 802-257-7300, www.buildinggreen.com/ecommerce/ebn.cfm?: *Essential* source about green building: methods, products, news, book reviews. Online by subscription; CD-ROM.

Smart Communities Network www.smartcommunities.ncat.org/: Resources, tools, links, "green" community success stories.

Who's Green: The Directory of Who's Green in the Design and Construction Field Ecotone LLC, Kansas City MO: Listings: firms (design, engineering, interior, consulting), green building organizations, nonprofits, green schools, and media.

Green Building Products: The GreenSpec Guide to Residential Building Materials A. T. Wilson et al., 2005 New Society Publishers, Brattleboro VT

Sustainable Construction: Green Building Design and Delivery C. J. Kibert, 2005 Wiley, New York

Green Building Project Planning and Cost Estimating: A Practical Guide for Constructing Sustainable Buildings A. Keenan and D. Georges, 2002 R. S. Means, Kingston MA: Cost data for green materials, components, and systems, special project requirements, financial analysis and incentives.

Regenerative Design Techniques: Practical Applications in Landscape Design P. Melby and T. Cathcart, 2002 Wiley, New York: Actually more about architecture than landscape.

Building for Life: Designing and Understanding the Human-nature Connection Stephen R. Kellert, 2005 Island Press, Washington DC: Proponent of "biophilic" design; criteria a bit vague, but inspiring.

Ecological Design Handbook F. Stitt (ed.), 1999 McGraw Hill, New York: Broad anthology of excerpts from other books.

Skinny Streets and Green Neighborhoods C. Girling and R. Kellett, 2005 Island Press, Washington DC: Good planning concepts.

Low-impact Development Design Strategies 1999 Prince George's County MD Dept. of Envir. Resources: Well integrated and illustrated; good section on public outreach.

Green Architecture Raj Barr-Kumar, 2003 Barr Intl LLC, Washington DC, www.barrarchitects.com/: Illustrates regional adaptations in many cultures.

Ecoregion-based Design for Sustainability R. G. Bailey, 2002 Springer, New York: Third in series (along with *Ecosystem Geography* and *Ecoregions*).

Planning and Design Strategies for Sustainability and Profit A. Pitts, 2004 Architectural Press, Oxford: International examples, businesslike attitude; mostly architecture.

The Not So Big House: A Blueprint for the Way We Really Live and *Outside the Not So Big House* Sarah Susanka (with J. Messervy), Taunton Press, Washington DC, various dates: See www .notsobighouse.com.: Trendsetting residential concepts combining sustainability and intimate spaces.

Construction

Search Terms: landscape construction || outdoor construction || construction || landscaping

Legal Daisy Spacing: The Build-a-Planet Manual of Official World Improvements Christopher Winn, 1985 Random House, New York: Probably the world's only *funny* book on landscape construction (hey, we tried)—and insightful, too.

Professional Land Care Network Herndon VA, 703-736-9666, www.landcarenetwork.org/cms/home.html

An Illustrated Guide to Landscape Design, Construction, and Management Gregory M. Pierceall, 1998 Interstate Publishers, Danville IL

An Introduction to Landscape Design and Construction Bartholomew J. Blake, 1998 Gower Publishing, Brookfield VT

Landscape Architecture Construction Harlow C. Landphair and Fred Klatt, 1998, 3rd ed., Prentice Hall, New York

Landscape Construction David Sauter, 1999 Delmar Publishers, Albany NY

Landscape Construction and Detailing Alan Blanc, 1996 McGraw-Hill, New York

Making Garden Floors: Stone, Brick, Tile, Concrete, Ornamental Gravel, Recycled Materials, and More P. Gilchrist, 2001 Lark Books, New York

Landscape Construction and Detailing: Articles in "Landscape Architecture" Magazine, 1910–1979 Bruce K. Ferguson, 1981 Vance Bibliographies, Monticello IL

The Handbook of Landscape Architectural Construction Maurice Nelischer, 1985, 2nd ed., Landscape Architecture Foundation, Washington DC

Public Works Research Institute (Japan) www.pwri.go.jp/: Environmentally oriented construction research, including roads.

Technology

Search Terms: landscape technology || technology

American Society of Agricultural and Biological Engineers 800-606-2304, www.asabe.org/: Publishes voluntary standards for machines, methods, materials; some relevant to landscape work.

Why Things Bite Back: Technology and the Revenge of Unintended Consequences Edward Tenner, 1996 Vintage, New York: Thought provoking, well documented on technology causing more trouble than it solves.

Chenier's Practical Math Dictionary Norman J Chenier, 1997 Chenier Educational Enterprises, Gladstone MI: A visual index makes it unusually easy to find formulas applicable to solving specific real-world problems.

Style and sustainability

Search Terms: sustainable living || sustainable home || eco living || eco friendly || biophilic design|| biomimicry

The Countryside Ideal: Anglo-American Images of Landscape M. F. Bunce, 1994 Routledge, New York: Analysis of attitudes toward look and function of US landscapes.

The Fractal Geometry of Nature Benoit Mandelbrot, 1983 W. H. Freeman, New York: Clear, revolutionary analysis of natural pattern as more than "random."

"The Experience of Sustainable Landscapes" Robert L. Thayer Jr., Fall 1989 *Landscape Journal*

"Toward a New Garden in Critiques of Built Works of Landscape Architecture" William MacElroy and Daniel Winterbottom, Fall 1997 *LSU School of Landscape Architecture* : On "infra-gardens."

Earth Easy Sustainable Living www.eartheasy.com/: Information on sustainable living, including live, grow, eat, play, wear, and give.

Eco-revelatory Design Exhibit University of Illinois Department of Landscape Architecture, www.gis.uiuc.edu/ecorev/: Exhibit catalog (special issue, *Landscape Journal*); fifteen projects, eight essays.

Emotional Design: Why We Love (or Hate) Everyday Things D. A. Norman, 2004 Basic Books, New York: Reminder that even sustainable design is not just functionality.

Last Child in the Woods: Saving Our Children from Nature-deficit Disorder R. Louv, 2005 Algonquin Books, New York: On human need for natural surroundings.

Planning, design, and management

Search Terms: land + (use OR planning OR management OR design) || land-use planning || landscape + (design OR management OR planning) || urban design

Clarence Stein Institute for Urban and Landscape Studies Cornell University, www.crp.cornell.edu/: Special interest in Ebenezer Howard and Garden Cities as influences on sustainability.

Planning Advisory Service http://www.planning.org/: Subscription-based research network.

Design with Nature Ian McHarg, 1995, reprint, Wiley, New York: Still the classic.

Environmental Management Handbook Sven-Olof Ryding, n.d.IOS Press, Amsterdam: International review of issues and technologies; summary for decision makers.

Risk-based Analysis for Environmental Managers K. A. Frantzen, 2002 Lewis Publishers, Boca Raton, FL

The Living Landscape: An Ecological Approach to Landscape Planning Frederick R. Steiner, 1991 McGraw-Hill, New York: Excellent planning-scale methods.

Best Development Practices Reid Ewing, 1996 American Planning Association, see www.planning.org

Conservation Design for Subdivisions Randal G. Arendt, 1996 Island Press, Washington DC

Deep Design: Pathways to a Livable Future David Wann, 1996 Island Press, Washington DC

Ecological Design Sym Van Der Ryn and Stuart Cowan, 1996 Island Press, Washington DC

Ecological Design and Planning Frederick Steiner and George F. Thompson, 1997 Wiley, New York

From Eco-cities to Living Machines: Principles of Ecological Design Nancy J. Todd and John Todd, 1994 North Atlantic Books, Berkeley CA

Green Development: Integrating Ecology and Real Estate Alex Wilson and Rocky Mountain Institute, 1998 Wiley, New York: A CD-ROM with case studies is also available.

Guiding Principles of Sustainable Design 1993 National Park Service Technical Information Center, Denver CO

Landscape Planning: Environmental Applications Wm. Marsh, 1997, 3rd ed., Wiley, New York

Our Ecological Footprint: Reducing Human Impact on the Earth M. Wackernagel and W. Rees, 1996 New Society Publishers, New York

Regenerative Design for Sustainable Development John T. Lyle, 1994 Wiley, New York

Social Consequences of Engineering Hayrettin Kardestuncer, 1979 Boyd and Fraser, New York

The Ecology of Place Timothy Beatley and Kristy Manning, 1997 Island Press, Washington DC

Time-saver Standards for Landscape Architecture: Design and Construction Data Charles W. Harris, Nicholas T. Dines, and Kyle D. Brown, 1998, 2nd ed., McGraw-Hill, New York

Earthscape: A Manual of Environmental Planning John Ormsbee Simonds, 1978 McGraw-Hill, New York

Recycling the City: The Use and Reuse of Urban Land R. Greenstein and Y. Sungu-Eryilmaz, 2004 Lincoln Institute of Land Policy, Cambridge MA

Construction Claims Monthly 800-274-6737, www.bpinews.com/const/pages/ccm.cfm: Newsletter of construction litigation, often environmental.

Landscape Architecture ASLA, Washington DC, 202-898-2444, www.asla.org/: Glossy project reportage; solid information on environmental practices.

Yes! Positive Futures Network, 800-937-4451, www.futurenet.org/: Quarterly, sustainability themed, urban design; nontoxic materials; watersheds.

Environmental Design Guide Royal Australian Institute of Architects Quarterly, EDG, www.architecture.com.au/i-cms/

Smart Communities Network www.smartcommunities.ncat.org/buildings/gbintro.shtml: Overview of green building, statistics, success stories, ordinances, links.

Environmental Organization Web Directory http://webdirectory.com/Science/Ecology/Environmental_Community_Living/

Planners Network www.plannersnetwork.org/: A good source of contacts for policy-level issues.

Planning Commissioners Journal 802-864-9083, www.plannersweb.com/

SmartGrowth Network 202-962-3623, www.smartgrowth.org/

Sustainable Communities Network www.sustainable.org/index.html

Virtual Library: Sustainable Development www.ulb.ac.be/ceese/meta/sustvl.html

Designer Shorts (Continuing Education) the Council of Landscape Architectural Registration Boards, www.clarb.org/ContinuingEducationRW.asp: Many courses relate to sustainability.

Greenmoney Journal 800-849-8751, www.greenmoney.com/: Quarterly; specifically includes green building, products, and energy.

Manufactured Sites: Rethinking the Postindustrial Landscape N. Kirkwood, 2001 Spon Press, New York

LandCadd 800-678-6565, www.eaglepoint.com/: Like other CAD, accurate quantities and simulations can improve sustainability.

Vectorworks Landmark, 410-290-5114, www.nemetschek.com/: Another landscape-specific CAD program.

Prairie Land Management 888-479-1760, www.habitatnow.com/: Restoration of marginal farmland.

Types of green landscapes

"Greening Federal Facilities" prepared by Alex Wilson and Building Green for US DOE, www.eren.doe.gov/femp/: All aspects of sustainable design, construction, and maintenance for government (including landscapes).

Sustainability on Campus P. Barlett and G. Chase (eds.), 2004 MIT Press, Cambridge MA: Curriculum and built-environment strategies.

Memorial Ecosystems 864-647-7798, www.memorialecosystems.com/: Green cemetery in Westminster SC.

Green Burial Council www.greenburialcouncil.org/: Nonprofit; ethical, sustainable burial process as means of facilitating landscape-level restoration and conservation.

"Toxic Burials: The Final Insult" Johnny P. Stowe, Elise Vernon Schnidt, Deborah Green, *Conservation Biology*, Dec 2001

"A New Option for Afterlife" EBN, Mar 1999

The Woodland Cemetery: Toward a Spiritual Landscape Caroline Constant, 1994 Byggforlaget, Stockholm

"A Green Way of Dying" Stephanie Ramp, www.newmassmedia.com/spring99/

"A Natural Death" William Thompson, LAM, Oct 2002, 74

Death Matters David Lee Schroeder, North Carolina State University, Master's Thesis, Spring 2002

Teamwork

Search Terms: sustainable collaboration || environmental collaboration || interagency OR teamwork

Growing a Business Paul Hawken, 1988 Simon and Schuster, New York: Both of Hawken's business books offer an important "ecological" alternative to the conventional dog-eat-dog view.

The Ecology of Commerce Paul Hawken, 1993 Harper, New York

Community-based planning

Search Terms: community-based planning || sustainability + teamwork

Community Stewardship Organizations (CSOs) 520-290-0969, www.sonoran.org/: Contacts, resources on forming CSOs to manage development.

Cultivating Community Success: Visions from the Heartland 1996 Heartland Center for Leadership Development, Lincoln NE, www.heartlandcenter.info

Divided Planet: The Ecology of Rich and Poor Tom Athanasiou, 1998 University of Georgia Press, Athens: Clearly links global economics and sustainability.

Streets of Hope: The Fall and Rise of an Urban Neighborhood Peter Medoff and Holly Sklar, 1994 South End Press, Boston

The Careless Society: Community and Its Counterfeits John McKnight, 1995 Basic Books, New York

The Ecology of Hope: Communities Collaborate for Sustainability Ted Bernard and Jora Young, 1997 New Society, New York

Toward Sustainable Communities Rachel Kaplan, Stephen Kaplan, and Robert Ryan, 1998 New Society, New York

Community and Consensus: Reality and Fantasy in Planning Howell S. Baum, 1994 Journal of Planning Education and Research, http://jpe.sagepub.com/

"How I Turned a Critical Public into Useful Consultants" Peter T. Johnson, *Harvard Business Review*, Jan–Feb 1993

"Rededicating Ourselves to Community" Jane E. Leonard, *Journal of Community Development Society* 25, no. 1 (1994)

Community-based Environmental Protection 202-566-2182, www.epa.gov/ecocommunity/

Community-based Resource Management, http://www.snre.umich.edu/ecomgt//collaboration.htm: Specific to Michigan, but useful examples.

Reclaiming Nature: Environmental Justice and Ecological Restoration J. K. Boyce et al., 2006 Anthem Press, New York

Principle I:
Keep Healthy Sites Healthy

The first rule of the tinkerer is to keep all the pieces.
—Aldo Leopold, quoted by E. O. Wilson, *Biophilia*

Every site resembles a living organism, and like organisms, sites vary in health. This chapter discusses what "site health" means, and methods for preserving it during construction. Like human health, site health is not easy to define in a simple formula. Prevention is usually more successful—and less expensive—than cure.

Protection of sites—particularly those with mature vegetation and healthy soils—is of increasingly critical importance because deforestation links to global climate change (see p. 14). Site protection can make local, cumulative differences.

Landscape construction that accidentally or deliberately damages a *healthy* site is doubly wasteful. While restoration methods can repair many site injuries, there is a point of no return, beyond which restoration is neither cost-effective nor ecologically sufficient. Mature trees needlessly destroyed in construction are not effectively "restored" by planting saplings, for example. Thus, the first principle of sustainable landscape construction is self-evident yet easily overlooked: *avoid harm to healthy sites.*

Protecting a healthy site requires care *throughout* the design and construction process, from initial reconnaissance through final cleanup. Sustainable *design* anticipates and integrates appropriate construction methods, influencing choices about siting, structures, and materials. The quality and coordination of such choices can make the difference between irreparable damage and minimal impact.

Discussed in This Chapter

Identifying healthy and unhealthy sites.
How site knowledge forms the basis for sustainable work.
Dealing with pre-construction impacts through teamwork.
General protection strategies applicable to any important site feature.
Protection of specific features like soil, vegetation, or water bodies.
Choice of construction equipment and construction planning.

What Is a Healthy Site?

"Health" is one of those conditions everyone knows when they see it, but which remains impossible to define completely. Despite this difficulty, it is important for both ecological and economic reasons to develop at least an operational definition of what "site health" means.

It is fairly easy to say when a site is *unhealthy*: stripped of topsoil by natural erosion or human carelessness, polluted by chemicals, supporting only a small percentage of the richness of plant and animal life found in the region, or overrun with invasive species, sick sites are often obvious eyesores.

Some site "illnesses" are brief ones, with quick recovery. A site drowned in sediment by a flood, or burned by a forest fire, may look unhealthy, but usually retains vitality and soon begins regrowth. In fact, many plant communities and soil types depend on such events for long-term health. A site that is healthy and has plentiful resources (water, soil fertility, sunlight) can recover from minor construction damage, too.

More serious ill health results when toxic chemicals are involved, or when soil is removed, massively eroded, compacted, or paved. Some plant and animal species invade the site in much the way that parasites, microbes, or even cancers invade the human body.[1]

The cumulative effect of small, normal stresses also affects site health. Individual factors like wind, temporary drought, or increased ultraviolet radiation can add up over time to weaken plant life that holds a site together. Human use of a site produces new stresses. A site that had limited resources to start with may be unable to adapt to added stress.

Like healthy humans, healthy sites are productive, have vitality enough to keep growing despite some stress, and generally have a satisfying "look" and "feel." The appearance of a site can tell much about its health. Some healthy sites, however, go through messy-looking phases, and some landscapes conventionally viewed as stylish conceal serious ill health. Conventional landscape aesthetics are not a reliable guide to site health. (See Figure I.1 and Figure I.2.)

Healthy ecosystems provide what have been called "environmental services," keeping air and water clean, improving local climate, and creating food—services on which human life depends.[2] Healthy sites also provide many amenities. Compared to landscapes cleared and flattened for convenience in construction, healthy sites have significantly higher property values (by at least 5–20 percent).[3]

Healthy sites are recognizable by several characteristics:

- They support *diversity* of plant and animal life adapted to the region and linked to one another in a web of interdependence.
- They are *seldom dominated exclusively by one species*, and especially not by species imported there by humans. (Criteria for agricultural sites are different, but crop monocultures are also unhealthy.)
- Their communities or ecosystems (soil, plants, and animals) are essentially *self-maintaining*, not de-

pendent on outside resources supplied by people.
- Their living species are *self-reproducing.*
- The geological portion of the site is *not changing too rapidly* to support the living community, nor poisoned or infertile.
- The site has sufficient vitality to *overcome* a variety of stresses.
- The community changes with age through a process called *succession.*

Succession is a regionally characteristic series of changes. Healthy meadow or bog may be superseded by healthy forest. Unlike invasion by imported species, succession is healthy. It is like the changes in a healthy human from infancy through adolescence, maturity, decline, and death—and in the case of plant communities, includes rebirth. Accelerating or holding back succession without weakening the site's health is one of the most sophisticated methods of site management. Excessively slow or fast succession, like unusual aging in people, can indicate ill health.

It is seldom up to a single construction or design professional to decide precisely how healthy a site is. However, if developers, designers, and contractors learn to *recognize* relatively healthy sites, such sites will be valued and protected more often. Recognition and protection of site health is increasingly required of landscape professionals.

Take a Role in "Pre-construction"

Prior to what is conventionally considered the beginning of either design or construction work, a great deal can happen to the site. The pre-construction actors are likely to be realtors, surveyors, developers, utility companies, and government agencies. Increasingly, projects stand or fall on the input of neighborhood groups as well.

Landscape professionals can influence most of these groups toward sustainable practice—but only if they form strong channels of communication and give input at the right time. Failing this, these same groups will act on the site, often by default, before landscape professionals are involved. Some standard practices—including hiring a landscape consultant

Figure I.1 Assessing site health visually can be misleading. This site fits the conventional image of landscape health, but it may use or pollute resources unsustainably. (*Photo:* Kim Sorvig.)

only at the last moment to "shrub up" an already completed design—attempt to disguise unsightly or unhealthy results. Although not easy, winning influence over land-use planning is critically important to sustainability. The teamwork required among landscape architect, contractor, architect (or other consultants), and client/user is a good place to start forging community connections.

Prevent "Pre-Clearance"

One very specific pre-construction practice is increasingly unacceptable in light of the clear links between vegetation loss and global warming (see p. 14). This is the practice of "pre-clearance"—bulldozing a site flat and removing all vegetation and much of the topsoil *before* putting up a For Sale sign. Although realtors clearly believe flattened sites are attractive to commercial buyers, pre-clearance is truly destructive. Convenient, perhaps, for a big box or parking lot, but what if a corporation wanted to create a model green headquarters? Much of the incentive, and many "environmental services," are now destroyed. We suspect that pre-clearance is an end run around development permit processes—if the site is cleared before the regulatory process begins, there is nothing left to regulate.

Sometimes pre-cleared sites lie naked and vacant for years, waiting for sale, planning, design, and construction. During that time, for absolutely no reason, all the air and water benefits of healthy plants and soils are lost.

Figure I.2 Messiness is commonly equated with ill health, but this site is growing back from flooding—an important part of a healthy life cycle in any floodplain. (*Photo:* Kim Sorvig.)

Site clearance should not only be kept to a minimum, but should not be done any longer *in advance* than truly necessary. Responsible, sustainability oriented developers will not pre-clear. Unfortunately, some conventional realtors and developers have to be threatened with legal penalties before they consider anything beyond their own interests. No site should *ever* be cleared until a *specific* master plan or design has been approved.

Do Your Homework First: Knowledge as Sustainability

Those who think that site analysis before design or construction is expensive need to consider the costs of ignorance, which are always far greater.

Figure 1.3 "Pre-clearance" destroys potential and actual site benefits, for reasons that aren't even commercially valid. (*Photo:* Kim Sorvig.)

There are two kinds of "homework" involved in protecting a healthy site. The information gained from each applies to every subsequent step of sustainable landscape work, from design through maintenance. The first involves attitude; the second, facts.

It is impossible to protect what you don't respect. Even with a strong love of nature, working on a site involves carefully setting priorities, and in many cases, reeducating clients and coworkers. Attitudes about preserving natural conditions have a strong influence on design and construction priorities. Is the desire for home soccer practice worth flattening the backyard? Is impressing the neighbors justification for using extra resources or replacing native plants with lawn? Choices like these are never easy and involve basic attitudes about human relationships to landscapes. This book's introduction includes thoughts about cultivating sustainable attitudes, as does the conclusion.

Between attitude and facts are concepts and models used to understand and organize complicated subject matter. Landscape ecology is one important concept whose influence continues to grow. Around 1994–95, at least five federal agencies developed land-management principles based on landscape ecological concepts.[4] These policies treat landscapes and ecosystems as nested systems at several scales, with fuzzy boundaries, interacting with other units to form the whole. A related conceptual system that is useful for understanding landscapes in a dynamic way is called complexity science, which studies and digitally models systems made up of many independent "agents."[5]

Even with respectful attitudes, protecting what you do not thoroughly understand is difficult. Information gathering is critical to sustainable work, from the earliest preliminary feasibility studies, through design and construction, and into maintenance. Data gathering, both informal *site reconnaissance* and technical *surveying*, benefits from a team effort, clear communication, and information sharing.

Reconnaissance should identify and evaluate site features *before* design begins. (In fact, this knowledge should inform selection of properties to develop, but rarely does.) Much reconnaissance is visual, observing and noting conditions without technical equipment. Published sources, such as soil and topography maps or land-use records, are also important in effective reconnaissance. Contractors usually carry out a separate reconnaissance just before bidding a contract. Ideally, their insights should be part of the design process, though this is rare.

Surveying with technical instruments is too often used only to establish ownership boundaries, general contours, and a few construction control points. GPS and GIS (see below) leave little excuse for not locating all major site features prior to starting design. Assuming that "design" means remaking the site without reference to anything existing is often at the root of inadequate surveying.

Whether done with survey instruments or camera and sketchbook, detailed site-specific mapping is a critical part of building sustainably. Homework left too late may be of poor quality or may be overridden by assumptions made before good information is gathered. Much conventional construction is undertaken from site plans that are nearly blank. Given clearer site data, designers can work with existing topography or trees, while contractors can prioritize site-protection zones and avoid hazards to construction.

Site-specific data has long been considered prohibitively expensive to gather using conventional survey methods. In this book's first edition, we noted the then-recent arrival of Global Positioning Systems (GPS) and Geographic Information Systems (GIS). GPS, for gathering ecologically important site information affordably with less site impact, and GIS, to store, analyze, and selectively map site data, have become standard tools. They have generated more, better, and cheaper site-specific information. Despite a few attempts to monopolize this information for profit, the overall result is better public access to site data.

Increasingly, online information sources are helpful site reconnaissance tools. (They should seldom become substitutes, however, for field observation.) Extremely valuable site information formerly only available in print—the US Soil Survey, climate data, geological diagrams, native and invasive plant lists—is available via the Internet. A wide variety of maps and air photos is also online, some updated almost in real time. For example, the University of New Mexico's Center for Rapid Environmental Assessment and Terrain Evaluation has redeployed military technology to turn satellite data into maps instantly. One projected use is mapping forest fires as they happen. Studies of vegetation change, flooding, and other quickly occurring processes are also in the works.[6]

Software for organizing and visualizing Earth data is improving rapidly. Google Earth provides views of most locations on the planet. It is beginning to be used as a central repository for links to other site-specific information. In theory, by clicking on a place on the Google Earth map, one can access site photos, as-built drawings, regional soil or climate data, or local history. The software has been used to expose "mountaintop removal" by coal companies in Appalachia;[7] it could as easily be used to link any site to full ecological data. While no systematic effort has yet been made, readily accessible "site-indexed" background information could be a quantum leap toward making sustainable design the norm rather than the exception. Microsoft's Virtual Earth, released in 2006, will probably spur competitive developments of online geographic information.

CommunityViz is a software add-in for GIS that produces 3D visualizations of "what-if" land-use scenarios. For example, specific house types can be drawn, and the "look" of new development using a mix of those house types at different densities can be portrayed. This promising program has two major landscape-related blind spots. Houses "plopped" on topographic surfaces do not reflect actual grading; and air photos draped over 3D contour maps show vegetation and site features two dimensionally, as if steamrolled onto the slopes. Not dealing realistically with two issues that so frequently make development ugly and unsound, CommunityViz's current version can actually mislead citizens trying to visualize acceptable growth. Until those defects are fixed, it remains a potentially green tool that leaves landscapes out.

"Agent-based modeling" (ABM) programs simple rules of interaction into large numbers of individual "agents" and produces remarkable simulations of complex systems. This is perhaps the most promising trend in realistically envisioning ecological and social processes. Easy-to-learn but robust software for ABM is "Netlogo," downloadable free; for understanding any process where many small forces over time produce large results, Netlogo is a powerful tool that few landscape professionals yet use.

Use Flexible, Accurate Visualization Tools

Having good survey data doesn't help much if it can't become visible in the design process. Although design graphics are well outside the scope of this book, it is worth noting that some are better suited than others to visualizing irregular existing site features like rock outcroppings or specimen trees. The choice of the right tool can directly affect the ability to transform sustainable intentions into on-the-ground success.

Software like SketchUp increasingly makes it easy to overlay digital field photos, hand sketches, and 2- or 3D wire-frame images. Measured perspective sketching techniques are very valuable for fieldwork and charettes at the client site.[8] Although skill with graphics is often dismissed by ecologically oriented designers as just a way of making pretty images, it can be an important link between the reality of the site and the proposed construction—a tool for site protection.

Locate Features During Site Reconnaissance

The best and most vulnerable features of any site should be inventoried early. Many will be items of clear ecological value; others will be historic or cultural; some may be of personal importance to the owner, client, or user group. All are likely to need protection during construction. A basic checklist includes:

- all trees, and any unusual or specimen plants
- meadows, groves, thickets, and other identifiable vegetation communities
- wildlife dens, breeding areas, and pathways, including seasonal ones
- streams, wetlands, ponds, and lakes
- soils: erodable, fragile, and especially fertile areas
- cultural features (archaeological, historical)
- items or locations of personal or sentimental importance to owners or users
- connections, links, and pathways among these features.

Responsible design firms will make such an inventory the first step in their work. Analysis of the site may reveal other reasons for protecting certain features: for example, a common and none-too-beautiful tree may need to be protected because it acts as a windbreak or moderates solar gain.

Pay Special Attention to Streams, Lakes, and Wetlands

The care of water bodies is a very specialized topic (Principle 4). Because of the difficulty, expense, and legal complications involved in restoring them, it is critical to *identify and protect* streams, lakes, and other wetlands at the earliest possible stage. In fact, the presence of wetlands should be researched before *buying* a property for any sort of development. Horror stories about wetlands regulation usually reveal an owner who didn't know, or didn't want to know, about site conditions. Despite regulation, many commercial land buyers still limit their site research to the proverbial "location, location, location." That is a mistake no designer or contractor can afford.

Once wetlands are identified, they need protection during construction. The techniques discussed in this chapter, particularly fencing to limit access, are used to safeguard wetlands as well as other site features. Because of their biological complexity and legal status, however, wetlands protection often requires go-

ing well beyond generic site-protection techniques. For this reason, protection of wetlands is discussed in its own chapter (Principle 4), along with other issues involving water.

At the site research stage, remember that wetlands:

- must be delineated according to legal definitions, not just a layperson's observations
- are highly susceptible to sediment, which erodes off of adjacent land surfaces (see "Preserve Healthy Topsoil," see p. 54).
- vary seasonally much more than most other landscape features, to the point of disappearing in dry periods
- have life cycles and may be "healthy" or "unhealthy," affecting decisions to protect them as they are or to restore them to better condition
- are linked to and influenced by off-site water sources, which need to be included in protection planning
- often require the addition of a specialist to the team
- can cause special difficulties for construction workers and machinery.

Even where no wetland exists on the site, protect the existing *drainage* patterns carefully. A featured grove or meadow, thoroughly fenced for protection, can die from flooding or drying if grading outside the fence redirects the flow of water. For sustainability, the movement of water on a site should be changed only with great care.

Tap Local Knowledge of Sites and Seasons

Contractors with years of experience in a specific region know that weather and seasonal changes can make or break a project. The same conditions dramatically affect the need for site protection. Erosion on recently graded soil may be minimal in most weather, until a summer rain squall or seasonal high winds sweep the soil away overnight. Frozen or muddy soils cause practical and engineering problems; equipment may damage wet soil that would be unharmed if worked when dry. Plants may be especially susceptible to breakage or root compaction during seasons of rapid growth, or may tolerate damage better when dormant. Seasonal vulnerability of endangered wildlife has delayed many public projects.

For sustainable construction, consider whether a change in construction *schedule* can minimize disruption. For example, in Bouctouche NB, work on a large boardwalk for Le Pays de la Sangouine was done in winter, with heavy machinery positioned on ice.[9] Working in the summer would have been more complicated *and* more disruptive to the river-dune-island site.

No book could possibly include appropriate advice for protecting all sites, in all seasons, for all aspects of construction. A growing literature on site conservation (or "geoconservation") is available, mostly from the United Kingdom. Local contractors often have a remarkable store of seasonal, site-specific knowledge, used to plan ahead for practical matters, scheduling around periods when the site will be inaccessible. If sustainable construction and protection of site features are recognized as goals, this local knowledge is invaluable in achieving results. Large national firms can do sustainable work if they subcontract local experts and heed their influence. The tendency of large firms to standardize all procedures must not overrule adaptation to local conditions. Applied globally and in all seasons, rigid standardization is incompatible with sustainable work.

Avoid Survey Damage

Although detailed site-specific mapping is often key to reduced construction impact, the *process* of site surveying can be the start of site degradation. Fortunately, new technology combined with new attitudes makes survey damage avoidable.

Manage Line-of-sight Surveys

Conventional surveying relies on a clear line of sight between a known point or "datum" and any point whose position is to be determined. Optical surveying instruments, including lasers, must be able to "see" in a straight, uninterrupted line from the instrument to the point being recorded. Sonar and ultrasonic instruments, which bounce sound off a target and back to the instrument, also require a clear shot at the unknown point. To ensure clear line-of-sight connections, surveyors clear brush and small trees with machetes or similar tools, a process known as "brashing."

Depending on region, climate, and vegetation, brashing can cause anything from minor injury to long-term harm. It is least critical in regions where vegetation grows back quickly, such as deciduous forest. Even in these areas, brashing, like careless pruning, can spread plant disease and may affect vegetation diversity, both in species and age distribution. In bioregions with fragile vegetation, brashing may be less necessary, but regrowth takes decades. Vegetation removal in linear patterns opens paths for soil erosion. Conventional surveys concentrate on lines, such as property boundaries, which arbitrarily cut across slopes or watersheds, thus increasing disruption.

Modern surveyors plan their fieldwork carefully in advance to minimize wasted time and backtracking. The same planning skills can minimize site damage from brashing, as well as from unnecessary vehicle access. In some cases, a well-planned survey can measure around an obstacle instead of removing it. Baseline-and-offset surveying can also decrease brashing under some site conditions.

Because much conventional development starts with total regrading of the site, existing site features, other than landmark-quality specimens, may seem unimportant to site crews. In the worst cases, surveyors, like other construction workers, thoughtlessly destroy any inconvenient item found on the site. If minimal site damage is an explicitly stated goal of the project, the survey team becomes an important ally in meeting that goal.

Use Alternative Survey Technology

Several methods of surveying that do not rely on line of sight are appropriate for landscape construction surveying. These include both high-tech and low-tech options.

Global Positioning

Global Positioning Systems (GPS) have been in the surveyor's toolkit for over a decade and have rapidly changed both processes and results. GPS field equipment consists of handheld, backpack, or vehicle-mounted units capable of receiving signals from satellites. These satellites continuously signal their location relative to Earth. By triangulating on several satellites at one time, the receiver unit computes and records its own Earth-surface location. GPS units guide commercial airliners and smart missiles, rental cars, trucking fleets, recreational hikers, and wildlife managers.

Basic GPS technology has not changed since this book's first edition, but GPS has become easier, cheaper, more accurate, and more widespread.[10] Survey results are digital and can be fed directly into computerized drafting, mapping, and analysis programs. If site design is done in CAD, drawings uploaded into the GPS field unit guide construction staking. GPS-gathered field information makes accurate "as-built" drawings and maps.

In terms of site protection, a major advantage of GPS is that Earth-surface line of sight is not required. In most cases, brashing can be entirely eliminated and access to the site is simplified. Anywhere the surveyor can carry it, a GPS unit can record horizontal and vertical location. (Dense tree canopy, very narrow canyons, or tall buildings may block communication skyward to the satellites.[11] Such obstructions can be worked around or surveyed with line-of-sight instruments.)

Three major types of GPS are available today. Handheld units, accurate to within ten feet (three meters), cost $100–$200, perfect for many general site-inventory purposes, as well as recreation and street navigation. (For all types, accuracy refers to *horizontal* measurement; vertical elevation is also measured, but typically is about half as accurate.) Mapping units are accurate to one yard/meter horizontally; these start around $2,500. Many are designed to collect data directly into GIS maps; for example, "ArcPad," a PDA-like device from ESRI, can display GIS maps and databases, update them on-site with user input, and record its own GPS position.

Survey-quality GPS is accurate to less than half an inch (one centimeter) horizontally, plus or minus. This degree of accuracy requires two units in a "differential" system (often called DGPS): one mobile, plus a stationary "base station" at a known point. By comparing satellite readings from the mobile unit to those taken at the known point, small deviations can be corrected. A differential system is "real time" when corrected data is beamed directly to the mobile unit in the field, rather than doing batch corrections back at the office after completing fieldwork. Such systems cost $30,000–$60,000.

A growing number of regions have the newest variant on differential GPS: regional providers set up fixed "reference stations," which correct mobile GPS readings for anyone within about a twenty-mile radius. The mobile units incorporate a cell-phone SIMS chip to communicate with the reference station. Subscription charges and password access are required, but the end user only has to have one GPS. This is likely to cut the investment for survey-quality GPS to about $20,000.

A similar concept, covering all US states, is WAAS (Wide Area Augmentation Service). Set up by the Federal Aviation Administration, it uses independent satellites to correct GPS accuracy. It is free and works even with many inexpensive GPS models. For site inventory, check whether your unit can be set to use WAAS; instruction manuals or an online search should provide this information.

For landscape professionals, there are several ways to take advantage of GPS technology. Most surveyors offer GPS, and contracts can specify it. A second option is renting (budget about $2,000 per week); setup, calibration, and data-file conversion may be included. Once set up, GPS software is simplified so fieldwork can be done by people not trained in surveying—for example, a botanist could produce very accurate tree inventories, a designer could walk and map desirable paths, or a contractor could locate construction hazards. A third option is to purchase GPS equipment and be trained in its use. This remains a big investment, and teaming with a skilled surveyor is often more productive.

GPS Project Examples

Design Workshop (Denver, Aspen, and Tempe) has used GPS on several projects where accuracy, environmental sensitivity, and speed of site analysis were important. At McDowell Mountain Ranch (Scottsdale

Figure 1.4 GPS units, often backpack sized, make surveying quicker, easier, and potentially less destructive to site vegetation. (*Photo:* Magellan Corp. ↄ)

AZ), new community trails had to be integrated with regional trails, and strict environmental laws were involved. Starting with rough sketches on a topographical map, landscape architect Stuart Watada leased a handheld GPS unit to refine trail locations and collect data on trailside vegetation and features. Design Workshop uses an inexpensive GPS unit to field verify potential home sites at large developments, and for early site planning in countries like Bolivia, where no published survey information is available.

For Anchorage (AK) Botanic Gardens, Jeff Dillon of Land Design North had GPS data collected by University of Alaska students. Existing vegetation and features were incorporated directly and accurately into design work. Dillon has also used GPS to lay out miles of ski trails in Anchorage parks.

Ohio State University's Center for Mapping has developed a "GPS van," which can produce a digital map, linked to video images, simply by driving through or around a site. A GPS unit pinpoints the location at which each reading or image was taken. Onboard computers compile this data into maps almost as fast as the van can drive. Combining GPS and stereo-photo methods, the van can locate any item it can "see" to an accuracy of ±14 cm (five inches). In other OSU research, semi-automated grading has been done with GPS controlling the bulldozer from digital maps of existing and proposed topography.

GPS has been welcomed in conservation work. Rob Corey, a landscape architect with the Natural Resource Conservation Service, produces "virtual landscape animations," which allow users to visualize land-use changes and then compute environmental-impact statistics from the images. GPS is important in collecting the data on which Corey's innovative system is based. In the Nature Conservancy's Parks in Peril program in Latin America, landscape architect Brian Houseal and colleagues use GPS to establish accurate legal boundaries for nature preserves and locate endangered plant communities. The information greatly increases the Conservancy's ability to win protection for remote, ecologically critical sites.

LASER 3D IMAGING

In our first edition, a system using laser as if it were radar (Cyrax) was noted as promising. Along with systems that stitch together photos from multiple angles, this high-tech system is widely used for fast surveys of buildings, bridges, and historic structures, as well as to coordinate spatial movements where digital effects mix with live-action moviemaking. Unfortunately, truly complex geometry, such as trees in an orchard or forest, are still beyond such technology to record accurately. It is suited to very fast modeling of open or cleared topography, rock faces requiring retention, or engineering structures. This, plus cost, limits its usefulness in landscape applications. Sustainable work may someday benefit from advanced tools that offer better understanding of the dynamics of each site, but not yet.

LOW-TECH, NON-LINE-OF-SIGHT TOOLS

While GPS looks to satellite technology to free itself from line-of-sight limitations, a much-simpler method relies on the oldest of all leveling tools: water. The tube level or hose level is available in several forms.◌ Like a surveyor's transit, it determines vertical level only; separate distance measurements make a complete survey. Where sight-line clearing must be minimized, and for some types of construction layout, it is an inexpensive and valuable tool.

In a U-shaped tube partially filled with water, the water surfaces in each of the arms of the U always lie at the same level. In a hose level, the U is replaced with twenty or more feet of clear flexible tubing. The water line at one end of the tubing is held at a known elevation, and the water at the other end of the tube adjusts to exactly the same level.

Hose levels can be used around blind corners, without clear sight lines, and at considerable distances across rough ground. They speed construction layout because no calculation is required: the two water lines are simply the same level. Laser equipment provides similar functions, but it is more costly and requires line-of-sight clearance.

Some manufacturers have added electronic sensors to the traditional tube level; an audible signal sounds when the ends of the tube are aligned. This allows one person to use a hose level more efficiently. Even these enhanced versions cost only about $50. If a site is free of visual obstructions, line-of-sight tools are more convenient for most surveying. But where clearing would be costly and intrusive, tube levels offer cost-effective site protection.

Another remarkably simple site-surveying tool is the "A-frame level," in use since ancient Egypt. Three light boards nailed together form a rough capital "A"; a mark is made at the center of the cross arm. A weighted string, like a plumb line, is hung from the top of the A. When the string intersects the cross arm exactly at the center mark, the two "feet" of the A are level. Walked across the land like old-fashioned drafting dividers, the A-frame quickly establishes a series of level points. For terracing and other erosion-control work, the A-frame can level earthworks or find contours quickly, without any math calculations, and without line-of-sight clearance.

Sometimes what needs to be measured is not the size or layout of the landscape, but the rate at which some aspect of it is changing. Some remarkably simple tools can serve this purpose. For example, rebar "benchmarks" (usually with bright plastic caps for visibility and safety) can be used to mark the edge of vegetative cover or the level of soil. Set deep enough that they can't move, such markers can reveal loss or movement of soil or plants between site visits. These simple measurements can be critically important for planning and performance monitoring of sustainable projects.

Minimize Utility Damage

Many modern landscapes are crisscrossed with buried and overhead utilities. Although some of these systems are invisible, constructing and maintaining them seriously alters the landscapes through which they pass.

Irrigation, site lighting, and storm-drainage lines are part of landscape construction, their functions landscape specific. Other utility systems, like sewage, power, phone, and cable TV, serve the buildings on the property. The site may also be affected by systems that serve larger communities (main power, sewer, or phone lines) or commercial interests (oil and gas pipelines), along with easements for such systems.

Landscape construction has direct influence over landscape-specific utilities. Landscape architects and contractors have also had significant effects on public-utility impact (below). The difference between planning carefully for utilities and dismissing them as necessary evils can be like night and day and is an important aspect of site protection.

Make Maximum Use of Narrow Easements and Trenches

Access is required to construct, maintain, replace, and repair utilities. Significant decreases in site impact can be achieved by reconsidering how utility access is pro-

Figure 1.5 The Egyptian A-frame is a simple, site-friendly way of establishing level and the fastest way to lay out points along a contour line. (*Photo:* Kim Sorvig.)

vided. Public utility easements are usually far wider than actual pipeline or cable. Rural utility easements cut across country, requiring their own access roads. In urban areas, utilities companies frequently dig up buried lines and keep street trees clear of overhead wires. Ways to decrease the impact of access in each case are discussed below.

According to the Edison Electric Institute, no one keeps national records of the total length or land area occupied by utility easements.[12] Pacific Gas and Electric (PG&E), as a single example, has 14,000 miles of electrical transmission lines. A fifty-foot-wide easement uses about six acres per mile. At this common width, PG&E's transmission lines alone could require as much as 80,000 acres. Multiply this across the continent and it is clear that utility easements have a major impact on landscape health nationally. Utilities are recognizing the potential for lessening these

impacts and for creating habitat corridors in easements. The Edison Institute, for example, publishes EPA-approved guidelines for maintaining easements.

REDUCE CLEARING FOR ACCESS ROADS

Access roads are required when utility lines do not follow existing transportation. Main branches of utility systems through rural areas or urban parks often have their own dedicated access roads, on top of pipelines or below overhead wires.

Easement clearing can often be narrowed.[13] Minimum clearance is usually a single lane for maintenance or construction vehicles with wide turnarounds at strategic points. Using the smallest and lightest possible machinery can further decrease the access space required. Decisions about machinery use are made at many levels, from corporate purchasing offices to the job supervisor renting extra equipment for an emergency. Landscape professionals have a variety of opportunities to influence these decisions.

Special construction techniques, such as trenchers that lay pipe or cable behind them as they go, can cut easement width dramatically. At Loantaka Brook Reservation in Morris County NJ, landscape architects Andropogon Associates challenged both conventional routing design and conventional construction methods for a gas pipeline through mature beech-oak forest. Space-saving methods of pipe installation, devised with the contractor, reduced a proposed fifty-foot right of way to thirty-four. Using a tracked loader specially adapted for the project, the contractors were able to replace slabs of vegetation-rich soil along the pipeline trench, guaranteeing revegetation.

In Loudon County VA, a developer installed a sewer line across park authority property. Two landscape architecture firms, HOH Associates and Rhodeside & Harwell, persuaded the county sanitation authority to reduce construction width from their standard seventy-five feet to thirty-five. With an arborist and engineer, they worked out three main guidelines for the project:

- Keep construction and final easements to thirty-five feet.
- Eliminate straight utility swaths longer than 1,000 linear feet. Follow topography and natural fea-

tures. (This principle is particularly important in steep or forested areas.)

- Keep openings in or out of woodlands—the points of greatest visual impact—as narrow as possible. In this project, the opening into the woods was pinched to ten feet.

These principles proved so successful that they became standard in Loudon County.

Utility easements should, wherever possible, be thought of and constructed as multifunctional space. Combining an easement with a public road, trail, or bike path is a common example, used in the Morris County project above. Combining utility easements with trails is an increasingly common way for park systems to pay for needed services. The Washington & Old Dominion trail in northern Virginia combines four major functions and "recycles" an older right-of-way. What began as a disused rail corridor first became a power-line easement. A paved trail was added, managed by the regional park authority. Later, sewer line and fiber-optic cable were installed under the trail; leasing fees ($250,000 annually) pay for trail maintenance.[14] The result is a much-needed recreation corridor. Sharing functions achieves more with less site disruption.

Utility corridors can share with wildlife, too. Their linear and interconnecting patterns can form wildlife corridors and habitat—*if* they are not ruthlessly cleared of all vegetation. Despite costs and impacts, mowing (or spraying) the entire right-of-way is still common practice. Even where a certain width of easement is legally required, clearing can be selective. Where easements are extra wide to allow for future expansion, clear only the area in actual use. Leave the access road grassed to reduce runoff and erosion. Except for the road itself, shrubs or small trees can be allowed to remain. As long as the road is kept drivable, clearing the location of a specific repair when it occurs is often cost-effective, compared with ongoing clearance of the whole easement.

KEEP URBAN UTILITIES ACCESSIBLE

In addition to sharing space with wildlife or bicyclists, carefully designed utilities can also share space

Figure 1.6 This easement, in Loudon County VA, is less than half as wide as the utility's standard. Note the site protection fence. (*Project:* Park Authority, HOH Associates, and Rhodeside and Harwell. *Photo:* Doug Hays.)

,with each other. Landscape contractors frequently lay irrigation tubing and low-voltage lighting cables in the same trench. The same concept applied to municipal utilities can save energy, simplify maintenance, and reduce space for easements. Excavation costs money and energy, both during initial construction and subsequent maintenance. Shared-trench construction reduces excavation and should be part of sustainable construction.

Not all utilities are suited for shared trenches. In particular, natural gas cannot run in the same trench as any electrical utility, including phone, cable TV, and low-voltage wires. The bending radius required for large pipes may prevent routing them with other utilities; consider designing the more flexible system to follow the less flexible. Similarly, gravity-flow systems have strict limits on slopes and lengths of run; other systems might follow their layout.

Shared trenching is most likely to work for "main" supply lines, because the starting and ending points of different utilities seldom coincide. For example, streetlights and fire hydrants are spaced differently along a street but are supplied by main lines running parallel to the street, which might be shared. With careful planning, some utility fixtures can be located together (streetlights sharing poles with electric lines, for example), reducing both materials used and space required. Such arrangements require clear cooperative agreements between utility companies for maintenance, future expansion, and similar issues.

Easy access to buried utilities can save materials and energy otherwise wasted. Locating utilities under roads saves easement space, but digging through asphalt or concrete pavement to repair lines is costly and disruptive. Patched pavement is frequently inferior to original construction, and excavated material contributes to solid-waste problems.

A European solution relies on interlocking pavers (like bricks with jigsaw-puzzle edges). Europeans call these concrete block pavers, or CPBs. Laid without mortar, they provide a strong paved surface that can be removed and replaced for access to buried utilities. Although initial cost is higher than sheet paving, lifetime savings on labor alone may justify unit pavers. From a sustainability perspective, almost no material waste is involved, because interlocking pavers can be pulled up and replaced repeatedly (or reused elsewhere). To excavate through solid paving requires heavy machinery, but to remove and replace unit pavers, smaller machinery or even manual labor is used. This not only saves energy but also decreases access widths. Lest anyone worry about strength, interlocking pavers support huge commercial aircraft at Hong Kong's international airport, Chek Lap Kok.

Interlocking pavers offer other practical and aesthetic advantages over standard sheet asphalt or concrete. Different colors can designate pedestrian crossings or make elaborate mosaics: for example, a miniature baseball diamond in multicolored block greets baseball fans at Anaheim CA's Edison Field. Streets surfaced with interlocking pavers give a traditional, cobblestone look to New Urbanist streetscapes; an example is Riverside Village in Atlanta, by progressive land management firm Post Properties.

Compared to mechanized sheet-paving methods, interlocking blocks may seem labor-intensive. European companies like Optimas ⊃, however, have developed small forklift-like tractors to pick up and place pavers about eighty at a time, plus tools for preparing the sand bed and edging. The same machine can pull up groups of pavers three feet square during maintenance, setting them aside for quick replacement. If ease of maintenance is included, interlocking blocks may actually use less labor than sheet paving over their life cycle.

Figure I.7 Interlocking pavers set on sand are easily removed and replaced for utility access, saving energy, cost, and waste. Some pavers also permit water infiltration. (*Photo:* Courtesy of Interlocking Concrete Pavement Inst. / David R. Smith. ⊃)

Edging required to keep interlocking pavers from moving sideways is often made of polyvinyl chloride (PVC). This is a material that should be phased out of landscape use wherever possible (see p. 252). For edging, many alternatives exist.

PLANT THE RIGHT STREET TREES AND PRUNE THEM RIGHT

Where overhead utility lines follow streets, they frequently conflict with trees, which get pruned away from the lines. Most affected are street trees, planted along roadsides at public expense and increasingly important to urban environmental quality. Utility crews have been notorious for butchering trees near their lines, a practice that fortunately is changing.

Prevention is the preferred solution. For new construction, utility lines should be placed where they will not conflict with trees. New plantings that cannot be relocated should use ornamental species that will not grow tall enough to touch the lines.

Where existing or poorly selected trees do conflict with utilities, thinning the tree *selectively* is in everyone's best interest. The temptation to lop the entire treetop like a hedge results in increased costs as well as environmental damage. Although lopping is initially quick and cheap, and requires little skilled labor, the tree will sucker vigorously at every cut, producing a dense thicket of branches. These fast-growing shoots soon threaten the utility lines again and must be trimmed every year or two. (Huge, tractor-mounted circular saws, buzz-cutting everything in their path, do a particularly destructive "drive-by" lopping.)

Selective thinning, by contrast, carefully removes those branches that extend toward the wires. Far fewer cuts are made; aggressive sprouting does not occur. For many species, thinning once every five years is sufficient to protect the utility. In the long run this makes thinning as cost-effective as lopping. Savings in transportation energy are high, because distance is a major factor in utility corridor tree work. Thinning is far less stressful on the tree, and much less likely to spread disease. Selective thinning done well is hard to see. Thus, without extra cost, thinning prolongs the life and appearance of valued trees, maintains their ability to filter air and provide shade, and reduces energy expended on line maintenance.

Increased awareness of costs and environmental issues has led many utility companies to contract tree maintenance with knowledgeable arborists. ⊃ Public disgust with the ugliness and ill health of butchered trees, as well as outrage at destruction of tax-financed street trees, has helped change older practices, a trend that landscape contractors and landscape architects should encourage.

Look Ahead to Make New Utility Technologies Less Intrusive

Cellular and wireless telecommunications utilities are a new concern for sustainability-focused landscape professionals. More than 22,000 transmission towers are already in place, and industry analysts expect another 125,000 or more as cellular companies battle for profitable markets.[15] Industry-sponsored federal law forbids communities from regulating tower placement or requiring shared towers. A few communities have succeeded in forcing cell companies to use existing steeples or towers or new decorative clock towers[16] to accommodate transmitters. Even this much compromise is the exception. With growing demand, towers and access roads are proliferating.

Cellular facilities rely on height to function and cannot be buried, making landscape integration awk-

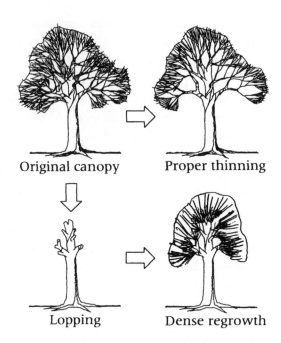

Original canopy   Proper thinning

Lopping   Dense regrowth

Figure 1.8 Dense tree canopies should be selectively thinned (top) to solve utility, shade, or view problems. Lopping or "pollarding" (bottom) disfigures the tree, and regrowth is denser than before. (*Illust.:* Craig Farnsworth.)

ward. Disguising the towers as trees[17] is not the solution, but cell equipment is ever more intrusive. One cellular tower may serve an area equivalent to hundreds of telephone poles, and in this sense saves resources. Towers are not *replacing* poles, however, but are built *in addition*. The ideal system would eliminate most poles and miles of wiring, with unobtrusive towers. Realistically, common easements and shared towers for telecom should be a policy goal.

One manufacturer, Phazar Wireless Antennas, makes boxlike cell antennas intended to be building mounted. The company will print a photo-based "Chameleon Covering" that matches the mounting surface—for example, a brick pattern—making the antenna all but invisible.

Technical alternatives to towers do exist. "Cable microcell integrators," or CMIs, are box antennas so small that they hang from existing utility poles, providing phone and data service over cable-TV wires, which already has nearly 97 percent coverage in the United States. About four CMIs can replace a tower system, often at 30 to 50 percent cost savings. Visual

Figure 1.9 Cell-phone towers, even when disguised as trees, mar the landscape visually and harm wildlife; access roads cause environmental disruption. (*Photo:* Kim Sorvig.)

impact is much less than towers, and CMIs can provide service in tower technology "holes." Educating designers and engineers that there are practical alternatives to new towers is one of the main challenges.[18] A major provider is Transcept.

Specify and Lobby for "Alternative" Utility Systems

Because utilities are shared services, their location, use, and maintenance are strongly influenced by legal agreements. Such agreements can be used to encourage environmental care.

Many subdivisions have covenants requiring buried utilities. Such covenants could include requirements for shared trenches, limited easement widths, and selective clearance and pruning. Community associations can use maintenance contracts to minimize utility damage.

Many public utility regulations date from a period in which the only concerns were mechanical efficiency, cost savings, and safety. Recent cellular regulations continue this tendency to favor utilities over public or environment. As older infrastructure decays, technical, cost, and safety concerns (not to mention Enron) are pushing utility issues to the fore.

Current laws favor centralized utilities, which require extensive infrastructure networks for distribution (electricity or natural gas) or collection (sewage, crude oil). These networks cost materials, energy, and maintenance. Constructing them laces whole regions with environmental disruption, temporary or permanent. Operational losses (leakage from pipes, voltage drop from cables) increase with distances. On-site alternatives avoid these problems.

Many "alternative" systems are local: for example, photovoltaic panels generate power at the point of use; constructed wetlands treat waste on-site. These "near-the-need" systems can eliminate distribution/collection infrastructure entirely, at least in theory. On-site power generation eliminates the 60 percent voltage drop losses common to grid electricity.[19] Similarly, on-site sewage treatment eliminates huge amounts of water used merely to transport waste. Some "alternative" systems have flexible infrastructure: for example, pressure-based sewage systems can follow topography in small trenches, unlike gravity systems.

In natural and historic parks, where overhead pylons and wires are forbidden, and buried cable is impossible for reasons of geology, safety, or cost, dispersed power generation, especially solar, gains an extra advantage. On-site systems, carefully integrated, are often the lowest-impact way to provide power to remote sites (see p. 268).

Two promising alternatives to utility power exist, but have been slow to market: fuel cells, which produce electricity by reacting hydrogen and oxygen; and micro turbines, which are generators fueled by natural gas (see p. 269). Widespread adoption of these on-site energy sources would transform landscape design and construction. Eliminating power lines may be a real possibility. Even a director of the Edison Electric Institute, a utility company group, has said that the era of big central power generation plants "is certainly over."[20] Hiding a generator in every back-yard will sorely test conventional landscape aesthetics, challenging sustainable designers to integrate decentralized "utility" structures into residential and public landscapes.

The policy bias *against* alternative, localized systems has decreased slowly, and an increasing number of professionals now design and build such systems. Even solar and wind power advocates, however, often overlook the problems of the grid. Several projects and landscape products that rely on "alternative" localized utilities are described in the sections on constructed wetlands (p. 189) and solar electricity (p. 265).

Physically Protect Site During Construction

Construction, even appropriate and sustainable construction, is a forceful process. The forces used in construction, whether small and cumulative or large and intense, can easily damage a site. Unintentionally backing a few yards too far with heavy equipment can irreparably damage fragile site features; so can a work crew's thoughtlessly placed hand-warming fire. Prevention means physically keeping construction activity out of protected areas, no matter what the project size.

In addition to protection against utility work and surveying damage *before* design or construction actually starts, careful decisions about what to protect must be made throughout the design process. As a goal, aim to keep clearing, grading, and other site disruption minimized: one model development guideline recommends that clearing extend no further than ten feet from the building footprint, and that construction access coincide with permanent roadways.[21] This may need adjustment in some regions. These protection goals, often backed up by covenants, actually raise property values; developers who think of site protection as a hindrance to business, or merely as lip service, are behind the times. (See discussion of Dewees Island covenants, p. 66.)

Carbon sequestration (p. 18) may make protecting existing trees directly profitable. Nor would it be any surprise if, in some jurisdictions at least, tree pro-

tection became mandatory, as it has been for decades in Europe.

Clearly Designate Protected Areas

Based on site inventory, all areas to remain undisturbed should be clearly marked on the plan *and* on site. This may require additional fieldwork, especially if the initial inventory was generalized or approximate.

It is important to mark protected areas on *all* construction plans before contract bidding begins. Site-protection requirements affect contractor procedures and costs. Requirements added after bids are accepted cause disagreements and are often disregarded. *All plan sheets* should include protected areas, so that subcontractors (who may only see the irrigation plan, for example) are clearly informed. Copies for the supervisor, the crew, and the office should *all* include these markings, as should any change orders. With CAD software, producing such documents is simple.

Areas to be protected are best staked out during a site walk with designer, contractor, and client all present. This allows decisions to be made in the field to protect *that* tree and *this* piece of meadow. On-site communication is much clearer and simpler than trying to work strictly on paper. As soon as the protected areas are located in the field, they must be fenced.

Modify Grading to Protect Site Features

Grading plans usually assume plane slopes at consistent grades. Especially on large projects and along roadsides, these regular computations can be "flexed" around important existing features. For example, even under AASHTO road design standards (which so many engineers treat as engraved in stone), regular side slopes can be "warped" to protect trees, rock outcroppings, or cultural features. What appears on the plan as a regular 3 percent slope might actually vary from 2.x percent to 3.x percent as it bends around site features. Working with contractors and engineers to make these adjustments costs almost nothing but can have a significant effect on site protection.

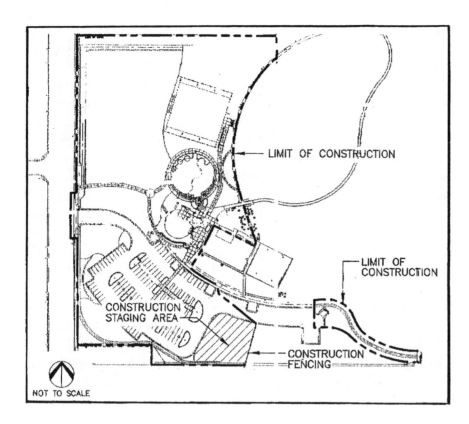

Figure 1.10 Fencing, protected zones, and staging areas should always be clearly marked on all plans. (*Plan:* Design Workshop.)

Fence Protected Areas and Maintain Throughout Construction

There is no substitute for temporary fencing to protect landscape features. Even conscientious crews can be tired and inattentive. Snow-fence or bright plastic mesh fencing will not physically stop a vehicle or even a determined pedestrian. But it provides a tangible, visible boundary, reminding construction workers to keep clear. More than one specimen tree has been saved by the sound of snow fence snapping as heavy equipment backed into it. Tree root systems, though invisible, need to be part of protection planning (see Figure 1.10); contrary to popular belief, roots don't extend straight down! To prevent overreaching by backhoes and loaders, place fencing six or more feet beyond the edge of the protected area.

Fencing must be erected before *any* other work begins, including site clearing. On densely overgrown sites, placing fence before clearing may be very inconvenient, but the risk of not doing so is great. At the least, fluorescent marker paint or flagging should be used around (not on) protected features to guide preliminary clearing, followed immediately by fencing.

Protection fencing should remain until all work and cleanup is complete—at an absolute minimum, until all heavy machines (including delivery vehicles) have left the site.

With few exceptions, all fenced areas should be *completely* off-limits. This includes foot traffic as well as machines. A dozen trips with a loaded wheelbarrow can compact some soil types enough to kill plant roots. Where there is foot access, crew members often dump buckets or mix and spill gas or chemicals. Plan site protection fencing so that there is no reason for any access during the entire construction period.

Limit On-site Stockpiling, Parking, Etc.

Even outside fenced protection zones, the whole site needs protection from some common construction activities. This protection is best accomplished by designating areas for certain uses, enforced by careful supervision. Specific areas should be established for activities such as:

- chemical mixing and disposal (even "harmless" chemicals can damage soils when concentrated)

- on-site parking (construction equipment, large or small, *and* private transportation); repeated parking compacts soils; oil and gas leaks contaminate soils
- fires (if permitted at all) must be contained and well away from vegetation
- cutting and drilling metal, plastic, concrete, some stone, and treated wood, which can contaminate soils, affecting pH and plant growth
- stockpiling of supplies (heavy weight can compact soil; chemicals can leak).

The need to stockpile materials on-site can sometimes be reduced by "just-in-time (JIT) delivery." Suppliers deliver materials just when they are needed for use. Common in factories, JIT delivery is not always feasible for construction materials. Where it is possible, however, reduced stockpiling can limit site damage and avoid loss, theft, or damage of stored materials.

Choose Staging Areas Carefully

Locations designated for construction activities are often called "staging areas" and may be as large or larger than the area of actual construction. Staging areas limit damage to other parts of the site by serving as sacrifice zones where soil compaction, spills, and other damage are concentrated. A thoughtfully planned staging area avoids treating the entire site as disposable (a worst-case situation that is unfortunately still common).

Where a busy road or path exists on the site, maintenance of uninterrupted vehicle or foot traffic is often a high priority, especially for businesses. Space for detours, in effect, expands the staging area. Careful planning limits temporary roads and paths, decreasing ecological and monetary costs.

The ideal staging area, from a sustainability perspective, is a future driveway, patio, plaza, or tennis court, already designed to be permanently "hard" landscape. Existing paving makes good staging areas, because dust and mud can be a serious problem, both on-site and for neighbors. Be certain that construction equipment is not too heavy for the pavement. In urban areas, permits allow public streets as staging areas.

Before an unpaved staging area is used, topsoil should be removed and stockpiled (p. 88). Unless the staging area is to become hardscape, it must be restored and revegetated once the project is complete, using stockpiled topsoil and appropriate restoration techniques (Principle 2). Soil compaction is almost inevitable in staging areas, which should be well away from important trees. Tilling to loosen compacted soil is usually necessary as part of restoration.

On large sites, it may be necessary to plan construction access roads. Where possible, use existing roads, or follow future permanent roadbeds. Temporary construction roads are extensions of the staging area. Their overall area should be minimized as far as possible. This must be balanced against total distance covered by machinery, an energy-efficiency concern. Within reason, the number of trips across the site should also be minimized. Crossing streams or wetlands should be avoided; special restoration will be required if crossings are unavoidable (Principle 4). Temporary roads generally require topsoil removal and restoration, as do staging areas.

Access needs are strongly influenced by the size of machinery used. Consider extra-small machinery (p. 272) and plan for the effects of working space (see Figure 10.2).

Preserve Healthy Topsoil

Topsoil, the top few inches in which 70–100 percent of all root activity occurs,[22] is a living part of every site, composed of billions of life-giving organisms interacting with organic materials and mineral components. Protecting soil during construction is one of the most fundamental sustainability practices— and one of the most easily overlooked. When not protected adequately, soils are easily damaged and must be restored (Principle 2). This costs both money and scarce resources and should be avoided wherever possible.

"In 1978, 80 million tons of soil were eroded from construction sites, and 169 million tons from roads and roadsides. . . . nearly 90% of this takes place on land under development."[23] The rate of erosion from construction sites is *2,000 times* (or more) greater than normal rates on healthy vegetated sites

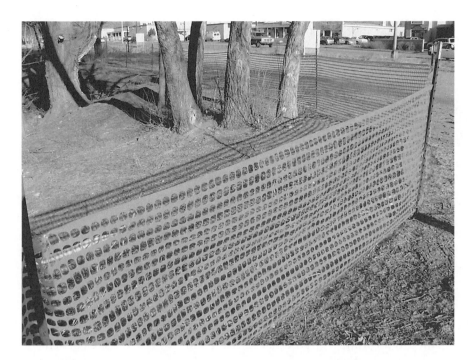

Figure 1.11 Fencing to protect site features is critical and should remain throughout construction. Much plastic fencing used today is at least partially recycled. (*Photo:* Kim Sorvig.)

(see Figure 6.19), equivalent to the worst erosion from mine sites. Although there has been some improvement in development practices since the time of these statistics, soil erosion caused by conventional carelessness is still a serious problem. Agriculture, mining, and forestry also cause major soil erosion—but as with all sustainability issues, each industry must do its part, not point fingers at others.

Saying that soil is alive is no poetic exaggeration. It is difficult to imagine the microscopic life teeming in healthy soil, but estimated numbers can help form a picture.[24] In just one pound of soil, there are more than 460 *billion* organisms; in a cubic yard of soil, something like 740 trillion; and in an acre covered with one foot of soil, the truly mind-numbing figure of 1,000,000,000,000,000,000 living things. This counts earthworms, but nothing larger. It has been said that if the nonliving part of the Earth's soil mantle were somehow vaporized, leaving living organisms undisturbed, the shape of the land would not change noticeably. Thus, treating soil "like dirt" is truly life-threatening behavior.

Avoid Soil Compaction

Healthy soil is permeable, with spaces between solid particles where water, air, and soil organisms can move. Soil compaction occurs when weight on the soil surface collapses these spaces, creating a hard solid mass. Compaction can result from a single intense force, or small repeated forces such as persistent foot traffic. Water, air, and roots may be completely unable to penetrate compacted soil, reducing or destroying its capacity to sustain life. The susceptibility of soils to compaction varies greatly by soil type and is an important reason for knowing the soils of each site before beginning work.

The sections on staging areas (p. 54) and on the choice of construction machinery (p. 278) discuss specific ways to decrease the danger of soil compaction. Compacted soil may already exist on the site due to previous land-use patterns. Compacted areas will need to be tilled, and often require adding amendments to restore fertility and porosity.

Protect Healthy Native Soils from Unnecessary "Improvement"

Soil is conventionally viewed simply as *more* or *less* fertile, with the goal always to "amend" or "improve" it toward more fertility. For sustainability, think of different *types* of soil fertility, not just different *levels*: that is, some soils have the appropriate type of fertility for rich grassland, while other soils have the right fertil-

Figure 1.12 Staging areas (this one is for a fairly small road project) can permanently damage an expanse larger than the site of actual work. (*Photo:* Kim Sorvig.)

ity for desert plants. This is not strictly a scientific concept, but does point out that fertility is directly linked to characteristics of ecosystems. Complex interactions between available minerals and a host of organisms (from microbes to grazing herds, from fungi to trees) are specific to each region, site, and soil type. Fertility is also influenced by how *long* this soil-creating interaction has been happening, and in what climate. Looked at in this way, raising the chemical fertility level of the desert soil may be an "improvement" if the goal is to grow grass, but is *detrimental* to the type of fertility that sustains native vegetation and animals.

Increased fertility can be inimical to native plants in other biomes than deserts. At Freedom Parkway in Atlanta, an overzealous contractor fertilized soil intended for common broomsedge (*Andropogon virginicus*) and other natives that thrive on depleted soils. Added fertilizer hastened growth of invasive weeds.[25]

Soil fertility is changed out of a desire to alter the plant community, usually toward agricultural crops or horticultural ornamentals. This is an important sustainability topic for two reasons. The process may be too energy and material intensive to be sustainable. Second, changing the ecosystem may have unsustainable results. Some soil amendments, especially heavily processed ones, concentrate in runoff and cause serious water pollution. Especially when existing soil is an undamaged local type, "improving" the soil may have negative effects. Appropriate uses of amendments in site *restoration* are discussed on p. 89–92.

Air pollution deposits significant extra nutrients (especially nitrogen and sulfur) in many "untouched" soils. The conventional impulse to add still more fertilizer is doubly wasteful in such cases. Even compost, which is almost universally a good idea for soil management, needs to be used with care on healthy native soils. It should not be imported from dramatically different sites. For instance, composted grassland vegetation will not support the best microorganisms for forest soils. Compost made from vegetation *similar* to what is being reestablished may *aid* the process with appropriate seeds and microbes. The balance of woody, dry, and green matter, as well as its age, should be matched to organic accumulations found on healthy sites. Leafy compost decomposes more rapidly than woodland compost. Replacing a layer of twigs and rotting logs with fully rotted and sieved commercial compost may satisfy a desire to tidy the site but actually changes the nutrient status for the worse.

Exotic plantings (for whose benefit the soil is usually improved) can bring a great deal of pleasure and beauty in a landscape. If they begin to outnumber native plants, loss of habitat, climate deterioration, and other serious problems can result.

For these reasons, healthy soils need protection. Limit the "improvement" of soil to carefully chosen areas. Specimen plantings that require high soil fertility can be grouped together in locations to provide most impact and pleasure. The remainder of the site can then retain unamended soils, an unirrigated water regime, and native plants. This design approach (cf. Xeriscape, p. 180) is likely to reduce resource and energy use, pollution associated with manufacturing and transporting soil amendments, and ecosystem disruption caused by overuse of nonnative plant species.

Amending only selected areas of soil is not a new technique. Planting beds and vegetable gardens are often selectively amended. Some extra planning and care is required. Selective soil amendment using small, light equipment may in fact help protect sites from compaction. Closely targeted soil fertilization using GPS (above) and computer-driven tractors is now an experimental technique in agriculture. Drip irrigation can also deliver exact amounts of liquid fertilizer to precise locations.

Many situations cause loss of soil fertility and create conditions where soil improvement *is* appropriate. Amending and improving soils that have been damaged or have lost fertility is an important goal of site restoration. Restoring damaged soil can re-create habitat, stop erosion, and even break down some kinds of pollutants. Unlike the questionable "improvement" of healthy native soils, restoring damaged soils to match regional norms is almost always a sustainable practice. See the following chapter for discussion of site restoration.

Save Every Possible Existing Tree—Even Just One

Existing trees are among the most valuable features a site can have, from both ecological and real-estate perspectives. While individual trees do not affect warming or greenhouse gases as much as forests do, they still provide localized temperature modulation, water, air, and soil protection, and CO_2 sequestration. Economically speaking, carbon sequestration may soon make every tree bankable. Their value is already well-known to experienced realtors, who always note "mature trees" as selling points (sometimes with comically differing definitions of "mature"). A well-maintained landscape is reported[26] to increase property value by up to 75 percent; merely mentioning "landscape" in real-estate ads sells properties 20 percent faster.[27] Yet damage to trees during construction is common, and often fatal; one study estimates such losses for a single medium-sized U.S. city at $800,000 annually.[28] This problem is entirely preventable, though often overlooked. For sustainable landscape construction, prevention is a must.[29]

Get Professional Evaluation of Existing Trees' Health

Tree species vary widely in lifespan. Individual trees also vary in health, affected by soil nutrition, disease, and physical injury. Ideally, clearing for construction would remove only those trees that were already in poor health or near the end of their life (leaving some of these for wildlife habitat). Although this ideal is seldom fully achieved in practice, careful planning can greatly reduce the number of healthy trees destroyed. Success requires evaluating the site's vegetation in detail.

If possible, existing trees should be mapped and their health evaluated before either design or construction begins, as part of the surveying and site inventory process. Both design (siting of new features) and construction methods (access and staging) affect the need for clearance. Designing a new structure to fit beautifully among ancient trees is of little use if construction requires removing those trees for access. Site-protecting construction methods should drive the design on sites with high-quality vegetation.

A professional arborist or tree surgeon is the best person to evaluate health and expected life of trees. Thorough evaluation requires knowing species characteristics and hidden signs of weak health. Determining the health of specimen trees may require climbing them with tree surgeon's equipment. Rough visual surveys of site vegetation are useful first steps, but specialized knowledge and equipment is required to make a reliable evaluation.

The cost of an arborist's evaluation, which conventional developers often avoid, is small compared to the value of trees saved (see Table 3.2). Consulting cost can be lowered by limiting the number of trees evaluated. To do this in a way that contributes to sustainability, set a "construction envelope" (see p. 65). Outside the envelope, *all* trees and other site features are to remain undisturbed; thus it is only necessary to evaluate in detail the trees *inside* the envelope. Laid out during site inventory, or at the early stages of conceptual design, envelopes reduce *both* costs and environmental damage and raise property values.

Although trees are the most prominent vegetation on most sites, the health of other vegetation may be equally important in some regions. Large cacti and shrubs, meadows, hedgerows, windbreaks, and groves strongly affect both site character and ecological function. The health, lifespan, and growing requirements of such features may also require professional evaluation. A botanist, forester, or range management expert may be the appropriate consultant.

One caution: arborists usually sell pesticide-spraying services. Some are like doctors who are too quick to recommend expensive, heavy-duty medicine. Cultivate working relationships with arborists who respect preventative approaches to tree health, and who practice Integrated Pest Management (see p. 329).

Evaluating trees and other plants is usually easier and more accurate when done during the growing season. Judging a plant's condition when it is leafless and dormant is not impossible but requires extra skill. A dormant evaluation is better than none, but where possible, plan for this task to occur at the proper local season.

Remove Trees Early, If at All

Where it cannot be avoided, tree removal should usually be one of the first construction tasks, along with fencing of protected areas. Although competent tree surgeons can drop a tree piece by piece in a very restricted space, there is always the risk of damage by falling timber. After construction, felling may destroy new work. Large branches or trunks can leave deep gashes in soil where they fall, and stump removal leaves a crater, so it is better to complete these tasks before site grading.

Removing felled logs raises several sustainability questions. In "sustainable forestry," logs are winched out of the forest to avoid tractor access. This limits soil compaction and clearing and is often practical for landscape construction.

REMEMBER THE HEALTH BENEFITS OF DEATH

An important option is not to remove dead trees, logs, or stumps at all. (Those that are in danger of falling must of course be trimmed or felled, but may be left lying.) Standing snags, in particular, are home to many species of wildlife. In an undisturbed natural system, decomposing wood fertilizes soil and nurtures young trees. These benefits are lost when dead trees are removed.

Stump and root removal, in particular, has conventionally been done with heavy equipment, extremely strong chemicals, and dynamite. Cost and environmental damage from these methods makes leaving dead timber in place even more attractive. Clearly, not all landscape design styles or construction methods can integrate relic timber. Richard Haag's mysterious, stump-strewn moss garden at the Bloedel Reserve near Seattle proves that a sustainable approach can produce great beauty from what is conventionally considered an obstacle.

Fence All Protected Trees Thoroughly

Around trees it is especially critical to exclude all traffic and to prohibit stockpiling, parking, and toxic materials. One common mistake is to pile excavated soil under a tree "temporarily." This can kill many species.

There is no foolproof way of knowing where an existing tree's roots lie. The horizontal zone of root spread "is not a neat and tidy radially circular or concentric pattern, but one that is strictly determined by the path of favorable subsurface conditions."[30] Rule-of-thumb practices should always be considered the *minimum* area to fence and protect. One such guesstimation is the "dripline," an imaginary line formed by projecting the edge of the tree's canopy onto the ground (see Figure 3.18). The *actual* root zone is irregular, and often two or more times the diameter of the dripline. Likelihood of major root damage decreases with distance from the trunk. Especially for very old, very large, or shallow-rooted trees, the protected area should be increased by at least 50 percent beyond the dripline.

Species like aspen, sassafras, or sumac spread in circular groves by underground runners. The runners extend far beyond the dripline of any individual trunk, joining what appear to be many trees into one plant (a "clone"). Damage to roots near one trunk can spread to other trunks. If possible, groves of any species should be fenced as a group, enclosing an area *twice the diameter of the grove* if there is any reasonable way to do so. This is especially important, however, with clonal species.

Trees that "weep" or trail branches near the ground may require an extra buffer space beyond the branches. Similarly, tall machinery used near trees is responsible for many unnecessarily broken branches.

Build with Great Care Under Trees

People love the sheltered space under a tree or within a grove, which by definition is within the dripline. This presents a special challenge. Seating, gazebos, and other construction close to trees are often important garden features. Such construction should avoid changes in drainage or permeability and be lightweight, set without foundations or on the least intrusive foundation possible, such as pilings. Work should be done by hand, because even the smallest lawn tractor can compact soil around roots or injure the tree's bark.

Pliny Fisk, of the Center for Maximum Potential Building Systems in Austin TX, has developed a highly unconventional foundation system to place even large buildings very close to trees. Auger-like soil anchors form the foundation, screwed into the soil with little disruption. If additions or remodeling increase the building's weight, anchor foundations can be screwed in deeper to provide extra holding power. Once it is no longer needed, the whole foundation can be unscrewed, leaving none of the long-term disruption of abandoned masonry foundations. A commercial system based on similar concepts, called Pinned Foundations, is gaining popularity, especially for wetlands use (see p. 164; also Figure 6.16). For any landscape structure requiring a foundation, these removable systems should be seriously considered.

Working closely around existing plants requires craftsmanship and care. The attitude of some conventional construction crews is a real hazard to existing plants. Part of widespread cultural carelessness toward nature, this attitude treats existing plants as inanimate obstructions rather than living specimens. It is not uncommon to see construction workers hack or tear off branches they feel are in their way, rather than tying them back, leaving jagged stubs that invite disease. Experienced contractors take the extra care required to build around existing trees, reaping improved profits and reputation, as well as a healthier environment.

Avoid Grade Changes near Trees

Ideally, no cutting, filling, or tilling of soil should occur within the protected area around existing trees. On some projects, however, financial and other pressures may mean a choice between grading around a tree or removing it entirely. Keep such changes to a minimum, and consult an arborist. As a rule of thumb, no more than six inches of soil can be added or removed within the dripline. (Even this is too much if it applies to the *entire* dripline area.) Trees "breathe" in large part through their roots, which take

up oxygen as well as water and nutrients. Building up soil can smother the roots, while removal of soil exposes them. If a lowered soil level causes water to collect around the trunk, many species will eventually drown.

Sometimes it is impossible to avoid grade changes around existing trees without abandoning construction altogether. In such cases, special soil-retaining structures called tree-wells and tree-walls can be built to give the tree a chance at survival. These structures enclose the dripline (or more), keeping the soil and the tree at their original level while the new grade steps up or down at the edges. On a slope, a well or wall may be semicircular, either protruding from the new slope or cut into it. Many decorative variations are possible. Drainage into and out of these structures must be carefully designed and constructed.

If buried pipes and wires cannot be kept out of the root zone, a counterintuitive rule applies. Place the line across the tree's *diameter*, tunneling carefully under one edge of the main trunk. Because roots generally spread radially, this tactic avoids cutting across them; trenches further from the trunk usually damage more roots.

Don't Half-save a Tree

Unless most of the above guidelines are followed, leaving a tree on a drastically changed site and expecting it to survive is mere pretense. Some species are more adaptable than others, but most require rigorous protection; err on the side of extra protection. Many ignorant or disreputable developers have "left" (rather than protected) a large tree on-site, only to have it die within a year or two. By that time, the developer has made the sale and can deny all responsibility, and in any case it is too late: the magnificent old tree can only be replaced, if at all, with a nursery sapling. Nothing about such a practice is sustainable.

Use Appropriate Construction Machinery

Mechanical construction equipment is a part of most landscape projects. Available equipment varies widely in size, weight, energy consumption, and clean or pollution-prone operation. Each of these factors af-

Figure 1.13 Sitting under trees seems to be an innate human desire. Furniture or construction under trees must use minimal foundations (if any); erosion from constant use is a concern, but paving is risky unless very porous. (*Photo:* Kim Sorvig.)

fects the site directly and influences the need for staging and access areas. Careful choices of equipment are essential in sustainable construction, especially for site protection.

Don't *Assume a Need for Heavy Equipment*

Most experienced contractors have encountered at least one project where machinery other than hand power tools was impossible to use: a back garden for a row house, with access strictly through the house, or a terraced landscape too steep to drive onto without extreme risk. A can-do attitude finds ingenious ways to complete such work without heavy machines. The same approach can serve a sustainable agenda.

Many of the world's most admired construction projects have relied on limited machinery. Thorncrown Chapel, in Eureka Springs AR, was deliber-

Figure 1.14 Thorncrown Chapel is a national treasure, in part because nonmechanized construction preserved its relationship to the woods. (*Project:* E. Fay Jones. *Photo:* Stephen Schreiber.)

ately designed by architect Fay Jones to be constructed with materials no larger than two men could carry.[31] This deliberate decision kept the chapel and surrounding forest in intimate contact, a prime quality of this beloved building. Fallingwater and many other Frank Lloyd Wright buildings were constructed without heavy machinery.[32] Many preindustrial landscapes and buildings, entirely constructed with hand labor and nonmechanized tools, are revered design ideals. Their enduring quality, health, and popularity can be attributed at least partly to the appropriate technology used in their construction.

Conventional construction workers often default to powerful, heavy equipment, a "we can, so we do" assumption. When planning a fleet of landscape construction machinery, it seems easier to purchase the biggest, most powerful tools, on the assumption that they can do any job, large or small. Sustainability requires matching the size and power of the machine to the job and the site. Mechanical "overkill" has many costs that are not accurately reflected by the monetary price of purchasing or operating a machine.

The larger and heavier the machine, the greater its turning radius, and as a result, the more cleared area it requires for working and staging. Heavier machinery also means greater soil compaction: the weight of the machine is concentrated through the relatively small area of wheel or track in contact with the ground. An average-sized car or small truck occupies about 16,500 square inches, but only 140 square inches of tire meet the ground, multiplying pressure per square inch by over 100 times. Balloon tires and tracks are designed to decrease per-square-inch ground pressure, lessening soil compaction, erosion, and vegetation loss.

Even on paved roads, AASHTO estimates that a tenfold increase in vehicle weight results in *five thousand* times the damage to the road.[33] A dump truck with dual rear axles, at about 30,000 pounds, wears down the road 5,000 times more than a private car at 3,000 pounds.

In Table 1.1, note that some vehicles, especially tracked ones, have lower ground pressure than a person exerts when walking. (Wheels or tracks churn the soil, however, so walking can still be less damaging.) In general, damage to soil is reduced by any decrease in mechanical power and ground pressure. Often, reductions can be made without compromising work. In other cases, benefits of doing the work must be balanced against damage done by heavier machinery.

Use the Lightest Machinery Available

To match the tool to the job, consider both traditional construction tools and newly refined modern machinery. Many of the former accomplish construction tasks without internal-combustion engines. The latter are miniaturized, efficiency-improved, motorized tools. Both approaches have benefits.

In many cities of the eastern United States, there are sidewalks made of huge slabs of granite, up to twelve feet square. These were hoisted into place, and set with remarkable accuracy, using a tripod of poles and a block and tackle. In the great gardens of Japan

Table 1.1:
Ground pressure of vehicles and pedestrians

Vehicle Type	Ground Pressure (psi)
Mars Sojourner	0.14
Tracked, small all-terrain vehicle	1.0
Cuthbertson tracked LandRover	1.9
Person standing, flat shoes*	2.5 to 3.3
12.5 ton Rolligon timber hauler (loaded)	3.2
Person walking or running	3 to 12
Low Ground Pressure Vehicle (legal definition, Canada)	5 or less
Person standing, in "sensible" heels	9 to 12
Bulldozer or military tank	10 to 80
Work trucks	18 to 36
Spike heels (standing weight on toes and heels)	26 to 33
Spike heel (120 lbs. on one ¼″ heel)	1,920

* Low value: 40 sq in both shoes, weight 100 lbs. High: 75 sq in, weight 250 lbs. The obesity epidemic is raising these averages. Pressures increase when pushing off to stand up, walk, or run.

and China, massive stonework was constructed with similar tools. This system is cheap, simple, portable, and energy efficient. To get equal precision in placing boulders and similar objects from a crane, loader, or backhoe requires unusual skill on the operator's part.

The traditional pole sling, carried on two people's shoulders with the weight centered between them, is a remarkably efficient lifting and carrying tool. Widely used in Asia, and in Europe and America until the 1800s, two- and four-person slings are an energy-efficient way of moving objects weighing several hundred pounds. They are especially useful for irregular-shaped items, where the main difficulty is not the weight, but getting a handhold. On awkward slopes, a sling or similar device may offer access where wheeled carriers cannot go. A recent innovation on the basic sling, the Potlifter ⊃, uses self-adjusting straps buckled to handles for easy attachment, allowing two people to lift almost anything bulky, up to two hundred pounds: B&B trees, large pots, boulders, garbage bins, or bagged materials.

"Ball carts" for ball-and-burlap trees are available in various sizes. Low slung like a furniture-mover's

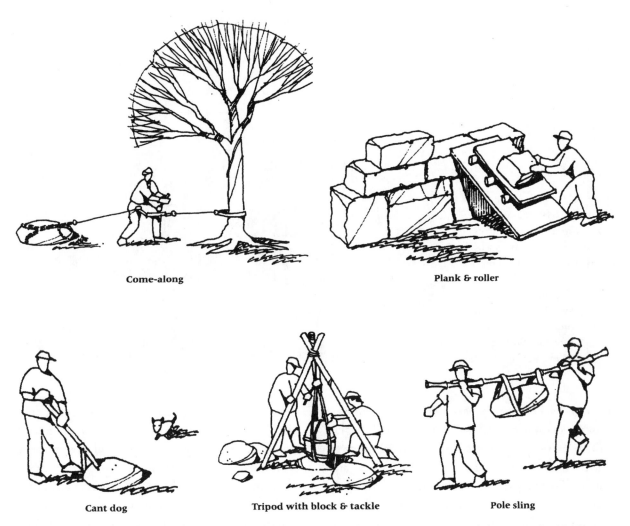

Figure 1.15 Traditional ways of moving heavy objects still work in landscape construction (often more flexibly than modern machines) and can reduce environmental costs. (*Illust.:* Craig Farnsworth, based partly on R. Daskam [Dubé and Campbell ⊃ Princ. 6].)

dolly, ball carts are also good for moving boulders and other heavy, irregular objects. Victorian horticulturists moved trees with root balls nearly six feet across in special tree-moving frames. Drawn by horses or large crews of workers, these frames were practical only on fairly flat land. (A modern relative is the TreeToad, a hand-operated, cart-mounted tree spade.) In Venice's canal-and-bridge environment, modified carts even negotiate stairways with ease.

Roller panels can also move large, heavy, irregular objects. A frame several feet long and a foot or more wide holds rollers every few inches—updating the technique that built the Egyptian pyramids. Winches and "come-alongs" can also drag heavy landscape construction materials into place, on the ground, on

skids, or on a ballcart or roller. Powered and hand-cranked winches are available for moving objects up to several tons. The Appropriate Technology movement has invented several innovative ways for a winch to replace a tractor in pulling a plow or tiller across a field. As long as fossil fuels remain artificially cheap, these tools will not replace trucks or tractors, but they are far more energy efficient and avoid most soil compaction.

Not all modern equipment is "heavy." Since the 1980s, construction machinery has become available in smaller and more efficient sizes. This trend has expanded considerably since the first edition of this book, and very small power equipment is widely available from suppliers and equipment rental agencies.

Figure 1.16 Col. Greenwood's Treelifter (1844) allowed one worker to transplant a thirty-foot tall tree. The "ship's wheel" cranked the axle, pulling up the lifting chains. In transit, the axle rotated independent of the chains. (*Illust.:* From "The Tree-Lifter," London, 1844; thanks to Tim Brotzman, Brotzman's Nursery, Madison OH.)

Tractors, backhoes, trenchers, and other common landscape machines are often half the size and weight of their 1970s counterparts. Powered wheelbarrows, walk-behind forklifts, and small "site dumpers" are available. These are maneuverable and light; their decreased weight increases efficiency. Several of these mini heavy machines are illustrated in figures 7.3 to 7.7, in the section on fuel consumption.

At Mill Brook in southern Maine, the team (a landscape architect, forester, and wetland scientists) needed least-destructive methods of reclaiming a sensitive eighteen-acre site. Noting that "standard methods of large-scale soil installation using bulldozers, excavators, etc. often trample or bury vegetation in the process," the team found a mulch spreader designed for steep slopes and reforestation areas. This "air spreader" caused minimal disturbance and applied soil evenly, following existing contours.[34] For a stream restoration project on Staten Island NY, small "power wagons" by Honda transported boulders down an erodable embankment. On sensitive sites, small equipment may be *more* effective than heavy machinery.

Hand-*carried* motorized equipment should also be considered in sustainable construction. The ability to move under power is necessary for trenching, grading, plowing, and very heavy loads. But in other tools, such as backhoes, augers, cranes, small mowers, or cement mixers, powered transportation is *not* essential to the machine's main purpose. Running a relatively small tool by connecting it to an engine large enough to move a tractor is not fuel efficient and may result in increased pollution. As fuel costs rise, self-propulsion will very likely be reserved for tools that truly require it.

A two-person motorized auger for digging post holes is a good example of a hand-carried machine. The handheld auger may be slightly slower than a tractor-mounted one, but can dramatically reduce soil compaction and the need for clearing. A muscle-powered post-hole digger is still more energy efficient but in some soils is unacceptably hard to use. The small engines used on hand-carried machines must be compared to larger engines case-by-case, because both fuel efficiency and pollution rates vary.

Similarly, not all heavy equipment is equally unsustainable in all uses. Given a suitable staging area, a crane may be used to "fly" heavy materials into a site, replacing trucks, barrows, or other wheeled machines, which would otherwise cross the site repeatedly. Concrete pumping systems are often used in this way. Such equipment can lift materials over protected parts of the site. Whether this should be considered "sustainable" depends on the energy efficiency of the individual machine, as well as the importance of preserving existing site features.

Related Design and Planning Issues

The pursuit of sustainability requires teamwork, and the issues involved often cross conventional boundaries between design, construction, and maintenance. Many approaches discussed in this chapter refer to design choices that link to construction methods. The following are some areas of site protection where, in practice, the designer, planner, and/or owner have more influence than the construction professional.

Advocate Sustainable Site Selection

Landowners (and designers if they are involved in identifying suitable sites for proposed projects) can protect healthy sites by simply *choosing other places to build*. In particular, prime agricultural soils are of exceptional importance to any sustainable society. The financial drive to subdivide such land is powerful but shortsighted, because it diminishes society's food reserves. Many communities limit building on such lands to ensure continued crop production, conserve habitat, and protect migratory corridors. Consultants may influence individual decisions to subdivide and develop; landscape professionals should support planning initiatives that encourage development on more appropriate land types.

Among these appropriate types of land for development, two stand out. One is the "hurt site" or "brownfield" (see Principle 2), where land damaged by previous use can be put to new use. This approach decreases demand for development on healthy sites. A second, sometimes overlapping idea is "in-fill development," which encourages development of the many leftover spaces found in most urban areas. Skill, commitment, political backing, and innovation by designers and contractors support these land-saving strategies.

Since McHarg's *Design with Nature* became influential in the 1970s, broad-scale planning has been used to protect many land types from inappropriate development. These include steep hillsides, fire-prone forests, and coastal beaches, to name only a few. Without appropriate site selection at both regional and individual scales, the construction techniques described in this book cannot be truly sustainable and can in fact cause great damage. (As noted in "Leaving the Landscape Out," pp. 7–8, site selection is a weak point of green building certification systems.) Site selection, and even unpopular limitations on the right to use certain categories of land, is an essential part of progress toward sustainability.

Collaborate with Community Stewardship Organizations

A relatively new type of nonprofit called a Community Stewardship Organization (CSO) can keep development from being the one-sided, divisive activity it so often is. CSOs are formally chartered partnerships among community groups, conservationists, government agencies, and potential developers. By anticipating how an area *could* develop, and balancing multiple interests about what *should* happen, CSOs tend to avoid adversarial situations. Involved citizens give the local environment—built and natural—better care. The CSO network links local (and potential) CSOs with experienced peers, seminars, tools, and concepts to help them succeed.

Lay Out Building Envelopes

Even if site selection is a "done deal" before the designer is hired, there are still ways to limit disturbance of a healthy site. One of the most useful is the "building envelope" concept. Based on careful site inventory, this is an area of the site within which all construction will be contained. This "envelope" is best located on already-disturbed areas, away from fragile areas, with views to the site's best features. It is sized to include the new construction as well as a carefully limited work zone. Everything outside the envelope is treated as a protected area during construction (see pp. 52, 66). Around the building, the envelope is either restored to native vegetation or planted with horticultural gardens, depending on owner preferences.

Since our first edition, building envelopes have become a familiar part of many landscape architects' repertoire. Protective covenants require each landowner to respect such envelopes in subdivisions like Desert Highlands (Scottsdale AZ, by Gage Davis Associates) and the similarly named High Desert (Albuquerque NM, by Design Workshop). Nonnative plants and constructed landscape features must be within the envelope; outside it, only native plantings are permitted. This approach balances the resident's desire for personalized outdoor space with the goal of preserving the native landscape as a community feature. The transition from garden to native landscape fits water-saving Xeriscape principles (p. 180) and enhances visual integration.

Promote Reasonable Grading and Clearing Regulations

Grading and clearing is regulated by law in many communities. This can be two-edged, however. One study found that only 40 percent of communities *enforced* their regulations with inspections; less than 20 percent set specific, measurable targets for how much of the site could be cleared.[35] The climate-change effects of removing healthy soil and vegetation make both voluntary and regulatory limits on clearance and grading imperative.

Grading limits can be too specific, resulting in site damage. Many communities set a *steepest* allowable slope. Because a gentle slope takes more horizontal distance than a steep one, such regulations may force removal of trees or features that could be saved if steeper grades were allowed (within limits of soil stability, of course).

In general, regulations of this sort should be *performance based*: they should set a clear goal, such as preserving a specific percentage of the vegetated area on a site, but avoid narrowly regulating the *methods* used to meet the goal.

Use Covenants for Site Protection

Covenants are contracts between private parties and can be more specific or flexible than governmental

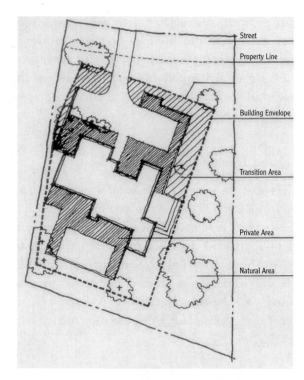

Figure I.17 Development "envelopes" can help integrate new construction with protected landscapes. (*Project:* Design Workshop. *Graphic:* High Desert Investment Corporation.)

zoning laws. Covenants and conservation easements can be used to protect traditional land uses, specific views or landmarks, habitat for particular species, or the character of a neighborhood or region. They can also prohibit certain types of development or construction. "Reversion clauses," which give the land back to the community or the donor if misused, can add teeth to covenants. (Misused, conventional covenants often enforce bluegrass lawns and penalize native plantings.)

Dewees Island, a residential development off the South Carolina coast, has been called by EBN "a model of what development can and should be."[36] The covenants used at Dewees Island will seem aggressive, even extreme, to those who think of themselves as "bottom-line" advocates—yet the project's return on investment will be *double* the investors' expectations. Clearly, something is being done right when good for the environment proves this good for business.

The Dewees covenants:

- limit total disturbance per site to 7,500 square feet, including house footprint, all paving, and utility easements; houses may not total more than 5,000 square feet, nor stand over forty feet tall
- require restoration of any temporary disturbance
- prohibit removal of any tree over 24 inches in diameter and require permit review for removal of *any* vegetation
- require native plants from a 136-species list
- limit driveways to twelve feet width and require all roads, driveways, and paths to be surfaced with sand, crushed shell, or wood chips
- allow only collected rainwater for irrigation
- permit only organic fertilizers and pest control, except for development-wide Integrated Pest Management mosquito control (purple martins and bats first, pesticides only if unavoidable)
- prohibit solid lumber larger than 2x12, metal or plastic siding, asphalt or fiberglass shingles, several types of insulation materials, and high-VOC paints and varnishes
- require a construction waste management plan, including sorted recycling of building materials
- prohibit garbage disposals and trash compactors as obstacles to recycling
- provide constructed wetlands for each house.

These covenants pull together many recommendations made in this book. Together with conservation easements, they have protected 65 percent of Dewees Island's 1,200 acres. A transfer fee of 1.5 percent on all lot sales supports environmental and community programs. The developer has invested in ongoing public environmental education in low-income communities nearby. Although covenants usually start out in wealthy developments, many of them can, do, and should trickle down into zoning standards that benefit whole regions.

Think of Landscapes in Zones

In any well-designed landscape, compatible uses and features are grouped in patterns for efficient use of space. Xeriscape explicitly extends this principle,

grouping plants with similar water requirements for irrigation efficiency. Designing zones of similar landscape maintenance can result in savings of time, energy, and materials. These principles are discussed in chapters on water and maintenance, but they have relevance to site protection too. Landscapes that combine similar uses into carefully designed zones can accomplish more in less area—leaving more of the site undisturbed.

Specify Site Protection in Contracts

Cooperation between owner, designer, and contractor is the best way to achieve effective site protection. By selecting contractors who are responsive and cooperative, and cultivating strong working relationships, designers and landowners can do much to ensure a healthy site.

Especially in public-sector projects, contractor selection is strictly by lowest bidder. Because the cheapest construction methods frequently rely on wholesale site clearance, low-bid selection often guarantees site damage. Especially in such situations, clear, strong specifications are essential to site protection. (As sustainability grows in importance, better site protection will hopefully become part of *standard* specifications, local and national building codes, and covenants attached to land deeds.)

Among the most important items to specify are:

- explicit methods of determining what areas are to be protected
- physical fencing of protected areas, in place before construction begins and removed at the latest possible date
- and strict limits on the activities noted above (pp. 53–54).

Because damage to existing landscape features, especially living plants, is usually irreversible, specifications *must* include financial motivation for protecting them. A positive incentive approach offers a bonus if all features are undamaged at final inspection. A liquidated damages clause sets financial penalties for damage. Without such financial motivation, site protection specifications lack teeth and will be ignored by those contractors who are ignorant or unconcerned about sustainability. It is often cheaper for a contractor to buy nursery stock and "replace" a mature tree than to pay a crew extra to work carefully around it. Contractual language and financial penalties can only go so far in overcoming this problem. Selecting and working closely with a contractor whose work is conscientious is far preferable. Fortunately, more and more contractors are becoming convinced of the value of sustainable practices and have the skills to protect construction sites from unnecessary damage.

Coordination and Follow-up

Protecting a healthy site requires coordination. Like a bad haircut, damage to a healthy site can't just be glued back. It must grow back, perhaps with the help of expensive restoration techniques, always with a requirement for time. Planning, surveying, design, physical protection, machinery use, cleanup, maintenance, and monitoring all play a role in keeping healthy sites healthy.

Because design, construction, and maintenance are conventionally organized as separate professions, monitoring and follow-up are often neglected. Ongoing attention is required to sustain those increasingly rare sites that have retained their health in today's stressed environment.

Resources

Keep Healthy Sites Healthy

Surveying and mapping

Search Terms: surveying OR mapping || land surveying || land mapping || GIS || GPS

Am. Soc. for Photogrammetry & Remote Sensing 310-493-0290, www.asprs.org/: Mapping, GIS, GPS, and related topics; membership.

National Society of Professional Surveyors www.nspsmo.org/: Publications, referrals to surveying firms.

GPS suppliers Magellan, 408-615-5236; Sokkia, 913-492-7585; Trimble, 800-874-6253

Tube level Zircon Corp, Campbell CA, 800-245-9265, www.zircon.com/: Commercial tube level with audible signal.

Navtech Books and Software 800-628-0885, www.navtechgps.com/: GPS books, software, educational items, booklists.

GPS Made Easy: Using Global Positioning Systems in the Outdoors Lawrence Letham, 1996 The Mountaineers, Seattle WA:

Instructions on using simple GPS for hiking, as well as field data collection and basic site reconnaissance. Glossary, supplier and book lists.

GIS for Environmental Management R. Scally, 2006 ESRI Press, New York

GPS Satellite Surveying Alfred Leick, 1995 Wiley, New York: Technical textbook.

GPS: A Guide to the Next Utility 1989 Trimble Navigation: Introductory volume on GPS.

GPS World www.gpsworld.com/gpsworld/: Monthly; rated listings of GPS models and new applications.

GIS.com www.gis.com/: Web site providing overview of GIS technology.

Cyrax 3D laser surveying Leica Geosystems, 925-790-2300, www.leica-geosystems.com/hds/en/lgs_5210.htm

Gradesetting: A Practical Handbook to Fit in Your Pocket Michael Smookler, 2005 American Printing, Burlingame CA: smookeythebear2000@ yahoo.com.

Site inventory and visualization

Search Terms: site inventory || site inventory method || site assessment || site assessment tools || site protection

Healthy Communities Environmental Mapping U.S. Department of Housing and Urban Development and U.S. EPA, Washington DC

GeoConservation Commission, Geological Society of London www.geoconservation.com/publications.htm: Books on landscape, site, and geological conservation.

Home Ground: Language for an American Landscape Barry Lopez (ed.), 2006 Trinity University Press, San Antonio TX: Wonderful "dictionary" of landscape terms, place names.

Ecological Networks and Greenways R. Jongman and G. Pungetti, 2004 Cambridge University Press, Cambridge

Landscape Perspective Drawing N. Dines, 1990 McGraw-Hill, New York: Still an essential skill for envisioning design.

Practical Ecology for Planners, Developers, and Citizens D. Perlman and J. Milder, 2005 Island Press, Washington DC: Basic ecological concepts linked to community issues.

CommunityViz software 802.367.6336, www.communityviz.com/

Orton Family Foundation www.orton.org/: GIS-based what-if visualizations; clarifies some landscape issues, distorts others.

NetLogo agent-based simulation software http://ccl.northwestern.edu/netlogo/: Tutorial at backspaces.net/tutorial/NetLogo/index.html.

ArcNews www.esri.com/arcnews/: Innovative GIS uses.

Measuring Landscapes: A Planner's Handbook A. Leitão et al., 2006 Island Press, Washington DC: Quantifying landscape patterns, functions, and flows.

"Getting to Know a Place: Site Evaluation as a Starting Point for Green Design" Alex Wilson, EBN, Mar 1998

USGS topographic maps 1-888-MAP-DEAL, www.usgs.gov/: Lists available maps, related products, retailers by region.

EPA Eco-regions maps www.epa.gov/waterscience/criteria/nutrient/ecomap.htm: Clear, detailed color maps show US regions based on ecological similarities, critical to sustainability.

American Digital Cartography 800-236-7973 ext. 2, www.adci.com/: Digital maps, including non-topographical types, such as urban maps showing road and street widths.

Maptech 888-839-5551, www.maptech.com/: Digital USGS maps; Terrain Navigator software, plus CD-ROMs with 200 USGS topographic maps per disk; automates calculations of regional distances and elevations; draws topographic sections.

Guide to a Plant Inventory at a Historic Property Margaret Coffin and Kristin Baker, 1998 Olmsted Center for Landscape Preservation, Boston

Advances in Historical Ecology William L. Balée, 1998 Columbia University Press, New York

Archaeologies of Landscape: Contemporary Perspectives Wendy Ashmore and Arthur B. Knapp, 1999 Blackwell Publishers, Malden MA

Breaking Ground: Examining the Vision and Practice of Historic Landscape Restoration 1999 Old Salem, Winston-Salem NC

Cultural Landscape Bibliography Katherine Ahern, Leslie H. Blythe, and Robert R. Page, 1992 U.S. National Park Service Cultural Landscape Program, Washington DC

Earth Patterns: Essays in Landscape Archaeology William M. Kelso and Rachel Most, 1990 University Press of Virginia, Charlottesville

Enduring Roots: Encounters with Trees, History, and the American Landscape Gayle B. Samuels, 1999 Rutgers University Press, New Brunswick NJ

Historic Landscape Directory: A Source Book of Agencies, Organizations, and Institutions Lauren Meier and Sarah S. Boasberg, 1991 U.S. National Park Service Preservation Assistance Division and Historic Landscapes Committee, Washington DC

History on the Ground M. W. Beresford, 1998 Sutton, Stroud UK

Landscape Assessment: Values, Perceptions, and Resources Ervin H. Zube, Robert O. Brush, and Julius Guy Fabos, 1975 Halsted, Wiley, New York

Landscapes and Gardens for Historic Buildings Rudy J. and Joy P. Favretti, 1997, 2nd ed., AltaMira Press, Walnut Creek CA

Landscapes in History Philip Pregill and Nancy Volkman, 1998, 2nd ed., Wiley, New York

Preserving Historic Landscapes: An Annotated Bibliography Lauren Meier and Betsy Chittenden, 1990 U.S. National Park Service Preservation Assistance Division, Washington DC

The Landscape of Man: Shaping the Environment from Prehistory to the Present Day Geoffrey and Susan Jellicoe, 1995, 3rd ed., Thames and Hudson, London

Site protection

Soil Mat Lifter Monroe Ecological Services, Heartlesville PA, 610-287-0671: A commercial version of the forest-sod lifting machine described above.

Caring for Our Land Carol Greene, n.d. Enslow Publishers, Hillside NJ

Checklist for Sustainable Landscape Management J. D. van Mansvelt and M. J. van der Lubbe, 1999 Elsevier, Amsterdam: European Union report AIR3-CT93-1210.

Connectivity in Landscape Ecology Karl-Friedrich Schreiber, 1988 F. Schöningh, Paderborn, Germany: www.usiale.org/lejlinks.htm; 1987 Conference Proceedings, International Association of Landscape Ecology.

Developing a Land Conservation Strategy George D. Davis and Thomas R. Duffus, 1987 Adirondack Land Trust, Elizabethtown NY

Greenline Parks: Land Conservation Trends for the Eighties and Beyond Marjorie R. Corbett and Michael S. Batcher, 1983 National Parks and Conservation Association, Washington DC

Landscape Ecology: Theory and Application Zeev Naveh and Arthur S. Lieberman, 1994, 2nd ed., Springer-Verlag, Germany

Landscape Protection: A Bibliography Mary A. Vance, 1988 Vance Bibliographies, Monticello IL

Making Educated Decisions: A Landscape Preservation Bibliography Charles A. Birnbaum, Cheryl Wagner, and Jean S. Jones, 2000, 2nd ed., U.S. National Park Service Preservation Assistance Division, Washington DC

Preparing a Landscaping Ordinance, Report No. 431 Wendelyn A. Martz and Marya Morris, 1990 American Planning Association Planning Advisory Service, Chicago

Protected Landscapes: A Guide for Policy Makers and Planners P. H. C. Lucas, 1992 International Union for Conservation of Nature; Chapman and Hall, New York

Protected Landscapes: The United Kingdom Experience Duncan and Judy Poore, 1987 Great Britain Countryside Commission, Manchester UK

Saving America's Countryside: A Guide to Rural Conservation Samuel N. Stokes, A. Elizabeth Watson, and Shelley S. Mastran, 1997, 2nd ed., Johns Hopkins University Press, Baltimore

The Economic Valuation of Landscape Change José Manuel L. Santos, 1998 Edward Elgar, Northampton MA

The Economics of Landscape and Wildlife Conservation Stephan Dabbert, 1998 CAB International, New York

The Funny Thing About Landscape : Cautionary Tales for Environmentalists Jay Appleton, 1991 Book Guild, Lewes UK

The Legal Landscape: Guidelines for Regulating Environmental and Aesthetic Quality Richard C. Smardon and James Karp, 1993 Van Nostrand Reinhold, New York

Wilderness by Design: Landscape Architecture and the National Park Service Ethan Carr, 1998 University of Nebraska Press, Lincoln NE

Land Development Checklist for Environmental Concerns Greater Grand Rapids Home Builders Association, Grand Rapids MI: 800-305-2021, www.hbaggr.com/.

U.S. Landscape Ordinances: An Annotated Reference Handbook Buck Abbey, 1998 Wiley, New York

Land Conservation www.lta.org/resources/index.html: Land Trust Alliance site lists books, legal decisions, nonprofits and trusts, links on legal and other aspects of land conservation.

Site protection: Vegetation

Search Terms: protection + (vegetation OR trees)

Preventing Construction Damage to Municipal Trees Milwaukee Forestry Division, Milwaukee WI: 414-286-8282, www.mpw.net/Pages/ops5.html: Detailed manual including sample specifications; for sale by the city.

Trees and Development: A Technical Guide to Preservation of Trees During Land Development Nelda Matheny and James R. Clark, 1998 International Society of Arboriculture, Champaign IL: 888-ISA-TREE, www.isa-arbor.com/.

Trees and Building Sites: Proceedings of an International Workshop on Trees and Buildings Dan Neely and Gary Watson, International Society of Arboriculture: conference proceedings, 31 May–2 June 1995

Vancouver tree bylaws Vancouver BC, www.city.vancouver.bc.ca/ commsvcs/planning/: Example of a thorough law governing protection of trees during construction.

Vegetation: consultants

Search Terms: biologist || range (scientist OR manager) || plant ecologist

Certified Arborists List International Society of Arborists, www.isa-arbor.com/

Vegetation: native plants

Search Terms: native plants || native vegetation || native landscaping

Guide to the Standard Floras of the World D. G. Frodin, 2001, 2nd ed., Cambridge University Press, Cambridge

Landscaping with Native Plants of the Southwest G. O. Miller, 2007 Voyageur Press, Saint Paul MN

Native Plant Revegetation Guide for Colorado Colorado State Parks, download from http://parks.state.co.us/NaturalResources/ ParksResourceStewardship/Revegetation/: Applicable to much of the Rockies.

EPA—Native Plants Page www.epa.gov/greenacres/: Benefits of native plants; many resources.

Plant Native www.plantnative.com/: General info, nursery directory, regional plant lists.

National Biological Information Infrastructure 703-648-6244, www.nbii.gov/: Gateway to government and private data about biodiversity, native plants.

Center for Plant Conservation www.centerforplantconservation .org/invasives/home.html: Source with good links regarding invasive plants.

Invasive Plants, Changing the Landscape of America: Factbook U.S. Government Printing Office, Washington DC: 866-512-1800, http://bookstore.gpo.gov/.

National Strategy and Implementation Plan for Invasive Species Management www.fs.fed.us/foresthealth/publica tions/Invasive_Species.pdf#search=%22National%20Strat-egy%20for%20Invasive%20Plant%20Management%22

Edison Electric Institute 202-508-5000, www.eei.org/: Information on electric utilities, with a clear industry slant. Guidelines for easement maintenance.

National Pipeline Mapping System www.npms.phmsa.dot.gov, ops.dot.gov, www.safepipelines.org, and www.pipeline101 .com: All offer information about utility pipelines.

The Forest Guild 505-983-8992, www.forestguild.org/

Manejo de Areas Silvestres Protegidas Colorado State University, welcome.colostate.edu/: Spanish-language training for forest protection.

Forest Trust www.forestguild.org/: Solid information on forest issues.

Utility impact

Search Terms: utility + (impact OR environment OR easement)

Interlocking Concrete Pavement Institute Washington DC, 202-712-9036, www.icpi.org/: Interlocking pavers, related machinery, suppliers and contractors; trade journal.

Cellular Tower Coalition www.cellulartower.com/: Alternatives to communications towers.

Cellular Telecommunications Industry Association Washington DC, 202-785-0081, www.ctia.org: Industry views; see also www.fcc.gov/.

EMR Alliance 212-554-4073, www2.cruzio.com/~rbedard/ emrall.html: Health concerns of electromagnetic radiation.

Municipal Research and Services Center www.mrsc.org/index .aspx: Concerns about cell towers; many other issues.

Transcept, Inc. 603-645-5581, www.wirelessnetworksonline .com/storefronts/transcept.html: Mini antenna for cell-phone systems; Manchester NH.

Energy generation

Search Terms: (energy OR power) + (generation OR production OR technology) _ renewable energy || photovoltaic || fuel cell || hydro power

Home Power magazine 800-707-6585, www.homepower.com/: Bimonthly.

Energy Information Administration www.eia.doe.gov/: Official energy statistics from the US government by source.

U.S. DOE Energy Efficiency and Renewable Energy www.eere .energy.gov/: Official U.S. resource for renewable energy.

Tools

Hand tools for landscape and arboriculture A. M. Leonard, Piqua OH, 800-543-8955, www.amleo.com/: Wide range of horticulture, arboriculture, and landscape tools, machinery, books, and supplies.

Potlifter www.potlifter.com, 888-644-4222: Cinch sling tool for lifting awkward round or bulky objects up to 200 lbs.

Principle 2:
Heal Injured Sites

And they shall build the old wastes and repair the waste cities, the desolation of many generations.
—Isaiah 61:4

In a consumer society, landscape development too often becomes a form of consumption. As development sprawls outward along an ever-expanding urban fringe, forests are leveled and farms destroyed to make way for cul-de-sacs, backyards, business parks, and, of course, acres of parking.

This paradigm must be rethought before this continent is paved from sea to shining sea. Instead of *consuming* virgin landscape to make places to live and work, think in terms of *recycling* existing sites. Degraded sites in cities and older suburbs can be rendered fit for new uses. At the same time, managed growth must preserve farms, forests, and natural areas surrounding cities.

There are various tested models of growth management; greenbelts and "urban growth boundaries" are probably best known. Such initiatives lie in the realm of politics and land-use planning, not landscape construction. But landscape construction that recycles existing sites has its own role to play in reinhabiting waste places.

The previous chapter describes methods of protecting undamaged sites and minimizing damage to them. Techniques in this chapter are useful in restoring sites (or portions of sites) damaged by prior use or during construction. These techniques may occasionally apply to healthy landscapes, but primarily offer help for abused landscapes—what most of us would consider wastelands. Fortunately, landscapes, like people, have a remarkable ability to heal, and numerous precedents exist for turning even wastelands into gardens.

Restoring sites that have lost vegetation and soil takes on new purpose and urgency with recent research that links such losses to global climate change (p. 15). Land restoration techniques to address most local climate-related issues overlap. Restoration that decreases wildfire danger, for example, is likely to decrease soil erosion, flash flooding, and drought as well.

Discussed in This Chapter

Types of sites requiring restoration.
Evaluating whether restoration is appropriate.
Social and organizational aspects of site restoration.
Structural restoration techniques.
Restoring soil to health.
Using plants in site restoration.
Restoration as the proper approach to wildfire dangers.
Getting professional help for heavy-duty site toxicity.

Turn Wastelands to Gardens

Urban and suburban landscapes may be degraded in various ways, from minor damage to Superfund sites. For this book, we consider three levels of damage, recognizing some overlap. In order of severity these are:

- derelict sites—damage to health and structure, but not particularly toxic

- brownfields, including contained landfills
- toxic waste sites.

Outside urban areas, sites are frequently damaged by vegetation removal or topsoil loss, by vegetation changes due to suppression of processes like fire, and by introduction of invasive species. Restoration of such "nontoxic" damage is discussed in the latter half of this chapter.

Arid regions present special problems for any kind of restoration, and for bioengineering, greenwalls, and greenroofs (see Principle 3). One promising resource is David Bainbridge's *Guide for Desert and Dryland Restoration*, just released in 2007 by Island Press. It covers techniques, tools, planning, and community issues, focusing on rather large-scale and mostly rural restoration—all invaluable in adapting the strategies presented below to areas of little rain.

Mend Derelict Sites

Every community has derelict sites, stripped of topsoil, littered with debris, and capable of supporting only noxious weeds. Buildings or paving cover some of these sites—"improvements" from a real-estate point of view—making them impervious. As such, derelict sites cause harm without necessarily harboring toxic waste: they prevent recharging of aquifers, seal off the soil, and support neither oxygen-replenishing plants nor wildlife. For derelict sites, soil revitalization may be enough restoration, permitting normal gardening techniques to work once more. Removal or reuse of structures is also realistic.

Reuse Brownfields

Brownfields are polluted lands—"the neglected sites of the postindustrial landscape," in the words of Harvard landscape architecture professor Niall Kirkwood, an expert on such sites. Brownfields go beyond derelict, usually suffering from polluted soil or groundwater or both.[1] Landfills can be considered deliberate brownfields. Some sources also refer to "greyfields," abandoned sites that are 50 percent or more paved or impervious,[2] which though not technically "polluted" are heavily damaged.

Landscape construction can play an active role in reclaiming these sites, usually in conjunction with engineering solutions. In addition to significant structural repair, plants that actively remove toxins ("phytoremediation") and "manufactured" soils are important techniques.

Kirkwood believes cleaning up brownfields could return landscape architecture to "the nineteenth-century vision that the landscape is the body and the lungs of the city. A lot of Olmsted's work," says Kirkwood, "was really environmental engineering. His Emerald Necklace [in Boston] is essentially a drainage project. Our roots [are] in issues of health, infrastructure, and open space—the Olmstedian concept of regenerating the city."

Recognition of brownfields' potential value was initially slow to dawn but today is growing rapidly. Early attempts at redevelopment were daunting: owners were liable for any site contamination, even if caused by previous users. Today, however, federal regulations have been streamlined, states like Massachusetts initiated their own brownfields-cleanup programs, and banks now lend money for sites previously deemed untouchable. In 1998 the *New York Times* estimated 6,500 brownfields in and around New York City alone; in 2007 it reported that restoring such sites was a chief priority of the city's economic development officials.[3] Nationally some 450,000 brownfields await return to productive use.

Get Specialist Help for Toxic Sites, Tanks, and Hazmats

On sites such as those covered by the EPA's Superfund, landscape construction is not the primary solution. Only after highly technical environmental engineering might surface landscape construction be appropriate. Remediation and restoration of sites at this level is outside this book's scope. For this category of injured sites, seek consultant help. Resources for Principle 6 also offer information on identifying toxic materials.

Removal of hazardous buried structures like fuel-storage tanks and remediation of heavily contaminated soils is a very specialized branch of construction. This work requires both special permits and special skills. It is critical to long-term sustainability that these

Figure 2.1 Brownfields take up large areas in most modern cities. Neither society nor the environment can afford this waste, and restoring the potentially toxic sites is a priority and a challenge. (*Photo:* Eric Carman.)

Figure 2.2 Restoration of mines, heavy industry, and Superfund sites requires specialized engineering, but should not exclude landscape concerns such as habitat and visual fit with surroundings. (*Photo:* New Mexico Department of Mining and Minerals.)

tasks be thoughtfully planned and skillfully carried out.

Any site remediation involving toxic materials is likely to require input from environmental engineers. The degree of engineering involvement *should* correspond to the severity of contamination. Current regulations, however, are written and administered largely by engineers, and sometimes exclude biological solutions. It is critically important to balance both types of approach in ways that meet safety requirements, minimize financial costs, and truly restore the site (rather than making it inert, safe but dead).

Landscape professionals can work to educate engineering colleagues and the public about biological site remediation. This must be done thoughtfully and diplomatically. No purpose is served by insisting on "natural solutions" that fail and tarnish the credibility of more careful site-specific approaches. Although bias against biological solutions is frustrating at times, landscape professionals *must* know when engineering help is truly the most appropriate solution.

Balance the Environmental Costs and Benefits of Restoration

Restoring landscapes costs money, energy, labor, and time. Hindsight is clear: avoiding contamination in the first place is much cheaper. But faced with undeniably injured landscapes, choices must be made. There are both economic and ecological limits to

what can be restored. For some sites, only full restoration to preindustrial conditions is worth doing; for others any remediation is better than nothing. Not all technologies are appropriate for all restoration sites, nor for the communities in which they exist. As with most sustainable practices, site specific is the key concept.

Site restoration is usually appropriate if:

- Disturbance resulted from human land use (construction, grazing, mining, logging, fire suppression, dumping, abandoned structures, off-road vehicles, regional economic decline, etc.).
- Use of the *restored* site can prevent developing or disturbing a *healthy* site.
- "Recruitment" (vegetation regrowth from relic seeds in existing soil or from adjacent sites) can be a major strategy.
- Restoration costs are likely to yield long-term savings by stopping erosion, rebuilding productive soils, buffering or treating noise or air or water pollution, or protecting threatened species. The crucial need to reduce global climate change is changing the equation significantly in favor of revegetation.
- Restoration is legally required, a condition for permitting land use, with costs borne by the parties who profit (e.g., mine restoration).

- The site has strong cultural significance, as in national and historic parks, or was significant before becoming degraded.
- Degraded forests, wetlands, estuaries, or aquifer recharge zones are involved.

Site restoration *may* be worth considering if:

- Disturbance resulted from disaster "provoked" by humans (landslides due to soil abuses, floods due to failed "flood control," etc.).
- Restoration will yield economic or aesthetic results valued by people (but of no particular ecological value).
- Restoration can create jobs, educate workers, or support local industry (a native-plant nursery, for example).
- Restoration involves community participation, increasing community cohesion and identity.
- Restoration educates community members about sustainability through planning, fieldwork, or activities at the completed site.

Site restoration is usually *not* practical or appropriate if:

- Disturbance resulted from natural processes not accelerated by humans.
- The site is so small that outside influences will overwhelm restoration.
- The true cause of disturbance is off-site, with no likelihood of cooperation from the source site's owner.
- The so-called restoration is cosmetic (disguising persistent problems, not self-maintaining).
- Restoration requires major use of materials whose removal damages other sites (e.g., wild-dug plants or imported topsoil).
- Restoration cannot be expected to sustain itself without long-term intensive maintenance, irrigation, or similar intervention. (Maintenance during establishment and minor periodic maintenance should be expected.)
- Restoration defers the real problem onto another site or into the future (in which case, it is probably cosmetic).

- Restoration may attract poaching, destructive or motorized site access, illegal use, or other problems, unless these can be monitored and prevented.
- Cost of restoration is excessively high, even when figured as life-cycle costs and taking environmental services, intangibles, and job creation into account.

Involve the Community in Site Restoration

Abandonment of defunct industries and deteriorated neighborhoods often makes site reuse a desperate need. Demolishing 800 vacant row houses at once, as happened in Baltimore in the 1990s, is unusual only in scale. There, reduced demand meant only a quarter of the housing would be replaced, leaving 600 lots to transform into green space.

Technical solutions to such challenges are invented, communicated, and used in social *context*. With infill development and neighborhood revitalization becoming common steps towards sustainability, we expect a growing percentage of the landscape professional's clients to be community groups, rather than top-down agency or commercial entities. Community-based recycling of derelict spaces isn't business as usual. The contractor or designer who wants to be part of this process will need to learn and adapt.

Know the Site's History

Restoring something implies going back to an original condition. For something as complex as a landscape, knowing what condition was "original" is not always simple. Sites are living, changing entities; both natural succession and human land use change every site over time.

It is important to distinguish between *historic* restoration, which attempts to re-create the site at a particular point in time, and *environmental* restoration, which attempts to restore site health. Both forms of restoration have their purpose, and overlap significantly. "Health," however, is a much more dynamic goal than period restoration. Consider the human equivalent: the health of a sixty-year-old can be restored; the sixty-year-old cannot be restored to being sixteen. (Landscapes can be set back in time, but re-creation is never exact.[4])

A person who recovers from ill health continues, once healthy, to age and change. So does an environmentally restored landscape. Suppose a forested site was developed, abused, and left derelict. Restoring it to health would primarily mean restoring its ability to support life. The restored parcel might look like a meadow and still be "restored" in health. It might also, given many years, use its restored health to grow back to forest. People could, of course, also choose to restore its health by planting forest trees. That would restore it both environmentally and historically, at an increased cost in resources.

Thus restoration requires both knowledge (What was the site before? How did it develop?) and decision (Is health the goal, or history? Are conditions in 1800 the target, or 1492?) In both knowledge and decision making, local community input is indispensable.

No matter what kind of restoration is planned, decision-making knowledge almost always includes history, of natural processes as well as of human land use. Resources from the fields of Historic Preservation and Historical Ecology are frequently helpful.⊃ Environmental and historic restoration may be separate goals; but the environmental past of a site is seldom separate from human influences. This is especially true of the derelict lands most in need of restoration, because that need is due to human abuse or neglect.

Start an Urban Barn-raising

Transforming, regenerating, and restoring neglected lands is crucial to restoring the *human* communities that have been abandoned on these unpromising sites. One individual who pursued land-and-community restoration was the late Karl Linn. Landscape architect, psychologist, and social activist, Linn was concerned about the decline of inner cities where shrinking populations or economies result in derelict land.[5] Conventional municipal-park landscaping generally fails or cannot be funded in such areas. Instead, drawing on experience of grassroots groups like New York City's Green Guerillas, Linn worked with inner-city residents to construct "neighborhood commons."

Linn proposed that derelict tracts be turned into urban farms or wildflower meadows, at least until further development. His methods rely primarily on natural plant succession, with help from humans, to improve soil and transform neighborhood appearance. Linn envisioned Newark NJ (often stigmatized as America's most squalid city) becoming "the Garden City of the Garden State," bringing together vast acreages of urban land with an ecological vision.[6] After relocating to Berkeley CA, Linn worked with community groups to create city gardens and farms in the Bay Area.

Community-based methods are critically important to urban restoration in particular. They parallel environmental protection efforts in less-developed countries, where participation of local and indigenous people has proved vital to success.[7] Clearly, they also link with the community-garden concept, a well-established movement in many parts of the world.

Follow the Lead of Community-garden Groups

One group Linn worked with is the San Francisco League of Urban Gardeners (SLUG), one of the country's most active community-gardening groups. SLUG's work crews have constructed numerous neighborhood gardens, plus San Francisco's only working farm, the four-acre St. Mary's Urban Youth Farm in low-income Hunter's Point. St. Mary's has utterly transformed a blighted inner-city site.

The site (adjacent to a housing project) had been used by contractors for dumping, littered with spoil dirt and waste concrete, soon followed by old refrigerators, wrecked cars, and household garbage. SLUG workers filled several sixteen-foot-long Dumpsters with debris. Today the site features thirty raised garden beds, nearly one hundred fruit trees, and herb gardens. These provide produce for residents' use, for distribution to food kitchens in other low-income communities, and for a cottage industry of salad vinegars, made by local residents. A composting operation produces and sells garden mulch from yard waste collected throughout San Francisco. While many urban Americans struggle with the concept of

Figure 2.3 St. Mary's Farm relinks urban residents with the land and their own skills. Most cities could benefit from similar community landscapes; where soil is not toxic, they produce food as well as social activity. (*Project:* SLUG. *Photo:* Karl Linn.)

food production, St. Mary's Urban Youth Farm is busy doing it.

The community-garden movement is quiet but widespread, a potent grassroots force for site restoration. Its thesis (quite foreign to this supermarket culture) is that food should be grown close to where people live. Thousands of community gardens thrive across the United States, most of them in major cities. In Philadelphia alone, 1,500 such gardens involve over 600 families in producing $1.5 million worth of food.[8]

European cities devote significant land to "allotment" gardens. A 1980 survey in England and Wales found only two main types of *urban* soils: sterile soils disturbed by construction, engineering, and dumping; and the fertile soils of community gardens. The survey described allotment-garden soils as "man-made humus soils . . . , dark well-structured topsoil from particularly deep cultivation (double digging) coupled with heavy organic manuring."[9] This is dramatic evidence that gardeners can reinstate site health in urban areas.

Despite their immense value, urban community gardens are seldom safe from development pressure. In 1999, for example, New York Mayor Rudolph Giuliani coerced community-garden and environmental groups into paying $4.2 million to ransom eleven acres of gardens they had revived from trash-strewn abandoned lots. Giuliani equated the gardeners' efforts with communism and did his best to create conflict with people on the eight-year waiting list for public housing. Like the environment-versus-jobs ploy, setting community landscapes against community housing is the worst sort of dishonesty and shortsightedness.[10]

Invest in a Garden Festival

The garden festival, more capital intensive and ambitious than a community garden, is nevertheless a valid restoration approach, widely used in Europe. Abused sites (both derelict and brownfield) are redeveloped as large, themed public gardens. Festival gardens operate like fairs for some months, then are "recycled" as parks or housing space. Essentially, such festivals create landscapes as a catalyst for reinvestment. Garden festivals were effective in rehabilitating bombed-out German cities after World War II, then applied to other European sites, including Britain's urban and industrial brownfields.[11] Despite high costs, they show how much can be accomplished quickly when society decides to reinvest in damaged sites.

Nearly all British garden festivals were constructed on industrially degraded sites. Liverpool Garden Festival (in the 1980s) was built on spoil tips from coal mining and inner-city garbage dumps. The "Nature

Figure 2.4 Peralta Community Art Gardens in Berkeley CA is a decorative meeting place made by neighbors from leftover land and materials. (*Project:* Community and Karl Linn. *Photo:* Karl Linn.)

in the City" portion of that festival, showcasing Britain's native plants, was built on an eighteen-acre mountain of garbage more than a hundred feet high.[12] "The people of Liverpool through the event were made aware," wrote one festival designer, "that you could transform a totally useless, severely polluted area of land into a major visitor attraction of international standing."[13]

Ebbw Vale in South Wales was also developed on a brownfield site. The 57-hectare (141-acre) site of this festival had been an air-polluting steel mill, with adjacent mines. The Welsh Development Agency reclaimed the site at a cost of twenty million pounds. The festival garden included a 5-million-gallon lake, a 120-foot waterfall, 33,000 trees and shrubs, and 550,000 flowers. *Landscape Design* magazine's description read: "Where there used to be satanic mills and furnaces there is now a fantastic array of lakes, gardens, floral displays, marquees, exhibitions, and fun rides." After the six-month festival, the landscape was developed as a business park.[14]

Garden festivals are costly and may fail to meet ecological goals. As fast-track projects they require installation of semi-mature trees and other plantings, trucked in from distant nurseries. Like other social issues affecting landscape reconstruction, decisions about speed of restoration are seldom simple. Instant landscape, however, manifests a commodity-driven

society. Emphasizing speed strongly affects choice of techniques and may rule out gradual, community-based reclamation. Instant plantings also can *mis*educate festival visitors, obscuring understanding of plant succession. A community that accepts the concept that built landscapes grow and evolve has an expanded range of cost-effective and ecologically sound restoration methods available.

Educating the public about landscape ecological processes is integral to the Earth Center in South Yorkshire, England. Although as big as many festival gardens, its stated mission is "to promote understanding of sustainable development and to help people become involved in the process of achieving it in their own lives." The Earth Center is built on a pair of abandoned collieries (coal mines) on the River Don, near Doncaster. It is the biggest landscape project in the United Kingdom based on sustainable principles—"to demonstrate," in the words of Andrew Grant, the landscape architect, "how regenerating land can provide rich opportunities for play, production of food, wildlife, and general public enjoyment."[15]

In designing the Earth Center, all decisions had to be justifiable in terms of sustainability. Materials specification required local materials, suppliers, and labor. This minimized environmental costs of transportation and bolstered the local economy. Many materials came from the site itself: for pedestrian paving, burnt coal shale—a pinkish by-product of historical coal-washing activities—produced an attractive surfacing at very little cost.[16]

Planting at the Earth Center was the antithesis of "instant landscape." Instead, "the Earth Center landscape is designed to make people look at, think about, and react to the issues that affect our future landscapes," says Grant. "It is to be a visual and ecological response to the process of regeneration on this site, and is deliberately planned to evolve and redefine its character well into the next century."[17] Plant succession and change is on display, contrasting not only with instant landscape, but also with attempts to "freeze" landscapes unchangingly through intensive maintenance.

Despite different methods, the Earth Center and garden festivals are public celebrations of the ability to regenerate blighted landscapes.

Make a Virtue of the Necessity for Landfills

Landfills, unlike other brownfields, are created deliberately to contain society's enormous quantities of waste. Once filled, they become environmental problems (and eyesores) if simply closed. If restored, landfills offer remarkable open-space opportunities—what might be called "postconsumer landscapes." Recycling these sites requires interagency cooperation, but may be cheaper than acquiring urban land for parks and recreation and can relieve development pressures elsewhere.

Recycling landfills is no substitute for waste-stream reduction. Entombing garbage within a clay liner, cut off from water and air, preventing natural processes of decay, is fundamentally questionable. As solid-waste authorities find more effective resource-recovery and recycling methods—or, for that matter, as consumers buy fewer throwaway products—landfills and landfill restoration may fade into history. Until then, reuse is better than abandonment.

Parks on landfills are not uncommon in the United States. One of the oldest is Virginia Beach VA's aptly named Mount Trashmore. Cambridge MA added 20 percent to its total open space with one landfill restoration, 55-acre Danehy Park. Featuring turf and naturalized plantings, this popular park also incorporated recycled "glasphalt" (see p. 234) in an ADA-accessible path.

A landfill project in Yarmouth MA, on Cape Cod, shows how many functions—ecological, social, and economic—a well-reclaimed site can serve. The designers of Danehy Park, Camp Dresser & McKee (CDM) have developed landfills as office parks, sports fields, and parking facilities, says Vice President John Kissida. The 57-acre landfill at Yarmouth, however, stands out for its integration of functions.

Federal and state regulators forced closure of Yarmouth's forty-year-old dump; among other problems, it was located in one of Cape Cod's scarce aquifer recharge zones. A community-based, participatory process created a golf course, park, bike path, and residential/construction/demolition waste recycling facility. Revenues from recycling and the golf course offset the cost. Effluent reuse provides nearly half the water (and fertilizer nutrients) for the golf course.[18]

Landfills have become golf courses in climates as diverse as Charlotte NC, Phoenix AZ, and St. Petersburg FL. Harborside International, on Chicago's South Side, is one of the largest (425 acres) and quite spectacular, comprising two eighteen-hole courses, a 45-acre practice facility, and a golf academy. Above the flat Illinois landscape, the site is a plateau built up of fly ash from a closed garbage incinerator. A recycled product provided fertility: processed sewage sludge from Chicago Metropolitan Water Reclamation District. Sinuous greens meander through tawny grassed mounds and steep hillocks where fescue and rye, unmown, wave in the unfailing breeze. Harborside has won several awards, including the 1996 Superior Achievement award from the American Academy of Environmental Engineering.

One of the world's largest dump sites, at 2,400 acres, is Staten Island's Fresh Kills landfill (the name, ironically, means fresh brook). The site is poised to be "refreshed" as New York City's most expansive open space. A draft master plan by Field Operations landscape architects (New York and Philadelphia) may be downloaded from the Fresh Kills Park website, www.nyc.gov/freshkillspark. The first recreation facility, Owl Hollow soccer fields, should be com-

Figure 2.5 At Quarry Hills outside Boston, a 130-acre closed landfill (in background) became 27 holes of golf. (*Project:* Quarry Hills Associates. *Photo:* Art Cicone.)

Figure 2.6 Harborside International golf course makes beautiful reuse of a landfill. Industrial buildings in the background show the context of this massive site restoration. (*Project:* Nugent Associates. *Photo:* Sally Hughes.)

plete in 2007, with other areas opening to the public by 2009. The New York City Department of Parks and Recreation will oversee construction, with an initial allocation of $100 million in capital funds.

Fresh Kills will undoubtedly be the country's largest, most elaborate landfill park, containing a memorial from World Trade Center rubble. Some unusual activities will be accommodated, like mountain biking and kayaking. Beyond notoriety or sheer size, Fresh Kills is important for scientific monitoring that provides hard data on the safety and cost effectiveness of structural restoration methods for landfills.

Understand Structural Issues of Landfills

Landfills are structurally unique in the built environment. Sealed to isolate the polluting materials abandoned in them, they are huge buried containers that cannot be moved and must not be punctured. The technology of capping and sealing landfills is well developed. Planting over such structures, however, requires unusual techniques. Some, like manufactured soil (p. 96), are widely applicable; others are specific to contained landfills.

Fear that tree roots might pierce the strictly regulated clay or plastic "cap," allowing dangerous gases

Figure 2.7 Fresh Kills on Staten Island, one of the world's largest garbage dumps, is being reclaimed as a twenty-first-century park. (*Project:* Field Operations. *Photo:* City of New York.)

to escape or rainwater to enter, has led some states to ban trees and plant landfills with unvarying swaths of turf. Research (some at Fresh Kills) suggests that banning trees is unwarranted.

Root penetration of a properly constructed cap is highly unlikely because:

- cap density physically prevents root penetration
- anaerobic conditions in and below the cap kill roots
- tree roots are concentrated in soil surface layers above the cap.[19]

A compelling reason to permit trees is to reduce landscape maintenance. Local trees will colonize unless actively prevented by mowing and herbicides, with energy and pollution costs. Trees also reduce erosion, a serious issue on landfills, where slopes may be 3-to-1 and 250 feet high. With shrubs and trees, landfills gain potential as wildlife habitat or corridors, not to mention visual variety. These benefits outweigh potential problems.

In the late 1980s the New York City sanitation department devoted six already-capped acres at Fresh Kills to testing. One goal was to determine whether the landfill could support anything approaching Staten Island's indigenous vegetation, which of course includes many species of trees.

The restoration team reshaped uniform steep slopes, interrupted every fifty feet by wide, flat benches, creating dune-like slopes that mimicked the island's coastal landscape. (Compare landform grading, Figure 2.9, p. 82.) They rescued plants from sites slated for development elsewhere on Staten Island: 3,000 shrubs, 523 native trees, and native perennial grasses and wildflowers.

Landscape architect Bill Young, one of the team members, advocated irrigating with leachate (water that drains from landfills, often picking up contaminants). This was controversial, but Fresh Kills leachate was tested and found to be within EPA toxicity limits. Because it could not be allowed to flow off the landfill, it was recirculated on site. Young notes that irrigating with leachate would be much more feasible if toxic items like batteries and household cleansers were eliminated from waste. Increasingly, landfills do require that such materials be sorted out (for reasons other than watering trees).

A team of restoration ecologists from Rutgers University was hired to monitor the Fresh Kills plantings. Test plots showed moderate tree growth and excellent shrub growth. Woody plants in "habitat islands" provided much-needed perching sites for birds, which reciprocated by dispersing seeds, spreading volunteer trees to other areas. Surprisingly effective, seed dispersal from the habitat islands boosted woody species from eighteen to fifty.

Perhaps the most important finding from the Rutgers Fresh Kills study, however, was that tree roots did *not* affect the clay cap.[20] Excavating selected trees, the Rutgers team found wide, shallow root systems. Planting directly in a sand/compost mix, with neither imported topsoil nor excavated "tree pits," may have encouraged horizontal rooting.

Even with these encouraging early findings, revegetating an area as large as Fresh Kills is a major challenge. Soils are thin and of poor quality, moisture levels are generally low but also highly variable, invasive species dominate, and there is little species diversity. Woody plantings, even from habitat islands, are unlikely to thrive everywhere, and other techniques will be tested. One is an adaptation of agricultural strip cropping. Fast-growing plants will be grown in contour furrows, then plowed into the soil to create "green manure," adding organic matter. This potentially cost-effective technique for improving poor soils on an industrial scale will be part of ongoing research at Fresh Kills.[21]

SUGGESTED PRACTICES FOR LANDFILL SITES
Build a multidisciplinary team early. For restoration of huge sites as amenity facilities, overlapping systems must be well integrated for environmental and human benefits.

Consider educational and interpretive design to shed light on the site's history. The way consumer society generates and hides waste is an important factor in long-term sustainability. Landscapes on landfills should not simply make those processes invisible.[22]

Grade the site using landform or stepped slope methods (below).

Plant in uniform soil cover, not pits. Pits can constrict roots and might force them into the cap.

If additional soil is needed, consider manufactured soil (below).

Plant trees for erosion control and habitat. Trees pose little risk to the cap and offer many benefits. Use turfgrass for active-recreation areas. Native grasses and wildflowers are also satisfactory.

Try bare-root stock or an on-site nursery. Allow seedlings to acclimatize to landfill microclimate and soils. Commercially grown trees, aside from being expensive, may not survive transplanting to landfill conditions.[23] Low-cost bare-root stock is sometimes available from government sources, usually mixed native and nonnative species, which should be carefully evaluated.

Plant "habitat islands" (above), from which no-cost seedlings spread.

Recognize Agricultural and Rural Restoration

Urban and industrial restoration projects are often dramatic, gaining media coverage because they restore lost services to downtrodden neighborhoods. Where they involve reuse of industrial ruins, they also are popular with the design avant-garde. In terms of sheer acreage, however, there is probably more restoration activity *outside* the city. Mine reclamation deals with sites similar to urban industrial land, but often at a huge scale. Reforestation of recent or historic timber clear-cuts can involve small armies of workers, as can range-land restoration after over-grazing.[24] Agricultural fields may seem benign, but many have suffered fertility and topsoil loss or worse abuse. They, too, are candidates for restoration, especially where created by draining wetlands (see Principle 4). Consulting firms such as Prairie Land Management have found that restoring native vegetation to marginal farm soils reliably increases efficiency and profitability.[25]

These site restoration projects have much in common with their urban cousins, but differ in scale and location. When hundreds or even thousands of acres are being restored, cost and practicality require simple methods. Some, like broadcast seeding, or prescribed burns in place of weeding or thinning, produce a naturalistic result. Other mass techniques result in functional landscapes: forests are restored for the next crop with one shovel-cut per seedling, hundreds per day. Highly designed landscape restoration might not fit rural settings.

Landscape architects and contractors may not often do this kind of large-scale, nonurban restoration, but should be aware of it. The County Extension is often a good place to find regional expertise in large-scale restoration.

Use Techniques Appropriate to Both Community and Site

As the previous sections illustrate, there is a very wide range of approaches to site restoration. Tiny lots may be repaired by the loving hands of a few volunteers. Where abandonment of a major industry has left huge gaps in the community, significant funding and professional work are required. Thus, the techniques described below must be adapted to the *community* as well as to the site.

Abandoned land often goes hand in hand with meager resources: such a community needs simple, inexpensive methods, cooperation, and patience. Compost and planting to restore soil health may initially be the only options. A surprising amount can be done with well-planned volunteer labor, however, and some intensive approaches can be scaled down. Inventive ways of funding such projects have been found by programs like the Massachusetts Heritage State Parks program or Philadelphia's linkage of public-art money to vacant site restoration.

Larger-scale restoration often involves agencies of the larger community—municipal, state, or federal. Creativity and inventiveness apply, but methods and funding are inevitably different. It is more difficult as an official agency or a nonresident investor to win the local support that makes did-it-ourselves projects so powerful. Nonetheless, truly public projects can take on problems too big for individual neighborhoods, and many succeed extremely well. It is critical to avoid moving in and taking over. Incorporate community-based planning and participatory design and expect to adjust to local standards. Community participation linked to serious reinvestment can be truly uplifting.

Thus the list of techniques that follows includes a range of approaches adaptable to various sites, community needs, and finances. Many successes in restoration have resulted from communities borrowing ideas and improvising.

Restore Landscapes Structurally

Although healthy soil and vegetation are the most evident goals of site restoration, it is often necessary to deal first with *structural* damage to the site. This includes site topography and drainage damaged by inappropriate grading or erosion. It also includes impervious structures that interfere with environmental functions. The unique structural issues of capped landfills, above, have parallels on other sites. Many emerging restoration methods address damage caused when structural forms fail to integrate with ecological dynamics.

Restore Environmentally Appropriate Grading

Grading changes the surface shape of the Earth. Conventional thinking assumes that such changes are purely a matter of human convenience and aesthetics. But recent evidence, both scholarly and practical, shows that Earth-surface forms are a critical *functional* part of the environment. Partly because modern society tends to see all natural patterns as "random," the irregularities of landform surfaces are conventionally viewed as unimportant, even as nuisances. Nothing could be further from the truth.

Most conventional grading is based on straight lines and planes, in plan, section, or both. Such grading produces level or near-level surfaces for human use and unvarying slopes on "in-between" areas (such as road cuts or embankments).

Until recently the acceptability of such large planar slopes was seldom questioned. Their grim shapes often raise public outcry because they are ugly, but engineers overrule these concerns with arguments about safety, slope failure, erosion, and cost. All of these, conventional thinking insists, require the mathematically regular patterns of conventional grading. The evidence suggests otherwise. Two alternatives are discussed in this section.

GRADE TO FOLLOW REGIONAL LANDFORMS
Horst Schor, whose Anaheim CA consulting firm specializes in what he calls "land-form grading," began questioning convention while a senior vice president of Anaheim Hills development company. "We, like every other developer," he says, "were taking natural (hilly) terrain and transforming it into rigid, mathematical shapes for building. It was a practice based on the idea: We've always done it that way." Public resistance to stark, ugly results was a heated is-

Figure 2.8 Conventional grading insists on uniform, planar slopes. Until recently, objections to this approach have been aesthetic, but recent research shows environmental disadvantages, too. (*Photo:* H. J. Schor.)

sue in Anaheim. Schor himself didn't like the looks of the engineered slopes.

His solution was to study and photograph natural hill forms across the world, and then retrain his team of designers, engineers, surveyors, and contractors to construct landforms based on geomorphic patterns. The bulldozer operator turned out to be key to success. Schor writes, "We finally had to go into the field and call a bulldozer operator off his machine, show him the drawings and photos and explain the ideas. 'Sure, I can do that. Why didn't you say that in the first place?'" was the response. [26]

The resulting slopes were carefully engineered but looked natural. Still, engineers and planning agencies were doubtful, if not hostile, at first. Engineers in particular predicted that naturalistic slopes would cause *increased* erosion. Schor proved them wrong by landform grading an experimental hill slope seventy feet high, deliberately leaving out all the drains and pipes usually required by code. After three years of unusually heavy rains and no maintenance, the land-formed slopes were un-eroded. Similar-sized conventional slopes were gullied and severely damaged by the same rains. [27] In California, where developed land is regularly washed away in landslides, Schor's grading practices had immediate practical appeal, and won professional and public acceptance.

Schor has carefully documented comparative costs of conventional and landform grading. [28] The first time a contractor is asked to do landform grading, costs of learning (and of resistance to learning) can push costs up 15 percent. Once the learning curve is overcome, however, surveying costs on average only 1 to 5 percent more than conventional methods, and design cost 1 to 3 percent more. Construction costs (once the contractor is experienced) are typically only 1 percent higher than conventional grading. (GPS surveying may help; see p. 43.)

Offsetting these costs are strong benefits. Construction costs were *reduced* by 20 percent on one project because landform grading required much less total earthmoving. Contractors often like doing landform grading because it does not require extremely tight

Figure 2.9 Landform grading creates forms that resist erosion by being in equilibrium and that increase habitat diversity and aesthetic appeal. Lifetime costs of creating and maintaining these forms is less than conventional grading. (*Project and Photo:* H. J. Schor.)

geometric control. Residential density on land-formed sites equals conventionally graded ones; commercial sites, which demand huge level pads, may be 1 percent fewer. Costly delays due to public opposition can be avoided. Buyers perceive landform grading as attractive, which can result in quicker return on investment, higher property values, or both.

Land-form grading has been shown to decrease erosion and fits well with scientific theory about geomorphologic evolution of natural slopes.[29] It clearly helps blend restored land with undisturbed areas. Compared to flattened slopes, land-formed slopes revegetate more quickly and cost effectively and offer a diversity of concave and convex, shaded and sunny, exposed and sheltered plant habitats.

Because of its combination of ecological and social benefits, land-form grading deserves to be a major part of sustainable construction. It is applicable both to site restoration and to work at the edges of protected healthy sites. "A willingness and an open mind to depart from old concepts are essential elements," says Schor. "Approving agencies must also be brought into the information dissemination process."[30]

Like porous paving (p. 211) or bioengineering (p. 114), land-form grading remains underused despite nearly twenty years of well-documented results. Rethinking, retraining, and overcoming entrenched resistance are one-time hurdles in each firm, agency, or community. (Schor uses clay models of typical landforms, along with slides of natural hillsides, to help both design and field workers get a feel for the desired results.) A more general change is also required: slightly increased upfront costs must be viewed as investments with rich, long-term payoffs, rather than as immediate gouges in the monetary bottom line.

GRADE LONG SLOPES IN STEPS

"Stepped slopes" are another effective approach that avoids some problems of conventional grading. Used on highway slopes in hilly topography from California to Appalachia, they are applicable to other grading situations. Essentially, stepped slopes are small horizontal benches, constructed during grading—modern versions of the terraced agricultural hillsides used for centuries by traditional societies.

Water collects on each bench, then drops to the step below, dissipating its energy. Because it flows slowly and puddles on each step, it has time to infiltrate, aiding plant establishment. Over time the steps do erode, but this only deposits loose soil on the benches below as rooting medium for seeds. Once plants have stabilized the slope, the steps are difficult to detect.[31]

Steps are typically cut at about two-foot vertical intervals; their width is proportional to the slope. They can be created during ordinary excavation by a bulldozer traveling in alternate directions so that material does not pile up at one end of the slope.[32] Step "tops" must be truly level or slope back into the hillside. Otherwise, erosion can actually be speeded.

Stepped slopes have costs comparable to conventional grading. On some projects costs are reduced because slopes are not fine graded after excavation. Change orders have added stepped slopes to contracts at no increase in price, according to one Federal Highway Administration engineer.[33]

Although designed to erode, stepped slopes must be able to stand long enough for stabilizing vegetation to become established. Caltrans erosion-control specialist John Haynes, with extensive experience with stepped slopes, has found that compost and mulch protect the soil while providing nutrients (see p. 92). The steepness of many California highway cuts has not prevented use of composts; Caltrans has applied wood-chip mulch on slopes up to 1.25:1.

GRADE SUBSOIL, NOT TOPSOIL

Whatever form grading takes, always grade *subsoil* to change site topography. Differences between subsoil and topsoil are discussed on p. 88; topsoil should usually be stockpiled and reapplied to graded or otherwise altered areas. The top surface of regraded subsoil must be several inches lower than the designed finish grade. This difference, usually about six inches, allows for topsoil to be re-spread; note that topsoil may expand or compact during stockpiling and replacement. The completed site has a blanket of topsoil over structural subsoil. Avoid mixing subsoil into topsoil during spreading.

A common problem of subsoils, including many urban soils, is compaction. Probably the best single volume on problems of urban soil is Phillip Craul's *Urban Soil in Landscape Design*, which describes ways of ameliorating compaction.⊃ These include deep water jetting and air injection to fracture compressed soil; fractures are then backfilled with some dry material such as vermiculite.[34] Applying humic acid will also loosen some soils.

Deep plowing or subsoiling, an agricultural technique for breaking clay "pans," is applicable to urban soils. Deep plowing shatters compacted soil, creating large pore spaces that aid water drainage, aeration, and root penetration. Two caveats: Subsoiling must be repeated every two to three years and cannot be used around trees and shrubs because of damage to the root systems.[35] On construction sites, a backhoe is often used for the same purpose as construction nears completion but before re-spreading topsoil and final grading.[36]

Balance Cut and Fill

Transporting soil is costly, in both money and energy (see p. 276). "Balancing" cut and fill, so that no soil needs to be trucked in or carted away, is standard practice for large engineering projects. This concept can contribute to sustainability and should be considered for all sites. Many construction projects, however, create large new impermeable surfaces (buildings, pavement), resulting in more topsoil than should be re-spread on remaining areas. Rather than placing topsoil to a depth which does not benefit plants on-site, it *may* be appropriate to truck the excess to another site where soil remediation is required. This should be a last resort, given energy costs and differences in soil chemistry or fertility. It is far preferable, wherever possible, to limit impermeable surfaces and to avoid contamination and other conditions that require remediation of soils.

In roadway construction, strictly balanced cut and fill can lead to raising or lowering the roadbed far beyond what is needed for safety. Although energy and cost savings result from not hauling the soil, excessively raised or lowered roads tend to disrupt natural drainage patterns, compromise traffic safety, and require increased maintenance. Sustainable construction should *first* minimize the *total* amount of grading, and then come as close as possible to balancing cut and fill.

NOTE: RE-GRADING AND WETLANDS

Poor grading often creates areas of standing water. If these ponding areas have persisted for a number of years, they may be legally classed as wetlands. Even if no regulatory situation exists, ponded water may be a desirable site feature or can become one with design help. Normally, however, badly engineered grading should be corrected as part of restoration.

Grading to eliminate *naturally* swampy or marshy ground is never sustainable, and usually illegal under the Wetlands Protection Act—a good example of how concerns for sustainability are changing landscape construction.

Remove Damaging Structures

Land restoration frequently involves *removing* existing structures. Most structures have environmental costs: they are designed to keep out water and wildlife, to block or absorb sunshine. These costs are offset by human benefits when a structure is in use. The same structure, abandoned or poorly used, has most of the costs without the benefits. Derelict houses in declining cities are one example of failed structures that hinder sustainable site use. On a much larger scale, the Army Corps of Engineers has demolished its own dams on some rivers where they disrupt river wildlife, especially the economically valuable salmon.

"Greenroofs" and "greenwalls" can turn unwanted structures into plantable surfaces (Principle 3). They provide air and water quality benefits and replace hot, sterile surfaces with habitat area.

REMOVE EXCESS PAVING

Paved surfaces, in the United States at least, almost seem to grow by themselves. A net *decrease* in paved area anywhere remains inconceivable to conventional thinkers. However, when a closed factory is renovated as shops, or a single firm takes over what was once several offices, parking needs may decrease. Many writers on sustainability envision major reductions in single-occupant vehicles.[37] Such changes call for restoration of paved areas.

Even where demand for parking has not decreased, pavement removal may be necessary. Many lots in current use are never be more than one-quarter filled, due to excessive planning formulas for parking requirements (see p. 201). Where land is affected by increased runoff and erosion, or by extremes of flooding and drought, successful restoration may depend on removing excess hard surfaces. For parking still in use, porous pavement may replace all or part of the impervious surface and biofiltration can infiltrate runoff on-site (see pp. 207–17).

On the Upper Charles River just outside Boston, impervious surfaces have been removed on a grand scale. Here, in the early 1990s, the Metropolitan District Commission (MDC) decided to reclaim several miles of abandoned, overgrown public riverbank as a greenway. For years, however, riverside businesses had encroached on the banks with impromptu parking lots. The MDC forced encroachers to pay for pavement removal, soil rehabilitation, and planting by landscape architects Carol R. Johnson Associates.[38] Removal of these paved areas restored the riverbanks to health and to their rightful use—a green riparian park for Boston's citizens.

Reducing runoff at the *top* of a watershed is usually more effective than trying to combat erosion with expensive engineering *downstream*. Ownership boundaries often hamper this approach, however. Watershed-wide cooperative control of stormwater, including removal or replacement of impervious paving on upstream sites, is an important trend.

Standard paving specifications require removal of all organic soils and placement of gravel "base course." These materials are highly compacted and chemically infertile. For revegetation, base course must be removed along with asphalt or concrete surfacing and the soil tested and revived before planting can be successful.

When paving is removed, conventional practice (or simply habit) is to dump the removed materials. Sustainability requires better practices. Both asphalt and concrete can be recycled using high- or low-tech methods (Principle 6); rubble is potentially reusable. Base-course aggregate is so cheap at present that it is seldom re-used. Demolished roads and buildings may become on-site material sources, as was done for the

Figure 2.10   The Upper Charles River was the site of miles of illegal paving. Note the ironic No Dumping sign. (*Photo:* Carol R. Johnson Associates.)

Chesapeake Bay Foundation's headquarters (Annapolis MD), sometimes called the world's greenest office building.[39]

REPLACE OVER-ENGINEERED DRAINAGE STRUCTURES
Conventional drainage practice focuses on quickly getting water away from desirable structures (especially buildings and roads), often at the expense of adjacent land and aquifers. Water considered "excess" is piped or shunted into ditches for delivery to a surface water body. This deprives land of infiltrated rainfall and increases erosion, sedimentation, and flooding. The true source of these problems may be the "drainage" structures themselves; restoration downstream may not be possible without removing them.

Figure 2.11   The same site, with paving, trash, and signage replaced by restored vegetation and public access. (*Project:* Carol R. Johnson Associates. *Photo:* Dan Driscoll.)

Many "hard" erosion and flood control structures deflect and concentrate the force of water onto other surfaces. Just beyond the hardened edges, soft soils erode quickly and undermine the structure, causing its collapse. In extreme climates, many municipally funded concrete drainage structures break down from undercutting and weathering *many years before* the bond issue debt is paid off.[40]

Where poorly planned grading *dams* natural drainage, stagnant water may produce anaerobic soil conditions and drowned plants. Examples are often seen along interstate highways. Where roads are raised on fill, cutting off drainage in surrounding low places, eerie dead forests stand like ghosts of misdeeds past.

Drainage methods should infiltrate more and harden less. These include bioengineering and appropriate planting (Principle 3), porous paving materials and infiltration structures (Principle 4), and land-form grading (above). Each may require removal of damaging structures first.

Restore Damaged Soils On-site

Once structural problems have been corrected, or if they are not an issue, restoring soil health is an important next step in most site restoration. Compaction may need to be reversed, or soil that has been hauled away or allowed to erode may need to be replaced—erosion rates on construction sites are disastrously high if not controlled (see Figure 6.19).

Urban soils are called "made land" for good reason. They are "produced by mixing, filling, or contamination of land surfaces"[41] and support little vegetation without help.

Methods of re-creating healthy soil range from simply adding organic material, to complete replacement with "manufactured soil." Unless the site has been stripped of all soil, sustainability is best served by methods that rebuild soil on-site. Only rarely should soil materials be imported in quantity, and never at the expense of another site.

Avoid "Topsoiling"

One of the most common—and most questionable—practices in contemporary landscape construc-

Figure 2.12 Rigid structures protect only the soil they can shield from water. Along the hard edges, erosive undercutting is actually increased. (*Photo:* Kim Sorvig.)

tion is "topsoiling." Some sites may truly lack topsoil, due to prior abuse. But more commonly, soil is imported on the assumption that on-site soils lack fertility—or that stripping topsoil and hauling it away is easier than stockpiling it.

In most urban areas, companies specialize in collecting topsoil from land under development and reselling it as "new" topsoil for *other* developments—a game of musical soils. The excuse is often that source sites are being disturbed anyway, so making off with their topsoil is no crime and saves it from destruction. The energy and pollution costs of transporting bulk soils, however, make good on-site soil management during construction the preferred alternative.

Importing soil also carries an *unseen* environmental cost—it often comes from developments that destroy productive farmland. Planning policies that allow this are unconscionable. "I feel strongly that landscape architects should never use the word 'topsoil' in specifications," says Vancouver BC landscape architect Cornelia Oberlander.

From a strictly practical standpoint, topsoil mixes have a significant disadvantage over sand plus compost (aka manufactured soil). Topsoil is usually of unknown origin and may contain near-inert subsoil, residues including pesticides, or depleted agricultural soil. In fact, the most likely time to sell soil is when its productivity declines.

Fortunately, alternatives to importing topsoil do exist. Where saving existing topsoil and reapplying it is impossible, try the soil restoration methods below before trucking in topsoil.

Stockpile Existing Topsoil

Depth of topsoil varies widely depending on soil type, from an inch or less in the desert Southwest to several feet in fertile farmland. Beneath it, subsoil contains far fewer organic materials and soil organisms. Subsoil can be thought of as primarily structural, while topsoil is alive.

The best way to preserve topsoil is to leave it strictly alone. Construction usually disturbs some areas, however, no matter how carefully minimized by planning and design. Prior to construction, topsoil should be scooped off all parts of the site that will be built on, as well as access paths and staging areas. As a practical rule of thumb, the top six inches are removed, but in unusually thin or deep soils this may vary.

Stockpile topsoil on-site in piles covered with breathable material. This slows drying, keeps down dust, excludes windblown weed seeds, and avoids mud, sedimentation, and erosion. On large projects, stockpiles are sometimes planted with a quick-growing crop of erosion-preventing groundcover.

Inevitably, many organisms in stockpiled soil die from lack of oxygen, drying, or other factors. Stockpiling longer than a month is particularly likely to kill the microorganisms on which soil health depends. Cases where construction cannot be phased to avoid long stockpiling are one of the few times when selling topsoil may be justified. Despite these concerns, and calls for reevaluation of how to protect topsoil that must be moved during construction,[42] stockpiling is clearly better than simply destroying topsoil. In order to keep soil organisms alive, observe the following suggestions.[43] The local Natural Resource Conservation Service or County Extension office may also provide advice on keeping stockpiled soil healthy.

- Make several small piles, not one large one.
- Depth of piled soil should be no more than six feet for sandy and four feet for clay soils.
- Keep piles moderately damp.
- Protect piles from wind and water erosion by covering or planting.
- Handle soil as little as possible, and stockpile as short a time as possible.

Figure 2.13   In this test pit, living organic topsoil contrasts clearly with light-colored subsoil. A precious resource, topsoil is only created from subsoil by major resource inputs, either from humans or from time. (*Photo:* Natural Resources Conservation Service.)

On large projects, the guidelines present a challenge of logistics and space. Nonetheless, studies by Caltrans have shown in no uncertain terms that topsoil reapplication works. On test slopes, where topsoil was reapplied after highway construction, plant growth after three years was 250 percent better than without reapplied topsoil—even with identical applications of nutrients, seeds, and erosion-control materials.[44] Under the even more demanding conditions of mine reclamation, "high sodium content, nutrient deficiencies, toxicities, and soil-water relationships were mostly alleviated by replacing topsoil."[45] There are limits, however: the same study found that two inches of replaced topsoil produced up to 70 percent as much grass regrowth as thirty inches.

One possibility to preserve topsoil and the "seed bank" found in healthy soil is to treat it like sod.

Andropogon Associates pioneered a modified front-end loader to scoop up huge sheets of intact soil and plants, on the Algonquin pipeline in Morristown NJ.[46] A similar machine is now commercially available. Small plugs of seed-bearing soil are commonly used to plant wetlands (see p. 165).

Grow Soil, Not Plants

Although it sounds quixotic, growing soil instead of plants is a watchword in organic agriculture, Integrated Pest Management, and natural turf care. The same should apply to landscape efforts.

With some four billion microorganisms in a teaspoonful of healthy soil, 60 percent or more of the metabolic activity in soil is microbial. Recycling organic materials, microbes allow soils to support plants—the mineral soil is just a structural matrix. The living parts of soil are responsible for binding mineral particles together, absorbing water, holding and releasing plant nutrients, and sequestering CO_2. The complex soil ecosystem suppresses excessive (disease) concentrations of any microbe species, maintaining itself dynamically like more visible ecosystems.

When soil organisms are few, or their populations are unbalanced and low in diversity, these beneficial processes are diminished. With less organic binder, soils erode more easily and hold less water and nutrients. In high concentrations, not balanced by other organisms, some microbes begin to act as pathogens, with plant diseases as visible results.

Construction, along with many other human activities, frequently diminishes soil health. Common landscape activities that can damage soil include topsoil removal; compaction by equipment or day-to-day use; mowing, pruning, and harvesting unless organic matter is returned to the soil; and "plant care" chemicals, not only pesticides, but also high-nitrogen quick-release fertilizers.

"Growing soil" means keeping the web of microorganisms healthy or restoring its health. Almost as a side effect, landscape plants, lawns, and crop plants thrive with reduced amounts of irrigation and fertilizer, and few or no pesticides.

Growing soil involves several simple techniques in coordination. These include correcting compaction and sometimes improving mineral soil structure; stopping the broadcast use of pesticides and high-intensity fertilizers; and restoring microbial life and organic content, primarily by adding composts and compost teas (see below).

Soil development in nature takes decades to centuries. Human efforts to grow soil need not take so long, but even so, it takes time. Compost tea sometimes produces results as quickly as chemical methods, and more lasting. In other cases, soil restoration may take two or three years in transition, during which the landscape may look scruffy. Convincing clients (and neighbors) that instant green is a deceptive short-term idea can be the most difficult part of the soils-first approach.

The negative effects on a regional scale of unhealthy soils, and positive effects of soil restoration, are profound enough that King County WA developed a program for the Seattle region called Soils For Salmon. This in turn has become a model for other regions to manage stormwater, pollutants, vegetation cover, and wildlife by focusing on soil health.

Franklin Roosevelt once said that "a nation that destroys its soil destroys itself." In the United States, where agricultural soil has lost more than 40 percent of its soil nutrients since 1860, this is not idle rhetoric.[47] The good news is that the region that invests in maintaining its soils reaps comprehensive environmental dividends, at less cost (in money, resources, and energy) than conventional methods of landscape "care."

Analyze Soil Both Chemically and Biologically

Since this book's first edition, sophisticated commercial soil testing services have become better known and used. Until relatively recently, soil analysis meant sampling physical sand-clay-loam structure and major chemical nutrients only. While this is useful information, it leaves out what is arguably the most important component of soil and the biggest factor in its health: the microbiological community of species that process and even create soil as part of their life cycles.

Truly modern soil analysis laboratories test soil microbiology and can recommend ways to bring soil flora and fauna into balance. Restoring microbiological balance to soils usually involves composts, which full-service labs also test. Two such testing services are Soil Foodweb, based in Oregon and with several labs worldwide, and BBC Laboratories, in Tempe AZ.

Sending soils for microbiological testing has sampling requirements that may be unfamiliar: be sure to check with the lab in advance. These are likely to include submitting accurate information on where and from what depth the sample was taken; express delivery on ice to ensure live microbes when tested; and deciding among several available types of testing. Tests to determine how to manage a specific soil for a specific "crop" (such as a turf-grass species) are simpler than those that give a more comprehensive picture of soil health in relation to its region. The latter are generally more useful to landscape projects, where single-crop plantings are less relevant. Simple tests can cost $25 per sample or less, with more complex ones ranging toward $75 each. Consultation is usually available to help interpret test results. For long-term maintenance, especially of heavily trafficked landscapes, routine testing shows what groundskeeping activities to prioritize; Battery Park's playing fields (p. 333) use this approach. Testing's relatively small investment yields big returns and should be part of most landscape projects, especially those that aim to restore damaged sites.

"Amend" Soil—But with Restraint

Particularly on abused urban sites, any topsoil worthy of the name may have been stripped away long ago or covered by rubble and fill. Even in the worst cases, however, existing soil properly amended may be better than commercially available "landscape" soil, according to Simon Leake, an Australian soils scientist.[48]

Apparently unpromising soils may actually be surprisingly viable. For example, "urban renewal" leaves large tracts of land strewn with demolition rubble. Research in Great Britain suggests that brick rubble can be amended as planting medium, particularly if it has lain on site for years. Soil-forming processes work on raw bricks and mortar to form a kind of stony soil.[49] Soil texture, drainage, and aeration are excellent. Nitrogen is typically deficient, although it may be rebuilt by nitrogen-fixing plants (or acid rain). Brick clay provides sufficient phosphorous, potassium, and magnesium; mortar offers calcium.

Other types of rubble, especially broken concrete, have fewer nutrients but so much calcium that the soil becomes alkaline. Concrete rubble is harder and denser than mortar or brick, and breaks down more slowly. Plastics, metals, woods (treated and untreated), paints, sealants, and petroleum fuels can be present in demolition debris in widely varied proportions. The unpredictable, spotty patterns in which debris may be scattered on a site make testing more complicated *and* more necessary.

Gardens on rubble are not easily created, nor always feasible. The above research suggests, however, that removing *existing* debris may not be the best or only way to rehabilitate derelict land. (This applies only to existing debris: responsible contractors must reduce waste and avoid leaving trash.) Rubble-strewn lots, a seemingly hopeless urban situation, show how biological processes and human practices together can resurrect damaged sites.

Materials and Energy for Soil Amendment

A wide range of materials is marketed for improving soils. Many are appropriate for use where existing soil is badly damaged. As noted on p. 55, however, it is possible to amend soil too much. As landscape architect Leslie Sauer puts it in *The Once and Future Forest*, "Researchers have shown repeatedly that fertilizer benefits weeds." *Decreasing* fertility and changing pH often favors native species.[50] Avoiding overfertilization is especially important on relatively undisturbed and healthy native soils. In general, the goal of restoration should be a soil with chemistry and fertility comparable to healthy regional soils. Regional variety allows for most reasonable landscape purposes.

Robert Nold, an expert on wildflowers of the Penstemon genus, puts soil amendment in regional perspective. "Dryland gardening, if it is to be successful," he writes, "must not attempt to compensate for 'inferior' conditions [by using] notions of 'soil improvement' left over from agriculture. Soils do not need to be improved—the plant choices do."[51]

Experts are not fully in agreement on the appropriateness of soil amendments, and indeed these practices are site or region specific. Some general guidelines can be stated, however:[52]

- Compost (rotted vegetative material) is the most universally valuable of all soil additives, a paradoxical substance that helps sandy soils hold water and clay soils release it. (See next section.) Compost tea, an increasingly important way of applying compost, has its own section, below.

- Sand is often specified to improve drainage. Impractical amounts, however, must be added to most clays. At least one-third of the final result must be sand; for an existing volume of clay, half that volume must be added. Smaller amounts of sand can bind soil tighter (as in adobe bricks). Add compost instead.

- Clay well mixed into sandy soil can readily improve its *structure*. Remember the farmer's adage: "Sand on clay, money thrown away; clay on sand, money in hand." Compost, however, is a better choice for *both*.

- Gypsum is useful on unusually calcium-deficient soils, or those affected by salt. Most Western US soils are already too alkaline to benefit from gypsum.

- Wood ash is useful on acid soils in the Eastern and Southern United States, but can increase existing pH and salt problems in Western soils.

- Peat moss is widely specified as a soil amendment. It can structurally improve drainage and water holding, but contributes little to living soil. Coir, from coconut palms, similarly provides drainage but few nutrients. Peat is harvested from wetlands in vast quantities and shipped long distances; many experts consider its use entirely unsustainable. Coir is sustainably produced, though shipping distances are long. Use compost instead, from local leaf litter.

- In many areas, soils today contain *extra* nutrients from acid rain and air pollution. Adding fertilizer may be unnecessary or harmful. A major nutrient from pollution is nitrogen; elevated levels encourage weeds.

- Some soils, especially if irrigated where evaporation is high, have high salt content. Avoid adding to this with salty fertilizers (fresh cattle and poultry manure, as well as ammonium nitrate and other high-nitrogen mixes).

- Microbes that decompose organic material require nitrogen. Amendments that are high carbon and low nitrogen (a "C/N ratio" higher than 20:1) cause microbes to *take* nitrogen from the soil to fuel their work. This can make nitrogen unavailable to plants until decomposition is finished. Amendments with high C/N ratios include horse manure, dairy (but not beef) cattle manure, straw, wood chips and sawdust, and some composts if not well matured. Such amendments may be good for high-nitrogen soils, or for woodland soils where leaf and twig litter naturally composts slowly. Elsewhere they should be used with caution.

- Many plants live cooperatively or symbiotically with soil organisms. Roots of such plants work in cooperation with mycorhizae (fungi that process nutrients and exchange them with the plant). If the correct symbiotic organism is not present in soil, these plants cannot survive. Mycorhizal "innoculants" are commercially available for some species. They should be used with expertise, however, because the wrong mycorhizae can displace beneficial ones native to the soil.

- Apart from composts, super-absorbent polymer granules can increase available moisture. One pound of such granules absorbs nearly fifty gallons of water; an almost bizarre amount of water disappears into dry polymer when mixed. Polymers in planting mixes reduce irrigation needs. Bare-root or live-stake bioengineering materials (Principle 3) can be dipped before planting directly into a slurry of the water-absorbent material. Salt holding by polymers has been a concern, but they have been widely accepted both in horticulture and in dryland reforestation.

Embodied energy and potential toxicity of soil amendments vary widely. Some amendments are simple materials like sand, clay, compost, or manure. Such materials are only toxic if contaminated, but energy to "mine" the materials and transport them can be significant. As noted above, topsoil should rarely be imported or exported. Toxicity by overusing fresh manure is a possibility. Unless carefully researched, "organic" may be a misleading or meaningless label on soil products. Other processed soil amendments range from simple ground limestone to completely artificial chemical fertilizers or water-holding polymers. A responsible approach to sustainable construction does not simply reject these materials because they are processed. Rather, each material must be analyzed for embodied energy, toxicity, and related concerns, and used accordingly. The number of available products continues to increase.

Even if soil-amending materials are energy efficient and nontoxic, widespread change in site soils may have undesirable ecosystem effects. Anyone who has overwatered or overfertilized a houseplant will understand this problem. In some regions of "poor" soils, increased soil fertility actually *decreases* the health and hardiness of native plant species. At the same time, it makes the soil more hospitable to weeds that are not picky about soil type. The result is unsatisfactory both horticulturally and ecologically, and increases maintenance.

To repeat an important point: soil restoration should usually aim to bring damaged soil back to conditions similar to healthy regional soils. In landscape use, this implies design based on native plants. Dramatically increased soil fertility should be reserved for the limited number of exotics planted as special accents in such designs.

Use Greenwaste and Other Composts

Compost for private yards or community-garden plots is everyday practice, but what about large-scale landscape construction? Some of the very largest-scale landscape projects—highway rights-of-way—routinely employ composted materials. A 1997 study by the University of Florida found that thirty four of the fifty state departments of transportation used compost on roadsides routinely or experimentally; the practice has only increased since.[53]

For large-scale projects, compost is usually applied hydraulically in a slurry, often mixed with uncomposted greenwaste. Compostable materials are countless: grass clippings and leaves from suburban back yards; chicken and livestock manure; brewer's waste; biosolids (composted sludge) from municipal sewage; trees chipped after felling; farm byproducts like walnut shells and peach pits; and chopped wood waste from demolished buildings.

The range of applications is equally wide: as a soil amendment, as mulch or topdressing, for erosion control, and as a planting-soil ingredient. Frequently noted benefits from compost include:

- better plant growth, with less fertilizer, due to balanced organic matter, slow-release nutrients, and microbial populations
- effective erosion control, slope stabilization, water-holding, and drainage
- fewer weeds, fewer herbicides (where used as mulch).

With compost, says Caltrans's Haynes, "you're effecting real soil improvement, since we often install landscape plantings in subsoil." Although the term "improvement" is used too casually about landscape practices, in the case of compost it is valid.

Compost has been a standard specification for Minnesota DOT (MNDOT) for fifteen years, completely replacing topsoil or peat moss. MNDOT uses 20,000 cubic yards of compost annually on roadsides, largely in planting trees and shrubs. DOTs in California, Florida, Illinois, Maine, North Carolina, Washington, and Massachusetts also report substantial—and successful—compost applications. Caltrans's wide use of compost fits California state policy of diverting recyclable materials from landfills.

These agencies have tested the performance of compost against results obtained from peat, humus, bark, topsoil, or fertilizer. Compost compares favorably in almost every trial. Caltrans finds compost to be as effective for slope protection as erosion-control blankets. Maine's DOT finds that turf grown on a fifty-fifty mix of compost and subsoil, with compost mulch, resists erosion better than grass grown on loam topsoil.[54] In short, compost has immense value on almost every landscape project.

Availability and Quality of Compost

In most urban areas there is a glut of yard waste. (If processed into boards, the volume of wood-like wastes is enough to replace all wood harvested for timber; see Figure 6.18.) In the past, this valuable organic matter was trucked to landfills, a practice increasingly banned by municipalities. Leaves and grass have made up as much as 18 percent of landfill volume, with another 7 percent composed of soil, rocks, and woody landscape waste.[55] Thus *one-quarter* of landfill volume could be eliminated by making good use of organic materials. With landfills bulging at the seams, the value of "greenwaste" has been recognized. California legislation in the 1990s required communities to reduce landfill greenwaste by 50 percent by 2000, a goal easily met by separating yard waste.

Many municipalities compost yard waste, for example Cleveland, OH.[56] Along with yard waste, Christmas trees, agricultural byproducts, scrap wood, animal manure, biosolids (see below), and food wastes from food services and restaurants are frequently composted. (In Vancouver BC, one composting firm makes high-quality compost entirely from restaurant wastes. Landscape architect Cornelia Oberlander's use of this product is discussed below.) Occasionally, mixing two kinds of waste can neutralize problems with both, similar to phytoremediation (below); for example, brewery waste consisting of spent yeast has been used to pull heavy metals out of computer-chip wastewater.[57]

Despite generally large volumes of raw "greenwastes," large-scale landscape use of compost can run into availability and quality issues. Several state DOTs have found it difficult to obtain compost in quantities required for highway projects. This can affect application rates and product quality. Hauling charges can be substantial for these bulky materials—particularly in large and sparsely populated states.[58] In such cases, environmental costs of energy use and air pollution must be carefully weighed against benefits of compost. Considering long-term health of plantings, reduced erosion, reduced chemical use, and decreased landfill disposal, however, transporting compost may still be environmentally viable, despite financial cost.

Specifications that spell out characteristics of quality compost are important in ensuring consistent product. Fortunately, model specifications do exist. One is the *Suggested Compost Parameters and Compost Use Guidelines* developed by the Composting Council.

Contaminants in and maturity of compost are the most common quality issues. Weed seed, heavy metals, salts, and other contaminants should be limited by specification. Some substances, such as small pieces of plastic or glass, pose no horticultural problem (see Manufactured Soils, below.) Of course, foreign objects that may cause injury to construction workers, to users of the site, or to wildlife must be eliminated. Special concerns when using compost on relatively healthy and undisturbed soils are noted on p. 90–91.

Compost that is not fully mature—that is, still decomposing—can steal nitrogen from the soil, depriving plants. The Washington DOT requires producers to provide maturity-testing kits with compost deliveries.[59] Soil testing labs that include microbiology analysis can also test compost and advise on modifying it to accomplish specific landscape goals. The US Composting Council, a trade organization, certifies compost after standard testing through their Seal of Testing Assurance (STA) program.[60] This voluntary program was formed with the explicit goal of avoiding state regulation; potential users of certified compost should read the testing standard to ensure that it meets their specific soil management goals.

There is no technical problem turning raw materials into compost. At present, more raw material is available than is collected or processed. In many areas, increased demand would help municipal governments fund increased compost production. Landscape professionals should make a commitment to putting this valuable product to use.

Use Compost Teas

Compost teas are one of the most interesting innovations of organic maintenance. Made from ordinary soil-like compost by "brewing" in water, teas enhance the microbial composition of the mix. As liquids, they are convenient to apply and quick to be taken up by plants. Compost teas are sometimes referred to as "effective microorganisms."[61] To be effective, they must be live and in the proper mix and concentration.

For compost tea, water is mixed with compost plus agents like soy, flour, kelp, fish emulsion, or molasses, which stimulate reproduction of specific types of soil microorganisms. The mixture is usually agitated with air to keep oxygen at optimum levels. Tea recipes are frequently based on biological soil tests (above). The finished tea is diluted in a water-to-tea ratio between 3:1 to 5:1. For turf, 50 to 100 gallons per acre are applied once a month. Foliar sprays are applied directly onto plant leaves (whose surface microbial populations are important to plant health). Foliar applications average one gallon per large shrub and four gallons per tree, adjusted per species. Horticulturalists have even developed a technique to inject teas into the sand joints of pavers around street trees.[62]

Compost tea must be brewed to match specific requirements and applied within a day after production. Commercial compost tea should be produced near the site, and generally remains the province of specialists. There are about twenty small US companies that brew teas to order. A Google search may help locate brewers in your region. Bottling compost tea may be a possibility, although effects on the living organisms are unpredictable. An alternative is brew-it-yourself; equipment to do so is available from several companies. A growing number of landscape and turf maintenance companies produce and apply their own compost teas.

Although compost teas are very popular, almost to the point of being faddish, they work best in a coordinated program of "growing soil." Such programs were discussed earlier in this chapter; their successful application to landscape maintenance is discussed in Principle 10.

Use Yard Waste On-site

Although municipal composting and use of compost in construction are desirable, most American yards would be healthier if yard waste were composted and reapplied *on-site* (see p. 331). As with most environmental technologies, on-site reuse also saves transportation and associated costs. If garden maintenance (and agriculture) becomes more sustainable, it is possible that current sources of greenwaste may decrease. In the meantime, however, municipal compost should be a mainstay in reclaiming damaged soils.

Plant "Green Manure" Crops

"Green manure" plants are aids for soil enrichment that farmers have known about for millennia. Grown on-site for one or more seasons, they are then tilled into the soil to compost. Most green manure plants are leguminous (pea family). Their roots fix nitrogen, available to later plantings as the green manure breaks down. For regionally appropriate green-manure practices, contact a local agricultural school or County Extension. Be sure to pick species not likely to become invasive—a few leguminous crops, such as alfalfa, spread aggressively in some climates.

Watch for Lead in Soils

Community gardens on derelict urban land must beware of lead. Although no longer used in consumer paints or gasoline, lead is not biodegradable and persists in soil. Sites near older buildings painted with lead, heavily traveled roadways, or service stations may be contaminated. Former industrial locations should always be researched carefully for persistent soil pollutants.

Community-garden sites where food crops will be grown should *always* undergo a soil test. For lead at levels less than 500 parts per million (ppm), the Ohio State University Extension recommends incorporating one-third organic material (compost or manure) by volume: twelve to sixteen cubic feet for a 100-square-foot plot. If lead levels are higher, build raised beds that separate planting medium from contaminated soil.[63] Raised beds are a convenient, traditional gardening method, favored for maintenance and handicapped accessibility, and common in European intensive vegetable cultivation. Whenever chemical residues are found, reconsider whether to use the garden for food plants. Decorative gardens are also an appropriate use of community allotments.

Heal the Soil with Biosolids

The urban environment produces many by-products in need of recycling. Few are more appropriate for use in restoring landscapes than "biosolids"—yet none is so underutilized. Many fears and misconceptions surround biosolids, processed from municipal sewage (yes, *sewage*). Although some concern is legitimate where food production is involved, for most other types of landscapes, biosolids are too valuable to waste.

Many traditional societies around the world prize composted human waste as fertilizer. Small-scale, on-site treatment, using composting toilets, constructed wetlands, and other "alternative" systems, is common—but not common enough—even in industrialized countries. Such systems are close to the source and relatively easy to keep free of chemical contaminants. In modern societies, however, sewage is too easily piped away underground, out of sight and out of almost everyone's mind.

At the other end of the sewage pipe, treatment plants used to simply dump the treated sewage. Beginning in the 1920s, the practice was recognized as neither cost effective nor environmentally intelligent. In 1926, Milwaukee began marketing the granddaddy of US biosolids products, and still the best known, Milorganite.

In 1988, federal law banned dumping municipal sludge in the oceans, narrowing disposal options for wastewater-treatment facilities. Landfilling and incineration are expensive and environmentally questionable. The 1988 ban created a full-fledged biosolids industry, products with names like Biogrow, GroCo, Nutramulch, and Technagro.

Increased biosolids availability has decreased costs—from $120 to $42 per ton in Florida between 1990 and 1994, for example.[64] Since supply is never-ending, some wastewater-plant operators even supply biosolids at no cost, especially for public-sector projects.

Not everyone concerned with the environment supports biosolids use. Despite extensive standards set by the US EPA, some biosolids contain heavy metals and contaminants dumped ignorantly or maliciously into sewer systems. These are of particular concern on food-producing fields. Many experts consider the EPA standards very low risk even for crops, but not everyone accepts these definitions. A 1998 proposal to allow foods fertilized with biosolids to be labeled "organic" raised serious public objection. Ordinary manufactured fertilizers, for which there are *no* standards, arguably pose far greater threats than biosolids; some even include toxic wastes merely relabeled as fertilizer.[65] (See "Toxics as 'Fertilizer,'" p. 257.) It is the authors' belief that when produced and used in accordance with EPA standards, biosolids are highly appropriate for *landscape* use, with the possible exception of aquifer recharge zones or little-disturbed, near-natural sites.

Biosolids are soil conditioners, essentially similar to compost, increasing water and nutrient retention in soil. Like compost, they improve soil tilth and boost fertility, with significant nitrogen, phosphorus, potassium, and beneficial trace metals. Used as mulch, often mixed with wood chips or yard waste, they control erosion—a multipurpose, low-cost soil amendment.

How safe are biosolids? The EPA recognizes two main classes, A and B.[66] Both undergo a process known as digestion, which reduces pathogen levels by approximately 99 percent and heavy metals to required levels. This produces class-B biosolids; application requires a state permit and site monitoring for up to a year.

Class-A biosolids are further composted, heat dried, or irradiated, sterilizing and deodorizing the product. Sea World of Ohio uses class-A "Technagro" on flower beds next to public walkways, stockpiling it for two weeks to dissipate any lingering odors.

The chemical composition of sludge varies greatly from one treatment plant to another. Because lime is sometimes used to stabilize it, pH may reach eleven, far too alkaline for most soils. Soluble salts and nitrates are not uncommon. According to one noted soil scientist, any contaminants can build up with repeated application, although they dissipate if application stops for several years;[67] a study on golf courses showed that metals did increase in grass tissues, but still below EPA-permitted levels.[68] Site remediation using plants (phytoremediation, p 103) or microbes (bioremediation, p. 105) removes very similar contaminants and might provide extra treatment for biosolids, before or after they are applied to landscapes.

Biosolids are not totally risk free; that claim cannot be made for commercial fertilizers either. Properly applied, they solve two major environmental problems—sewage disposal and soil fertility—with minimal health or environmental risk. One caveat: quality compliance varies from one *producer* to another, or at different times. Bob Rubin, professor of agricultural engineering at North Carolina State University, has conducted extensive research in landscape applications of biosolids. He recommends buyers and specifiers ask their state regulatory agency these questions: What facilities in the state are producing class-A pathogen-free biosolids? Has the agency analyzed nutrients, salts, metals, and other elements in those products? Which producers consistently comply with state and EPA guidelines? Such information, available in every state, identifies producers of quality products.

Satisfactory biosolids products may not be available in quantity in every locality. If no local options exist, the cost of transport may be more than that of the biosolids (see energy costs, Principle 7). Life-cycle costs may make even imported biosolids viable, and availability continues to spread.

BIOSOLIDS PROJECT EXAMPLES

Applying biosolids on the White House lawn sounds like a contractor's nightmare or partisan political joke. Nevertheless, the White House has used biosolids. In the late 1980s 825 tons of ComPro—biosolids from Washington DC sewage composted with lime and wood chips—were applied to the south lawn for compaction. The head White House groundskeeper reported no problems. A few blocks away, 6,000 tons of biosolids were applied to the National Mall's Constitution Gardens. The Washington Monument, Mount Vernon, and Dumbarton Oaks are other sites in the nation's capital maintained with biosolids. Washington-area landscape architect James Urban specified ComPro for the National Geographic Society headquarters. (Despite what humorists might predict, Washington's sewage is relatively benign; it has few of the heavy metals that plague waste in historically industrial cities like Boston.)

Seattle Parks and Recreation landscape architect Barbara Swift specified biosolids for Discovery Park, a 500-acre expanse degraded by years of logging and farming. On a fourteen-acre demonstration area, two inches of class-B biosolids from King County's waste-water-treatment plant were spread and tilled to fifteen-inches depth. Project manager Kevin Stoops notes that odors dissipated quickly when exposed to air and sunlight. Shifting winds led to neighbors' complaints late in the process; after that, the city switched to a class-A mixture. The site now exhibits

luxuriant growth, says Stoops. Parks and Recreation obtained the biosolids free, realizing enormous cost savings over other fertilizers.[69]

In general, Washington State has led other states in biosolids application since the mid-1970s, when Seattle's world-famous Gas Works Park was treated with class-B biosolids. Mountains to the Sound, a greenway initiative along Interstate 90, used biosolids to revegetate highly visible logged slopes and logging roads along a scenic mountain corridor, while in Everett, biosolids were tested for wetlands restoration.

Elsewhere, use of biosolids sometimes encounters public resistance. Kentucky DOT has been apprehensive about biosolids' potential for fouling water supply, and Minnesota DOT only uses biosolids in pilot projects. Wyoming DOT tried to use biosolids but encountered backlash that forced them to stop—even though the product in question easily met EPA standards. States like Massachusetts, however, are moving confidently ahead with biosolids, while in Nebraska, farmers use it as fast as it is made.[70]

A darker form of resistance to biosolids comes from entrenched conventional interests. Producers of wood mulch and fertilizers see any form of compost as cutting into their markets; at least one attempt to legislate roadside use of biosolids was "shot down by chemical industry lobbyists."[71] Special-interest resistance really argues in *favor* of biosolids. Public and professional education is key to its appropriate use.

Manufactured Soil

Many derelict sites have fill and rubble where topsoil should be, while landfills and highway cuts may be soilless, their huge size prohibiting imported topsoil. To cover Fresh Kills landfill with as little as twelve inches of soil would require 104,551,200 cubic feet, or nearly five million tons. The question at such scales is where to get that much topsoil. ("Excuse me, can you spare five million tons?")

That question can be answered by another: Why not recycle discarded materials to reconstruct a dump? Manufactured soil does exactly that—and not only on landfills. Although its seems an oxymoron, manufactured soil is technically quite feasible and often the ecologically responsible option. The constituents of soil—its mineral, organic, and chemical components—can be assembled mostly if not entirely from recycled materials. (Familiar household "potting soils" combine inorganic perlite and vermiculite with organic peat or compost.) Once the mix is applied, microorganisms and plants complete the "manufacturing."

Phil Craul, the author of *Urban Soils*, has taught at Harvard's Graduate School of Design and is a leading interpreter of soils science to landscape professionals. Craul has consulted on many projects using manufactured soils and written guidelines for specifying them. Here is Craul's definition of manufactured, or as he calls it, "sustainable soil": "Sustainable soil is comprised entirely of recyclable products, alone or in a mixture with derelict soil material, the latter useless without supplementation. It contains few, if any, non-renewable resources."[72]

Soil components are usually available on or adjacent to even the most abused sites. Examples include the following:

- sand from river dredgings
- recycled ground glass
- washings from aggregate plants
- certain smokestack fly ashes
- derelict soils such as mine tailings (selectively)
- fine-ground till from glacial deposits
- any composted/recycled organic material.[73]

The soils Craul envisions would *not* include sand specifically mined for the purpose, only the types of materials listed above. In most cities, says Craul, "you've got all the components you need for making soil—and it's all recycled."

A futuristic article about agricultural soils for space colonies led Craul to use ground glass. Lunar dust, noted the article, resembles ground glass, a possible silica matrix for man-made soils. "If they can use that stuff on the moon," mused Craul, "why can't we use ground glass as a matrix here on Earth?" He soon learned that others were thinking along similar lines, using ground glass as a sand substitute in drainage, from a landfill near Syracuse NY to septic drain fields in Washington State. "So there's a movement afoot," says Craul. Design of manufactured

soils, however, is still new, and few professionals are experienced.

Manufactured soils could make inner-city restoration feasible where little if any topsoil remains. Sasaki Associates proposed to demonstrate manufactured soil at the Washington Monument, collaborating with Craul. His biggest project, coming close to the idea of recycled materials exclusively, is a National Park in Boston.

MANUFACTURED SOIL PROJECT EXAMPLES
Spectacle Island, gateway to Boston Harbor Islands National Park, opened in 2006 with public access by ferry. The 105-acre island served as a landfill, capped with clay, for two million cubic yards of contaminated spoil from Boston's Central Artery tunnel. Craul and Boston landscape architects Brown & Rowe calculated that 582,000 cubic yards of topsoil would be needed to cover the island. To find that much soil, says Craul, "we would have had to strip all the remaining farms in Suffolk County," which neighbors Boston.

Instead, topsoil was manufactured. The first ingredient was stone grit, derived from the glacial till of which the island is composed. Other materials were barged over from the mainland: coarse sand from New Hampshire, and compost. Obtaining the inert till and sand proved relatively straightforward. The compost was another matter: 21,000 cubic yards were needed. The Rochester NH firm of AllGro was contracted to supply a mixture of 70 percent brewery waste and 30 percent biosolids.

The brewery waste ran out during the project's first phase, replaced by 100 percent biosolids. Because of the volume needed, AllGro had to contract for much of it from other processors in the region. Shipments arrived full of large sticks and wood chips—low-cost bulking agents that settle inconsistently as the wood decomposes. Quality fluctuations are symptomatic of compost industry growing pains. Far from arguing against compost or manufactured soils, they indicate need for better specifications and monitoring of delivered products.

With manufactured soil in place, the island was bare and without seed sources. Brown & Rowe protected the 3:1 slopes against erosion with multilayered

Figure 2.14 Spectacle Island in Boston Harbor is a recreational landscape salvaged from a toxic dump. (*Project:* P. Craul with Brown and Rowe. *Photo:* Massachusetts Turnpike Authority.)

plantings in bands along contours. Deciduous trees and shrubs were underplanted with grasses and legumes to stabilize slopes and increase water retention while the woody plants matured. Heights and densities alternated to counter winds buffeting the site. The plant list was somewhat experimental; the designers chose self-seeding, naturalizing plants, knowing some would thrive and others not. "Basically we designed for low or no maintenance," Rowe recalls. During establishment, sprinkler irrigation pipes and two water cannons were employed. Water was barged to a large tank on the north drumlin. By the summer of 2002, irrigation was no longer needed. The wisdom of installing a wide range of species has been confirmed: the plants are beginning to form a forest and give shape to the island.[74]

Other projects for which Craul has designed soils include cover on underground parking beneath Boston Commons; South Cove at Battery Park City, Manhattan; and J. Paul Getty Center, Los Angeles. The Fresh Kills revegetation (above) used manufactured soils, with ratios of between 3 and 4 parts sand to 1 part compost, depths varying from 1 to 2.5 feet. Discarded, chipped Christmas trees also provided organic mulch.

Suggested Practices for Soil Restoration

- Cardinal principle: *Wherever possible, avoid removing or bringing in topsoil.*

- Use soil analysis services to understand site soil and to plan any amendments. Analyze not only chemical components, but also microbes and soil organisms. Consult a soils scientist.
- Amend to match healthy regional soil types, not agricultural ideals. Use regional plant species rather than widespread soil amendment and irrigation.
- Wherever possible, stockpile topsoil from construction areas on-site and re-spread as soon as possible.
- Where there is only fill dirt on site, amend that to create viable soil rather than bringing in topsoil. Add compost or plant restorative plants.
- Specify *recycled local* soil amendments and erosion-control materials if possible.
- Get over your inhibitions about biosolids and help clients get over theirs. Promote this material (within limits noted above) to turn waste into a resource.
- Become knowledgeable about biosolids production and standards. Locate reliable local producers through appropriate state agencies. Use class A to avoid odor, class B for less public sites.
- For soilless sites, or if on-site soil must be removed due to contamination, consider manufactured soil.
- Once restored, ensure good soil maintenance (Principle 10). Inappropriate irrigation and fertilization can *damage* soil fertility.

Restore Regionally Appropriate Vegetation

Restoring site soils is essential to reestablishing healthy vegetation. The process, however, is two way. Vegetation interacts with mineral earth, microbes, and climate to produce regional soil types.

Without appropriate revegetation, few sites can properly be called restored. Landscape architects often use native plants, both for restoration work and in garden design, placing new demands on landscape contractors. Although a few contractors and nurseries specialize in native plants, the authors' experience is that most *construction* professionals still need to develop knowledge and skill to work successfully with these species. Standard construction often fails to create site conditions that favor native plants (sometimes quite different from conditions favored by human users).

Site restoration is not just about replanting appropriate species, but also about control and removal of inappropriate plants. Some derelict sites are literally green, due to an unhealthy mix of weedy plants. Restoring such sites requires attention to changed soil, grading, and drainage patterns that invited weedy species. Thoroughly eradicating aggressive introduced plants also requires methods not common in conventional work.

There are many books on site restoration using native species.⊃ Because restoration is specific both to region and to the type of site damage, no single book or resource can detail all practices. The following is an overview of main issues affecting construction professionals.

Remove Invasive Plants and Restore Native Succession

In purely economic terms, invasive plants, imported by people and allowed to overrun fields and forests, do an estimated $140 billion worth of damage annually in the United States.[75] This problem has become much more widely recognized, and perhaps bigger, since our first edition. The federal government's National Invasive Plant Management Strategy, drafted in 1996, estimated that 4,600 acres of public lands *per day* are lost to noxious weeds in the Western half of the United States alone, reducing both economic yield and ecological viability of these lands.⊃ Removal of these invasives, and restoration of diverse native plant communities, is expected to be the largest public-works project *ever* undertaken. It is a task that could largely have been prevented, in hindsight, if horticultural and agricultural plant introductions had been more carefully screened for invasive characteristics.[76]

Of the several thousand nonnative species that have naturalized (adapted to survive without human help) in North America, only about 10 percent (four hundred species) are truly invasive. "Invasive" has varied definitions (and some critics), but it essentially means a plant that not only survives where introduced by humans, but takes over and damages significant parts of the local ecosystem.[77]

Two examples show that the concept of invasives is complex, but that the damage done by such plants is real. Tamarisk, or salt cedar (*Tamarix* sp.), like about 60 to 85 percent of invasive species in the United States, was deliberately imported as an ornamental plant.[78] Two circumstances made it invasive. First, two separate tamarisk species from Asia and the eastern Mediterranean "met" for the first time in cultivation and hybridized, becoming tougher and spreading more vigorously.[79] Second, major water projects dammed Western US rivers and sharply decreased reproduction of native cottonwoods. The hybrid tamarisk then invaded these river areas—up to 90 percent of such habitat in many Western states.[80] It can live in salty soil (often produced by irrigation) and "sweats" salt onto its leaves, which it drops. Its leaf litter makes topsoil too salty for other plants.

Ironically, after getting its foothold thanks to water-supply dams, salt cedar has proved to take up huge amounts of water. One estimate is that, throughout the West, the invader sucks up 800 billion gallons a year *more* than the native plants it replaced. Eradication of this one species from the arid West is estimated to cost $500 million.[81]

A second example is spotted knotweed (*Centaurea maculosa*). Seed was accidentally imported in alfalfa in the late 1800s. It has now spread to almost every American state and Canadian province. In Montana alone, it covers 4.5 million acres and costs ranchers an estimated $40 million annually.[82] Even among invasives, it is unusual in forming monocultures, completely enveloping huge swaths of landscape. Most animals except sheep find it inedible; its dominance of some valleys has actually changed elk migration patterns.

Spotted knapweed releases a soil toxin. In its native Europe, other plant and insect species have evolved ways of coexisting, but North American plants have not had the centuries necessary to adapt. Worse, even if knapweed is physically eradicated, soil toxicity remains.

These examples show that each invasive species is a unique problem. Not only do invasives change vegetation communities, but they have varied detrimental effects on hydrology, soil erosion and sedimentation, nutrient cycling, and wildfire susceptibility.[83] Remedies require both ecological and historic knowledge, and clear evaluation of environmental and economic damage. Climate change may favor some invasive species and curb others. Species like tamarisk and knapweed are truly destructive to existing ecosystems, not just a threat to some romantic concept of nature. The main question is what degree of removal or control can feasibly be achieved.

In addition to the federal task force, most states and some local jurisdictions have agencies attempting to control invasive species. The Forest Service, the National Park Service, and the Natural Resources Conservation Service have their own programs. The ASLA has a National Policy Statement on Nonnative Invasive Species on its Web site.

Removing invasive plants has not been without controversies. Although control of human-introduced invasive *animals* is widespread and based on exactly the same principles, part of the public has a much harder time accepting that plants can be considered undesirable. Except for obvious threats like kudzu or porcelain berry, plants don't appear "aggressive" or destroy other species as obviously as predatory animals do. Diseases that invasive plants might spread are never as frightening as animal diseases threatening livestock or human health. Plants, to many people, are just green backdrop; any species will do.

A prime example of this dilemma was a raging controversy over proposed restoration of oak savannah and tallgrass prairie near Chicago around 1996.[84] The restoration would have removed some areas of naturalized—that is, human-introduced—forest, dominated by sugar maple and the impenetrable invasive shrub, European buckthorn. Thanks in good part to sensationalist press coverage by writers whose biological knowledge was pitiful,[85] the public attacked the restoration process and eventually stopped it.

This is clearly not an issue this book can resolve. However, design and construction professionals involved with landscape sustainability in any form, but especially with site restoration, need to be aware of the potential for such controversies. Approach restoration via community-based planning, educating the public about benefits of restoration and problems of invasive plants, and listening carefully to what they value about both native and nonnative landscapes. The pressing need to increase vegetative cover as a brake on climate change (see p. 14) is likely to influence restoration processes and politics. Ability to sequester carbon gives an objective measure for restoration cost-benefit decisions. Careful analysis might favor leaving nonnative woods alone; planting native vegetation; or planting whatever species are available—probably decided case by case. Age, species type, growth rate, and (probably) degree to which a planting fits the web of ecosystem interconnections are all likely to affect carbon uptake. Restoration of self-sustaining forests seems likely to get a major boost from this concern.

The remainder of this section discusses practical issues involved in controlling invasive plants and restoring native vegetation. Landscape designers and nursery operators will probably see more bans on some invasive ornamental plants.[86] Design and construction professionals concerned with sustainability can expect to see removal of invasives and reintroduction of native species as a new source of work, requiring new knowledge and practices.

Removing invasive plants is hard work. One mower manufacturer advertises a list of "the Toughest Weeds in America." Of these, fully 50 percent were introduced from Asia or Europe, while others have become weeds only after being accidentally or deliberately transported outside their original range.[87]

Figure 2.15 The curving floodplain (center right) of this New Mexico river has lost all native vegetation to two invasives, Russian olive and salt cedar. (*Photo:* Kim Sorvig.)

Invasive plants can either cause or result from site damage, and figure prominently as targets of restoration projects. (For discussion of what constitutes a "native," and how they are used in new planting, see "What Is A Native?," p. 142.) Invasion by weedy plants often indicates other disturbance, such as overgrazing, soil erosion, declining water table, or pollution. Correcting these problems is essential to restoring healthy plant communities. Some invasives, however, actively displace all other species and must be physically removed before the soil or desirable plants have any chance of recovery.

Conventional plant removal, called "grubbing," tends to be hit or miss, the largest plants ripped out with heavy equipment or sawed down. Eliminating invasive plants is not so simple: these species are among the world's most vigorous. Many can resprout from a small piece of root left behind in the soil, or multiply explosively from a few seeds. Ridding an area of invasives may require careful hand labor, such as forking the soil, to remove roots or tubers. Some invasives can be eliminated by changing soil conditions to favor native plants, requiring unusually careful analysis of soil nutrients and knowledge of plant metabolism.

In the case of truly damaging invasives, selective use of herbicides may be essential. (Some federal attempts to eradicate invasives have "crop dusted" with herbicides, both ineffective and dangerous.) Workers on selective-removal projects will need to be familiar with advanced techniques of herbicide application,

such as ultra-low-volume targeted application. Considerable plant identification skill will be necessary. Full eradication of invasive species often requires repeat visits in different growing seasons. Most of these practices are unfamiliar to conventional construction crews.

Replanting diverse and appropriate native plant cover also requires new skills and knowledge. While horticultural plants are commonly selected because they transplant or propagate easily, native plants demand a much broader range of nursery skills. For example, many natives can only grow in cooperation with specific soil organisms. Regional native plant societies often have excellent information on propagating and planting native species.

In contrast to horticultural care for *individual* plants, native plant restoration usually involves management of *communities*, and of *succession*. A plant community is a group of species that grow closely and codependently together, usually supporting an identifiable animal community. Every plant community undergoes succession, a series of changes in the composition of the community over time. Succession is considered to "start" from bare ground, whether exposed by natural events like fires or landslides, or cleared by humans. Small nonwoody plants usually pioneer bare ground, especially on poor soils. Over time, these are crowded out by shrubs, small trees, and eventually (if soil fertility, water, and sun permit) by forest. Ecologists originally considered the forest or other "climax community" as the end of succession, but more recent work shows that succession is frequently set back a stage, or even restarted, on a given site. This idea is extremely useful in site management.

The stages of succession (for example, the change from meadow to shrubland) are fairly distinct for most regional vegetation. Each stage requires certain conditions before it can develop and can be set back by other conditions. As an example, for woodlands to take over from shrubs, a high level of organic matter is often required, left in the soil by earlier meadow and shrubland plants. Many tree species only germinate in shade, which must be provided by their shrubby forerunners in succession. Thus, shade and organic soil might be human *management strategies* for hastening succession toward its forested phase. Similarly, changing soil pH, or burning a meadow annually, can "set back" succession, so that woody plants cannot occupy meadow territory. In fact, these ways of managing succession were widely used by preagricultural cultures, for example, burning the Great Plains to favor grass for the buffalo.

Some stages of succession are more desirable, socially, than others: many people favor meadows and woods over the big-shrub stage called "oldfield." It is crucial to note that, although native shrubs may be "invaders" in a native meadow, this is an entirely different process than invasion of an ecosystem by imported species. As just outlined, native invaders are frequently set back by natural disasters, or by aging of the community; in the process, other native species have their day again. When imported invasives take over, all other plants may be permanently suppressed, to the point of extinction. For example, the floodplain in Figure 2.15 will never see native cottonwoods again unless massive human effort eradicates the imported tamarisk and Russian olive that have overrun it.

Professional restoration skills, including work with native plants, are likely to be in demand as sustainability grows in importance. For most designers and contractors, collaboration with a native-plant nursery is the most practical route to this knowledge.

Follow Field-based Planting Patterns

Restoration planting is best based on *patterns* of plant growth that occur naturally in the region. Natural plant patterns are often seen as random, disorderly, and too irregular to reproduce (compare issues in landform grading, p. 82). In addition, many designers, influenced by avant-garde artistic theories, have developed deep-seated prejudice against any "mimicry of nature." As discussed in "Sustainability, Substance, and Style," pp. 19–26, nature mimicry *as cosmetics* over socially objectionable structures is a questionable practice. Practical experience, however, indicates that *pattern* is as important as species composition, soil condition, or microclimate to long-term health of plant communities.[88] In site restoration, by definition, getting the pattern right is fundamental.

Leslie Sauer, in her book on forest restoration, *The Once and Future Forest*, urges, "Plant in patterns that you have observed on the site or in analogous habitats."[89] Sauer and her colleague at Andropogon, Carol Franklin, have for years taught a simple method: field-sketched mini maps showing growth patterns of regional trees and shrubs. Selecting a little-disturbed grove of trees, pace off distances and draw, on graph paper, a roughly scaled plan of the major plants. The plan is like a designer's planting plan, but derived from naturally occurring patterns. It should show approximate trunk size of each tree and a dotted line representing the canopy—which will seldom, if ever, be perfectly round, because trees growing in groups compete for space and sunlight. A file of such sketches is a model on which to base landscape plantings. Computer modeling of succession, using agent-based or fractal methods, could also simulate regional patterns (p. 41). Used this way, naturalistic patterns are not "greenwash," but critical to survival and ecological function of plant communities.

Construction professionals and nursery employees are frequently responsible for laying out planting plans on site. Conventional attitudes treat accurate planting layout as optional, "close enough for convenience." For sustainable construction, careful adherence to well-patterned plans is a must. Although it is easier to locate and measure points along straight lines, planting crews need to relearn skills of laying out irregular, but not random, patterns. Baseline-and-offset measurement is one such skill; GPS could also be used.

Match Plants to Restoration Purposes

In restoration work, plants serve both general purposes of stabilizing and enriching soil, and more specific purposes like reattracting wildlife or processing toxic soil materials.

PLANTS FOR WILDLIFE RESTORATION

Reintroducing wildlife is a frequent motive for land restoration. Plants and wildlife in any region are a co-evolved community, depending on one another for survival. Some plants (or their fruits), however, may attract *undesirable* wildlife, either pests like rats, or desirable animals, such as bears, too wild to coexist well at close quarters with humans.

For wildlife restoration, plant species and patterns must match animal preferences. A simple and well-documented example: the three North American bluebird species are attracted to sassafras, cherry, dogwood, and juniper trees. Bluebirds are reluctant to nest unless surrounded by a clearing nearly one hundred feet across, which forms a barrier to their most aggressive competitor, the house wren.[90] Thus, a large dense *grove* of their favorite species would fail to attract nesting bluebirds while a *single tree* planted in a meadow might succeed.

Restoration projects intended to attract wildlife must be designed with detailed knowledge of the whole community and consideration for human impact. Constructing such landscapes offers unique challenges. Designer, contractor, scientific specialists, and client must work closely to achieve success.

Phytoremediation for Brownfields Cleanup

Correctly chosen, plants can be active workers in remediating many kinds of pollution. This approach is called phytoremediation. It has great but largely untapped potential for hundreds of thousands of brownfields that litter the North American landscape.

In innovative phytoremediation efforts, the United States lags far behind Europe. Early work was actually catalyzed by environmental artists like New York sculptor Mel Chin. In 1989 Chin teamed with US Department of Agriculture agronomist Rufus Chaney, who was experimenting with pollutant-absorbing plants. Because little was then known about increasing plants' uptake of toxins, Chaney suggested that Chin's artwork be configured as a scientific testing ground.

Chin's site was Pig's Eye landfill (St. Paul MN), contaminated with heavy metals. Here Chin and his team created Revival Field, a 3,600-square-foot garden. The design was a circle within a square.[91] Walkways formed an X and contained ninety-six test plots with various plant species. Three years of digging up plants each spring to analyze their metal content showed Chaney that Alpine Pennycress was best at extracting zinc and cadmium. In 1993 Chin and Chaney collaborated again in Palmerton PA, and as

Chin started a third such garden in Baltimore in 1998.[92] Other artists, such as Stacy Levy, have created beautiful and educational artworks that also rehabilitate toxic sites.

Where artists or landscape professionals aren't involved, cleanup is typically viewed as an engineering problem, ignoring biological or horticultural possibilities. Some approaches that have been tried on brownfields are not just prosaic, but brutal—sealing the entire site with paving, encasing the soil in concrete, or vitrifying it (turning it to glass with high-voltage electrical probes). Trucking the soil off to be cleansed by chemical and mechanical processes and returned, even if effective, drastically raises remediation costs, economic and environmental. These brute-force "solutions" often cost society all future productivity of the land.

For some situations, harsh engineering methods are unavoidable. Everywhere else, phytoremediation offers significant benefits to the environment, to the public, and to the landscape industry, which is well qualified to learn such work.

The basic concept of phytoremediation is familiar in constructed wetlands for water treatment (see p. 189). In wetlands, aquatic plants take up pollutants and cleanse water, often outperforming conventional treatment. Pollutants typically remain in the plants, periodically harvested as toxins build up in their tissues. In many cases, the toxic materials have industrial value and can be reclaimed. Constructed wetlands could, in fact, be called aquatic phytoremediation, because the same processes are at work.

Today phytoremediation is being developed for a range of substances considerably more toxic than the stormwater or sewage typically treated in wetlands. Briefly, phytoremediation is:

- useful against a wide variety of pollutants: crude oil, solvents, pesticides, landfill leachates, and such metals as chromium, mercury, and lead
- generally best for relatively low concentrations in upper soil layers
- solar powered, unlike energy-intensive mechanical methods
- far cheaper to install, maintain, and operate than other decontamination methods, although slower

Figure 2.16a,b Phytoremediation of a petroleum-contaminated site in Wisconsin. First photo shows willows at planting; second, after one year. (*Project:* Geraghty and Miller. *Photo:* Eric Carman.)

($80 per square yard or $1,000 to $6,000 per acre, or 4 to 32 percent of other methods[93])
- aesthetically pleasing.

New species are constantly emerging for phytoremediation. Tumbleweed and Jimsonweed take up radioactive waste; watercress has been genetically engineered to detect land mines. Salt-tolerant species might remediate soils made saline by desert irrigation.[94] "Phytomining" even uses plants to extract gold and nickel from marginal ores.

"Public acceptance of a phytoremediation project on a site can be very high, in part because of the park-like aesthetics, shade, dust control, and bird and wildlife habitat," notes Steve Rock, an engineer with the EPA's National Risk Management Laboratory. "There is a widespread intuitive agreement that a site covered in vegetation is less hazardous than a bare abandoned lot. When the plants are growing the site

is apparently being cleaned."[95] Of course, healthy growth is not a perfect indicator of improved health and must be backed by instrumented monitoring.

Phytoremediation operates through three principal mechanisms: by extracting, containing, or degrading contaminants.[96]

Extraction takes up and accumulates contaminants into shoots and leaves. (Phytoremediation experts like to compare plants to solar-powered pumps bringing contaminants out of the soil.) Harvested, the plant removes the contaminants from the site. Plant tissue may be dried, burned, or composted under controlled conditions, sometimes reclaiming the extracted chemical. *Phytovolatilization* extracts pollutants from soil or water, converting them into gaseous form that breaks down safely in air.

Containment uses plants to immobilize contaminants permanently. Certain trees, for example, can sequester large concentrations of metals in their roots. Although harvesting and carting away whole trees is impractical, the contaminants at least no longer circulate within the environment. *Hydraulic containment* uses deep-rooted (phreatophytic) species to keep contaminated groundwater from spreading, while *phytostabilization* keeps soil contaminants from moving through the soil.

Degradation breaks down or digests contaminants—principally hydrocarbons and other organic compounds—so that they are no longer toxic. Degradation often occurs in the root zone through microbial or fungal interactions, chemical effects of roots, or enzymes they exude. Degradation also occurs in the plant itself. Degradation may also convert a chemical from a water- or fat-soluble form (easily taken up by animals and people) to insoluble forms that pose little danger.

Phytoremediation is no cure-all, nor effective on all sites. It is generally limited to sites with low overall pollutant concentrations and shallow pollutant distribution. Most phytoremediation plants also seem to require a soil-chelating chemical (one that binds metals to itself, allowing plant uptake). Recent research, however, isolated a gene that allows *Arabidopsis thaliana* (a relative of Alpine Pennycress) to produce its own chelating chemical—and could be bred into other plants.[97]

A relatively new science, phytoremediation still invokes suspicion from some regulators. Certainly, valid questions have yet to be answered. What happens in the food chain if wildlife consume leaves or shoots of phytoremediation plants? How is air quality affected if plants pull pollutants out of soil and release them via evapotranspiration? More research is needed to answer such questions.

Alan Christensen, a landscape architect from American Fork UT who has studied brownfield remediation, raises another question: "What if you could plant trees to get rid of the contamination, and at the same time use the trees as landscape buffers or to create shade for parking lots and buildings?" Despite one National Park Service pilot project reportedly begun in Charleston SC, this idea has yet to be implemented, and results would be very long term.

The number of plants that can remediate a specific contaminant is limited; there may not be *any* frost-hardy shade tree with yellow summer flowers that can degrade cadmium. Capacities and hazards differ for every contaminant or plant species. We urge more designers and contractors to examine the possibilities for permanent phytoremediation doubling as parks.

BIOREMEDIATION

A related strategy is bioremediation: use of soil bacteria and microorganisms to cleanse pollution from soil or water. Like phytoremediation, it is a low-tech, environmentally sound approach that harnesses a benign force of nature—microorganism enzymes—to biodegrade pollution.

Bioremediation is already a mainstream approach to toxic site cleanup. It is widely used on petroleum spills and has proved successful against toluene solvent, naphthalene moth repellent, and pentachlorophenol fungicide and wood preservative. Especially if a chemical resembles natural substances, there is a good chance that a microbe can be found to metabolize it. Both government agencies and for-profit consultants are expanding bioremediation capacities.

Petroleum leakage from old, corroded underground storage tanks is a widespread environmental problem. Minnesota's DOT uses bioremediation for routine remediation of gasoline, diesel, and used motor oil, according to senior environmental engineer Brian Kamnikar. Indigenous soil bacteria treat petroleum as a free lunch, a source of energy. MNDOT accelerates natural biodegradation by mounding up contaminated soil ("biomounds") and adding nutrients (typically sheep manure). MNDOT adds moistened wood chips to reduce the soil's density, provide moisture, and keep oxygen flowing, thus promoting aerobic bacterial activity. MNDOT has successfully reused decontaminated soil, after testing, as topsoil on highway-construction projects—completing a cycle that turns a problem back into a resource.[98]

At the federal level the EPA is actively promoting bioremediation and has published field-testing results. The National Ground Water Association offers courses in what it refers to as "natural attenuation" of soil and groundwater pollution. Bioremediation consultants can be found via the Internet; the Web has played a significant role in the growth of bioremediation.

Bioremediation is not a panacea for all hazardous wastes. For example, in mixed wastes, heavy metals may kill bacteria that could metabolize the organic pollutants. Bioremediation is particularly valuable for dispersed, dilute soil contamination. In soils that air cannot readily penetrate, anaerobic conditions can hinder the process; relatively simple aeration methods, such as using blowers or compressors to pump oxygen into the ground, may enhance bioremediation.[99]

Perhaps the greatest appeal of bioremediation is its low cost. According to one summary on the Internet, "The cost of restoring the burgeoning global inventory of contaminated ecosystems is virtually incalculable.... Bioremediation ... is a safe, effective, and economic alternative to traditional methods of remediation."[100] Like many sustainable strategies, bioremediation is based on services that the environment has been providing to humans throughout history. A 1999 study found that bacteria living in lake- and stream-bottom mud can remove 35–85 percent of two carcinogenic water pollutants.[101] As emphasized in the section on soil preservation (p. 87), microorganisms exist by the billions in soil and are among the best-known defenses against pollution. Bioremediation is simply advancing human ability to make specific use of what the Earth has been doing for eons.

Restore Forests and Coexist with Wildfire

Until very recently, wildfire was not a landscape professional's concern. Several factors have combined to make it one today. Homes in wild places like forests and mountains are increasingly popular and feasible. Population growth is pushing development into new lands, some covered with "fire-adapted" vegetation that *requires* periodic burning to reproduce or compete with other species. Flight from cities perceived as dangerous and suburbs perceived as boring has motivated a new back-to-nature exodus. Instant communication, telecommuting, and four-wheel drive allow living comfortably in the wilds. Around and even within many cities and towns, residential development is colliding with relatively undeveloped forests, creating what is called the Urban Wildland Interface (UWI) Zone or, more bluntly, the Wildfire Danger Zone.[102]

The second factor in making wildfire a landscape issue is what ecologist George Wuerthner calls "a century of failed forest policy."[103] This policy, with Smokey the Bear as its mascot, suppressed all fires to protect timber interests, scenic parks, small towns, and a few homesteads. Suppression, however, produced overly dense stands of small trees that, when they do burn, do so explosively. Years of drought have dangerously amplified this situation.

Thus, exurban development has collided not just with forest, but with unhealthy, tinderbox forest (Figure 2.17). It is for this reason that wildfire is a landscape-scale *restoration* issue.

In 2000 a spectacular wildfire started when a National Park Service preventive burn got out of control. Public outrage focused on the federal government, which predictably threw money and regulations at the problem.[104] These regulations make wildfire an issue for landscape professionals, especially when trying to work sustainably.

Regulations imposed in UWI areas typically focus first and foremost on vegetation clearance, which fire activists call "fuel reduction." These regulations typically require removing 60 to 80 percent of vegetation for at least 30 feet around every structure, and in some cases over *600* feet. The only plants allowed are those considered fire resistant, almost always nonnative, irrigation-dependent species. Similar clearing is required for ten feet on either side of driveways, which must often be widened to urban standards: twenty feet wide and all weather, which for practical purposes means paved. These regulations are often retroactive, requiring removal of existing landscape plantings. In some jurisdictions, authorities have the power to carry out clearance and add the bill to property taxes; a citizen can thus lose ownership of property for not clearing it.

The federal government offers millions of dollars for state and local fire departments that institute such policies, and a massively funded publicity campaign called "Firewise." As *Audubon* magazine put it, "The press and politicians called fire season 2000 'a natural disaster.' The fires were natural, but the 'disaster' was how much the United States spent to fight them."[105] San Diego landscape architect Jon Powell declares that in many places "the fire marshal has become the only land-use authority."

Clearly, such regulations severely limit or prohibit many standard landscape practices. Of much greater concern is the sustainability effect of so much clearance and prohibition of native vegetation. Typical clearance requirements, applied to a 2,500-square-foot residence and quarter-mile-long rural driveway, removes most vegetation from over 1.25 acres.[106] In an average-sized county, total annual fire clearance could be over 45 *square miles*, or nearly 3 percent of total land area.[107] This amount of clearing would generate enough greenwaste to cover an acre five feet deep (20,000 tons or more), most of it hauled to landfills.

The unintended consequences of Firewise clearance requirements are major:

- increased runoff and topsoil loss, and with it, loss of organic soil and soil water retention capacity
- exposure of soil to direct sun, with heating and drying (and further soil loss)
- changes in microclimate that trend toward warming and drought—and thus toward *more frequent and more intense wildfires.*

Figure 2.17 In fire-adapted ecosystems, structures must adapt. Plastic fencing melted and the house (right rear) narrowly escaped (San Diego area). (*Photo:* Kim Sorvig.)

In fact, "fuel reduction" is cumulatively the same as deforestation, and has the same effects on regional and global climate (see p. 14 and Figure **0.3**). *Clearance aimed at fire prevention contributes to drought, making wildfires worse.*

What should landscape professionals do? Primarily, work to create regionally specific and well-reasoned fire policies.

- Emphasize that fire policy must be *coordinated* with other environmental management: storm-water and erosion, water quality, soil health, water conservation, restoration of wooded areas and grasslands, and reduction of greenwaste in landfills.

- Object strongly to fire codes imported word for word from other regions. The attempt to apply pine-forest fire codes to chaparral was one reason that 2002 fires in southern California did extreme damage despite code-compliant clearance.[108]

- Explain that clearance is ineffective against wind-blown flames and flying embers. ⊃ US Forest

Figure 2.18 The "Firewise" focus on clearing fire-adapted forests merely gives a false sense of security. This sign barely avoided being burned down in the 2002 San Diego–area conflagrations. (*Photo:* Kim Sorvig.)

Service fire researcher Jack Cohen states that "the evidence suggests that wildland fuel reduction for reducing home losses may be inefficient and ineffective."[109]

• Work to focus protection policy on fire-resistant buildings, especially metal or tile roofs, which are known to be far more effective than clearance. A nonflammable roof increases a structure's odds of surviving wildfire from 19 percent (no preventive measures) to 70 percent. Vegetative clearance can at best add another 20 percent and often fails to add any safety. Fire-resistant glass and paints are increasingly available. Not only materials but design details offer important protection against fire.

• Recognize that vehicles and power tools frequently spark wildfires; consider shared transport in UWI areas. Ensure all developments have two access/escape routes. Use single-lane-with-pullout designs on private driveways to provide safe access while minimizing runoff. Push fire departments to use the smallest reasonable vehicles.

• Where vegetation clearance is essential, be sure cleared plant material is returned to the soil by burning, chipping, or composting. Alternatively, use goats or other browsers that eat young woody material, recycling plants as manure.

- Be very cautious of proposals to use thinnings commercially, because this permanently removes large amounts of organic material. Commercial use of small-diameter thinnings can benefit local economies, but only if managed for long-term sustainability.
- Similarly, "salvage logging" (removing standing dead trees after a fire) has long been justified as reducing future fire danger. A June 2007 study shows clearly that this is not the case: areas salvage-cut and replanted burn up to 61 percent more intensely in subsequent fires than areas left to natural regrowth.[110]
- Where possible, design firebreaks for whole communities or clusters of houses, based on healthy grove-and-meadow patterns. Wetlands, sports fields, and other features can do double duty as community firebreaks.
- Work toward restoration of the health of whole forests, including periodic fires.[111] "Mimic Nature's Fire," both in vegetation patterns and planned fire schedules.[112] When fires occur at regular intervals, they tend to be less intense, to burn in patchwork patterns that increase species and habitat diversity, and to leave older trees as seed sources. Less intense fires are also far easier to control.

Wuerthner points out that fires are like floods: many small ones occur each year with little damage, but the "100-year fire" is also inevitable in fire-adapted ecosystems. In a given year, one or two "megafires" account for 90 percent or more of acreage and structures burned, says Wuerthner.[113] Policy and design for development in fire-adapted landscapes needs to acknowledge this distinction. Controlling the many small fires is feasible. Stopping megafires is only possible, if at all, with what a contributor to Wuerthner's book calls the "Fire-Military-Industrial Complex."

Because clearance is costly, environmentally destructive, and often entirely ineffective against wildfire, landscape professionals should resist fire ordinances that rely primarily or exclusively on vegetation removal. Ultimately, clearance is politically expedient, giving the appearance of preventive action,

but creates a false sense of security. (See Figure 2.18.) Fire-resistant construction plus forest restoration is by far the more sustainable goal, and one that landscape professionals should advocate.

Resources

Heal Injured Sites

Site restoration

Earth Island Institute 415-788-3666, www.earthisland.org/: Published Karl Linn's booklet *From Rubble to Restoration.*

Society for Ecological Restoration 520-622-5485, http://ser.org/: Excellent source; library of publications; links to consultants.

Beyond Preservation: Restoring and Inventing Landscapes A. Dwight Baldwin, Judith De Luce, and Carl Pletsch, 1994 University of Minnesota Press, Minneapolis

Environmental Remediation Construction Industry Institute, 512-232-3000, www.construction-institute.org/script content/Index.cfm, RS48-1: Inexpensive overview of three detailed CII publications on site-contamination management.

The Landscape Restoration Handbook Donald F. Harker, 1999, 2nd ed., Lewis Publishers, Boca Raton FL (CRC Press): Extensive native plants maps and species lists covering the whole United States.

Foundations in Restoration Ecology D. A. Falk et al., 2006 Island Press, Washington DC

Land Planning and Design for Land Reclamation Bibliography Bruce K. Ferguson, 1982 Vance Bibliographies, Monticello IL

Landscape and Surface Mining: Ecological Guidelines for Reclamation Gerhard Darmer and Norman L. Dietrich, 1992 Van Nostrand Reinhold, New York

Practical Handbook of Disturbed Land Revegetation Frank F. Munshower, 1994 Lewis Publishers, Boca Raton FL (CRC Press)

Restoring Our Earth Laurence P. Pringle, 1987 Enslow Publishers, Hillside NJ

The Ecology of Woodland Creation Richard Ferris-Kaan and British Ecological Society, 1995 Wiley, New York

The Once And Future Forest: A Guide to Forest Restoration Strategies Leslie Sauer, 1998 Island Press, Washington DC: Excellent source on restoration, focused on Eastern forests.

The Historical Ecology Handbook: A Restorationist's Guide to Reference Ecosystems D. Egan et al., 2005 Island Press, Washington DC

The Tallgrass Restoration Handbook: For Prairies, Savannas, and Woodlands Stephen Packard and Cornelia Mutel, 2005 Island Press, Washington DC

NOAA Landscape Restoration National Oceanographic and Atmospheric Administration, www.csc.noaa.gov/lcr/: Good information; shows how strong the link is among landscape, oceans, and atmosphere.

Fire, Fuel Treatments, and Ecological Restoration: Conference Proceedings 2002 US Department of Agriculture, Forest Service, 2003 Rocky Mountain Research Station, Fort Collins CO

Inventing Nature: Ecological Restoration by Public Experiments M. Gross, 2003 Lexington Books, Lanham MD

Nature by Design: People, Natural Processes, and Ecological Restoration E. Higgs, 2003 MIT Press, Cambridge MA

Handbook of Ecological Restoration M. R. Perrow and A. J. Davy, 2002 Cambridge University Press, Cambridge

Wildlife Restoration: Techniques for Habitat Analysis and Animal Monitoring M. L. Morrison, 2002 Island Press, Washington DC

Forest Landscape Restoration: Building Assets for People and Nature: Experience from East Africa Department for International Development, 2002 IUCN, Glanz Switzerland

The Sunflower Forest: Ecological Restoration and the New Communion with Nature W. R. Jordan, 2003 University of California Press, Berkeley

Ecological Restoration, North America Society for Ecological Restoration and University Wisconsin Arboretum, 1999 University of Wisconsin Press, Madison WI

Restoring Nature: Perspectives from the Social Sciences and Humanities P. H. Gobster and R. B. Hull, 2000 Island Press, Washington DC

Prairie Land Management Sedan MN, http://habitatnow .com/index.htm: Good information on restoration of marginal farmland.

Restoration and Reclamation Review http://horticulture .coafes.umn.edu/vd/h5015/rrr.htm: University of Michigan Horticultural Science Department online journal, overseen by Susan Galatowitsch; many case studies.

Greyfields into Goldfields http://cnu.org/search/publications: Congress for New Urbanism on remaking failed mall sites; Web site recently reformatted; search for report by topic.

Invasive Alien Species: A New Synthesis H. A. Mooney et al. (eds.), 2005 Island Press, Washington DC: Part of a series by SCOPE (Scientific Committee on Problems of the Environment).

Nature Out of Place: Biological Invasions in the Global Age J. Van Driesche and R. Van Dreische, 2000 Island Press, Washington DC: Readable, well-documented; includes many invasive plants (many books focus on animal invaders).

Center for Plant Conservation www.centerforplant conservation.org/invasives/home.html: Good links on invasive species, laws.

Union of Concerned Scientists www.ucsusa.org/: Web site has major sections on invasive species, global warming.

Brownfields

Search Terms: brownfields || site contamination OR cleanup || greyfields || Superfund || pollutants

Dealing with Dereliction: The Redevelopment of the Lower Swansea Valley Rosemary D. F. Bromley and Graham Humphrys, 1979 University College of Swansea, Swansea UK

Sustainable Brownfield Regeneration in Europe: Improving the Quality of Derelict Land Recycling B. Butzin and H. P. Noll, 2005 Ruhr-Universitat Bochum, Germany

Derelict Britain John Barr, 1969 Penguin, New York

Derelict Properties: Scale and Scope of an Urban Environmental Problem Craig E. Colten, 1995 Illinois Department of Energy and Natural Resources, Springfield IL

Brownfield Center at Carnegie Mellon 412-268-7121, www.ce .cmu.edu/Brownfields/

Brownfields Center of Excellence for Sustainable Development: Land Use Planning Strategies www.smartcommunities.ncat .org/landuse/brownf.shtml

Brownfields GAO reports Government Accounting Office, http://searching.gao.gov/query.html?qt=Economics%2C+ grants+for+re-use+of+brownfields.&charset=iso-8859-1&col=audprod&amo=9&ady=28&ayr=2005&bmo=9&bdy =29&byr=2006: Economics, grants for reuse of brownfields.

Brownfields Wisconsin www.dnr.state.wi.us/org/aw/rr/ rbrownfields/: Describes the Wisconsin Brownfield Initiative with general information, financial resource info, and redevelopment tools.

Environmental Aspects of Real Estate Transactions: From Brownfields to Green Buildings J. B. Witkin et al., 1999 American Bar Association, Environment Energy and Resources Section, Chicago

A Guidebook for Brownfield Property Owners L. Breggin, 1999 Environmental Law Institute, Washington DC

Brownfields: A Comprehensive Guide to Redeveloping Contaminated Property T. S. Davis, 2002 Section of Environment, Energy and Resources, American Bar Association, Chicago

Redeveloping Brownfields: Landscape Architects, Planners, Developers E. G. Geltman, 2000 University of Michigan Press, Ann Arbor

Brownfields Redevelopment: Programs and Strategies for Rehabilitating Contaminated Real Estate M. S. Dennison, 1998 Government Institutes, Rockville MD

Brownfields Law and Practice: The Cleanup and Redevelopment of Contaminated Land M. Gerrard, 1998 M. Bender, New York

Tackling the Tough Toxic Waste Problems: CERCLA, RCRA, and Brownfields, an ABA Satellite Seminar 1998 American Bar Association, Chicago

Turning Brownfields into Greenbacks: Developing and Financing Environmentally Contaminated Urban Real Estate 1998 R. Simons and Urban Land Institute, Washington DC

Brownfield Sites III: Prevention, Assessment, Rehabilitation, and Development of Brownfield Sites C. A. Brebbia and U. Mander, 2006 Wessex Institute of Technology, UK

Green Pages Global Directory for Environmental Technology http://eco-web.com/: Listing 4,000 international waste-management and energy products, services, organizations.

Grading

Search Terms: land grading || grading drainage || grading landscape

H. J Schor Consulting Anaheim CA, 714-778-3767: Landform grading consultation for mines, development.

Erosion Measurements on a Smooth and Stepped Highway Slope John Haynes, Caltrans Engineering Services Center, Sacramento CA, 916-227-7109

"Stepped Slopes: An Effective Answer to Roadside Erosion" John Haynes, *Landscape Architect and Specifier News*, Feb 1990

Overview of Engineering Techniques to Reduce Grading California Coastal Commission, http://ceres.ca.gov/coastal-comm/web/landform/attach3.html

Compost and mulch

Search Terms: compost || mulch || vermicompost || organic garden || compost tea

Clean Washington Center 206-443-7746, www.cwc.org/: Standards and information on composting.

Composting Council Holbrook NY, 631-737-4931, www.compostingcouncil.org/: Standards and information on composting.

Compost Utilization by Departments of Transportation in the United States Donna Mitchell, 1997 University of Florida Departments of Environmental Horticulture and Soil and Water Science, Gainesville: Full text at http://edis.ifas .ufl.edu/pdffiles/EP/EP05000.pdf#search=%22Compost %20Utilization%20by%20Departments%20of%20Trans portation%20in%20the%20United%20States%22.

Composting Ohio State University Extension factsheet, http:// ohioline.osu.edu/hyg-fact/1000/1189.html

Australia Mulch Network www.mulchnet.com/: Interesting way of matching mulch supply with users.

US Composting Council www.compostingcouncil.org/

Growing Solutions Inc. http://growingsolutions.com/: Compost tea brewing equipment.

SoilSoup Inc. http://soilsoup.com/: Compost tea brewing equipment.

Biosolids

Search Terms: biosolids || composted OR treated "sewage sludge"

Northwest Biosolids Management Association Seattle WA, 206-684-1145, www.nwbiosolids.org/: Source of information on Washington's innovations in biosolids use.

Water Environment Federation Alexandria VA, 800-666-0206, www.wef.org/: Health and regulatory aspects of biosolids.

Biosolids Recycling: Beneficial Technology for a Better Environment (EPA 832-R-94-009) EPA Center for Environmental Publications, 800-490-9198, www.epa.gov/ncepihom/: Primer on biosolids use in the landscape.

Soils

Search Terms: soil || soil profile || soil science || soil testing

Urban Soil in Landscape Design Phillip Craul, 1992 Wiley, New York: Detailed and complete source; specific to landscape.

Soil Science Society of America www.soils.org/: Soil news and publications.

Soil Survey Natural Resources Conservation Service, 402-437-5499, http://soils.usda.gov/: Soil types of almost all US regions identified, mapped over air photos; capacities include bearing strength, infiltration rates, and vegetation suitability.

Soil amendments and manufactured soil

Search Terms: soil amendments || soil enhancer || manufactured soil || soil microbes

Western Polyacrylamide Castle Rock CO, 303-688-3814: Manufacturer of super-absorbent soil amendment; has studies on effectiveness.

Worm's Way 800-274-9676, www.wormsway.com/: Catalog sales of soilless, hydroponic, and other growing media and low-toxic pest control products, tools.

Manufactured Loam Using Compost Material Michael S. Switzenbaum, Phillip J. Craul, and Tom Ryan, 1996 University of Massachusetts Transportation Center, Amherst: Specifications.

Developing Biosolids Compost Specifications Phillip J. Craul and Michael S. Switzenbaum, *BioCycle*, Dec 1996, www.jgpress.com/biocycle.htm

Phytoremediation

Search Terms: bioremediation || phytoremediation

A Citizen's Guide to Phytoremediation US EPA National Center for Environmental Publications and Information, 800-490-9198, www.epa.gov/ncepihom/

Plants to the Rescue A. Maureen Rouhi, *Chemical & Engineering News*, 13 Jan 1997, http://pubs.acs.org/cen/

Phytoremediation bibliography www.rtdf.org/: Currently lists 1,171 journal articles, abstracts, and books.

Phytoremediation: Using Plants to Remove Pollutants from the Environment Ilya Raskin American Society of Plant Biologists, 301-251-0560, www.aspb.org/INDEX.cfm : Good primer on phytoremediation.

Phytoremediation of Hydrocarbon-contaminated Soil S. Florenza et al., 2000 Lewis Publishers, Boca Raton FL

Phytoremediation of Contaminated Soil and Water N. Terry and G. S. Banuelos, 2000 Lewis Publishers, Boca Raton FL

Phytoremediation of Toxic Metal: Using Plants to Clean Up the Environment I. Raskin and B. D. Ensley, 2000 Wiley, New York

Phytoremediation and Innovative Strategies for Specialized Remedial Applications B. C. Alleman and A. Leeson, 1999 Battelle Press, Columbus OH

International Journal of Phytoremediation CRC Press, Boca Raton FL

Biochemical Mechanisms of Detoxification in Higher Plants: Basis of Phytoremediation G. I. Kvesitadze, 2006 Springer, Berlin

Metal-contaminated Soils: In Situ Inactivation and Phytorestoration J. Vangronsveld and S. Cunningham, 1998 R. G. Landes, Austin TX

Phytoremediation: Methods and Reviews N. Willey, 2006 Humana Press, Totowa NJ

Introduction to Phytoremediation National Risk Management Research Laboratory, Office of Research and Development, 2000 US EPA, Washington DC

Plants That Hyperaccumulate Heavy Metals: The Role in Phytoremediation, Microbiology, Archaeology, Mineral Exploration and Phytomining R. R. Brooks, 1998 CAB International, New York

Phytoremediation: Transformation and Control of Contaminants S. C. McCutcheon and J. L. Schnoor, 2003 Wiley-Interscience, New York

Bioremediation and Phytoremediation of Chlorinated and Recalcitrant Compounds G. B. Wickramanayake, 2000 Battelle Press, Columbus OH

Applied Bioremediation and Phytoremediation A. Singh and O. P. Ward, 2004 Springer, Berlin

Bioremediation

Search Terms: bioremediation || phytoremediation

US EPA http://clu-in.com/: Actively promotes and reports bioremediation field testing.

USGS Bioremediation Page http://water.usgs.gov/wid/html/ bioremed.html: Defines why bioremediation is necessary and discusses how it works.

Bioremediation: Theory and Practice Katherine H. Baker and Diane S. Herson, 2005 McGraw-Hill, New York

Wildfire

Search Terms: UWI || WUI || Urban Wildland Interface || Wildfire

Firefree Association 888-990-3388, www.firefree.com/: Fire-rated paint, et cetera.

Mimicking Nature's Fire: Restoring Fire-prone Forests in the West S. F. Arno and C. E. Fiedler, 2005 Island Press, Washington DC: Practical, ecosystem-specific approaches.

The Wildfire Reader: A Century of Failed Forest Policy George Wuerthner (ed.), 2006 Island Press, Washington DC: Excellent mix of myth busting, fire ecology, and practical policy.

In Fire's Way: A Guide to Life in the Wildfire Danger Zone Tom Wolf, 2000 University of New Mexico Press, Albuquerque NM: Pragmatic techniques and info beyond just clearance.

"Will Wildfire Ravage Our Profession?" Kim Sorvig, LAM, Dec 2001

"Crying Fire in a Crowded Landscape" Kim Sorvig, LAM, Mar 2004

The Book of Fire William H. Cottrell, 2004 Mountain Press, Missoula MT: Clear, concise graphic concepts.

Principle 3:
Favor Living, Flexible Materials

He that plants trees loves others beside himself.
—Thomas Fuller, 1732

In 2000, we wrote of "a quiet revolt against conventional approaches to erosion control, known as biotechnical erosion control or bioengineering." For this second edition, we are happy to report that the revolt has spread.

Bioengineering combines living and inert structures into something stronger and more flexible than either. These *living structures* reinforce vulnerable interfaces between soil and water, especially on steep slopes, streambanks, and shorelines. In researching our first edition, we were hard pressed to find a dozen practicing experts. Today, a Google search for "biotechnical erosion control" produces 50,000 hits. These include established and new firms, books and best-practice guidelines, even specialized software. Perhaps most encouraging, state and local agencies have Web pages dedicated to biotechnical approaches. At least part of the official world is recognizing these methods, in addition to or instead of conventional rigid engineering.

So far as we can determine, there have not been major changes in the *techniques* of bioengineering. This is hardly surprising, because existing techniques are mature and well tested. Although a specialist consultant should almost always lead any bioengineering project, basic knowledge of these methods belongs in the repertoire of every landscape professional.

The rigid structures of concrete and steel, which are the twentieth century's technology of choice for controlling erosion, are barely a century old. By contrast, bioengineering is a modern adaptation of age-old "green" technology. For centuries before the industrial revolution, constructed banks were held in place by grading and terracing, by pervious walls of local stone, and by dense-rooted plantings.[1] These tested systems were rejected by conventional engineering, insistent that rigid structures were always cheaper, more durable, safer, and mathematically more predictable.

Detailed observation has shown, however, that these conventional claims obscure problems *caused* by rigid erosion- and flood-control structures. Hard, engineered structures certainly have their place, but as a one-size-fits-all standard they trigger the problems they were designed to solve. Concrete ditches and pipes transform precious rainwater into a problem to be whisked away. Wherever it is shunted, stormwater becomes a concentrated and destructive force and fails to nourish the ground or replenish the water table. Hard structures, especially flood-control ditches, preempt wildlife habitat. Engineered for "safety," they traverse many cities—lifeless, armor-plated canyons, usually posted with "Danger" signs.

Bioengineering and its close relatives are closely related to sustainable use of water (Principle 4). Live surfaces may be applied to building walls and roofs as well. Increased acceptance of these techniques reflects a new—or renewed—respect for an essential landscape component: living vegetation.

Discussed in This Chapter

Controlling slope erosion with the strength of living plants.
Using "greenwalls" to retain slopes and clothe buildings in growth.

Revitalizing wasted acreage on the skyline with planted "greenroofs."

Designing and building appropriate structures for sustainable planting.

Selection, substitution, and handling to ensure plant survival.

Native plants for sustainability.

Hold Slopes in Place with Biotechnical Erosion Control

Biotechnical Erosion Control (BEC) includes a wide array of applications, almost all using certain plants' remarkable ability to sprout from freshly cut twigs stuck in soil. The most vigorous are willows, poplars, or dogwood; the authors have literally seen poplar fenceposts sprouting leaves. These are the live materials of bioengineering. When cut, they have neither roots nor leaves, making them almost as convenient to work with as wood stakes—yet they are alive, and within days or weeks are beginning to weave new roots deeply into the soil.

Perhaps the purest form of BEC is *soil bioengineering*, a simple system in which live woody cuttings and branches provide both structure and growth. Mulch and natural or synthetic fabrics also play a major role, preventing surface erosion until cuttings leaf out. Once the cuttings take root—usually within one growing season—they provide long-term slope stability and are self-repairing and self-maintaining.

BEC does not rule out hard structures, however. Inert structures of concrete, wood, metal, or plastic—through which plants grow and water drains gradually but freely—are important in bioengineering. Greenwalls (next section) are related live-plus-hard techniques, along with a whole menu of vegetated structural approaches.

Biotechnical methods recall one of this book's themes—that many supposedly "outdated" traditional techniques warrant reexamination. Twig-and-wattling erosion control has been in use for millennia in widely different cultures. In the 1930s, Works Progress Administration (WPA) and Civilian Conservation Corps (CCC) workers repaired gullies and restored stream banks with native stone and cuttings from local plants.[2] Modern bioengineering was pursued most energetically

in German-speaking countries, spreading to North America in the 1970s. Specialized supplies for some forms of bioengineering are still imported.

Bioengineering provides:

- a flexible, self-sustaining, self-repairing structure
- cheaper installation and maintenance than hard structures, in most cases
- greater strength than standard surface plantings, due to deep burial of cuttings, and interwoven stems, roots, and geotextiles
- a practical alternative where heavy equipment cannot be used
- wildlife habitat, air and water filtering, and other functions of plants.

Bind the Soil with Living Plants

Some common soil bioengineering techniques are:

Live stakes (sturdy cuttings an inch or more in diameter) can be tamped directly into slopes with a mallet, typically two to three feet apart. Live stakes provide initial structural slope protection (similar to rebar in concrete); rooting, these systems further stabilize the soil; sprouting leaves intercept stormwater before it hits (and erodes) the ground.

Wattles and *brushmattresses* ("woven" pads of live branches) are staked to slopes for coverage.

Fascines (tied, linear bundles of branches or whips) are buried lengthwise in trenches along contours to reduce surface erosion and stabilize slopes. (Some companies refer to these as wattles, too, but fascine is the preferred term.)

Brushlayering places branches perpendicular to contours on excavated terraces. The terraces are backfilled with soil, covering the branches except for the tips. When the branches take root, the tips leaf out.

Live crib walls, boxlike structures of interlocking live logs, backfilled with alternating layers of soil and branch cuttings, can stabilize the toe of a slope. Roots of cuttings extend into the slope, providing structural support.

Control Surface Erosion with Mats and Mulches

New BEC slopes need some form of cover until plants take root, either erosion-control nets, blankets,

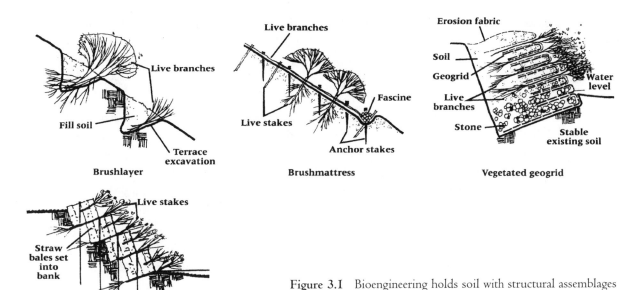

Figure 3.1 Bioengineering holds soil with structural assemblages that later root. Correctly installed, these resilient solutions often outperform rigid structures at less cost. (*Illust.:* Craig Farnsworth, based on R. Sotir and Stan Jones.)

and mats, or organic mulches. Both work primarily by blunting the force of raindrops, which dig into bare soil surfaces. Both have proven effective, but mulching, in most cases, is by far cheaper. Mulch can slow runoff moving across the surface, but the structure and weight of a mat may be more effective under such conditions.

MATS AND BLANKETS

Although the range of commercial mats and blankets has increased since this book's first edition, selection criteria remain unchanged.

Biodegradable products are usually preferred. Typically they comprise fibers such as jute, straw, wood, excelsior, or coconut fiber (coir). Pins and stakes secure blankets to the slope; biodegradable examples are North American Green's Bio-STAKE and Eco-STAKE, made of lumber scraps. Like mulches, biodegradable mats add organic nutrients to the soil.

For extremely steep or erodable slopes, some practitioners prefer products bound together with long-lasting synthetic fibers (see project examples, below). Avoid plastic or similar meshes likely to trap birds or mammals. Biodegradable mesh could trap

Figure 3.2 Lakeshore stabilization at Whiskeytown CA. Soil wraps are being constructed on top of brushlayers. (*Project:* Salix Applied Earthcare. *Photo:* John McCullah.)

Figure 3.3 Three weeks later, willow twigs are sprouting between wrapped soil layers. The willows will be at water level once the lake is refilled. (*Project:* Salix Applied Earthcare. *Photo:* John McCullah.)

animals, but is easier to gnaw or break and eventually disappears.

"Landscape architects, like engineers, are too ready to use manufactured products," says John Haynes of Caltrans, a longtime BEC practitioner. "All these products have their niche and can be very effective in the proper application; but some of them are pretty darn expensive. We need to be looking at locally available, inexpensive materials for use in erosion control." For large-scale highway-construction projects, even inexpensive blankets cost ten times as much per acre as tackified straw mulch from local sources.

Mulches and Composts for Slope Stabilization

Except for unusual soils or extreme conditions, consider composts, biosolids, and proprietary "soil tackifiers" applied directly to soil or mixed with straw or other fibers. Loose wood chips will protect a surface against rainfall as long as running water is not channeled under them. For erosion control, all types are usually applied as slurry, using hydro-seeding machinery.

Tackifiers of guar gum are environmentally preferable to asphalt-based ones; asphalt's fumes are moderately toxic and it can contaminate soil. Polymer tackifiers have various formulas; each should be evaluated for biodegradability.

The many uses of compost are discussed in more detail in Principle 2. Further information on these practices is available from Caltrans. ⊃

Evaluate and Monitor Each Site Carefully

When is bioengineering appropriate for a project? Landscape architect Andrea Lucas of Berkeley CA, who has wide BEC experience, recommends it for any steep slope subject to excessive runoff. "If you see a long, cut slope with rills occurring," says Lucas, "this is the perfect place to reduce runoff velocities by adding contour wattles and contour straw rolls." Hillsides already planted with standard techniques but continuing to erode are also prime candidates, as are banks of streams and lakes (p. 166). Extremely steep slopes or abrupt grade changes may require a "greenwall," the bioengineered version of a retaining wall (see below).

Lucas recalls bioengineering initially being presented as a foolproof miracle cure. Despite continued enthusiasm, Lucas warns against taking that view.

As part of her research for a graduate degree, she visited bioengineered streambanks across California. All had eroded at least 20 percent after bioengineering was installed. This does not mean that BEC is invalid, says Lucas, but that it requires monitoring and maintenance for the first few years—patching unexpected gullies in particular. Follow-up makes the difference between success and failure—and increases expertise for future projects.

Bioengineering cannot always stand alone against major off-site influences, such as expanded upstream pavement and increased runoff. Bioengineering provides structural solutions as *part* of watershed-wide water and erosion management. Bioengineering adds living and structural strength to eroding slopes. In addition, it slows and absorbs runoff, unlike conventionally armored slopes. Surface roughness, irregularity, and permeability relate directly to landform grading (p. 83), Permaculture (p. 173), and near-the-source solutions (p. 157). Used together, these concepts reinforce each other.

There is a growing body of information in English on bioengineering techniques, including computer programs for planning. One of the foremost authors of bioengineering books, as well as an active consultant (see projects, Figure 3.6), is Robbin Sotir, of Marietta GA. Sotir emphasizes that even though bioengineering is straightforward in concept, success depends on adjusting to complex site-specific conditions, and requires well-honed ecological expertise. Lucas seconds this: "As a designer or practitioner you need to respond to each site individually," she says. "Along with the specific plants you choose, soils, compaction, slope angle, amount of sunlight, runoff forces that the site must weather—all affect the design." Sotir, who has tirelessly championed bioengineering in the United States, has seen many enthusiastic do-it-yourself bioengineering projects fail because seasonal or regional conditions were overlooked, plants were misidentified, or cuttings were harvested at the wrong time.

Bioengineering is usually cheaper than hard alternatives, but more expensive than hydro-seeding. Compared to simple planting, it involves more grading, filling, or extra-deep plantings; some methods are hand-labor intensive. Where labor is scarce or high priced, bioengineering becomes less cost competitive.

Bioengineering is also knowledge intensive for design services and on-site supervision. Nevertheless, says Lucas, bioengineering "is always cheaper than building a concrete wall."

To evaluate specific BEC products or approaches, observe a completed one-or-two-year-old installation. Erosion-control publications, manufacturers, consultants, and agencies may provide a list of projects and contacts in your area; the federal government has sponsored hundreds of demonstration projects. Locations and other particulars may be scattered, though Web searches make them easier to find. Examples below and in Principle 4 give some idea of the diversity of existing installations.

Figure 3.4 Brushlayer installation can be done by hand or aided by equipment. (*Project and Photo:* Biohabitats Inc.)

BIOENGINEERING PROJECT EXAMPLES

Many state highway departments use BEC on at least some types of work. John Haynes has used BEC techniques on many Caltrans projects and has compared various approaches on test plots. On a 1.5:1 slope with highly erodable soils near Redding CA, Haynes employed "brushlayering" (defined above). On bulldozed terraces, willow stems were laid twenty per yard; backfilling was also by bulldozer.

Four weeks into this 1993 project, a major storm dumped fifteen inches of rain on the test site. Some slopes treated with erosion-control fabrics failed, but the willow cuttings held. Those slopes suffered some gullying—a problem that could have been avoided, Haynes feels, if he had specified about three times as many cuttings as were actually used. The results of Haynes' test plots are summarized in *Proceedings of the 1994 IECA Conference*, available from the International Erosion Control Association.

Brushlayering also stabilized a large mudslide on slopes from 2.5:1 to 1.5:1 near Pacifica CA, above a residential area. Andrea Lucas collaborated with BEC pioneer and author Andrew Leiser. In addition to brushlayering, Lucas planted rooted seedlings of native pine and cypress, and seeded the slope with an erosion-control mix of grasses, perennials, and annuals. Although installed during California's rainy season, the work immediately reduced sediment transport dramatically, Lucas reports, and continues to perform well.

In gullies, watercourses, and drainage channels securing fill is particularly difficult; soil tends to liquefy during storms and flow downhill. At Sanders Ranch in Moraga CA, one drainage ditch, though lined with pieces of concrete, was eroding ever deeper with each storm. Lucas began stabilizing it with "burritos" (fill soil wrapped in geotextile). At the edges of these devices, the crew buried locally gathered live willow cuttings with only the tips exposed. These quickly rooted, tying fill, geotextile, and existing subsoil together as a strong flexible channel.

Side banks were seeded with fast-growing annual grass and perennial native bunch grass, covered with geotextile blankets. Stout willow "live stakes" two to three feet deep, plus cables, held the geotextiles to the ground to withstand storm flows. Storms soon after installation are a risk that must be anticipated by design. A storm struck the Moraga project one month after installation during an El Niño winter—and the system held.

Robbin Sotir has tirelessly educated the public about alternatives to standard engineering, even working as a mediator where brute-concrete projects raised public outcry. She has built scores of projects across the United States, even in desert areas. Her Crestwood project (below) is an excellent example of how bioengineering *combines* techniques to fit a site, or even specialized conditions within a site.

At Crestwood condominiums (Houston TX), twenty-foot banks were eroding into Buffalo Bayou (a shipping channel leading to Houston's port). Virtually all the techniques diagrammed in Figure 3.1 were used to stabilize this bank. At the toe of the slope, rubble wrapped in erosion-control fabric provided a

Figure 3.5 Fabric anchored with logs, live stakes, and fast-sprouting grass, in place only a few weeks when this storm struck, survived with no losses. (*Project and Photo:* Andrea Lucas.)

strong footing above and below mean water level. Above that, the main slope was held with vegetated geogrid—soil wrapped in fabric or stronger plastic grid sheets or both, with layers of branches between soil layers. Fascines and bare-root plantings were used at transitions: between rubble and geogrid, and along the top of the slope. Carefully monitored since construction, the slope shows no sign of moving. Bayou sediment is now trapped by vegetation and deposited, gradually building even more strength.

Even Walden Pond, ur-environmentalist Henry David Thoreau's home near Concord MA, has benefited from BEC. Annually 80,000 visitors come to swim or sightsee. By the late 1990s the pond was suffering from severe bank erosion. Using live staking, coir mats, and cellular containment systems (see p. 124), Walker Kluesing Design Group of Cambridge MA reconstructed 3,800 feet of pond edge, bank, and path. The project won a 1998 Boston Society of Landscape Architects award.

SUGGESTED PRACTICES
• Employ an experienced practitioner.
• Tailor techniques to topography, plant species, and site conditions.
• Consider greenwalls (below) on steep slopes.
• Options may be limited on rocky or gravelly slopes, or in arid regions.

• Where possible, obtain cuttings of native species locally. (Be sure to obtain owner permission. Do not harvest on ecologically sensitive sites.)
• Protect the project, especially exposed soil and existing vegetation, using methods from p. 52.
• Be sure structures can withstand storm flows before plants root, or divert runoff until vegetation is established.
• Maintain bioengineering like any other planted work, for at least a one-year establishment period.[3]

Make Vertical Structures "Habitat-able" with Greenwalls

What can hold up a truck, protect a prince, foil graffiti—and clean the air too? It's not the Incredible Hulk; it's the "greenwall."

These strong structures with a green face resemble bioengineering on near-vertical slopes.[4] Viewed from another angle, they apply the greenroof concept (below) to the rest of the building. Greenwalls are an important use of flexible, living materials for functional purposes.

Understand Advantages of Greenwalls

Jon Coe is a persuasive advocate of greenwalls. His Philadelphia firm, CLR Design, used them in zoo ex-

Figure 3.6a,b,c Bioengineering techniques form a flexible toolkit, often used in combination, as in stabilizing this bank at Crestwood (Houston TX). Note the large stump, left as added protection, visible in the before, during, and after photos. (*Project and Photo:* Robbin B Sotir.)

hibit design.[5] But Coe sees much wider possibilities for the greenwall. "Contemporary technology," he says, "spends inordinate effort to stifle biological succession on built surfaces. What if we set out to design structures that *welcomed* plant growth?"

Greenwalls offer compelling alternatives to structures of concrete, metal, or wood. A vegetated surface suits many aesthetic preferences; it deadens and diffuses noise, makes graffiti impossible, cuts heat and glare, slows rainwater, traps air pollutants, and processes CO_2, while providing food and shelter for wildlife. Most greenwalls use small, light elements, installed without heavy equipment. Reduced materials, no formwork, and (for some types) no footings save money and resources. Most deal flexibly with unstable soils, settling, deflection—even earthquakes. Careful attention to irrigation and microclimate is richly repaid. Various designs are discussed below, from residential to heavy duty.

Know the Types of Greenwall

Greenwall systems have been based on many concepts. Not all are commercially available in the United States; some can be built with on-site materials. Some of the main structural *concepts* (see Figure 3.7) are:

block—engineered with gaps where plants root
　　through the wall.
crib wall—concrete or wood elements stacked
　　"log cabin" style.
frame—stacked interlocking O- or diamond-
　　shaped masonry (mostly in Europe and
　　Japan).
trough—stackable soil-filled tubs (retaining or
　　freestanding).
gabion—stone-filled wire baskets, strong but
　　permeable.
mesh—like mini gabions, holding a thin layer of
　　soil to a surface.
cell—flexible, strong honeycombs filled with soil,
　　also used horizontally.
sandbag—geotextiles wrapped around soil;
　　formally called "vegetated geogrid."

Two definitions: *Geotextiles* are woven or felt-like synthetic filter fabrics. *Geogrids* are stronger sheets that look like plastic construction fencing. Geogrid is also (confusingly) a trademark for a type of cellular honeycomb. Several good publications give further detail on methods and definitions.⊃

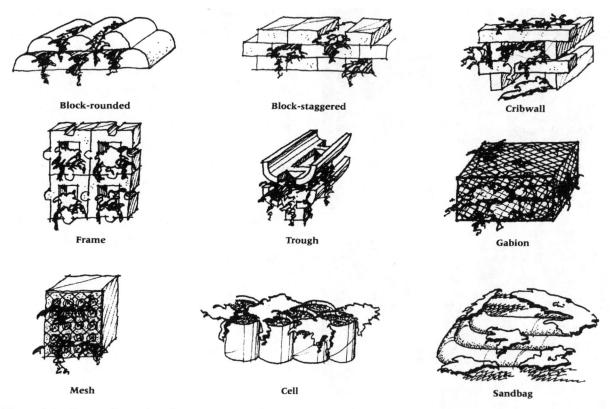

Figure 3.7 Greenwalls combine bioengineering with a variety of hard structures; several basic concepts are diagrammed here. (*Illust.:* Craig Farnsworth.)

Greenwalls derive their strength *primarily* from their inert elements; planting protects the surface and adds some strength. This contrasts with soil bioengineering; they are often combined as part of systematic whole-site design. With many materials to choose from, it is essential to get technical assistance from manufacturers and specialists. Costs are often 25–50 percent less than cast-in-place concrete, but analyze case by case.

Greenwalls are as effective for slope retention as conventional structures. Add their soil, stormwater, and vegetation benefits, and they clearly perform *better* in landscape construction than impervious, monolithic retaining walls.

Newly planted greenwalls require maintenance; weeds may move in before plantings establish, or if plantings fail. At least a year's monitoring and maintenance should be planned for any new greenwall. Mulching and other preventive measures should be carefully considered. Once weeds are present, hand removal or selective herbicide use may be unavoidable. With proper design and vigorously established plant-

ings, however, a mature greenwall requires less maintenance than hard surfaces—especially if graffiti is an issue.

Greenwall structural systems, discussed here for outdoor use, can be used indoors for air quality and soothing ambience, or in zoo or botanical displays. Lighting, watering, and fertilization need adjustment as with other forms of indoor horticulture.

Build Plantable Masonry Structures

The simplest plantable retaining structure is a drystone wall. Constructed against the toe of a slope by stacking local stones, these one-rock-wide walls require considerable skill to lay.[6] If rocks are readily available nearby, such walls are particularly attractive.

Drystone must usually not exceed six feet in height. For taller structures, gabions (rocks encased in heavy galvanized wire mesh) are an alternative. Usually, the empty basket is set up and filled on-site; moving prefilled gabions requires heavy equipment. Gabions may be stacked in a battered arrangement, tilted into the

Figure 3.8 Gabions cause fewer problems than impervious walls because they allow water to seep through. Over time or by design, gabions can support vegetation. (*Photo:* Kim Sorvig.)

slope. They can look mechanical and raw, but soil can be added to establish vegetation over them.[7]

Crib walls are somewhat more sophisticated—open faced, interlocking wood or concrete beams embedded in the slope. Normally battered to improve stability, crib walls may be vertical with appropriate foundations. Plants grow through openings between beams. Preserved wood is often used (see p. 254 for concerns). As mentioned earlier, "live" crib walls may be assembled in the field from living logs, then filled with soil and fast-rooting cuttings.[8] These persist because they are living, rather than toxic.

Where walls must be extremely high or nearly vertical, concrete may be a better choice. Concrete "logs," notched for stacking, resemble parking wheel stops in size and shape. Short walls of this kind can be built with hand labor.

Green Troughs

Imagine earth-filled bathtubs with slab legs in a tapering stack up to sixty feet tall. Each trough has holes in the bottom, forming a continuous soil core throughout the wall and allowing moisture to reach each level. The proprietary Evergreen system offers a narrow footprint, and can be freestanding, planted on both faces for noise or security (an example surrounds Jordan's royal palace). To retain soil or rock faces, trough units stack against the surface. Philadel-phia's Synterra used a 600-foot Evergreen wall along the Blue Route expressway. Affected neighbors favored its appearance, and after testing, the Pennsylvania DOT used similar walls elsewhere, according to Synterra principal Bill Wilson. The National Park Service used Evergreen for huge earthworks at Cumberland Gap Tunnel. Trough units are sixteen feet long, weighing up to 3.5 tons without soil. Unlike other greenwall systems, they can only be installed with heavy equipment.

Tessenderlo Group, an international chemical manufacturer based in Brussels, has produced a similar trough wall—but made of PVC. Known as EKOL, it is used in Europe as a sound wall. It would certainly be lighter for installation than concrete troughs. Our concerns about PVC (p. 252) make it hard to evaluate this idea. Recycling PVC is seldom feasible, and some consider the concept a sham. If EKOL achieves real recycling of this controversial plastic, it may be a good thing.

Greening the Block Wall

Any wall can be *draped* with trailing or climbing plants, rooted above or below it. True greenwalls have plants growing *through the surface*, which requires soil spaces. Two basic designs achieve this: leaving out blocks in each course, or rounding the corners of each block.

Figure 3.9 The Evergreen "trough" greenwall serves both as retaining wall and as noise wall on Philadelphia's Blue Route (I-476). (*Project and Photo:* Synterra Ltd.)

The so-called "S-block" system, a European product distributed by US licensees, leaves out occasional blocks. The blocks' S or Z shape and weight lock courses together, so missing blocks don't compromise strength. S-blocks require poured footings, and must slope at least ten degrees. In earthquake-prone California, these walls withstand Richter-7 tremors, settling tighter afterward.

Verdura blocks, recently patented by Soil Retention Structures (Oceanside CA), are small, trough-like blocks with elliptical front faces; planting spaces occur at the rounded corners, into soil behind. A fish-scale texture provides interest until covered by growth. A similar system, known as Hercules (St Louis MO), uses a face shaped like an *m*, planted at both sides and in the middle.

Standard block systems, like Keystone, Anchor, or Rockwood, are plantable if terraced. Attempts to put planting "pockets" on the face of such blocks (without root access through the wall) have fared poorly, resulting in root-bound plants and awkward irrigation.

Unanchored, some block systems can be fifty feet tall. Anchoring is done by geogrid sheets, pinned to the blocks and buried behind the wall. This is a variation on the "sandbag" system, described in more detail below. Geogrid anchors, with or without block facings, are standard fare in heavy-duty civil engineering, giving them a clear track record for stability.

Use Flexible Soil Support Systems

An entirely different concept for greenwalls relies on flexible materials rather than masonry to make soil stand upright. Mesh, honeycomb, or fabric, these flexible materials are filled with soil. The weight of the soil prevents the support material from moving, and support keeps the soil from slumping.

Experiments with Mesh

Bill Bohnhoff, landscape architect and owner of Invisible Structures, notes that turf can grow in soil less than an inch deep. Invisible Structures manufactures recycled plastic landscape products, including Grass-pave and Slopetame, a mesh of two-inch-diameter rings held in a flexible grid. The grid is usually pinned to the top of a slope and rolled down, then filled with soil on-site; it may be "prevegetated" in a greenhouse. Bohnhoff speculates that it could hang vertically on structural backing or cover a "sandbag" system with a kind of reinforced sod.

An ultrathin greenwall made of wire mesh, System Krismer is used in Europe but not the United States. The mesh is pinned to rock, concrete, or soil, and filled with soil-gravel mix using hydro-seeding equipment. Another mesh system, Terratrel, from Reinforced Earth Co., is normally used for temporary soil retention, but might be adapted for greenwalls. Metal structures are likely to amplify heat and cold, affecting some species.

One addition to the repertoire since this book's first edition is GreenScreen, a modular system of galvanized welded-wire panels surrounding two or three inches of "captive growing space." GreenScreens are double-sided trellises; plants root below, in the ground or a planter. It is neither a retaining wall, nor a "true" greenwall. Rather, it is what the name says: a screen system that can completely or partly cover structural walls, or be used as a freestanding (but not load-bearing) space divider. It is also available as cylindrical columns or traditional fan trellises. One variant, combining a lightweight wheeled planter with a GreenScreen, is dubbed the "Rolling Bush."[9] Panels may be "prevegetated" for instant effect, and maintained by switching out panels showing deteriorated growth. Similar systems are used in Europe.

GreenScreen's Web site lists recommended plants, mostly nonwoody vines, plus succulents (like those for greenroofs). The plant list suits moderate climates; other regions would need adaptation. Like any freestanding landscape wall, these screens face climate extremes: depending on compass orientation, one side may be in full sun while the other is completely self-shaded, with severe temperature, moisture, and wind exposure differences.

The great majority of projects illustrated on GreenScreen's Web site are in their home state of California and in Florida, probably the most favorable climates for such a system. Photos of other installations in Arizona, New York, Texas, and Maryland show rather sparse growth, probably because installations were new.

Firms like EDAW and SWA have used custom-fabricated GreenScreens to create vegetation-covered gazebos and shade structures. GreenScreens have also been integrated with signage and lighting. By covering or replacing hard surfaces with plants, this system combines visual novelty with environmental benefits: purification of air, microhabitat creation, and decreased heat retention. GreenScreen does not appear to be appropriate, as greenwalls are, for soil erosion or stormwater management.

GreenScreen was innovatively used at the National Wildlife Federation's headquarters in Reston VA, designed by HOK. GreenScreen panels cover the south-facing windows, mounted about four feet out from the facade. By using deciduous vines in these trellises, the building is screened from solar gain in summer and open to solar heat in winter. This takes the concept beyond mostly cosmetic planted surfaces (as at Universal Studios in California, or the recently opened Quai Bronly Museum in Paris) and into the arena of significant energy savings through design.

Sandbag Variations

At zoos in Seattle and Rochester, Jon Coe developed a simple, cost-effective greenwall. Reinforcing fabric is laid down wider than the wall's footprint. A one-foot layer of soil is placed on the fabric; the extra width is then folded over the soil. More layers of fabric folded around soil are added, stepped to final height. Soil weight holds fabric, and fabric holds soil. If the height-to-width ratio exceeds about 2:3, fabric is pinned to the ground or structure; footings are sometimes needed. Geogrid may be wrapped around fabric-lined "bags" for extra strength. The wall face is seeded or turfed; woody seedlings or cuttings are planted through the fabric. At Seattle's Woodland Park, grass covered the wall immediately, with Arctic Willow taking over by the third year.

Coe layers geogrid and porous mat together, or uses Enkamat Type S, which fuses grid and mat into a single sheet. He avoids "the ziggurat look" of a stepped face for two reasons. In zoos, kids who climb

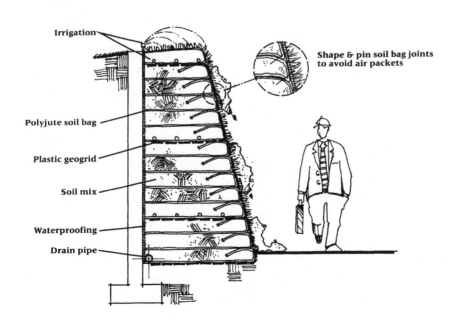

Irrigation

Shape & pin soil bag joints
to avoid air packets

Polyjute soil bag

Plastic geogrid

Soil mix

Waterproofing

Drain pipe

Figure 3.10 A greenwall against a structure, designed for zoo use by CLR Design. The same concept used for bank stabilization is called vegetated geogrid (3.1). (*Illust.:* Craig Farnsworth, based on Jon Coe.)

the steps risk falling off—and being eaten. Secondly, sharply stepped angles can produce root-killing air pockets. So Coe's workers soak the finished wall, then beat the face flat with shovels.

Landscape architect Kevin Kleinhelter used a similar system for Post Properties (Atlanta GA), whose management emphatically values landscape as a prime client attraction. Using Tensar's Sierra system (geogrid stabilization with plantable-mat surfaces) Kleinhelter avoided massive concrete retaining walls that didn't fit Post's landscape-focused marketing philosophy.

For exhibits, sandbag greenwalls can simulate nature or historic sod construction (CLR used them to re-create Kodiak Island pit houses). In other settings, greenwalls could be ornamental, patterned with colored sedums or blooming displays. One limitation: fabric-reinforced systems rely on fill weight and wide footprint. For this reason, they are best used on fill slopes or to cover built walls. If used on cut slopes, significant extra excavation is required, affecting existing vegetation and offsetting greenwall benefits.

CELLULAR CONTAINMENT

These polyethylene-sheet honeycombs fold flat for shipping, expanding when pulled like crepe-paper holiday decorations. Once staked at the edges, the expanded cell sheet is strong enough to walk on while being filled with soil. Each cell is about eight inches square, available in two-inch to six-inch depths.

A single layer of cells can blanket an existing slope for stabilization; filled with gravel, it substitutes for paving; with perforated sidewalls, it stabilizes stream crossings. To make a greenwall, cell sheets are laid horizontally on top of one another, stepping upward as steeply as 4V:1H. Edge cells, exposed by the stepping structure, are filled with planting soil; the remaining cells, with gravel. The polyethylene edge of each layer remains exposed, but is quickly covered by plants.

At Crystal Cove State Historic Park, near Newport Beach CA in a historically certified landscape, undercutting by a creek and the ocean threatened the Pacific Coast Highway. Landscape architect Steve Musillami replaced the highway's original vegetated fill slope with Geoweb, a Presto cellular product. Fill-

Figure 3.11 Cellular containment materials are flexible honeycombs filled with soil or gravel. A single layer can form a drivable surface; stacked as shown, cells form a greenwall. (*Photo:* Webtec. ⊃)

ing cells with local "duff" soil produced a healthy mix of native plants from seed. By steepening the slope, Musillami widened the creek bed to accommodate the real source of the problem: increased runoff from upstream development. The landscape architect's solution went far beyond the rip rap suggested by highway engineers—and did it in record time. The cell material, Musillami says, easily installs to curves, without massive formwork or heavy equipment. Presto cites a similar creek-bed project that flooded ten feet deep without damage.

Some greenwalls benefit from underdrains; Musillami used one to return water to the stream. At Minnesota's Grass Lake, state highway engineers underdrained a cellular greenwall to keep potentially polluted road runoff out of the lake. The engineers noted that the geocell (Terracell by Webtec) avoided disruptive excavation, resisted road salts better than concrete, and softened vehicle impact in accidents.

Design for Greenwall Maintenance

Many design choices go into a successful greenwall:

- Microclimate on any vertical surface depends on compass orientation and is usually severe—hot/sunny, cold/shady, or alternating daily.
- Soil mix and plant selection are critical.
- Irrigation can be sprayed onto the wall, channeled down from the top, or (using drippers) run on or

Figure 3.12a,b Greenwalls can reduce the "footprint" or horizontal extent of a high bank by steepening it. This approach protects Crystal Cove State Park (California) from increased upstream runoff—shown during and after construction. (*Project:* California State Parks, Steve Musillami. *Photo:* Alan Tang.)

behind the face. For trellis-like systems, irrigate the soil, not the climbing vegetation.

- Be sure to plan for maintenance during plant establishment.
- Especially if the greenwall covers a building, plan scrupulously for maintenance of the underlying structure.

Turn Barren Roof Spaces into "Greenroofs"

Of all strategies cited in this book, none has seen more dramatic growth since our first edition than greenroofs (aka ecoroofs). In the late 1990s, greenroofs were rapidly emerging in northern Europe, especially Germany. At that time, however, we could not find a single example on a major US building.

Today there are scores of fine examples, and not just on "alternative" buildings: the greenroofs on Chicago's City Hall and Ford's truck factory at Rouge River MI show how far this technology has come. According to Greenroofs for Healthy Cities (GHC), the US greenroof industry's main association, 2.5

million square feet of greenroof were constructed in the United States in 2005. Greenroofs even put in an appearance at the 2002 Philadelphia Flower Show, winning a Best of Show prize for Temple University's landscape architecture and horticulture department.

Nonetheless, by European standards the North American greenroof movement is just starting. "We're still in the very early stages," confirms Steve Peck of GHC. Two and a half million square feet sounds impressive, but by comparison, Peck notes, "Germany averages eleven to twelve million square feet of greenroof construction per year," with a population roughly one-third of the United States.[10] Germany's density, size, and relatively uniform climate may have helped, but progressive cultural attitudes have Europe outstripping the United States in many types of sustainable construction.

Promote Greenroofs' Environmental and Economic Benefits

Every contemporary city has, in the words of Toronto environmental designer and author Michael Hough, "hundreds of acres of rooftops that for the most part

Figure 3.13 Lightweight, "extensive" greenroof covers Peggy Notebaert Nature Museum in Chicago. (*Project:* Conservation Design Forum. *Photo:* Andrea Cooper, Conservation Design Forum.)

lie desolate and forgotten." Hough's description conjures a city in decline, yet is true even of economically vibrant cities: at ground level, they are lively, but at roof level, lifeless.

Conventional roofs are severe microclimates, impervious to water, exposed to high winds. Every square foot of sterile roof corresponds to a square foot of life missing from the ground surface, linked to various urban environmental problems, and even to global warming (see p. 14).[11] Greenroofs have great potential for reversing these problems, as Hough and Vancouver landscape architect Cornelia Oberlander have long advocated.

Requirements of greenroofs are relatively modest, yet environmental benefits are considerable:

- Improving buildings' thermal insulation.
- Reducing the urban "heat island" effect, by absorbing less heat.
- Reducing glare and reflected light pollution.
- Producing oxygen, absorbing carbon dioxide, and filtering air pollution.
- Storing carbon.
- Providing wildlife habitat, especially for birds.
- Absorbing up to 75 percent of rain falling on them, thus slowing runoff.[12]

About eighty cities in Germany promote greenroofs by regulation or incentive, according to Peck. "Their primary motivations are stormwater management, urban heat-island reduction, and provision of green space," he says. In Germany, builders must provide new green space equal to the amount dislocated through construction. Greenroofs are usually a good way to comply.[13]

Greenroofs also make economic sense: they protect conventional roofs from ultraviolet (UV) radiation and temperature extremes—the two main sources of roof-membrane degradation. Roofing materials like Bituthane are vulnerable to UV breakdown; a greenroof completely shields such waterproofing materials from light, often doubling (or more) their service life. On a conventional asphalt roof, temperatures may fluctuate 170°F over the course of a year. Greenroofs dramatically decrease this. The Chicago Department of Environment found that on a 100-degree day, the surface temperature of a blacktop roof reached 165°F, while a greenroof was only 85°.[14] Greenroof insulation can cut summer cooling costs by half, and winter heating by 25 percent.[15] Both savings—energy and membrane lifecycle—have environmental and economic benefits.[16]

The oddest rationale for greenroofs appeared in the *Los Angeles Times* recently: "Thanks in part to the surging popularity of Google Earth—a bracingly new, if detached, way to interact with the built environment—rooftops are shedding their reputation as forgotten windswept corners of the urban landscape and moving toward the center of architectural practice."[17] In this case, aesthetic visibility is driving sustainability, which is certainly the exception rather than the rule!

Understand Greenroof Definitions, Approaches, and Materials

As greenroofs become more widespread, it is important to be clear what distinguishes them from conventional "roof gardens." Despite some general similarities—soil and plantings on top of a building— the two are quite different in intent and execution.

Conventional roof gardens typically are used like street-level gardens. Shrubs and trees are often included. These require deep soils and irrigation, resulting in two structural options: reinforce the whole roof, or grow plants in containers. The former is costly and in some cases structurally impractical; the latter limits planted surface area and, with it, limits environmental benefits. Conventional roof gardens may be "better than nothing" environmentally, but energy and materials costs must be carefully considered. We would certainly not discourage home owners from rooftop container gardening, but landscape professionals should think honestly and rigorously before justifying conventional roof gardens as sustainable. While rooftop Edens are delightful to the favored few who have access (including birds), they are too costly to help the urban environment as a whole.

Greenroofs, by contrast, are not intended for regular access, and generally do not feature woody plants. This keeps them lightweight, covering the entire roof with a continuous layer of specialized growing medium, as thin as 50mm (about two inches), supporting low-maintenance vegetation. In concept they are lightweight, modern sod roofs, updating centuries-old tradition.

This different intent is reflected in different structure. First, greenroofs require relatively modest additional load-bearing capacity and may be retrofitted to many existing roofs. Second, they do not require flat roofs, but may be installed on slopes up to thirty degrees. On steeper roofs, greenwall techniques could be adapted. Third, they require little or no irrigation (except during establishment and in some harsher climates). Fertilizer, if any, should be formulated for healthy minimal growth.

Greenroofs use materials found in conventional roof gardens, but in dramatically different configurations. They consist of waterproof membrane, insulation layer, drainage layer, and growing medium, sometimes referred to as "substrate." Insulation may be above or underneath the waterproof membrane; insulation above waterproofing is far easier to salvage if the roof is replaced. On roofs pitched five degrees or more a drainage layer is not needed.

Greenroofs *hold stormwater on the roof* rather than sending it down gutters into storm drains. Thus, every greenroof requires reliable waterproofing, properly coordinated with architectural and structural design. Different methods of waterproofing not only affect reliability, but also how easy it is to detect and repair any leaks that may develop. Sheet waterproofing laid loose on the roof deck may allow leaks to migrate long distances. Fully adhered waterproofing solves this problem, but can cause difficulties at expansion joints and structural edges. Some European greenroofs incorporate sophisticated leak detectors.

Roots penetrating waterproofing would cause leakage. A PVC sheet is often added below the substrate to prevent this; given PVC's environmental difficulties (see p. 252). HDPE sheeting is preferable. Some systems incorporate copper-based root-killing barriers. This has been questioned both because of copper's toxicity, and because the chemical effect is likely to wear out long before the rest of the greenroof.[18]

Greenroof soil conditions differ markedly from conventional roof gardens, which rely on deep, high-quality soil. Greenroofs generally make do with poor and relatively thin growing medium, adequate for sedums, grasses, wildflowers, and other tough small species.

Growing media specifically manufactured for greenroofs are at last available in North America. No one substrate is suitable for all sites, however. Some

Figure 3.14 A greenroof ready to plant, showing porous-aggregate lightweight planting mix. (*Project:* Emory Knoll Nursery. *Photo:* Ed Snodgrass.)

designers develop their own regionally adapted mixes. Expanded shale, a widely available lightweight material of which the brand Permatill is an example, is often combined with sand and humus (recommended by author Ted Osmundson, who uses 9:9:2 proportions). For sedums in some climates, pure sand may be sufficient. Cornelia Oberlander has successfully used one-third sand, one-third pumice, and one-third Humus Builder, a food waste compost that adds an extra dimension—recycling—to greenroof benefits.

Rubble and other on-site materials might be crushed as the basis of substrate, thereby avoiding the double environmental cost of hauling rubble away and fresh materials back. Crushed brick waste and concrete are among substrate materials (mixed with organics) that have been used in Europe.

Some mixes incorporate hydro-gels for water retention. There is some question how long these products will last in a roof environment, where replacement is physically difficult and costly. Another question concerning greenroof mixes is how best to protect lightweight soils from wind erosion, especially during establishment.[19] Erosion control blankets have been used for this purpose; tackifiers might also be appropriate.

What plants do well in thin, nutrient-poor greenroof substrates? Begin by looking at plants that spontaneously colonize local hard surfaces, including roofs never intended to support plant life. Many gravel roofs are colonized over time with mosses and stonecrop.[20] Develop a list of regional drought-resistant plants. At least one US nursery now specializes in such plants: Greenroof Plants, in Street MD.[21] Its founder, Ed Snodgrass, coauthored a greenroof planting manual.⊃ For arid regions, there is still a great need for research and testing of soil and plant combinations suitable for greenroofs, greenwalls, bioengineering, and constructed wetlands. Properly planted, greenroofs need little or no irrigation, except during extended dry spells.

Like their cousins, the greenwalls, greenroofs can be invaded by weeds if poor establishment or maintenance leaves bare soil exposed. Many invaders are weeds that cause problems wherever they grow. Most greenroofs, however, approximate a meadow, successionally replaced in most regions by shrub or tree communities. Shallow, nutrient-poor soil mixes prevent shrubs and trees from thriving for long—but not from sprouting in the first place. Although a few woody ground covers fit right in, removing woody seedlings is a necessary greenroof maintenance task.

GREENROOF PROJECT EXAMPLES

So many greenroofs have been built in the last several years that it is hard to choose which to discuss. The leading cities in the greenroof movement are Chicago

Table 3.1

Ecoroof cost example (based on European experience)

Materials	*$ / sq. ft.*
Fleece layers	$0.45
Root protection mats	$0.74
Waterproof seal	$0.74
Soil mixture	$0.60
Plants and seed	$0.30
Total	$2.83

Plus incidentals: sealants, clamps, connectors, edge lumber, etc.
Contractor fees not included.

Additional options:

Heat insulation	$1.49
Drainage layer	$0.52

Based on Stephanie Beckman et al., *Greening Our Cities: An Analysis of the Benefits and Barriers Associated with Green Roofs* (Portland: Oregon State University Press, 1997), 44.

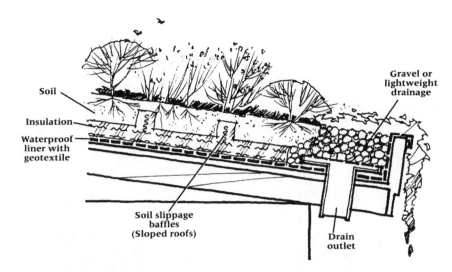

Soil

Insulation

Waterproof
liner with
geotextile

Gravel or
lightweight
drainage

Soil slippage
baffles
(Sloped roofs)

Drain
outlet

Figure 3.15 Unlike conventional roof gardens, greenroofs are light enough to retrofit on existing structures. (*Illust.*: Craig Farnsworth, based on Re-Natur.)

and Portland OR, both of which have policies promoting this landscape type. Most US greenroofs today are retrofits; this will change as greenroofs are incorporated into new buildings.

The greenroof atop Chicago's City Hall is probably the most widely publicized US greenroof. This pioneering example cools the building considerably, but its design was too expensive to be widely replicable.[22]

One of the Windy City's most impressive greenroofs—and a more affordable model—is the Chicago Academy of Sciences' Peggy Notebaert Museum. This 17,000-square-foot retrofit illustrates various concepts: "extensive" design (shallower soils, ground-cover-type plants) and "intensive" (deeper soils, taller prairie grasses and wildflowers).[23]

The roof section most visible to the public, a 2,400-square-foot intensive demonstration completed in 2001, is the only irrigated area. In 2003, when more funds became available, the museum added two extensive greenroofs to cover its large south and north wings. These were designed to weigh no more than 22.5 pounds per square foot when saturated, well within the building's structural capacity. On the existing roof, waterproof membrane was installed, followed by root barrier and moisture-retaining fabric—all manufactured by Sarnafil, one of several new North American greenroof suppliers.⊃ An inch of gravel followed by two and a half inches of lightweight soil mix were blown onto the roof from trucks below. The roof was hydro-seeded with wildflowers, native grasses, and sedums, and

hand planted with sedum cuttings. Hose bibs were installed to permit watering in case of drought—Chicago has long, hot summers.[24]

At 10.4 acres, the Ford Motor Company's Rouge River truck plant (Dearborn MI) is North America's largest greenroof, motivated by the stormwater discharge needs of the huge factory. The greenroof is one component of architect William McDonough + Partners' natural stormwater management system, which includes a network of underground storage basins, porous pavement installations, wetlands, retention ponds, and swales.

Ford undertook a lengthy series of greenroof trials with the Michigan State University (MSU) horticulture department. They finally chose the XeroFlor system, in which mats of sedum are grown in a very thin substrate—just 2 cm (3/4 inch)—and then

Figure 3.16 Ecoroofs are an update on traditional sod roofs—an example of revisiting past technologies to meet sustainability goals. (*Photo:* Kim Sorvig.)

Figure 3.17 Montgomery Park Business Center (Baltimore) boasts a thriving lightweight greenroof. (*Project:* Katrin Scholz-Barth. *Photo:* Kai-Henrik Barth.)

installed. This system—the lightest and thinnest system available in North America—weighs 9.7 pounds per square foot fully saturated. Fewer species can withstand such conditions, basically limiting the choice to sedum; thin-medium greenroofs may require ongoing irrigation. In MSU's trials, this system retained 66 percent of rainfall; commercial gravel holds only 25 percent.[25] A Ford representative esti-

mates, "We ended up paying about twice as much [as a conventional roof], but it will last twice as long."

Baltimore's Montgomery Park Business Center makes a central feature of its retrofitted 30,000-square-foot, three-inch-thick greenroof. Installed in August 2002, it was designed by Katrin Scholz-Barth, a Washington DC greenroof expert. The project was driven by strict regulations on nonpoint-source stormwater pollution affecting Chesapeake Bay. The developer's proposal qualified for a $92,000 EPA grant[26]—an example of incentives for greenroofs. Once fully vegetated, the roof is expected to reduce runoff by 50 to 75 percent. Remaining roof and parking-lot runoff is collected in a 30,000-gallon underground cistern and reused for flushing toilets.

This roof consists of a single-ply PVC waterproof liner, covered with 2.5-inch insulation board, and two geotextile layers that keep soil from migrating downward and washing out. Sloping 7 percent, the roof provides gravity flow without a drainage layer. The planting medium (15 to 25 pounds per square foot, saturated) consists of 75 to 85 percent expanded slate, plus composted mushroom substrate from a nearby farm. The expanded slate, which puffs up like popcorn when heated in a rotary kiln, was mined in North Carolina.[27]

Monitor Greenroof Benefits

An astonishing eight-acre rooftop landscape in Salt Lake City shows that evaluating greenroofs is complex. Conifer-forested terraces climb the north and east walls onto the rooftop of the Conference Center of the Church of Jesus Christ of Latter-Day Saints (LDS, or Mormon). Sweeping off to a meadow framed by mountain views on the west, the roof drapes hanging gardens along south-facing ledges.

Designed by Philadelphia-based Olin Partnership, it is a stunning example of planting on a structure.[28]

The LDS design was driven by a religious vision and regional aesthetics, not primarily by sustainability. By sheer size, it must have stormwater, air-purification, habitat, and insulation value, though no monitoring is done to substantiate this. But in Salt Lake's climate, it requires irrigation, seriously offsetting environmental gains. (Intensive greenroofs, if any, suit arid areas and are being tested from Albuquerque to Los Angeles.) The LDS garden's drama also came at high initial cost: the auditorium roof, already a huge clear span, required extra steel to support full-size trees, shrubs, and pedestrian access.

Greenroof pioneer Charlie Miller of Philadelphia says that comparing greenroof benefits is "a mess." "There is little attention being devoted to investigating the variables that control the potential benefits," he says. "The same greenroof will provide different benefits depending on the climate in which it is installed, the elevation of the structure, whether or not it is irrigated or fertilized, and so on."

As an engineer, Miller associates greenroofs with building performance. "I would like to see greenroofs and green facades, as well as ground-based landscape management practices, come of age as building systems." Designs based on current knowledge, then monitored, are essential for the next generation of North American sustainable design, and not only for

Figure 3.18 The LDS Convention Center in Salt Lake City supports lush "intensive" roof gardens, even forest. (*Project:* Olin Partnership. *Photo:* Craig Widmier.)

greenroofs. Research is increasingly available to back claims of sustainable design (for example, German greenroof data), but reliance on anecdotal evidence still leaves much room for improvement.

Europe's head start on greenroofs makes projects there worth watching; some are well monitored, tracking almost twenty years of performance.[29] Amsterdam airport's extensive green terminal roof, and Ecover's greenroof on their green products factory, are well-documented examples; Ecover's used treated effluent for occasional irrigation.[30] Ecover's home page contains project information, including lessons learned from a few repairable problems. In Britain, researchers are testing greenroofs designed to purify wastewater like constructed wetlands.[31]

Early North American greenroofs should also be revisited in pursuit of documentation. Our first edition reported on Library Square, a Moshe Safde high-rise in Vancouver BC with a greenroof by Cornelia Oberlander, and Tom Liptan's modest homemade retrofit greenroof in Portland OR. This ten-by-eighteen-foot greenroof was actually monitored for performance—as all greenroofs should be at this stage of the industry's development. Liptan reported that a 0.4 inch rainstorm produced only three gallons of runoff (7.5 percent of the forty gallons that fell on the roof). Overall, the roof retains 15 to 90 percent of precipitation. Intense storms saturate it; after a two-inch storm, runoff flows slowly for two days. Plants thrive without irrigation. This sort of specific, observation-based information is needed for greenroofs in each bioregion. Where no full-scale greenroofs exist locally, Liptan's approach offers a quick, cost-effective, low-risk feasibility assessment.

Suggested Greenroof Practices

- Think of *every* roof, especially if large, as a greenroof candidate.
- Understand waterproofing, insulation, and structural requirements.
- Specify lightweight growing medium from locally available ingredients. (See" Manufactured Soil," p. 96.) Where feasible, use recycled ingredients. Do not make the mix too fertile. Use the shallowest soil layer that will support herbaceous plants.

Figure 3.19 The ecoroof atop Ecover's headquarters helps meet the company's goal of a green factory producing green products. (*Project:* Ecover. *Photo:* Peter Malaise.)

- Select drought-tolerant, shallow-rooted regional plants.
- If possible rely on rainfall alone. If necessary, irrigate with gray water, treated effluent, or water harvesting (Principle 4).

Although not strictly "landscape" practices, incentives encourage sustainable techniques like greenroofs. Designers and developers can help draft and lobby for ordinances that fit their region. Many US cities offer greenroof incentives. These include density bonuses (developments with greenroofs can build more square footage than otherwise permitted) and accepting greenroofs toward fulfilling requirements for open space, landscaping, permeable surface, en-

Figure 3.20 Even small-scale ecoroofs decrease runoff, support habitat, and clean the air. Tom Liptan replaced his conventional garage roof with this one. (*Project and Photo:* Tom Liptan.)

ergy efficiency, or stormwater management. Minneapolis, for example, will reduce utility fees for buildings with features that improve stormwater quality or reduce quantity—and greenroofs do both. Tax credits, low-interest loans, and outright grants are also possible; fast-track or "streamlined" permitting, which risks slipshod plan review, is nonetheless a common incentive.[32] To explore policy tools and precedents, start with the Greenroofs for Healthy Cities Web site. ⊃

Construct for and with Plants

Much of the "hard" construction of any landscape is created to support or control plants. Landscape plants represent a significant financial investment, whether purchased, transplanted, or protected on-site. Healthy plants, and the construction that keeps them that way, are essential to functional, ecological, and aesthetic success of built landscapes.

The US urban forest is in severe decline and needs restoration. John Cutler, landscape architect with Houston's SWA group, points out that amid alarm over tropical deforestation, "the media is basically ignoring the equally disturbing disappearance of our urban forests."[33] In the past decade, the largest US cities have lost a total of 3.5 *billion* trees, according to the advocacy and research group American Forests. Cutler notes many new neighborhoods have *no* trees because "developers don't want to spend the extra money." American Forests offers a useful tool, GIS-based CityGreen software,⊃ that tracks existing or proposed urban forests and quantifies their environmental and economic benefits.

As vegetation's many crucial roles in sustainability are recognized, plant-friendly construction methods are more important than ever. Despite the fact that these methods are long established, *careless* planting still wastes millions in money, materials, and energy. Many plants of all sizes are unavoidably removed during construction—damaging any more by carelessness or poor planning is utterly wasteful. The city of Milwaukee WI, for example, estimates its *annual* street tree losses from poor construction practices exceeds $800,000.[34] Milwaukee publishes a thorough manual to help avoid this destruction.

The purchase cost of a landscape plant is far outweighed by value it adds to the environment. The Michigan School of Forestry has estimated the value of a single mature tree at $162,000—based solely on quantifiable services it provides.[35] Other values, such as wild bird habitat, or aesthetic and historic worth, are hard to put in dollars, but cannot be disregarded. Computer software, and a manual for legally defensible tree appraisal, can help; the Council of Tree and Landscape Appraisers (CTLA) offers such aids. Contact the International Society of Arboriculture⊃ for regional experts.

Table 3.2 compares initial costs of landscape plantings against some estimates of their true worth. These figures vary by region as well as species and age; historic and cultural values are also reflected.

Cornell ecologist David Pimentel estimates the economic value of environmental services provided by nature to humans at $320 billion for the United States and $2.9 trillion globally—*not* including the value of agricultural crops.[36] A US Forest Service scientist estimates urban forests save the US about $4 billion annually by moderating climate.[37] Three trees, properly located around a home, can cut air-conditioning energy use by half; planting about seven million trees (a medium-sized urban forest) could eliminate demand for 100 megawatts of power-plant capacity. Trees slow runoff enough that San Antonio TX plans to increase urban tree cover by 8 percent as an alternative to a $200 million stormwater facility.[38]

Clearly, plants contribute greatly to sustainable environments, and sustainable construction must be done *with plants in mind*. Botanical expertise—general plant biology and ecology, protection on-site, and cultivation requirements—is essential on landscape teams. A surprising number of landscape architects have only cursory plant knowledge; fortunately, many plant specialists can provide this expertise.

Guaranteeing plantings makes it in the *contractor's* interest to select, transport, handle, and maintain plantings properly. Careless hard construction practices, such as compacting soil or burying debris in planting pits, can kill plantings. Sustainable structures often require innovative construction skills.

Inappropriate species substitutions for specified plants can undo the intended function of plantings,

Table 3.2
Comparison of costs and values of landscape plantings

Service, Value, or Cost	Amount	Notes
Purchase or replace nursery stock up to 6″ caliper size	$25 to $750	Varies regionally; based on informal survey of nurseries
Cost to install and establish one tree	$75 to $3,000	Through second year; based on CTLA rule of thumb, two to three times initial cost of tree
Annual maintenance investment, one tree	$0 to $75	Informal estimate of likely costs
Oversize replacement (> 6″)	9″ = $955 to $5,725 36″ = $15,270 to $91,620	CTLA, $15 to $90 per square inch of trunk cross-section area
Oxygen production, one mature tree	$32,000	Mich. Forestry
Air pollution control, one mature tree	$62,000	Mich. Forestry
Water cycling and purification, one mature tree	$37,500	Mich. Forestry
Erosion control, one mature tree	$32,000	Mich. Forestry
Energy saving (heating and cooling adjacent structure), one mature tree	$26,000	50 years times annual $520 (40 percent of EPA heating/cooling national average; equivalent to 10.7 million Btu savings per home)
Insurance limit for one tree under ordinary property-owner policy	$500	Informal survey of several policies
Litigation value of one tree destroyed	$15,000	1981 Arlington VA US tax court case on record
Annual losses of trees caused by construction in Milwaukee WI	$800,000	R. J. Hauer, R. W. Miller, and D. M. Ouimet, "Street Tree Decline and Construction Damage," *Journal of Arboriculture* 20, no. 2 (1994): 94–97.
Annual energy savings of entire US urban forest	$4,000,000,000	Rowan Rowntree, USFS—no other information; cited at http://www.treelink.org

or the substitutes may not thrive. Substituting cheaper, easier-to-find non-natives for specified native species is especially inappropriate. (Even experienced designers and contractors need help from nursery professionals when substitution is necessary.)

Construction professionals should not assume that the designer never makes mistakes about planting design. Planting structures require buildable, maintainable, well-dimensioned designs; some contractors have considerable experience with such structures. From the pre-bid meeting through the last change order, the contractor may spot problems that the designer may not have noted, or that are site-specific. Challenging the design may be tricky; a team approach focuses on protecting plantings, not egos.

The following sections give some plant-focused guidelines about structures and handling. Always modify general rules in light of regional experience. Unusual climate conditions, soils, and plant species may require additional or different care.

Follow Up-to-date Planting Structure Guidelines

Alan Blanc, a British lecturer and author on landscape construction, had a sense of humor about his topic. His term for undersized street-tree pits was "dog-graves" (really tiny ones were "chihuahua-graves.") The image is morbid, but appropriate. Without adequate soil *volume* for roots and nutrients, and adequate *surface* for water and air to pass through, even the toughest plant is doomed to die, leaving its pit empty and grave-like.[39]

Their roots severely cramped, some street trees wither, while others rebel, heaving and cracking the oppressive pavement. Controlling errant roots with barriers may save sidewalks, but further stresses trees. That stress is extreme: Jim Patterson, retired National Park Service soils scientist, once saw three successive street-tree plantings die, finally replaced with artificial trees—which soon rotted away in "the most hostile environment we know," an ordinary streetscape. Older conventional tree-planting specifications focus on squeezing plants into minimum space. Because clients demand maximized buildable and rentable area, the landscape industries continue to build lethal, undersized planting structures. Sustainable practice does not waste trees where they cannot survive and makes survivable space for plants a priority.

Several special structures in which to plant urban trees have been developed. These are the focus of the following section.

Street Tree Structures

Inadequate planting structures are a leading cause of urban street-tree deaths: the average lifespan of urban trees has been estimated as low as two years, and few experts give them longer than ten years to live.[40] These are trees that could live fifty years or more in suburban settings or in the wild. Clearly, this epidemic is an economic and environmental disaster. As one expert puts it, "Elaborate and expensive designs are produced and installed only to have the plant materials succumb to some malady even before the grower's guarantee expires."[41]

What is "adequate" soil space for a tree? A widely accepted *minimum* is 300 cubic feet, that is, a pit 10′ × 10′ × 3′ deep. This is much more than many street trees ever get, yet it is truly adequate only for trees whose *mature* trunk diameter (DBH) is less than 6 inches. For a 24″ DBH tree, about 1,500 cubic feet of soil is recommended—a pit about 22′ × 22′ × 3′ deep. (Increased *depth* is of little value to most trees,

because root growth stays mainly in the top foot of soil.)

The relationship between tree canopy and soil volume can be expressed by a rule of thumb: *the volume of root space (cubic feet) is roughly 1.5 times the area under the canopy (square feet)*. (See Figure 3.21.) This relationship is "the most critical factor in determining long-term tree health," according to James Urban, an Annapolis MD landscape architect and national street-tree expert.[42] Some plants probably use more than this volume in the wild; many can survive on less. As a general principle, the *more root volume is reduced* from this ideal, the *more stress* the plant must cope with, and the *more maintenance* it requires. Avoidable stress and maintenance are costly and unsustainable.

Above ground, plants may be domed, columnar, or pyramidal; root volume also varies in shape. A narrow columnar tree does not necessarily have a deep, narrow root system. The "dripline" concept is handy, but seldom accurately represents actual roots. Because roots taper and fork as they grow away from the trunk, the dripline usually covers a majority of the largest roots.

Available root volume may be even less than it appears at the surface. Utility lines frequently run through tree pits; steam lines are lethal, but all utility lines steal root volume. Flared footings, bedrock, and other invisible barriers may rob even more. Many trees survive only by sending roots immense distances, following any line of soil weakness and permeability. This stresses the tree and can result in heaved sidewalks, broken planters, and clogged sewers. (Contrary to popular belief and marketing, few trees actively attack foundations except when severely root-bound.) The conventional bias is toward protecting structures, and unnecessarily destroys many trees as a result. Relatively few tree species are capable of attacking masonry. Most "problem" species are "gross feeders" whose roots follow the soil surface, thus requiring extra-broad planting areas. In new construction, such trees should not be planted near structures.

There are proprietary physical or chemical barriers to stop the spread of roots. Unless the plant can spread in other directions (which may cause problems elsewhere), the barrier is merely another reduction of root space, producing increased stresses. Barriers are

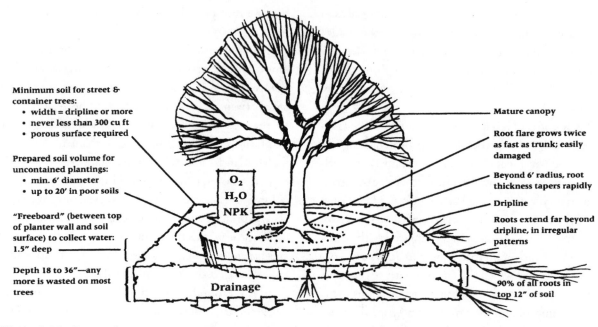

**Minimum soil for street &
container trees:**
- width = dripline or more
- never less than 300 cu ft
- porous surface required

**Prepared soil volume for
uncontained plantings:**
- min. 6' diameter
- up to 20' in poor soils

"Freeboard" (between top
of planter wall and soil
surface) to collect water:
1.5" deep

Depth 18 to 36"—any
more is wasted on most
trees

O_2
H_2O
NPK

Drainage

Mature canopy

**Root flare grows twice
as fast as trunk; easily
damaged**

**Beyond 6' radius, root
thickness tapers rapidly**

Dripline

**Roots extend far beyond
dripline, in irregular
patterns**

**90% of all roots in
top 12" of soil**

Figure 3.21 Root-volume requirements for trees. Recent research indicates the minimum soil volume, especially for contained plantings, is greater than conventional standards provide. (*Illust.:* Craig Farnsworth, based on James Urban et al.)

usually short-term solutions at best and, especially for sustainable construction, a last resort. Avoid placing structures and vigorous-rooted trees too close together. Make sure that water, irrigation, stormwater, and sewer pipes do not leak in root zones, attracting roots toward the leak and eventually into the pipe. ("Frost free" faucets, which intentionally release water below the standpipe to avoid freezing, need special consideration near trees.)

Reduced root volume can have several effects. The most striking example is bonsai, in which root pruning dwarfs the aboveground plant. Bonsai can be kept alive and healthy for hundreds of years, but only with devoted maintenance. (Bonsai are regularly turned out of their pots for root care; don't try this with the average street tree!) The stress of inadequate planting space makes trees short-lived, highly vulnerable to pests, diseases, and storm injury.

Despite new research-based standards, widely published in the *Graphic Standards* and other references, many horticulturists, landscape architects, and contractors are *still* using outdated planting details, especially for containers or limited spaces. Current standards recommend significant increases in volume per tree, and introduce two alternatives to street-tree

"pits." These are "continuous trenches" and "root path trenches," illustrated below.

Soil under pavement is deliberately compacted for engineering support of sidewalks or traffic lanes. This creates a wall around conventional pits, often as hard

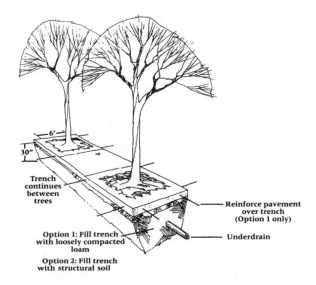

6'

30"

**Trench
continues
between
trees**

**Option 1: Fill trench
with loosely compacted
loam**

**Option 2: Fill trench
with structural soil**

**Reinforce pavement
over trench
(Option 1 only)**

Underdrain

Figure 3.22 Continuous trench plantings gain enough root space to survive in urban settings. The trench may be filled with loam (reinforced paving is required) or with "structural soil." See Figure 3.23. (*Illust.:* Craig Farnsworth, based on James Urban et al.)

Figure 3.23 Continuous trench plantings can unify a streetscape. Paver joints are open to admit air and water. (*Project and Photo:* Henry Arnold.)

as concrete. The continuous trench stretches from tree to tree, under paving strengthened by reinforcement, greatly increasing soil volume available to each tree. It requires slightly different sidewalk construction details, which any experienced contractor can readily learn. Variations on the design are used for plazas, sidewalk plantings, and other urban situations.

The Root path trench leads roots out of the pit in small radial trenches, about 4 inches wide by 12 inches deep. Each trench contains a drainage product, a plastic "waffle" core wrapped in geotextile, which brings both water and air through the length of the trench. Surrounded by good planting soil, this air and water source provides conditions roots need to grow; thus roots follow the trench. Beyond the narrow trenches, soil does not need to be replaced wholesale, but must be good enough for roots to spread eventually.

"STRUCTURAL SOIL" FOR URBAN PLANTINGS

In addition to redesigning structures in which urban trees must survive, there have been attempts to redesign soil itself. Various forms of "structural soil"

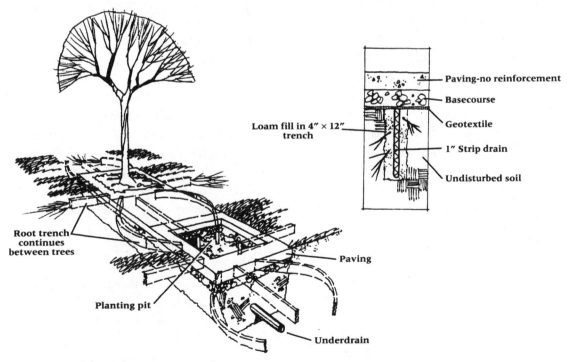

Figure 3.24 Root path trenches require less excavation than continuous trenches, yet provide air and water "paths," which lead root growth. Pavement reinforcing is also eliminated. (*Illust.:* Craig Farnsworth, based on James Urban et al.)

attempt to protect root zones from compaction, while supporting sidewalk traffic. The term "structural soil" covers several materials:[43]

- natural "compaction resistant" sandy loams
- sand-based "Amsterdam tree soil"
- lightweight porous-aggregate mixes
- crushed-stone-and-soil mixes.

In the first edition of this book, we gave crushed-stone-based structural soil a cautious thumbs up. Since that time, however, serious controversy has emerged over this material. Cornell University's Urban Horticulture Institute (UHI) catalyzed the debate by *patenting* its crushed-stone structural soil recipe, called "CU-Soil."[44] Even structural soil advocates have deep doubts about patenting a mix that cannot work without adjustment for local conditions and that has been tested for only about a dozen years. Among others, street-tree guru Jim Urban and soil scientist Phillip Craul have expressed reservations about the patented mix.

Phil Craul ran a thirty-year test of a sand-based mix at the Syracuse (NY) College of Forestry. Trees planted in it withstood 115-mph winds that toppled trees in ordinary soils; brick paving over the mix neither heaved nor sank, even under snow-removal equipment. "The main reason I'm critical" of UHI's exclusivity, says Craul, "is that there's a long-tested, cost-effective alternative that works." Sand mixes, he says, are horticulturally better, structurally almost equal, and far less costly than CU-Soil.

Henry Arnold independently developed what he calls "air entrained soil." The aggregate he uses is internally porous; minerals like expanded shale or slate, heated until they swell like popcorn, are similarly used for greenroof soils. Arnold uses 50 to 65 percent porous aggregate, 5 to 10 percent organic matter, plus loam topsoil; the mix is adjusted for each site. Many of Arnold's installations have been in place for over twenty years (thirteen years before UHI published their recipe); he reports vigorous trees under heavy foot traffic. He points out that structural soil mixes require aeration and underdrainage and that pavement over structural soils should be pervious. Any landscape professional who understands soil basics can specify his nonpatented system.[45]

In concept, structural soil using crushed stone is simple, even elegant. An open matrix of stone provides support; soil for root growth fills voids in the matrix. To ensure stability of both support and void space, the stone must be angular, locking together under pressure.

For maximum voids, the stone is sieved to close size tolerances with only traces of smaller or larger particles. This is called "open grading," "gap grading," or "no-fines sorting," and is important in other soil mixes and in porous concrete and porous asphalt paving (p. 211).[46] Proportions must be carefully controlled, and the soil portion must be sticky enough not to sift out of the matrix during placement.

UHI's specification for structural soil starts with 100 lb crushed stone, sized $3/4$ to $1^{1}/_{2}$ inch. To this are added 20 lb clay loam and .03 lb ($^{1}/_{2}$ oz.) of an artificial copolymer (hydrogel) tackifier. Moisture content should be about 10 percent. The mix is placed in 6″ layers and compacted to 95 percent, sufficient to support heavy-duty paving.

UHI's early experiences convinced Director Nina Bassuk that ordinary landscape contractors couldn't guarantee quality, so UHI patented their mix, requiring licensed installers. Although Bassuk credits thirty-five projects in twenty-two states to license-enforced quality control, the CU-Soil *patent* has probably caused as many problems as it has solved.[47]

"Everybody wants to use the stuff, but how can you patent a base-course material?" asks David Dockter, managing arborist for the city of Palo Alto CA, a strong advocate of structural soils. Indeed, those happiest with UHI's system seem to be people who, like Dockter, have adapted the formula to their region, with or without help from UHI. Where suppliers or city ordinances have enforced the patent word for word, dissatisfaction is common.

Michael Mills, consulting arborist with Vancouver's DMG Landscape Architects, has probably installed more structural soil than any individual in North America. Like Dockter, he credits UHI, but has significantly modified the mix for British Columbia's wet climate. Water-holding hydro-gels were useless in Vancouver; Mills eventually substituted a binder called Soil Stabilizer. He's not sure how necessary it is, but because "the first question from engineers is always, how do you keep it from separating," it remains in his mix.

In UHI's original mix, the soil to stone ratio is 1:4. Mills uses a gravel-yard machine called a "cone separator," which removes flat stones that sieves can't catch, and achieves a 1:3 mix with more space for soil, aeration, and drainage. This innovation has widespread potential.

In Palo Alto, Dockter found that CU-Soil needed 50 percent more clay, low in silt to prevent clogging. It took Dockter's Cornell-licensed supplier several tries to find the right material, and supplies are limited. Regional availability, says Dockter, "is a tough one."

Regional problems can be aggravated by "boilerplate" specifications written into local codes. Bernie Jacobs (of Jacobs Ryan, Chicago) underscores how inflexibility can backfire. After what Jacobs calls "a real hard sell," Chicago-area planners wrote CU-Soil into municipal ordinances, enforcing them retroactively on already-designed projects. Crushed limestone was used, based on UHI's experience in New York, but Illinois limestone is much softer, affecting soil pH. Lime-intolerant trees had already been purchased for Jacobs' project, but the contractor claimed (incorrectly, according to UHI) that changing stone would infringe the patent. Here the patent was misused to *prevent* adaptation.

UCLA Berkeley landscape architecture professor Patricia Lindsey, who studied at Cornell, also advocates designing structural soil mixes regionally. "There is no one perfect compaction-resistant, aggregate-based tree soil mix," she writes in an article outlining the mix-design process. The list of "Street Trees Appropriate for Use in Structural Soil" published by UHI's Bassuk is quite limited, and heavy on imported horticultural species.[48]

CU-Soil excels in one regard: it can be compacted above 95 percent "Proctor density," the standard test level required for base course under highway and industrial paving. The fact that the other mixes score only 85 to 90 percent compaction is less a technical concern than a matter of professional politics. US sidewalks, viewed as minor adjuncts to roads, are built to codes set by engineers, copied from highway specs. In Europe, where streetscapes are better valued, sand base mixes compacted at 85–90 percent are almost universal. Acceptance of these proven standards would permit a much wider range of solutions. According to Bruce Ferguson, 85 percent compaction is becoming near standard for use under porous pavement, where excessive compaction defeats permeability.[49] Unfortunately, many US planners and engineers still insist, "We want thirty-year sidewalks, and don't care if we have to replace the trees," as Jacobs reports.

Engineer-friendly compaction may distinguish CU-Soil, yet its "horticultural viability remains untested," says Mills. Amsterdam soil and porous-aggregate mixes have thirty-year track records. The oldest CU-soil installations are about twelve years of age; UHI published initial results in 1995. Since that time, says Jim Urban, "it has been embraced as almost a fad, a panacea for trees in urban areas. We just don't have good science on what happens to tree roots going through this mix long-term."

To study root growth, UHI and Palo Alto researchers dug up trees grown one or two years in structural soil. Roots showed vigorous, long, thin growth, kinked from squeezing around matrix stones. Dockter found eighteen inches of new root growth after one year. Roots also tended downward, away from pavement, which should prevent heaving. According to proponents, plantings in CU-Soil always outperform those in conventional pits, but their methodology, especially of early testing, has been questioned.[50]

Arnold's air-entrained installations have been revisited periodically and appear to be robust.[51] They indicate that structural soil based on porous aggregate and carefully designed for drainage and aeration can seriously improve urban tree survival. They suggest that gels and other additives may be unnecessary, at least in some regions.

The key question, though, is long-term documentation. Craul has seen several recent cases of trees dying, apparently of root strangulation, in mixes based on the CU-Soil spec.[52] Although small roots and young trees thrive in short-term tests, Craul fears that mature roots may become too big to fit through voids—a problem that will only appear over time.

Bassuk counters that failures are only due to improper mixes or procedures. "People typically think the mix is too stony, and add extra soil," she says, which interferes with stone-to-stone locking. The mix then settles, producing compacted stony soil. Skimping on depth is another risk. UHI recommends 24 to 36 inches depth; one failed test, says Bassuk, used only four.

Structural soils have real promise and need real testing. But in an applied profession like landscape architecture, how should such things be tested, and how much testing is enough? Horticultural testing in particular can't be hurried: as one urban forester puts it, "It still takes a hundred years to grow a hundred-year-old tree."

Until many different species have been tested to maturity, structural soil users are beta testing an experimental method, says Urban. Especially for landscape sustainability, testing and verification is critical. Inflated claims can doom an otherwise worthwhile product in the fickle court of public opinion. Jacobs suggests the structural soil debate is a wake-up call for landscape architects. In an increasingly quick-fix world, "We need a Green Industry Review Process," he says.

Urban plantings are critical to the environment in which an increasing percentage of humanity lives. Pit and soil innovations may considerably improve tree survival. The main reason such systems are needed, however, is a social one: the value of urban land is so inflated that landowners refuse to allow adequate space for plantings. Special systems like continuous trenches and structural soil are resource intensive. Changing social expectations to recognize trees as essential to healthy urban places would be truly sustainable; special engineering for squeezed trees is a distinctly second choice.

Recommended Street-tree Practices

- Advocate adequate planting volume for urban trees.
- Advocate compaction requirements appropriate to traffic type and volume, not "boilerplated" from vehicular paving standards.
- If clients refuse to allocate sufficient space, or regulations interfere with doing so, consider specially engineered urban planting methods.

- Use continuous and root path trenches independent of structural soils, or in combination.
- Always analyze and design for soil aeration and drainage.
- For structural soil, specify "or-equal" clauses to include CU-Soil without excluding other variants. Test structural soil locally; specify what works best.

Planters, Raised Beds, and Containers

Growing any plant in a container or planter is more stressful than planting the same species in the ground. Limited soil volumes tend to dry out, heat up, or freeze quickly, and can easily become waterlogged or nutrient deficient. Containers are most often set on hard surfaces, amplifying temperature and exposure. These stresses make container plants particularly hard to sustain, especially if containers are undersized.

Container plants require water and air. If the container has sufficient "freeboard" (see Figure 3.21), it may collect enough rainfall to sustain the plantings. Otherwise, irrigation is required. Container plantings without adequate irrigation are generally an unsustainable waste. Drainage for excess water must also be built in.

Similarly, plants that require maintenance they will never get cannot be part of a sustainable landscape. Containers usually require *increased* maintenance, but are frequently located in inaccessible places, making maintenance nearly impossible. Contractors' practical experience can often help landscape designers avoid such costly mistakes.

Updated Standards for Uncontained Plantings, Too

Trees and shrubs have been planted using the same standard details since roughly 1900. Even where containers are not involved, these standards have changed[53]—but are still frequently reproduced from old books, cut and pasted onto blueprints, and taught in university courses.

In particular, the size and shape of planting holes has grown. An older standard of "twice the width of the root ball" is now considered a *minimum*. In good soils, a shallow pit just six inches deeper than the root ball, but at least six feet wide is now preferred. In

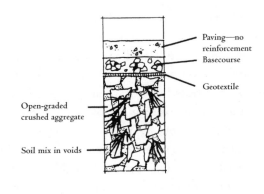

Figure 3.25a,b Structural soil resists compaction by incorporating crushed stone; soil fills voids, providing space for roots, air, and water. Diagram (b) shows components; paving over structure soil may be porous. (*Photo:* J. Grabosky.)

poor, clayey, or compacted soils, pit width goes up dramatically, to fifteen or twenty feet.

The bottom and sides of the pit must be roughened. Clay soils particularly will glaze when dug, creating "virtual container" conditions. In slow-draining soils, space for good soil *below* the root-ball level helps prevent waterlogging. Soil for filling the pit should be amended with compost or other organic matter up to about 5 percent by weight. Making the soil too rich can discourage roots from leaving the pit—and voila, virtual container again. Mycorrhizae (fungi symbiotic with plant roots) are important in many planting mixes, purchased commercially or incorporated from native leaf litter and soil. Grade the surface to form a water-collection saucer, but not so deep that water stands.

Many experts now feel that staking and wrapping the trunk of trees is to be avoided. In addition, the tree should be oriented in the same direction it was growing in the nursery. This is not just a reference to the old horticultural jokes about "green side up." Rather, it means marking the north side of each tree in the nursery, and turning that side northwards when planting it on-site.

Select Sustainable Species (and Substitutes)

Landscape architects select plants for aesthetic and practical reasons: color and flowering season, or capacity as a windbreak or shade tree. When sustainability is a goal, these reasons must be balanced carefully with environmental costs of planting and maintenance. Resource costs can vary greatly between different species. When *substituting* because the specified plant is unavailable, basic understanding of ecological issues is essential.

Every species of plant evolved in, and is adapted to, a fairly specific region with its own range of soils and climate. Individual species are also "coevolved" to depend on other species of plants, animals, insects, fungi, and microbes in their community. Some species are very narrowly limited to exact growing conditions, while others, informally known to plant ecologists as "wides," are adaptable within a broad range of conditions.

When people plant landscapes, they must help plants survive in one of two basic ways. The conventional approach is to *provide the conditions* that each plant requires—watering, shading, warming, even cooling the garden environment to match conditions where the plant evolved. The second approach is to *select plants that are adapted to conditions* similar to the new landscape. These plants tend to survive in the new location with little maintenance. Thus the second approach is generally more compatible with sustainability.

One way of ensuring well-adapted landscape plants is to select species that grow nearby without human assistance—the *native* plants of a region. There is some controversy over how to define "native" (see p. 142), and their maintenance performance is not conclusively documented. Nonetheless, a growing number of professionals have found that landscapes based *primarily* on native species save water and other resources. This is not an argument for using natives *exclusively*. Exotic or non-native species, adapted to similar conditions, are used in many regional gardens as specimen or accent plants.

Few if any plants, including natives, are "no maintenance" in a built landscape. Even the most hardy natives are stressed by being transplanted. Isolated from the diversity of their coevolved ecosystem, and placed in close contact with human activity and human chemicals, even native plants require care. This is especially important during an establishment period of one or two years after planting.[54] After that time, natives require less maintenance than most exotics—but not "zero maintenance." The only zero-maintenance landscape is solid concrete, and even that will begin to break down after about thirty years.

Because they are adapted to a range of conditions, "wide" species are among the easiest to match to new sites. Most common horticultural species are "wides," because they survive in many settings. Some of these species, however, adapt *so* easily to new conditions that they become invasive, disrupting native ecosystems and causing extinction of unique regional species. Loss of regional species and ecosystems, like high maintenance of poorly adapted imports, is a serious sustainability issue. It is also a tragedy for design, since the results are homogenous around the globe.

Native plants, ironically, are not as easily available in nurseries as globe-trotting imports. As a result, it may take *more* work to locate a native species, and to find an appropriate substitution when the specified native can't be found. Some natives require specialized planting techniques. Contractors and designers committed to sustainable landscape construction *must* be prepared to go the extra mile, and in particular, to communicate extremely clearly about substitutions.

In general, if a specified plant is native, the substitution should also be. If a suitably similar native can't be found, then the substitution should be well adapted to survive without extremes of artificial maintenance. Non-native species that are invasive under local conditions should *never* be specified for outdoor use. (Nursery catalogs often refer to "naturalizing species"; their ability to naturalize is an environmental problem if they spread rapidly and aggressively.)

Trying to match these sustainability concerns to desired form, color, flowering season, and so on is not easy. In some regions, such as the desert Southwest, no substitutable species may exist. For example, except for river and mountain areas, the Southwest lacks "canopy" trees. In such cases, we believe design should change to achieve sustainability, not the other way around. Those who have mastered the art of native-plant gardening produce stunningly beautiful landscapes that eloquently tell the story of their region. This regional awareness in turn contributes to sustainable attitudes about specific places.

What Is a Native?

At first glance, it seems simple to define which plants are native to a region, and which are not: a native grows someplace naturally and always has—right? But this apparently simple issue provokes one of horticulture's hottest controversies.[55] This book is not the place to throw more fuel on that fire, but native plants are an important part of sustainable landscape construction. Without respecting native species, it is difficult to protect or create self-sustaining, diverse plant communities.

Several criteria can be used to distinguish native plants, but no single one will define them:

- The species *reproduces* in the region, without human intervention.
- The species *survives* in the region without human care (irrigation, fertilization, removal of competitors, or other maintenance).
- The plant shows distinctive *local variations* that it lacks when growing in other regions.
- The species *coevolved* with and depends for survival on regional plant and animal species.
- The plant (or its ancestors) was not transported to the region by humans, purposefully or accidentally.

The basic concept of a native plant is not overly complicated. It has practical value in maintaining healthy ecosystems, not to mention a sense of regional place. Scholarly and geographic *certainty* about what is native is hard to achieve, however, and controversy has been surprisingly bitter. Landscape professionals can benefit from considering some of the difficulties in pinning down the concept.

- Plants do extend their ranges without human help, dispersed by wind, tides, or animals. However, like species extinction or soil erosion, dispersion is a naturally occurring process that has been dramatically and selectively speeded by human actions.

- Prehistoric and precolonial people frequently managed the plant communities around them, for example using fire to keep grasslands from being overtaken by shrubs and trees. The "managed" species, however, both those favored and those hindered by management, usually remained parts of the native plant community; only their balance was changed.

- Prehistoric and precolonial people also introduced seed from distant regions, usually for food. Relatively few imported crop plants colonized aggressively or survived without cultivation, unlike the many weedy invaders imported by colonial settlers.

- Defining the "region" can be difficult. For example, Red Fir (*Abies magnifica*) is found in the Sierra Nevada mountains, at elevations of 6,000– to 9,000 feet. Saying that the species is native to the Sierras, which few would dispute, is still risky: there are many areas in the Sierras above or below the species' altitude range where it would never grow well. Stating that a species is native to a *political* region (for example, a state) is even more misleading. Red Fir is considered an *Oregon* native, because it grows in the southern edge of the Cascade Mountains there, yet its current range includes less than 5 percent of Oregon's land area.[56]

- The "range" of a plant is a snapshot in time. During the most recent Ice Age, Red Fir grew at much lower elevations and further south than it does today, and may have been totally absent from areas where it now thrives. Climate change due to greenhouse emissions is likely to redraw range maps of many species dramatically.

None of these points, in our opinion, seriously discredits the idea that coevolved, self-sustaining plant communities are critical to sustainability. Natives should be planted and protected *at every opportunity*. The alternative is an anything-goes horticulture favored by critics of the native-plant movement. Historically, that type of horticulture is responsible for many of the four hundred species of invasive plants now threatening vast areas of US ecosystems (see p. 99). A working definition of "native," even if not perfectly precise, is appropriate—and necessary—for sustainable landscape construction.

For landscape purposes, the most appropriate snapshot or baseline for native plants is fairly clear: just before modern colonization and industrialization began their trend toward unsustainable environments. In the United States, this list would include plants growing here between the end of the Ice Age and the arrival of European settlers. This is clearly not a "pure" historical or botanical yardstick. Rather, it is a value-driven choice reflecting the goal of reestablishing *self-maintaining* plant communities that conserve environmental resources and regional diversity.

From a practical landscape perspective, there is no need for a vendetta against non-native plants. Only those non-natives that are invasive should be eradicated or prohibited or both. The remainder should be used sparingly, with consideration for their higher resource demands and lower value to coevolved regional species.

Using primarily native species is often hindered by official and commercial attitudes. Many municipalities maintain officially approved plant lists. Some lists are based on native and regionally appropriate species. More often, unfortunately, the lists were drafted long ago, aimed at avoiding "messy" seeds, keeping branches away from utilities, protecting sidewalks from "terraist" roots, or preventing allergies. Commercial horticulturists, often advisors on these lists, saw (and some still see) no profit in native plants. The lists are now changing in many areas to promote drought-tolerant species.

One other commercial hindrance to native species is nursery stock grading. Standards rate uniformity of growth and form above most other considerations. Because many native plants never produce lollipop forms even under ideal conditions, they may be ruled out by default when Grade One Fancy stock is specified. There are times when uniformity is desirable—but be careful not to let it exclude valuable species unintentionally.

Designers interested in applying the idea of native species can get a clear, graphic, and scientifically based resource in Robert G. Bailey's trilogy of Ecoregion books.⊃ These explain the concept thoroughly, map out major species and ecosystems that make up bioregions, and relate region to design.

Handle with Care

Besides requiring appropriate structures and conditions to support them, landscape plants need careful handling during the "unnatural" moving and planting process. Observing a few guidelines can cut losses—financial losses for the contractor, and waste that affects sustainability on a larger scale.

These guidelines are relatively common knowledge—conventional nurseries and contractors follow them for business reasons. When sustainability is a goal, these points increase in importance. Energy and materials costs involved in preparing, transporting, and planting nursery stock may be estimated roughly using data in Principle 7.

CHOICE OF NURSERY STOCK

Landscape plants are supplied by nurseries in temporary containers, balled in burlap ("B&B"), or bare-root. They may also be transplanted directly from one site to another. The choice among these options significantly affects energy and labor costs, and plant survival rates, all of which are environmental issues worth considering.

Bare-root stock must be protected from drying; even a few minutes of exposure to air and sunshine can kill roots. Moist sawdust or wet paper, often under plastic sheet, hold in moisture.

Handle bare-root plants while dormant; this restricts the planting period. Refrigerated storage keeps plants dormant longer, but has serious energy costs.

Bare-root plants are least expensive, in resources and dollars. Survival rates are reasonable, especially when plants are fairly small.

Containers and burlapped root-balls protect plants during transplanting, with generally higher survival rates. This is offset by resource costs of containers, and extra transportation weight. Be sure the ball or container size complies with or exceeds minimum industry standards.

Most containers are plastic; some are metal or wood. Resource issues are discussed in Principle 6.

Large mature plants, in great demand for landscape use, are always B&B or container; they cannot survive as bare-root. Large specimens represent long growing time and, like old-growth forests, are becoming rare and expensive.

On-site transplanting may save plants located in construction zones. Hand-dug transplants are usually bare-root. Root-balls of transplants can be burlapped; this requires skill and must be done in season.

"Tree spades," large truck-mounted machines that lift trees, soil and all, provide the only option to save most mature trees. They represent significant energy costs and may risk compacting soil very near new planting pits.

All plantings, regardless of method, require significant time to recover from "transplant shock." Smaller stock recovers more quickly and usually "catches up" in size with larger plantings that take extra seasons to resume full growth.

MOVING AND STORAGE

Highway speeds generate wind, which along with sunshine and high temperature can wither plants rapidly, especially if recently dug or repotted.

In winter, wind-chill affects plants in transport, creating freeze-dry or frost conditions even when temperatures are not below freezing.

Plants in transport should *always* be completely covered with opaque tarps; in summer, spray the load before tarping. Do not use clear plastic; it has a greenhouse effect, and polyethylene blackens leaves.

Spray chemical anti-transpirants on leaves to slow water loss into the air, both in summer and winter.

Enclosed delivery vans, covered trucks, or semi-trailers protect plants, and can double as on-site storage. Enclosed vehicles *must* be ventilated to prevent overheating, and heated to avoid freezing, especially while parked.

Ideally, deliver and plant all in one day. Realistically, weather, available labor, and incomplete hard construction require just-in-time delivery or careful on-site storage, partially shaded and protected from wind.

For longer storage, or in hot, dry, or very cold weather, consult a nursery professional. "Heel in" roots or root balls with loose soil or moist sawdust, water regularly, and mist leaves.

PLANTING PRACTICES

Comply, *at a minimum*, with up-to-date industry standards.

For bare-root plants, spread roots in the planting pit. Place the plant on a cone of soil.

Dipping bare roots in super-absorbent polymer slurry increases water availability during the critical period after planting.[57]

Rough handling of container and B&B plants cracks soil away from roots. Never lift B&Bs by stem or trunk; use the wire cage, or nursery hooks.

Most contractors remove containers at planting, but it is not uncommon to see dying plants buried in their containers.

Slide plastic and metal containers off the root ball, sterilize, and reuse. If containers must be cut off, try to recycle them.

Remove wire from B&Bs to protect soil wildlife and future gardeners.

Cut back burlap around trunks. Leaving burlap at the trunk may stabilize the newly planted tree for the first year, after which it should be removed.

Disassemble and reuse wood from large-stock boxes (but not in new boxes, because of potential for spreading diseases).

Loosen or cut strangling container-bound roots before planting.

Set plants at the same depth indicated by the "nursery line," a color change on the trunk. Collect water toward or drain water away from the plant by regrading surroundings or adding soil amendments, *not* by "planting high" or extra deep.

Completely fill soil around roots. Air pockets commonly kill new plantings. To avoid them, water-in the plant immediately and thoroughly.

Use root stimulants and vitamins, especially vitamin B, to help the plant recover from stresses of being moved; apply immediately at planting.

Fertilize the plant only after it establishes new roots, based on local experience with soils, climate, and species. Conventional contractors usually fertilize at planting, to save a trip.

Mulch planting surfaces about three inches deep to hold moisture, but keep mulch several inches from the trunk itself.

Sod, bulbs, seeds, and potted herbaceous stock must be selected, handled, and maintained with equal care as larger plants.

WILDFLOWERS

Meadow-like wildflower plantings have become popular for naturalistic, low-maintenance gardening. Not all commercial wildflower mixes are composed of natives; work with local suppliers, and carefully evaluate species.

Home owners and professionals often assume "wild" flowers require no maintenance. As with other native plantings, this is not true.

For most sites, do *not* deeply till soils prepared for wildflowers. Loosen the top inch of soil. Deeper tilling releases dormant weed seeds.

Don't bury seed too deeply. Follow supplier recommendations. Many wildflower seeds should simply be broadcast, then rolled or tramped in.

Protect seed from birds during germination with mesh or mulch.

Keep seed evenly moist during germination, even for dryland species.

One wildflower supplier points out that the main cause of failure is *impatience*, followed by incorrect site evaluation, improper soil preparation, and inadequate early maintenance.[58] This reminder applies equally to all plantings, not just wildflowers.

Maintain New Plantings

Even with careful planting, many landscape plants die within their first year or two. Some losses are unavoidable, but many are due to inadequate maintenance. Watering, pruning, protection from extreme weather, and pest and disease monitoring are especially important during this "establishment period." Yet this is the time when these tasks are *least* likely to be done, at least in landscapes built under contract.

Unlike home-owner plantings, residential or commercial contract planting is often completed long before the buildings are occupied. Between planting and occupancy, *no one* may remember to do maintenance. For new plantings, this can literally be a matter of life or death. Watering, particularly critical just after planting, may be forgotten; plumbing may not be hooked up, or irrigation may not be programmed. Post-move confusion may keep clients from noticing the landscape for weeks after occupancy. The result: dead or stressed plants, remedial maintenance costs, and loss of "environmental services" that plantings were supposed to provide. Such waste is unacceptable in landscapes designed for sustainability.

To avoid this undesirable situation, contractor, designer, and client must plan in advance for maintenance responsibility. Some landscape design firms provide a written landscape maintenance schedule as part of their services; a few do scheduled maintenance as part of the contract.

Every client's needs and abilities are different—when they will move in, whether they do maintenance themselves or hire groundskeepers—but the common factor is a transition period when responsibility passes from contractor to client. Because the landscape construction contractor is already familiar with the plantings, and is in many cases responsible for guaranteeing them, that contractor is best positioned to ensure plant survival during the establishment period. It is the authors' conclusion that planting contracts should include complete maintenance services *for the first two growing seasons after planting*. By that time, the guarantee on plants has been fulfilled, the client is in occupancy, and the contractor can hand over an established maintenance program or bid to continue services.

To cover two growing seasons, maintenance contracts for spring plantings must run 18 months; for fall plantings, 24. Including such long-term maintenance requirements in construction contracts is *not* common practice. It certainly increases initial client cost and requires landscape construction contractors to do (or subcontract) horticultural maintenance. Lack of maintenance, however, is the most common cause of unsatisfactory landscape performance. Such failures are costly in dollars and environmental waste-

fulness. Good maintenance *during* the establishment period almost always decreases maintenance needs *after* that period by establishing strong plants from the start—a form of preventive medicine. Planning and paying for competent maintenance up front is a cost-effective investment in sustainability (Principle 10).

Organic Maintenance

"Organic" or "natural" gardening has become well-known and popular, both for food crops and decorative gardening. Many excellent reference works are available (p. 337). Many are home oriented, and not all organic practices can easily be used with large-scale landscapes or paid labor. Decreasing toxic chemical use in *all* landscapes, however, clearly benefits sustainability. Energy costs of synthesizing, transporting, and applying chemicals are also of concern.

The conventional separation between construction and maintenance sometimes blurs this issue. Likewise, many professionals who maintain commercial and institutional landscapes continue to opt for machinery and chemicals. The authors strongly believe that the design, construction, and maintenance of built landscapes at all scales benefits from keeping organic gardening principles in mind.

Some information on landscape-scale organic maintenance is included in Principle 10. Related information on composts and compost teas, important in organic maintenance as well as construction and restoration, is found in Principle 2.

Evaluate Turf: The Green, the Bad, and the Ugly

In general, almost any vegetation contributes to sustainability. Turf, the three-quarter-inch fuzz that covers more than 30 million acres of the United States, may be the exception, a sustainability paradox. As author Ted Steinberg puts it in his excellent book *American Green*, "Grass by itself can indeed prevent soil erosion and stormwater run-off, but the quest for perfect turf is another story altogether."[59]

In our first edition, we did not devote much space to controversies over turf, which often appears to be America's number-one cultural landscape. Books like Virginia Scott Jenkins's *Lawn: History of an American*

Obsession offer in-depth coverage of this contentious topic, so we decided not to dwell on it. Today, however, the emerging trend toward *artificial* or *synthetic* turf requires a hard look.

Severe and prolonged drought has been widespread in many parts of the country between our first edition and today.[60] First among responses of drought-stricken municipalities are limits on landscape irrigation and outright bans on new landscape planting, especially turfgrass. While this may be unfair to the landscape industry and potentially counterproductive (lost vegetation eventually makes drought more severe), these water constraints have had unavoidable impacts. Among these have been increased use of native plants and Xeriscape, but also replacement of living turf with plastic.

For home owners, water restrictions plus no-maintenance fantasies make artificial turf very attractive. For similar reasons, many communities have installed artificial sports fields, dog runs, and road medians; maintenance costs go down to one-tenth or -twentieth of live grass, water use theoretically drops to zero, and playing surfaces become all weather and all season, an alluring economic justification.

It requires a deeper look to evaluate whether artificial or living turf is "greener." An excellent source of information, and one on which the following discussion draws extensively, is Jessica Boehland's article in April 2004's EBN.[61]

Living turf is huge business. Upward of $40 billion is spent annually on US lawn care, with three-quarters of a million going to seed for new installations. Turf cumulatively covers an area larger than Pennsylvania. Six million tons of fertilizer plus 70 million pounds of pesticides are applied to lawns each year. Home-owners, many of whom would not eat a vegetable grown with poisons, typically apply lawn pesticides at *ten times* the rates used by farmers on crops. Overuse is leading to resistant pests and increased dosages. Runoff from yards is the single largest source of water pollutants in many urban areas. Lawn irrigation consumes an estimated 60 percent of urban water in the Western United States and 30 percent in Eastern US cities. Overwatering escalates growth, thus increasing mowing and greenwaste, and contributing to fungus growth, which in turn

increases pesticide use. Mowing lawns uses hundreds of millions of gallons of gas yearly and puts out 5 percent of US total air pollutants. Gas mower noise reaches 90 decibels, beyond levels known to cause hearing damage. Finally, 31 million tons of yard waste are generated annually, accounting for 17 percent of municipal solid waste in the average US city.

Artificial turf eliminates many of these problems. Ideally, it requires no water, fertilizer, or pesticides. In practice, artificial playing fields are often hosed down twice a day because they heat up. Water is used to wash dirt, blood from sports injuries, and the like off plastic grass. Persistent weeds will also grow through artificial turf, requiring pesticide treatment. Still, none of these equals what living grass requires.

Artificial turf, when it first appeared under the name Chemgrass in 1964, was stiff plastic mounted to asphalt or even concrete. Sports injuries on early fake grass were high. "Second generation" artificial turf uses smaller, softer plastic blades, "infilled" between stems with sand and recycled rubber chips. This is far softer than early versions, and due to absolute regularity, artificial turf surfaces are now considered safer for players than divot-pocked, worn living turf.

Although artificial turf avoids many problems of living lawns, it has few of living turf's environmental benefits—such as they are. Living turf, even monocultures of locally ill-adapted species, is living. It produces oxygen and cleans air, like any living plant. It can trap half a ton of airborne dust a year and, like bioswales (p. 208), filters pollutants from stormwater. It also dramatically decreases soil erosion because its roots stabilize soil. Turf is up to 14°F cooler than bare soil on a hot day, 30°F cooler than asphalt. It reduces ambient noise by 8 to 10 decibels.

Artificial turf, by contrast, is inert, in many ways a form of paving. It does not produce oxygen, and worse, it often outgasses VOCs (volatile organic compounds, found and regulated in paints and plastics). If it filters stormwater at all, the process is passive, without biological breakdown.

Permeability (to water and air) of many artificial turf products is limited. Most manufacturers' information and marketing gloss over this extremely important point. Even for permeable products (especially those with granular infill), ground beneath fake turf is at least compacted, often paved, to guarantee that it doesn't move. A new form of artificial turf, patented in 2004, features "horizontal drainage": an impermeable bottom membrane, a permeable layer that shunts water to the edges, and artificial turf on top. The South Nevada Water Authority accepts artificial turf as the water-saving equivalent of mulch, but only if it is permeable.

Thus, although it protects surfaces from precipitation, artificial turf does not actually stabilize soil. Like paving, artificial turf is probably vulnerable to being undermined by flowing water. Like pavement, it sterilizes soil if it excludes light, water, and air. Even types that permit some water infiltration may be air-impervious enough to create anaerobic conditions that harbor potentially nasty microbes. Impervious artificial turf concentrates runoff (and pollutants) rather than infiltrating it.

Artificial turf is promoted for airport runway edges, where elimination of wildlife is desirable for safety. The Web site of Air FieldTurf states bluntly that artificial turf "does not support food, water or shelter—which wildlife depend on and build their habitats about."[62] For runways, this is logical, but the antithesis of sustainable landscapes.

Artificial turf is 5 to 15°F hotter than grass in hot weather. (The higher figure is equivalent to bare soil.) Artificial turf appears green from ordinary viewing angles, but from above is nearly black because of ground rubber "infill," which greatly increases heat holding.

Artificial turf, like any plastic, is susceptible to breakdown by ultraviolet radiation. This effect is most pronounced in the arid, sun-drenched regions where drought makes artificial turf seem most attractive—at least to those who are too homesick for temperate lawns to appreciate desert flora. Sunlight in the American Southwest is intense enough to make plastic trash bins crumble in a couple of seasons. Thus, while many brands of artificial turf have an eight-year warranty, they may not last that long in the places where drought inspires their use. Living lawns, properly maintained, can last many decades.

Living lawns *can* be created and maintained more organically. In 2003, for example, New York City's Battery Park City Authority completed playing fields grown without conventional pesticides or fertilizers. Instead, organic soil nutrition products like compost tea (p. 93) maintain healthy soil, and thus, healthy turf. Soil nutrients and microorganisms have to be regularly monitored. IPM (Integrated Pest Management) keeps pesticides as a narrowly targeted last resort. Using native or regionally adapted species, and allowing lawns to go dormant with normal seasonal changes, such lawns meet most purposes of turf, while avoiding the worst problems of excessive water and chemical usage.

Ultimately, the question of which is greener may have to be answered, "Neither." It may be that the *idea* of turf—the perfect surface, nature subservient to human geometry—is the problem, not whether that surface is grass or plastic.

Although turf is living, it is misleading to call it "natural." "In most places, flawless carpets of green simply cannot be grown in an environmentally benign manner," says one scientist quoted in EBN.[63] Natural meadows are seldom grass monocultures, nor an even, ground-hugging height. A natural meadow, furthermore, almost always is an early stage of succession, quickly invaded by woody plants. Preventing this—also known as maintaining the lawn—requires heavy inputs of labor, energy, and materials. Almost none of the fifty or so grass species used for US turf are native to North America.

Artificial turf, however, only avoids problems of living turf—it does not really offer benefits unless one assumes that turf-like expanses are inevitable. This assumption is perhaps the final criterion for judging both artificial and living turf. As Jessica Boehland succinctly notes in EBN, "By maintaining flawless living greenscapes, we teach that the control of nature is possible. Worse, we teach that it is to be expected."

Landscape architects such as Capability Brown and F. L. Olmsted bear considerable responsibility for popularizing turf lawns as essential parts of the American scene, as do gardening organizations and magazines. The fact that a layer of shaggy impervious plastic can substitute for turf may be the best indication that the idea itself needs to change, and that landscape professionals who care about sustainability must advocate that change.

Count on Plants to Sustain

Plants are the only truly "productive" organisms on Earth, the ones that trap solar energy as photosynthesized food. All the rest of the world's creatures rely entirely on plants for food and fuel, with rare and bizarre exceptions such as sulfur-eating, geyser-dwelling microorganisms. Globally, one plant species in eight is on the verge of extinction, while in the United States nearly one-third of known species are threatened.[64] The destruction of rainforests and oceanic algae are well-known threats to global sustainability. What is less widely considered is that every tree damaged in "developing" land contributes to the same problems—and every tree planted offsets them, however slightly.

Planted trees serve many functions that decrease other resource use. They can perform a number of functions better than any technological equivalent yet invented. Because of their essential role in making life possible, as well as the social and financial costs of raising them, cultivated plants are too valuable to abuse. Sustainability requires that the very best of human horticultural knowledge become a universal standard for landscape work.

Resources

Favor Living, Flexible Materials

Bioengineering

Geosynthetic Institute (GSI) 610-522-8440, www.geosynthetic-institute.org/: Academic and industry membership group, research geotextiles and geogrids.

Bestmann Green Systems Salem MA, 978-741-1166 and 508-741-1166: Suppliers, consultants: erosion control, bioengineering.

Robbin B. Sotir and Associates Marietta GA, 770-424-0719, www.sotir.com/: Consultant, author on bioengineering.

Bioengineering for Land Reclamation and Conservation H. Schiechtl, 1980 University of Alberta Press, Edmonton, Canada

Soil Bioengineering for Upland Slope Protection and Erosion Reduction Natural Resource Conservation Service, 1992 National Technical Information Service, 888-584-8332, www.ntis.gov

Use of Vegetation in Civil Engineering N. J. Coppin and I. G. Richards, 1990 Construction Industry Research & Info. Assn., Butterworths Publishers, Boston

Vegetation in Civil and Landscape Engineering D. H. Bache and I. A. MacAskill, 1984 Granada Publishers, New York

"**A Soft Approach to Erosion Control**" James L. Sipes, Feb 1999, LAM

Firms and Organizations: Bioengineering, Wetlands, Erosion Control, and Ecological Restoration

The Bioengineering Group, Inc., Salem MA, 978-740-0096, www.bioengineering.com/

BioDraw 3.0 and ErosionDraw 5.0 software from Salix Applied Earthcare, 800-403-0474: Interactive video of methods, with CAD standard-details.

Biotechnical and Soil Bioengineering Slope Stabilization: A Practical Guide for Erosion Control D. Gray and R. Sotir, 1996 Wiley, New York

Biotechnical Slope Protection and Erosion Control D. H. Gray and A. T. Leiser, 1982 Van Nostrand Reinhold, New York

Designing for Effective Sediment and Erosion Control on Construction Sites J. Fifield, n.d. International Erosion Control Association, www.icaa.org. : Includes biotechnical and vegetation methods.

Erosion control

International Erosion Control Association Steamboat Springs CO, 800-455-4322, www.ieca.org/: Publishes books, other information.

Use of Organics in Erosion Control John Haynes, Caltrans Engineering Services Center, Sacramento CA

Erosion Control **magazine** International Erosion Control Association, Santa Barbara CA, 805-682-1300, www.erosioncontrol.com/ec.html

ECMDS 4.1 (Erosion Control Materials Design Software) North American Green, 800-772-2040, www.nagreen.com/: Also erosion control suppliers/consultants.

MOSES (Modular Operational Soil Erosion System) National Soil Erosion Research Lab, 765-494-8673, http://topsoil .nserl.purdue.edu/nserlweb/index2.html: Calculates soil erosion under a wide variety of site conditions and uses.

Greenwalls and greenroofs

Search Terms: greenwalls || ecoroofs || greenroofs || roof gardens

Re-Natur Gmbh Ruhwinkel, Germany, 0 43 23/90 10-0, www.re-natur.de/index.php5: Consultant with 20 years' experience in greenroofs, constructed wetlands, natural swimming pools, and biological pest control; German and English.

"**The Vertical World of Greenwalls**" Kim Sorvig, 1999 LAM: Project examples and further information on greenwalls.

Ecover www.ecover.com/: Organic household product manufacturer, with large ecoroof.

Green Roof: Ecological Design and Construction Earth Pledge, 2005 Schiffer Publications, Atglen PA

Roof Gardens: History, Design, and Construction Theodore Osmundson, 1999 W.W. Norton, New York

Building Green: A Guide to Using Plants on Roofs, Walls, and Pavements Greater London Authority, 2004: Full text at www.london.gov.uk/mayor/strategies/biodiversity/docs/Building_Green_main_text.pdf.

Greenwalls: cell type AGH Industries (TX), 817-284-1742; Fluid Systems (Aurora IL), 504-393-1804; Presto Products (Appleton WI), 800-558-3525; RK Manufacturing (Ridgeland MS), 800-957-5575; Webtec (Charlotte NC), 414-769-6400

Greenwalls: mesh type Invisible Structures Inc (Aurora CO), 800-233-1510; Reinforced Earth Co. 800-446-5700

Greenwalls: plantable block Hokanson Block (Sacramento CA), 916-452-5233; Modular Concrete Systems (MCS) (Vista CA), 727-945-1864; Soil Retention Systems (SRS) (Oceanside CA), 760-966-6090; Hercules/St. Louis Retaining Wall (St. Louis MO), 314-389-6416: Hokanson and MCS are licensees of the "S-block" system. SRS currently serves only the Southwest United States.

Greenwalls: grid/textile-wrapped Akzo Nobel Geosynthetics (Netherlands), 31 26 366 4600; Huesker Geotextiles (Charlotte NC), 800-942-9418; Tensar Earth Technologies (Atlanta GA), 800-828-5126

EKOL trough recycled greenwall Group Tessenderlo Rue de Trône 130, 1050, Bruxelles, www.tessenderlo.com/contentNS4.asp: Green/noise wall made of recycled PVC; not marketed in the United States.

Evergreen Wall Systems (trough) Norcross GA, 800-234-3119: Concrete trough greenwall/noise-wall system.

Eco-Wall Zeller International, www.zeller-int.com/

Greenroofs for Healthy Cities http://greenroofs.org/ or http://greenroofs.ca/: Main US greenroof association; info, contacts, and events.

www.greenroofs.com/: Site by Atlanta landscape architect L. Velasquez.

Planting Greenroofs and Living Walls Nigel Dunnett and Noël Kingsbury, 2004 Timber Press, Portland OR: www.timberpress.com or 800-327-5680

Greenroof Plants: A Resource and Planting Guide Edmund C. Snodgrass and Lucie L. Snodgrass, 2004 Timber Press, Portland OR

Emory Knoll Farms www.greenroofplants.com/: E. Snodgrass's nursery, Street, MD, specializes in greenroof plants.

Greenroof Case Study series, LAM: Many articles since 1998.

American Hydrotech www.hydrotechusa.com/: Greenroof supplies.

Sarnafil www.sarnafilus.com/: Greenroof supplies.

Xero Flor America, LLC www.xeroflora.com/: Greenroof supplies.

GreenGrid modular green roof www.greengridroofs.com/: Preplanted, recycled-plastic modules; can include irrigation, walkways.

ASTM standards for greenroofs www.astm.org/, 2002

StaLite Permatill greenroof medium 877-737-6284, www.stalite.com/: Expanded slate for greenroofs, structural soils.

Plants: valuation

American Society of Consulting Arborists (ASCA) 301-947-0483, www.asca-consultants.org/: Consultant references.

Building Greener Neighborhoods: Trees as Part of the Plan National Association of Home Builders, 1992, 800-368-5242, www.nahb.org/

Guide for Plant Appraisal Council of Tree and Landscape Appraisers (CTLA), 9th ed.: Methods and formulas for legally defensible valuation of landscape features.

American Forests Washington DC, 202-737-1944, www.americanforests.org/: CITYgreen software (calculate urban trees' economic, ecological value) and Personal Climate Change Carbon Calculator.

Plantings

Irrigation and Green Industry Network 818-342-3204, www.igin.com/: Virtual trade show of urban forestry and landscape professional groups.

ASLA Invasive Plant Guide www.asla-sandiego.org/content/plantguide.html: LA-specific, what-to-do plant guide for invasives.

Urban Forestry bibliography Dr. G. Kuchelmeister, Tree City Initiative, Illertissen, Germany, http://ag.arizona.edu/OALS/ALN/aln42/kuchelmeister.html: Lists thirty-five books specifically on value and effects of urban trees.

Requiem for a Lawnmower: Gardening in a Warmer, Drier World S. Wasowski and A. Wasowski, 2004 Taylor Trade Publishing, Lanham MD

Plant Materials in Urban Design: A Selected Bibliography J. Wayne Pratt, 1986 Vance Bibliographies, Monticello IL, title #A1575

Plantings: native plants

Search Terms: (native OR regional) + planting OR plants || plantings "native plants" || native plants design

Cooperative Extension USDA, located at county government offices and/or local agricultural college, 202-720-7441, www.csrees.usda.gov/: For each state or region; often an excellent source of local expertise on plants and other landscape issues.

Landscaping with Native Trees Guy Strenberg and Jim Wilson, 1995 Publishers Ltd.: For Eastern United States; for other areas, check local bookstores, botanic gardens. Many garden books steadfastly refuse to list plant origins.

Plant for Natural Gardens: Southwestern Native and Adaptive Trees, Shrubs, Wildflower, and Grasses Judith Phillips, 1995 Museum of New Mexico Press, Santa Fe: Good source for region much neglected by horticulture writers.

Landscaping with Wildflowers: An Environmental Approach to Gardening Jim Wilson, 1993 Houghton Mifflin, New York

Revegetation with Native Species: Proceedings, 1997 Society for Ecological Restoration Annual Meeting L. K. Holzworth et al., 1999 US Department of Agriculture, Forest Service, Rocky Mountain Research Station

Native Trees, Shrubs, and Vines for Urban and Rural America: A Planting Design Manual for Environmental Designers G. Hightshoe, 1988 Van Nostrand Reinhold, New York

The Native Plant Primer Carole Ottesen, 1995 Crown/Random House, New York

The Natural Habitat Garden Ken Druse and Margaret Roach, 1994 Clarkson N. Potter Publishers, New York: Good information in coffee-table format; Druse's other books are also excellent, and show how much exciting design can be done with what some call "boring weeds."

The Wild Lawn Handbook: Alternatives to the Traditional Front Lawn Stevie Daniels, 1995 Macmillan, New York

Field and Forest: A Guide to Native Landscapes for Gardeners and Naturalists J. Scott, 2002 Blackburn Press, Caldwell NJ

Wild About Wildflowers (CD-Rom) Tom Huggler, 800-735-3476, http://http://www.wildflowersmich.org/sales/sales.htm /: How-to for using native alternatives to lawn; video, image library; links.

Weeds of the Northern US and Canada F. Royer and R. Dickinson, 1999 University Alberta and Lone Pine Publishing 1999, Alberta: Identification guide.

Plantings: structures

Search Terms: planting structures || plantings "trellis" || planters || street tree

"Sidewalk Design for Tree Survival" M. Evans et al., Mar 1990, LAM

Selected literature: root control methods Dr. Kim D. Coder, Mar 1998, UGA Cooperative Extension, www.caes.uga.edu/extension/

Horticultural Products

Search Terms: (horticulture OR garden OR yard OR landscape) + supplies

Green Net: Company-Product-Service Database www.greennet.net/
Horticultural manufacturers list www.yetmans.mb.ca/manufacturers.html

CPULS: Continuous Productive Urban Landscapes—Designing Agriculture for Sustainable Cities A. Viljoen, 2005 Architectural Press, Oxford: Crops in cities to reduce transport, restore connectedness.

Principle 4:
Respect the Waters of Life

A mighty mercy on which life depends, for all its glittering shifts water is constant.
—Donald Culross Peattie, 1950

Water covers nearly 70 percent of the globe, and makes up almost 99 percent of the human body. Essential to life, it is also a powerful force of change and destruction. Despite its global presence, far less than 1 percent is fresh water suitable for sustaining land animals and plants.[1] In Ambrose Bierce's wonderful phrase, "Water occupies $2/3$ of a world made for Man—who has no gills."[2]

Besides regional and seasonal water *scarcity*, water *quality* is threatened by pollution. Even in such apparently waterlogged and water-surrounded places as Florida, scarcity of fresh clean water is a serious issue.[3] Paul Simon (the US senator, not the musician) has predicted that wars over oil will soon take second place to wars over water.[4] Drought and increased flooding spread simultaneously over whole continents, their occurrence linked both to air pollution[5] and global climate change (see p. 15). Even places that receive increased precipitation often lose available water, due to high runoff, violent storms, higher evaporation rates, or changes in seasonal arrival of moisture.[6]

If any single issue seems likely to push landscape sustainability into the foreground of public awareness and to change professional practice, that issue is water. Since the first edition of this book, the seriousness of water problems (which have been there all along) has become far more evident. Consumers, businesses, and government agencies have taken active interest in what were once fringe concepts—rainwater harvesting, bioengineering, or constructed wetlands. In addition to better acceptance of existing solutions, water conservation has driven technological innovation in the irrigation industry. Even the civil engineering and regulatory community is slowly changing, although it remains far too dominated by the pave-and-pipe paradigm.

Construction affects water and water quality in many ways. By changing natural patterns of water movement, structures and paving can change water from a life-giving force to a destructive one. During construction work, sediments and pollutants enter water on or near the site. Collecting and distributing water for human use also affects the site's hydrology—and that of its neighbors. Carefully planned landscapes can compensate for some of these changes.

Water is well-known as a poetic metaphor for patient, slippery, flowing power, gentle yet unstoppable. Yet the conventions of engineering frequently take a confrontational stance toward water—as if it could be pinned down by brute force. Conventional texts on landscape construction continue to indoctrinate students with ideas like "Water causes scouring action when left uncontrolled."[7] Destructive water flows, ironically, result more often than not from human attempts at control. Unlike hard construction materials, water *never* responds well to heavy-handed methods. It must be worked *with*, like plants, people, or any living thing.

This chapter looks at ways of protecting the most critical resource of all.

Discussed in This Chapter

Understanding natural water patterns.
Protecting surface water features, such as wetlands, lakes, and streams.

> Restoring water bodies that have been damaged.
>
> Special techniques for balancing human water needs with regional conditions:
> "harvesting" and storing water
> getting more out of each drop with graywater
> efficient irrigation, and new savings through "smart controllers"
> stormwater purification by vegetative and mechanical means.

Work with the Site's Water Regime

Water is more a system than a substance. Using water sustainably, and protecting natural water bodies, begins with understanding this system. Although it is possible to think of a pond as an object, its boundaries are muddy, and its connections to other objects are many. The pond (perhaps the simplest form of surface water) cannot be properly protected just by fencing it, as a tree or historic sculpture might be. Protecting water features means understanding their links to larger patterns.

For this reason, we have given water protection a separate place in this book, rather than treating it as part of site protection. The techniques discussed in Principle 2 are *part* of protecting water on-site. What differs is how these techniques are applied to the web of water, a web that weaves together rivers and wetlands, evaporation and rainfall. In this web, surface waters are linked to one another, to underground aquifers and springs, to water vapor and precipitation, and ultimately to the oceans. Protecting any part of this system is valuable in itself, and also contributes to conserving the health of the whole. For maximum benefit, protection of water bodies needs coordination throughout each watershed or river-basin.

Respect Natural Drainage Patterns

Because river geometry is complex, many people still think of stream channels as random in shape and location. Nothing could be further from the truth. Each channel where water runs, and each pocket where it col-

lects, matches the quantity and speed of water that normally flows through it. A similar relationship between shape and capacity is simpler to see in roadway design: a four-lane avenue with distinct turn lanes can handle more and faster traffic than a two-lane street where turning cars wait in traffic. Likewise, the shape of any landscape feature touched by water is dynamically related to the way water flows there. So is its location. For construction, the important point is this: change the shape and you change water's performance, how much soaks in to benefit soil and plants, and how much runs off or collects. Too much or too little of either can dramatically change the site, sometimes overnight, sometimes over many invisible years.

Three major factors interact to determine how water performs on a site. These are:

- the *quantity* of water itself
- the *material(s)* over which it runs, including vegetation
- the *shape*, particularly the steepness, of the surface on which flow occurs.

A small quantity of water running on porous soil at a gentle slope will mostly be absorbed. On the same material and slope, a large quantity (from a huge storm, or hard surfaces upstream) will erode the soft soil quickly. Surfaces stabilized by vegetation erode more slowly, as do hard surfaces. Hard materials are vulnerable, however, where they meet softer soils.

Construction can change any of these three factors. Impervious surfaces shed water, concentrating water quantity. Soil materials are compacted, loosened, and amended. Grades are changed, and plant cover removed or altered. Once the dynamic balance between these factors is changed in any part of the system, all links in the water-web must readjust toward new balance. This readjustment happens gradually all the time in natural watersheds and is a key concept in construction involving water.

Planning for water on a site demands understanding local patterns that have evolved over centuries. This is site-specific and region-specific, but there are several key questions to ask. If you cannot answer these yourself, or don't understand what they imply, get specialist help. Water is too important to ignore.

From where does water come to the site, and where does it go from the site? Even standing water has a source and a destination, if only rain and evaporation.

- Does on-site runoff move in sheets, or in channels? Are surfaces hard or porous, and where does water spill from one kind of surface to another?
- Where does standing water accumulate, and why? How are standing and moving water linked?
- Regionally, what are the shapes of river systems? Do they branch like trees at acute angles, or make sudden right-angle changes in direction? Large-scale patterns often indicate that geology is shaping the drainage, making it hard to construct new channels "against the grain."

If there is any kind of stream, creek, or river on the site, or affecting it, the following questions also need answers:

- Does the channel meander (bend from side to side)? This indicates a stream that is slowing and dissipating excess energy. Its force may be due to steep slopes or to increased volume from upstream. Straightening the meanders is ill advised; forceful flow will cause erosion and flooding until meanders are reestablished. Working upstream from meanders involves different conditions and methods than working downstream.
- Is the stream cutting away its banks, or depositing soil? Cutting indicates high volume and speed. Expanding into a larger channel, water slows and drops sediment. Planting or stabilizing areas of cut requires a different approach than areas of deposition.

Besides answering such questions in the present, it is important to respond to changes over time. Upstream, development may increase runoff, or agriculture and industry may divert water. An example of a response to upstream development is Crystal Cove (pp. 124–25). Monitoring development proposals may forestall some problems. (Downstream changes usually have less impact, although wells or dams affect whole regions.)

Accept Regional Limitations of Water Supply

Conventional water management imports and exports water hundreds of miles by pipe or ditch for municipal, industrial, or agricultural use. Since our first edition, water conflicts have increased: farmers versus cities versus river-restorationists, for example. Areas lacking political defenders lose their water. Water is diverted from regions, particularly undeveloped mountain areas, said to have "excess" water, to supply demand in locations that have used up their local supply. Water is impounded in reservoirs before it can "wastefully" run away downstream. Clearly, this affects the ecosystem from which water is taken, or to which it no longer flows. The smaller the quantity of water and the shorter the distance diverted from natural flows, the less likely to do harm.

Regional water management has stark impacts on landscape-related businesses and land-users. Particularly in the Western United States, municipal water conservation ordinances, in response to drought, typically target horticulture first. The 2002 drought, for example, cost landscape industries in Colorado two thousand jobs and $60 million in revenue.[8] In response, many landscape-related firms *increased* revenue by providing drought-tolerant plants, Xeriscape designs, and water-saving maintenance.

Thus, although water management and policy may seem a planning issue, it impacts and is influenced by site-specific construction. Demand for water is affected by where and how people build. Conventional water features, like fountains, can be great sources of pleasure, but ostentatious designs waste water—often imported, purified water. Modern recirculating technology combined with traditional designs get stunning effects from tiny amounts of water.

Demand for water is also affected by plantings. Minimizing water import/export is a strong argument for gardening with native plants (pp. 141–44). In some regions, the native-plant list may not include plants for every use. For example, in the high desert, there are simply no native "shade trees" except along water courses; upland trees are small and shrubby. Cottonwoods planted on dry mesas around Albuquerque require imported water, even though the

Figure 4.1 This Guadalajara convent garden makes elegant, sparing use of water for tranquility. Roof drains replenish the pool. (*Project:* Arq. Alfonso Peniche-Banisteros. *Photo:* Kim Sorvig.)

plant is technically "native." The region's Indians created shade structures of brushwood. Many beautiful Southwest landscapes have adapted this idea instead of shade trees, truly respecting the regional water regime.

Deal with Stormwater near Where It Falls

When rain cannot infiltrate the ground where it falls, it becomes runoff. Runoff supplies water in most natural streams, lakes, and wetlands, but *excessive* runoff causes problems for humans through flooding and erosion. With increased runoff comes a dramatic increase in water pollution. Loss of infiltration due to development is one of the single most serious barriers to sustainability.

Fortunately, since the first edition of this book, stormwater issues have gone public. Revisions to the Clean Water Act require stormwater management on virtually every construction project. This necessity

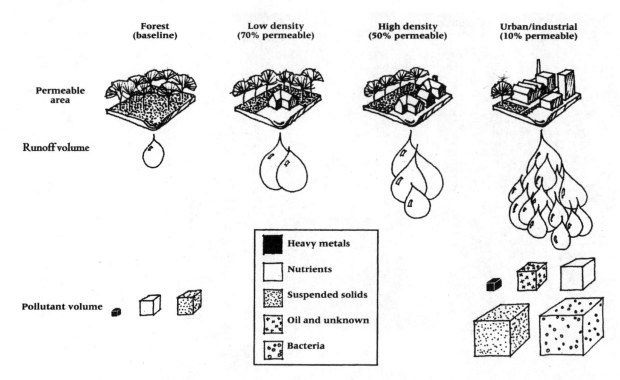

Figure 4.2   As impervious development reduces infiltration, the volume of runoff increases dramatically, as does pollution. Even nutrients, harmless in forest runoff, become serious problems at higher concentrations. (*Illust.:* Craig Farnsworth, based on data from Groesbeck and Streifel.)

poses intriguing opportunities to transform runoff into design features. Stuart Echols and Eliza Penny-packer, of Penn State University's landscape architecture department, call this strategy "artful rainwater design"—combining the utility of stormwater management with the amenity of rich place making.[9]

Many techniques are available for controlling runoff, but their success depends on one simple principle: *control runoff near its source.*

The farther runoff travels, the faster it moves as increasing volumes move together in a steady flow. Speed and volume give water erosive and sediment-carrying force. Thus, controlling water quality and runoff damage "is most easily and economically achieved if stormwater management *starts at the point that water contacts the earth*."[10]

Many specific techniques in this and other chapters follow this close-to-the-source strategy. These include bioswales (p. 208) and water harvesting (below). For dispersing water or collecting it, a single centralized system almost always adds pipes, pumps, and other hardware, which dispersed, close-to-source systems do not require. Other infrastructure (sewage treatment, below, or power generation, p. 51) is also most resource-efficient if *decentralized*—that is, close to the resource or to the point of use, or both.

In water management, there are two reasons why this principle is not followed. A landowner may have no influence on upstream neighbors and must deal with runoff they have neglected. For this, there is no simple cure. Second, conventional practice favors massive solutions instead multiple ones; conventional wisdom believes larger structures offer economy of scale. Particularly for runoff control, this is a false economy, considering only capital costs, ignoring performance and maintenance. Several small infiltration devices in the upper part of a watershed are more effective than a single large one in a lower location. At the lower spot, fast-moving water will not infiltrate as effectively, and the sediment it carries will clog the drainage structure much more quickly.

Where runoff is controlled early, slower speeds and lower volumes also allow bioengineering to be

Figure 4.4 More effective than a single massive dam, a series of small check dams stop and infiltrate water throughout a stream or gully. Only the highest floods overflow spillways. (*Photo:* New Mexico Department of Mining and Minerals.)

Figure 4.3 Contour-line infiltration trenches, plus check dams in the gully at bottom, stop erosion and raise soil moisture in this permaculture project in arid New Mexico. (*Project:* Arina Pittman. *Photo:* Kim Sorvig.)

especially in the West, for "smart irrigation" retrofits (see below).

These three general strategies—know the patterns, accept regional supply, and deal with water near its source—underlie all the specific techniques discussed below.

used effectively (Principle 3). Despite bioengineering's modern track record and ancient pedigree, engineers sometimes dismiss it because performance calculations are more complex than estimates for hard structures,. New methods of computer simulation and modeling (see pp. 39–41) offer potential for persuasive calculation of such "soft" approaches. Designers, contractors, and even some engineers are increasingly recognizing that "small and close to the source" is the key to sustainable water management.

One study suggests that, at least in the Eastern United States, every gallon of water properly managed on-site saves at least two dollars in engineering costs downstream.[11] This "avoided cost analysis" has persuaded many municipalities to offer incentives for close-to-the-source water management and,

Figure 4.5 Straw bales pinned to the ground provide temporary control of erosion and sedimentation. (*Photo:* New Mexico Department of Mining and Minerals.)

Understand, Protect, and Restore Natural Wetlands

Wetlands may well be the most unique and challenging kind of site for landscape work. Part land, part water, wetlands are often in the news, often misunderstood. Conventional landscape work, not long ago, needed no knowledge of what wetlands were, how to recognize them, or how they function. Today, even though the majority of wetland work is still done by specialists, almost everyone in the construction-related industries knows: watch out for wetlands. Landscape professionals need to go further, because wetlands health is closely linked to sustainability of human land use.

Scientific and practical aspects of working with wetlands have changed only gradually since the first edition of this book. What has changed more rapidly is acceptance of their importance—despite an adversarial stance from property-rights and industry groups emboldened by the Bush administration. The net result is greater willingness among construction professionals, with some irresponsible exceptions, to respect wetlands and make them a positive part of the human landscape.

Despite controversy over their legal definition, it is not difficult to understand what a wetland is. According to international wetlands consultant Donald Hammer, wetlands are places that are *wet enough long enough* each year to produce *oxygen-poor soils* favoring *specially adapted plant species*.[12] Contrary to popular misconceptions, wetlands are not constantly wet. They are transitional zones, or "ecotones," between land and water, both spatially (edges where land meets water) and over time (land and water in the same place at different seasons). Understanding this shifting, transitional character is essential to working with wetlands. Misunderstanding this, or trying to force wetlands to fit stable-state expectations, fueled controversy over wetlands regulation.

Wetlands are a critical link in the water web, crucial to food webs and habitat diversity. US wetlands are home to 190 amphibian species, 270 birds, and 5,000 plants, many of which can survive *only* in wetlands. Of all US endangered species, 26 percent of the plants and 45 percent of the animals are wetlands species.[13]

Recognize "Services" Provided by Wetlands

The many ways wetlands serve humanity warrant their protection:

- filtration: purifying water and trapping sediment; biodegrading many pollutants
- aquifer recharge: wetlands are often porous gateways to groundwater
- floodwater overflow basins: wetlands slow stormwater
- economic productivity: some of the richest and most diverse ecosystems, wetlands influence fisheries and other industries. Estuaries (wetlands where fresh and salt water meet) are particularly productive
- recreation and aesthetics: enlightened developers increase property values by including protected wetlands as amenities.

Wetlands have provided free "services" to humans since prehistory and are cost effective today, even when constructed. For example, Ed Garbisch of Environmental Concern, one of the first wetlands specialists, could provide coastal erosion control with a strip of salt marsh created for 17 percent of the cost of stone revetments.[14] For sewage effluent treatment, wetlands are built for one-tenth of conventional facilities' cost, and are simpler and cheaper to operate.[15]

A wonderful example of what can be accomplished in protecting and conserving wetlands is the Crosby Arboretum, a Mississippi State University facility in Picayune MS. Architect Fay Jones, curator Ed Blake, and landscape architects Andropogon (Philadelphia) made the wetlands accessible to visitors through carefully planned construction. The result carries a message of hope for sustainable construction on unusual sites—and is a supremely beautiful place as well.

Know the Issues Before Working in or near Wetlands

"Homework first" is especially critical in wetlands. Wetlands are a resource from which sustainable development, design, and construction benefit. Careful planning is required to do so without diminishing or endangering the resource for the future.

Figure 4.6 Crosby Arboretum epitomizes the beauty, as well as ecological and educational value, of wetlands. (*Project:* Ed Blake, Andropogon, Fay Jones. *Photo:* Ed Blake.)

To work successfully in or around wetlands, both ecological and legal understanding is essential. Major issues are summarized here.

UNDERSTANDING AND RECOGNIZING WETLANDS

Scientists recognize over 100 types of wetlands: marshes, swamps, bogs, mangroves, and seasonally flooded bottomland forests.[16] While design and construction professionals can recognize wetlands generally, classifying wetlands and understanding their particulars usually requires specialist advice. An ideal team would include a wetland ecologist/botanist, hydrologist, soils specialist, and landscape architect with strong engineering skills.[17] Some projects need wildlife specialists, geologists, and experts in environmental education, recreation, and cultural archaeology. Much of this expertise is available through governmental and educational institutions. The National Hydrography Dataset, a GIS-based map of the nation's watersheds, water resources, and pollution sites, became available in 2000. Such online information leaves little excuse for approaching wetlands without thorough understanding.

To restore or create a wetland, observe natural wetlands in the region. This is no place for aesthetic theories that condemn mimicking nature. Wetlands consultant Hammer emphasizes that "the created wetland must closely imitate natural systems adapted to that region if it is to succeed without excessive operating and maintenance costs."[18] Diversity of species and habitat, and varied, fractal physical forms, are *functional* essentials.

Several general points are critical to wetlands protection and restoration:

Wetland plants *tolerate* flooding that would kill dryland plants, but more and deeper is not always better. Like all plants, wetland species require air and sunlight; most have at least their leaves above water. Species that grow underwater require *clear* water to get sunlight. Many wetland plants need *alternating* flooding and drier conditions. Too deep or too long inundation can stress or kill wetland species.

In natural wetlands, alternating flood and dry states control nutrient availability, set up conditions for germination, influence wildlife behavior, and keep weedy invaders out—especially important in newly planted wetlands. Built or restored wetlands require precise water-level control and seasonally draining the basin. Use a "stop-log" or "flash-board," an adjustable spillway formed by boards or logs set into a vertical channel in a dam. (See Figure 5.6.) Valves only control flow volume, but stop-log spillways set water *level* directly and simply.

Any natural wetland is a temporary landscape feature. Ecological succession changes wetlands to drier communities, as sediment fills the basin and creates soil. Built wetlands are only prevented from disappearing over time by management practices.

Essential information for any wetlands work includes source(s) of water supply, "hydroperiod" (seasonal water-level changes), soil type(s), plant species, adjacent land uses, and project objectives.

Wetlands, like most natural systems, usually serve multiple functions. To truly "replace" or "mitigate" destruction of existing wetlands, the replacement must match *all* the functions of the original.[19] For constructed wetlands, a single function may be primary, but secondary functions offer large returns for small investments. For example, constructed waste-water-treatment wetlands in places as diverse as Arcata CA and Minot ND include wildlife habitat and environmental education. Such "secondary" functions increase public acceptance and value of wetlands.

Legal and Political Issues

Most US states have lost between half and 90 percent of precolonial wetlands area.[20] Wetlands were first protected under US law in the 1970s, although hunting groups, concerned about waterfowl, had been restoring wetlands earlier. State and federal laws responded to wetlands' value and rapid loss. Before wetlands regulation began, 700 square miles (nearly 450,000 acres or 180,000 hectares) of wetland were destroyed *per year*. After regulation, that rate dropped to 300,000 acres annually, and today is about 100,000 acres.

Important though these reductions are, wetlands continue to be lost, and construction professionals should be aware of two concerns. First, present losses are slowing, but past losses are far from being restored. Second, successes in slowing wetlands loss have been mostly agricultural; losses due to development and construction have declined very little, and now make up 80 percent of the total.[21]

Protection of wetlands remains a priority for sustainability, on a par with protecting rainforests. The construction industry and landscape professionals especially need to do everything possible to reduce impacts on wetlands.

Filling and draining wetlands, once common practice, is largely prohibited. Erosion and sedimentation

requirements enacted in 2003 include *permanent* soil stabilization (almost always by revegetation) of any project *disturbing more than one acre*.[22] Many conventional developers see such laws as restricting their freedom to build on what were once cheap lands, and some contractors complain wetlands interfere with just doing their job. While frustration is understandable, wetlands are too important to sustainability to allow negative attitudes to destroy them. Fortunately, these attitudes continue to change for the better.

Some conflicting laws and definitions exist; the focus of much current legislation is to make wetlands regulation more consistent nationally, more responsive to regional differences, and more straightforward.[23] Legal definitions have moved close to Hammer's (above), while developers and the public are learning to understand and recognize these transitional areas *before* damage and regulatory penalties happen. Although there have been horror stories about making mountains out of mud-puddles, wetlands protection deserves everyone's support.

Wetlands "Creation" and Brokering

Legislation protecting wetlands often permits their destruction if they are replaced on another site. This process is called "mitigation." Brokering (also called "mitigation banking") goes one step further and allows developers to trade rights to destroy and mitigate wetlands across projects.

Some mitigation wetlands have succeeded in replacing wildlife and plant habitat, water filtering, and recreational and amenity value. Others, as reported in several studies, replace less area than was destroyed and create a completely different type of wetland (23 percent were essentially "tanks," steep-sided ponds built for ranch livestock). Only half are ever monitored for function. Permits, justified by these inadequate "replacements," allowed destruction of endangered species habitat "in most states evaluated."[24] There is strong doubt whether even the best created wetland is interchangeable with a natural one.[25]

A major concern is whether re-created wetlands can function as aquifer recharge zones. Aquifers—porous underground reservoirs between impervious soil or rock layers—recharge where surface water gets into the porous layer. Such zones are usually low areas where water collects—that is, wetlands. Unless a wetland is re-created in very similar conditions, it will be unconnected to groundwater and offer no recharge.

Wetlands are also related in complex but logical ways to surface drainage patterns. Wetlands linked to flowing water serve as flood dispersal basins. Susan Galatowitsch, of Iowa State's Landscape Architecture Department, points out that (in prairie regions) a wetland area must equal at least 0.5 percent of its watershed to be effective for flood control.[26] Location relative to streamflow is also critical.

Especially for recharge and flood control, mitigation wetlands of different size, location, or type may fail to replace functions. Such mitigation is primarily decorative and can disguise environmental damage.

Proponents of brokering argue that it allows regional planning, restores the most valuable wetlands in larger units rather than piecemeal by each developer, and provides profit motives for protecting wetlands.[27]

By the EPA's own analysis, wetlands brokering seldom re-creates functions or values of the destroyed wetland.[28] Rather, it is located on land the developer can acquire cheaply enough to make the trade worthwhile. In highway construction, ordinary route-planning difficulties make wetlands removal very attractive. Highway engineering does not preclude ecologically appropriate wetlands mitigation, but in practice acts against it.

Proposals for mitigation banking are often linked to stricter function-for-function replacement. Even advocates of wetlands creation and brokering, however, acknowledge that "our ability to replace functional values, with a few exceptions, is limited because of our poor understanding of these functions ... [and even] existing information has often not been used."[29] Most forms of environmental "banking" and "brokering" raise similar questions: are they convenient ways to allow continued destructive behavior by paying a remote price?

Neither mitigation nor banking of wetlands is indisputably sustainable. *Restoring* wetlands on sites where they previously existed has much higher chances of success. Simply in terms of energy and materials, *conserving* an existing wetland is more efficient than either creating or restoring it. Protection

of these important ecosystems is *always* the preferred alternative.

Protect Wetlands During Construction

Many general site protection techniques (Principle 1) are used in protecting wetlands. The main difference is that wetlands will almost certainly connect off-site in one or more directions. This requires extra care and ingenuity when restricting access. Nonetheless, preventing construction traffic from entering or crossing wetlands is very important.

If there is no alternative to crossing a stream or wetland, temporary access must be provided, removable without damage on completion. Some work can be carried out from boats and other specialized equipment.⊃ (Launch or landing sites still need protection or restoration or both.) If land vehicles must cross a wetland, protect bottom soils from being churned by wheels, tracks—or feet. Use temporary bridges, planks, mats, or removable structures filled with gravel. Dumping gravel directly into wetlands forms a passage, but is hard to remove.

Banks of any water body are especially susceptible to damage and require protection well beyond actual crossings. Temporary shoring may be an option. Banks attract people and animals, sometimes causing inadvertent damage. Expect to rebuild and replant the banks at the end of the project.

Construction runoff must be prevented from entering wetlands, or at least filtered through straw bales, sediment fencing, or other standard erosion and sedimentation (E&S) controls. Natural rates of erosion can increase by a factor of 2,000 during construction, unless controlled (Figure 6.19), often washing into water bodies. Polluted runoff threatens streams and wetlands. However, Dawn Biggs, a Virginia landscape architect with strong experience in wetland and stream management, notes that wetlands are resilient at water purification (see bioremediation, pp. 103–6). Potentially more serious than chemical pollutants are dense sediments that choke wetlands, and mechanical soil disturbance that admits invasive species.

Certain stages of work (site clearing or paving, especially) can lead to temporary danger of flooding.

Figure 4.7a,b,c The Nichols Arboretum (Ann Arbor MI) creates beauty from stormwater management structures. The sequence shows construction and planting of stepped pools to control runoff. (*Project:* The Nichols Arboretum. *Photo:* Robert E. Grese.)

E&S controls, designed for severe storms, *must* be in place before such work. Even wetlands designed to hold floodwater cannot be suddenly inundated during their establishment period. It may be critical to deal with problems of the whole watershed before attempting to protect or restore a wetland.

Use Wetlands-specific Protection Strategies

Wetland conditions may need special protection techniques.

- Soil compaction risk is generally greater on saturated soils than dry ones.
- Wet zones should have generous buffers, above and beyond what would be fenced for dry site features.
- Plan for seasonal variations in precipitation, water table, and flooding. These, as well as tidal motion, can dramatically change wetlands during construction.

Use Low-impact Construction If Building in Wetlands

Nature centers, water recreation facilities, and other special projects may require construction *in* a wetland. This involves specialized techniques and materials.

Work in standing water stirs up bottom sediments. Sedimentation curtains, hung from floats, keep muddied water within the construction zone, and out of other waters. These function like filter fencing on land, but form a boundary between two areas of water.

Structures built in or at the edge of wetlands are best supported by minimal-footprint foundations. Pilings are commonly used, as is a newly patented system called "pinned foundations" (below, and see Figure 6.16). These minimize disruption, permit water motion around the structure, and work with unstable wetland soils.

Pilings are available in many forms and materials. Tubular forms driven into the soil and filled with concrete are common; a conical plastic mold called Bigfoot creates quick and economical footings for tubular concrete pilings, with minimal excavation. Wood pilings are also widely used. Rot resistance is important, but beware of toxic preservatives, which can leach into the water (see p. 254). Some woods,

like elm, are rot-resistant if they *remain* underwater; in ancient ports, centuries-old pilings of such woods have been found in perfect condition. These timbers rot only if alternately wet and dry (as in fencing or decking). Not all species of naturally rot-resistant wood will function well when submerged.

Recycled "plastic lumber" is also used for waterside construction, despite some structural limitations (Plastic Lumber, p. 239). It is waterproof, rot proof, and cannot leach, making it a good choice for wetlands construction.

Boardwalks have traditionally provided dry-footed access into wetlands. Treated lumber may contaminate water and kill wildlife.[30] Well-designed boardwalks leave spaces between boards, permitting precipitation and light to the area underneath; aquatic life can be excluded by lack of light.

At Juanita Bay Park in Washington, landscape architects Jongejan Gerrard McNeal used two different methods of supporting boardwalks.[31] One, requiring considerable skill, was to lay logs across the wetlands as grade beams. The contractor had to match variable-thickness logs to the ground surface, without digging, to keep upper surfaces level. The second system, for wetter ground, was to drive two-inch steel pipe as pilings. This avoided heavy equipment: one worker with an air hammer and scaffolding installed the pipes. Cross-tie pipes were added for stability, plus 4×12 beams. Both support systems were decked with ACZA-treated lumber, clearing the ground by eight-

Figure 4.8 Boardwalks can make an art form of the necessity for minimum disturbance in wetlands. This is at Spring Peeper marsh in the Minnesota Arboretum. (*Project and Photo:* Fred Rozumalski.)

een inches so that visitors would think twice about stepping off.

An innovative foundation system for sensitive sites is the "pinned foundation," from the company of the same name in Gig Harbor WA. Grade beams or short aboveground wooden posts are fitted with metal brackets. Through slots in these brackets, the "pins" (four- to eight-foot-long sections of galvanized pipe) are driven by hand or jackhammer into the ground at diagonal angles. The structure's weight locks the pins into the slots. They can be pulled up, adjusted, or removed with minimal site disturbance. Pinned foundations can be placed even closer to existing trees than conventional pilings. Another adjustable, removable system is auger foundations, developed by Pliny Fisk (p. 59).

Pinned Foundations has recently developed two variations on this system. One, the "Diamond Pier," is essentially a precast concrete footer with holes for pins and a bolt on top for attaching one four-by-four post. The second, called Low-Impact Foundation Technology or LIFT, attaches the metal pin-sockets to formwork, casting them into on-grade concrete foundation walls. After removing the forms, pins are driven through the sockets to anchor the walls, with conventional construction on top. Pin spacing is engineered for each structure. The on-grade system uses 20 to 30 percent less concrete than conventional foundation walls, according to the manufacturer. Pinned systems greatly reduce site disturbance, compaction, and grading for drainage, and have applications beyond wetland areas.

Floating walkways, where feasible, are assembled in segments, off-site; one section is placed from the bank, providing a platform for placing the next, and so on. If sized for a crew to move by hand, very little site disruption occurs. Such a system was used by Bruce Dees & Associates, at the Hood Canal (Washington) Wetlands Project. Styrofoam-stuffed used tires may serve as floats if sealed to prevent waterlogging or degrading into the wetland.

Restore Damaged Wetlands

Wetlands damaged or drained by prior land use can be restored; these techniques may apply to post-construction repairs or to creating new wetlands. Reconstruction takes advantage of existing links to aquifers, streams, and ponds, and taps remnant soils as a "seed bank" of dormant wetland species. A restored wetland is much more likely to function as a recharge zone or flood basin than one created at a site of convenience.

First, reestablish water flows and levels. If the original level is known, this may be simple, but more often a specialist must determine what level to restore. In wetlands drained for agriculture, removing or altering drainage structures may be enough, with plants and animals soon reestablishing themselves.

On other sites, a dam or dike may be needed, usually constructed of earth, often with a clay core, and welded wire mesh buried in the center to exclude burrowing animals. A "stop-log" (p. 159 and Figure 5.6) in the dike sets normal water level. The flood spillway is a separate "emergency exit"; in wetlands under twenty acres, design for the ten-year storm. A grassed spillway, reinforced with geotextile, is preferable to concrete in cost, functionality, and appearance.[32]

Once the surface level and rate of water flow are known, grading may be needed. The basin should not be steep sided, even if deep water exists in the center. A broad shallow basin offers the widest area and diversity of plantable shore.

Figure 4.9 The T-shaped opening in this wetland structure sets the water level. Small rises in level flow out through the "trunk" of the T; if major flooding raises the level higher, the top of the T permits faster drainage. (*Project and Photo:* Rick Scaffidi, EQR.)

Grading must be unusually accurate, because wetland plants require precise water depths. Because the water surface is always horizontal, it is the basin bottom that determines water depth. Zones of different depth support diversity of species. Stepped horizontal terraces work better than sloped grading. A very small slope (as little as .05 percent) can cause a major difference in depth over one hundred yards, so that the same plants cannot survive throughout the zone.[33]

During grading, wetlands soil should be stockpiled *underwater* to preserve seeds, tubers, and anaerobic chemical conditions. Some artificially created wetlands require a liner of bentonite clay or waterproof sheeting. The liner is covered with 16 to 24 inches of soil for planting. Either an artificial liner or a natural impervious surface can be punctured by careless construction work, causing the wetland to fail.

Another reason for care during grading is that soil disturbance invites invasion by aggressive aquatic plants like Giant Reed or Loosestrife. Once established, they can be difficult or impossible to weed out, actively displacing native species. Invasive species (sometimes deliberately planted) are responsible for decline of many existing wetlands; creating a haven for them defeats the purpose of restoration. In general, select wetland species native to the region and suited to the specific type of wetland.[34]

Wetland planting techniques are specialized. Only a few species float freely; most must be rooted in the bottom even if their leaves or flowers are above the surface. When replanting existing wetlands, plants or seeds are often weighted and dropped from a boat, a technique that has mixed success. Where possible, flooding the wetland and then draining it produces ideal muddy planting conditions. Tubers, seedlings, and "live stake" cuttings may be planted by hand or with specialized machinery. Furrows, cut across the direction of water flow, can speed planting. In soft soils or where wildlife are feeding, plantings may need to be anchored and protected with erosion control matting or biodegradable mesh.

When previously existing wetlands are restored, planting may be unnecessary. Seed of wetland plants can survive for a decade or more in drained or filled soils, germinating once wetland conditions are restored. Soil "cores" collected from nearby wetlands

Figure 4.10a,b,c This constructed wetland was (a) excavated to careful depths required by wetland plants, then (b) lined. Planted with marsh-tolerant sedges (c), the completed wetland treats graywater organically for re-use, reducing this Michigan convent's water use by half. (See p. 202 for project description.) (*Project and Photo:* Veridian Landscape Studio.)

are sometimes used to seed restored or new wetlands. Extreme care must be used in collecting cores not to damage the donor site. Small cores (a few inches across) should be dug in a scattered pattern, leaving undisturbed soil to support regrowth.

Managing water level is critical to plant establishment. After planting, the water level needs to keep

Table 4.1

Plants to avoid (or use very cautiously) in wetlands.

Botanical Name	Common Name(s)
Eichornia crassipes	Water Hyacinth
Lysimachia sp.	Purple Loosestrife
Melaleuca quinquenervia	Melaleuca, Bottlebrush
Phalaris arundinacea	Reed Canary Grass
Phragmites australis	Giant Reed
Salix sp.	Willows (some shrub and tree forms)
Tamarix sp.	Tamarisk, Salt Cedar
Typha latifolia and T. angustifolia	Cattail

pace with plant growth. Hammer describes water management schedules for various newly established wetland types, in some cases filling and draining the wetland weekly. After establishment (two to five years) management needs decrease, but annual or seasonal manipulation of water levels is still common.[35]

The final aspect of restoring wetlands is monitoring and adjustment. Flows and levels, plant and animal establishment, and water quality should be recorded. Final field adjustments of inlet and outlet grades may be needed. Responsibility for these adjustments must be carefully spelled out in specifications. Wetlands construction exemplifies the teamwork, coordination, and inclusion of long-term maintenance essential to sustainable landscape work.

Detailed site-specific planning is essential to wetland design, construction, and maintenance. Few wetland creation and restoration techniques should be attempted without specialist help.

WETLAND RESTORATION PROJECT EXAMPLES
Las Vegas NV doesn't seem like a wetland sort of place to most visitors (although many do take a soaking). But the Las Vegas Wash, which empties into Lake Mead, had 2,000 acres or more of wetlands as recently as the 1970s. Used for sewage effluent discharge, as much as 1,600 tons per day, the Wash lost all but 10 percent of those wetlands.

Las Vegas drinks from Lake Mead, and in 1998 the EPA found bacterial pollution and traces of rocket fuel in the lake, which galvanized the county government into action. Early in 1999, they unveiled a plan

to build fifteen erosion-control dams, with wetlands behind each one, and trails expected to attract a million visitors a year. The restored Wash today offers clean drinking water to Vegas residents (those who don't follow W.C. Fields about drinking water). Called Clark County Wetlands Park, these reconstructed wetlands have interpretive exhibits, a small visitor center, and a theater. Interior Secretary Bruce Babbitt called the plan "a model for the West," and the park has been welcomed by local residents. Harvard landscape scholar Robert France recognized it as one of the most innovative wetlands projects in the world in 2001.

Spring Peeper marsh, at the Minnesota Arboretum near Minneapolis, won an ASLA award for original educational design. Simple color-coded stakes show how water depth coincides with vegetation types (see p. 167). Wetlands need interpretation because they are so rare and misunderstood; the good news is that they attract and educate people so successfully.

Restore Rivers and Streams to Full Health

Eroding stream banks are an environmental problem close to many people's backyards, degraded by two main forces: first, channelization, culverting, and burial to make watercourses fit human development patterns; and second, massively increased stormwater runoff from impervious urbanization. In many communities degraded streams have catalyzed local restoration projects.

Restoration is much more complex than simply stabilizing eroding banks. Holistic restoration takes into account the entire watershed and how water entering the stream has been affected by development. According to Tom Schueler, executive director of the Center for Watershed Protection, simply repairing the bank—even by environmentally progressive methods—is little more than a short-term fix. "A lot of people have been doing that kind of work because, quite frankly, it makes for great before-and-after pictures," says Schueler. "I don't mean to imply that it's just cosmetic, but that alone is not stream restoration. It's stream-bank stabilization."

Stream restoration entails a considerable learning curve, but many aids exist: a growing how-to literature, courses and workshops, and environmental ac-

Figure 4.11 At Spring Peeper marsh, lines of color-coded stakes show water-depth contours, and coincide with vegetation changes. Wetlands are prime sites for education and interpretation. (*Project and Photo:* Fred Rozumalski.)

tion groups. Much of the real work involves regional design and policy measures that reduce impervious surfaces (see Principle 5).

Keith Bower's design/build firm, Biohabitats (Towson MD), has increasingly worked in stream restoration. "Stream restoration doesn't start in the stream channel," Bowers says. "It starts in the watershed. If you just patch a stream, that improvement may be blown away in the next big storm. You have to recapture some of that off-site flow and try to release it

slowly." Thus, restoring upstream wetlands may be essential; the Center for Watershed Protection calls upstream ponds and wetlands "a watershed manager's most reliable tool ... to successfully improve a stream's overall operating health."[36] (Treat major parking lots as "headwater" sources.) Best results are achieved by looking at the whole watershed and all the communities—human and ecological—in it.[37]

The overall goal, says Bowers, is to "get the water into the ground as fast as possible in as many places as possible," through infiltration. This is easiest in new design, but applies to retrofits, too. Control stormwater runoff from existing paving *before* it enters the stream, and do so prior to restoring stream banks. Otherwise, problems will return periodically.

One leading stormwater expert, University of Georgia landscape architecture professor Bruce Ferguson, emphasizes that flood control basins must be selectively sited, or they can do active damage. A watershed-wide plan is the only way to determine proper locations. Basins sited at random or uniform locations fail on two counts: overflow from these ponds may join downstream to create a delayed flood; and infiltration at wrong locations may never reach groundwater, nor seep back into streambeds to replenish "base flows."

Local policies often mandate a detention basin on every site. This, however, produces excessively numerous and wrongly located basins, according to several studies cited by Ferguson. Such basins actually *increase* flooding downstream and seldom reduce storm flows to predevelopment levels.[38]

To avoid these problems, runoff must be infiltrated (not just detained) into drier soils in the upper watershed. Basins should be designed as diverse wetlands (above) rather than simple holding tanks, with water-level control devices and grading for varied depth. Engineers and regulators increasingly see the benefits of such design; watershed-wide management, however, transcends property boundaries and still causes consternation.

With stormwater infiltrating and base flows normalized, restoration of the stream itself can finally be addressed. To bring back some semblance of the structure, function, and dynamics of the predevelopment stream often requires regrading the banks, and even the streambed.

Two patterns of stream dysfunction are common. In *incised channels*, erosion cuts (incises) into the bed; in *aggrading channels*, the stream fills with silt, becoming broad and shallow without pools or riffles. Incised channels generally reflect increased flow volume from upstream; they may also be caused by increased speed, if the streambed is lowered downstream (into a culvert, for example). Aggrading streams reflect decreased speed, blockage downstream, or increased amounts of sediment from upstream erosion.

In general, an incised channel needs to have the volume and speed of flow decreased, and banks strengthened. An aggrading channel needs deposits cleaned out, and more steady flow. The source of the sediment (often an incised channel upstream) may require repairs, too.

There are several approaches to bank erosion. Conventionally, riprap or "river rock" is dumped down the banks. At best, this offers local, short-term relief, often accelerating trouble elsewhere. Riprap is easily swept away by floods and provides no resting and feeding places for fish (as shade and roots of vegetative stabilization do). It is unsightly, neither tidy nor naturalistic; the stone is seldom local, and its out-of-place color exposes it as imported, often over long distances. (Strategically placed boulders can help restore a stream's natural structure of pools and riffles.)

Most restorationists recommend plant cover, not riprap, to stabilize stream-bank soils—bioengineering in a specialized, partly submerged use. As in other forms of bioengineering (Principle 3), hard but permeable structures (crib walls, gabions, etc.) are used in extreme situations. (An unusual approach, described on p. 236, combines rubber tires with tree saplings to rescue collapsing banks.)

Branches, roots, or even entire tree trunks are widely used stabilizers. The Missouri Department of Conservation has perfected whole-tree revetments, cabled along stream banks. The trees are salvaged, from development, road building, or after storms.

Live trees also protect stream health. Streams and rivers in many parts of the world are buffered by forests, or were before development. Streams with wooded banks have channels that are cooler, shallower, and up to four times as wide as streams running through pastures or meadows. Replacing tree cover restores channel form, increasing habitat as well as resilience to pollutants, according to the National Academy of Science's Stroud Water Research Center (Pennsylvania).[39]

Most bioengineering materials and methods (p. 114) are useful for stream restoration; the number of suppliers has grown significantly. Biodegradable fabric blankets hold streambanks and streambeds until plant growth is established. At the toe of the bank, where water and soil meet, rolls or "biologs" made of

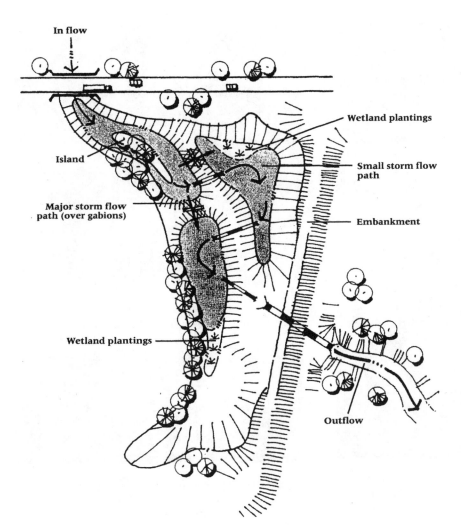

In flow

Island

Major storm flow
path (over gabions)

Wetland plantings

Wetland plantings

Small storm flow
path

Embankment

Outflow

Figure 4.12 Ponds at the headwaters of Wheaton Branch hold stormwater, infiltrating part and slowly releasing it into the stream. (*Illust.:* Craig Farnsworth, based on Center for Watershed Protection and Loiederman Association.)

coconut fiber have proved effective. For extensive bank restorations readymade products can be expensive. The University of Oregon, stabilizing a stream bank on campus, put design students to work assembling and installing cost-effective soil-filled "burritos." This may be an option for cash-strapped community groups.

One bioengineering technique that California stream restorationist Ann Riley and many others recommend is live willow or cottonwood stakes. Riley calls these "the underused workhorses of restoration," reinforcing soil like rebar in concrete, and far better than riprap (which she considers a last resort).[40] For tall banks, live stakes can be driven through straw-bale walls to root—another technique used at the University of Oregon.

Bioengineering consultant Robbin Sotir often uses plants alone (mostly willow cuttings) to stabilize

stream banks while providing excellent wildlife and aquatic habitat. Such techniques are attractive for a number of reasons. Materials are often available at little or no cost from the site, or from other client- or contractor-owned property. Unable to find a qualified consultant locally, the Oregon DOT had to bring Sotir all the way from Georgia for one project. Even so, the bioengineered solution has resisted major flooding and was probably more cost-effective than repeated hard-engineering failures.

Stream Restoration Project Examples

"Conventional stream and river practices," says Ann Riley, create "community blight where natural resources once existed."[41] This observation was reflected in the history of a meandering woodland stream in Silver Spring MD, Wheaton Branch. With

Figure 4.13 University of Oregon landscape students fabricated "soil burritos" of fabric, soil, and chicken-wire for a campus restoration, demonstrating a simple, inexpensive method. (*Project and Photo:* Professor Stan Jones.)

Figure 4.14 Students installing "burritos" and brush-layer to stabilize the stream bank. (*Project and Photo:* Professor Stan Jones.)

time, its highly urbanized watershed 55 percent impervious, Wheaton Branch took cascades of new runoff. Years of such torrents reduced it to a broad, shallow channel with eroding banks and scant vegetation, its cobbled bed buried beneath inches of silt. Aquatic life was reduced to two pollution-tolerant species.

Today Wheaton Branch again meanders between densely vegetated banks; whole trees buried, roots outward, stabilize the bank. The water runs clear, scouring the cobbles clean. Plentiful small fish and crayfish dart in pools and riffles created during restoration.

The interagency project[42] is the first phase of restoring Sligo Creek, of which Wheaton Branch is a tributary. Rather than simply "patching" eroded stream banks, the team is addressing Sligo Creek's entire 13.3-square-mile watershed. Interconnected

ponds detain runoff, allowing pollutants and sediments to settle out, then gradually release water into the stream. Wheaton Branch's streambed was reconfigured with stone "wing deflectors" and log weirs; banks were rebuilt and reinforced; and the riparian zone was revegetated with shrubs and trees. Finally, fish were reintroduced by a "bucket brigade" of neighborhood volunteers. Monitoring indicates that aquatic life—perhaps the best indicator of water quality—is flourishing.

At Wheaton Branch, upstream runoff was accepted as a given—a common, realistic approach, but not inevitable. Repairing uplands infiltration to restore a stream is an opposite approach, and at least in theory, is more cost effective and lasting.[43] A truly holistic approach requires both mending upland problems and rebuilding stream structures.

Figure 4.15 Stone deflector in restored Wheaton Branch unobtrusively guards the stream bank from floods. (*Project:* Washington Council of Governments. *Photo:* Walt Callahan.)

One guru of stream restoration is hydrologist Dave Rosgen, of Colorado-based Wildland Hydrology. Rosgen is the author of a profusely illustrated book classifying the many different types of streams according to morphology. At the risk of oversimplifying, Rosgen's scientifically based approach restores a stream's ecological functions by re-creating its natural dimension, pattern, and profile. This may involve excavating an entirely new channel for a disturbed stream, requiring more room than is available in many dense urban situations. Combined with upstream runoff reduction, the end result should approximate a predevelopment stream.

A Staten Island restoration project demonstrates just how challenging it can be to renovate urban streams to anything resembling original ecological structure and function. Sweet Brook, one of Staten Island's major streams, alternates between aboveground fragments of natural channel and underground storm sewers, a common urban condition. One aboveground segment flows through a quarter-mile wooded valley alongside Sweetbrook Road, but its source is a culvert. Only manhole covers mark its upstream corridor, and it empties into another culvert. The valley—a designated open space that also included private homes—is "a little remnant, an island in an otherwise man-made environment," says Dana Gumb of the New York City Department of Environmental Protection (DEP).

Receiving far more water from the culvert than its narrow channel could possibly handle, the stream regularly flooded the valley, tearing out a pedestrian bridge and turning Sweetbrook Road into a linear lake. In 1995 the DEP moved to restore the valley segment as part of its Staten Island Bluebelt program, a watershed-scale effort to infiltrate stormwater. Bluebelt planners argued successfully that restoring natural systems was cheaper than installing storm sewers, thus guaranteeing good funding.

Sweet Brook's tight, urbanized situation precluded most current stream-restoration principles—treat the whole watershed, control runoff at the headwaters, excavate a new "natural" channel. Even though the stream was part of a 12,000-acre watershed, there was not even room to construct a retention basin directly upstream to slow stormwater.

A technical compromise was developed. Normal "base flows" would run in the restored aboveground channel, while a device called a flow splitter diverted storm flows into large new pipes below Sweetbrook Road. To restore the visible channel, dumped rubble was removed, flood-damaged retaining walls were rebuilt, native stone reshaped the streambed, and native plants—including ferns long absent from the island—were reintroduced.

The six-acre, quarter-mile corridor restoration cost $1.1 million. "Whether such projects are worth the investment is widely debated," says Richard Claytor, principal engineer with the Center for Watershed

Figure 4.16 Tons of accumulated sediment were removed from Sweet Brook and used to fertilize the restored banks. (*Project:* New York City Department of Environmental Protection. *Photo:* Dean Cavallaro.)

Figure 4.17 Sweet Brook after restoration, just downstream from the previous photo. (*Project:* New York City Department of Environmental Protection. *Photo:* Dean Cavallaro.)

Protection. Pointing out that stream restorations in fragmented watersheds are not uncommon, he cites Strawberry Creek on UC Berkeley's campus. It, too, says Claytor, is in pipes above and below the restored, "daylighted" segment.

Claytor considers such projects "less valuable than a continuous stream. Aquatic exchange of plant and animal species is severely limited, so it has limited value from a biological standpoint. But it has great value as an educational resource. It sharpens nearby residents' ability to appreciate the watershed."

At Maguire Avenue, another Staten Island Bluebelt project, a 250-foot stretch of stream had become a drainage ditch. Armoring the road simply created extra erosive power, and the channel undercut and collapsed the pavement. Creative Habitats (White Plains NY) used gabions to stabilize the steep banks. Gabions, bioengineering's method of last resort according to Riley, are still "softer" than solid concrete. Boulders and fibrous "biologs" slowed the flow of water. Within a year, the banks were revegetated and protected from further collapse.

A small but growing number of landscape architecture firms undertake such restoration, but most still require consultant help. There are many more stream, shoreline, and wetland restoration specialists since the first edition of this book; check the International Erosion Control Association.⊃ Many con-

sultants are also suppliers of specialized products like mats or wattles. This is not necessarily a conflict of interest, because localized knowledge is often essential in producing appropriate supplies.

Collect and Conserve Water

Reducing human use and waste of water protects natural water systems. Conflicts between diverting water for human use and leaving it in-stream to support aquatic life are increasingly common, especially in the Western United States. Much is at stake if rivers or aquifers dry up from overuse. Not only biodiversity and habitat, but human survival depends on water, much of it diverted from distant sources. Conserving water, through a wide range of techniques, is necessary in its own right, essential to protection of wetlands and streams, and important in keeping water supplies clean.

Harvest Water from Roofs and Landscapes

Water harvesting means close-to-source collection and storage of rainwater from roofs, paved surfaces, and landscapes. Roof collection was common in older US homes, often filling basement cisterns. In 1997 the American Rainwater Catchment Systems Association estimated there were about 250,000 roof

Figure 4.18 Erosion undercut pavement at Maguire Avenue and prevented plants from reestablishing. (*Project:* New York City Department of Environmental Protection. *Photo:* Dean Cavallaro.)

systems in the United States;[44] they are common in Australia and the Caribbean.

Harvesting from ground surfaces has an even longer history. Ancient Israelites, Chinese, Pueblo Indians, and Australians (both aboriginal and recent settlers) have used landscape water harvesting to survive. Variations on terracing, usually small scale, and low stone walls or check dams infiltrate water at strategic points in a watershed. This traps fertile sediment and moisture in some of Earth's most arid environments. Shallow ditches roughly following contours (often called "key lines") are also used to gather sheeting water into linked hillside ponds.

The results of arid-land water harvesting can be startling: stopping gully erosion, raising the water table, and greening the desert without artificial irrigation. In recent years, such techniques have been revived and somewhat systematized by Australian author Bill Mollison, under the name Permaculture. Many techniques from this agriculturally focused system of sustainable construction are adaptable to landscapes.[45]

Evaporation and precipitation "distill" rainwater, so it is free of many surface-water pollutants. It is "soft" water, holding few minerals and no municipal chlorine or fluorine. Unless contaminated by materials on the collecting surface, its purity makes it desirable for drinking; many plant species prefer

Figure 4.19 Maguire Avenue after installation of gabions, boulders to deflect culvert outflow, and plantings. (*Project:* New York City Department of Environmental Protection. *Photo:* Dean Cavallaro.)

rainwater irrigation. (For purifying harvested water, see p. 188.)

In roof systems, stainless steel, along with tile, terra cotta, and slate, are frequently used. Color coatings, solder, and fasteners may contain lead, making them inadvisable for drinking-water collection; metals may leach from galvanized roofing. In irrigation for ornamentals, this may or may not be a problem. Where rain is frequent and plentiful, as in the Caribbean, limestone roofs sweeten the water. In any less-wet climate, the porous stone surfaces would collect impurities and grow algae, bacteria, or mold. Wood shingles share these problems of porosity, and if treated with preservative should not be used on collector roofs. Asphalt (with gravel, or as shingles) may contaminate water, and the rough surfaces hold dust; spray-foam roofing must be evaluated per material.

Any paved surface can be a water harvesting collector, but not for drinking water. Asphalt can produce contaminants; most other paving materials are relatively inert. Paved surfaces collect residues from air pollution, spills, automotive sources, Dumpsters, and industrial processes. Paved non-vehicular or lightly trafficked surfaces are generally suitable for water harvesting. Runoff from potentially polluted surfaces (driveways, Dumpster pads, etc.) should be routed through a vegetated biofilter (Principle 5, p. 208) before flowing to final use. Lawns, unless maintained with excessive pesticides, also serve as collecting surfaces, although like any porous surface they yield less runoff.

Perhaps the simplest form of water harvesting for landscape use is simply grading the site to drain toward planted beds or ponds. Permaculturist Ben Haggard of Tesuque NM used this approach for the landscape of New Mexico's first Energy Star–compliant house. In a region where annual precipitation averages about twelve inches, Haggard's design supports mature shade and fruit trees without supplemental water.

The volume of water collected by any surface— paved, roofed, or planted—can be calculated using standard engineering formulas, treat the resulting volume as a *resource* rather than a nuisance. The same formulas make it possible to size collection basins. Without careful planning the collected water may drown some plants while others parch. Planting beds, which are low points in such a design, must be sized to prevent water standing in them. If ponds are to collect water, size them to accept the ten- or twenty-five-year storm and provide spillways to avoid washout.

Most water-harvesting research focuses on drinking water. For landscape irrigation, which can consume two to three times as much as indoor uses combined, potable purity is not needed; heavy metals and lead should still be avoided. Collecting enough for all irrigation is desirable, but difficult unless use is reduced. Even as a backup irrigation source, water harvesting makes good sense, reducing use of pumped groundwater or treated municipal supply. Even in Arizona, demonstration homes have shown that harvested water supplemented by graywater can meet irrigation needs.[46] Water harvesting is also extensively used at Lady Bird Johnson Wildflower Center in Austin TX.

Water harvesting turns impervious surfaces into assets; irrigation becomes a form of close-to-source infiltration. The combination may, as in the following example, moderate both peak flows and seasonal water availability. Water availability in the local ecosystem as a whole increases with infiltration.[47] Concerns about (and Western US laws against) harvesting as "taking" water are mostly misguided. Intense water harvesting could delay in-stream flow, especially if sent into sewers after use rather than infiltrated. Local small-scale water harvesting for on-site infiltration benefits sustainable communities.

WATER HARVESTING PROJECT EXAMPLES
Parque da Cidade in Oporto, Portugal, offers an intriguing example of contemporary water harvesting to maintain water levels in a man-made lake through Portugal's six-month dry season. Project engineers initially specified plastic lake liner on the premise that the sandy soil would not hold water. Instead, landscape architect Sidonio Pardal and a hydrologist sited fifty infiltration basins throughout the park. Some are grassy swales, others edged with city-salvaged granite. The basins interrupt overland flow during Portugal's rainy season, collecting rainwater that slowly infiltrates. This groundwater reaches the lake during the dry season, taking months to seep from the infil-

Figure 4.20 Rainwater from a roof drain is caught in a gravel basin and routed to furrows in the garden at the Denver offices of designer Bill Wenk. (*Project and Photo*: Bill Wenk.)

tration basins. Almost no drains or pipes were used, because speeding up flow was undesirable. The approach is worth trying in similarly wet/dry climates, like California.

Even major downtown areas have places to capture and conserve rainwater. Combining design with ecological principles can create extraordinary urban places that celebrate rain's beauty and life-giving effects. In a number of recent design competitions, using only harvested water has been a major selling point.[48]

Thirty projects that address rainwater environmentally and artfully were studied by Stuart Echols and Eliza Pennypacker (Penn State University landscape architecture department). One of these projects is called "10th@Hoyt," a Pearl District urban apartment courtyard in Portland OR, designed by landscape architect Steve Koch. Copper downspouts convey runoff from the building roof to tall, thin, concrete structures resembling skinny ziggurats, stepping down and cantilevering over raised concrete basins filled with round river rocks. In two of these stepped aqueducts, Cor-Ten steel sheets perforated by colored glass dots spread the water cascading onto the river rock, hard counterpoints to lush planting. The spreaders are lit from below, making the glass dots glow at night. In this inward-oriented, private oasis, thanks to the "chutes and ladders" conveyance system, *visitors can watch rainwater flow.*

At 10th@Hoyt, captured rainwater is stored in a buried 4,000-gallon cistern for up to thirty hours, then slowly released to the city stormwater system. Some recirculates to steel fountains in the courtyard. It might have been more educational to spill water into planting beds, visibly sustaining vegetation. Nevertheless, this project incorporates many principles of artful rainwater design:

- Make rain visible as it flows through the system.
- Incorporate a cistern or other receptacle to handle overflow.
- Use rainwater for irrigation or other needs.
- Design the flow system artfully for sound, reflection, and aeration.[49]

Figure 4.21 Collected on the Portland Water Pollution Control Lab's roof, water spouts from scuppers in rhythmic jets. (*Project*: Robert Murase. *Photo*: Tom Liptan.)

Figure 4.22 The 10th@Hoyt courtyard (Portland OR) makes rainwater visible and artful en route from roof to cistern. (*Project:* Steve Koch. *Photo:* Stuart Echols.)

Infiltrate Water Simply On-Site

Until the mid-1990s, a focus on *getting rid of* water virtually displaced the many varieties of water infiltration devices. European texts on landscape construction were well ahead of most US counterparts (an exception being Ferguson's work). For example, a standard British text from the *1970s* contains no less than four detail drawings for infiltration devices, plus calculations showing how large a land area each can drain in normal soils.[50]

On-site infiltration may be overlooked because it is so simple. It relies on two basic principles: slowing or holding water flow, and increasing soil permeability. Both are easier to achieve close to the source of water, because large volumes or fast flow are harder to hold and require extreme porosity to infiltrate quickly.

Bioswales (p. 208) use vegetation and gentle gradients to slow and infiltrate water. Wetlands (whether natural, restored, or constructed) slow and hold water due to topography and vegetation, and frequently are major infiltration sites. Porous paving over a reservoir provides on-site infiltration (p. 211). Water harvesting, sometimes put into storage, often has direct infiltration as its goal. Check dams, terracing, key-line trenches, and many other techniques of bioengineering and Permaculture hold water in small, even tiny, reservoirs from which it soaks into the soil. Conventional retention basins do the same thing, though generally on an overcentralized scale.

Two structures especially designed for infiltration are the French drain and the "soakaway." Conventional construction recognizes these only as minor weapons in the arsenal of water control. For sustainability, they should be everyday tools for making peace with water and winning its benefits.

The French drain is simply a pit or trench, filled with rubble or gravel. The rubble should be graded, large at the bottom to small near the top. Over the smallest gravel, several inches of soil match the original surface. Modern French drains are lined with filter fabric, which permits water to move through the rubble, while keeping out sediment that would eventually fill the voids.

Prior to invention of filter fabric, French drains had to be dug up and cleaned of silt, or replaced, every few years. Conventional concrete catch basins can also be overwhelmed by silt, but are somewhat easier to clean. Silting, however, really indicates that the structure is serving a quickly eroding area; more structures, closer to the source, may solve this. A single drain for a large area may seem economical, but only in terms of initial costs. Shorter flow lines, and

Figure 4.23   Close-up of 10th@Hoyt stormwater conveyances. (*Project:* Steve Koch. *Photo:* Stuart Echols.)

vegetated surfaces for the flow, significantly cut maintenance costs due to siltation.

Soakaways are quite similar to French drains, but usually receive water from a small drainpipe or downspout rather than overland flow. Some soakaways are rubble filled, while others are called "dry-wells." Infiltration occurs through unmortared stone walls and an earth floor. Without rubble, soakaways hold a larger volume of water. Unlike French drains, they are usually covered with a grate or manhole. If incoming water is very silty, a conventional silt trap can be added. Like wells, dry wells may pose accident dangers. Where this is a concern, the filled soakaway or French drain with filter fabric may be a better choice.

In soils with ordinary drainage and rainfall typical of Britain, a 60-cubic-foot-capacity soakaway can infiltrate runoff for about 2,200 square feet (1.6 cubic meters for 200 square meters). Larger soakaways collect from areas almost 100 feet square.[51] This gives an idea of the small scale appropriate to these methods. For larger areas, terraces or check dams may be simpler and cheaper.

A number of commercially available drainage systems use filter fabric around a core with large voids (usually waffle-like plastic). In effect, they provide a French drain in the shape of a pipe, very useful for collecting and filtering sediment-laden water. Old-fashioned perforated pipe serves some of the same purposes, but may clog with sediment. Filter drains are important in some updated tree-planting standards (Principle 3) and valuable in water harvesting. For harvesting, similar "wrapped waffle" materials are available in modules, for example AquaStor, for constructing updated versions of the French drain.

Store Water for Later Use

One common complaint about water harvesting results from underestimating required storage volume. Precipitation usually comes in one season and must be held for use in another. Thus, the total *season's* accumulation determines the size of storage tank needed. Most people are surprised by how much water can be harvested from a single storm, and tend to skimp on storage.

Harvested water can be stored in tanks above or below ground, or in ponds. Ponds lose too much to evaporation to make efficient irrigation holding tanks and are unsuitable for drinking water. These limitations may be offset, however, if ponds also serve for raising fish, for solar collectors with a heat pump, for slowing flood flows, or as decorative features.

Tanks are available readymade in metal, fiberglass, plastic, or precast concrete. They can also be built on-site from stone or ferrocement (thin cement over steel-reinforced mesh). Wood tanks should be of sustainably harvested lumber. If located aboveground, tanks should be opaque; sunlight promotes algae growth. Buried tanks must be heavy duty, but have the advantage of protection from freezing. Not all tank materials are suitable for drinking water. Energy and toxicity in manufacture should be considered as well (see Principles 6 and 7).

Tanks and box culverts installed under paved areas are increasingly common as developers try to maximize space, conserve water, and manage runoff. To some extent, these substitute for "reservoir porous paving" (p. 211). In a few places (for example, Houston TX), dense clay soils virtually prevent infiltration, and tanks may be important in managing storm flows. With safeguards against collected pollutants, water from tank storage may be reusable as non-potable irrigation.

Use Pumps If Needed

Where possible, gravity-flow water systems are most energy efficient. Harvested rainwater, however, is normally stored lower than the collecting surface; if this is a roof, gravity flow into the same building's plumbing is unlikely. Careful placement of roof collection storage tanks might make ground-level gravity *irrigation* possible. Water pressure for modern irrigation is hard to achieve using gravity unless tanks are in high locations.

For these reasons, water harvesting often requires pumps. Water pumping is one of solar electricity's most efficient uses (see p. 265) common in agriculture and at remote campgrounds. For water supply, it is cheaper to store water than electricity—that is, pump to a high tank during sunny periods, supplying users by gravity, rather than pumping on demand using storage batteries. Decorative fountain pumps can be solar powered; sunshine intensity could regulate pumped volume, creating a climate-responsive fountain. For a solar pump to operate constantly, it needs batteries.

There are many types of pump design. Look for low energy usage, good service life, and low maintenance. Many suppliers offer pumps designed for solar power, or even paired with PV panels as kits. DC-powered pumps can be operated directly from solar panels without an inverter, keeping systems simple.

Irrigate Intelligently and Sparingly

The irrigation industry has undergone major changes since the first edition of this book, to the extent that some experts consider irrigation systems more than five years old obsolete.[52] Fortunately, these changes have substantially improved irrigation's alignment with water conservation.

In writing about irrigation in the first edition, it was difficult not to treat it as fundamentally unsustainable, deeply associated with bluegrass obsession.[53] Apart from drip irrigation, most of the industry seemed unrepentantly devoted to unlimited water.

Today, by contrast, the irrigation industry is outpacing the landscape professions in walking conservation's talk. Perhaps the handwriting on the wall has been more blunt about water issues than other aspects of landscaping. Faced with a choice between changing direction or shriveling away, irrigation industry associations, manufacturers, and contractors have made water conservation a priority.

As a result, many of the idealistic and even radical ideas suggested in our earlier edition are now incorporated in new technologies and advocated as best practices. Artificially redistributing the Earth's waters to fit market demands will always raise sustainability issues, but landscape irrigation today involves a serious conservation ethic.

Change Attitudes, Incentives, and Technologies

The quantity of fresh water on Earth is a fixed amount,[54] of which some is made unavailable by water pollution and drought. Much available water is essential to nonhuman life forms and in that sense "spoken for." Yet human demand is growing. In many countries, population growth is outstripping water supply; US "lifestyle improvements" have increased water usage *four times* as fast as population growth, doubling every twenty years since 1900.[55] In addition to actual scarcity, water infrastructure is becoming inadequate to meet demand in many regions.

As water has become an international resource concern, this has affected irrigation. Usage restrictions have become common, many targeting landscape irrigation first. In the 1990s, costs of water in the United States rose an average of 23 percent, and as much as 400 percent.[56] This has forced real efficiencies and generated heated debate about irrigation's role.

Landscape uses a major portion of US water, but far from the largest. Landscape irrigation consumes 30 to 50 percent of municipal water in many areas, and in dry regions or hot months can account for 75 percent.[57] Cities use about 21 percent of the US total; at 30 to 75 percent of this, landscape use is 6 to 16 percent of the national total. Industry uses 10 percent; the remaining 69 percent goes to agriculture.

Two issues differentiate landscape irrigation from industrial and agricultural use, however. First, unlike either agriculture or industry, much landscape irrigation unnecessarily uses *treated* municipal water. Second, agriculture and industry use water for tangibly productive purposes. By contrast, landscapes are considered ornamental, their benefits far harder to quantify than crops or manufacturing. Thus, when drought or supply problems arise, there are realistic reasons to target landscape irrigation before agriculture or manufacturing. Restricting the relatively small landscape industry, rather than take on larger ones with more clout, is also politically expedient.

As a result, "the first reaction to drought and water shortages tends to be . . . 'shutting off the taps'" for landscape use.[58] This is arguably unfair and may risk destroying environmental services from planted landscapes, such as heat-island abatement and runoff control. Studies from Australia and New Jersey also suggest that when on-again-off-again water restrictions are lifted, water consumption increases 4 to 10 percent over pre-restriction levels.[59]

Instead of waiting for droughts and shutting off irrigation, proactive jurisdictions mandate certain types of irrigation equipment, such as drip systems and efficient controllers. California offers rebates of several hundred dollars for such installations and by 2010 will require all new irrigation systems to have "smart" controllers and meet other efficiency criteria (see below).[60] The EPA announced, in October 2006, a new program called WaterSense to certify water-conservation products, services, and specialists.

As stated in our first edition, irrigation means addition of water above and beyond normal precipitation. Although some irrigation techniques save water compared to others, *all* irrigation requires extra water. The *baseline* for evaluating *ecological* costs and benefits of irrigation should always be the unirrigated landscape and its natural water regime.

This does not mean that irrigation should be excluded from sustainable design. Rather, irrigation should be used where it can produce outstanding results in resource-efficient ways. Truly saving water requires considering all options, from irrigating with surplus water to eliminating irrigation for most or all of a site. Comparing relative efficiency of different irrigation systems is not, by itself, sufficient to make a landscape sustainable.

Water efficiency is not just a matter of technology, though. "The most important feature of a water-conserving landscape is the preservation of as many existing [native] trees and shrubs as possible."[61] Thus the issues and techniques raised in Principle 1 are critical to water conservation. This constant interlinkage of good practices cannot be overemphasized. The first step toward truly sustainable irrigation is to plan and design a landscape that *minimizes the need for water*.

Design Xeriscapes for Real Water Savings

Xeriscape designs landscapes to use water efficiently. This system, trademarked by the Denver Water Department and the National Xeriscape Council, promotes seven basic principles, corresponding to many themes of this book.[62] They are:

- planning and design
- soil analysis and improvement
- practical areas of turf
- appropriate plants
- efficient irrigation
- mulching
- proper maintenance.

These principles (which, taken individually, are not new to gardeners) are all essential to the system. Xeriscape's central concept, however, is that plants with like water requirements are grouped together, and that water-intensive plants are reserved for locations of maximum effect. Exotic, water-hungry specimen trees might be used at focal points. A small, drought-tolerant lawn might be a special feature. Moving away from the house, however, planting zones contain more drought-tolerant plants. On larger properties, only a reasonably sized garden contains irrigated plants; outside that zone, the native landscape predominates. In the native zone, any plantings are species that survive without watering once established.

Clearly, this concept offers far greater water savings than irrigating the entire lot, no matter how efficiently. With efficient irrigation technology where any is used, Xeriscape gardens live up to their name: "xeric" means dry.

Like native-plant use in general, Xeriscape requires changes in attitude, encouraging people to see well-adapted plants as beautiful. Too many (laypeople and professionals) still assume that only certain horticultural varieties have merit, and that all others are scruffy weeds. Xeriscape encourages attention to the qualities that make a place unique. This attitude is critically important to sustainability.

A simple approach to water efficiency, emphasized by Xeriscape and many other systems, is organic mulch. (Inorganic mulches, like gravel, can protect soil moisture, but lack other benefits.) In addition to increasing soil fertility, applying two to four inches of mulch as part of regular maintenance dramatically decreases evaporative water loss (see Principle 10).

Healthy soil produces healthier plants while demanding or wasting far less water. Before increasing site irrigation, test and maximize existing soil's ability to store water and release it to plants. Recall that excessive soil "improvements" are counterproductive in some regions (p. 55).

Install Water-efficient Irrigation Technology

The main forms of irrigation are flood, spray, and drip. Flooding a field or bed requires the least equipment, but is labor intensive. Spray can use simple hoses and fittings, which are easily moved and aimed, although dragging hoses is many a gardener's complaint. As a result, buried pipe with fixed spray heads and automated controllers is popular. Drip irrigation delivers water to precise points on the ground, or even underground. Like buried spray systems, it requires considerable pipe runs, but can easily be automated.

Comparisons of water efficiency between these three systems are straightforward. (Ease of maintenance and other issues may be more awkward.) Flood and spray systems lose significant amounts of water to evaporation, and spray systems waste water by over spraying unless very carefully installed and maintained. Micro-spray systems have been developed that suffer less loss, but still more than drippers. Compared to older aboveground systems, drip saved up to 90 percent of water used; despite important recent improvements in spray technology, drip continues to outperform spray by 30 to 65 percent.[63] Instead of going to waste, nearly 95 percent of water supplied by drip is delivered where plants need it.[64]

Water-efficient design is not more costly than conventional landscapes. In fact, at least one study concluded that for two equivalent landscapes, one water conserving and the other conventional, the low-water design's overall operational and maintenance costs were less than *half*, including labor, fuel, pesticides, fertilizer, water, and energy. Because operation and maintenance represented 80 percent of each landscape's total cost (design and construction representing only 20 percent), this difference is significant.[65] One reason for these savings is that over- or underwatering affects soil and plant health, contributing in turn to costly erosion and soil subsidence and requiring more pesticides, water, fertilizer, and staff attention.

In this book's first edition, only drip irrigation systems were covered in any detail because we considered them the main mode of environmentally responsible irrigation. In general, this is still true. Aboveground irrigation, however, has been enough improved, and controllers have taken such a predominant position in efficient irrigation, that they warrant expanded coverage.

Irrigation work involves specialized skill, and many landscape companies subcontract it. (Those who do both often say, resignedly, that landscape is a sideline to their irrigation business.) This section focuses on sustainability of irrigation systems. For basic design principles, and equipment details, consult irrigation-specific reference books, software, and manufacturer catalogs.

Use Controllers and Sensors for Efficiency

Controllers, when this book first appeared, were time clocks, some fancier than others, occasionally equipped with a sensor to override the clock in rainy or windy conditions. These controllers were important attempts at water conservation, but have truly been supplanted by a new generation of "smart controllers."

Even when irrigation hardware is highly efficient, immense waste occurs if the system runs when evaporation is highest, during rainstorms, or on saturated ground. Few people can remember to turn irrigation on and off at precisely the right times. The best times for residential irrigation are often when people are asleep or not home. Time-clock controllers were the first attempt to solve this problem.

Weather, however, doesn't happen on a clock schedule. From one day to the next, a site's soil moisture, relative humidity, temperature, light levels, and wind can vary dramatically. All affect how much moisture is in the soil, and how much a given plant actually needs.

Irrigating at the same time every few days actually has had the unintended and unexpected consequence of making water waste *worse*. A number of studies have shown that set-and-forget time-clock controllers apply up to *twice as much water as is actually needed* by landscape plants. (An attentive person hand watering does far better, wasting only about 10 percent.[66]) Water needs are complex; convenient, predictable settings give very poor conservation results.

Older clock-type sensors can be made more efficient in two main ways (if it is not possible to replace them). Rain and wind sensors can override clock settings to avoid obvious waste. Many older controllers also allow "seasonal adjustment": after programming the "peak" month, usually July, clock schedules are adjusted for other months as percentages of peak (e.g., September might be 65 percent of the July setting).

Smart controllers achieve far great water efficiency by basing irrigation times and amounts on actual environmental conditions. They do this in three basic ways:

The simplest single indicator of actual growing conditions is soil moisture. When sensors register soil moisture below a set threshold (due to depletion by plants, or hot, dry conditions), the controller opens valves until the threshold is reached. If the soil is moist from rain or earlier irrigation, the sensor-linked controller stays off. Similarly, as plants slow their moisture uptake in late fall, or begin uptake in early spring, sensors ensure reduced irrigation. Some soil-moisture systems have a single sensor, giving an overall picture of site conditions; others have a sensor for each valve or zone. An example is the Watermark controller from Irrometer.

"ET controllers," available from most manufacturers today, use evapotranspiration (ET) data to determine when and how much to water. (In the 2000 edition of this book, we noted this data was available in California for computing irrigation *design*. It is now available throughout the United States and used directly by the controller.) Older ET controllers relied on built-in databases of past seasonal ET levels and guesstimated current conditions. Newer models download current ET values from regional weather stations daily, or even hourly. Some compare current data to a database before "deciding" whether to water. Transmitted-ET controllers receive information from weather stations dozens of miles from the irrigation site. Computerized interpolation estimates current weather on a half-mile (1 km) square grid. In some areas, especially arid regions where irrigation and conservation are most critical, even a half-mile difference can mean totally different weather.

Integrated multisensor systems put a mini weather station at the irrigation site, calculating ET values from site-specific information. Some models use relative humidity (RH) and temperature to predict rainfall (RH rises dramatically before storms and remains high afterward). In theory, local data provides most accurate control. One integrated multisensor system is WeatherMiser, by Terragreen Irrigation.

The ongoing revolution in communications not only makes downloading of ET data possible, but also has produced "central controllers" using two-way communication to manage multiple irrigation sites remotely. (This concept was pioneered in the 1990s by LEIT solar irrigation controllers, noted below.) Sites may be linked by radio, cellular, phone, dedicated hard wiring, Internet, or wireless connections. Many of these require monthly subscriptions. Remote sites are programmed from the central computer, operate independently, and send back local status updates. For irrigation companies or large institutions, this can significantly cut fuel usage by reducing site visits.

Many recent controllers offer leak detection and electrical troubleshooting. Useful for single-site systems, this is essential for centralized control of multiple sites. Leaks can consume huge amounts of water. According to the Boulder (Colorado) Energy Conservation Center, 5 percent of average residential use is wasted via leaks.[67] With US residential use at around 250 gallons per day,[68] leaks waste some 4,500 gallons annually per household.

Smart controllers significantly improve water conservation. By replacing a clock-only controller (without changing the rest of the system), 50 percent of water waste and 70 percent of irrigation runoff can be eliminated.[69] An increasing number of jurisdictions either require or offer rebates for smart controllers.

No controller can completely overcome poor design, inadequate plumbing, or negligent maintenance (some can detect such problems). "Smart" controllers come very close to applying exactly the irrigation that scientific tests show plants need. This is an impressive achievement—and also means that further improvements in efficiency are not likely to be easy.

Make Drip Irrigation First Choice

Drip technology was already highly efficient as of the first edition of this book. Although it has continued to evolve, the changes are aimed at overcoming drip's reputation (largely undeserved) for being "complicated." The broad principles relating drip to sustainable practice have changed relatively little.[70]⊃ These are:

In-line emitters (built into the supply tube every few inches) are most reliable. Most manufacturers offer standard spacings (twelve or eighteen inches); some offer custom-spaced tube.

Other drip types are useful for some conditions, including emitters that "punch in" to the supply tube wall or connect via small "spaghetti tube." Some can be disassembled for cleaning. Porous or "leaky" pipe, in which water oozes through the whole tube wall, is used in some drip systems.

Pressure-compensating emitters adjust for supply pressure, topography, and pressure drop over distance, increasing efficiency.

Self-cleaning emitters are preferred. The most common design uses turbulent flow to clean the dripper. Some drippers are impregnated with root-inhibiting chemicals to prevent clogging; longevity of these chemicals varies. Drippers exposed to strong sunshine may become caked with evaporated mineral salts.

Table 4.2
Leaks consume surprisingly large amounts of water.

leak size		water waste (gallons/month)	equivalent water use if not wasted
drops per minute:	60	192	
	90	310	1 average household for 1 day
	120	429	
length of smooth stream:	3"	1,095	1 super-efficient household for 1 month
	6"	2,190	
	9"	3,290	
opening diameter:	1/32"	6,300	1 average household for almost 1 month
	1/16"	25,000	
	1/8"	100,000	1 average household for more than 1 year
	3/16"	225,000	1 church, hotel, or retail store for 1 year
	1/4"	400,000	1 acre turf irrigated for 6 months, or a 100-student elementary school for 1 year

Assumes line pressure at 60 psi. Sources: Drip rates, California Urban Water Conservation Council, "Practical Plumbing Handbook," 2001, www.cuwcc.org. Equivalent uses, City of Santa Fe (New Mexico) Planning Department, 2001 pamphlet.

Filters are essential, upstream from all valves, even with self-cleaning drippers. So-called Y-filters are preferred over straight-in-line designs, providing a larger filter surface and simplifying draining and cleaning, which can even be automated.

In addition to pressure-regulating drippers, each valve should have a master pressure regulator.

Backflow preventers are required on all irrigation, and may be especially important where harvested water or graywater (below) supplement tap water.

Drip irrigation relies strongly on zones of similar water need—the Xeriscape concept. Although much has been made of drip systems delivering water to individual plants as needed, in landscapes (as opposed to containers) the system actually waters a zone. Putting each *plant* on an individualized watering schedule would require separate valves and pipes per plant.

Individualized water delivery has misled many designers into placing a single dripper per plant, which irrigation author Robert Kourik refers to as "water bondage." Kourik recommends that emitters be on a zone-wide grid, uniformly watering that area.[71] Grid spacing needs to match plant types, rates of percolation, and spread in local soils. Another approach where grids are awkward (e.g., rock gardens) is

"hubs" that supply several easily adjustable spaghetti-tube drippers. Each hub is fed by a riser from a buried supply line; the hubs are not movable, but the drippers are.

Drip systems can be buried successfully, but extra care is required; the emitter tubes, which must be near the surface to deliver water, tend to heave up out of the ground, possibly due to frost action. (Supply tubes without emitters can always be buried.) Attaching emitter tubes to buried mesh has been suggested, but seems likely to harm soil wildlife. A better approach is to stake the system before burying it, using landscape staples (those with a kink in each leg hold better than plain ones). Rainbird offers tube joint fittings with attached stakes.

Even with self-cleaning emitters, some models clog easily if buried. Under lawns, drippers may need to run briefly every few hours to keep grass roots from growing into emitters.[72] A buried drip system, however, is completely below ground and unlikely to be damaged by surface traffic or vandalism. One improvement that would be extremely valuable in drip tubing and fittings would be built-in or clip-on metal markers to allow buried lines to be traced magnetically.

Unburied drip systems can be an unsightly sprawl of piping, but for full efficiency, surface drippers should be covered by mulching. As long as the owner is committed to regular mulching, drip systems stay invisible. By leaving them on the surface, pipes remain accessible, reparable, and adjustable. Adjustment is important as plants mature or site usage changes. No other fully automatic irrigation system can easily be moved.

Drip's inherent efficiency can be defeated by poor design or maintenance, or by an ineffective controller. Coupled with smart controllers, however, drip remains the system of choice for water-conserving irrigation.

Consider Spray and Rotor Systems

Conventional aboveground irrigation includes impact heads, spray nozzles, and rotors. Impact heads, originally developed for agriculture, cover large areas; spray heads put out a sheet of water in circular or part-circle patterns; rotors put out one or more rotating streams of water. Recently, "rotary nozzles" have been added: small rotors that mount on spray-head risers. Bubblers can flood the ground, generally used for trees and shrubs.

All aboveground hardware suffers evaporative losses that drip systems avoid. They also require careful aiming and maintenance or they put water where it is not wanted—on fences, sidewalks, windows, or plants that don't need it.

Aboveground hardware has gradually improved in several ways. Low-volume and ultra-low-volume systems are available; they lose less water, and more heads can be put on a single line or zone. Spray patterns have been made more accurate, and include rectangular coverage. One prototype nozzle, developed in 2004 by Dr. Prasada Rao of California State University, can be adjusted for radius and trajectory in several directions, producing irregular patterns to fit awkward spaces. This potentially useful fitting does not yet appear to be commercially available.[73]

Pressure regulation is important for spray heads. If line pressure is higher than the head is designed for, it will produce rapidly evaporating mist and overspray.

Spray heads can clog, but are fairly easy to clean. They have moving parts, however, while drippers do not. Risers and pop-up heads are easily broken or damaged. Flexible mountings between supply line and riser have improved spray-head survival of foot or mower impact. Regular readjustment to keep spray heads vertical and high enough to clear surrounding vegetation is essential to maintain performance and avoid ponding or runoff.

Aboveground systems often drain from the lowest head in each zone after shutoff. Many manufacturers have added check valves to prevent this. The valves will also prevent geysers from broken, vandalized, or stolen heads.

Some landscape professionals believe that combining micro-spray with drip produces a humid soil surface, microbe populations on periodically wetted leaves, and water to break down mulch. The authors have been unable to confirm this theory, but would welcome further information.

Carefully designed and maintained, aboveground irrigation fixtures can be efficient, especially with smart controllers. However, evaporative loss as water sprays through the air or runs across the ground can only be reduced, not eliminated. For water conservation and sustainability, drip systems should be favored unless there is a compelling—not just convenient—reason.

Remember Other Irrigation Options

Some irrigation suppliers now offer "root-watering" fixtures,[74] primarily for trees and large shrubs. These are tubes, three or four inches in diameter, from the soil surface to root depth, usually a foot or two. Plain pipes have been used in this way for years, filled periodically from a hose. The updated version is filled by the automatic irrigation system. For some species, and with a separate valve controlling only them, root waterers may have value and conserve water.

A low-tech option is the "TreeGator drip irrigation bag," a heavy fourteen- or twenty-gallon plastic sack that drip irrigates one tree for up to ten hours. Careful placement of the bag is important: with all but small trees, it is a mistake to place it next to the trunk. Compared to hose watering, Treegators reduce evaporative loss and runoff. The manufacturer estimates that this system cuts weekly watering visits from four to one, and laborer time per tree from fifteen minutes to two. By this estimate, labor cost is only 3 percent of that for hose watering, and some fuel costs may be saved. Average wholesale price is $17.50 per bag. The manufacturer suggests that landscape contractors save enough on labor that they can use the bags to establish plantings, then give them to the client.

Hose watering is an often-overlooked option. Professionals profit on irrigation systems, but should not forget that for some situations (occasional watering of tough species or early establishment), hose watering is a reasonable, water-conserving alternative.

Use Non-potable Water for Irrigation

Non-potable water can and should be used for irritation. Very few plants benefit from treated water; chlorine and fluorine harm some species. Infrastructure and treatment costs are significant. Many manufacturers offer non-potable pipes and fittings (usually color coded purple). These are identical to conventional components, except where valves and filters must be redesigned to avoid clogging or attack by impurities in non-potable water.

Aim for Energy-efficient Irrigation Systems

Controllers, sensors, and valves all require electricity. A few models run on 9V batteries. Manufacturers like Photocomm, Hardie, Heliotrope-General, and DIG (which purchased Altec, formerly Solatrol) have developed solar-powered irrigation systems. These take advantage of photovoltaics' greatest benefit: flexible location. Solar-powered controllers have proved popular with streets and highways agencies for irrigating road medians and other non-electrified areas. One large California developer, McMillin Properties, installs Photocomm solar controllers temporarily at new sites during the vulnerable period before utility power is turned on. Solar-powered controllers can be located close to valves, decreasing wire runs and reducing both voltage-drop and materials costs.

Solar irrigation controllers are available both for retrofitting and new construction. Most non-solar

Figure 4.24 This large Photocomm solar irrigation controller uses an inverter to provide 110V AC power to standard valves. (*Photo:* Photocomm/Golden Genesis Co.)

systems use solenoids held open by constant electrical current and closing when current stops. Supplying constant current has until recently only been possible with utility power; solar panels could not generate enough electricity. So-called latching solenoids are much more energy efficient: they open on a brief energy pulse and close with a second pulse. Whether a latching solenoid can be retrofitted to a standard valve depends on the model of each.

Photocomm incorporates an inverter in their PV unit. DC power is converted to 12 or 24V AC, which powers most standard irrigation. Developed at the instigation of Tucson landscape architect Mark Novak, these power units look like medium-sized transformer boxes.

DIG's LEIT (light energized irrigation technology) system uses extreme low-voltage latching solenoids. To use LEIT on an existing system, all solenoids must be replaced. A pulse of 3.5V energy operates high-efficiency valves and moisture sensors. Solar-generated power is stored within the parking-meter-sized controller, without separate storage batteries. The system will operate in light conditions equivalent to a bad winter day in Alaska. An option called LEIT-LINK allows remote-control operation of any number of controllers by FM radio, potentially saving fuel energy for site visits.

Costs of these solar systems are significant, sometimes two or three times the cost of conventional controllers. They are most cost effective for new,

Figure 4.25 Small, solar powered, and radio controlled, LEIT irrigation controllers can save electricity as well as fuel used in site visits. (*Photo:* Altec Co. [now DIG Corp.].)

rather than retrofitted, work. Depending on the site, savings may well pay for these costs. Savings are primarily from installation, operating, and maintenance costs, not from the electrical bill, but may still represent energy savings.

At one time, Solatrol advertised its solar-powered irrigation controller with a photo montage of irrigation on the moon. Theoretically, this clever image is possible now that lunar water has been discovered. It also is a reminder, however, that solar-powered irrigation makes it easy to bring irrigation to truly remote sites, where irrigation may be quite inappropriate. Used with good judgment, solar irrigation can significantly increase irrigation efficiency.

Reduce Materials Use in Irrigation Systems

Pipes, valves, and components of irrigation systems "embody" energy in their manufacture. This concept is discussed in Principle 7 and relates to other environmental impacts, such as toxic materials, introduced in Principle 6. Relative energy and material costs of irrigation is important to long-term sustainability.

Irrigation is a significant user of PVC and other plastics. PVC is a controversial material (see p. 252). Organochloride materials, of which PVC is one, are highly toxic during manufacture and disposal, and

many experts have called for phasing them out. Solvents for PVC and other plastics pose health risks for installers. Thus, irrigation designers and contractors have a stake in how these materials are used.

Materials impact can be reduced by cutting the amount of material used, and by using materials with low embodied energy and toxicity. Reusing or recycling materials also reduces overall environmental costs.

The irrigation system that uses the least *materials* is simple flooding. In old-fashioned agriculture, this was done with nothing more than soil channels cut with a hoe. Labor intensiveness, evaporative losses, and imprecise application offset savings in materials.

Although it is popular to bury them, spray irrigation, and to a lesser-extent drip systems, can be based on a single supply hose moved around the landscape. Crawler sprinklers were once the only "automated" systems, still common for home use. Large parks sometimes use movable metal irrigation pipes. These use less piping than buried systems, but involve high labor costs. Home owners do not like to move hoses constantly; moving large-scale pipes requires tractors. The Treegator system, discussed above, uses material-efficient movable bags.

Buried controller-driven systems eliminate labor and save water. They crisscross the site with pipes, however, which must connect every head to a valve. Wires must link the controller to each valve; if the valve box is distant, this uses significant materials. Material costs for subsurface drip are reportedly 10–15 percent greater than for buried sprinklers; here, costs probably reflect resource consumption. Installation, however, was reported by the same author to be 10 percent *less* for buried drip than for buried sprinkler with its more-complex assemblies of risers, pop-ups, and so on.[75]

Embodied energy of plastic pipe is about 20,000 Btu per foot, and some plastics have toxic ingredients. Copper wire ranges from 500 to 1,700 Btu per foot, depending on gauge.[76] These factors, along with monetary cost, make efficient irrigation layout important. Connecting a set of points with the fewest and shortest connectors is a classic mathematical riddle called the "random walk." New research has recently proposed computerized solutions to this puzzle.[77] These algorithms might be combined with pipe-sizing and pressure-drop software to optimize irrigation layout.

One recent development is irrigation material recycling. At least one manufacturer, Netafim, will accept bundled used tubing of any brand. Contractors and suppliers should take advantage of this program; land-owners should investigate whether they can participate or take old irrigation materials to suppliers.

Follow the Irrigation Association's BMPs

The Irrigation Association (IA) offers training as well as informative literature (much of it online). Among IA publications are extensive best management practices and practice guidelines for irrigation.[78]

The IA has been a positive force in moving the industry toward water conservation and sustainability. Although the guidelines cover other topics, the following IA recommendations relate to sustainable practice.

- Start with site analysis.
- Encourage non-potable water use.
- Make avoiding runoff a priority.
- Specify equipment by make and model to ensure compatibility.
- Design sprinklers/emitters in any zone to have the same water delivery rate.
- Ensure that line pressure matches heads and emitters.
- Field test actual system performance after installation, and periodically.
- Maintain and adjust system parts regularly.
- Provide each client with information and instructions, not just hardware.

One important concept embodied in IA guidelines is the "Drought Response Plan." Designers should plan each system so that in a drought, it can be set to distribute minimal water to high-priority plants while sacrificing low-priority ones (such as lawns, which can be replaced far faster than mature trees). Also called "Water Budget Deficit Design," this proactively minimizes the impact of almost-inevitable water shortages and restrictions.

Drought response planning goes beyond irrigation. Reducing fertilizer slows growth, reducing water needs, as does increasing mower height. Mulch and soil-health practices reduce irrigation, as can Integrated Pest Management (see p. 329). During drought, careful monitoring for stress-induced plant health problems is extra critical.

Don't Expect Miracles

The Irrigation Association's emphasis on drought planning underscores one reality: irrigation efficiency can make big differences, but is not a cure-all.

For now, smart controllers, efficient hardware, careful design, and conscientious maintenance can, as some irrigation advertising suggests, "conserve water without sacrificing landscape design." The efficiency of these systems, however, appears to be approaching a maximum. Once efficient systems become standard, irrigation technology may not be able to offset rising water demand and population growth any further. Therefore, landscape professionals have a strong stake in regional, national, and global water conservation initiatives. Without these larger solutions, even maximally efficient landscape irrigation could once again become the first use of water to be prohibited.

Reuse Graywater

Graywater means all "used" household water except from toilets. If biodegradable soaps are used, laundry wastewater may be included. (Some definitions exclude kitchen water, for fear of food particles.) Graywater systems use separate plumbing from "blackwater" sewage pipes, allowing reuse. Graywater typically amounts to 60 percent or more of household wastewater; using it "twice" offers significant savings.[79] Although some systems use graywater to flush toilets, the most common use is landscape irrigation. Graywater is the most common source for non-potable irrigation.

Concerns have been raised about health and safety of graywater, which is banned under some building codes. Australian researchers concluded, however, that there was little evidence for disease spread from graywater in ornamental landscapes.[80] Few disease organisms will survive once applied to soil. In 1992 California established a US precedent by allowing untreated graywater for landscape irrigation. Since then, many jurisdictions have followed suit. Especially for owner-occupied single residences, and where volume is small, restrictions on graywater are being lifted. Home owners can often install their own systems (as simple as fitting a hose to the washing-machine drain).

Graywater should be applied directly to soil or mulched surfaces for quick absorption; some overcautious standards require that it never "daylights," for fear that ponding, spraying, or residue on plants could expose people to pathogens. With proper filtration, surface driplines covered with mulch are the best no-daylight graywater design. Alternatively, graywater drip can be buried in the top three to six inches of soil. Deeper burial puts the water below plant roots, and below the soil organisms most effective at breaking down impurities. (For these reasons, many experts believe that the California code requirement for nine-inch burial is a mistake.[81]) As a precaution, graywater should not be used for vegetable gardens. If used with drip systems, graywater needs filtration to remove materials that clog emitters.

Home owners must be informed and willing to maintain graywater systems. Filters and tanks need periodic cleaning; gloves, eye protection, and a simple mask should be worn (decomposing materials could in theory cause health risks). The household must adapt to alternative cleaning solutions; paints, solvents and other toxic materials must be kept out of graywater. Powdered detergents high in sodium, bleach, boron, or softeners can build up in soil and must be avoided. Acid-loving plants dislike graywater, often alkaline from soaps, according to Sacramento's *Water Conservation News.* Thus, graywater may be of limited value if site soils are already alkaline.

An even greater water savings is possible by eliminating water-flushed toilets entirely. By substituting a composting toilet, *all* wastewater is graywater. Especially in arid climates, this may be a more sustainable solution than using water to flush, then building a constructed wetland to purify the water. These options must, as always, be evaluated using site- and user-specific criteria.

Purify Water at Every Opportunity

Conventional thinking has centralized water-purification processes in large facilities relying heavily on chemical processes. Conventional treatment tends toward a one-size-fits-all approach: contaminated water in, drinking water out. The dark side of conventional centralized treatment is that it makes water quality "someone else's problem," almost encouraging local abuses of rivers and lakes on the assumption that water dirtied *here* can be fixed *over there.*

Several alternatives exist. Although large-scale treatment for drinking water is likely to continue (and even increase, with desalinization plants), near-source approaches should be part of the toolkit. A number of these are within the landscape realm.

Bioswales and small-scale stormwater filtration for use with paving are discussed on p. 208. The following sections note several other water-cleansing methods for harvested rainwater, swimming pools, and piped stormwater retrofits, and constructed wetlands for stormwater and industrial wastewater.

Purify Collected Water for Drinking and Swimming

Collected water may need to be purified, although for landscape use this may be unnecessary and even wasteful. Water is purified by physical filtration, ultraviolet (UV) light, or chemicals. For sustainability, chemicals should be a last resort; for irrigation, chemicals are harmful to soils and plants.

Physical filtration ranges from simple screen or sand filters to high-tech ceramic filters. Ceramic filters are commonly sold for camping (see Real Goods, p. 196) and can remove bacteria and viruses sized less than one micron. Similar systems can be installed at the faucet. For drinking/cooking water, filter-as-used may make more sense than treatment in storage. Filters require periodic cleaning or replacement or both.

For drinking-water systems, "roof washers" or "first-flush" diverters reroute the first few gallons of stormwater, which carry dust and contaminants, before allowing water into storage. There are many designs; some can be adapted to pavement-based water collection.

Solar power is a trusted technology for purifying water supplies in the Third World, and at some US campgrounds. Photovoltaic power can run standard ultraviolet purification systems; these require significant energy—80 kWh per year or more.[82] Filter the water first, to remove particles that hide microorganisms from UV light. With carefully designed storage, perhaps in dual tanks, water can be pumped and purified during the day, eliminating the need for storage batteries.

A related application is a floating swimming-pool purification system manufactured by Floatron. This unit ionizes water in which it floats, eliminating chlorination. A 12-inch unit can treat 50,000 gallons continuously. Another swimming-pool purification option is the "natural swimming pool," of which there are many thousand in Europe, both private and public. Such pools are ponds designed with open water at their centers for swimming, and constructed wetlands (see below) around their edges that continually purify the water.

Test Modern Hardware for Cleaner Piped Stormwater

Pave-and-pipe stormwater "control" contributes to pollution and is not a recommended practice. Piped systems, however, remain an article of faith among engineers, and many cities, large institutions, and even national parks have legacy systems of stormwater pipes.

Over the past decade, engineering ingenuity has been applied to making stormwater cleaner in the pipe. The engineering solutions, predictably, are mechanical and chemical. As such, they are frequently more costly to install and maintain than the many vegetative and wetland methods described in this book, and appear to fall short of drinking-water-standard output that wetlands achieve.

Nonetheless, faced with existing piped systems or where no other solution is workable or permitted, some of these relatively new devices are worth considering.

Mechanical water-cleaning systems replace or can be inserted into older catch basins or stormwater system components. In general, they are called "storm-water separation or filtration devices." Using inflow and outflow pipes at different levels, filters, baffles, and vortex flows created by the shape of the device, such in-pipe systems are widely available. According to manufacturers' claims, they remove oils, fats, suspended solids, nutrients (fertilizers, etc.), metals, and other pollutants. Effectiveness, again according to manufacturers, ranges from 80 percent upward. Even in stormwater trade journals, however, there is debate among engineers as to which devices work best, or even at all.

Chemical treatments for stormwater are also available. Like mechanical systems, these have costs and consequences not found with vegetative and soil filtration.

Related systems for improved septic-tank performance are also available, for example the Pirana and SludgeHammer systems. ⊃ These may be relevant to constructed wetlands for sewage treatment (below), most of which rely on septic tanks to remove solids.

Landscape professionals concerned with sustainability should be aware of these engineered water-cleansing systems for two reasons. One is as a last resort, where lack of space or budget, regulatory insistence, or heavy-duty pollutants truly require such systems. The second reason to know these systems is to challenge their use on projects where sustainable solutions are more appropriate. A good source of information on these products, as well as for consultant help, is the trade magazine *Stormwater.* ⊃

Let Constructed Wetlands Treat Water

Constructed wetlands are beautiful water gardens with a new ecological twist: they transform sewage effluent into growing medium for plants—and the plants, in turn, filter the effluent, turning it into water fit for swimming and fishing. Natural wetlands have provided similar services to humans since prehistory, yet people still find the concept novel—half treatment mechanism, half nature center. In fact, constructed wetlands form a bridge between two main issues of this chapter: sparing use of water supply, and restoration of water bodies.

As Alex Wilson, editor of EBN, notes, "Constructed wetlands can become valuable assets to the

Figure 4.26 Treatment wetlands in raised beds are the focal point of gardens at the Albuquerque home of green architect Paul Lusk. (*Project:* Paul Lusk. *Photo:* Kim Sorvig.)

landscape around buildings, especially if we call them 'flower beds.' It is quite conceivable that within a few years it will be landscape professionals who deal with wastewater treatment, not sanitary engineers."[83]

Constructed wetlands are more widespread than many people realize. When the subject comes up, the famous Arcata CA wetland is typically the only one mentioned; there are, however, probably over one thousand functioning constructed wetlands in the United States, with more under construction each year.[84] The EPA actively promotes their spread as an alternative to conventional sewage and stormwater treatment.

Constructed wetlands are fairly straightforward, although various configurations exist. Modern wetlands for sewage/stormwater treatment originated in Germany in the 1960s, introduced to the United States in the 1980s. Constructed wetlands are shallow ponds, often divided into "cells." Wastewater flows over gravel substrate supporting vegetation.

Plant roots, and the many microorganisms that live in the root zone, actively filter and absorb pollutants. Mechanical equipment (other than a pump) is not involved.

Some waste treatment terminology: *primary* treatment removes solids, *secondary* treatment removes most remaining pathogens, and *tertiary* treatment "polishes" the effluent. "Tertiary treated effluent" is water clean enough to swim in, irrigate with, or discharge into lakes or streams, often exceeding standards for municipal drinking water. Wetlands can provide all three stages of treatment, but most of today's constructed wetlands in the United States are tertiary only. A fair number provide secondary treatment, and a primary-treatment wetland on the border between California and Baja California was proposed by students of visionary landscape architect John Lyle.[85] Solids are removed before reaching any wetland by a pretreatment unit (often an ordinary septic tank). For larger systems, mechanical primary systems are used, like those found in conventional sewage-treatment plants.

There are two design options for constructed wetlands: (1) "subsurface flow," in which water flows *beneath* gravel through which emergent wetland plants grow, and (2) "surface flow," in which water is visible among the plants, closely resembling a natural wetland. Subsurface-flow wetlands are often recommended for applications near housing or office buildings. Water is never at the surface, and some designers take this to mean less risk of mosquito breeding, odor, or human contact with effluent. Wetlands

Figure 4.27 The "business end" of any treatment wetland is the root zone and the billions of microorganisms that live in its complex geometry. (*Project:* City of Albuquerque and MFG. *Photo:* Michael D. Marcus.)

Figure 4.28 Increasing clarity is visible in water from Arcata CA's constructed wetlands, sampled at progressive stages of wastewater treatment. From left: inflow to system; outflows from oxidation pond, treatment marsh, and enhancement marsh. (*Photo:* Professor Joe Meyer, University of Wyoming.)

expert Donald Hammer, however, states that hiding the effluent under gravel is less reliable than surface-flow designs. As he puts it, "The latest designs ... are quite simply [returning to the initial concept] that patterned constructed wetlands after natural wetlands. [These] have proven to be the least costly to build, have higher removal efficiencies for a wider variety of pollutants, [and] are less costly and complex to operate."[86] Surface flow also provides greater wildlife habitat and is more feasible in poorer communities with most to gain from simple waste treatment. As far as the authors can determine, both designs are legitimate alternatives and should be compared for site-specific advantages.

A typical subsurface system is one to three feet deep, with impervious (plastic or concrete) bottom and sides, filled with gravel and planted with wetland species. With the wastewater out of sight below gravel, small-scale subsurface-treatment wetlands are easily integrated into housing, park, and office landscapes. One prototypical subsurface wetland, at Indian Creek Nature Center in Cedar Rapids IA, lives up to Alex Wilson's image as a "flower bed." Designed by North American Wetland Engineering in Forest Lake MN, it treats all sewage from the visitor center. The wetland has become locally popular for its show of aquatic plants and wildflowers. It is clearly not an objectionable feature—the deck overlooking the wetland is a favorite place to hold weddings.[87]

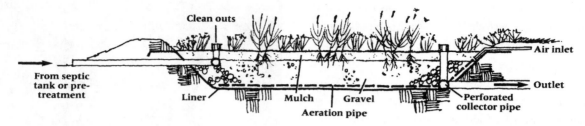

Clean outs

Air inlet

From septic tank or pretreatment

Outlet

Liner   **Mulch**   **Gravel**   **Perforated collector pipe**

Aeration pipe

Figure 4.29   Constructed wetland (subsurface type; surface-flow type would have water at surface instead of mulch). Treatment wetlands discharge to infiltration basins, irrigation systems, leach fields, surface water, or tanks. (*Illust.:* Craig Farnsworth, based on NAWE [North American Wetland Engineering].)

Despite some people's reluctance to do so, surface-flow constructed wetlands can also be installed quite close to buildings—for example, at the Crosby Arboretum. A small pond system provides *secondary and tertiary* treatment for the site's two public restrooms. It was designed by Mississippi-based scientist Bill Wolverton, a pioneer in natural sewage treatment. When the director of the arboretum, landscape architect Ed Blake, saw Wolverton's design concept—a standard engineer's rectangle—he asked, "Can we loosen this up a bit?" With Wolverton's consent Blake reconfigured the treatment pond as a naturalistic river meander. The resulting pond fits seamlessly into the arboretum landscape, an amenity in full view of all visitors—who learn from interpretive guides that it treats on-site sewage.

Constructed wetlands can fulfill many functions in addition to water purification. Two wetlands built several years apart by the town of Gilbert AZ (a suburb of Phoenix) make an excellent case study of the *process* of multi-function design. The wetlands are fine examples of their type, but more importantly, variations in public perception and team approach between the two projects are a valuable lesson.

Comparing these two projects is easier because the same firm worked on both, in different capacities—the multidisciplinary Sacramento CA firm of Jones & Stokes. Landscape architects Joe Donaldson and Sheri Brown were involved in habitat restoration and interpretive exhibit design for both projects. Donaldson in particular speaks of wetlands experience reinvigorating professional practice.

In the early 1990s, Gilbert's wastewater reclamation complex built the Cooper Road Recharge Ponds, a series of shallow ponds designed for the single engineering purpose of recharging groundwater. After

Figure 4.30   Indian Creek Nature Center (Cedar Rapids IA) illustrates Alex Wilson's vision of constructed wetlands doubling as flowerbeds. (*Project and Photo:* NAWE.)

the boxy, functional ponds were already laid out, the town saw an opportunity to create urban habitat for birds, bats, and other fauna, and was able to get funding from the state game-and-fish department. Jones & Stokes was hired to enhance the ponds' habitat value. Donaldson planted riparian and marsh plants around the banks and upland species on levees, with assistance from desert-plants purveyor Wild Seed and community volunteers. Although not able to alter the basic pond layout, Donaldson and Brown constructed nesting boxes, and added interpretive exhibits and a ramada (shade structure) for visitors. Despite their initial functionalist layout, the Cooper Road Ponds garnered a Governor's Pride award for environmental leadership, as well as the Arizona Planning Association's 1994 Best Project Award.

Perhaps more important for the continuing story, habitat and interpretation won the approval of Gilbert residents. When the opportunity arose for another recharge facility in a 130-acre park, the town again turned to Jones & Stokes, with one important difference: this time landscape and restoration specialists managed the multidisciplinary team from the start. Engineers, as well as local landscape architect Carol F. Shuler, became part of the team.

The result of public support and consistent planning is clear. Named the Riparian Reserve, the park is a highly visible feature, beside the public library where two main bike paths intersect. Permanent marshes, wildlife islands, roosting structures, and varied wetland and upland planting are managed as an urban wildlife sanctuary. At nearly seventy acres, the recharge ponds restore significant lost habitat. Xeriscape design and botanic-garden exhibits of rare Sonoran plant communities make this an educational as well as recreational center. The public had been convinced: multifunction wetlands have much greater value than single-function ponds.

One issue raised by the Gilbert ponds is that of access. Interestingly enough, there is no consistent standard for access around wastewater ponds. Some facilities allow visitor access to *secondary* treatment ponds. The much better treated Cooper Road ponds are fenced. At the Riparian Reserve, the town weighed benefits of education and recreation against risks of liability. Because this facility infiltrates tertiary-treated

Figure 4.31 Cooper Road Ponds treat wastewater, support waterfowl, and attract birdwatchers. The square ponds were already excavated when landscape architects were called in. (*Project:* Jones and Stokes. *Photo:* Joe Donaldson, ASLA.)

water, they decided in favor of public access. Similarly careful planning could open many more wetlands to amenity use.

Consider Wetlands for Industrial Wastewater

Nature's filters can purify some of humanity's least "natural" water wastes, from mining and manufacturing. Wetlands absorb phosphates, nitrates, and other toxins through phytoremediation (p. 103). There is a growing literature on industrial treatment wetlands, and an increasing number have been built near factories and mines.

One highly visible treatment wetland is the award-winning Living Water Garden, covering six acres along the banks of the Fu-Nan River in Chengdu, western China. This elegant example of environmental education is the core of an urban park, growing out of a larger water-quality improvement project. The garden draws 200 cubic meters of water from the Fu-Nan each day, removes bacterial pollutants and heavy metals, and returns the water to the river. This is not meant to have an appreciable impact on a river the size of the Fu-Nan; major improvements can be achieved only by reducing pollutant emissions. People go to Living Water Garden for relief from an intense urban setting, and the park seduces them into learning about natural water purification. The impact of Living Water Garden lies in its effects on the

Figure 4.32 Coordinated by landscape architects from the start, Gilbert AZ's Riparian Reserve will go beyond its Cooper Road predecessor to create a full-fledged public park. (*Project:* Jones and Stokes. *Photo:* Joe Donaldson, ASLA.)

thinking of the people of Chengdu: increased awareness of environmental issues and pride in progress the city has made toward resuscitating the river.[88]

The principle of respecting water comes full circle, like the hydrological cycle itself. When water is wasted, shoved aside as a problem, or contaminated, humans and the environment both suffer. When humans work thoughtfully with water, even contaminated water, it repays them in health, in livable surroundings, and in recreation and learning.

Resources

Respect the Waters of Life

Wetlands

Search Terms: wetlands || freshwater wetlands || saltwater wetlands || wetland ecology

Management of Lakes and Ponds George William Bennett, 1985 Krieger Publishing Company, Melbourne FL

Shoreline Protection Study: A Report to the Wisconsin State Legislature 1996 Wisconsin Department of Natural Resources, Madison WI, 608-266-2621, www.dnr.state.wi.us/

Enhancement of Ecologic and Aesthetic Values of Wetlands Associated with Interstate Highways Carl A. Carlozzi and Kenneth L. Bergstrom, 1971 University of Massachusetts Water Resources Research Center, Amherst: www.umass.edu/tei/wrrc/, 413-545-2842: Old, but specific to wetlands and highways.

The Future of Wetlands: Assessing Visual-cultural Values Richard C. Smardon, 1983 Allanheld Osmun, Totowa NJ

Wetlands International +31 (0)317 478854, www.wetlands.org/: Global organization (NGO) dedicated to wetland conservation.

National Wetlands Inventory www.fws.gov/nwi/: US Fish and Wildlife Service page with national wetlands data, maps, and publications.

National Wetlands Research Center www.nwrc.usgs.gov/: US Geological Survey wetlands page including general info, maps, data, and the NWRC library.

Natural Swimming Pools: Inspiration for Harmony with Nature M. Littlewood, 2005 Schiffer Design Books, Atglen PA, www.schifferbooks.com: Heavily illustrated overview of wetland-pool concept; short on specifics.

Expanding Horizons www.expandinghorizons.biz/: Natural swimming pools.

Total Habitat www.totalhabitat.com/: Natural swimming pools; downloadable technical manual.

US EPA constructed wetlands site www.epa.gov/owow/ wetlands/watersheds/cwetlands.html: Many good links.

Constructed Treatment Wetland System Performance Database http://firehole.humboldt.edu/wetland/twdb.html: Joint project of Humboldt University and US EPA.

Wetlands restoration

Search Terms: wetland restoration || wetland mitigation || wetland protection

Marsh Master II amphibious work vehicle Coast Machinery, 604-556-2225: 1,500-lb. load with 1-psi ground pressure.

Wetland Planting Guide for the Northeastern United States: Plants for Wetland Creation, Restoration, and Enhancement Gwendolyn A. Thunhorst and Dawn Biggs, 1993 Environmental Concern, St. Michaels MD

Creating Freshwater Wetlands Donald A. Hammer, 1997, 2nd ed., Lewis Publishers, Boca Raton FL (CRC Press), 800-272-7737

Lakes and Ponds J. T. Tourbier and R. Westmacott, 1992, 2nd ed., Urban Land Institute, Baltimore

Mitigation Banking: Theory and Practice L. Marsh, D. Porter, and D. Salvesen, 1996 Island Press, Washington DC

Riparian/Wetland Research Expertise Directory (SW USA) Barbara Tellman, 1995 University of Arizona, Tucson, and Roy Jennison, US Forest Service, Fort Collins CO

Statewide Wetlands Strategies: A Guide to Protecting and Managing the Resource 1992 Island Press, Washington DC

An International Perspective on Wetland Rehabilitation B. Streever, 1999 Kluwer Academic Publishers, Boston

Wetlands Wm. J. Mitsch and James G. Gosselink, 1986 Van Nostrand Reinhold, New York

Wetlands: Mitigating and Regulating Development Impacts D. Salvesen, 1994, 2nd ed., Urban Land Institute, Baltimore

Wetlands Restoration Links by State and Local Governments www.epa.gov/owow/wetlands/restore/links/: Lists agencies involved in wetlands restoration nationwide.

Wetland Drainage, Restoration, and Repair T. R. Biebighauser, 2007 University Press of Kentucky, Lexington

Handbook for Restoring Tidal Wetlands J. B. Zedler, 2001 CRC Press, Boca Raton FL

The Do's and Don'ts of Wetland Construction, Creation, Restoration, and Enhancement E. W. Garbisch, 2002 Environmental Concern, St. Michael's MD

Construction in wetlands

Pin Foundations Inc. Gig Harbor WA, 253-858-8809, www .pinfoundations.com/: Nonintrusive foundations.

Bigfoot Systems 800-934-0393, www.bigfootsystems.com/: Footings for concrete tube pilings.

Stream restoration

Wildland Hydrology Fort Collins CO, 970-568-0002, www .wildlandhydrology.com/: Courses and publications, consulting.

Applied River Morphology Dave Rosgen, 1996 Wildland Hydrology, www.wildlandhydrology.com, 970-568-0002

Nine Mile Run Briefing Book (draft) Rocky Mountain Institute and Studio for Creative Inquiry, 1998: Unpublished; may be available from RMI, www.rmi.org, 970-927-3851; or SCI, www.cmu.edu/studio/, 412-268-3454.

Restoring Streams in Cities Ann Riley, 1998 Island Press, Washington DC

"Streambank and Shoreline Protection" chapter 16 in *Engineering Field Handbook*, 1996 Natural Resources Conservation Service, Washington DC, 202-720-9155

Water Bioengineering Techniques for Watercourse, Bank and Shoreline Protection H. M. Schiechtl and R. Stern, 1997 Blackwell Science, Malden MA

Bioengineering for Stream-bank Stabilization Rutgers University Continuing Professional Educational, New Brunswick NJ, 732-932-3000 x512: Three-day, hands-on course.

Stormwater

Search Terms: stormwater || stormwater management ||runoff ||erosion sedimentation || hydrology

The Center for Water and Watershed Studies University of Washington, Seattle WA, 206-543-6920, http://depts .washington.edu/cwws/

Center for Watershed Protection Ellicott City MD, 410-461-8323, www.cwp.org/: BMPs for stormwater control, watershed-based zoning, vegetative stream buffers, and permeable parking.

Watersheds: A Practical Handbook for Healthy Water G. G. Beck and C. Dobson, 1999 Firefly Books, Willowdale ON

Permaculture Institute of Southern California Bill Roley, Laguna Beach CA, 949-494-5843, DrRoley@aol.com

Water Resources Protection Technology Joachim Toby Tourbier, 1981 Urban Land Institute, Baltimore

Introduction to Stormwater Bruce K. Ferguson, 1998 Wiley, New York

Land Development Provisions to Protect Georgia Water Quality David Nichols et al., 1997 University of Georgia School of Environmental Design and Georgia Department of Natural Resources: Available as a PDF at www.uga.edu/sed/

publications/other/ga_developement_water_quality_study
.pdf: Good sample guidelines, translatable to most regions.

Model Development Principles to Protect Our Streams, Lakes, and Wetlands Tom Schueler, 1998 Center for Watershed Protection, Ellicott City MD, www.cwp.org/

Site Planning for Urban Stream Protection Tom Schueler, 1995 Center for Watershed Protection, Ellicott City MD

Start at the Source Tom Richman, 1999 Bay Area Stormwater Management Agencies Association, Oakland CA, 510-622-2326, www.basmaa.org/ or www.scvurppp-w2k.com/basmaa_satsm.htm

Stormwater Infiltration Bruce K. Ferguson, 1994 Lewis Publishers, Boca Raton FL (CRC Press), 800-272-7737

Stormwater Strategies: Community Responses to Runoff Pollution P. Lehner, G. Clarke, D. Cameron, and A. G. Frank, Natural Resources Defense Council, New York, www.nrdc.org/: Case studies.

Urban Watershed Protection Reference Guide bibliography 1996 Center for Watershed Protection, Ellicott City MD, www.cwp.org/

Watershed Protection Techniques Center for Watershed Protection, www.cwp.org/: Quarterly; case studies, methods illustrated; summer 1995 issue on urban stream restoration features an extensive annotated bibliography.

"The Failure of Detention and the Future of Stormwater Design" Bruce K. Ferguson, Dec 1991, LAM: Documents necessity of regionally coordinated infiltration.

Watershed Academy www.epa.gov/owow/watershed/wacademy/its.html: Publications and courses on watershed management.

Scientific Software Group 866-620-9214, www.scisoftware.com/: Stormwater management and design software.

Stormwater **magazine** www.stormh2o.com/: Information, ads, contacts: engineering aspects of stormwater management.

Water harvesting, storage, and purification

Search Terms: water harvesting || water storage || water purification || rain barrel || ponds

Real Goods 800-762-7325, www.gaiam.com/realgoods/: Products and information.

The Home Water Supply: How to Find, Filter, Store, and Conserve It Stu Campbell, 1983 Storey Communications/Garden Way, Pownal VT: Pragmatic and thorough guide to water supply, from geological sources to cisterns, pumps, and purification; relatively conventional "homesteader" attitudes, some not very green.

Planning, design, and management

Water in the Garden : Design and Installation of Ponds, Fountains, Streams, and Waterfalls James Allison, 1991 Little, Brown, New York: Conventional water features; many are adaptable to sustainability goals.

Elements and Total Concept of Urban Waterscape Design Henshubu, 1990 Grafiksha, Tokyo

Waterstained Landscapes: Seeing and Shaping Regionally Distinctive Place Joan Woodward, 2000 Johns Hopkins University Press, Baltimore.

Graywater

Search Terms: greywater OR graywater (or as two words or hyphenated)

Building Professional's Greywater Guide Art Ludwig, 1995 Oasis Design, Santa Barbara CA, www.oasisdesign.net/: Detailed decision-making criteria, pro and con; conceptual system layouts; analysis of detergents for compatibility.

Graywater Use in the Landscape Robert Kourik, 1991 Metamorphic Press, Santa Rosa CA, www.metamorphic.com/press.htm

Xeriscape, Permaculture, and related strategies

Consumptive Water Use by Landscape Plants: A Brief Sourcelist for Landscape Architects Anthony G. White, 1980 Vance Bibliographies, Monticello IL pub. # A319

Drought-tolerant Plants: Waterwise Gardening for Every Climate Jane Taylor, 1993 Prentice Hall, New York

Southwestern Landscaping That Saves Energy and Water E. Gregory McPherson and Charles M. Sacamano, 1989 University of Arizona Cooperative Extension, Tucson pub #8929

Taylor's Guide to Water-saving Gardening 1990 Houghton Mifflin, New York

Water Conservation in Landscape Design and Management Gary O. Robinette, 1984 Van Nostrand Reinhold, New York

Water-conserving Gardens and Landscapes John M. O'Keefe, 1992 Storey Communications/Garden Way, Pownal VT: Includes plant selection list, drip irrigation guide, region/zone maps.

Water-efficient Landscape Guidelines Richard E. Bennett and Michael S. Hazinski, 1993 American Waterworks Association, Denver CO, 800-926-7337, www.awwa.org/waterwiser/

Waterwise Gardening Kathryn Stechert Black, 1989 Sunset Books, Menlo Park CA

Water-wise Gardening Peter Robinson, 1999 American Hort. Society guides; DK Publishers, New York

Water-wise Gardening : America's Backyard Revolution Thomas Christopher, 1994 Simon and Schuster, New York

Xeriscape, Water-conserving Gardens Carol Kopolow, 1994 National Agricultural Library, Beltsville MD

Indigenous Permaculture Center, Traditional Native American Farmers Association Tesuque NM, 505-983-2172

Permaculture Drylands Institute Santa Fe NM, 505-983-0663, www.permaculture.org/

Irrigation

The Irrigation Assn. Falls Church VA 703-536-7080, www.irrigation.org/: Standards, referrals, product search engine, forum for posting questions.

American Society of Irrigation Consultants (ASIC) Rochester MA, 508-763-8140, www.asic.org/

Water Wiser Clearinghouse American Waterworks Association, Denver CO, 800-926-7337, www.awwa.org/waterwiser/

Drip Irrigation for Every Landscape and All Climates: Helping Your Garden Flourish, While Conserving Water! Robert Kourik, 1992 Metamorphic Press, Santa Rosa CA, www.metamorphic.com/press.htm

Office of Water Use Efficiency Irrigation Page California Department of Water Resources, www.owue.water.ca.gov/landscape/faq/faq.cfm: Answers to common irrigation questions.

The Complete Irrigation Workbook: Design, Installation, Maintenance, and Water Management Larry Keesen and Cindy Code, 1995 Franzak and Foster, Cleveland OH

Irrigation Business and Technology The Irrigation Association, Falls Church VA, 703-536-7080, www.irrigation.org/: An irrigation trade magazine that "tries to be proactive" about environmental issues.

CIMIS (California Irrigation Management Information System) California Department of Water Resources and the University of California at Davis, 530-756-0778, www .ceresgroup.com/: ET statistics for California by county.

US Water News www.uswaternews.com/

Landscape Irrigation Science Program California State Polytechnic University, Pomona, 888-2DAYS AG, www.csupomona .edu/~lis/aboutprog.html: First US accredited program.

Office of Water Use Efficiency California Department of Water Resources, www.owue.water.ca.gov/landscape/faq/faq.cfm: Useful site for common irrigation questions.

Netafim 888-638-2346, www.netafim.com/: Recycling of used and scrap irrigation tubing (any brand).

Irrigation controllers and sensors

Irrigation controllers and sensors Weathermatic, Garland TX, www.weathermatic.com/; Tucor, Wexford PA, www.tucor.com/: Two companies offering advanced sensors and controllers.

Irrometer Co. 950-689-1701, www.irrometer.com/: Watermark soil moisture module

WeatherMiser Multisensor Terragreen Irrigation, 877-948-3772, http://weathermiser.com/

Solar controllers for irrigation Photocomm, 602-948-8003; Toro Company, 619-562-2950

LEIT (DIG Corporation) 800-322-9146, http://digcorp.com/: Bought Altec, formerly Solatrol; markets LEIT compact solar irrigation controllers.

Constructed wetlands

Search Terms: wetland construction || constructed wetlands || treatment wetlands || biological water treatment

Waste as a Resource in Regenerative Design for Sustainable Development John Lyle, 1994 Wiley, New York: Good introduction.

Constructed Wetlands for Wastewater Treatment Donald A. Hammer, 1989 Lewis Publishers, Boca Raton FL (CRC Press), 800-272-7737: In-depth look at wetlands technology.

Constructed Wetlands for Wastewater Treatment and Wildlife Habitat 1993 US EPA, Washington DC (EPA832-R-93-005): Full text at www.epa.gov/owow/wetlands/construc/: Seventeen case studies; well-illustrated introduction to US systems.

Constructed Wetlands for Water Quality Improvement Gerald A. Moshiri, 1993 Lewis Publishers, Boca Raton FL (CRC Press), 800-272-7737

Constructed Wetlands in the Sustainable Landscape Craig Campbell and Michael Ogden, 1999 Wiley, New York: Authors are principals of Southwest Wetlands and pioneered wetlands in desert United States.

EPA wetland site US EPA, www.epa.gov/owow/wetlands/: Overview of wetland science and policy and links for restoration.

Pirana ABG Inc. 800-426-3349, www.piranaabg.com/: Makers of aerobic bacterial generators and mechanical agitators for septic tanks.

Principle 5:
Pave Less

Little by little, roads eat away at the hearts of mountains.
—Gary Lawless, *First Sight of Land*, 1990

The United States paves more area each year than the Roman Empire did in its entire existence. In the 1990s the average was about 30,000 linear miles per year. The US Department of Transportation counts a total of 8,295,171 "lane miles" of public highway, as of 2002.[1] Assuming an average 12-foot lane width, plus 4 feet for shoulder and other auxiliary areas, one lane-mile equals 84,480 square feet, or nearly two acres. The total—16.1 million acres—is more than enough paved area to cover Massachusetts, Connecticut, Rhode Island, New Jersey, and Delaware. Add to this an estimated 4.7 million acres (1,921,582 hectares) devoted to parking in the United States.[2] It is easy to see that paving is an environmental issue of colossal proportions.[3] The US road network is "perhaps the biggest object ever built."[4]

Widespread paving is a very recent phenomenon. Even a century ago, the normal condition of city streets was a muddy morass (recall, for example, Sherlock Holmes's deductions from clay on urban trouser cuffs); many rural roads were still "paved" with logs. All that changed in the mid-1800s, when "macadam" (compacted stone bound with asphalt) was introduced by a Scottish contemporary of the fictional detective. The past hundred years have seen paving cover unprecedented areas. By the early 1970s paving was referred to as "the nations' biggest publicly endowed business."[5]

For all its popularity and functionality, paving has been implicated in a wide range of ecological problems. Most paving materials create surface stability by excluding water from the soil, causing serious difficulties. Soil absorbs rainfall and nurtures flora,

fauna, and humans, but impervious surfaces increase runoff, causing erosion and flooding, depleting soil water, and contributing to siltation and water pollution; any and all of the above contribute to drought and vegetation loss. Modern construction has created such vast nonporous areas that many communities are being forced to limit creation of new impervious surfaces.

Parking lots, for example, constitute an ever-increasing blight on the American landscape. As metropolitan areas sprawl away from transit-friendly cores, surface parking becomes the urban fabric's common denominator. From the air, parking is *the most visible feature* of many communities. This hardening of the American landscape shrinks the biologically productive surface of the Earth, replacing cornfields, meadows, forest, or desert. Moreover, "paving the planet" (as it has been called) consumes nonrenewable resources both in building the lots and in fuel to truck materials to the site. Asphalt, the material for most parking lots, is a complex mix of hydrocarbons, mixing and application of which is a air-polluting act in itself. Asphalt has been shown to have adverse health effects on workers exposed to its fumes.[6]

Parking lots can directly affect microclimates and overall city climates. Since the automobile conquered America, summer temperatures in urban areas have risen two to eight degrees Fahrenheit hotter than surrounding rural areas.[7] Surface parking is the prime land use in most American cities, making parking a major factor, if not *the* main factor, in this "heat-island" effect—not to mention spiraling land costs.

Low-speed roads—suburban residential streets, in particular—are often wider and more impervious than necessary. Thirty-six feet or more is a typical width, making streets the largest single impervious surface in the subdivision. The total width of the average residential street has increased by 50 percent since World War II.[8] Blanket application of standards for high-speed, high-volume highways to low-speed, low-volume streets has created unwanted pavement in thousands of urban neighborhoods and rural byways. Overbuilding of roads has serious sustainability (and safety) implications and has even been challenged by several national *engineering* organizations.

The most egregious impacts of over-paving have to do with stormwater.[9] Conventional parking lots, for example, seal off enormous areas of soil, preventing rainwater from soaking in and replenishing crucial groundwater resources. Concentrating rainfall, paving and subsurface drainage systems send erosive torrents of runoff into local streams. Erosion, sedimentation, extremes of flooding and drought, and habitat loss are among the results—a central problem for sustainable landscapes, and repeated, of necessity, throughout this book.

There are many practical, well-tested alternatives to over-paving. Many have been known for almost as long as the automobile—yet are ignored in conventional design predicated on ever-increasing road speed, volume, and "convenience." Highway and parking engineers cater to such social demands, which today are changing. Interestingly, much of the most positive change is "top down": from the Federal Highway Administration to the Institute of Transportation Engineers, official research and design standards are focusing on the benefits of better integration of roads with community, ecosystem, and scenery.

Since our first edition, "context-sensitive" roadways and traffic calming have been officially accepted by many transportation authorities; what was once an all-cars-all-the-time attitude has broadened. A few states have been slow to catch up; county and local public-works departments harbor more than their share of dinosaurs. Individual engineers remain resistant, fearful that they might be liable for not following set-in-stone standards, despite (literally) an act of Congress that says otherwise.[10] Today over-paving remains one area of landscape design and construction where the *main* culprit is outdated,

unthinking habit—stoutly defended by industries with vested interests, and by a society still addicted to cars.

Discussed in This Chapter

Planning and policy strategies to reduce paving requirements.

Design options to decrease paving area and its site impact.

Techniques for infiltrating more of the runoff from pavement.

Infiltration to reduce pollution potential of pavement runoff.

Porous and partially porous paving materials.

When it's most appropriate *not* to pave.

Reducing the heat-sink effect of paved areas.

Plan and Design to Reduce Paving

Although this chapter will focus on building parking lots and streets with fewer environmental impacts, the crying need in North America is to *reduce the total area of paving*. This constitutes an enormous challenge to planners, designers, and policy makers for the simple reason that parking is generally regarded as a universal good. American cities are built around auto use, with destinations so spread out that walking from home to the grocery store is no longer possible.

Where driving is the only option, congestion soon follows. In major US metro areas, a given trip takes 30–50 percent longer during peak hours; the average commuter spends 54 hours annually waiting in standstill traffic (that's $1\frac{1}{4}$ work weeks); and idling in traffic jams wastes 60 to 120 gallons of gas per driver per year.[11]

Many urbanists are reviving pre–World War II patterns of development—walkable communities effectively served by mass transit.[12] This goes against many national habits, but is successfully promoted by Walkable Communities, the Congress of New Urbanism, and others, a movement sometimes called Neo-Traditionalism. Aiming for livability rather than accepting suburban sprawl or urban jam, these models treat streets as public spaces primarily for *people*, shared with cars where needed.

Urban growth boundaries (UGBs) are a related planning strategy to rein in sprawl, encourage infill, and increase urban density, thus reducing need for paving. A well-known (if sometimes controversial) US example is Portland OR. In 1976 politicians and planners took the unprecedented step of drawing such a boundary around Portland and prohibiting expansion beyond it. The UGB has not completely abolished sprawl—housing prices have risen, and Portland still has strip malls and cookie-cutter subdivisions. Such development, however, is all within three to eighteen miles of Portland's compact, walkable downtown, on which an exemplary light-rail system converges.

Walkable-density ideals have received a real boost, where paving is concerned, from skyrocketing materials costs. Between 2000 and 2005, the cost of asphalt paving rose 37 percent according to the US Bureau of Labor.[13] This has promoted "pavement preservation" (preventive maintenance) and recycling of roadway materials and made governments more cautious (slightly) in undertaking new paving. Unfortunately, it is still true, as the Foundation for Pavement Preservation notes in a 2001 Federal Highway Administration report, "There has always been more management interest (and Federal funding) for building new roads than maintaining existing ones."[14] Even if vast paving operations were sustainable, building them and then *not* maintaining them is clearly not.

A tradeoff exists between compactness and green open space: Densely compact communities are walkable, with fewer miles of street per person; overall, the ratio of impervious to planted areas is high. Communities with high proportions of green open space have decreased stormwater problems but are less dense, requiring more miles of traffic infrastructure and more trips per person. One solution is "skinny streets and green communities," the title of a useful book on these planning choices.⊃

Several specific policies are valuable for avoiding unnecessary paving and decreasing negative effects of existing pavement.[15] These include:

- Density Zoning: local policy based on number of units per acre (or percentage of acreage devoted to structures) works better than minimum lot sizes, allowing flexible adaptation to site topography.
- Cluster Development: several buildings centered in open space, rather than each in the center of its separate lot, can greatly reduce infrastructure costs, including paving.
- Combined Land Uses: zoning that allows residences, shops, and workplaces to coexist makes walking, biking, or public transit realistic; often forbidden by existing zoning laws.
- Impervious Surface (IS) limits: cap the percentage of site area that can be impervious (both paved and roofed areas, existing and new); at 10 percent IS or less, streams and other hydrological features of the area can be considered protected; above 10 percent, impacts will require mitigation, and at 30 percent IS, ecosystem degradation is almost inevitable. In urban areas already far over this threshold, incentives for reducing impervious cover can be effective.
- Street-width limits: set a maximum, reversing laws that require minimum widths. Besides reducing total paving, narrower lanes give Context-Sensitive Design and traffic-calming benefits (below).
- Planted islands: paving traffic islands is no use to drivers; replaced with permeable, planted surfaces as a matter of policy.
- Isolate pollutant-collecting pavement: separating runoff from gas stations, car washes, dumpster pads, and other pollutant "point sources" keeps stormwater on ordinary streets much cleaner.
- Label storm drain inlets: knowledge of where pavement runoff goes can decrease public dumping of pollutants onto pavement and into drains.

Truly paving less begins at the policy level. Some of the above policies aim at existing problems, but the most important are forward-looking. The central intent of policy must be to *establish growth management that encourages denser development and decreases automobile dependency.* Construction methods can help, but only a concerted effort can create compact cities. Decreased paving will be both *result* and cause of more people traveling by foot, bicycle, rail, or bus.

Put New and Renovated Development on a "Parking Diet"

Even cities that are fundamentally auto-oriented can reduce parking. In 1996 Olympia WA completed large-scale research, the Impervious Surface Reduction Study, aimed at reducing need for new parking and decreasing environmental impacts of new or existing paving. The study carefully documented effects of runoff from roads and parking on Olympia's water quality and quantity, and articulated a set of strategies with the remarkable goal of *smaller and fewer parking lots in future developments* throughout the city.

To accomplish this intent, which flies in the face of current development practices, a central strategy is to get developers to *size parking lots to reflect real needs.* Olympia's study uncovered a fact that applies across the United States: developers routinely *oversupply* parking to meet a single "peak-day" (or even "peak-hour") projection—the height of the Christmas retail rush, for example. In Olympia, parking supply was *51 percent above nonpeak needs.* Retailers fear that without this excess, customers will be turned away for lack of parking. In Olympia, this fear proved groundless. On those peak shopping dates, the study team surveyed thirty-one parking areas, representing fifteen different commercial uses. Eighteen of the lots had less than 75 percent occupancy rates *during their peak periods.*

Armed with such data, Olympia formed new policies.[16] One is *to encourage cooperative or shared parking.* This combines parking quotas for land uses with different hours of operation—a church and an office, for example, or a movie theater and a paint store. Shared parking works best for long-term tenants whose parking needs do not fluctuate much over time. It may require legal agreements between neighboring tenants; local governments should actively promote such agreements. Shared parking is already working in some cities, Oakland CA among them, according to the Institute of Transportation Engineers, which endorses the practice.[17]

A related principle is to enforce the *maximum* amount of parking for any land use. Typically, local governments enforce *minimum* parking requirements. Many developers and designers, who have struggled to fit in required parking spaces at the expense of site amenities, would welcome an enforced-maximum approach. Minimum parking ratios confer license to over-pave. Suburban office parking is routinely over-supplied by one-third.[18] Townhouse developers commonly provide the actual spaces required, *plus 103 percent*—fully *double* what anyone needs. The Center for Watershed Protection recommends parking codes that impose a maximum number of spaces unless compelling data clearly justifies more.[19] Oympia's new parking code requires developers to build according to "median" parking ratios that reflect day-to-day use.

Mass transit lowers paving demand by reducing the number of vehicles driven and parked. For developments close to a bus or rail stop, regulations should reduce the number of parking spaces. This may be controversial; getting US car users onto mass transit has never been easy. A number of communities have nevertheless encouraged or required developers to reduce parking when mass transit is available. These include Chicago; Hartford CT; Montgomery County MD; Albuquerque NM; and, of course, Olympia.[20] When Portland OR added 20,000 new seats to its sports stadium, it did not add a single parking space: a light-rail stop served the arena. (Excellent mass transit is obviously essential to such a solution.)

On a smaller scale, Seattle landscape architects Berger Partnership prescribed a "parking diet" for Washington's Department of Ecology headquarters in Lacey WA. The agency's original proposal called for 1,150 parking spaces, nearly one per employee. This would have claimed 4.5 acres, more than twice the building's footprint. In the final design, parking used just over 1 acre. The number of spaces was slashed to 900, and stacked in a land-saving garage. The new design challenged employees to adjust their commutes, but also served, in the words of partner Tom Berger, as "a model for what the Department of Ecology should expect from other planners." Besides cutting runoff, the reduced parking footprint made it easier to put the main building close to bus and foot access. In the garage, the closest spaces were reserved for car poolers; not even the director got a free space. Still, the farthest spaces in the garage were closer than most surface parking would have been, and state officials call the experiment a success.[21]

"Parking diets" offer major opportunities for site restoration. In Monroe MI, the historic convent campus of the Immaculate Heart of Mary order was being renovated. Landscape architects Rolf Sauer and Partners were actually able to change the campus's zoning by showing that carpooling and shuttles had reduced on-site parking needs. The sisters also convinced the local bus line to add a stop. These changes eliminated *more than 300 parking spaces*. Some roads were converted to pedestrian paths, others demolished, along with old parking areas, and converted to wildflower meadows and stormwater wetlands (Figure 4.10).[22]

Mark Childs, author of *Parking Spaces*, notes that every driver who parks is also a pedestrian. He advocates improved design of parking that accommodates pedestrian and public-space possibilities. Childs's book details many methods, plus insights into the history and social perception of parking in the United States.

Questioning assumptions about the *need* for parking is becoming more feasible, as the previous examples show, but still requires careful and persuasive planning. Fortunately, literature and assistance is increasingly available from sources like the Institute of Transportation Engineers, the Center for Watershed Protection, and the city of Olympia.

Parking reduction is largely a task for local government. Planners and designers should advocate and implement such policies wherever possible.

Take Advantage of "Context-sensitive Road Design"

Road standards can be even more difficult to update than parking policies. Over-engineered roadways, and standards that enforce overbuilding, have many of the same environmental impacts as excessive parking. Oversized roads also have negative effects on traffic safety and diminish the quality of life for communities through which they pass. Since about 1998, however, a major change in US attitude and policy has at last developed serious momentum. This is "Context-Sensitive Design" (CSD; or CSS, context-sensitive solutions; or CS³, context-sensitive and sustainable solutions). Where past policy explicitly designed for the safety and convenience of motorists and no one else, CSD gives communities and environments through which a road passes equal consideration.[23]

CSD is a very positive change, wholeheartedly adopted by many transportation departments throughout the country; some states have full-time CSD staff, often landscape architects. Unfortunately, some agencies still ignorantly or deliberately disregard CSD. Smaller jurisdictions, such as counties, are often the worst offenders. Chronically under funded, they resent CSD and environmental protection as imposed costs, and are extra-paranoic about imagined liability.

In Santa Fe County NM, for example, Sorvig has documented county road projects with *no* stormwater management or revegetation at all, resulting in destructive soil erosion of over a foot per year on adjacent private property, despite strict regulations requiring no net increase in runoff leaving any site.[24] Many public-works agencies get away with such negligence, for which any other agency, developer, or private landowner would be severely fined. What highway departments call "erosion control" merely armors the right-of-way, still dumping increased runoff onto the neighbors.[25] Road "improvements" remain so popular, however, that such damage often goes unchallenged, especially at the local level. Landscape professionals can hasten change, especially if they seek allies among young progressive engineers, who are often frustrated with outdated official attitudes.

One important policy change related to CSD concerns tranportation department funding. Strict separation of capital design and construction costs from operating budgets defeats attempts to analyze life-cycle costs (see Principle 7). Some DOTs use this split deceptively: during design, the public is promised that issues like revegetation will be done by the maintenance branch (and are then dropped). Many sustainable design techniques are vetoed because the design engineers cannot require the maintenance necessary to make these techniques work.

Legalize Narrower Streets and "Traffic Calming"

"Traffic calming," closely allied to CSD, improves roads safety for everyone, motorists and others alike.

Designed to motivate drivers to slow down and be attentive, traffic calming has been gaining acceptance in the United States; in Europe, Canada, and Australia, it has a thirty-year track record. Traffic calming originated from safety concerns, but also has significant environmental benefits, especially where it results in narrower roadways.

Conventional street and road statutes, although often imposed by local agencies, tend to be carbon copies of state and federal requirements more suitable for major highways. Ironically, at the Federal Highway Administration (FHWA), the Institute of Transportation, and many state agencies, progressive research has cast doubt on older requirements for extra-wide, straight, flat roads. Updated standards, including the FHWA's computerized Interactive Highway Safety Design Model, are available, but many local governments continue to enforce design standards decades out of date. Local agencies often adopt the American Association of State Highway and Transportation Officials (AASHTO) guidelines, which the local engineers enforce far more inflexibly than do most state DOTs. These standards are often presented to the public as cut-and-dried matters of safety: the "AASHTO Green Bible," as it is called, is (wrongly) considered by many engineers to be completely mandatory and inflexible. Although actually specifying acceptable *ranges* of design criteria, AASHTO standards are usually interpreted as requiring widening, flattening, and straightening of all roads, everywhere.[26] The assumption, however, that bigger roads are always safer (like the assumption that more parking is always better) is increasingly questioned, even by otherwise conventional agencies and professional organizations.

Where did bigger-is-safer come from? American society (with industry encouragement) has demanded that an exploding number of private vehicles should always be able to drive door-to-door at full speed. This single-minded focus on speed and capacity has disguised crucial safety issues. Current research shows that the real cause of most accidents, serious ones especially, is *speed itself*, and that wide, straight, flat roadways encourage drivers to speed. Conventional engineering has struggled to make *speeding* as safe as it can be, which is not actually very safe at all.

Traffic calming takes a different approach. In the words of Robert A. White, a Norwich VT landscape architect who consults on traffic calming, "measures that reduce lane width, introduce roadside 'friction' features like street trees, and prominently define pedestrian crossing points can [significantly reduce] roadway speeds—from 20% to 50% reductions depending on the technique and location. It has been shown that similar safety improvements can reduce crashes by as much as 80%, and those that do occur tend to be less severe."[27]

Traffic calming relies on self-preservation instincts, rather than on fear of punishment. "Most drivers adjust their speed more readily in response to road and traffic conditions than to speed limit signs and the often remote possibility of enforcement penalties. 85% of drivers tend to adopt a sensible speed for prevailing road conditions. [Drivers] unconsciously respond to the physical cues presented to them."[28] Thus, making a road narrower (or even making it *look* narrower with grassed shoulders or roadside shrubs) is something highway designers can do to get drivers to observe safe speeds. Recognizing that no amount of design can "idiot proof" a road puts responsibility back where it belongs: on the 15 percent of drivers who speed, rather than on the designer or public agency that built the road.

Robert White considers traffic calming as "a set of roadway design tools and principles where *community values* as they relate to traffic management are more fully represented and integrated into the actual roadway design." Streets and roads once again become multipurpose spaces. Narrower roads release space for bike lanes, walkways, and bridle paths; in residential neighborhoods and small business districts, streets become truly public; on scenic highways, conflicts between tourists and local drivers are reduced.[29] Traffic calming provides practical methods of achieving these "neo-traditional" goals. Conventional design and exclusive use by automobiles remains appropriate for freeways and major highways. For any road where access cannot be limited, however, the multiple-user approach is safer, less disruptive, and frequently cheaper. Traffic calming projects are eligible for funding under federal "intermodal" or multi-use transportation acts.[30]

"Traffic Fatalities and Injuries: Are Reductions the Result of Improvements in Highway Design Standards?" is a critically important 2001 paper by traffic researcher Dr. Robert Noland. Traffic injuries and fatalities *have* gone down during the past few decades; it is an article of engineering faith that this is due to flatter-wider-straighter improvements. By sophisticated analysis of statistics from all fifty states, Noland shows that the reductions *actually* result from better vehicle-safety design, increased seatbelt use, demographic decline in 15-to-24-year-old drivers, and greatly improved emergency response and medical triage for injured motorists. The traffic engineers' claim that their bigger roads are safer may be an innocent mistake, but it is false.[31] In fact, to quote the paper, "as arterial and collector lane widths are increased up to 12 feet or more, traffic fatalities and injuries *increase*."[32]

For rural roads, recent FHWA research from Turner-Fairbank Highway Research Center has shown that "9-ft lane widths have lower accident rates than 10-ft lanes with narrow shoulders, at least partly due to reduced vehicle speeds." The report suggests that it is *safer* to retain existing 9-foot lanes unless a community can afford dramatic widening of both roadway and shoulder.[33]

Alex Wilson, in an EBN summary of traffic calming, notes several compelling facts. Traffic calming techniques reduce collisions by anything from 51 to 94 percent. Slowing traffic decreases pedestrians' chances of being killed: 83 percent fatality at 44 mph, only 37 percent at 31 mph, and less than 4 percent at 15 mph. (Similar reductions apply to motorist risks.) Calming from 56 to 48 mph decreases noise as much as 90 percent. Reductions in crime (due to more pedestrians) have also been credited to traffic calming, as have increased property values: 63 percent for residences, and for commercial properties, 80 percent increase in occupancy and an astonishing 967 percent increase in average rents.[34]

Those landscape professionals who deal with streetscapes and roadsides should remember a simple summary of the reasons for traffic calming:

Wider + flatter + straighter = faster driving
Wider + flatter + straighter = inattentive driving
Faster + inattentive = more dangerous

As one traffic official put it, "Roads aren't dangerous; drivers are." Traffic calming and Context Sensitive Design try to influence the most effective safety device in every car: the person behind the wheel. The safety and community benefits of traffic calming are clearly of concern to landscape professionals—especially those who are tired of being steamrolled by outdated arguments in favor of overbuilt roads.

A closely related trend is banning motor vehicles from selected streets on specific days, or permanently, to encourage pedestrian and bicycle use. Begun in Bogota, Colombia, the "ciclovia" (bike road) is widespread in Latin America and Europe; more than twenty US cities have adopted it to date.[35]

Traffic calming has been bitterly attacked by special-interests like the American Road and Transportation Builders Association (ARTB). ARTB took the position, *despite a 63 percent increase in federal funding* for highway construction between 1993 and 1999, that "environmental and community extremists" were out to deprive road builders of their livelihood.[36] Although such associations represent part of the construction industry, contractors and designers concerned with sustainability need not feel too much sympathy for the poor starving highway-construction lobby. Like developers who produce 50–100 percent more parking than necessary, the ARTB treats paving as an unqualified good—and for their pocketbooks, it clearly is. For society, less is more, and more can be lethal.

Community Benefits of Narrower Streets

Narrowing roads is the traffic calming technique with clearest *environmental* benefits. For safety, *visual* narrowing, even an illusion created by painted lane lines, is effective for slowing traffic. To have an environmental effect, the narrowing must be physical, reducing the amount of paving material and decreasing impervious surface.

Retaining existing, narrower roads saves construction and maintenance costs. Because older rural roads tended to follow topography, simply repairing them avoids the environmental destruction common to so-called road improvement. Where a road is on a side slope, small increases in paved width are drastically magnified by wider-cut-and-fill slopes to either side.

On a 30 percent side slope, adding just one foot on either shoulder increases fill by two-thirds, and widens the road-construction "footprint" by ten feet. For one inch of rainfall, the two-foot added pavement width increases runoff by nearly 700 gallons per mile of road.

Conventional residential street standards frequently call for two 12-foot lanes plus 6-foot shoulders, totaling 36 feet. National engineering organizations now suggest that residential streets can be as narrow as 22 feet in neighborhoods that generate fewer than 500 daily trips (about fifty homes).[37]

Compared to the 36-foot wide standard, a 22-foot street saves nearly *1.75 acres* (75,000 square feet) of paving *per mile*. Assuming a city block of 700 × 500 feet, or about 8 acres, the 22-foot street on all sides saves nearly an acre. That land savings can be used for open space, stormwater or wetland functions, or additional lots. At the same time, the narrowed streets reduce infrastructure costs both for paving and for utilities. By slowing traffic, they also protect children, pets, and pedestrians.

In most states, local governments have the option to permit narrower streets, and communities such as Bucks County PA and Boulder CO have done so. One of the most important achievements of New Urbanist communities like Seaside FL and Kentlands (near Washington DC) is using narrower streets than the nationwide norm.

Unfortunately, in many localities, narrow streets are still *illegal* under local or DOT codes. Broad streets

Figure 5.2 Narrow streets enhance livability of older cities, especially in Europe. Recent U.S. developments use narrowed streets to save land and infrastructure costs, and to protect watersheds. (*Photo:* Kim Sorvig.)

were portrayed by early civic booster as patriotic and sanitary; today, emergency access is often the argument.

Traffic calming in fact causes little delay for police and ambulances; delays for larger fire-trucks average 5 to 20 seconds,[38] compared to delays of 10 to 20 *minutes* commonly caused by sprawl distances.[39] Delays vary by traffic calming technique. Only speed bumps, raised intersections, and large roundabouts, however, cause as much delay as ordinary stop signs. Mini traffic circles, which eliminate stop signs, often *reduce* delays at intersections, actually lowering pollution from idling, stopped vehicles.[40] Traffic calming also reduces the frequency and severity of accidents; this cuts emergency vehicles responses overall, so the effect on public safety is definitely positive. Challenges to narrowed streets on the basis of the "right to drive" or "right to park" are entirely outweighed by public benefit; even some drivers' groups say these attacks on traffic calming smack of conspiracy theory and lack credibility.[41]

Standards that ban well-designed narrow streets are outdated and should be seriously reconsidered. Appropriately narrow streets restore a sense of community to places deadened by the dominance of the car. For sustainability, the Center for Watershed Protection recommends narrower streets as principle number one in its model development principles.

AASHTO published "A Guide for Transportation Landscape and Environmental Design" in 1991; as

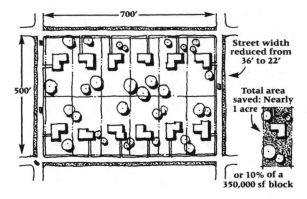

Figure 5.1 One acre of developable or protected land is saved by reducing street width from thirty-six feet to twenty-two feet around an eight-acre city block. (*Illust.:* Craig Farnsworth.)

of late 2006, it is undergoing extensive revision by landscape architect Donal Simpson of HNTB (Charlotte NC). Following these guidelines and educating engineers about context sensitivity can give landscape professionals real leverage to improve the often dismal community impacts of roadways and streets.

CONSIDER THE CRITTERS

Roads affect not just human communities, but animal and plant communities as well. "Road ecology" is a rapidly emerging science devoted to understanding impacts of roads on ecosystems. It is a strongly cross-disciplinary outgrowth of landscape ecology; the well-known landscape ecologist Richard Foreman has been a pioneer. Research centers and databases of techniques are being developed at the University of California at Davis, Montana State University, and North Carolina State University; transportation agencies like AASHTO, FHWA, and the Transportation Research Board sponsor research and maintain their own programs.

The findings of road ecology confirm concerns that observant drivers, environmentalists, and designers have had for years.[42] Roads interrupt the flow of ecosystem processes and fragment populations. They cause mortality, disease, and suppressed reproduction in both plants and animals within a zone fifteen to twenty times as wide as the road itself. In addition, roads are primary vectors for the spread of invasive species.[43]

Two aspects of road ecology are expanding horizons for applied landscape work. These are roadside habitat management and wildlife crossings.[44]

The Surface Transportation Policy Project (STPP), a Washington DC think tank, notes that public highway right-of-ways occupy 12 million acres of land, and that there are 90,000 miles of road on public lands. "Transportation agencies are land managers on a grand scale," according to STPP, which recommends that all roadsides should be revegetated with their original vegetation communities.[45] Hedges to block wind and snow (instead of fences) provide extra wildlife habitat; decreased mowing and seasonal mowing schedules increase habitat value. Road structures like bridges can be modified to provide nesting sites and hunting perches for birds.

Wildlife crossings have put road ecology in the news, and landscape professionals are frequently involved, collaborating with wildlife specialists. Wildlife crossings, which are still experimental, vary according to the species expected to use them. Crossings have been developed to protect deer, elk, moose, foxes, panthers, badgers, gophers, tortoises and turtles, frogs, toads, snakes, and alligators. A number of Web sites share ideas and track projects. One such site, www.wildlifecrossings.info, is especially useful because it attempts to standardize terms for the structures and includes clear sketches of each major type. These types are:

- Wildlife Overcrossing: a bridge-like overpass for animals (sometimes called ecoducts or bio-bridges), or a traffic tunnel under natural or naturalistic crossings.
- Wildlife Underpass: a road bridging the wildlife corridor; or a soil-floored culvert or tunnel for animals.
- Wildlife Barriers: fences, jersey barriers, or walls (including noise walls doing double duty) that funnel animals to crossings, and in-road barriers similar to "cattle guards" (grate-covered pits across the road where it passes through fencelines).
- Escape Structures: one-way gates and ramps for animals accidentally trapped inside barrier fences.

For easily caught animals in small numbers, radio collars have been successfully used to trigger flashing lighted signs when an animal enters the roadway. Infrared beams can detect large species like moose and elk without collaring, but specific knowledge of crossing locations is essential.

The cost of wildlife protection varies widely, offset by accident costs. The Virginia Transportation Research Council found that even structures costing hundreds of thousands of dollars saved the state money if they prevented between three and nine deer-auto collisions annually. Deer, elk, and moose collisions cause hundreds of human deaths and tens of thousands of injuries yearly; property damage, road cleanup and repair, and other costs add up to many millions of dollars. A 2003 lawsuit held Arizona liable for not providing wildlife protection on Interstate 40, awarding a driver $3.1 million. Wildlife value to hunting and tourism provides other economic incentives, if ethical and ecological arguments are not enough.

Use Techniques That Reduce Runoff from Paving

Even where planning and design efforts reduce the total area of roads and parking, some new paving is inevitable. Its environmental impact can and should be limited by appropriate choice of materials and methods.

A good starting point for this discussion—in opposition to the prevailing tendency to pave every piece of ground in sight—is "Haag's Theory of Softness." Propounded by Seattle landscape architect Richard Haag, this simple principle states that *no ground surface should be any harder than absolutely necessary for its function.* Paving, for instance, should not be used where crushed stone will do, nor crushed stone where a path of bark chips is sufficient. Many conventional paved areas are much harder than function requires them to be.

Softness is not necessarily literal—porous concrete, for instance, is quite hard. The same principle can be restated for permeability: *no ground surface should be any more impervious than necessary.* Any technique or material that works *with* environmental dynamism, rather than resisting, is "softer" than conventional engineering.[46]

Just Say No to Paved Parking

This concept is self-evident, yet almost radical: *not all parking areas need to be paved.* In fact, many lightly used parking lots are much improved (from a sustainability standpoint) by simpler surfacing.

Professor Bruce Ferguson, an expert on stormwater management, says that crushed aggregate was common for surfacing until the 1930s, but now largely abandoned. Crushed oyster and clam shells are used in some regions in a similar way. Both persist where over-engineering is not mandatory. In the upscale suburban community of Medford Village NJ, this humble paving material formed part of a township-wide stormwater infiltration plan by environmental planner Ian McHarg. Seeing crushed stone used with consistency and sensitivity in historic Medford, Ferguson "really concluded that gravel pavements had a future."

Although it may be porous, not just any gravel will do. Technically "gravel" is rounded small stones, washed by a river; for loose surfacing, it is highly unstable. Crushed stone, which interlocks under pressure, is preferable despite the extra energy costs of producing it. In specifying crushed stone, Ferguson notes, coarser grades drain more readily; finer grades are more walkable and ADA-accessible. Open grading (sorting so all particles are the same size, aka "no fines") improves drainage and reduces dust; it is important in porous asphalt or porous concrete (see below).

Figure 5.3 Porous parking is separated from standard driving lanes. This stormwater management tactic can also create strong aesthetics. (*Project:* Spaceplan (arch.); Petrus (pervious paving). *Photo:* Bruce Ferguson.)

Like most materials, crushed stone should be used selectively. Best suited for relatively low traffic, it is commonly used in parking stalls served by asphalt travel lanes, with adjacent grassed swales to handle overflow from large storms. Gravel surfaces on clay soils can become highly compacted and impervious under traffic, offering little stormwater advantage over asphalt.[47] Six inches of aggregate is a minimum depth; use a filter fabric or geotextile under the stone to keep it from mixing into soil. The surface layer will almost always become compacted as cars pack the top stones; hand raking yearly will restore porosity. Contain the loose materials on either side with substantial edging, or incorporate cellular containment (p. 124) or meshes similar to those used for grass paving (see below).

Stone chips or screenings are widely used for pedestrian surfaces in parks. Many famous European gardens, such as the Tuileries in Paris, are "gravel" surfaced. Henry Arnold used such surfacing, supported by air-entrained soil (see Figure 5.4), at MetroTech plaza in Brooklyn.

For garden paths and very-low-use areas, organic materials such as bark chips or mulch can be used as a truly soft surface, possibly combined with cellular or mesh support. Some (but not all) are acceptable for handicapped access when properly designed. All must be maintained and replenished.

Make Gutters and Curbs Permeable

Many municipal standards require a concrete curb and gutter along both sides of any residential street. Curbs collect and concentrate pollutants deposited on paving by spills and from the air. Conventional road drainage usually dumps these into the nearest stream.

To avoid this, in most residential neighborhoods it makes sense *not* to add curbs and gutters—a seemingly simple design strategy, but one that may require a variance from the municipality. If curbs are absolutely required, add multiple openings that allow water to flow through the curb, into grass (or, if possible, into bioswales, below). Gutters of brick laid on sand can also infiltrate a considerable amount of precipitation.

Infiltrate Road and Parking-lot Runoff in Bioswales

Beyond (or instead of) the curb, install grassed or vegetated areas called "bioswales"—linear, planted drainage channels. A typical bioswale moves stormwater runoff as *slowly* as possible along a gentle incline, keeping precipitation on-site as long as possible to soak into the ground—contrary to conventional engineering practice. At the lowest point of the swale there is usually a raised drain inlet taking any over-

Figure 5.4 Stone screenings over air-entrained soil at MetroTech in Brooklyn create a permeable surface with the feel of traditional French public spaces. (*Project and Photo:* Henry Arnold.)

flow to storm sewers. This is insurance, however, because well-designed bioswales completely infiltrate all but the most intense storms. Bioswales plants and soil microbes cleanse runoff, a simple form of phytoremediation (p. 103).

Bioswales for road drainage are common (and in some counties, mandated) in the Pacific Northwest. In Vancouver WA, more than five acres of bioswales at Heritage (a planned-unit development) were configured as roadside park with handsome plantings, winning a Portland/Vancouver Metro Area Stormwater Design Award. Bioswales can enhance streetscapes, rather than looking like ditches.

Bioswales function particularly well in parking lots, where stationary cars often drip pollutants. Such plantings also improve the pedestrian environment. At Portland's Oregon Museum of Science and Industry (OMSI), a demonstration project features seven bioswales where the raised parking-lot medians would typically be. The OMSI bioswales improve water quality by filtering pollutants from the museum's 800 parking spaces before runoff enters the Willamette River. Quite unlike conventional catch basins and sewers, OMSI's system actually protects the river.

Designed by Murase Associates, OMSI's bioswales are graded to a very gentle incline, retaining water rather than hurrying it out of sight. River rocks and small wooden check dams at thirty-foot intervals cause water to pond, giving it time to soak into the soil. Native wetland plants—cattails, bulrushes, and iris, among others—further slow the water while biologically breaking down pollutants. Contaminants that escape this gauntlet are attacked by soil microorganisms. Thus filtered, the stormwater seeps through the subsoil into the water table. Raised drain inlets were installed, but in practice rainwater rarely gets that far.

The city's Bureau of Environmental Services asked OMSI to build the bioswales, prompted by pioneering work on grassed bioswales at the University of Washington. Tom Liptan, a Bureau landscape architect, felt the idea should be tested in Portland, and OMSI management agreed. "Stormwater should be part of the landscape architect's design palette," says

Figure 5.5 Bioswale at OMSI filters, slows, and infiltrates runoff from parking. Raised grate overflows to storm sewers only in very heavy storms. (*Project:* Robert Murase. *Illust.:* Jeff Foster, Portland Bureau of Environmental Services.)

Liptan. "We need to be much more involved in the water that falls on a site than most of us are currently." Liptan notes that conventional details for parking lots raise landscaped area *above* curbs, mounded so that any rainfall runs off onto the pavement—exactly the opposite of bioswales.

OMSI directed the project engineer to pitch the lot so that it would drain *into* the medians between parking rows, where the swales would be; most lots are pitched *away* from the median strips. Murase Associates designed the richly planted swales, using native plants in lieu of turf, as an "exhibit" to reveal water falling on the site. To widen the swales, the Murase team convinced the engineers to cut nearly two feet off each parking stall (only 16.5 feet). Computer stormwater modeling indicated the swales would hold runoff *longer* than the engineer had calculated, fully infiltrating 0.83 inches of rainfall in a twenty-four-hour period. This is sufficient for 75 percent of all the storms that fall on Portland, says Liptan. The computer model estimates that the swale's topsoil captures 60 percent of suspended solids in the runoff; with a few improvements Liptan expects 90 percent pollutant capture. The parking design won an honor award from an Oregon consortium of municipal governments.

Not surprisingly, visitors to OMSI often ask whether the swales are breeding grounds for mosquitoes. "They don't hold water," is Liptan's response. "The water drains into the soil quickly enough that mosquitoes are not an issue." This might not be true on all sites, Liptan cautions; much depends on the soil and its permeability.

Most encouraging for the future of such projects, the OMSI parking-lot design saved $78,000, compared to a conventional lot, catch basins, and drainage system. This cost savings has helped Bob Murase market the bioswale concept to several Portland-area clients. One is the Bureau of Environmental Services itself, which practiced what it had been preaching and installed bioswales at its new Water Pollution Control Laboratory (Figure 5.5). There, bioswales not only capture runoff from the parking lot but from the laboratory's roof as well. The building has no gutters; instead, scuppers extend from the roof and send water spurting in graceful trajectories to land in a rock-lined bioswale several feet from the edge of the building. The Water Pollution Control Laboratory has already won several important awards, regional and national.

Bioswales are gradually appearing at other sites around North America. One is the new School of Architecture and Landscape Architecture at Penn State University.[48] Such functional systems on university campuses can also provide on-site demonstration of ecological principles for students.

Figure 5.6 This bioswale, part of Glencoe School's green street in Portland OR, uses check dams, a "flash-board" level-setting device in the weir, and overflow drain to treat and infiltrate stormwater. (*Project:* Portland Bureau of Environmental Services. *Photo:* Kevin Robert Perry and Portland Bureau of Environmental Services.)

With or without bioswales, it is a good idea to break up paved areas so that they drain to unpaved areas rather than to other paving or to storm drains. "Directly Connected Impervious Areas" (DCIAs—paved surfaces that drain straight from one to the next) should be minimized in design.[49] It is especially important that the "first flush" of rain off paving, which carries most surface pollutants, go to a grassed or vegetated area. If stormwater is routed first to a bioswale, and only enters a drain system if ponding is deep enough to reach an overflow outlet, most first-flush pollutants are kept out of further flows, and broken down.

Use Porous Paving Materials

Paving can be made permeable so that infiltration occurs *through the surface of the paving itself.* (Not all alternative paving materials are porous. For soil cement, glasphalt, and plasphalt—using recycled glass or plastic as aggregate—see Principle 6.) Porous paving comes in several forms.

PorOUS ASPHALT AND CONCRETE
Porous paving combines surface stability with permeability. Since the 1970s, landscape professionals have been pioneers in its development and use. Although gaining acceptance, it is not as well-known as it deserves to be. Considering how often the profession is involved in (and frustrated by) pavement design, familiarity with these materials is a must for being "part of the solution" rather than part of the problem.

Since the first edition of this book, porous asphalt and concrete have become considerably more accepted and used. An increased number of asphalt and concrete suppliers have at least some experience with porous versions of their material; a few actively promote porous paving.

One major step toward full integration of porous materials into mainstream practices was the publication, in 2005, of Bruce Ferguson's handbook *Porous Pavements.* ⊃ This book finally offers the documented detail necessary to make porous paving understandable and acceptable to clients, engineers, and regulatory agencies, including information on suppliers and existing projects.

Figure 5.7   Even at as ceremonial a place as Washington DC's National Cathedral, porous pedestrian paths fit in while protecting the site. (*Project:* Andropogon Associates. *Photo:* Peter von Pawel.)

Porous asphalt and porous concrete are similar materials that go by a variety of names: no-fines paving, pervious paving, permeable paving, and per-crete (for "percolating concrete"). Stone aggregate is held together with either asphalt or Portland cement; high-tech versions have used epoxy binders. The aggregate must be angular crushed stone, usually $3/8''$ in size, carefully sorted to exclude all the "fines" (sand-sized particles) that normally fill voids between larger stones. Without fines, voids make the material porous. (The same concept creates root space in "structural soil," Figure 3.25.)

Whether held together with asphalt or cement, porous paving is strong enough for parking, pedestrian use, and some road surfaces. The asphalt version was originally developed for airport runways, where it prevents dangerous surface ponding. Many state highway departments use it for road surfacing, and asphalt plants routinely carry it, specified as "open-graded mix," "popcorn mix," or "porous friction coat." As a surface over conventional impervious paving, it gets water off the road quickly (the focus of conventional pavement engineering), but does nothing to solve runoff, erosion, or infiltration problems.

In order to affect these issues, the porous surface material must be underlaid with a bed, or "reservoir," of larger aggregate surrounded by filter fabric. The reservoir supports the porous surface and holds precipitation until it can percolate into the soil. The reservoir may be as shallow as nine inches on some well-drained soils.

During construction, temporarily extend the filter-fabric edges aboveground (like erosion-control fencing), to keep *all* sediment out of the reservoir. Using crushed rock open graded to about two inches in size, almost 40 percent of the reservoir's total volume will be water-holding voids. A "choker course" of half-inch gravel is laid on top of the larger stone to even the top surface. Keep heavy equipment out of the excavation; if unavoidable, drive only on previously placed layers of stone and minimize the number of trips. Folding the temporary "fence" fabric onto the top of the reservoir, the porous pavement (either asphalt or concrete based) is then laid.

For porous asphalt, binder is about 6 percent of the aggregate's dry weight, and the porous course about three inches thick. It is slightly flexible and will withstand freezing and thawing. In hot weather, vehicle tires that repeatedly take the same path may rut the surface (as they will on any asphalt paving). Thus in warm climates, and for constant in-and-out traffic, porous concrete may be a better choice.

Porous concrete uses Portland cement binder in a ratio of four or four-and-one-half parts aggregate to one part cement by weight. This layer is usually five inches thick for ordinary vehicular traffic, and thicker for heavier use. Porous concrete is frequently laid directly on compacted soils in areas with very good soil drainage. It will withstand heavier and more repeated loads than porous asphalt, and it does not soften under heat. Concerns are often raised about freeze-thaw damage. Water drains so quickly through porous asphalt or concrete that ice never forms either in the paving or on the surface. A large reservoir enhances this effect. Air-entrained or otherwise strengthened concrete mixtures can also combat freeze-thaw problems, although concrete additives are frowned on by many in the green building movement. In all, Ferguson considers freeze damage and frost heaving extremely rare.

Both the mixture and timing of porous concrete must be carefully controlled. The contractor must keep to the narrow range of a 0.34 to 0.40 water/ cement ratio. With too much water, the cement runs off the aggregate and seals the bottom of the layer; with too little, material bonding is weak. Porous concrete must be placed within sixty minutes of mixing, finished immediately, and covered with plastic sheeting within twenty minutes of placement, to cure for three to ten days.

The technique of porous asphalt over a reservoir was first researched in the 1970s by Edmund Thelan and Fielding Howe of Philadelphia (the latter a practicing landscape architect). Since then, firms such as Cahill and Associates, Resource Technologies, and Andropogon Associates⊃ have not only completed significant porous designs, but have won several awards for them. An example easily accessible to the public is at the Morris Arboretum (Philadelphia PA).

Reservoir porous paving reduces both runoff volume and concentration of overland flow. This decreases disruption of on-site groundwater recharge and slows downstream erosion and siltation. While water is percolating through the porous system, significant amounts of water-borne pollutants may also be filtered. On some soils, microbes will further neutralize contaminants during infiltration.

In addition to its ecological advantages, porous paving can save construction, real-estate, and maintenance costs—a clear example that working *with* natural systems yields economic benefits. These cost savings happen because porous paving serves two purposes at once—or perhaps more precisely, in the same place.

Porous-paved surfaces absorb rainfall near where it falls, making the storm drainage system for the site significantly smaller and simpler. Considered strictly as a paving material, porous paving may cost 10 percent more than conventional asphalt. By doubling as a stormwater system and eliminating storm drains, however, it may be 12 to 38 percent cheaper overall.

A second, greater savings occurs where a porous paving reservoir substitutes for stormwater detention or retention basins. Land area otherwise required for basins is freed for other uses—to create more buildable space, which can offset several times the added paving cost; or to conserve site features that would otherwise have been destroyed. In Lower Merion PA, Cahill and Associates was able to create porous tennis courts over reservoirs, an amenity that met stormwater management regulations.

A third advantage is reduced maintenance costs, particularly where snow removal is significant. Snow that falls on porous paving melts quickly and drains into the pores. Only after heavy snowfall will any removal be required, and dangerous surface icing can be virtually eliminated.

Soil around any porous installation must percolate at a minimum rate of a half-inch per hour and should contain no more than 30 percent clay. The reservoir bottom must be at least three feet above bedrock or water table for unimpeded drainage. If clay lenses or other impermeable barriers exist on-site, the reservoir must either be well above them or deep enough to reach permeable soils. On sites sloping 3 percent or more, terrace paved areas so that the bottom of each reservoir remains relatively level; extra depth at the lower side, however, may be needed in some cases.

The size and depth of the reservoir must be designed to fit site conditions: soil permeability, slope, and the local design storm. (Cahill and Associates uses a computer program to do this.) The reservoir must be sized to accommodate the water generated by the design storm and to hold it long enough to percolate into that specific soil. Some conditions (and nervous authorities) may require underdrains or overflow pipes set to catch water if the reservoir fills. Ferguson's book shows a variety of overflow solutions.

Runoff from roofs and nonporous pavement may also be directed into the reservoir, assuming it is sized accordingly. This water thus reenters the groundwater-recharge cycle. Sediment-bearing runoff, such as flow from wooded areas, should not discharge directly onto porous paving. It may, however, be channeled or piped into the reservoir via bioswales, sediment traps, or filter-fabric once sediment is removed.

With all its advantages, why hasn't porous paving become a standard material? The primary reason appears to be resistance from some engineers and regulators. Porous paving goes against conventional "pave-and-pipe" notions of stormwater management. Moreover, successful design requires more sophisticated site-specific data than standardized pipe sizing; in particular, soil, bedrock, and groundwater characteristics must be tested and respected. As with any

new technology, porous paving has a learning curve and requires educating both clients and colleagues.

Among concerns raised by engineers and planners, the fear of clogging is most common. Unfortunately, some "tests" of porous paving were reportedly built on unsuitable soils and at toe-of-slope locations where clogging was virtually assured. Yet initial porosity is far in excess of any storm event (1,000 inches per hour), and most researchers have found that proper design, installation, and maintenance can prevent loss of porosity over time. In one test, an inch of loose fine material was applied to a porous concrete surface. The pavement never became less porous than turf, and full porosity was easily restored by cleaning with a device called a HydroVac.[50] Porous asphalt may lose surface porosity in areas deformed by traffic; drilling compacted areas with a small bit can restore performance. A relatively minor loss of porosity occurs in all porous materials over the first four to six years and should be assumed in design calculations; even after this loss, porous surfaces still infiltrate no less than 200 inches per hour, still far more than any normal regional precipitation.[51]

Underdrains, overflow drains, and edge drains have been installed on some systems in case the reservoir should ever clog and cease to percolate. Cahill and Associates states that in more than twenty-five years of experience with porous paving, these added features have had only one real purpose: not to deal with clogged or overfilled pavement, but to deal with the "clogged" thinking of skeptical planning commissions.

Most designers familiar with the material recommend porous paving, especially asphalt, for areas of lighter traffic where repetitious movement will not be severe. Employee parking, generally once-a-day in and out, is an example. Main traffic lanes are paved with ordinary asphalt. Porous paving can also be used for many light vehicles, such as golf carts or bicycles, for pedestrians, and some sports surfaces. Increasingly, these limits are giving way to improved design and materials, so that porous pavement can at least be considered for almost any use.

Porous paving should generally not be used where site soils or bedrock drain very directly into a vulnerable aquifer, or where particularly toxic pollutants are likely to be deposited on the paving. The gravel reservoir and ordinary soils filter ordinary pollutants well enough that this is not a widespread concern. If the subgrade is mostly fractured rock, however, or if the water table is high, consult with soil scientists and hydrological experts before using porous paving.

In our first edition, we recommended research into improved binders, and since that time, stronger asphalt and concrete binders have begun to be used. Epoxies have also been used for binders, but primarily on roofs. The perfect binder would have improved strength, flexibility without permanent deformation, and resistance to temperature extremes, and reasonable cost. Even as implemented today, porous paving is a fully mature method of resolving many of the conflicts between transportation and the environment.

PAVE WITH GRASS

Grassed paving systems allow turfgrass to grow through permeable, structural cells that support the load of vehicles. A variety of commercial products are available, including large sheets of plastic mesh, precast open concrete blocks, and form systems for casting concrete cells in place.

Figure 5.8 Porous concrete, shown here, and porous asphalt support vehicles but permit water to infiltrate rapidly. (*Photo:* Florida Concrete and Products Association/Dennis Graeber.)

The environmental benefits of grassed paving can be considerable. According to one manufacturer's study, every 1,000 square feet of grass paving infiltrates nearly 7,000 gallons per ten inches of rainfall, which would otherwise be runoff; converts enough CO_2 to oxygen to supply 22 adults for a year; provides significant cooling (equated to 1.7 tons of air conditioning annually); and recycles more than 400 pounds of plastic.[52]

Grassed paving is somewhat limited in its applications because grass will not survive constant daily traffic. (Grass for parking stays healthy if used not more than about one day a week—less in dry climates.) It is excellent for emergency fire lanes and temporary overflow parking. But as the Olympia study documented, many more parking areas receive temporary use than is generally supposed. Sports arenas, for example, are typically used on one or two days a week; grassing the entire stadium parking would greatly reduce the need for storm drains (see project examples).

An active operating plan may increase grass-paving's capacity. A large grass-paved area can be divided into two or more subareas, using fences or barriers (permanent or temporary). By alternately using and resting the subareas, each can be given a chance to recover from wear. This works especially well for overflow parking where, for example, the *whole* area is only needed occasionally, but filling the lot to *half* capacity is fairly common. Base plans on realistic, not speculative, numbers.

"Grass" paving systems do not have to be filled with sod. A number of ground covers, such as thyme or chamomile, will flourish in some climates. Fine gravel, oyster shells, or other permeable materials can substitute for grass where frequent parking is expected (or in climates in which grass does not readily grow). Such materials provide strength and permeability without worrying about the health of grass. At least one paving-systems manufacturer, Invisible Systems, manufactures a system, Gravelpave[2], designed to be filled with a gravel mixture. This system was employed in 1999 as part of a demonstration project for the headquarters of the Riverside/Corona Resource Conservation District in Riverside CA. (Gravelpave[2] is only one of the innovative materials used at the center; others include car stops made of recycled tires.)

A drawback of grassed paving is its cost, which can be higher than that of solid asphalt or concrete parking lots. In fact, the Olympia study found that concrete grass pavers average two to four times the per-square-foot cost of asphalt. A parking area with 20 percent grassed pavers would cost approximately 60 percent more to install than an equal all-asphalt area. But the Olympia study found that permeable paving systems are less costly to maintain over time than asphalt.[53] Moreover, the initial expense of grassed pavers may be deceptive because it does not take into account the *reduced* need for storm drains and sewers. Subtracting the cost of such drains, the overall cost of grassed systems (like porous concrete or asphalt) may actually be lower than conventional, impervious paving.

Three general types of grassed paving systems exist:

Poured-in-place systems such as Bomanite's Grass-crete consist of steel-reinforced concrete and are typically the most expensive systems. They require skilled workers to install.

Precast concrete pavers resemble interlocking concrete pavers (p. 49) and provide rigid structural support. Typical pavers are heavy and require equipment for hauling and lifting. Precast and cast-in-place concrete systems have a lattice- or checkered-appearance, concrete grid framing areas of grass. This can be very attractive in some designs and may help make it clear that the area is for parking.

A large number of the available systems are *plastic pavers*, some manufactured from recycled plastic.[54] Although they do not have concrete's rigidity, these flexible pavers conform to irregular surfaces. They appear to support grass growth better than the thick-walled concrete cells if moisture is scarce. Plastic grid systems come closest to disappearing entirely under the grass, giving the appearance of ordinary lawn. Invisible Structures, founded by Denver landscape architect Bill Bonhoff, makes all its products of recycled plastics. Invisible Structures grass pavers have been tested up to 5,700 psi bearing strength when filled; the empty structure will support over 2,000 psi.

In general, it is better to use a mix of sand and water-absorbent polymer as grass-paver growing medium than to use topsoil. Topsoil usually is loamy or clayey and will compact. Sandy fill is also most permeable. Porosity of the system depends strongly on the native soil underneath it. Over clay or loam soils, 50–80 percent of rainfall may run off (compared to 95 percent from hard pavement); over sandy soils, runoff from grass paving can be as little as 15 percent.

A key requirement of grassed paving is maintenance. This includes mowing, which is important because tall grass matted down by vehicles can decrease porosity. People are less likely to park if grass paving does not appear stable and well cared for.[55] Invisible Structures states that snow can be plowed off their systems if inch-thick skids are attached to the snow-plow blade. An irrigation system is also recommended even in areas of high rainfall to counter stresses of compaction, shallow rooting space, oil drips, and, with concrete cells, heating and water wicking by the concrete.[56] Maintenance costs appear to be comparable to or less than for conventional pavement, although such comparisons are hard to make. Durability is likely to vary with soil type and climate.

In choosing between different grassed systems, evaluate ease and weight of installation, durability, grass growth and maintenance issues (preferably by comparison of projects in your regions), and finished appearance.

GRASSED PAVING PROJECT EXAMPLES

Grassed paving is well suited for periodic "event parking"; the City of Miami used a recycled-plastic system for new parking stalls at the Orange Bowl, with conventional asphalt driving lanes.

"Overall, it's working out really well," says Enrique Nuñez, a landscape architect with Miami's Department of Community Planning and Revitalization. Nuñez confirms that grass pavers have helped to eliminate runoff; the site has a conventional stormwater system as a backup.

Because much retail parking is only used at peak periods, grass paving may be appropriate for areas not used day-to-day. Westfarms Mall (Farmington CT) seized this opportunity. When the mall proposed adding 4.7 acres of parking, primarily to accommodate the Christmas rush, the local zoning board pointed to a percentage green-space requirement. A grass paving system of recycled plastic pavers enabled Westfarms Mall to get its parking while meeting the green-space quota, and without enlarging existing storm drains. Although this particular project incorporated tree plantings, too, grass paving is certainly a minimal form of "green space," and the authors cannot recommend it as a way to *get around* planted-area regulations. Converting excess *existing* parking to grass paving would be more appropriate; removing the excess altogether, better yet.

Olympia WA tested the effectiveness of grassed paving in a demonstration project: a public-school parking lot from which storm runoff regularly flooded adjacent athletic fields. An 8-foot-wide, 2.5-foot-deep infiltration trench was dug along the edge of the lot and backfilled with porous sandy gravel. Honeycomb-like cellular containment units, filled with a gravel and soil mix, bear parked cars while allowing rainwater percolation into the trench. For quick vegetative cover, turf was installed over this. The soil mix was designed to hold enough water for grass to survive.

Post-construction evaluation was done for forty-eight days, of which thirty-four were rainy. Ponding on the athletic field occurred on only six of these days, a marked improvement. Parks and Recreation vehicles drove over the test; tire tracks were found on several occasions but did no irreparable damage to the lawn or to infiltration.[57] People tended not to park on the area, however, apparently averse to driving on grass. Turf, a loose carpet over such a system,

may have looked unstable, a problem that grass-in-cells avoids.

UNIT PAVERS ON PERMEABLE SUBGRADE

Another potentially permeable surface uses unit pavers (set as individual pieces, rather than poured as a continuous sheet). Such pavers themselves are not permeable, so they must be laid on permeable material: sand, crushed stone, or stone screenings. If set on concrete—as unit or interlocking pavers so commonly are—the resulting surface is no more permeable than the concrete.

Unit pavers are time-honored materials in many older cities: the brick that makes the undulating historic sidewalks in Washington DC or Philadelphia so appealing; the hexagonal pavers used in New York; or even flagstone, granite setts, or cobblestones. Interlocking concrete pavers in many styles and colors also provide some percolation. (Because permeability is not their primary environmental benefit, ICP systems are discussed in Principle I.) Some unit pavers are cast with spacers on each edge, which automatically creates extra-wide joints, while maintaining paver-to-paver contact for stability. These "spaced" systems are probably the most permeable of any unit paver, unless precast grass pavers are included.

Figure 5.9 Gravelpave² uses recycled plastic grids to stabilize gravel. Similar plastic or concrete grids strengthen grass paving or combat slope erosion. (*Photo:* Invisible Structures.)

Figure 5.10 Overflow parking at Westfarms Mall uses Grasspave² instead of impervious asphalt. (*Photo:* Invisible Structures.)

Figure 5.11 Traditional granite setts being laid on sand in Philadelphia's historic district. Joints are somewhat permeable if not mortared. (*Photo:* Kim Sorvig.)

Because percolation actually takes place in joints between the pavers, joint width and fill becomes critical. A Cornell University study[58] recommends:

- small pavers, to maximize total joint area
- thicker pavers to increase rigidity
- $1/4$-inch wide joints; wider reduces stability
- joints lower than the walking surface to increase infiltration
- coarse, sharp sand bound with bitumen (a sort of miniaturized porous asphalt) as permeable joint filler
- extra joint filler after initial settling, to avoid finer debris that blocks porosity
- coarse, lightly compacted base course for under-drainage.

Similarly, the National Concrete Masonry Association recommends *not* compacting sand under interlocking concrete pavers. Ferguson has found that joint fill coarser than sand is more permeable and stable.

As with porous paving, above, unit paver permeability may decline over time as joints become compacted by traffic and filled by debris. This decline levels off after about five years, leaving considerable permeability.

For landscape architect Henry Arnold, the major benefit of such systems is that easy percolation supports healthier plantings and cuts irrigation costs. As an example, Arnold used colored concrete unit pavers

set on a bed of finely crushed stone in downtown Atlanta's Peachtree Plaza. This beautiful walking surface collects and infiltrates water, helping to irrigate plaza plantings. (See Figure 5.13.)

On Sensitive Sites, Scatter the Parking

One problem with expansive parking lots is that they require leveling landforms and clearing vegetation. For forested and other sensitive sites, scatter the parking throughout the site, keeping disturbance small-scale. The Simmons Mattress Company outside of Atlanta used this strategy successfully for 200 parking spaces. Instead of the typical monolithic lot, Robert E. Marvin & Associates created "woodland parking" throughout the forest. A sinuous one-way driveway connected one- to three-space clusters. Flexible layout required much less cutting of trees and disturbance of the forest floor; the one-lane access kept total paving equivalent to a single lot for similar numbers of spaces. Stormwater from the slender roadway and small groups of parking spaces runs directly onto the woodland floor (there are no curbs or gutters) and soaks in. (See Figure 5.14.)

This approach requires much more detailed siting and staking than a single lot. It requires extra care during construction, preferably with small, light machinery. Landscape contractors who forgo the convenience of grading a single large space will gain satisfaction from very attractive results and reduced environmental impact. A reputation for care brings repeat business and an edge over more conventional competitors.

One objection to the scattered approach is that, because the parking is so dispersed, an employee may have to walk farther from her or his car to the building. The authors say: Get over it! Like the "right-to-drive" arguments mentioned above, this objection has little merit. Dispersed parking should be tried at many more low-density sites where trees or other site features need to be preserved.

In general, even where preservation of site features is *not* a major issue, it is advisable to break up any paved surfaces into smaller units so that each can drain to an adjacent unpaved area. By reducing runoff-flow distances for near-source infiltration, this

Figure 5.12 In small-scale, low-traffic areas, unit pavers can even support wildflowers. (*Project:* R. and V. Sorvig. *Photo:* Kim Sorvig.)

system protects the site's water regime, a concept discussed in more detail on p. 211. Breaking up level surfaces also reduces grading significantly. On hillsides especially, parking lots, roads, and trails should be terraced. This requires subdividing the parking, and separating roads and trails into independent parallel lanes, a technique beautifully used in parkway design.

Install "Green Streets"

An important innovation in managing runoff from paving is the "green street." A green street, essentially, is one that cleanses and infiltrates its own stormwater through a coordinated combination of techniques similar to those in this chapter. A green street decreases stormwater burden on both sewer systems and streams.

Figure 5.13 Henry Arnold has used open-jointed unit pavers at large plazas in Atlanta GA, Brooklyn NY, and Newport NJ, usually with extra aeration vents. (*Project and Photo:* Henry Arnold.)

Figure 5.14 Dispersed parking for Simmons headquarters reduced disruption and infiltrates runoff near its source. (*Project:* Robert Marvin Associates. *Photo:* Bruce Ferguson.)

In concept, green streets work like bioswales. Water runs down the street in the gutter and drops into a series of planted basins for cleansing and infiltration. Vegetated, porous areas divide impervious surfaces (see DCIAs, above); for example, they are typically inserted between sidewalk and street. Excess can flow into a conventional storm sewer during heavy storms.

Green streets can be new streets or retrofits. Typically, their many elements are shoehorned into existing urban fabric: wrapping around elementary schools, wedged into boulevards, growing at grocery-store entrances, and planted in residential parking zones. They are *constructed ecological networks* designed to treat urban stormwater.

Not unexpectedly, green streets are most frequent in the rainy Pacific Northwest. Portland OR has installed several as ongoing demonstrations. All are capable of infiltrating at least two inches per hour and have measurably reduced impacts on the larger stormwater system. They are generally low maintenance, requiring occasional sediment removal and annual plant trimming. Soil quality is monitored for heavy metals (currently within safe levels). These demonstrations show that the concept works, and if applied on a citywide, master-planned scale could be significant for stormwater management.

Kevin Perry, a landscape architect formerly with Portland's Bureau of Environmental Services, suggests four key concepts for green streets:

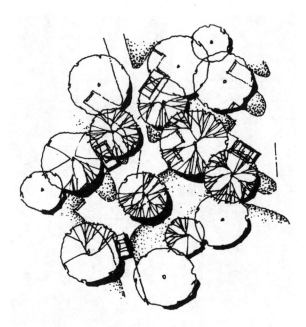

Figure 5.15 Plan of Simmons dispersed parking shows small graded areas integrated with the existing site, rather than one large flattened area. (*Illust.:* Craig Farnsworth, based on Ferguson.)

- Manage Water at the Source: Infiltrate water where it hits the ground. Green streets reduce downstream flows by at least 80 percent; that much less water reaches the next pipe, basin, or treatment facility.
- Manage Water at the Surface: Avoid pipes, which are expensive to install, and can clog or freeze. Overland conveyance is easier to install and maintain, and allows evaporation, use by plants, and infiltration.
- Let Nature Do the Work: When plants and soil slow runoff, filter minerals, and prevent erosion, costs for construction and operation of infrastructure such as treatment plants are reduced.
- Create Community Assets: Pipes and catch basins don't do anything for anybody except the dubious service of whisking away water. Green streets bring beauty to urban neighborhoods, make pedestrian crossings safer, and calm street traffic.[59]

Green streets exemplify multifunctional and geometrically complex design, increasingly recognized as a core concept in sustainability. Conventional streets and drain pipes are designed with simplified geome-

tries to optimize one exclusive function (flat surfaces for vehicle movement, simple cylinders for water removal). Like ecosystems, green streets are a step toward approximating ecosystems' geometric complexity, functional openness, and diversity. (See p. 24.)

Cool Asphalt with Planting and Albedo

Conventional parking lots, as noted above, are major contributors to urban "heat islands." Black asphalt is particularly heat-absorbing. Concrete and some other light-colored paving materials reflect more sunlight, absorbing less heat. Dark brick and stone, and colored concrete, may be almost as heat-absorbent as asphalt. (Meg Calkins gives surface reflectivity index [SRI] values and other heat-island data for fifteen materials; conventional asphalt ranges from zero—black—to 6; concrete and colored asphalt, from 35 to 85; LEED gives a credit for SRI over 29.[60])

Grass paving is significantly less absorptive of heat than any hard surface. If the climate is not too harsh to support grass, this alternative paving can cut heat retention. Initial test results indicate porous paving, with its built-in air space and moisture, holds less heat than conventional paving.

Reducing the *amount* of paving should always be the first consideration where heat is an issue. Where a hard-surfaced lot is essential for a project, however, the EPA recommends two ways of reducing the heat increases from paving.[61] The first is to plant shade trees—a seemingly simple move. Some city tree ordinances, however, actually ban true shade trees in favor of small convenient species. Vine-covered trellises can be an alternative, but the magnificent street trees of older cities shade more area more economically.

The second EPA approach is to increase pavement's reflectiveness (or "albedo"), thus reducing heat absorption. Too much reflectance equals glare and must also be avoided. Given the prevalence of asphalt (nearly 75 percent of all US paving), and the fact that its oily composition makes it hard to paint or stain, methods of lightening these surfaces take on particular importance for sustainability.

Fortunately, asphalt can be lightened in several ways. Specify light-colored aggregate and fines in asphalt mixes; although surfaces are initially black, wear exposes this aggregate. Many conventional "blacktop" roads are in fact the color of local aggregate. Ensure that neither construction workers nor maintenance staff apply the conventional pure-black "wearing coat," often done routinely for a new and tidy look. Light-colored aggregate can be used for porous as well as nonporous asphalt.

Color-coating for asphalt developed as a decorative system, but has environmental possibilities. Slurry seals, composed of sand, cement, and acrylic-polymer binders, have been developed to adhere to the slightly oily surface of asphalt. These can be almost any color; light-colored coatings make asphalt paving less heat-absorptive.[62] These coatings are often used with metal templates that, pressed into the hot asphalt by a vibratory roller, produce surface patterns: brick, cobblestone, even custom logos or artwork. Normal cracking of the asphalt is reduced because template-compressed areas act as expansion joints, while the coating seals out water. The first installations in the United States, made in the early 1990s, have required much less routine maintenance than conventional asphalt.

The main environmental reason to consider these coatings is to reduce heat absorption. To the extent that these coatings reduce maintenance and extend the life of asphalt, they save resources. They may also solve the difficulty of trenches cut through paving for utility repairs: using templates, trenches can be recoated to match original work. Coatings do not address asphalt's imperviousness, nor health problems that exposure to hot asphalt can create.

Coatings, which can be applied by ordinary laborers, add 30–50 percent to the price of plain asphalt. Similar in appearance to patterned concrete, they cost 50–80 percent of high-end stamped concrete systems like Bomanite.[63]

In addition to coatings, asphalt can be colored in the hot mix. Provided by Asphacolor (Madera CA), this relatively new process was used for Los Angeles Union Station. Heat-island reduction was not apparently a goal of this project, but probably occurred incidentally.

Bagged colorant is batch mixed with asphalt and aggregate at the plant; as with coatings, almost any color can be produced. Compared to ordinary asphalt, mixing is slightly slower, more coordination is required, and extra cleanup is necessary before mixing other colors or plain asphalt. Only the top 1 to 1.5 inches of paving are usually colored. Costs are somewhat higher than asphalt-coating systems, but still less than colored concrete. Because it is integral to the mix, the Asphacolor process may wear longer than coatings. It offers some interesting design pos-

Figure 5.16 "Green streets" (like Siskyou St., Portland OR) collect water from wider areas with parking, and infiltrate it in "bump-out" planted areas that also help traffic calming. (*Project:* Portland Bureau of Environmental Services. *Photo:* Kevin Robert Perry and Portland Bureau of Environmental Services.)

Figure 5.17 Decorative color coatings for asphalt can lighten the surface, decreasing heat-island effects. Integral color, mixed into hot asphalt, is also becoming available. (*Photo:* StreetPrint, Scott Hind.)

sibilities in combination with contrasting colored aggregate and is the only way that *porous* asphalt could be colored.⊃

Asphalt is one of the cheapest ways of meeting society's massive demand for paving and likely to remain a major component of the built environment for a long time to come. Being able to achieve color more cheaply than colored concrete may actually expand the marketplace for asphalt. Whether these decorative systems can make asphalt paving significantly more sustainable remains to be seen. They clearly affect the heat-island problem, however, and may somewhat reduce asphalt maintenance and replacement. Like any impervious paving, colored asphalt requires runoff management.

As we stress throughout this book, technical solutions to sustainability problems can only succeed if paralleled by social changes. This is particularly true anywhere cars are involved, as with paving. Creative and high-quality work by landscape designers and contractors is one of the best hopes for raising public awareness and acceptance of new paving methods. Museums, nature centers, and educational institutions, as well as national and regional parks, have environmental goals and offer high-profile opportunities to showcase sustainable methods. Sustainability is also a concern in more and more corporate boardrooms; projects for such clients offer different avenues to educate the public about paving less.

Resources

Pave Less

Over-paving

Search Terms: paving excessive || impervious surfaces ||parking quotas

Asphalt Nation: How the Automobile Took Over America and How We Can Take It Back Jane H. Kay, 1997 Crown/Random House, New York: Overview of history of paving in the United States; despite the title, not focused only on asphalt.

Paving

Search Terms: paving || paving materials || pervious paving || permeable paving

Portland Cement Association Skokie IL, 847-966-6200, www.cement.org/: Publishes and consults on concrete use.

Porous paving Andropogon Associates, 215-487-0700; FL Concrete and Products Association, 407-895-9333; National Aggregate Association, 301-587-1400; National Asphalt Paving Association, 888-468-6499

SF-Rima wide-joint unit pavers SF Concrete Technology, Mississauga ON, 905-828-2868, www.sfconcrete.com/about _us .html: Unit pavers held apart and sturdy by joint spacers on all sides.

Grasspave², Gravelpave² Invisible Structures Inc, Golden CO, 800-233-1510, www.invisiblestructures.com/: Recycled-plastic, porous alternatives to paving; notable for being owned and run by a landscape architect.

Impervious Surface Reduction Study Cedar Wells, Dir., Olympia WA, Public Works Department, 360-753-8362, www.ci .olympia.wa.us/citygovernment/dept/pw/

Grass Paving Systems James Sipes and Mack Roberts, Jun 1994, LAM

"Porous Paving" Kim Sorvig, Feb 1993, LAM: Article introducing porous asphalt and concrete.

Parking Supply Management 1997 Federal Transit Administration, Washington DC: www.fta.dot.gov/ Search site for "parking supply."

Shared Parking Planning Guidelines 1995 Institute of Transportation Engineers, Washington DC, 202-289-0222, www.ite.org/

Bureau of Transportation Statistics www.bts.gov/: Numbers and databases on all modes of transportation in the United States.

Porous Pavements B. K. Ferguson, 2005 Taylor and Francis, Boca Raton FL

"Impervious Surface Coverage" Chester Arnold and James Gibbons, Spring 1996, *Journal of the American Planning Association*

International Parking Institute www.parking.org/: Answers to common questions about parking.

Parking Spaces Mark Childs, 1999 McGraw-Hill, New York

Riverside/Corona CA conservation district www.rcrcd.com/: Innovative planning and technologies of interest.

Taylor's Weekend Gardening Guide to Garden Paths: A New Way to Solve Practical Problems in the Garden Gordon Hayward, 1998 Houghton Mifflin, New York

Rubber Paving Association www.rubberpavements.org/: FAQ page especially useful.

Roadway design

Search Terms: traffic calming || context sensitive design || roundabouts || speed bumps

Greenways: A Guide to Planning, Design, and Development Loring Schwartz, 1996 Island Press, Washington DC

Interactive Highway Safety Design Model FHWA Turner-Fairbanks Highway Research Center, www.tfhrc.gov/: Interactively simulates, evaluates road design, driver behavior, speeds; incorporates "traffic-calming" concepts.

Lying Lightly on the Land Curators Timothy Davis and Joseph Roas, National Building Museum, Historic American Engineering Record, and Federal Lands Highway Office, 202-272-2448, www.nbm.org/: Exhibit on park road design and construction; alternatives to over-engineered roads; online exhibit at www.nbm.org/Exhibits/past/2000_1996/Lying_Lightly.html.

Center for Livable Communities Sacramento CA, 916-448-1198, www.lgc.org/: Useful publications, including *Streets and Sidewalks, People, and Cars: The Citizens' Guide to Traffic Calming.*

US Transportation Research Board http://rip.trb.org/: Look for "Research in Progress" listings; includes many native-plant revegetation projects, wildlife and road ecology methods, and context sensitive strategies.

Context Sensitive Solutions www.contextsensitivesolutions.org/: Many free downloads, including FHWA's "Flexibility in Highway Design."

Surface Transportation Policy Project www.transact.org/: Look for "Second Nature: Improving Transportation Without Putting Nature Second"; nationwide network of 800-plus planning, community development, and advocacy organizations.

"Development and Nature: Enhancing Ecosystems Where We Build" EBN, Feb 2001: Includes great checklist; "Wildlife Habitat Enhancement of Developed Land."

Traffic calming

Traffic Calming Library Institute of Transportation Engineers, 202-289-0222, www.ite.org/traffic/: Searchable library of articles on traffic calming—issues, methods, devices, law, etc.

TrafficCalming.org www.trafficcalming.org/: Includes overview, effectiveness, and measures for traffic calming.

Slow Down, You're Going Too Fast!: The Community Guide to Traffic Calming 1998 Public Technology Inc., Washington DC

"Traffic Calming Ahead!" Alex Wilson, Mar 2003, EBN

Traffic Calming: State of the Practice 1999 Reid Ewing Institute of Transportation Engineers, Washington DC: Downloadable comprehensive guide to traffic calming at www.ite.org/.

Take Back Your Streets: How to Protect Communities from Asphalt and Traffic 3rd ed., 1998, Conservation Law Foundation: Available online at www.clf.org/; search site for title under publications; full text now appears to be online.

Heat islands

Asphalt color coating DecoAsphalt (CA) 877-332-6277, www.decoasphalt.com/; Integrated Paving Concepts (Canada), 800-688-5652, www.streetprint.com/: Asphalt patterning and coating systems with potential for albedo use.

Asphalt: integral colorants 866-506-3554, www.asphacolor.com/

Cooling Our Communities: A Guidebook on Tree Planting and Light-colored Surfacing Hashem Akbari, 1992: Lawrence Berkeley Laboratory report LBL-31587, US Government Printing Office, 866-512-1800, http://bookstore.gpo.gov/

Biofiltration

Search Terms: bioswales || vegetated (swale OR filtration) || biofiltration

Road ecology

Search Terms: "road ecology" || wildlife crossings || vehicle wildlife accidents

Road Ecology Center http://roadecology.ucdavis.edu/: Informative Web site on wildlife ecology and roads; many affiliated scientists.

Road Ecology: Science and Solutions Richard Foreman et al., 2003 Island Press, Washington DC: First comprehensive book on this recent science.

The Ecology of Transportation: Managing Mobility for the Environment John and Julia L. Davenport (eds.), 2006 Springer, Berlin

Corridor Ecology: The Science and Practice of Linking Landscapes for Biodiversity Conservation Jodi A. Hilty et al., 2006 Island Press, Washington DC

AASHTO Center for Environmental Excellence www.environment.transportation.org/: TERI database tracks and shares new transportation and environmental research ideas.

Center for Transportation and the Environment (CTE) www.itre.ncsu.edu/CTE/: North Carolina State University, Institute for Transportation Research and Education.

Federal Highway Administration: Easy Ways to Help Wildlife Along Roads www.fhwa.dot.gov/environment/wildlife protection/: Many case studies and ideas.

The Wildlife Crossings Toolkit www.wildlifecrossings.info/: USDA Forest Service searchable database of case histories, mitigation measures, and articles.

International Conference on Wildlife Ecology and Transportation (ICOWET) www.dot.state.fl.us/emo/sched/icowetiii.htm: ICOWET annual proceedings.

Western Transportation Institute 406-994-6114, www.coe.montana.edu/wti/: Road ecology program.

Australian Research Center for Urban Ecology (ARCUE) www.rbg.vic.gov.au/research_and_conservation/arcue/conservation/selected_road_ecology_references: Good international bibliography on road ecology.

Principle 6:
Consider Origin and Fate of Materials

Nature resolves everything into its component elements, but annihilates nothing.
—Lucretius, 57 BC

One theme of this book is that inappropriate landscape design and construction—such as over-paving or invasive plantings—damages sites. Even landscapes that seem perfectly harmonious with their sites, however, can impact environments far *beyond*. Pliny Fisk, codirector of the Center for Maximum Potential Building Systems in Austin TX, illustrates this: "One can disturb a site to the least possible degree and be causing utter havoc on Earth at the same time—because of what you're *bringing to* that site. Let's say that landscape architects are going to do a large paved area and they decide to use granite pavers quarried in Minnesota. There's a good chance that the granite is shipped to Italy, sliced up, sent back and delivered to Houston, or wherever the building site is. That's an incredible imposition on the well-being of this planet."[1]

Fisk is referring, of course, to energy costs (and concomitant air pollution) required to move that granite around the globe. *Materials* used in landscapes have many such impacts. Extraction of raw materials for landscape products has environmental and energy costs, including impacts from polluting factories far from the site. Even debris hauled off site has impacts—energy costs of removal and space taken up by landfills.

While designers have become increasingly aware of sustainable techniques, the majority of landscape projects still specify virgin materials. "Such landscapes, no matter how sensitive they are to the ecology of a site, are still destructive," says Kathleen Baughman, a landscape designer in Portland OR, "for they promote the continued environmental degradation associated with resource extraction."[2]

Almost every construction material is extracted from somewhere. Some extraction processes are more destructive than others; some products are renewable or reusable. Hidden costs can be high, from nonrenewable petroleum products used in asphalt, to destruction of rainforests for tropical hardwoods—or, for that matter, felling of domestic redwoods for decks and site furniture. This chapter focuses on recognizing hidden costs of landscape materials, and hazards to land-owners and landscape workers.

Realistic alternatives do exist: local materials, reused or recycled materials, and materials found on-site. Acceptability of these materials was growing rapidly when the first edition of this book was released: a contest to win a custom home built of "top-of-the line recyclables" attracted *seven times* as many entries in 1998 as 1997.[3] These trends continue: wider acceptance of alternative materials, and more detailed materials research. Alternative materials are now viewed by many landscape professionals not as limitations, but as opportunities, not only imposing lesser burdens on the planet, but also inspiring some of today's most creative landscapes.

Discussed in This Chapter

Eight basic guidelines to simplify choice of sustainable materials.

Using on-site and local resources.
Recycled products for landscapes.
Recycling construction materials.
Recognizing and avoiding toxic materials.
Impacts of transportation, mining, and other general processes.

Note to readers of the first edition: After careful consideration, the appendix covering 49 basic construction materials has been made available online at www.SustainableLandscapeOnline.com. We hope this provides wider access to the information; it allows updating this edition without massive expansion in bulk.

Recall Some Simple Guidelines

As a simple set of operational rules, consider this short list of principles from Maurice Nelischer, a landscape architect in Guelph, Ontario:[4]

- Whenever possible, specify locally produced products.
- Use less-processed materials (rough-sawn or air-dried lumber, for instance).
- Perform a rough audit of energy required to mine, produce, ship, and install materials. See Principle 7.
- Explore recycled materials. Specify reusable materials—for example, stone, brick, or concrete pavers rather than poured concrete.
- Avoid petroleum-based materials whenever possible. Asphalt and many plastics are indispensable in a few uses, but not for every purpose.

These guidelines offer a starting point. Some additions to the list:

- Use durable materials and designs.
- Minimize use of materials that are toxic, either on-site or during manufacture or disposal.
- Offset CO_2 at every opportunity. Lock up carbon by using wood durably; Fisk speaks of "CO_2 balancing" a project's materials. Use living materials (plantings or bioengineering) that take up CO_2 while serving structural purposes.

Let Reuse Be Re-inspiration

Recycling is worthwhile for simple pragmatic reasons. But like necessity, it can be a source of invention, inspiring both designers and users of landscapes.

The uniqueness of specific places has been diluted

Figure 6.1 Landscapes that reuse neglected materials can be a much-needed source of pride and identity in a homogenizing world. (*Photo:* Kim Sorvig.)

by modern communication and transportation; many people feel adrift in a featureless landscape of convenience. Reusing castoff materials is a link to other people and times, giving a deeply desired sense of continuity. The results may be as quiet as "character" from worn, used stone, or as blatant as an old tractor planted with petunias. Large or small, tasteful or garish, reused materials have an identity that can't be bought new.

Use Local, Salvaged, or Recycled Materials

The simplest single way to cut down material impacts is to obtain them locally. Trucking one ton of material one mile typically uses between 2,000 and 6,000 Btu; air freight can easily use twenty times this energy.[5] Fuel consumption for transporting materials from afar can be greater than energy used to extract and manufacture the items. Rising fuel costs make local materials economical.

Figure 6.2 "Recycling" a power turbine into a picnic umbrella (New Zealand) saves no materials, but humanizes a massive postindustrial artifact. At this scale, reuse and recycling can be both whimsical and transformative. (*Photo:* Kim Sorvig.)

Not only is long-distance transportation an energy cost, but fuel combustion is a primary source of pollution and greenhouse gases. For every mile less between supplier and site, nonrenewable fuel resources are saved, and emissions that cause health problems and contribute to global warming are reduced.

Some materials are easier to obtain locally than others. Steel, for instance, is produced in a few centralized factories, while cement or brick are frequently manufactured locally. Buying from your local steel mill is not often an option: production efficiency requires centralization. For other materials, such as lumber, it may be possible to find a local supplier, but conventional business practices (such as supplying all US lumber from the Pacific Northwest or Georgia) keep local materials artificially expensive. Distant or foreign ownership of local material production can also distort costs. Intense demand from China for construction materials is destabilizing prices. Monetary cost is often a misleading indicator of environmental costs, and sustainability requires better true-cost estimating of materials.

Salvaged or reused materials are often local, serving twice for roughly the same energy cost. Clearly, some salvage methods use so much energy that they offer no real environmental savings, but the bulldoze-and-dump approach uses as much and wastes more. Salvage work is typically done by hand or small power tools, more renewable human energy, and less nonrenewable mechanical energy.

Recycled materials are *remanufactured* between first and second use. Careful analysis is required to know which materials are environmentally cost-effective to recycle. Popularly equated with sustainability, some forms of recycling do not save enough energy to be environmentally sound. While aluminum can be remanufactured using a fraction of new production energy, other materials cannot. Collecting and transporting materials for recycling may evaporate net energy savings. For some materials, recycling can only produce a second-rate material; this is called "downcycling." For example, plastics pure enough for medicine containers generally are not recyclable. Recycling, like salvage and reuse, does keep materials out of landfills; sometimes this is reason enough to recycle even when energy savings are borderline.

Participation in recycling programs fluctuates dramatically. Nineteen states dropped glass recycling altogether in 2001; overall recycling was stagnant at about 30 percent of total volume of consumer trash. Even the easiest products—aluminum cans—were only recycled about half as much as they could be between 2001 and 2003. If a community recycles a large amount, recycled materials may flood the market, making them less valuable; recycling then becomes costly, rather than profitable or breakeven. Worst of all, the rate at which Americans dispose of trash is 80 percent higher today than it was in 1960—and most studies show that the more people recycle, the more trash they also produce.[6] These are issues far larger than the landscape industry, but affect many landscape practices.

The market for recycled materials is also unstable. Aluminum scrap, for example, dropped dramatically in 2003, but hit an eighteen-year high price in 2006, according to the Institute for Scrap Recycling Industries. In the mid-1990s, recycled newsprint was worth $100 a ton; in 2003, it had fallen to one-tenth that value. Metal recycling prices, at their highest, can induce *theft* of landscape items. Aluminum bleachers, park benches and irrigation pipes, steel highway guardrails, light-rail tracks and railroad spikes, copper down-spouts, all have been stolen—even power lines, which have electrocuted several would-be thieves.[7] As natural resources become scarcer through unsustainable use, they change social behavior, often negatively.

In some cases recycling and reuse may *converge*. For example, yard waste has made up about one-fifth of municipal solid waste, and more in some areas; many jurisdictions now ban it from landfills (see p. 331). If used as mulch and soil builder, greenwaste is seldom considered "recycled" in the same sense as recycled plastic. Yet greenwaste uses the landscape as the *medium* of recycling. Renewability, too, happens in the landscape. Wood is the only really renewable construction product, with the exception of a few plant-based paints and varnishes.[8] Renewability depends on proper management of forests or fields so that these can continue to produce resources.

Sustainable use of materials has many complexities, and the well-known slogan "Reduce, Reuse, Recycle" needs to be understood as a list *in priority order*. Using less materials, reusing them in their present form, and finally recycling them is a sustainable path. When recycling, or even reuse, becomes an excuse to continue using more materials, or to use materials with extremely poor environmental records, it makes a mockery of hopes for sustainability. Likewise, using a locally produced but highly toxic material is of little environmental benefit.

For better or worse, environmental choice of materials is seldom cut and dried. As Sandra Mendler points out in HOK's *Sustainable Design Guide*, these choices will become easier the more professionals practice them. "It took about 100 years to arrive at a generally accepted set of 'rules' to deal with basic issues of safety in 'modern' buildings.

We must now move forward by focusing on sustainable design as our 19th century predecessors emphasized life safety."[9]

Use On-site Materials

If using local materials follows "close-to-source" principles, then the closest source is the site itself. The great majority of materials for traditional construction—soil, wood, or rock—were from the site or very nearby. Limitations on locally available materials played a strong role in development of regional technologies and design styles. For example, the high deserts of the Southwestern United States and Mexico have tall trees only in limited mountain areas. This led directly to adobe—earth from within the building's footprint, in many cases—as the main building regional material, with timber reserved for roof beams and lintels.

Far from being just a constraint, these local materials awakened creative design: Southwestern adobe has become one of today's most popular and imitated styles. With creativity, a wide range of on-site materials may be productively reused in landscapes. In an era when the homogenizing effects of industrial, Modernist design are widely regretted, creative use of on-site materials offers not only environmental benefits, but artistic rebirth.

BOULDERS, STONE, BRICK, AND TIMBER
As well as earth and plants, many sites contain stone, either cut or rough, bricks, or old lumber. Mario Schjetnan, a Mexico City landscape architect, made extraordinary reuse of on-site volcanic stone at Malinalco golf club south of the capital (Figure 6.3). The stone—some of it sizeable boulders—was unearthed during excavation. Instead of reinterring it at great cost, Schjetnan constructed massive stone walls to define the entry, and a spacious entrance plaza built entirely of smaller stones. The project won an honor award from the American Society of Landscape Architects in 1998. (Another Mexican landscape featuring on-site volcanic stone is Luis Barragan's famous Pedregal.)

The stones at Malinalco were placed by hand—a labor-intensive process not replicable in nations with

Figure 6.3   Stone from site excavation, reused in walls and paving at Club de Golf Malinalco, makes a stunning argument for inventive use of site "waste." (*Project:* Mario Schjetnan. *Photo:* Courtesy of Grupo de Diseno Urbano.)

high labor costs. Social issues are part of construction, and designers and builders must evolve reuses that fit their own societies.

On-site rubble can be used in developed countries, though. In Oslo, Norway, demolition permitted creation of a garden court in a historic area. Landscape architect Rainer Stange transformed roof tiles and other rubble into retaining walls. Following the former buildings' footprints, the walls are a ghostly reflection of history, restating the recycling concept. Steps were made of reused stone curbs. Tiles and

other salvaged materials fill plantable gabions, while for contrast, clean high-tech metal trellises tie the space together. Careful selection of climbing plants, one species per wall, helps orient users to this charmingly offbeat garden (Figure 6.4).[10]

Demolition rubble can be reconstituted as paving surfaces. At the Institute for Regenerative Studies, broken concrete slabs were pieced together and cemented to form a new driveway and parking area. This reduced new cement requirements significantly. Asphalt is directly recycled on-site by modern road

machinery; concrete recycling is developing, though still not common.

Elsewhere in this book we argue for removing old paving and structures and restoring soil underneath. But where the structure can be adapted, or where energy costs of removal are high, it may make more sense to leave such structures in place and "recycle" them. An example is Monnens Addis Design in Berkeley CA, where a defunct warehouse was rehabilitated as a graphic-design studio. The owners wanted a garden, but the only available spot was the former loading dock, covered with a concrete slab eight inches thick. Landscape architect Jeffrey Miller chose

an unusual strategy: instead of demolishing the slab, he built the garden atop it.

Cost was an obvious factor; transporting and dumping demolition debris has become a significant expense in most cities. But beyond this pragmatic consideration Miller believes in reuse of on-site materials. "I've found that if you can leave things where they are," he says, "you're not spreading more junk around the planet."

Miller punched through the slab to create planting pits for four weeping acacia trees, a queen palm, and two species of bamboo, using a diamond-blade saw. Cement from the holes was piled against the

Figure 6.4 Salvaged during demolition, roof tiles form curbs and gutters, and fill gabion-like planted walls in this urban garden in Oslo, Norway. Crushed tile surfaces paths, and serves as concrete aggregate. Stone, too, is second hand. (*Project:* Snøhetta Landskapsarkitekter. *Photo:* Rainer Stange.)

building to create raised, planted seating areas. Compacting the rubble mechanically by vibration, Miller filled any voids with gravel and sand, and finally added eighteen inches of soil. The striking results can be seen in Figure 6.8.

ADOBE, SOIL CEMENT, AND OTHER EARTHEN MATERIALS
Mud, that most elemental of materials, has been used in dozens of cultures, not just the familiar Santa Fe Style. Ironically, architects and historians are more

likely to be aware of this than most landscape professionals. Although scarcely familiar in contemporary landscapes, earth-building techniques are intimately linked to landscape history.

Historically, the earliest Persian gardens and Babylon's Hanging Gardens were probably earth walled. North Africa and the Arab world have a vibrant mud-building tradition with arches, domes, and incised decoration. The Great Wall of China is cored with rammed earth; many of Japan's most sophisti-

Figure 6.6 This unpromising site was reborn as a garden—without major demolition. (*Photo:* Jeffrey Miller.)

Figure 6.5 Broken concrete, reused in slabs or crushed as aggregate, demonstrate John Lyle's concepts at the Institute for Regenerative Studies. (*Project and Photo:* John Lyle.)

cated gardens are mud walled, often whitewashed. Even in rainy European climates, each country has its earthen architecture: "cob" and "wattle-and-daub" in England, *leichtlehm* in Germany, or *pise* in France; some emigrated to the colonies, where examples still survive.

A few landscape architects use earth structures today, appreciating its sculptural, geomorphic flexibility, plus the unparalleled intimacy it creates, site specific and understated. Albuquerque landscape architects Baker Morrow and Bill Hays have used adobe blocks for garden shelters, walls, seating, even patio pavement. In New Mexico's dry climate, adobe will last nearly twenty years without even a coping. Russell Beatty, a California landscape architect, uses rammed earth for garden walls. The firm of Cochran and Delaney used rammed earth walls based on South African tradition in their African Healing Gar-

den in San Francisco. Although earth building is almost never taught in landscape courses, it is energy efficient, nontoxic, and self-recycling.

Technically, only sun-dried bricks of earth are "adobe."[11] Other earth-building includes "puddled" or "coursed" adobe, a poured-in-place approach. Rammed earth tamps a form full of relatively dry, cement-stabilized earth; "pressed adobe" is rammed blocks; and "stabilized" adobe is the old-fashioned sun-dried brick, with a little asphalt emulsion added. *Adobe quemado* is a porous, low-fired brick, made on-site, typical of Mexico and parts of Arizona.

Soil cement is ordinary soil mixed with a few percent Portland cement. Many examples survive from "New Deal" public works and national parks structures, most still in good shape today. For soil paving that blends aesthetically with the site, several companies offer binders or stabilizers. These save importing bulk materials. The resulting surface is impervious, with runoff problems similar to asphalt or concrete.

Many but not all types of soil can be used for earth building. High organic content and shrink-swell soils should be avoided. The National Bureau of Standards even has a formula: 17 percent clay, 24 percent silt, 19 percent coarse (angular) sand, and 40 percent fine sand. More than 30 percent clay causes shrinkage cracks; added straw can help and adds slight tensile strength. About 10 percent water is the right consistency for forming adobes, while rammed earth is better at 7 percent. Stabilization uses either asphalt (about 4 percent) or cement (not more than 6 percent) to slow water absorption and surface

Figure 6.7 The Monnens Addis renovation in progress. (*Project:* Miller Co. *Photo:* Jeffrey Miller.)

erosion of blocks. The compressive strength of adobes ranges from 300 to 600 psi, strong enough for arches and carving. Rammed earth is considerably stronger.

Construction with adobes is wonderfully flexible. Just about any item can be embedded (from tiles to mailboxes); existing trees are often simply flowed around. The material seems to evoke artistic improvisation (Figure 6.9).

To shelter a free-standing landscape wall, an Asian- or Spanish-style tile coping projecting beyond the wall face is best. Concrete caps actually accelerate erosion of the softer wall below. A waterproof foundation is also advisable. Traditionally, though, permanence in earth construction is achieved using the technique that makes Taos Pueblo the oldest continuously inhabited structure in North America: a new skin of mud plaster every couple of years.

One interesting variation on adobe is on-site firing, invented by Iranian-born architect Nader Khalili. By placing simple oil-fired burners inside a domed adobe house (or, for landscape walls, under ceramic-fiber blankets), the whole structure is fired and glazed. Khalili has also experimented with self-hardening sandbag walls, and other resource-efficient building methods.

Adobe is *both* the most expensive building material (if made commercially and trucked to the site) and the cheapest—if done by hand on-site. One study

showed that for 1.5 gallons of gasoline, a dozen standard bricks can be fired and transported—or ninety adobes can be made using an on-site machine. Each adobe has the same volume as a dozen common bricks, and is ninety times as energy efficient. Hand-pressed adobes require so little fuel energy that they hardly register on the embodied energy scale.

Unstabilized earth-built structures also self-recycle: as long as they are maintained and used, they are lasting and solid, but once abandoned, they slowly return to the earth.

Earth building does pose one sustainability problem: the sandy loam soils that work best for adobe may also be the best agricultural soils an arid region has to offer. Stabilized adobe takes soil out of agricultural use for much longer, similar to fired bricks. Ideally, only poor soils from the building's footprint should be used for earth building.[12]

Find and Reuse Off-site Salvage

When materials are not available on-site, nearby sources are worth finding. Municipal greenwaste is one example (p. 92). Any salvage that slows the endless stream of waste going to landfills is worthwhile. Another significant component of the waste stream —construction and demolition debris—comprises anywhere from one-quarter to one-third of municipal waste. Metal, wood, glass, brick, and concrete are

Figure 6.8 The finished Monnens Addis garden gives no hint of its former derelict status. (*Project:* Miller Co. *Photo:* Jeffrey Miller.)

often recycled, yet are also *reusable* landscape materials.[13] If they can be sourced locally, such materials can be reconfigured in artful landscapes *without* resource-intensive industrial recycling.

STONE

Reused stone may be particularly applicable for public projects: public-works departments often stockpile granite curbing and other used stone elements. Salvaged stone was used evocatively at Parque da Cidade in Oporto, Portugal (Figure 6.11). Sidonio Pardal, the park landscape architect, reused salvaged granite to construct retaining walls and other structures, including faux ruins. One such "ruin" overlooks the park's lake, resembling the remains of some fabulous palace; in it are irrigation controls for the park. Many other structures, in a variety of styles, could be constructed with salvaged stone. Not all landscape designers approve of "fake" features, although reused materials lend themselves to fantasy.

Figure 6.9 Adobe is one of the most flexible materials to work with, and inspires site-specific construction that celebrates existing features like this tree. (*Photo:* Kim Sorvig.)

The presence of salvaged, durable stone can lend a remarkable sense of history and place to new landscape work.

TIMBER

The challenge in using salvaged materials is not simply to make do with second-hand resources but to create visually powerful design and compelling places. Landscape architect Marjorie Pitz accomplished this when she constructed The Sacred Circle, a temporary (1998) AIDS memorial, in Loring Park Minneapolis MN. Her budget was only $2,500. "My project involved significant structure, which made the jury wonder if it would be possible to pull it off with such a limited budget," notes Pitz. "The use of salvaged materials made it feasible."

The Sacred Circle consisted of twelve "tree trunks" made of salvaged utility poles, donated by the local utility after removal from another Pitz project site. Pitz's concept was to wrap the poles with saplings to symbolize AIDS victims cut down in their prime, but she was reluctant to cut trees of value to anyone. She was able to locate, through her network of colleagues, a farm outside Minneapolis on which willows were being removed to restore native prairie. The property owner had lost a cousin to AIDS and was happy to see the saplings salvaged. Finding the poles and saplings required a certain amount of scouting, compared to the more usual route of obtaining materials through a salvage dealer.

CRUSHED GLASS

Crushed glass, or cullet, is a versatile recycled material. It can replace sand or gravel in many applications; its inherent beauty suits it to many decorative purposes. Even high-end projects, such as Los Angeles County Museum and Mandalay Bay Hotel in Las Vegas, have used recycled glass in their landscapes.[14]

Cullet is used in concrete, asphalt, and other paving mixes; as a fill material to replace aggregate; and as an ingredient in tiles and similar remanufactured products (p. 239). Glass for all landscape uses is tumbled to smooth away sharp edges.

"Glasphalt," replacing aggregate and sand with crushed glass, has been used in pedestrian and bike paths, parking areas, and even roads—up to 10 percent glass without instability or cracking. Cullet cannot be used without other aggregates because it is not as strong as crushed rock.[15] New York City, through a joint venture between its departments of sanitation and transportation, has made a commitment to using glasphalt in all repaving projects.

A glasphalt bike/pedestrian path leads to the top of the artificial hill at Danehy Park, a former landfill. (See p 78.) Merle Ukeles's project combined community involvement, recycled materials, and artistic intent, recalling sacred Indian mounds. Twenty-two tons of glass were mostly collected by schoolchildren and community groups; a Washington manufacturer donated ten tons of scrap stained glass, normally considered unrecyclable, and a New York mirror manufacturer donated surplus. Because the state of Massachusetts had never used glasphalt, it requested testing at New York City's glasphalt plant.[16]

Figure 6.10 Earthen landscape construction graces hundreds of historic sites, including Japan's most refined gardens. (*Photo:* Kim Sorvig.)

One caveat in specifying glass for paving is a small potential for contamination—not from the glass itself but from lead off wine bottles. Producers are required to test periodically for contamination; in properly handled cullet, lead should not be a problem. Test projects in King County WA have not detected appreciable lead leaching.[17]

Coarse recycled cullet is used as fill material. For drainage trenches, Glass Aggregate Corporation makes a cullet product called Redpak. It consists of cylindrical geotextile sacks filled with glass, placed end to end in a trench, which is then backfilled. The concept is similar to French drains (Principle 4) or reservoirs used under porous paving (Principle 5). Geotextile sacks filled with crushed glass are also used for erosion control.

Using glass in trenches and sacks nullifies its inherent beauty. It is an attractive replacement for gravel in walkways and garden borders, used at 1994's Jardin Encore recycling exhibit in Seattle. (See below and

Figure 6.11 A "recycled folly" in Parque da Cidade, made of stone salvaged around the city of Oporto, Portugal. Many salvaged materials are becoming expensive because of demand for their weathered appearance. (*Project:* Sidonio Pardal. *Photo:* Lynn Miller.)

Figure 6.12.) Intriguing and semitransparent, cullet comes in green, amber, and clear; more exotic blues and reds are sometimes available. For walkways, the King County (WA) Commission for Marketing Recyclable Materials recommends screened glass, one-quarter to one-sixteenth inch, a consistency somewhat like coarse sand.

Tires

Worn-out rubber tires are familiar decorative elements in vernacular landscapes, used as planters or to define a rural driveway. Increasingly, however, scrap tires—whole, shredded, or reconstituted into entirely new products—are finding functional landscape uses, such as stream-bank and slope stabilization; check dams; surfacing material; marine construction; and as an ingredient in rubberized asphalt. These uses may slightly deflate the monstrous national glut of scrap tires, which increases by 280 million each year.[18]

Scrap tires, laid flat and buried into a slope, can create low garden terraces. Up to several feet high they can be built without reinforcement.

The Oklahoma Department of Environmental Quality, concerned about stream-bank erosion and more than three million waste tires in 200 illegal dumps, is promoting a single solution to both problems: armoring stream banks with tires. This approach not only reuses waste, but is also lower in cost and simpler to build than riprap or concrete bank stabilization. Tires for such projects are locally obtained from gas stations, tire dealers, and junk yards, minimizing transport. At least eighteen projects have been built, varying from 300 to 4,750 feet in length, protecting roads, bridges and oil pipelines threatened by collapsing stream banks.

Overall, about 500,000 waste tires have been used in these projects.[19] Two to ten rows of car or truck tires are used, depending on bank height. Cost is low, typically $20 to $30 per linear foot. For one demonstration project near Weatherford OK, 1,800 feet of stream bank were stabilized with ten rows of tires for $70,000—about $39 per foot, but far less than the estimated $550,000 for regrading and riprap. Installation requires little skilled labor or machinery; in Oklahoma, it is typically done at no cost by work-release prison inmates. Where inmate labor is not available, such projects could conceivably be installed by community volunteers.

Bank construction is quite straightforward. Rows of tires are placed along the water line lying flat; tires ascending the bank are placed upright. Cables tie each row together, anchored into the ground using deadmen (buried logs) at fifty-foot intervals and at least fifty feet back from the bank. Little or no stream-bank grading is required. After installation, silt settles inside the tires, further anchoring them. Over time, most are completely buried, forming a new and more stable bank. Native black locust is planted in these banks for its fast-growing fibrous root system.

Figure 6.12 At the Northwest Flower and Garden Show, Jardin Encore is primarily made of recycled materials, including glass, wood, and iron. A new exhibit each year promotes recycling in the landscape. (*Project:* King County Commission for Marketing Recycled Materials. *Photo:* David McDonald.)

In Pima County AZ, Stuart Hoenig, professor of agricultural and biosystems engineering at the University of Arizona, along with engineer Joshua Minyard, directed construction of a check dam made of 2,000 passenger-car tires. Five layers of tires were placed on their sides, held together by plastic bands, reinforced by quarry rock between each layer, and anchored to the arroyo sides like a conventional concrete structure. Funded by the state and approved by the Army Corps of Engineers and Arizona Department of Water Quality, the project shows institutional acceptance of "alternative" technology. Construction costs, including labor from the county probation service, to-

taled only $6,000. The dam was installed in 1997; a year later, vegetation had begun to grow in the arroyo for the first time in years, and a road upstream no longer washed out as previously.[20]

Tires are available baled, stacked like straw-bales for construction. Sliced sideways like bagels, tires have been laid under lawns to retain water. They can also be reused as flotation materials for docks, marinas, and wetland boardwalks. Topper Industries of Battle Ground WA uses discarded tires this way and finds them cheaper than other floats. According to Topper, nothing leaches from tires; they are biologically inert, making them ideal as floats in sensitive wetlands.[21]

Other interesting products made from scrap tires are turning up on the landscape market. In New South Wales, Australia, Tyredrain Australia has patented a system for drainage channels from half sections of recycled tires, much cheaper than concrete channels. Tyredrain is seeking to license the idea in other countries. In Fort Dodge IA, Dodger Enterprises promotes whole, cut, and shredded tires for varied landscape uses. One-inch tire chips spread on bare soil can control wind erosion and hold moisture and heat for seed germination. Dodger also offers cut-out sidewall rings to protect bare slopes. On slopes of 3:1 or less, the rings are simply laid next to each other. On steeper slopes they can be tied

Figure 6.13 Tires and broken concrete achieve unexpected elegance as terraces at the Institute for Regenerative Studies. (*Project and Photo:* John Lyle.)

Figure 6.14   Check dams reuse waste tires to stabilize an arroyo in Arizona. Tires in trench form a footing for the dam at the upper level. (*Project and Photo:* Stuart Hoenig and Joshua Minyard.)

Figure 6.15   Strapped in place, tires form a strong flexible structure that traps sediment and eventually supports plants. Some systems incorporate live staking. (*Project and Photo:* Stuart Hoenig and Joshua Minyard.)

together as a blanket. Grass grows through and between them.[22]

None of these tire structures are particularly beautiful, at least until completely overgrown, and will not please believers in pristine landscapes. However, they show one environmental problem solving another. This mimics natural systems in a very fundamental way—a high rate of reuse, leaving very little as "waste" in the long term.

Specify Remanufactured Materials

Recycled materials specifically for landscapes are widely available today. What distinguishes them from products discussed above is energy to recycle the material, rather than reuse it. A good introduction to the breadth of recycled landscape materials is *The Resource Guide to Sustainable Landscapes* by Wesley Groesbeck and Jan Streifel.

This 425-page catalog of landscape-related products lists more than 2,000 products by CSI section. Most include some recycled content. The book's purpose is to list "sustainable products and materials that are energy-efficient, ecologically safe, and support healthy landscapes and gardens." Suppliers, more than 1,300 of them, are listed from the English-speaking world, plus Germany and Mexico.

Among those items explicitly listed as recycled are glass-brick pavers; asphalt, rubber, and rubber-asphalt pavers and patching materials; lumber; used brick; reclaimed stone; plastic lumber; tile; resilient flooring; exterior paint and lacquer thinner; and tire structures. More than fifty exchanges and stores carrying used building materials, for profit or nonprofit, are also listed. "Plastic lumber" lists 25 manufacturers and another 50 suppliers. By comparison, in 1992 when Sorvig wrote an early LAM article concerning plastic lumber,[23] there were less than half a dozen brands. By 2006, plastic lumber has become universally available, even from large home-improvement chains.

The *Resource Guide* offers clear proof that recycled or environmentally friendly materials are available today for almost any landscape purpose. Although the *Guide's* criteria for what makes a product sustainable are not spelled out, no one reading this useful volume could argue that products for sustainable landscapes are merely a futurist's dream.[24]

PLASTIC LUMBER

Plastic lumber—a wood substitute from recycled milk jugs—has become a familiar landscape feature, most commonly as plastic benches and picnic tables. To some people, plastic lumber lacks the beauty of real wood, but it has distinct advantages.

Plastic lumber is biologically inert—it does not give off toxins, in contrast to preservative-treated woods. This recommends it for use in such sensitive landscapes as wetlands. In wetland boardwalks and overlooks, recycled plastic may be especially appropriate, and environmental permitting agencies are increasingly favoring such uses. (Some plastic lumber, however, is PVC; see concerns, below.)

The fact that plastic can last virtually forever has been a major environmental problem. Plastic lumber turns this into an advantage. It does not rot, splinter, peel, or suffer insect damage. It never needs painting, will not bow or warp with age, and requires minimal maintenance—advantages that offset its initial cost, higher than that of wood. It is very durable, provided it is kept from high heat and is UV-stabilized (ultraviolet light degrades most plastics outdoors).

Plastic lumber provides new, productive uses for some of the immense quantities of throwaway plastic—and saves trees from being cut for lumber. Despite plastic lumber's advantages, its use was hampered for years by lack of reliable data on its strength, shear properties, and other performance criteria. That changed in 1997 when the American Society for Testing and Materials (ASTM) approved a number of testing methods to ensure uniform standards for plastic lumber.[25]

One researcher identifies three grades of plastic lumber currently available:

Purified plastic lumber (such as Durawood and Duratech) uses a single postconsumer plastic such as high-density polyethylene (HDPE). Other factors being equal, single-plastic lumber provides consistency. See table 6.2.

Commingled plastic lumber (such as Hammer's Envirowood and Earth Care products) are made with two or more plastics and are generally cheaper. They are potentially variable in physical properties.

Composites (such as Lifecycle, Trimax, and Trex) are manufactured by mixing sawdust or other fibers with plastic. Composites are stiffer than pure plastic lumber, with rougher textures. In rare cases, composites may absorb moisture or suffer insect damage.[26]

Plastic lumber does have some disadvantages. The first is cost: on average, two to three times that of pine lumber. (Lifecycle costs may more than offset this; timber scarcity also affects wood pricing. See p. 286) Second, plastic lumber is considerably heavier than wood; supports must be designed accordingly. Third, plastic lumber contracts and expands much more than wood and may deform in hot weather. Finally, plastic lumber is much more flexible than wood. In applications like boardwalks, plastic boards must be spaced closer together than wood to minimize sagging. For use as beams and other structural elements, research strength and deflection carefully. Flexibility can be turned to advantage, and many suppliers feature images of sweeping curved decks and inventive patterning.

It has been said that plastic lumber is not usable for posts or structural supports. For decks overlooking the Upper Charles River outside of Boston, however, landscape architects Carol R. Johnson & Associates (CRJ) specified supporting piers of recycled plastic lumber to avoid leaching into wetlands along the river. Bruce Leish of CRJ notes that the designers did not use plastic lumber for beams or joists for fear it would flex too much, but the plastic piers have caused no problems.

Working with plastic lumber is generally similar to working with wood: it can be sawed, drilled, and fastened with staples or nails.[27] Expansion can loosen nails, so nuts and bolts or screws are recommended. Unlike wood, most plastic lumber cannot be glued.

Plastic lumber is the most common use of recycled plastic in the landscape, but not the only use. Many grass-paving systems (see p. 214) are recycled plastic. The entire Invisible Structures (Aurora CO) line of landscape products is recycled plastic. A relatively unusual recycled plastic is "plasphalt," combined like "glasphalt" as a paving material.

RECYCLED GLASS TILE

In addition to minimally processed cullet, glass can be refired in tiles and pavers. Stoneware Tile Company (Richmond IN) manufactures colorful pavers with 70 percent recycled glass content. New Design (Seattle WA) makes recycled glass tiles with a rugged, weathered look. Syndesis (Los Angeles CA) manufactures tile from glass in combination with other waste products such as sawdust and metal shavings. Such decorative products are becoming available at specialty stores.

Garden ornaments may also be crafted from recycled glass. These include decorative garden lanterns, manufactured by New Design. Glass block is available from recycled glass in standard shapes and sizes. Finally, limited-production art glass ornaments are hand blown from recycled material in some small shops. To the artist's hand and eye, glass—new or recycled—remains an inspiration.

CRUMB RUBBER

Discarded tires can be used whole or with minimal processing, as described above. Recycling rubber entails more intensive processing. Many discarded rubber products are ground into "crumb" rubber, resembling coarse sand in texture, then remanufactured.

Crumb rubber has found a number of landscape uses, primarily for surfacing. "Rubberized asphalt" (p. 317) mixes crumb rubber with asphalt; although more expensive than conventional asphalt, it is durable and elastic, reducing road maintenance and noise. Several companies process crumb rubber into resilient surfaces for athletic, safety, and playground use. These greatly reduce injury from falls in high-risk play areas, but are fairly expensive. Loose rubber "mulch," reconstituted mats, or poured-in-place resilient materials are available, in varied colors, with flexible rubber edging to contain it on-site.

Loose crumb rubber is also proving its worth as a trail surfacing material. Polk City FL ground 10,000 scrap tires to surface the 49-mile Withlacoochee State Trail—the first time crumb rubber has been used for a trail, according to the Rails-to-Trails Conservancy. In Georgia, a sloping hundred-yard trail at Tallulah Gorge State Park was paved with ground tires donated by the manufacturer, Phoenix Recycled Products, to see how it would withstand heavy usage. The trail, which is wheelchair accessible, is resisting erosion. Georgia's Spalding County has ground scrap tires for a pedestrian trail at Airport Road Park;

Figure 6.16 Recycled plastic lumber piers support decks along the Upper Charles River near Boston. Metal "pinned foundations" cause almost no site disruption and can be removed or adjusted easily. (*Project and Photo:* Carol R. Johnson and Associates.)

elderly users in particular like the trail because it is smooth and easy on their feet. The county received a $100,000 waste reduction grant from the state for this experimental project.[28]

OTHER RECYCLED MATERIALS

Plastics, glass, and rubber are the most common and visible recycled materials in landscape use today. Some other remanufactured products are not as easily recognized. Steel and aluminum are regularly recycled in large quantities; although we have not discovered any landscape-*specific* recycled products, much metal used outdoors certainly contains recycled elements. Metals are particularly good for recycling in at least one sense: the recycled material is closely

Figure 6.17 Glass fish swim in elegant recycled tile, part of the annual recycled garden exhibit staged by King County WA. (*Project:* King County Commission for Marketing Recycled Materials. *Photo:* David McDonald.)

equivalent to virgin metal, not the case with many plastics, for instance.

Concrete is crushed and recycled as aggregate and for other uses, keeping this bulky and slow-to-degrade material out of landfills. Asphalt is also recycled; it is unique in that the recycling machinery comes to the asphalt. These large machines mill the surface off an existing road, reheat and mix the asphalt, and lay it down as new paving. It is unclear how energy efficient this process is, but it clearly makes good use of another material that not long ago was discarded after a short service life.

Recycle at the Job Site

Every construction job generates scrap material. Even when using salvaged and recycled products, cutting, fitting, and finishing leave scrap: cutoff boards, whole overestimated items, sawdust, surplus concrete and mortar. Construction machinery produces used blades and spent oils. Construction workers drink from disposable aluminum cans and Styrofoam cups, and buy lunch-wagon meals variously wrapped.

Setting up simple job-site waste sorting is an effective first step for recycling construction materials. On small residential jobs, this may take little more than some bins—just a couple more than for home use. For large jobs, one or more Dumpsters, possibly with internal partitions, may be required. Be sure to locate these in the staging area where they can be hauled out without site damage at the end of the project.

Properly sorted construction leftovers can be taken to municipal recycling centers in some regions, but others prohibit this. Some commercial recyclers will buy construction salvage. A growing number of communities have special construction recycling programs.⊃ Many include a site set aside for *exchanging* construction salvage: those who have usable excess leave it; those who can use materials take them. An alternative to a physical exchange site is a newspaper or Web listing system: those who have materials list them, and others list what materials they need. Civic-minded newspapers, sometimes in cooperation with local government, businesses, or social service organizations, donate space for these free listings.

Starting a construction recycling program takes time and has upfront expenses. One approach to funding such a program is analyzing costs *avoided* by keeping construction materials out of landfills. Even a relatively small exchange program can keep a ton or more a week out of the local dump. Encouraging reuse and avoiding waste are goals appropriate to public-private partnerships. Contractors benefit by reducing their landfill fees; the community benefits by not paying for constant expansion of landfills.

Evaluate Environmental Costs When Choosing Suppliers

Making sustainable choices among sources for similar materials is a big assignment and can be confus-

ing. Concise rules continue to evolve. Meanwhile, we can suggest several approaches worth trying.

Evaluate the *distance* between supplier and end-user, and the number of intermediate deliveries involved. Does your wood come from California or Brazil? Is it sawed where it is felled, at your supplier, or transported to Michigan or Michoacán for processing?

Evaluate the mode of transport. Are logs floated to the sawmill or trucked (or flown whole to Japan)? If the supply chain has several links, evaluate each. Differences between diesel and gasoline trucks, or between relatively fuel-efficient ships and less-efficient air or land modes, can be significant. Finding out what transportation a supplier uses is not easy, but is information worth seeking.

Evaluate CO_2 production and sequestration. One rule of thumb: for every billion Btu of energy consumed, $1/8$ pound of CO_2 is released. This applies best to electrical power; availability and accuracy of data for specific practices and materials continues to improve slowly.⊃

Evaluate embodied energy, a concept discussed in more detail in Principle 7. (Rough energy-cost numbers for landscape materials are at www.SustainableLandscapeOnline.com.) Like CO_2 figures, what is currently available is limited but useful, likely to be updated and improved by ongoing research.

Evaluate toxicity of materials over their life cycle. In most cases this cannot yet be done quantitatively, but should at least be considered in a reasoned way. (This information is also online, as above.)

Evaluate each source. Many manufacturers and suppliers are just as green as you are; at the other extreme, many still resist all environmental responsibility. Ask about factory safeguards and mitigation, and about energy awareness. Favor those suppliers who will at least make an honest attempt to discuss these issues, and who are taking appropriate steps to reduce their environmental impacts.

Use Sustainably Harvested Renewables

Wood is America's renewable resource, the slogan reads. Clearly, wood is the only major construction material that is grown, rather than mined. Like recycling, using renewables is a very popular concept and in general worthy of support. But it, too, has limits that must be respected.

The primary limit is the *rate or speed* of renewal. *Given time*, forests can and do renew themselves. Historically, the entire US East Coast was logged by colonists, farmed, then abandoned as small family farms became uneconomical. Today's forests are evidence of renewability—and required a hundred years or more to reach their current size. For forests as well as people, time is the great healer.

If demand for wood is too great and too impatient, the rate of harvesting outstrips regrowth. Quick harvesting limits the size of wood a forest can produce: where old-growth forests once yielded huge beams, forestry today hurries to harvest two-by-twelves. With hasty harvesting, or where destructive methods are used, forest health declines. Eventually there comes a point of no return, meaning that at least in that location, the living ability of renewal is lost. Push a renewable resource too far, and it faces at least local extinction.

In an un-logged forest, dead timber is recycled into soil by insects, fungi, microbes, and periodic fires. This complex natural composting determines how much new growth the forest can produce. Removing timber removes soil-renewing materials; too much removal without some replacement depletes forest soil, like any other. Perhaps the most striking example is tropical rainforest: so much organic material is embodied in living trees, and so little stored in the soil, that carting away timber often leaves a brick-like, near-sterile soil called laterite. If forest is to renew itself on such soil, it will be over millennia, if at all.

For these reasons, the fact that wood is renewable does not give license for unlimited use—contrary to marketing of timber as *infinitely* renewable. Renewability fits into the Reduce/Reuse/Recycle equation as a form of recycling. As long as reduced use and salvage are the first-choice strategies, using renewables is a valuable concept.

Three major ways of managing renewable resources for long-term sustainability affect today's market. These are salvaged wood, sustainable harvesting certification, and substituting waste for wood.

Salvage Wood Where Possible

Although mangled framing lumber still is landfilled with other bulldozed waste, salvaging wood during demolition is becoming more common. Wood from the 1940s or before is particularly valued; harvested from healthier, older trees, it is often denser and stronger than any new lumber sold today. The wood salvage business mostly markets "antique" wood to high-end custom homes, at prices beyond reach for landscape use.

Salvage for landscape use is complicated by several factors. Outdoor timbers suffer from rot, termites, and other insects; they may also be hard to extract from concrete footings. Nonetheless, naturally decay-resistant landscape woods (tropical hardwoods and redwood, in particular, threatened by past overuse) should be salvaged where at all feasible. Similarly, preservative-treated lumber can be reused with care and should be salvaged because there is no environmentally responsible way to dispose of it (see p. 254).

Specify Sustainably Harvested and Processed Wood

As this book's first edition was being published, a major step toward sustainably harvested wood was announced. The world's largest lumber retailer, Home Depot, phased out all wood products from old-growth forests and required sources to be certified as sustainably managed. Environmental groups such as the Rainforest Action Network, as well as Home Depot's own staff, predicted the move would compel the rest of the market, including contractor sales, to follow. Home Depot did not expect its prices or availability to be directly affected by certification.[29] Since 2000, demand has changed lumber pricing so much that measuring the cost, if any, of certification is difficult.

Several organizations certify sustainable lumber. Certification takes into account basic issues of harvest rate and forest health, as well as whether previously untouched forests are cut, or whether clear-cutting is used. Carefully managed methods like "shelter-wood cutting," which selectively takes trees to maintain health, size, and diversity of the whole forest, are usually required for certification. The use of waste-reducing sawmill tools, such as thinner blades and more efficient chippers, is often a consideration; the US Forest service estimates that such techniques reduce wood waste by 33 percent.[30]

Specifiers must become familiar with different certification groups and their criteria. Like the various seal-of-approval systems that have emerged for consumer goods and health foods since the 1970s, wood certification is likely to produce both reputable and superficial claims of sustainability. For this very valuable system to work, informed specifiers must support reputable certifying groups.

One particular conflict over wood certification is worth noting. The foremost sustainable wood certification process, and we feel the most reputable, is the Forest Stewardship Council's program (FSC). Competing with it is the Sustainable Forestry Initiative (SFI), established by the American Forest and Paper Association. There are two major differences. FSC requires independent third-party verification that forest practices meet the standards, while SFI allows producers to self-certify.[31] In addition, FSC has a "chain-of-custody" approach, so that products made with wood from certified forests can also be certified. The SFI approach stops at forest certification. Many US government agencies, as well as other specifiers, have adopted FSC standards.[32]

Substitute Straw and Other Wastes for Wood

Various wastes, such as straw, paper, and waste wood, can substitute for new lumber. Direct use of straw bales as a construction material is one example. Plastic lumber is another, especially composite forms incorporating wood waste. Wallboards manufactured from straw, primarily for interior use, are yet another.

US production of lumber, including plywood, was about 65 million tons in 1993. That same year, almost 155 million tons of waste from straw, paper, wood, and woody materials like nut shells were available; plastic waste added another 15 million tons. Wheat and rice straw alone equaled the total tonnage of lumber produced.[33]

Clearly, if all these wastes could substitute for wood, lumber production could cease for nearly three years without being missed. Just as clearly, these substitutes cannot really replace *all* uses of lumber. Besides, these wastes are in demand for ethanol, compost, and other environmentally important products. So-called waste materials, however, offer significant opportunities to slow timber use and protect the renewability of forests.

One example of a thoughtful waste-for-timber substitution is plastic lumber production by the AERT company (Junction TX). AERT's product is a composite of recycled PET plastic with juniper fibers, a by-product of pressing scented oil from juniper wood. AERT manages lands from which juniper is harvested for eventual reforestation by more valuable hardwood species.[34]

Avoid Toxic and Nonrenewable Materials

Reducing, reusing, and recycling materials gets more benefit at less environmental cost. In addition, some materials must be handled correctly, and others used sparingly if at all, to avoid costly hazards to human health and the environment.

An important addition to Nelischer's guidelines (p. 225) is whether a material is hazardous, and if so under what circumstances. Toxic materials can threaten construction workers, as well as anyone using the finished landscape. Hazards to the larger environment are not always visible on-site. In many instances, contractors or designers can act directly to reduce toxic exposure. In other cases, the combined influence of environmental professionals and their industries is required to affect pervasive or hidden hazards.

Toxic and hazardous materials affect landscape construction differently from effects in buildings. Radon is a good example. It is an indoor hazard, but a normal outdoor condition.[35] If trapped in unventilated buildings (or mines, where it was first noticed), concentration makes radon hazardous. This does not justify dismissing concern about radon, however. "Even too much water will kill you" is a posture that seldom promotes rational debate, let alone sustain-

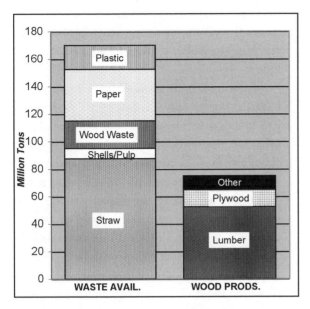

Figure 6.18 Wood Products and Possible Substitutes Annual Tonnage. (Based on data from P. Fisk.)

ability. It is critically important to know *at what point* a substance becomes toxic, and if this point is unknown, to err on the side of caution.[36]

Responsible professionals must analyze how and where a material will be used, as well as how it is produced, transported, disposed of, or recycled. A few landscape materials (below) are so hazardous that their use is truly unsustainable. More frequently, toxicity is one important consideration among many in comparing material life-cycles. (See Table 6.1.)

Anticipate Hazards from Prior Land Uses

Sites never developed for modern use seldom hold hazardous materials. In rare cases, site geology may produce hazards. An example is serpentine, a rock toxic to plants and humans. At Potrero Heights, a hillside housing development in San Francisco, prominent soil-filled retaining walls are a response to serpentine bedrock. Initial plans calling for terraced grading were abandoned on discovering serpentine, which releases toxins when excavated. Such hazards, however, are uncommon.

On brownfields and similar sites, toxic materials may be present before landscape construction ever begins. Recognizing hazardous materials in the field requires a great deal of experience. The following sections can help with basic knowledge, but clearly not with real-world identification. If contamination is suspected, hire a consultant.

Demolition or remodeling of structures may release hazardous materials. These can include not only landscape-specific materials (below), but also lead paint or asbestos from old buildings, or PCBs from abandoned utility transformers. Lead used in flashing is found in old roofing waste and in antique garden-wall copings. Building demolition is messy; interior materials may well become part of the landscape. Thus, some materials that play no part in normal landscape construction can be site hazards.

If there has been *dumping* on the site, be alert for an even greater range of hazards. Illegal dumping is common, often affecting remote sites with no history of previous use—sites that may look pristine at first glance—as well as urban lots. It is very difficult to predict what might be in these dumps. Often it is merely household trash (which can still contain many toxics) that some ignoramus refused to take to a landfill. Some illegal dumping is deliberate criminal disposal of industrial or medical hazardous waste, dumped to avoid regulation, and could be truly deadly. Owners of farms and small businesses, ignorant of hazards, used to dispose of wastes on-site. Public awareness has decreased this kind of dumping, but it still goes on. Pesticides, oils, solvents, old vehicles, and batteries may have been buried in such private dumps, sometimes in quantity. Neither illegal nor small-user dump sites are usually documented, unlike larger industrial sites.

If the site has ever been used industrially, be on the lookout. Soil and water can be contaminated by pollutants settling out of air around a factory, by leaching from stockpiles, or by tanks leaking, as well as by deliberate on-site disposal. Industrial pollution frequently spreads to neighboring sites; air or water pollutants can move long distances. Fortunately, public records usually indicate types of past land use at industrial sites, which can help predict hazards.

The following industrial operations are common sources of heavy metals, some of the more dangerous soil contaminants:

- electroplating (cadmium, chromium, nickel)
- battery production or use (cadmium, lead, nickel, zinc)
- paints and painting (cadmium, chromium)
- mining (arsenic, copper, nickel)
- metal production and products (chromium, copper, lead, mercury, zinc in brass and for galvanization)
- pesticides and preservatives (arsenic, copper, mercury)
- rubber production (zinc)
- petroleum and coal (arsenic)
- plastics (cadmium)
- fire brick (chromium)
- fly ash (copper)
- fertilizers (copper).

A number of manufacturing catalysts may leave traces of mercury. Nickel and lead traces can be carried and deposited by rain or air, far from their industrial sources.[37] A wide variety of industrial and household products may leave organochlorides and volatile organic compounds (VOCs). Some agricultural chemicals are very persistent, including DDT (banned in 1973, but still used against much-feared insects like tussock moth); old orchards often used arsenic or cyanide pesticides.

While actual remediation of hazardous sites is a task for specialists (see p. 72), landscape architects and contractors need to know what "red flags" to watch for. Removing found contaminants can add thousands of dollars to a project and subjects workers to hazards. *Failure* to remove such pollutants can harm workers and end-users, leaving owner, designer, and builder open to lawsuits. It is far cheaper and smarter to investigate the possibility of existing hazards before work begins. Some basic methods:

- Check available records, such as land title, historic zoning maps, and other legal documents, for clues to land use over the past century. Watch for industrial uses, as well as agricultural ones.
- Carefully inspect the site for signs of dumping. On previously undeveloped sites, refuse is usually aboveground. If previous use seems likely to have generated hazardous wastes, look for ground dis-

turbance or peculiar vegetation patterns. Try to imagine a convenient and accessible dump site, and how (or whether) people might have tried to hide it.

- Field-testing kits are available for early warning of hazards. For example, Labware Safety Supply⊃ lists kits to detect lead, PCBs, or chlorine in soils; other kits reveal liquid toxics. One test (in a kit of six to ten) costs about five dollars, a small price if it avoids a serious problem. Advertised as requiring no special training, they indicate in five to ten minutes whether hazards are above or below a safety standard, usually by an unmistakable color change. No substitute for specialist analysis, such tests can give a quick reading of potential hazards.
- If *anything* indicates serious contamination, get advice from specialists in hazardous waste mitigation. Trying to remove wastes yourself can subject you and your client to red tape and costs at least, and prosecution at worst.
- If you work in areas where many contaminated sites are found, investigate whether you or your client can be insured against unforeseen costs and liabilities related to cleanup.

Lest anyone think that these "engineering" matters are too complex for landscape architects, consider the Boston firm whose principals are Nina Brown, Clarissa Rowe, and Alison Richardson. They have developed, almost accidentally, a specialty in design for contaminated sites. In urban areas, it is hardly necessary to seek out such projects: many sites, especially those left to the public as open space, are blessed with fruits of industry and illegal dumping. Brown & Rowe has uncovered buried car-battery dumps, extensive engine-oil spills, and, on one project, the threat of biological-warfare-agent anthrax. Taking it all in stride, the three partners often interpret site history as part of their designs. (They usually collaborate with environmental specialists; see p. 72.)

Be Aware of Direct Hazards from Construction

The list of products, including building materials, suspected of causing health problems for people is a long one. Most research done on such toxicity,

Table 6.1

Organic and heavy-metal chemicals common in building materials.

Chemical (and synonyms)	Found in
VOCs	
1,1,1-Trichloroethane (methyl chloroform)	Solvent in paints and degreasers
1,2-dichlorobenzene (ortho-dichlorobenzene)	Solvent; fumigants and insecticides; dyes; metal polishes
4-PC (4-Phelylcyclohexene)	Solvent; penetrating agent
Acetone	Solvent; lacquers; inks; adhesives; tool cleanup
Acrolein	Herbicides; used in polyurethane and polyester production
Acrylonitrile (vinyl cyanide)	Paints; adhesives; dyes; pesticides; used in plastic production; mixed with wood pulp as "synthetic soil"
Benzene	Very common in production of synthetic chemicals, especially plastics
Carbon tetrachloride (perchloromethane)	Metal degreasers; fumigants; rubber solvent; banned in household-use products
Ethylbenzene (phenylethane)	Solvent in resins; used in styrene production
Formaldehyde (oxymethylene)	Glues, and thus in wood composites, plywoods, and glulams; plastic resins; dyes; preservatives; fertilizers; urea-formaldehyde is least stable, longest outgassing, and cheapest form
Isophorone	Solvent, especially for polyvinyl and other resins; pesticides; specialized lacquers
Methyl ethyl ketone	Solvent in lacquers, paints, adhesives, inks, thinners, cleaners; peroxide of MEK is fiberglass hardener
Methyl isobutyl ketone	Solvent in paints, paint removers, lacquers, adhesives, cleaners; acrylic and vinyl coatings
Methylene chloride (dichloromethane)	Paint removers; degreasers; foams (blowing agent); used in plastic production
Naphthalene (tar camphor)	Dyes; fungicides; moth and animal repellents; cutting fluids and lubricants; coal tar; resins
Phthalate esters	Soft plastics, as plasticizer; hardener for resins; dyes; insecticides (examples: DEHP; phthalic anhydride)
Styrene	Used in production of plastics; synthetic rubber and latex (for adhesives and paints); polystyrene glazing; and Styrofoam
Tetrachloroethane (perchloroethylene)	Degreasers for metals; paint removers; varnishes; insecticides; herbicides; used in production of other chemicals
Toluene (methylbenzene)	Solvent; paints, coatings, plastics, plastic adhesives, cleaners, fuels
Trichloroethylene	Degreasers; paints; fumigants
Vinyl chloride	Used in plastics production, especially PVC; adhesives
Xylene (dimethylbenzene)	Solvent; paints, lacquers, resins, rubber cements, fuels
HEAVY METALS	
Antimony	Lead batteries; bearings; solder; pigments in paints, dyes, stains; metal alloys
Cadmium	Pigments; metal coatings; brazing rods; ceramic glazes; NiCad batteries; electrical parts
Chromium	Pigments for glass and paints; metal and plastic plating; alloys
Lead	Old paints; solder; batteries
Mercury	Mercury-vapor lamps; batteries; electrical controls; mirror plating
Nickel	Alloys; welding; electroplating; batteries

Sources: List from HOK, *Sustainable Design Guide*; synonyms and "found in" data based on Hawley's *Chemical Dictionary*.

however, refers to *indoor* air quality.[38] Many chemicals, including some naturally occurring ones, are hazardous when trapped within walls and concentrated; adequate ventilation is the main user precaution. Since landscapes are by definition open-air places, hazardous chemicals are quickly diluted outdoors, greatly reducing *direct* risk to users.

Use of toxic materials in landscapes, however, raises different questions than the same materials used indoors. In the early days of environmental awareness, a popular slogan decreed that "Dilution is the Solution to Pollution." This has proved shortsighted. The very openness that lets toxic chemicals dilute into air also means that they are free to move beyond the site. Some biodegrade, but others accumulate in ever-increasing quantities in air, water, or soil. Increased levels of global pollution parallel increasing allergies, respiratory diseases, and other chronic conditions, not to mention climate change.[39] The *outdoor* use of chemicals known to be hazardous *indoors* may contribute to regional pollution levels even if they do not pose immediate threats to users.

Some individuals suffer from Multiple Chemical Sensitivity (MCS), believed to be severe allergic reaction to chronic pollution. Very small quantities of chemicals, or materials not affecting most other people, cause mild to severe symptoms in MCS sufferers. Design for MCS has produced many advances in knowledge about "healthy building materials." Lists of such materials are available from a number of books and on the Web; one book even includes sample specifications organized by CSI division.

Relatively few *outdoor* construction materials cause symptoms even for people with MCS. Large areas of hot asphalt are a concern. Preemergent herbicides or broad-spectrum insecticides sprayed around foundations and under unit pavers can affect indoor air quality.[40] Problem materials for MCS indoors may be fine outdoors; conversely, some MCS-safe materials are not weatherproof. Nonetheless, these nontoxic materials deserve consideration in landscape construction.

In 2006, the Architectural and Transportation Barriers Compliance Board, who oversee the Americans with Disabilities Act's demands on design, weighed in on green building—negatively. The Board attacks greenroofs because possible leaks or inevitable leaf drop *could* increase indoor molds, and because "plants can emit volatile fumes and pollen"; they consider brownfield redevelopment inappropriate for children or the elderly, essentially dismissing the ability to clean up any site; and they even blame indoor plants, not only for attracting bugs, but for the use of Raid! This is single-focus special-interest advocacy gone far afield indeed.[41] Green building's general reduction of pollution (including greenhouse gases that directly raise pollen levels) clearly outweighs these localized complaints, even for people with disabilities, let alone for the whole planet.

Many landscape materials are in direct soil contact, or unprotected from weather. Either situation may leach toxic materials into soil; taken up by plants, these could enter the food chain. Because of such risks, some outdoor materials may need to be *more* completely nontoxic than their indoor counterparts, just as brick exposed to weather needs to be more durable than interior grades.

Minimize Invisible Hazards Off-site

In addition to on-site hazards, some materials cause environmental problems either during manufacturing or disposal. Even materials completely nontoxic in use may present serious problems at the beginning or end of their life cycle. For genuine sustainability, these invisible issues cannot be ignored. In fact, for most common *landscape* materials, research for this book leads us to believe that direct toxicity to users is minor compared to hazards of extraction, manufacturing, and disposal.

Manufacturers of basic building materials, like the rest of society, have changed in response to environmental concerns. Many are sincerely committed to reducing environmental impact of their products. Others have improved their records only under threat of regulation. Overall, most basic US industries have made significant improvements in efficiency and pollution control within the past few decades. These improvements have been offset, and even overwhelmed, by increased consumption of goods and depletion of resources due to population pressures. (Humanity has used more raw resources since 1950 than in all prior history, and the trend continues to increase.[42])

Not even the most conscientious manufacturers can prevent all toxic releases. Spills and accidents during transportation of hazardous materials can release toxics, as can natural disasters, sabotage, and human error. Facilities that *release* little or no pollution to the environment may still expose their own workers to serious hazards. Landscape professionals share a responsibility with other citizens to ensure that foreseeable pollution problems are prevented and that unforeseen problems are kept to a minimum.

Resource extraction is a related off-site issue. Timber and stone, for instance, are nontoxic materials, but conventional forestry and mining practices have caused widespread environmental damage. Transportation of materials causes pollution. These general production processes, which are very much taken for granted by society, have serious impacts, part of the environmental cost of materials.

IMPACTS OF GENERAL MANUFACTURING PROCESSES
The following processes contribute to environmental costs of most construction products. (More detailed information and source citations are now posted at www.SustainableLandscapeOnline.com).

Electrical generation is a major source of CO_2, about 1.5 lb. per kilowatt-hour (from coal). According to Amory Lovins of the Rocky Mountain Institute, converting a *single* light bulb from incandescent to compact fluorescent saves 57 watts of energy. Over its lifetime the efficient bulb eliminates about one *ton* of CO_2, seventeen pounds of SO_2, and other pollutants. If the electricity source is nuclear, the same bulb change eliminates generation of 25 grams (nearly an ounce) of plutonium, a deadly nuclear byproduct.[43]

Fuel combustion (industrial and vehicular) produces volatile organic compounds (VOCs), sulfur and nitrogen compounds ("Sox and Nox"), CO_2, and carbon monoxide. Diesels produce particulates. Fuel mining has its own impacts.

Petroleum production generates toxic and nontoxic drilling sediments, and air pollutants. Petroleum fuels are burned to drill and maintain wells. Oil spills, poorly designed pipelines, and access roads seriously disrupt habitat. Drilling may disrupt groundwater.

Mining can elevate soil erosion rates (see Figure 6.19) up to 2,000 times what occurs in stable

forested land.[44] Some kinds of mine tailings give off toxic leachates, poisoning or clogging waterways. Physical site disruption, especially by pit mining, is difficult if not impossible to restore fully.

Logging elevates normal forest erosion rates by up to 500 times. Reduction of forest areas decreases global ability to process CO_2. Burning of slash and waste produces air pollutants. Overharvesting decreases biodiversity; even commercial productivity suffers from monoculture "reforestation."

Construction itself elevates normal erosion rates by up to 2,000 times, causing roughly the same degree of added soil and water problems as mining.

Disposal of materials can release toxic leachates (landfills) and fumes (incinerators). Bulky or nondegradable materials consume landfill space, increasingly at a premium.

In part because of these general impacts, and also because materials and manufacturing methods vary widely, it is important to consider the entire product life-cycle when deciding on building materials or construction methods.

Use and Advocate Life-cycle Analysis (LCA)

Life-cycle analysis (LCA) takes into account the entire sequence of material production, use, and disposal/reuse. (See Figure 7.8.) At each life-cycle stage, energy consumption, toxicity, resource depletion, potential for misuse, and other factors are accounted for. Comparisons are made between whole life-cycles, rather than between materials at the point of use. Examples include the Center for Resourceful Building Technology's *Guide to Resource Efficient Building Elements*, the AIA's *Environmental Resource Guide*, and a checklist for materials selection developed by EBN.[45] Each offers guidelines for determining whether a product is in tune with sustainability over its life-cycle.⊃

Pliny Fisk points out that many LCA approaches are manufacturer-specific and suffer from limited data. While he supports the overall idea of "cradle-to-grave" analysis, his own research is based on national statistical databases that make it possible to look at the life-cycle of all materials of a specific kind, not just products from a few manufacturers. A study using national data was published in the 1980s

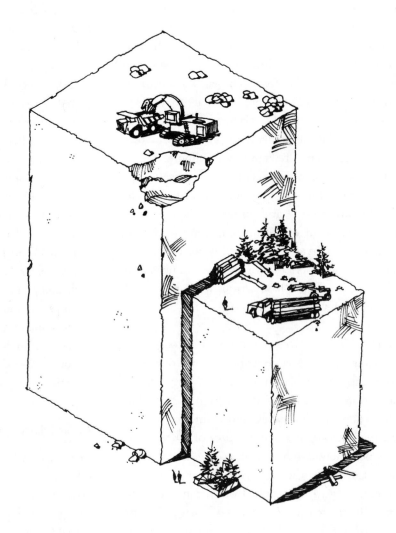

Figure 6.19 Erosion from healthy forests averages 0.0375 tons (seventy-five pounds) per acre per year. Logging raises this five hundred times, while mining and construction raise it two thousand times. (*Illust.:* Craig Farnsworth.)

by Stein and others. Still often cited, its data were collected in the late 1960s. Fisk's work, called *Green Baseline* and *Green Balance*, offers a method of computing up-to-date, detailed, and nationally averaged information.[46]

Although LCA (which in the broad sense includes Fisk's work) is probably the best basis for materials selection, there are difficulties applying *existing* LCA studies to landscape construction. Most existing research has focused on life-cycles related to *buildings*. Basic materials are used differently in landscape applications; their life-cycles may not be comparable to the same material as a building component. In trying to make LCA information accessible to architects, many authors have also focused on building "assemblies" such as structural insulated panels or complete framing systems. These are seldom relevant to landscape construction.

In the first edition of this book, we called for landscape-specific studies of materials, covering their whole life-cycles as used outdoors. Although much greater attention to these issues has been paid in landscape publications since 2000, full-scale original studies of this type remain rare. We are posting basic information about toxicity and energy of landscape-specific materials on the Web (see above) in hopes that wider availability of this information will encourage landscape professionals and researchers to develop life-cycle studies of landscape materials in greater depth.

Construction and maintenance materials are being evaluated as part of governmental "environmentally preferable purchasing" (EPP) programs. "Biobased" products, such as oils, alternative fuels, and paints, are often encouraged by EPP standards, and used in landscape maintenance (see p. 328).

Know General Toxicity Issues by Material Type

Publications on toxicity are mostly organized by technical names of chemical ingredients. It is possible to look up DEHP or 1,1,1-trichloroethane, but not to find out what each is used in, much less look up "plastic pipe" or "oil-based paint." We have tried to remedy this situation in two ways: by giving an overview of toxicity and hazard issues specific to landscape materials, and by compiling a list of materials under names more recognizable to design and construction professionals.

This section *summarizes* hazards and concerns associated with basic landscape materials. Many minor hazards, important for particular sites or clients, are not noted. Detail on forty-nine common materials (the first edition's appendix) is now online (see p. 225). That information is organized *by material*, and notes main ingredients or emissions associated with each. Situations when a material may pose special risks (such as accidental fires or improper disposal) are also noted.

For some materials, and for most chemical ingredients, Material-Safety Data Sheets (MSDS) from suppliers provide extreme detail. Use the online list to identify main ingredients that pose hazards, and then read the MSDS for each ingredient. Several Web sites make MSDS information available.⊃

Published information indicates that most landscape construction materials, in the forms to which end-users are exposed, are *relatively* nontoxic to humans. Their toxic effects on regional environments are not well understood. All construction materials require proper use and disposal, and continued improvement in handling and emission control by manufacturers. Alternative materials with fewer toxic effects are becoming increasingly available for many types of products.

Of the landscape materials reviewed, only two (PVC and wood preservatives, below) are of such en-

vironmental concern that serious calls have been made to ban them outright. Controversy over these materials is discussed in the next section, along with a scandal concerning toxic materials relabeled as fertilizers.

Coatings, adhesives, and solvents expose users to hazardous fumes during application and curing. These "volatile organic compounds" (VOCs) have been reduced considerably in recent formulas, but still can harm both the user and the broader environment. More than 50 percent of all US use of paints and coatings is for construction work.[47] Some types of specialized outdoor paints (pavement marking or survey "flagging" paints) have unusual formulas, for example to allow use during freezing weather. Such proprietary formulas are often secret, concealing possible dangers.

Postconsumer disposal, accidental fires, and spills present problems for many plastics, coatings, preservatives, adhesives, and solvents. Improper and illegal disposal is one facet; officially approved disposal has also been criticized, especially incineration and waste-as-fuel in cement kilns and other industrial facilities.

Many plastics, coatings and preservatives, adhesives, and solvents, as well as a few metals and fertilizers, have toxic chemical ingredients, precursors, or by-products. Factory mitigation processes control many of these risks adequately, or are making progress toward doing so. Product specifiers have many opportunities to influence suppliers toward safer production and complete disclosure of product and production risks.

Conventional mining and lumbering create extremely serious environmental problems (see p. 248); impacts vary from firm to firm. Sustainable forestry and mine reclamation are becoming more widespread and should be universal.

Be Aware of Landscape Plastics

Many types of plastics have landscape uses, either in construction or in landscape furniture and furnishings. An unscientific survey of catalogs, home centers, and garden stores produced Table 6.2, a list of landscape objects, by the type of plastic from which they are made.[48] Many plastic landscape products are not marked with any information to allow identification of component materials.

Avoid Three Controversial Materials

PVC and conventional wood preservatives are toxic enough that reputable organizations, both industry and environmental groups, have called for phasing them out of general use.[49] Such calls, and controversy around them, have increased since this book's first edition. The PVC industry has responded defensively, often heatedly so. By contrast, wood-preservative manufacturers have taken initiative to develop less-toxic products, with varied results.

A third controversial landscape material is fertilizer. As detailed below, the Associated Press has reported heavy metals, toxic chemicals, and radioactive waste being relabeled as fertilizer—without any actual processing, and no regulation.

Landscape professionals as major users of PVC, preserved wood, and fertilizers have a responsibility to know the hazards associated with these materials, and to make informed decisions about using them. Yet many practitioners remain ignorant of these issues, or have been unable to locate and learn to use safer alternatives that are available.[50]

Further detail on these materials is cited in the on-line appendix.

Polyvinyl Chloride (PVC and CPVC)

PVC and CPVC are regarded by many environmentalists as the most dangerous plastics produced. These same materials, and the base material chlorine that forms 57 percent of PVC by weight, are highly profitable for their producers, and easy for installers. Industry-funded studies and industry marketing materials claim that PVC is perfectly safe. We are forced to agree with the director of Ball State's Land Design Institute, who cautions, "Cast a wary eye toward research funded directly or indirectly by the PVC industry."[51]

Solid PVC is relatively (though not completely) harmless, but other stages of its life cycle raise major environmental concerns. PVC is a polymer (a chain of molecules called monomers; the monomer is vinyl chloride, the polymer *poly*vinyl chloride). CPVC, also known as PVDC, is a form of PVC made more heat-stable by adding extra chlorine.

Of the nearly 14 billion pounds of PVC produced annually, 50–75 percent is used in construction, much of it for irrigation and drainage pipes and other landscape products; see table 6.2. Production is growing, especially in the less-regulated Third World. Greenpeace alleges that as DDT, PCBs, CFCs, and other deadly organochlorides were banned, the industry hyped PVC to ensure a market for chlorine, 30 percent of which now goes to PVC manufacture. Billions of pounds of PVC are discarded each year; Greenpeace estimates that over 300 million tons of PVC waste, which is not biodegradable, was in the world waste stream by 2005.

To make PVC more rigid or flexible, a variety of additives are used; these may form 60 percent by weight of a PVC product, and include serious pollutants like lead, cadmium, and tin.

PVC remains very popular despite its dangers, for several reasons. The primary reason is familiarity; it is required by many local building codes, despite preferable alternatives. More rigid than many other plastics, it is easily made flexible with additives. Tensile strength is high, keeping PVC pipes from bursting under pressure. It is easily joined by glue fittings, unlike other plastic- or metal-pipe systems. It is relatively cheap in today's economy (although energy intensive to produce, and thus susceptible to energy-cost increases).

End-use issues: Chlorine compounds and additives including lead have been reported to leach from PVC pipe into water supply. The state of California requires labeling of all "vinyl" garden hoses (vinyl is essentially PVC with plasticizers) as follows: "This product contains chemicals known to cause cancer and birth defects or reproductive harm. Do Not Drink From This Hose." PVC is banned for food containers.

End users can also be affected by gases if PVC accidentally burns or smolders, as when wiring insulated with PVC overheats. PVC in the World Trade Center caused a dioxin cloud that hung over Manhattan after 9/11. Designers of tunnels, ships, and other enclosed public spaces routinely specify non-PVC-coated wiring because of the danger of toxic smoke.

The Institute of Horticultural Research (Wellesborne UK) has documented that DBP, an additive used in PVC greenhouse glazing strips, kills or

Table 6.2

Plastics used for landscape products—an unscientific survey.

	♻ 2: HDPE	♻ 3: PVC †	♻ 4: LLDPE	♻ 5: PP	♻ 7: other (see note*)
IRRIGATION	watering cans supply pipes (incl. pressurized) hose reel carts and hose pots flexible downspouts	garden hoses drip tube ("spaghetti") supply pipes drainage pipes extendable downspouts	drip tube ("spaghetti") laser soaker hose non-pressurized pipe		irrigation heads (ABS)
FURNITURE	floating lounge chairs picnic tables	"wicker" furniture arbor with benches "leather" upholstery umbrella fabric closed-cell foam floats and pool lounges		outdoor furniture	"bentwood" rocker (resin) "wicker" furniture (resin) "cast-iron" furniture (resin) outdoor upholstery (acrylic)
HORT. USES	planters bins planter with trellis fake terracotta pots nursery pots artificial turf turf reinforcers	trellises arbors lattice lawn edging root barriers artificial turf		fake terracotta pots nursery pots	fake terracotta pots (foam resin) propagation trays ("polymer") planters (resin) arbors (resin) planters (fiberglass)
STORAGE	bins			boxes and bags	storage sheds (resin)
WORK CLOTHES	hard hats	work gloves rain and chemical-spray clothing work boots			
CONSTRUCTION SUPPLIES	"landscape plastic," clear and black sheets tarps most plastic lumber duct tape powder-coated metal some geotextiles	coated metal cable, wire, and screen tarps flagging and barricade ribbon some plastic lumber some geotextiles some adhesives		construction fence tarps	
ELECTRIC		light fixtures electrical conduit junction boxes, etc. electrical tape			
GREENHOUSES		corrugated clear panels glazing strips			greenhouse windows (polycarbonate) clear greenhouse fabric (polyethylene reinforced with nylon mesh)
OTHER	basketball backboards chain-link privacy slats composting bins powder-coated CL fence and posts some signage	inflatable pools pool covers pool toys some pond liners dock structures fencing pickets, rails, posts, and gates vinyl-coated CL fence vinyl grill covers some signage		doormats, "jute"-look and other mailboxes	in-lawn alligator and other ornaments (resin)

*The only landscape use found for PET (♻ 1, polyethylene terapthalmate) and PS (♻ 6, polystyrene) was in pots for nursery growing. Polyethylene has many forms: only PET, HDPE (High Density), and LLDPE (Linear Low Density) have recycle numbers, above. PEX (cross-linked polyethylene) is stronger than PE and occasionally used in pipes. Others seldom if ever found in landscape use are UHMWPE and HMWPE (Ultra-High and High Molecular Weight), VLDPE (Very Low Density), and MDPE (Medium Density).

† The use of the 3 symbol allows PVC to be sorted from other plastics. The symbol does not mean that PVC is feasibly recyclable. For environmental problems with PVC see p. 252.

injures plants at low airborne concentrations. The institute documents such damage to greenhouse crops since the 1930s.[52] Outdoor landscape plants are less likely to be damaged.

Production issues: Despite industry improvements, PVC and CPVC still risk release of dioxins and other highly toxic chemicals during manufacture and transport. Many common additives are neurotoxins or carcinogens. Ingredient vinyl chloride is a known carcinogen; incomplete polymerization can leave leachable traces of this monomer in PVC. Liquid vinyl chloride is the glue used by PVC installers, such as irrigation contractors; workers with vinyl chloride have extremely elevated risk for liver cancer. The US EPA's National Toxicology Program rates liquid vinyl chloride as "ultrahazardous"; a 2005 emergency law banned its transport through Washington DC.

PVC's main ingredient, chlorine, is hazardous; production requires intensive use of electricity.

Factors that reduce/offset risks: Strictly regulated manufacture has reduced production risks, but cannot affect disposal or accidental hazards. There is no question that PVC has great practical and commercial value, but there is serious doubt that the risks are worth it. "The environmental community generally wants to see a phase-out or banning of [organochloride compounds, including PVC and its ingredients] except for essential uses."[53] Many national and municipal governments, plus a significant number of multinational corporations, have restricted use of PVC and mandated alternatives.

Renewability/recyclability: PVC is not recyclable to any significant degree; Greenpeace states that less than 1 percent of all PVC is recycled, and almost no PVC construction materials. They allege that PVC recycling was promoted by industry to avoid regulation, using claims that were often flatly false. Possible, but rarely practiced, is CPVC recycling. If recycled at all, PVC is "downcycled to manufacture inferior products such as garden benches and sound barriers along highways."[54] Much of this small amount of recycling is shipped to developing countries, where worker and environmental protection is weaker than in the United States. In many ways, PVC garden furniture may prove to be the landscape industry's overseas sweatshop scandal.

Burning PVC for disposal releases chlorine compounds, dioxins, furans, and heavy metals. PVC in waste has been said to account for half of the chlorine in incineration fumes, and in many countries it is the main source of lead and cadmium in air pollution. Chlorine-based chemicals (organochlorides, chlorofluorocarbons, PCBs, DDT, dioxin, and others) are strongly implicated in cancer, reproductive disorders, species loss, and ozone depletion. When PVC is incinerated, resulting chlorine by-products are themselves toxic wastes; if stabilized by adding inert materials, these often exceed the bulk of the original PVC.

Alternatives: Several other plastics are less toxic in manufacture and easier to recycle or dispose of than PVC. Various forms of polyethylene (PE) are suitable for pipes, furniture, plastic lumber, and other common products. ABS plastic is considered a slightly less environmentally damaging material, but not a general PVC replacement. Traditional materials like metal and clay, although less convenient and with energy and cost disadvantages, may need to be reconsidered for drainage pipes.

Landscape use of HDPE has been tested by Seattle Parks Department, EDAW (Fort Collins CO office), and Cahill Associates. In general, polyethylene is comparable to PVC in materials cost, but not as widely available. Installation can cost twice that of PVC, because contractors are unfamiliar with fuse-welding of PE (which actually produces less leak-prone waterlines). Like other "learning-curve" costs, this should not be an excuse: the more PE is used, the more labor costs will fall. In some cases, like catch basins and inlets, PE requires product redesign to achieve PVC's structural strength. PE, however, is more resilient, more UV resistant, and less likely to fail with age or extreme cold than PVC.[55]

Wood Preservatives

Since this book's first edition, the wood-preservative industry has been in a state of rapid change.[56] This is due to several factors: a partial ban on industry-standard CCA preservative (chromated copper arsenic) in 2004; introduction of alternatives with varied performance; and economic battles as producers scramble to grab market share.

Wood preservation is a knotty problem: it can dramatically prolong life of renewable woods, but introduces serious pollutants. As Alex Wilson, editor of EBN, notes, there is no getting around the fact that "preservatives are designed to kill. [Preventing wood decay requires] finding the right balance between toxicity to the problem organism and safety to us and the environment."[57] Finding that balance has become even more complex since CCA was removed from much of the market for environmental reasons. As with PVC, preservatives pose relatively minor *user* health hazards, but serious manufacturing, contractor/installer, and disposal problems.

Annual US production of treated woods is about 8.4 billion board feet (20 million cubic meters), just over 20 percent of total softwood production both in volume and cost. How much is used in landscapes is uncertain, but outdoor uses far outnumber interior ones. Some 60 billion board feet (140 million cubic meters) of CCA-treated wood installed since the 1970s are now reaching the end of their service life. (Yes, even treated wood eventually breaks down.) Because "there is no environmentally sound way to dispose of [CCA] treated wood,"[58] this huge waste volume poses major—and growing—disposal problems.

Main types of treated wood are discussed in this section; only four can be expected to work reasonably well in fully exposed, wet, or ground-contact situations.

Oil-based preservatives: Pentachlorophenol ("penta") and creosote still each account for about 10 percent of US treated wood. Penta combines two toxic chemicals (chlorine and phenol); creosote and its parent material, coal tar, are also toxic. Their use is limited by smell and difficulty sealing or painting over them; they are most common on utility poles, railroad ties, and fence posts, sometimes reused in ornamental landscapes. In general, they are best avoided.

Water-based copper preservatives: CCA and its arsenic-free relative, ACC (acid copper chromate), were industry standards. Both raised concern about human health (via skin contact), leaching into soil and water, and disposal. In 2004 the EPA banned CCA for high public-contact uses like playgrounds and decks; it is still used for foundation sills, pilings, piers, guardrails, sound-wall posts, and fenceposts, and it is almost universal for wood installed in saltwater. ACC

is discontinued; the EPA proposed reviving it, but retreated under public pressure in January 2007.

These bans have spurred a quest for kinder, gentler copper formulations. The two most common "second-generation" products are ACQ (alkaline copper quat, "quat" being quaternary ammonia) and copper azole. These are environmentally preferable to CCA, containing neither arsenic nor chromium. High hopes, as of this book's first edition, have been tempered by problems. The new preservatives contain higher percentages of copper, not as well bonded to the wood (fixed by chromium in CCA/ACC)—more copper to leach, and more likely to do so.

Copper, the main fungus and insect killer in these formulas, is highly toxic to aquatic life and plants and causes human health problems. "Fixing" copper-based preservatives in pressure-treated wood is essential to performance and safety. At 70°F, fixing takes about three days; at 50°F, nearly two weeks; near freezing, it may not occur at all. Because wood is often shipped "wet" immediately after treatment, check how, where, and at what temperature it was stored at the sales yard. Use extra caution working with water-soaked pressure-treated wood.

ACQ and copper azole are more corrosive to metal fasteners than CCA, despite improvements by reformulation. Galvanized or stainless-steel fasteners are required.

The new copper preservatives are not usually guaranteed for ground-contact use, suggesting that manufacturers do not expect them to perform well in this situation—marketing claims notwithstanding. They appear to be safer for end-users, but problems in manufacturing, installation, and disposal remain. The AIA concluded that the most serious environmental hazard of CCA was potential spills during transportation or production; the newer formulas still involve some hazardous ingredients, posing risks to treatment workers and anyone sawing or drilling copper-treated wood. Incineration puts preservative chemicals into the air; ash from this process concentrates toxic substances and greatly increases their leachability.

Of particular concern to landscape professionals is chipping waste wood for mulch. In theory, treated lumber is kept separate; in practice, it is hard to sort treated from untreated wood when weathered. Discarded after long service and chipped, wood leaches more easily than whole new treated boards. Less than 0.1 percent copper-treated wood in wood mulch can leach enough to violate safety standards. Nearly 6 percent of wood construction waste is treated; the potential for contaminating mulch is great.

As with PVC, a main ingredient in mainstream wood preservatives is produced by a powerful industry, in this case copper. Industry preference for copper-based preservatives limits research and marketing for other types, while the EPA's current industry-friendliness contributes to "copper's hegemony," according to EBN's Tristan Roberts.

Borate preservatives: Boron is relatively safe for humans, provides good control of both fungi and insects, and is long tested. Unfortunately, it is very water-soluble and mostly unsuitable for outdoor use. One exception may be "ES+Wood," from Wood Treatment Products, which binds boron to wood with a polymer and offers a forty-year warranty covering ground-contact use. Roberts remains skeptical that any borate can survive seriously wet exposure.

Silicate preservatives: Sodium silicate is inexpensive and abundant, presents few hazards in manufacture, use, or disposal, and has long been used as preservative, although not for exterior wood. A new silicate preservative called TimberSIL, from Timber Treatment Technologies (TTT), won a "Top Ten Products" award in 2004 from Building Green, publishers of EBN—but is still struggling to reach market. TimberSIL surrounds wood cells with glassy silicate that keeps water, insects, and fungi out *structurally* rather than by poison. It offers a forty-year, full-exposure warranty. Where available, its price is comparable to ACQ; price is expected to drop once widely marketed.

TimberSIL's problems follow a common pattern for sustainability-driven initiatives. Contracted manufacturing facilities, accustomed to simpler pressure treatment with poisons, had precision troubles with silicate application. In addition, the EPA (allegedly urged by competitors) put TTT in a catch-22: it investigated TTT for making pesticide claims about a material not registered as a pesticide—when sodium silicate is so non-toxic it cannot qualify as a pesticide!

These appear to be "learning-curve" issues. TimberSIL is currently manufactured in South Carolina,

but is developing licensing and distribution agreements. It will probably be 2008 before it is available nationally. Although primarily lab tested, the product promises the preservative holy grail: wood protection without poisons.

Other preservatives: Evaluate individual products; few of the following types have outdoor uses.

So-called organic preservatives (meaning carbon based, not wholesome and healthy) are agricultural pesticides in solvents for wood treatment. The solvents give off VOCs (volatile pollutants). Because the agricultural chemicals are already EPA registered, their adaptations as wood preservatives can slip through regulatory loopholes.

Heat treatment hardens and dries "thermally engineered" wood, limiting insect and fungus access. It is somewhat brittle and little suited to outdoor use.

Chemically modified wood infuses wood with chemicals ("acetylization" derives from vinegar; "furfurylization" from plant-based alcohol). This changes the wood's molecular structure. This Scandinavian technique is unlikely to reach US markets and in any case is not well suited to outdoor use.

Finally, futuristic nanotechnology uses beads of preservative so tiny (one hundred nanometers, or about four millionths of an inch) that they pass through microscopic pores in wood cells. This can put preservative where it cannot leach—possibly *increasing* disposal problems. In any event, like most nanotechnology predictions, this remains experimental.

Alternatives to preserved wood: Some woods naturally resist decay and insects. Tropical hardwoods (teak, ipe, etc.) should be used only if Forest Stewardship Council certified, and with careful consideration of transportation energy. Domestic softwoods (cypress, redwood, northern white and western red cedars, and yellow pine) are moderately resistant, but supplies, especially of most-resistant old-growth heartwood, are limited or gone. Most such woods are now obtained through salvage. Several species (black locust, honey locust, and osage orange) are very resistant, but too small to provide dimensional lumber. Laminating these woods is possible; exterior-grade products might result.

A second alternative to preserved wood is plastic lumber (p. 239). Although essentially rot and insect proof, 100 percent plastic "lumber" is unsuitable for structural use. Wood-plastic composites incorporate wood fibers and can be used structurally in some cases. These materials have already become widespread for decking, a major substitution for treated wood.

Recommendations: There is no one-size-fits-all way to extend outdoor life of lumber. The following are options, roughly in priority order:

- Design to *avoid* wood in wet or soil-contact locations. Local stone footings, and sometimes concrete or steel, are substitutes. Question whether a permanent structure is necessary; other design solutions could meet functional and aesthetic demands.
- Evaluate whether protection is required from fungus, insects, or both, and whether wood will be soaked or buried. Less-toxic protection against specific threats may be easier than blanket protection.
- Consider resistant woods, with sustainable harvest certification, or salvaged.
- Consider plastic and composite lumber if not limited by structural requirements.
- If treated wood cannot be avoided, use the least-toxic type suitable for the purpose. Because disposal is a major problem, durability and life-cycle interacts significantly with toxicity issues.
- Ensure that any treated wood is installed with care. This includes skin and breathing protection for workers and proper job-site cleanup. Strictly follow manufacturer instructions for fasteners and for treatment of field-cut surfaces.
- For many treated woods, sealing with paint, stain, or varnish will improve resistance and longevity, and reduce user-health risks, if any.

When disassembling any wood structure, make a serious attempt to separate treated from untreated wood. *Reuse* treated wood to avoid disposal. Verify what happens to wood wastes locally before dumping treated wood. Landfills vary widely in the United States; many dumps are not constructed to isolate heavy metal leachates such as those from treated lumber waste.

Toxics as "Fertilizer"

In 1997, the mayor of the small town of Quincy WA led an investigation for local farmers. Cattle had sickened; crop yields were declining. The farmers discovered that toxic waste was being repackaged and sold to them *as fertilizer*. *Seattle Times* reporter Duff Wilson pursued the investigation, finding examples of this practice nationwide. Wilson later documented the scandal in a book, *Fateful Harvest*.⊃ An Oklahoma uranium-processor licenses its radioactive waste as a liquid fertilizer. Pulp mills in Washington spread lead-laced waste on livestock grazing land. Two Oregon steel mills put a powdered waste into silos under federal hazardous waste permits and take *the exact same material* out of the silo for sale as fertilizer. While most industrialized nations regulate fertilizers, the United States does not. State governments do so inconsistently, leniently, and with little testing or enforcement.

Findings by Wilson and the Washington-based nonprofit Environmental Working Group show that over 600 toxic-waste-producing companies in 44 US states were involved in this shady but legal practice. These included smelters, chemical companies, mining, cement, waste incinerators (some handling medical wastes), wood-product firms, and other heavy industries. Over 450 firms in 38 states received the waste; some were fertilizer manufacturers, while others were farms. Between 1990 and 1995, some 270 million tons of wastes were shipped, some directly to farms, the rest relabeled as fertilizer, usually with minimal processing. The repackaged wastes contained cadmium, lead, arsenic, radioactive materials, and dioxins.

Thanks to the *Seattle Times* report, there was a flurry of activity in 2001 that culminated in 2002 with slightly stricter EPA regulations for a narrow portion of the problem: zinc waste recycled as zinc fertilizer. Since then, the issue seems to have been swept under a rug. Contaminants in fertilizers are still not regulated or tested federally, nor tracked, nor revealed on product labeling. The EPA considers fertilizers under their "land disposal" rules, as if farm fields were equivalent to landfills. The American Association of Plant Food Control Officers has attempted to set consistent state standards. Unfortunately, its rules accept heavy metals in fertilizers at levels that *average* 469 percent of levels allowed by the state of Washington, for example.[59]

Ironically, the scandal originates from the 1976 Resource Conservation and Recovery Act. Intended to encourage recycling, this law failed to distinguish between harmless recyclable "waste" and toxic by-products. This is no simple matter. Some industrial waste products, such as unbleached paper slurry, may actually provide beneficial plant nutrients without toxic contamination. But merely by stating that a material is a "product," it immediately becomes exempt from hazardous-material regulations. In a few cases, toxic materials have even been labeled as "organic" when sold as fertilizer.[60]

The extent of selling toxic materials to the unwitting public remains murky. The practice is certainly unethical; at the very least labeling should be required. Industrial toxic waste likely has higher concentrations of harmful materials than treated sewage sludge (see p. 94)—yet it is biosolids that have been subject to public outcry, while repackaged industrial waste goes unchallenged.

As users of considerable quantities of fertilizer, landscape professionals would be well advised to keep abreast of this issue and to lobby for truth in packaging (at least) for all fertilizers. Those who *apply* fertilizers are at most risk from toxic exposure. If concentrated toxic materials are in fact being passed off as fertilizers, it is in the landscape industry's self-interest, not to mention environmental and public health, to demand that the practice be stopped.

Fertilizer, with potential effects on the food chain, has been the major concern. The Resource Recovery Act's advocacy of recycling, however, has also allowed toxic waste to be incorporated in building materials such as asphalt, cement, glass, roofing materials, and noise barriers, as well as in combustible fuels. Landscape construction uses virtually all of these products, and contaminants in them affect the landscape. This abuse of the concept of recycling is something that landscape professionals need to expose and oppose.

Prioritize Hazard-reduction Efforts

We draw the following conclusions about ways for landscape professionals to lessen environmental impact of materials they use.

- Focus on proper *disposal, salvage, and recycling* of construction materials, *reducing fuel use*, and *influencing manufacturers* toward nontoxic processes and accident prevention. Relatively few outdoor materials are directly hazardous to end-users; end-use issues are probably *not* the area in which professional attention can produce greatest results.

- Reuse materials creatively, and create jobs and markets by doing so.

- Support technical and social efforts to reuse and recycle construction materials. Fairly small changes in disposal and recycling of construction materials could produce real results.

- Analyze and reduce transportation, equipment use, and other fuel consumption (Principle 7). Fuel use, rather than materials hazards, probably contributes most to environmental impact of landscape materials.

- An increasing number of manufacturers have recognized the social and economic value of nontoxic processes and materials. Landscape professionals should support those whose claims can be documented.

- Select FSC-certified sustainable wood whenever possible.

- For plastics, give preference to manufacturers who use mostly recycled plastic, and who label each product (better still, each distinct piece of a product) with the recycle symbol and plastic-type number.

- Use the product with the fewest known end-use effects on human health and environment. Use products with known hazards only where no practicable alternative exists. Even minor effects may be cumulative or may interact with other pollutants.

- Avoid PVC and conventional wood preservatives wherever they are not absolutely essential.

- Work to ensure that landscape products, including fertilizers and "downcycled" materials, do not become a clandestine "sink" for toxic wastes.

Current information, including this book, is not sufficient to give landscape-materials selection a truly sound environmental basis. Information about architectural materials and indoor air quality, although more readily available, should be used cautiously as a guide to outdoor conditions.

There is a definite need for authoritative, accessible information on *landscape* products and their environmental impacts. The landscape professions should fund production of such information, preferably in LCA or similar format. Individual landscape professionals should work to convince suppliers that accessible information is to everyone's advantage.

Resources

Consider Origin and Fate of Materials

Recycled, Re-seen: Folk Art from the Global Scrap Heap Charlene Cerny and Suzanne Seriff, 1996 Harry N. Abrams, Inc., and the Museum of International Folk Art, Santa Fe NM; 505-992-2611: Wonderful overview of recycling as art and as livelihood for much of the world's population; exhibition catalog, richly illustrated; two chapters devoted to recycled landscapes by folk artists.

Materials

Search Terms: landscaping materials || landscape construction materials

Athena Institute www.athenasmi.ca/: Research organization on materials and energy.

Center for Maximum Potential Building Systems 512-928-4786, www.cmpbs.org/: Pliny Fisk, codirector; exceptional information on materials, energy, economics of sustainability.

Construction Specifications Institute 800-689-2900, www.csinet.org/s_csi/index.asp: Research and standards on specifying materials.

A Guide to Estimating Landscape Cost Gary O. Robinette, 1983 Ctr. for Ldscp. Arch. Educn and Rsch, Van Nostrand Reinhold, New York: As a guide, this book is less dated than standard annual price summaries.

Biocycle magazine 610-967-4135 ext. 22, www.jgpress.com/biocycle.htm: Devoted to composting and recycling; the March 1998 issue discusses uses of crumb rubber.

Chemical glossary Chemical Abstracts: Download current publications catalog to find glossary and other resources.

Plumbing Claims Group (Polybutylene) 800-490-6997, www.spencerclass.com/index2.htm: Information on why PB is no longer manufactured in the United States.

Plastics industry associations 202-974-5200, www.socplas.org/, 202-974-5200, and www.bpf.co.uk/ (UK): Recycling code system; industry views on PVC, environmental regulation.

NIST Building and Fire Research Lab (National Institute of Standards and Technology), www.bfrl.nist.gov/: Materials research; also fire and disaster studies—many publications, software, links.

Ecology of Building Materials Berge, Bjørn, 1992, Norwegian ed., 2001, English ed. Butterworth-Heinemann, Oxford: Materials origins, manufacturing, uses, environmental considerations.

Materials selection

Search Terms: "material selection"

The Environmental Resource Guide: American Institute of Architects Joseph A. Demkin, 1994–98 Wiley, New York: Loose-leaf, with annual supplements; exceptional detail on materials, life-cycles, and energy.

EBN Product Catalog Environmental Building News annual loose-leaf directory, http://energy-efficient-products.ebuild.com/default.asp, www.ebuild.com/: Now online by subscription.

Environmental by Design Kim Leclair and David Rousseau, 1992 Hartley and Marks Ltd., Vancouver BC: Focused on interior materials and IAQ, but useful because it includes Canadian and European products.

Green Building Resource Guide J. Hermannsson, 1997 Taunton Press, Newtown CT: Primarily for buildings, but useful for CSI-format and price comparison indexes.

Guide to Resource Efficient Building Elements Tracy Mumma, 1997, 6th ed., Center for Resourceful Building Technology, www.crbt.org/index.html, 406-549-7678

Resourceful Specifications: Guideline Specifications for Environmentally Considered Building Materials and Methods Larry Strain, 1997 Siegel and Strain Architects, Emeryville CA, www.siegelstrain.com, 510-547-8092

Constructability Concepts File Construction Industry Institute, 512-232-3000, www.construction-institute.org/script content/Index.cfm: Mainly engineering, but some related concepts on materials efficiency and on-site remediation.

Environmental Design and Construction magazine 248-244-6258, www.edcmag.com/: Bimonthly, mostly buildings; good annual buyer's guide.

Landscape Architect and Specifier News Landscape Communications Ltd., 714-979-5276: Trade magazine; valuable for ads, annual product guide, and Landscape Online; articles tend toward advertorial.

CITES (Convention on International Trade in Endangered Species) US Fish and Wildlife Service, www.cites.org/: Lists endangered timber species and other natural products that should not be specified.

Masterspec Landscape Architecture Specifications ARCOM Systems, 800-424-5080, www.arcomnet.com/arcom indexstill.html: Not specifically green, but useful.

National Park Service Sustainable Design and Construction Database Sally Small, 1994 National Park Service Technical Information Center, www.nps.gov/

Resources for Environmental Design Index (REDI) Iris Communications, 541-317-1626, www.oikos.com/: Frequently updated database of products.

Making Better Concrete: Guidelines to Using Fly Ash for Higher Quality, Eco-friendly Structures B. King, 2005 Green Building Press, San Rafael CA

Materials: on-site

Search Terms: materials + "on-site"

Earth-building innovations Nader Khalili Cal-Earth foundation, 760-244-0614, www.calearth.org/: Information on site-fired earth housing and other low-tech, high-result building methods.

Stabilized soil pavement Stabilizer, 800-336-2468, www
.stabilizersolutions.com/: Bonds soil in place for paths, etc.

Stabilized soil pavement Soil Stabilization Products,
www.sspco.org/: Bonds soil in place for paths, etc.

Natural Stonescapes: The Art and Craft of Stone Placement R. L. Dube
and Frederick C. Campbell, 1999 Storey
Communications/Garden Way, Pownal VT: Practical advice;
cultivating a sense for unusual stone.

Materials: recycled

Search Terms: material + (recycled OR reused OR remanufactured)

Reuse of whole tires Stuart Hoenig, 520-887-3815: Article
about his thoughts on old tires, http://composite.about.com/
library/PR/1999/blua3.htm.

Recycled plastic greenwalls EKOL Belgium,
www.tessenderlo.com/contentNS4.asp: Recycled plastic as
park benches, tables, flower troughs, molded paving slabs,
fencing, and traffic islands, motorway sound barriers.

Impact-Post 800-863-6619: Plastic lumber in railroad-tie sizes.

The Resource Guide to Sustainable Landscapes Wesley Groesbeck and
Jan Streifel, 1996 Environmental Resources Inc., Salt Lake
City UT: Listing of some 3,000 landscape products with
recycled content or other environmental benefits.

Caltrans and Recycled Transportation Products
www.ciwmb.ca.gov/ConDemo/Roads/CalTrans.htm:
Online article on specifying recycled materials for surface
transportation.

Netafim www.netafim.com/: Recycling of used and scrap tubing
(not just their own brand).

FreeCycle groups www.freecycle.org/: International nonprofit,
free exchange via web; 3,975 local volunteer-moderated
groups; 3,261,119 members.

Sustainable wood

Search Terms: sustainable wood || bamboo construction ||
certified wood products || sustainable forestry

ProSilva Europe
http://ourworld.compuserve.com/homepages/J_Kuper/
page1_e.htm: Information on sustainable forestry and related
issues from Europe.

Ecoforestry: The Art and Science of Sustainable Forest Use A. Drengson
and D. Taylor, 1997 New Society Publishers, Gabriola
Island BC

Good Wood Directory Certified Wood Product Search, www
.certifiedwoodsearch.org/searchproducts.aspx; Good Wood
Trade Directory, www.aboutgoodwood.info/trade.asp

The Forest Certification Handbook Christopher Upton and Stephen
Bass, 1996 St. Lucie Press, Delray Beach FL

Woods of the World database 1996 Tree-Talk Inc., Burlington,
VT: wow@together.net CD-ROM with photos, or diskettes
without; encourages use of plentiful but unknown woods.

Cascadia Forest Goods www.cascadiaforestgoods.com/: Sustainable forest products supplier.

BambooLiving.com www.bambooliving.com/construction.html:
Information on bamboo construction.

Construction waste management

Search Terms: construction waste management || construction
waste reduction

International Solid Waste Association (ISWA) RecycleNet
Corporation, www.recycle.net/recycle/assn/; ISWA info,
www.eco-web.com/register/00840.html: Copenhagen,
Denmark; (+45) 32 96 15 88

*WasteSpec: Model Specifications for Construction Waste Reduction, Reuse,
and Recycling* Judith Kincaid, Cheryl Walker, and Greg Flynn,
1995 Triangle J Council of Governments, Durham NC,
www.tjcog.dst.nc.us/regplan/wastspec.htm, 919-549-0551

Construction Materials Recycling Guidebook Pamela W. Laner, 1993
Metro Council of St. Paul, MN, www.metrocouncil.org,
651-602-1140: Full guide available at
www.p2pays.org/ref/24/23737.pdf.

Residential Construction Waste Management: A Builder's Field Guide Pe-
ter Yost and Eric Lund, 1997 National Association of Home
Builders, Washington DC, 800-368-5242, www.nahb.org/:
Free thirty-page booklet.

Hazard identification

Search Terms: hazards identification || toxic materials identifica-
tion

Soil Contamination: Think First, Dig Later! Construction Industry Institute, 512-232-3000, http://www.construction
-institute.org/scriptcontent/Index.cfm: VC-404, ninety-
minute video; other reports and videos also sold.

The Home and Land Buyer's Guide to the Environment Barry Chalof-
sky, 1997 Center for Urban Policy Research, New Brunswick
NJ, www.policy.rutgers.edu/cupr/, 732-932-3133 ext. 555

Toxics A to Z: A Guide to Everyday Pollution Hazards John Harte,
Cheryl Holdren, Richard Schneider, and Christine Shirley,
1991 University of California Press, Berkeley: Lists about
one hundred of the most common toxic materials, plus noise,
and discusses health effects; lists are by common name; covers
a few construction materials and many solvents and other
ingredients.

What Remodelers Need to Know and Do About Lead 1993
National Association of Home Builders, Washington DC,
www.nahb.org, 800-368-5242

Lab Safety Supply Inc. 800-356-0783, www.labsafety.com/:
Toxics test kits; safety data on industrial chemicals, processes,
and regulations.

**Water Quality Information Center of the National Agricul-
tural Library** www.nal.usda.gov/wqic/Bibliographies/

Pollution-preventing Landscape Management www.epa.gov/
nps/MMGI/Chapter4/ch4-6.html: Lists ways in which landscapes contribute to pollution, and how to avoid these.

1996 Toxic Release Info (TRI) Public Data www.epa.gov/tri/:
Lists events in which toxic materials have been released into
the environment.

Guide to Cleaner Coating Technologies US EPA, http://
es.epa.gov/program/epaorgs/ord/org-coat.html: Clear
discussion of various coatings, environmental issues, and
alternatives.

MSDS-Search 877-673-7123, www.msdssearch.com/: Free Web site with one million Material Safety Data Sheets.

US EPA www.epa.gov/epahome/search.html: Searchable site for pollution and many other environmental issues.

Greenpeace PVC campaign and database www.greenpeace.org/international/campaigns/toxics/polyvinyl-chloride/pvc-products/: Detailed information on PVC issues and products; database at see also www.greenpeace.org/australia/ or www.greenpeace.org/usa/ and search for PVC (each site has different articles).

Fateful Harvest: The True Story of a Small Town, a Global Industry, and a Toxic Secret Duff Wilson, 2001 HarperCollins, New York: Reports relabeling of toxic waste as fertilizer.

"Factory Farming: Toxic Waste as Fertilizer in the United States 1990–95" Environmental Working Group, www.ewg.org/: Report (avail. online) on relabeling of toxic waste as fertilizer.

American Association of Plant Food Control Officials www.aapfco.org/: Works for fertilizer standards.

Materials: nontoxic or alternative

Search Terms: chemical sensitivity || building materials "nontoxic" OR alternative OR healthy

Green Seal 202-872-6400, www.greenseal.org/: Environmental standards for paints, caulks, adhesives, plus general environmental publications.

Soy Safe 866-359-9401, www.soysafe.com/: Nontoxic paint stripper, adhesive remover, graffiti remover, driveway cleaner, lubricants.

Prescriptions for a Healthy House Paula Baker, Erica Elliott, and John Banta, 1998 InWord Publishers, Santa Fe NM: CSI-format listings of materials healthy enough for IAQ for chemically sensitive people.

Bio-Form nontoxic form-release agent Leahy-Wolff, Bellwood IL, 708-432-0020, www.leahywolf.com/:

Safer wood preservatives (ACQ) Chemical Specialties, 800-421-8661, www.treatedwood.com/; ACQ info, www.treatedwood.com/products/preserve/: Other manufacturers with similar products not marketed in the United States are Osmose Corp. (Copper citrate), Hickson Co. (Copper Azole), and Kodiak Inc. (CDDC).

Healthy Building Network www.healthybuilding.net/: Links to: PVC-Free Pipe Purchasers' Report, PVC-Free Alternatives Database, "Environmental Impacts of PVC Building Materials," and USGBC report on PVC.

Life-cycle analysis

Search Terms: life cycle analysis || life cycle assessment || life cycle costing

"The Big Picture: Life Cycle Analysis" Rob Goldberg, May 1992, *Academy of Natural Sciences* 215-299-1000, www.ansp.org: Good article on abuses of LCA if not kept in perspective with other regional factors.

Principle 7:
Know the Costs of Energy over Time

The law of conservation of energy tells us we can't get something for nothing, but we refuse to believe it.
—Isaac Asimov, 1988

Energy is the core of life, central to doing, living, building. Since the "energy crisis" of the late 1970s, design and construction professionals have been keenly aware of energy issues: energy-saving lights and appliances, efficiency standards for heating and cooling, and the ever-increasing costs of fuel. Energy efficiency can sell a property, and inefficient use of energy can sink a construction business. Yet despite energy's increasing importance in building design and construction, it is still rare to find energy conservation principles systematically applied to *landscape* construction.

Architecture 2030, the group that has put designers into the forefront of the attempt to reverse global warming (see p. 14), estimates that nearly 50 percent of *all* energy used goes into constructing, operating, maintaining, and decommissioning buildings.[1] This and similar estimates worldwide have given architects the impetus to tackle climate change through professional efforts.

The role that landscape construction plays in these energy estimates is unclear, since landscape work is sometimes but not always reported as part of architectural statistics. If landscape construction consumes even *one-fortieth* of what building construction does, however, this would be 1.25 percent of the US total—comparable to some estimates of energy used in constructing highways (1.64 percent) or single-family residences (1.19 percent).[2] It is well beyond the scope of this book to attempt accurate estimates of *total* landscape-industry energy use. Landscape construction clearly consumes enough, however, to make energy analysis and conservation worthwhile.

Energy analysis, although its methods are still evolving, is a skill that will be as essential as cost es-

timating to designers and contractors in the very near future. As decisions about which material, what design, what machinery become increasingly interlinked and complex, energy costing offers the clearest available baseline for these hard choices. At present, energy studies are rough-and-ready, generalized, occasionally even misleading. In the evolution of knowledge about energy in construction, landscape professionals have real opportunities both to benefit and to contribute.

Construction "represents a huge, relatively long-duration energy investment";[3] currently, this investment is mostly gambled, rather than managed. Any landscape professional who wants to work sustainably will gain great advantage by keeping current with emerging energy-planning methods.

The authors hope to encourage construction, design, and planning professionals to *help develop* practical methods and reliable standards for energy evaluation. Even more than when our first edition was released, fuel prices, oil wars, and climate change underline the need to rethink how energy is managed.

Discussed in This Chapter

- How energy affects landscape construction.
- Ways to make better, more energy-conscious decisions about landscapes.
- The difference between energy consumed in *using* a landscape ("operating energy") and energy used to *construct* a landscape (fuel energy for construction machinery, and "embodied energy" in construction materials).

- The emerging field of *embodied energy analysis*, a relatively new concept whose uses (and limitations) every environmentally conscious designer and contractor needs to understand.
- The use of *life-cycle costing* to make thorough long-term cost estimates (energy and/or dollars) for construction materials and methods.

Understand How Landscape Energy Use Is Different

Throughout this book, we have pointed out differences between *building* construction and *landscape* construction, differences that have important environmental consequences. Energy use, too, differs between indoor and outdoor construction: types and total amounts used, as well as where and when. To understand why landscape professionals need to concern themselves with energy issues, it is essential to understand these differences.

Know the Types of Energy in Construction

Because energy plays so many roles in life, it is not surprising that the word has multiple definitions. Only two or three definitions are specifically important in talking about energy in construction.

It takes energy to produce construction materials, to install them, and to operate the site or structure once completed. To discuss these uses of energy clearly, we will use the following terms:

Operating energy (also called end-use energy) refers to power used in day-to-day functioning of a completed project. A common example is energy for heating and cooling buildings. In landscapes, operating energy includes electricity for irrigation valves and controllers, or for outdoor lighting.

Fuel energy (sometimes called inherent or specific energy) is the energy that a material can give off when burned. It is different from embodied energy (below), and applies only to materials that have practical value as fuel. For example, a one-pound piece of pine lumber might produce 2,600 Btu (British thermal units) when burned;[4] embodied energy (for felling and saw-

ing) would be about 2,776 Btu for the unprocessed board; planing, drying, and glue-laminating it could bring the embodied energy to as much as 6,788 Btu per pound.[5]

Fuel energy, and efficiency of transforming it into useful work, is a factor in computing both operating and embodied energy. Fuel efficiency for construction machinery is one area in which landscape contractors can directly affect both their operating costs and environmental impacts.

Embodied energy refers to energy used to *produce* materials. Energy is required to mine or extract raw materials, to refine and combine them, shape them, and, in complex products, to assemble the parts. Between each step, the material may be transported, at an energy cost. Transport from factory to construction site also uses energy. Embodied energy sums up all these energy inputs, usually in terms of energy per pound (or other unit) of material. Energy costs of disposing or recycling the material are important, but sometimes neglected, in embodied energy. For a whole construction *project*, embodied energy totals all energy inputs for materials, processes, and waste.

Embodied energy has a number of synonyms: embedded energy, process energy (which emphasizes factory processes and often excludes transportation), and energy intensity. Energy intensity emphasizes the relative level of energy required to produce a unit (weight, volume, size, etc.) of material. The same term, unfortunately, is used by the US Department of Energy and others to mean the amount of energy used to produce a *dollar's worth* of product.[6] Although this energy-per-dollar idea has its own uses, it should never be confused with energy-per-*material* figures. Architects have also used "energy intensity" to mean per-square-foot *operating* energy of buildings.[7] Because of these confusions, we feel that "embodied energy" is the most consistent term for energy in materials production.

Differentiate Energy in Buildings Versus Landscapes

In buildings, large amounts of energy are used for *operation*; 60 percent of the running costs of the building can readily be saved through efficiency in heating and cooling.[8] There is a trade-off, however: improved operating efficiency usually requires upfront invest-ment in better construction and materials. Low-cost developments, for example, skimp on insulation to keep sale prices low; increased heating and cooling bills are the result. For poorly insulated houses, op-erating energy costs are so high that total energy to *produce* the structure is only about nine times the en-ergy to *operate* the building for a year. By comparison, a house built to today's best efficiency standards can be operated for nearly eighteen years for the energy-price of its materials; one year of operation equates to less than 6 percent of the energy embodied in con-struction.[9] Unfortunately, "spec building" means that the developer's interests (low upfront investment to maximize profit) conflict with the end-user's interests (better, alternative construction to minimize life-cycle operating costs).

Thus, in *building* construction, investing extra in the *embodied* energy of materials, such as insulation or double-pane glass, gives large savings in *operating* en-ergy.

In constructed *landscapes*, the relationship between operating and embodied energy is quite different.

The major operating energy costs of buildings are either absent or greatly reduced in landscapes. Me-chanical heating and cooling are rarely used outdoors, and insulation is not a consideration. As a result, if energy embodied in construction is compared to an-nual operating energy, the *ratio* is much larger for landscapes than for buildings. Thus, better landscape construction, at a higher cost in embodied energy, is unlikely to yield as dramatic a savings in *operating* en-ergy for landscapes as the 60 percent quoted above for efficient buildings.

Some types of operating energy are certainly part of today's landscapes. Outdoor lighting, like its in-door equivalent, has been greatly improved for energy efficiency, and LED lighting appears to promise even greater efficiency. This environmentally important subject is discussed in Principle 8. Irrigation con-trollers and valves (see p. 181) have been redesigned for energy efficiency and water conservation.

Other "outdoor appliances" also use energy: gas grills, poolside conveniences, gate openers, or foun-tain equipment, to name a few. When purchasing or specifying such landscape items, energy efficiency sel-dom seems to be a client concern. Outdoor appli-ances are viewed as luxuries, and there is a peculiar human tendency *not* to expect efficiency from luxury items. Nonetheless, a few manufacturers are starting to design outdoor appliances to use less energy in op-eration. Energy consumption figures for such items, however, are still scarce.

The machines used in maintaining landscapes, such as lawnmowers, chipper shredders, and chain-saws, can be considered as operating energy costs. Be-cause they are similar to construction equipment, however, their energy requirements are discussed in the section below on machinery and energy.

Save Energy in the Landscape

Any net energy savings is significant in sustainability, and where possible, the energy consumed in using landscapes should be minimized. However, the amount that can be saved by reducing landscape *op-erating* energy is limited. Much greater potential en-ergy savings can be accomplished in three areas:

Site design strongly influences operating energy ef-ficiency of *buildings*⊃: shade or windbreak plantings, solar orientation, rainwater management, and many other well-known techniques use landscape as part of green buildings, essential to the struggle against global warming. These design approaches are not de-tailed in this book, but relate directly to many tech-niques and materials of sustainable construction.

Carefully planned machinery use, both on-site and for transportation, can result in significant energy sav-ings. Total machine fuel energy use on any project is strongly affected by choices: between local suppliers and distant ones; among options for bringing work-ers to the site; and between heavy or light equipment and hand tools. Energy consumption estimates and guidelines for making such choices are given in the following section.

Significant savings are possible by analyzing land-scape materials' embodied energy and life-cycles. Each of these topics is discussed in a section of this chapter, which concludes with specific energy-saving suggestions for landscape construction.

Manage Energy for Machines, Tools, and Labor

Landscape construction makes use of a wide range of tools, from very heavy equipment to simple hand tools. Some, like dibbles or planting-sticks, have been in use since prehistoric times; others, such as bulldozers and laser levels, have come into existence only in the last few decades, a mere second in the long day of human existence on this planet.

In thinking about how energy is invested in landscape work, it is important to recognize that the *tools* of landscape construction also differ from those for building construction. Neither set of tools is better; they are simply suited to different jobs. Sitework today relies on large motorized machines; building construction other than sitework uses different, and in general fewer, heavy machines. A vast array of hand power tools is used in building construction; many are too specialized or too easily damaged by weather to be used regularly outdoors. Landscape construction frequently uses simple hand tools; many sites are remote from power supplies, and variability of terrain, site size, and other outdoor conditions often requires the great adaptability of hand work. The differences between these two tool-sets, especially in their balance of powered and non-powered tools, means that the energy economics of landscape construction cannot be optimized by an approach based solely on architectural work.

A simple comparison shows the impact that choice of landscape equipment can have on energy consumption. A modern scraper (or earthmover) can move 20 cubic yards of soil a distance of 200 yards in less than 2 minutes. The same task would take a full day for eight workers using picks, shovels, and the kind of backpack baskets still common in the Third World. The machine, with a 450-hp engine, would have used 0.9 gallons of diesel fuel, or about 7,560 Btu. The eight laborers would use about 20,000 Btu to accomplish the work.[10] Although the machine's direct energy cost is less than that for human labor, indirect costs and problems change the equation significantly.

In industrialized countries, speed of work is highly valued, and true energy costs are disguised by artificially cheap fuel prices and high labor costs. There is no question that the machine is faster—almost 240 times faster. But for sustainability, other considerations compete with convenience, speed, and monetary cost. In the earthmoving example, diesel is a nonrenewable source of energy that produces pollution. Oil exploration, drilling, refining, and transportation cost energy to produce energy—adding at least 3 to 20 percent to the amount directly used. The workers' food is readily renewable and all their waste is biodegradable.[11] In addition, the scraper is composed of many tons of steel and other energy-intensive materials. Its size and weight damage the soil and limit its use to large unobstructed sites.

Few if any industrialized societies would willingly move back to manual labor for all tasks. This is not the only way, however, to cut energy costs. Choosing the most appropriate sources of energy and types and sizes of machinery, as well as prioritizing hand labor where it is effective, offers significant energy savings and site protection (see pp. 60–64).

Try Alternatives in Generating Energy

Energy for tools used in construction, manufacturing, and homes is *generated* in a variety of ways, each with implications for sustainability and for the landscapes in which people live and work. The most common sources of construction power are gasoline and diesel, plus "grid" electricity generated from coal, hydro, and nuclear plants. Portable gas-powered generators are also common at job sites, along with gas or electric air compressors.

Solar (photovoltaic, PV) and wind-generated electricity increasingly provide power to homes and some businesses; with rising oil costs, PV is increasingly being adapted in power sources for construction work, and small wind generators probably could be as well.

LEARN TO DESIGN FOR ALTERNATIVE POWER
"Alternative" power generation links elegantly to landscape design. Unlike large utility networks that intrude on site-specific design, solar, wind, and even small-scale hydro generators are small landscape elements that can and must integrate into individual

sites. Alternative generation uses site conditions—sun, wind, water—that landscape professionals already know how to analyze and work with. Few landscape architects will ever design a power plant, but many have been involved in site-scale energy generation.

Analysis of site suitability, and proper siting, is essential for alternative power. Photovoltaic panels vary in tolerance for shading; wind turbines vary in the minimum wind speed at which they can generate, and the maximum their blades or bearings can withstand. Site analysis also determines whether a specific system is cost-effective: for example, in most regions, the cost of running new utility wires any significant distance is greater than that of buying and installing alternative generators. With photovoltaics, for instance, this breakeven distance is between 200 and 900 yards.[12]

Detailed thought must be given to each component in relation to the whole system. Wind and hydro are turbine generators, their output a function of speed. Wear on moving parts, and noise, must be considered. Solar panels have no moving parts, but take up more space, and their output rating is different (see below). For all systems, output, storage capacity of batteries, and "loads" using energy must be carefully matched. Most alternative generators produce direct current (DC); alternating current (AC) requires an "inverter." Controllers to protect generators and batteries from voltage extremes are frequently needed.

Most alternative generators work only part-time: when the sun is bright or wind is strong. (One interesting, if expensive, development is Blue Sun's wind turbine with solar cells embedded in its surfaces, generating whenever there is either sunshine or wind.) Storage batteries stash power for "off" times. Unlike car batteries, designed for high power for a short cranking period, storage batteries must supply power in small doses over long periods. "Deep-cycle" batteries can be fully discharged repeatedly and still recharge. The battery "bank" must be sized for expected load. Most batteries contain pollutant chemicals; careful manufacturing, use, and recycling is essential.

Photovoltaic generation is the newest and most different of such systems, so we offer a few more de-

tails. It is also widely used for outdoor lighting and other landscape-specific power.

As recently as 1954, Bell Labs scientists were overjoyed to get 6 percent efficiency from newly developed solar cells; their one-kilowatt panel cost more than one million dollars. Today's one-kilowatt panel is two or three times as efficient and has a price of a few thousand dollars. Top experimental efficiency has exceeded 30 percent.[13] New forms of PV include "roofing" (tile, metal, or shingle); thin see-through films applied to windows, harvesting power and screening the interior; and flexible, even rollable films that, though still low-efficiency, have promise as portable chargers for landscape tools and other devices. Organic films have been experimentally "grown" without toxic chemicals. Rising efficiency and falling cost make solar power a reality for many applications unthinkable a decade ago.

The two major types of PV materials are cells and films. Crystalline cells, usually about three inches round or square, are soldered together in series and sandwiched under glass into a "panel" or "module." Subtypes are single-crystal, multi-crystal, and dendritic; each has its own efficiencies and limits. Thin-film, the other main type, also has subtypes; the best known is "amorphous silicone," common in solar calculators and watches, identifiable by long stripes rather than distinct cells. Efficiency is half to two-thirds that of cells. Groups of panels, of either type, are "arrays."

Each panel is rated in watts of electrical output, under Standard Test Conditions (STC wattage).[14] Actual operating conditions can be very different. Cloudy weather or shading decreases PV output. Most panels also lose about a half percent efficiency for each degree Celsius hotter than 25°C (77°F). Cooler operating temperatures *increase* efficiency, somewhat offsetting shorter winter daylight hours.

Location of panels is critical. Crystalline panels must be completely unshaded, and protected from vandalism; thin-film panels are less susceptible to either. (One California dreamer was caught stealing roadside call-box PV panels to heat his hot-tub!) Large, flat panels are susceptible to wind and must be securely mounted; some mountings incorporate sun-tracking mechanisms, increasing efficiency.

For truly remote sites, PV offers immediate savings; for others, initial cost is offset by near-zero operating costs. At Cholla Campground, a US Forest Service (USFS) facility near Phoenix AZ, landscape architect Kim Vander Hoek and her colleagues saved an estimated $435,000 in upfront costs by using solar power for everything: lights, water pumping and purification, even a power hookup for the campground host's motor home. Public-sector landscape architects dealing with remote, protected sites are in the forefront of solar landscape design. Albuquerque's Colleen Friends, responsible for a Parks and Recreation project that chose solar lighting and irrigation, puts it succinctly: "Without photovoltaics Tramway Trail wouldn't have been lighted."

PV systems are completely silent, nonpolluting, and highly reliable. (Federal transportation agencies are converting safety signals, including runway lights, to solar power.) PV has a long lifespan (at least twenty to thirty years); periodic cleaning of panels and checking batteries is the only routine maintenance.

In 2006 a photovoltaic incentive was reinstituted in Los Angeles, after Reagan-era neglect. Owners can get three to four dollars per watt to install PV arrays on homes and businesses. Clearly, this technology increasingly makes both environmental and economic sense.

No power technology is without problems. The clear glass or plastic components take energy to manufacture; cheap plastic panels have degraded in ultraviolet light in some regions. "Doping" cells (sensitizing them to light) uses hazardous chemicals, as do batteries; both are contained, and careful recycling lowers risks. Poor performance in PV systems is usually linked to incorrect site analysis, design, installation, or excessive client expectations.

Technical assistance and supplies are available from a growing number of solar consultants and manufacturers.⊃ The Solar Energy Industries Association lists nearly 400 members nationwide. The Photovoltaic Design Assistance Center offers a clearly written handbook with step-by-step worksheets on designing custom systems. Real Goods Trading Company (now Gaiam) offers components from many manufacturers, design assistance, and their *Alternative Energy Sourcebook.*

Figure 7.1 Solar electricity for lights and other uses saved hundreds of thousands in utility installation at Cholla Campground, near Phoenix. Operating costs are near zero. (*Project:* USFS. *Photo:* Kim Vander Hoek.)

EVALUATE TOOLS AND THEIR ENERGY SOURCES

Each way of generating energy starts a chain of events leading to its final use by a tool or machine. Some of these chains are long: coal burned at a power plant heats steam, is converted into electricity and transmitted through utility wires, then runs an electric motor to compress air that powers actual tools. Other chains are very short. Internal combustion engines, for instance, convert fuel energy directly into mechanical energy. Each time energy is converted from one form to another (solar to electric, combustion to mechanical, etc.) there are losses, because no conversion is completely efficient.

For in-depth analysis, all forms of energy should ideally be measured by a common yardstick, one that allows for conversion losses. Howard Odum and his associates quantify the energy value of solar radiation or of nuclear-generated electricity in terms of "fossil-fuel equivalents." Although Odum's conclusions about "alternative" energy sources seem dated, anyone interested in a thorough introduction to energy costs and their effects on society and the environment would do well to start with his book *Energy Basis for Man and Nature,* a classic since 1976.⊃ Odum's methods are particularly useful in putting day-to-day energy use into long-term policy perspective.

In thinking about energy and sustainability, what matters most is resource depletion and pollution from energy use. In many ways, this simplifies evaluation of energy consumption by specific tools.

Specific details of efficiency that affect tool *design* (for example, what percentage of the energy theoretically available from exploding gasoline actually reaches a tractor's tires) are less important for the tool user than the *total amount of fuel consumed* while the tool is in use. It is this total amount that affects the environment directly—and which most directly affects the pocketbook. This total use is what construction professionals need to reduce.[15]

The tables in the following sections give *rough* energy usage rates for machines and tools of many kinds. To interpret these rates, the source or type of energy must be considered. We have made the following assumptions:

Gas, diesel, and gas/oil engines consume fuel directly. Energy use for the machine or tool is based on fuel used per hour, converted for ease of comparison to one of the standard units of energy, the Btu. (To convert to the metric unit, the joule, multiply Btu by 1,055.)

Electrical tools running from utility power are part of a system that, as a national average, *loses 60 percent of energy generated*, due to transmission loss. At the beginning of this energy chain, fuel is burned to produce 2.5 times as much electricity as ever reaches the user. This does not mean that electrical tools are necessarily inefficient. It does mean that, in comparing effects on the environment, electrical tools must be evaluated in terms of energy *generated*, rather than energy used "at the plug." The tables below give an at-the-plug figure for each tool, followed by the same figure multiplied by 2.5 to include transmission losses.

When an on-site generator is used, its total fuel use is a better gauge of environmental impact than measuring the electricity used by tools connected to it. A 10,000W generator running a 700W drill is consuming fuel based on generator capacity, not on the attached tool; it also consumes fuel while the tool is idle. Thus, for sustainability, it is important to evaluate the number of hours of fuel consumption *by the generator*, rather than trying to add up use by all the individual tools.

Air tools should also be evaluated by fuel usage *of the compressor*. Gas-powered or tankless compressors run constantly. Electric compressors with tanks run only when tank pressure drops, which is efficient but more difficult to estimate; based on experience, assess how many minutes per hour the compressor motor actually runs. Thus, tables include only compressors, not specific air tools.

Alternative power sources, such as solar and wind, are essentially "free," because no fuel is used or pollution generated. (Like any power generating equipment, resources are used in *building* PV panels or windmills; these "second-order" resources are not usually considered in energy analysis, but will eventually need to be. Some "clean" power sources incorporate toxic materials, a difficult trade-off that needs deeper recognition.)

If installed on a site as the first step in construction, permanent solar or wind generators can provide construction power. They generate relatively low wattage and require an inverter to produce AC. Since this book's first edition, *portable* solar power for contractor use has become a real, though still little-known, option. In 2000 such systems were essentially homemade; we reported that one contractor had developed a way to recharge 12V cordless tools from a solar panel on his truck. EBN editors advised anyone modifying tools for this purpose to wait until the warranty ran out![16]

Today, at least two companies that we know of offer vehicle-mounted or portable PV generators. Soltek Powersource has a team devoted to mobile-fleet PV systems. These usually integrate with vehicle electric systems, recharging the vehicle battery and powering hand tools, laptops, and such. SolarOne takes a different approach, offering PV panels and batteries on a bicycle-wheeled cart. Such systems charge constantly during daylight hours, providing many hours of power for off-grid sites. Costs depend on wattage and battery capacity, in the two- to three-thousand-dollar range.

PV has potential for special landscape maintenance equipment, such as solar-powered trash compactors (p. 328).

Since 1975 several US patents have been issued for wind generators attached to vehicles, the most recent in 2005. The idea sounds promising, especially for contractors, but we have been unable to find any commercial product of this type.[17]

Fuel cells have been long predicted, but slow to arrive. They are about 40 percent efficient, up to 80 percent if "waste" heat produces steam or hot water (compared to central power plants at less than 30 percent). General Motors unveiled a prototype pickup-mounted fuel cell in August 2001.[18] From 2002 through 2006, DaimlerChrysler produced fuel-cell-powered public buses for the European Fuel Cell Bus Project; 36 buses were tested under real-world conditions in ten European cities, plus Beijing and Perth, Australia.[19]

"Micro fuel cells" have been under development by computer giants like Toshiba and NEC. Prototypes operated a laptop for several hours on fuel cartridges as small as one ounce (25 ccs). If they are ever commercially viable, either regular or micro fuel cells could provide tool power for remote sites, with no point-of-use pollution. At present, they remain too expensive to market. Nor have "micro turbines," generating electricity from natural gas, become widely affordable. Rising oil prices could soon affect both.[20]

Energy Use: Heavy and Self-propelled Machinery

Usually adapted from agricultural and engineering machinery, landscape equipment looks tiny compared to truly *heavy* equipment. Mining-industry trucks, for example, may weigh 200 *tons* empty and carry 300 tons; there are 3,500-horsepower excavators that move 60 tons at a scoop.[21] Nonetheless, thousands of smaller landscape construction machines do add up. Their combined energy usage, as well as their effect on the soil (see Table 1.1), makes them important targets for energy efficiency and appropriate use.

Some rough estimates of energy use by various types and sizes of machinery are given in tables below, along with data that can be used for doing your own estimates. These are *rough* estimating tools only, and do not reflect specific performance of specific models. More accurate information, by brand name and under specific work conditions, is available, but these rough averages may be of equal value for several reasons. Fuel consumption varies with condition and age of equipment. Engines operate most efficiently at optimal RPM and full loads—but in the field, these conditions cannot be maintained con-

stantly. Fuel consumption also varies with soil hardness, surface conditions affecting traction, outdoor temperature, and elevation. Thus an average figure may be more useful than detailed specifics in *planning* for energy efficiency across a whole job.

To estimate energy consumption, it is necessary to know how much energy is burned up with each gallon of fuel, and how many gallons are used to run a given machine for a time or distance. The following tables give rule-of-thumb figures.[22]

Nichols and Day, in their respected reference *Moving the Earth*, give fuel-usage factors, in *gallons* used per horsepower per hour (Table 7.2).[23] Based on Table 7.1, these are converted to *Btu* per horsepower per hour, which makes comparison between different engine types easier.

To use these figures, multiply the number in the table times the machine's horsepower to determine gallons of fuel or Btu consumed per hour.[24] For example, a 30 hp gas-powered tractor would use 30 × 10,000 Btu for each hour of operation, or 300,000 Btu. Hours of machine work required for particular jobs is given in standard estimating references like Means or Spons. If the Means book says that the task you are estimating requires a small tractor for nine hours, total energy use for that task would be 2.7 million Btu.

These figures are for ordinary machinery and average conditions. For extremely well-maintained equipment and light work, *subtract* 25 percent for

Table 7.1
Fuel type and energy.

Fuel Type	Energy Produced in Use Btu/gallon	Weight per Volume* lbs/gallon
DIESEL	140,000	7
GASOLINE	125,000	6
2-STROKE GAS/OIL MIX‡	125,000	6

* Machinery manufacturers and engineers usually chart fuel usage in pounds per hour of operation. Use these factors to convert pounds to gallons.
‡The figure for gasoline is used as a round number, since the usual gas/oil mix (50:1) is primarily gasoline.

Table 7.2

Average fuel and energy consumption per horsepower hour.

Fuel Type	Gal/Hp-Hr	Btu/Hp-Hr
DIESEL	.06	8,400
GASOLINE	.08	10,000
2-STROKE GAS/OIL MIX	.09	11,250

Note: An arithmetic error in the first edition gave diesel more advantage than it actually has. This has been corrected in this edition.

diesel and 13 percent for gasoline (including two stroke). For poorly maintained machinery and difficult conditions, *add* up to 75 percent for diesel and 25 percent for gasoline. If manufacturer's data for a specific machine is available, Nichols and Day recommend using 80 percent of rated full-load fuel consumption. Such information must be converted first from pounds to gallons, then to Btu.[25]

Table 7.3 gives *rough* energy estimates for various types of machinery, based on fuel consumption factors in Table 7.2.[26] Machines listed were selected as representative of *types*—not specific models—used in landscape construction. The listing is not comprehensive, and tends toward *smaller* machines of each type. (Larger machines, less common in landscape work, may be estimated if horsepower and fuel type are known, using the method just described.) For each listing, horsepower, weight, and capacity figures are derived from real machines; closely similar models were averaged. Fuel usage, in Btu, was then estimated using Table 7.2.

These figures are intended *only* for project planning and general strategizing about machine use. Like most figures in this chapter, they will seem inaccurate to manufacturers and engineers used to very precise, model-specific fuel consumption estimates. These figures should certainly not be confused with thorough documentation of specific machines under specific conditions. Rule-of-thumb generalizations like the Nichols and Day factors used here are what allow *field users* to make better decisions. Rough as they are, the estimates in Table 7.3 are a first step in an important process: gathering *and refining* information to help con-

struction practice change in response to sustainability concerns. (Further data at www.SustainableLandscapeOnline.com.)

EXAMPLE OF MACHINERY EVALUATION

The example of the scraper and the workers, given at the beginning of this section, shows one form of comparative thinking about energy options. Another example might be: excavating a particular job requires 4 hours with a mini skid-steer loader, and 2.25 hours with a standard-sized skid-steer. The smaller machine is 16 hp and gas powered, while the larger is a 60 hp diesel.

Table 7.3 lists the mini-machine at 160,000 Btu per hour of operation, the larger at 504,000 Btu/hr. Thus, although the larger machine is nearly twice as fast, it uses 1,134,000 Btu for the whole job, almost twice the mini-machine's 640,000. Other factors affect such decisions: if tight access slows the larger machine, its total fuel/energy consumption will be still higher. If the mini-machine is at another job fifteen miles away, while the larger machine is two miles away in the contractor's yard, the advantage may go to the larger machine. Furthermore, energy considerations could be overridden by an imperative need to avoid soil compaction, so that only the smaller machine would be appropriate.

Monetary costs will frequently appear *totally unrelated* to energy-based comparisons. This is a symptom of a society that underprices fuel energy and overvalues speed. The decision to sacrifice some money savings to save energy is an ethical choice, and no one would argue that it is easy. Without considering energy, however, decisions about sustainability become complete guesswork. These figures are a first step toward informed decisions.

THE SPECIAL ROLE OF MINI MACHINERY

For landscape construction around valued existing features, small machinery makes great sense. Whether protecting a site from soil compaction or grading dispersed parking among trees, mini-machines are second only to hand labor in minimizing damage and maximizing flexibility. Compared to their heavy relatives, mini-machines:

Table 7.3

Energy consumption estimates for heavy landscape machines.

MACHINE TYPE	Capacity or Rating	Operating weight (lbs)	hp	Fuel	Est. Btu's per hr
Tractors and "Tool Carriers"					
Tractor, Compact (range = 16 to 40 hp)	8 cf 1400 lb. bucket	4,000	30	D	252,000
Lawn Tractor (range = 10 to 20 hp)	light duty only	635	13	G	130,000
Backhoe Loader	5,000 lb. lift	14,000	75	D	630,000
Backhoe Loader	7,500 lb. lift	22,600	100	D	840,000
Wheel Loader	.85 cy	10,000	40	D	336,000
Wheel Loader	2.0 cy	15,000	90	D	756,000
Wheel Loader	5.0 cy	51,000	250	D	2,100,000
Dozer	.75 cy	8,710	40	D	336,000
Dozer	1.4 cy	13,500	70	D	588,000
Dozer	4.0 cy	27,000	120	D	1,008,000
Mini Skid Steer (stand-behind)	750 lb./ 3.85cf	1350	16	G	160,000
Skid-steer Loader	880 lb. lift	3,100	30	D	252,000
Skid-steer Loader	1,750 lb. lift	6,200	60	D	504,000
Site Dumper	2,500 lb. haul	1,200	13	D	109,200
Mini Excavator (track)	.03 cy	1,700	8	D	67,200
Mini Excavator (track)	1.5 cy	3,600	23	D	193,200
Mini Backhoe (wheeled, not self-propelled)	.04 cy	1,300	8	G	80,000
Road Grader (small)	10 ft blade	11,000	35	D	294,000
Road Grader (medium)	12 ft blade	28,000	125	D	1,050,000
Compactor (double drum type)	50" wide	5,400	33	D	277,200
Compactor (rubber tires)	50" wide	9,300	45	D	378,000
Asphalt Road Reclaimer	full lane × 15"	32,000	350	D	2,940,000
Trucks					
Pickup (small/import) (avg. 22 mpg, or 5,700 Btu per mile)	½ ton	4,400	142	G	1,420,000
Pickup (full size) (avg. 13 mpg, or 9,600 Btu per mile)	¾ or 1 ton	6,400	270	G	2,700,000
Dump Truck, Flatbed, etc. (avg. 8 to 11 mpg, or 12,750 to 17,500 Btu/mi)	2 or 2½ tons	30,000	350	D	2,940,000
Specialized Machinery					
Chain Trencher	36" deep cut	720	11	G	110,000
Chain Trencher	60" deep cut	4,000	32	D	268,800
Wood Chipper (portable)	home use	140	5	G/O	56,250
Wood Chipper (mobile)	lt. comml use	1,200	20	G	200,000
Wood Chipper (mobile)	hvy comml	7,500	116	D	974,490
Stump Cutter/grinder	small	1,060	25	D	210,000
Brush Mower	26" blade, cuts 1.5" stems	230	8	G	80,000
Curb-laying Slipform or Extruder	asph or concr	2,700	20	D	168,000
Motorized Wheelbarrow/Rough Terrain Forklift	1,500 lb.	560	8	G	80,000

Note: This table has been corrected for this second edition.

- require far less clearing for access (see Figure 10.2)
- use less fuel (though efficiency per unit of work varies)
- may produce less pollution (again, compare case by case)
- are lighter to transport, saving fuel
- are manufactured from smaller quantities of material
- may exert less ground pressure than a person walking (Table 1.1)
- do tasks beyond human strength or endurance, without "overkill."

Size, weight, fuel efficiency, and maneuverability are criteria for choosing among machines for site work; contact manufacturers for this information.⊃ Intelligent tool-design choices are also important, like the decision that self-propulsion isn't a requirement for all backhoes (Figure 7.7). Machines that have a wide range of attachments (see Figure 7.3) sacrifice some mechanical efficiency, but often are more resource-efficient overall than ultra-specialized machines.

Several mini-machines are illustrated below, embodying some or all of these criteria.⊃ The number of companies offering mini-machinery for purchase or rental, and the number and type of attachments for such machines, has grown greatly since this book's first edition. Examples include two new small machines from Bobcat (www.bobcat.com/). One is a "mini track loader," a walk-behind tractor with rubber tracks; 36 inches wide and (without attachments) less than 70 inches long, it has the usual complement of tools: sweeper, auger, buckets, pallet fork, tiller, trencher, and scraper. The other, Bobcat claims, is the world's first loader to offer *both* skid-steer and all-wheel steering. Steering the tires reduces ground disturbance and tire wear; skid-steering minimizes turning radius. While these innovations are valuable to sustainable firms, it is still notable that none of the marketing material includes even rough fuel-usage estimates; neither do recent brochures from John Deere or from DR (mowers, powerwagons, chippers, etc.). Far from even nodding to sustainability, DR's advertising extols "busting through entire stands" of brush and small trees.

Several companies market all-electric machinery. These are quiet and pollutant free at the point of use. (Grid power to charge the vehicle has pollutant costs, of course.) Most are tractor-like, or powered carts, generally under 15 horsepower (but with the high torque typical of electric motors); attachments are similar to those for gas tractors. Running a full work-day on a charge is common; recharge times vary. A few have AC inverters into which corded tools can be plugged in the field. At least one, the Sun Horse, a walk-behind machine with varied attachments, has a built-in solar panel.

Energy Use: Small Power Equipment

In 2000, as the first edition of this book was going to press, both the US EPA and the California Air Resources Board (CARB) initiated stricter standards for two-stroke engines on outdoor power equipment. At that time, Jim Elmer of Tanaka America/ISM characterized the two-stroke engine industry as being "where cars were twenty years ago," that is, largely unconcerned about fuel consumption or emissions.[27]

Tiny engines with fuel tanks measured in ounces might seem environmentally harmless, but an example puts this in perspective. "For most models," Elmer noted, "you produce less pollution driving your car 2,500 miles than running your chainsaw for an hour." Multiply this by approximately ten million

Figure 7.2 Some "heavy equipment" isn't. The small Bobcat excavator is about seven feet tall by three feet wide. Compared to the larger excavator shown, weight and fuel use are about 10 percent. (*Photo:* Kim Sorvig.)

Figure 7.3 This mini skid steer, from Ramrod, fits where larger machines can't, and has an unusually wide range of attachments. Size generally corresponds to decreased fuel use and ground pressure. (*Photo:* Ramrod Equipment.)

Figure 7.4 "Site dumpers" can be an efficient compromise between hand labor and full-size tractors. (*Photo:* Kim Sorvig.)

Figure 7.5 Motorized wheelbarrows, like this Honda PowerWagon, can do heavy work with decreased site impact, as in Sweet Brook's restoration. (*Project:* NY DEP. *Photo:* Dean Cavallaro.)

Figure 7.6 Articulated steering, as well as small size, means this roller can work around existing site features instead of obliterating them. (*Photo:* Kim Sorvig.)

Figure 7.7 Not all machines need to be self-propelled. Trencherman backhoes, by NorthStar, are towed to work; the bucket levers the machine around the site. (*Photo:* Northern Tool and Equipment, manufacturer of NorthStar machinery.)

small engines sold per year, and both fuel use and pollution become significant.

By 2005 hand gas-powered tools produced 70 percent less emissions than similarly rated 1990 models and in many cases used 30 percent less fuel. Redesign eliminated much of the lubricating oil that passed through the engine unburned, improving both efficiency and emissions. A conventional small engine used 600 hours would consume 117 gallons of fuel mix; post-2000 engines should require only 94.[28] This savings equates to savings of nearly 3 million Btu for a single machine.

Also in 2000, the EPA required small engines to be labeled as meeting federal emissions requirements. Labels provide no engine efficiency or emissions information—simply that it is EPA certified. Nor is performance information part of most power-tool marketing literature. Many small-tool manufacturers resist discussing efficiency. They feel they have been unfairly targeted, and have not received credit or publicity for improvements that have been made.

Despite the improvements, CARB says that a 2006 mower emits 93 times the smog-forming compounds per gallon of fuel as a 2006 car.[29] In 2007 CARB will institute third-tier regulations on two-stroke engines. The Outdoor Power Equipment Institute (OPEI) characterizes the 2007 regulations, which it publicly supports, as requiring 40 percent reduction in exhaust emissions and 90 percent in evaporative emissions from fuel tanks and lines. The regulations are expected to require catalytic converters on new two-stroke engines.

The 2007 CARB regulations met with heavy attack led by Briggs and Stratton, raising dubious concerns about fire danger from catalytic converters.[30] OPEI, to their credit, lobbied the EPA to produce a consistent national standard matching California's, so that equipment need not be specially manufactured for California. Those standards are still under consideration.

Energy efficiency of small power tools is especially difficult to rate, for several reasons. For handheld tools like chainsaws, both throttle speed and workload vary widely during a single use. Others, like lawnmowers, run at relatively constant speed. Additionally, although power ratings for gas and electric are both in horsepower, different rating systems are used, with electric motors rated conservatively, and gas engines rated "as high as honestly possible."[31]

Given these difficulties and the changing market, the following table of estimates (Table 7.4) should be used judiciously. It is based on an average figure for two-stroke fuel consumption per horsepower (Table 7.2), which is fast being improved. For the time being, a conservative estimate is appropriate to sustainability concerns, since many tools currently in use are older models.

Electric tools are listed below in their own table (Table 7.5). Energy-consumption estimates will have more meaning among tools of the *same* type (electrical or gas) than *between* types, though these rough figures may still have some value for basic planning.

Air compressors, powered by either gas or electricity and used to power other tools in turn, are also listed separately (Table 7.6). According to Dave Moorman of Ingersoll-Rand tool company, a basic rule of thumb for *portable* air compressors is that they require about 1 hp to produce 4cfm of air. The Compressed Air and Gas Institute gives a much wider range, but this includes large stationary industrial compressors.[32] Efficiency varies considerably with altitude, which directly affects ambient air pressure.

A few gas-powered electrical generators, their rated output, and fuel consumption based on horsepower are given in Table 7.7.

Finally, for landscape maintenance, energy use can be estimated per acre (Table 7.8), based on work by Helen Whiffen, Agricultural Energy Specialist with the University of Florida. Although these figures were based on Florida conditions, they can serve as a model for information that should be public knowledge in every region.[33]

Energy Use: Hand Tools and Labor

Unlike many industries, landscape construction still relies on human labor, often the most efficient way to get landscape jobs done. Hand labor is economical for landscape work where limited access, awkward terrain, irregular materials, or artistic care are involved.

As a round figure, an adult male human's base energy use is about 300 Btu per hour, or on the order

Table 7.4

Energy consumption estimates for small gas landscape tools.

TOOL TYPE	Capacity or Rating	Operating weight (lbs)	hp	Fuel	Est. Btu's per hour
Compact stump grinder	Small full duty	180	9	G	90,000
Horticultural sprayer, trailer type	55gal, 500psi, 3gpm	130 empty	3.5	G	35,000
Lawn aerator	26"W	200 + ballast	4	G	40,000
Lawn edger	Heavy duty	65	3	G	30,000
Pressure washer	3 gpm cold wtr	74 to 130	5.5	G	55,000
Rototiller	26"W, 8"D	200	8	G	80,000
Lawnmower	30" cut	40	7.5	G	75,000
Sod cutter	18"W	325	5.5	G	55,000
Sprayer, backpack	3 gal tank	30	5	G	50,000
Auger, 1-person	12" max bit	19	2	G/O	22,500
Auger, 1-person	10" max bit	26	3	G/O	33,750
Auger, 2-person	10" max bit	53	3.8	G/O	42,750
Blower, backpack	405cfm, 1950mph	28	2.8	G/O	31,500
Blower/shredder, handheld	130mph	12 to 18	1.2	G/O	13,500
Chainsaw	12"	11	2.2	G/O	24,750
Chainsaw	24"	16	3.1	G/O	34,900
Cutoff saw, handheld	12" blade	26, plus blade	3.5	G/O	39,380
Cutoff saw, handheld	14" blade	32, plus blade	4.8	G/O	54,000
Hedge trimmer	17"	11	1.2	G/O	13,500
Lawn edger	Light weight	13	.9	G/O	10,130
Line trimmer		8.5	1.05	G/O	11,820
Power pruner (chain type)	10"	18	.9	G/O	
Rototiller, mini	12"W, 10"D	20	2.0	G/O	23,630

of 2,500 Btu for a working day.[34] As shown above, only a few of the smallest electric motors will run for an hour on less than 500 Btu of energy, while almost all petroleum-fueled machines use 10,000 Btu per hour or more. Virtually all machine energy produces pollution and comes from nonrenewable resources. Human (and draft-animal) energy is derived from agricultural products, which are among the most quickly renewable resources; wastes are easily biodegradable. In addition, a 180-pound man wearing size-ten shoes puts about two pounds per square inch pressure on the soil. When a self-propelled machine has a "ground pressure" of less than 5 psi, manufacturers start advertising the fact.

Thus, although energy comparisons between human and machine are more thought provoking than scientific, any work done by hand provides clear sustainability payoffs. Some hand tools amplify muscle-power. Investing in such machines literally leverages human efforts, often producing better projects, paying off in reputation and financially too. An example is the Tree Toad, a hand-powered tree spade for transplanting nursery stock up to 450 pounds. Digging blades are driven into soil with a slide hammer (a tube with handles, used to drive steel fenceposts); the tree is lifted with a hand-cranked jack; a long-handled handcart moves the lifted tree "in the earliest wet Spring, even in areas that no other machinery can access."[35] Costing less than one-tenth of most powered transplanters, Tree Toad uses human power to real advantage in landscape work.

A final note on human energy use: "Thinking," says energy expert Vaclav Smil, "is an enormous energy bargain." Not only does brain activity require only about 5 percent of the base energy expenditure of staying alive, but that energy use stays the same

Table 7.5

Energy consumption estimates for electric landscape tools.

TOOL TYPE	Capacity or Rating	Operating weight (lbs)	hp or Watts ‡	pwr*	Est. Btu's per hour †	
Chainsaw	12″ bar	7	1600W	AC	(5,470)	13,675
Lawnmower	30″ cut	25	6 hp	AC	(16,000)	40,000
Chop saw (stand mounted)	14 in	35	1800 W	AC	(5,660)	14,150
Disc grinder	4.5 in	5	780 W	AC	(2,450)	6,125
Horticultural sprayer, trailer type	15gal, 40psi, 1.4gpm	53 (empty)	180 W	DC	(570)	1,425
Power pruner (chain type)	8″	12	1.25 hp	AC	(3,190)	7,980
Submersible pump	90gph, 2 ft head	1	5 W	AC	(16)	39
Submersible pump	1800gph, 20 ft head	10	130 W	AC	(410)	1,025
Submersible pump	300gph, 15 ft head	6	220 W	AC	(690)	1,725
Submersible pump	520gph, 15 ft head	7	300 W	AC	(945)	2,360
Submersible pump	2750gph, 15 ft head	10	700 W	AC	(2,200)	5,500
Winch	550 lb.	90	½ hp	AC	(1,275)	3,190
Winch	2,000 lb.	14	.6 hp	DC	(1,530)	3,825
Winch	1,900 lb.	230	1.5 hp	AC	(3,825)	9,560

*All are 120V AC or 12V DC.

‡ Energy consumption for electrical tools is based on watts where known, or hp if wattage is unavailable.

† Electrical tools show two estimates, both converted to Btu/hr: The first, in parentheses, is usage by the tool "at the plug" without transmission losses. The second factors in 60 percent losses between generating plant and user; that is, 2.5 times as much energy is generated as is used at the plug. If using an on-site generator or photovoltaics, see Evaluate Tools and Their Energy Sources, p. 267.

whether zoning out or thinking furiously.[36] In energy terms, it costs nothing to think things through carefully—yet the result can be massive savings in both labor and equipment. Think about it!

Energy Use: Transportation

Transportation touches all aspects of construction efficiency. Materials, machinery, and workers are transported to the site. Energy use for all these movements is a significant part of the energy cost of the whole job.

Fuel to move materials and run machines gets more attention, but worker commutes should not be forgotten. Tractor-trailers are much more efficient per ton of material moved than passenger cars or small trucks. Although many older trucks guzzle diesel at a rate of 6 mpg, "for a compact car to get the equiv-

Table 7.6

Energy consumption estimates for portable air compressors.

COMPRESSOR TYPE	Capac Rating	Wt	Cfm @ 90 psi	hp	Fuel	Est Btu/Hr	
Two stage shop model	30 gal	440	18	11	G	110,000	
Twin tank wheeled	20 gal	167	6.5	5	AC	(12,750)	* 31,875
Twin tank wheeled	10 gal	235	18	9	G	90,000	
Twin tank wheeled	8 gal	139	10	5.5	G	55,000	
Single tank	3 gal	25	2.9	1.5	AC	(3,825)	* 9,560
Tankless	Lt duty	15	1.8	.75	AC	(1,915)	* 4,790

*See note on electrical ratings, Table 7.5.

Table 7.7

Energy consumption estimates for portable electric generators.

Electrical Output			Engine Fuel Estimates	
Watts max	Amps	hp	Fuel	Est Btu/Hr
1,000	7.5	2.5	G	312,500
2,700	20	5	G	625,000
4,400	35	8	G	1,000,000
10,000	80	16	G	2,000,000
12,000	110	20	G	2,500,000

Table 7.9

Transportation energy consumption per ton of material per mile.

	Btus/Ton/Mile	
	Low	High
Boat	350	540
Train	680	820
Truck	2,340	6,140
Plane	37,000	?

alent mileage based on a fuel consumption *per ton mile*, the compact car would have to get almost 500 miles per gallon."[37] Passenger cars use a couple tons of machine to haul a hundred-and-some pounds of passenger—a classic example of using more power than the job requires. Large trucks running empty, however, still get 6–10 mpg while hauling only their driver, a situation that responsible companies avoid if at all possible.

Most researchers agree that one of the most important steps a construction professional can take to reduce environmental impact is to cut down transportation and fuel costs. Table 7.9 makes it clear why this is critical in materials transport.[38]

Transportation of workers is a significant part of the total energy used by the landscape professions. Job-sites tend to be far from either the firm's offices or the workers' homes.

Compare these numbers against those for site machinery (Table 7.3), power tools (Table 7.4), or embodied energy of materials (see p. 279). The average energy consumption for one hour's use of the large machines listed is about 95,000 Btu. A crew member who drives alone to the site in a car getting 20 mpg uses the same amount of fuel every fifteen miles. Average for an hour's use of a gas-powered hand tool is around 12,000 Btu. The same employee uses that by driving two miles.

Notice also that getting the employee with the 20 mpg car to take one rider lowers the energy per passenger mile *more* than getting him or her to drive (still alone) in a new car getting 35 mpg. A *car-pooling policy* can be a construction company's most effective energy-saving tool.

With construction sites frequently located on the suburban fringe, miles add up rapidly—twenty or

Table 7.8

Energy use in landscape maintenance.

Maintenance Type	Energy Use per Unit	Energy Use per Acre	Annual Energy Use
Mowing, gas mower	86,650 Btu/hr.	125,000 Btu per mowing	1.25 to 2.5 million Btu per acre per year
Mowing, electric mower	40,000 Btu/hr.	60,000 Btu per mowing	600,000 to 1.2 million Btu per acre per year
Irrigation (municipal water)	18 Btu/gal.	n/a	16 million Btu per acre per year
Fertilizer (for lawns)	2,700 Btu/lb.	n/a	2.16 to 7.2 million Btu per acre per year
Pesticide (for lawns)	n/a	0.625 to 2.5 million Btu per application	n/a
Trees (water + fertilizer + pesticide)	n/a	n/a	0.5 to 1.0 million Btu per tree per year

Source: Based on Whiffen, Helen H. "Landscape Maintenance Takes Energy: Use It Wisely," *Energy Efficiency and Environmental News* (University of Florida Extension), Feb 1993. Units conversion by authors. Items marked n/a were not noted by Whiffen.

Table 7.10

Transportation energy consumption per passenger mile.

MPG →	20	25	30	35
↓ Number in Vehicle	Btu per passenger per mile			
1	6,250	5,000	4,000	3,500
2	3,125	2,500	2,000	1,750
3	2,000	1,700	1,350	1,175
4	1,550	1,250	1,000	875

Gasoline vehicles. Fuel only. To allow for all energy used to make travel possible, multiply these figures by 175 percent. Howard T. Odum and Elizabeth C. Odum, *Energy Basis for Man and Nature* (New York: McGraw-Hill, 1976)

thirty miles each way is not uncommon. At such distances a six-person crew, each in a 20 mpg car, racks up 2.25 *million* Btu per day; that equals 11.25 million Btu per five-day work week. That energy would power three pieces of heavy equipment all week, assuming the average noted above. It would also be enough energy to produce five tons of common brick, or five hundred pounds of steel. (This is *without* factoring in energy costs of vehicle maintenance or highway infrastructure, which Odum estimated at an additional 75 percent of fuel energy.[39])

As a society, Americans tend to overlook transportation costs—a difficult habit to change, even for oneself. No matter how well-intentioned, a professional cannot truly stake a reputation on "green building" while commuting many miles daily in a single-occupant four-wheel-drive pickup. Transportation alternatives are hard to find, especially in newer cities and the West, but are every bit as important as green practices adopted at the site.

Much of the energy embodied in materials comes from transportation. For example, brick used 350 miles from the factory uses as much energy in transportation as was used to produce the bricks.[40] Obviously, ignoring transportation energy distorts decisions like "Is brick appropriate as a material at this site?" For this reason, one of the most consistent sustainability recommendations is to *specify local materials*.

Many specifiers already choose suppliers in part based on transportation distances, but international sourcing is still common. Monetary costs of shipping, plus rising fuel prices, are incentives to choose local products. Owners of large trucks can calculate fuel savings for various improved technologies at www.epa .gov/smartway.

Car-pooling involves quite different incentives, requiring "green" businesses to put their money where their principles are. Fuel costs for getting to the job-site are commonly borne by workers; saving fuel saves the *company* no money and may in fact cost money. Having all employees report to the main office and then go to the site in company vehicles is not always efficient routing.

Mapping software may help. By entering employee home locations and project sites just once, such software can easily compute travel distances. "Logistics" programs save major transportation companies billions of dollars, hours, and fuel gallons by computing efficient routing. The same programs could provide decision-making support about suppliers as well. Even CAD or GIS systems, already in most design and contracting offices, might be modified for this purpose.

Save Energy and Money with Machinery and Tool Guidelines

The following suggestions, although not ironclad, are a starting point for saving energy by careful planning about machinery:

- Plan! Conventional contractors may get by with seat-of-the-pants fuel-usage decisions; no one concerned with green building can afford such guesswork. Gasoline at three dollars per gallon makes planning a survival skill.
- Cut job travel miles and fuel costs by any means possible. Company-sponsored car-pooling is one option. Regular tune-ups of company vehicles should be standard practice. One famous design-build architecture company, the Jersey Devil, moves onto the site in Airstream trailers for the duration. Choose your own methods, but decrease work-related transportation.
- Use hand labor where it is reasonable to do so. Take pride in hand-work's quality, eco-friendliness,

and health benefits, rather than focusing only on speed and ease of power equipment.

- Use the *most efficient* tool for the job. If that tool is engine powered, balance low fuel consumption with speed.
- Use the *lightest* machinery that will do the job. Manufacturers and tool rental companies are offering more and more mini-machinery.
- When buying or renting power tools large or small, insist on information about fuel consumption per hour, pollutant emissions, and ground pressure. Give your business to companies that provide this information willingly. Understand and use the information in planning.
- Look for innovative ways of generating energy—solar, wind, and fuel-cell power sources, and battery tools—for mobile construction crews.

Embodied Energy—Why Do We Care?[41]

Embodied energy, as discussed at the beginning of this chapter, is the total energy used to produce something—either a single material, a complex product, or a whole project. It is a critical factor in understanding, achieving, or evaluating sustainability. In addition, being able to present energy and materials choices rationally is increasingly important in persuading clients, regulatory agencies, and the public that specific construction plans are well justified.

A general diagram of energy inputs adding up to embodied energy is shown in Figure 7.8. For some materials, inputs shown may be repeated or skipped. A simple "raw" material like landscape boulders or sand might only involve energy from extraction, transportation, and placement. Embodied energy of steel or aluminum bars would involve extraction, smelting ore, shaping the bars, plus transportation (during processing as well as from factory to site). If further manufactured into tubular fencing, energy used in making tubes and assembling fence panels would be added, as would energy to erect the fence on-site.

Embodied energy is usually expressed in terms of *energy per unit* of product, just as cost estimates are based on cost-per-unit or cost-per-quantity figures. Energy is most commonly stated in Btu or in joules

(the metric/scientific standard); calories and watts are also used as energy units. Thus the embodied energy of builder's sand might be in Btu/ton or in kilojoules/cubic meter; for metal ingots, in kilocalories/pound; and for fencing, in Btu per linear foot or per panel of fence. Conversion tables can be found under "measurements" in dictionaries or *Architectural Graphic Standards*; excellent shareware called Master Converter is also available.⊃

Tables of embodied energy values specific to common landscape materials were included in our first edition, along with an essay, "Limits of Embodied Energy Methods Today." In order to make the information more widely available, these have been posted at www.SustainableLandscapeOnline.com, and the printed versions below have been simplified to save space. We *strongly* recommend reading this whole chapter before trying to use the tables, because interpretation and comparison of these statistics requires care.

Benefit from Embodied Energy Analysis

In concept, embodied energy is straightforward. Embodied-energy analysis has many potential benefits for designers and builders, though only part of this potential is currently feasible. In theory, embodied energy figures can be used to compare environmental impacts of widely differing materials and designs, revealing trade-offs that do not show up in economic or engineering analysis.

Embodied energy is more *objective* than price as a measure of comparative product value. Accurate value comparisons in construction are critical to everyone—client, designer, and contractor—yet market prices are frequently misleading indicators of value, especially environmental value. Distorting effects of local and international markets, artificial price subsidies, inflation, and buyer psychology can be set aside in energy analysis. (See adobe, p. 230, as an example.) Once underlying or intrinsic value is established by energy analysis, financial value can be better understood, too. The authors suspect that "energy accounting" will one day be the most accurate way to predict business expenses, profits, and losses, as essential a tool for contractors and designers as monetary cost-estimating is today.

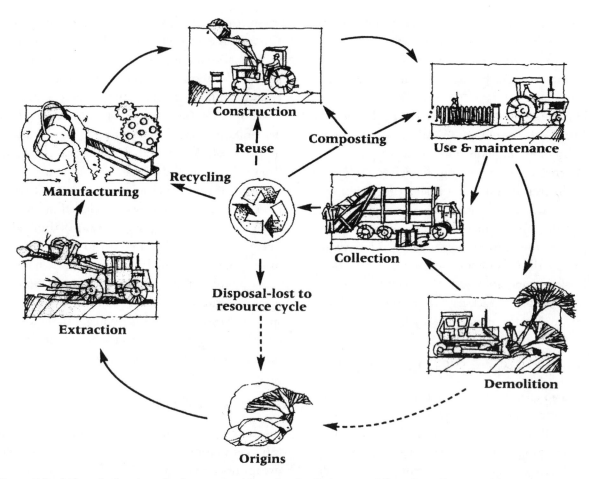

Figure 7.8   Life-cycle flowchart: landscape materials and embodied energy. (*Illust.:* Craig Farnsworth.)

Energy is a *common denominator* in all manufacturing and construction, making complex apples-and-oranges decisions much easier. If you need to compare the environmental impact of two functionally equivalent designs—say, a cast-in-place concrete wall built with gas-powered machines versus a wood fence made with air-powered hand tools—energy analysis is the most meaningful measure available. Questions like "steel studs versus wood framing" get a new and important perspective from knowing that steel is relatively high in embodied energy per pound, and that wood is relatively low. (Strength, durability, and re-cyclability must also be factored in.)

Fuel burning to produce energy is a major source of pollution, so embodied energy is a rough-and-ready *indicator* for materials that pollute. For example, about 55 kg of CO_2 is released for every gigajoule (billion joules) of energy produced by burning natural gas (a relatively clean fuel).[42] Thus, if I mega-joule (million joules) of natural-gas-generated energy is required to produce a ton of some material, its embodied energy (I mj/ton) also represents 0.055 kg (about .125 lb) of CO_2 emissions per ton. Fuels vary in how much pollution they release, and not all pollution is accounted for in fuel consumption. As a general rule, higher embodied energy means higher pollution during production.

Operating energy efficiency has been regulated since the 1970s, making dramatic changes in building design and contracting. Landscapes, using little operating energy, have largely been ignored. As energy efficiency in *all* aspects of construction becomes more critical, *embodied*-energy standards will probably affect landscape materials and construction. New Zealand, for instance, studied the feasibility of embodied-energy standards as part of national code (rejecting it as not *yet* practical).[43] Similarly, in 1993 the US government considered a "Btu tax"; the measure was not politically acceptable, but similar initiatives are likely to succeed as both energy costs and global temperatures continue to rise. (Al Gore's proposal to tax carbon emissions is, in effect, a Btu tax.)

ENERGY ACCOUNTING AND SUSTAINABILITY

Energy accounting is as complex as economics—no more and no less. There is one major difference, however. Most modern societies monitor money and trade; in industrial societies, this monitoring is a huge industry. By contrast, accurate and detailed monitoring of energy has not yet become a priority, and tools, methods, and institutions for this task are far from fully developed. As a result, available statistics on embodied energy are sometimes confusing and hard to compare. Is this an unavoidable limitation?

Energy accounting today *is* rather complex and inexact (see online information). Critics argue that this will always be the case. The authors disagree. These limitations would be overcome if energy statistics were collected with the same diligence that monetary and trade statistics are. Technology to collect energy data exists, at least in basic form. The ability to predict, plan, and make decisions would quickly and dramatically improve, for businesses, for individuals, and for society. Accuracy would increase, and "voodoo economics" would decline.

CONSTRUCTION INFLUENCE ON THE ENERGY FUTURE

Why consider this issue in a book on construction? Like any technological advance, energy analysis will only develop if there is a demand for it. That demand will come from those most directly affected by energy costs—those whose livelihoods make them energy power-users. As Architecture 2030 has publicized, construction and design decisions affect nearly half the world's energy use. Our professions cannot single-handedly create demand for accurate energy estimating and tracking—but our influence will be significant.

The Athena Sustainable Materials Institute, a major embodied energy research organization, states bluntly: "Building construction, renovation and operation consume more of the Earth's resources than any other human activity. This generates millions of tonnes of greenhouse gases, toxic air emissions, water pollutants, and solid wastes. No other sector has a greater impact on the global environment or faces a greater obligation to improve its environmental performance."[44]

Landscape designers and planners need to expect to choose materials at least partly on embodied energy considerations. Software to aid this process is under development. Landscape contractors will need new skills to implement energy-conscious designs; they will have to understand embodied energy when proposing substitutions for specified materials. In order to stay competitive in a sustainable economy, contractors will also need to manage energy efficiently. Although it is an unfamiliar concept to most landscape professionals today, embodied energy is an idea whose time is coming soon—some would say, should have come long ago—and for which there is good reason to be prepared.

Know the Embodied Energy of Landscape Materials

More than half a dozen major studies have been published with extensive tables of embodied energy for construction materials. Many others have been commissioned for in-house use, but not published.[45] Increasingly, the resulting statistics are available online. None of these studies focused specifically on *landscape* construction materials. At www.Sustainable LandscapeOnline.com, we have posted embodied energy values derived by comparing ten published studies.

These figures help compare energy costs of various materials, designs, or suppliers. If you intend to use these numbers directly, be sure you:

- Read this *entire* chapter and the text on the Web site, which discusses issues of comparability.
- Use Life-cycle analysis (below) to account for the effects of time.
- Base final materials decisions on the guidelines at the end of this chapter and on your own good judgment, not on energy figures alone.

The essay "Limits of Embodied Energy Methods Today," posted at the Web site, briefly discusses methods and assumptions used by these studies, and regional conditions that influenced the statistics. It also discusses variability between figures for the same material in different studies. Finally, it gives methods used in the online compilation, important in interpreting and using those figures.

Embodied Energy Estimating Example

An example of how the tables of energy statistics might be used is shown in Table 7.11 and described below.

You have decided to build a five-foot high garden wall, using either handmade adobe or straw-bale construction, with identical footings in either case.

Calculate the volume of the wall. Note that standard straw bales are 4 inches thicker than adobe blocks, so the bale wall's volume is larger. Assume a wall length of 100 feet.

Convert volume to weight, multiplying density times volume for each material. (See Table 7.13.)

In Table 7.12, unstabilized adobe (listed as Earth) has embodied energy of 172 Btu/lb; baled straw is 103 Btu/lb. Multiply these times the total weight for each material. It appears that the bale wall, being much lighter per volume, uses less than 2 percent of the energy required for adobe.

Straw bale construction, however, requires stuccoing. For stucco, calculate a volume, convert to weight, and compute embodied energy.

Stucco requires metal wire or lath. This material is listed by area, and can be looked up directly, showing 52,100 Btu/sf. Multiply the area of wire used by this amount.

Adding stucco and lath to straw bale shows that adobe uses less than 15 percent of the energy for straw bale.

The analysis could go further. Steel reinforcing is optional, adding much embodied energy; you might decide on bamboo stakes as reinforcing.

The above assumes that the adobes were made by hand on site. If they were transported, you would need to look in Table 7.9, where trucking is shown to use an average of about 4,000 Btu per ton per mile. The wall weighs about 28.5 tons. If the supplier is 20 miles from the project, this adds 2.28 million Btu

to energy for adobe. The total is still only about 18 percent of energy for straw bale, even without calculating transportation for the bales.

However, if someone insists on stuccoing the adobe . . .

This example shows how similar energy estimation is to money estimation; it also shows that job- and site-specific inclusions or exclusions make a great difference in which material is most energy efficient. Factors like durability, distance to source, and so on must also be taken into account.

Not Energy Alone

Analysis of energy requirements is a strong baseline for comparing construction materials and methods. Though potentially far more realistic than price comparison, it must still be used in combination with other factors. These include:

Strength in proportion to weight or cross-section shows how much of a material is required to accomplish a structural function; a tiny amount of a high-energy material may be more energy effective than a large amount of a low-energy material.

Durability and service life, which tell how long a material can perform its function before being replaced or recycled, and thus, how often energy investment must be repeated.

Resource scarcity and renewability: glass is high energy, but sand to make it is more abundant than petroleum to make clear plastics. Neither is renewable.

Reusability and recyclability: re*using* a material in its existing form requires only transportation and installation energy for the second use. For some materials, re*manufacturing* saves a high proportion of new production energy; aluminum can be recycled for as little as 5 percent of the energy needed to refine new ore.[46] Not all materials are equally recyclable. Some materials are themselves recyclable, but fasteners or adhesives interfere with reuse or recycling.

Toxicity: in addition to air and water pollution generated by energy use, some materials are inherently toxic or require toxic chemicals in production. See Principle 6.

Other design considerations: materials that degrade under ultraviolet light are unsuitable for exposed out-

Table 7.11
Worked example of simple embodied energy comparison.

Wall volume				
length	100 ft			
height	5 ft			
std. width	(in feet)	× 500 sf=		
adobe (14″)	1.2	600 cf		
straw (18″)	1.5	750 cf		

convert to Weight				
	lb/cf	× volume	total	
adobe	95	600	57,000	lb
straw	8	750	1,125	lb

Basic Embodied Energy				
	Bt/lb	× weight	total	
adobe	172	57,000	9,804,000	Btu/100 LF
straw	103	1,125	115,875	Btu/100 LF

Rqd for straw only				
½″ stucco	1,150	sf surface	46	cf stucco
	145	lb/cf	6,670	lbs stucco
	860	Btu/lb	5,736,200	Btu for stucco
wire lath	1,150	sf surface		
	52,100	Btu/sf	59,915,000	Btu for wire

Total Embodied Energy		
adobe	9,804,000	Btu/100 LF
straw	65,767,075	Btu/100 LF

door use, no matter how energy-efficient they may be. Another example is steel: energy-efficient for uses requiring strength, it can be corroded by some soils, affecting its suitability for in-ground fittings. To overcome this, steel may be coated—but the energy cost of doing so must be accounted for.

Although it is beyond the scope of this book to give comprehensive information on each of these factors, it is clear that they must be considered in materials selection and energy analysis. A promising approach to this type of multifactor analysis is usually known as Life-cycle Analysis, or LCA, which is discussed on p. 249. There do not appear to be any landscape-specific LCA studies at this time.

A simpler method called Life-cycle *costing*, which can address some life-cycle issues without the exten-

sive expertise required for LCA, is discussed in the following section.

Use Life-cycle Costing to Justify Sustainable Design

Life-cycle Costing (LCC) is a relatively simple tool for apples-to-apples comparisons of design and construction options. It was first developed for financial comparisons such as return on investment, but can easily be used for energy comparisons as well. Unlike its similarly named cousin, Life-cycle analysis (LCA), it does *not* deal with resource scarcity, pollution issues, or in any detail with recyclability. Nonetheless, LCC is a respected technique, and ready to use today, while LCA and embodied-energy analysis are still

Table 7.12

Embodied energy of selected landscape materials by weight.

Materials by Weight	CSI	Avg Est Btu/Lb.	Materials by Weight	CSI	Avg Est Btu/Lb.
Earth	2.3	172	Steel, mild, galvanized	5.1	15,652
Earth, stabilized 5% concr.	2.3	241	Steel, stnls, coldroll bar	5.1	193,000
Paving, bitum, 1.5″(wearing surf only)	2.7	1,242	Steel, stnls, coldroll sheet	5.1	138,000
Fertilizer (ammonia)	2.9	27,596	Steel, stnls, hotroll bar	5.1	157,000
Fertilizer (phosphatic)	2.9	32,373	Steel, stnls, hotroll sheet	5.1	89,800
Fertilizer (superphosphate)	2.9	2,701	Steel: Recycled	5.1	4,647
Aggregate, crushed stone	3.0	929	Zinc	5.1	22,145
Aggregate, river stone	3.0	9	Zinc, galvanizing /kg steel	5.1	1,204
Sand	3.0	16	Metal expanded lath	5.7	12,000–
Cement, dry powder	3.1	3,062			33,000
Concrete, readymix	3.1	656	Steel common nails	5.9	34,000
Lime, hydrated	3.1	4,406	Steel HS bolts	5.9	26,600
Mortar (hydrolic & masonry cements)	4.0	860	Lumber, hardwood, airdry	6.0	215–602
Adobe block, bitumen stablzn	4.2	123	Lumber, hardwood, kilndry	6.0	1,054
Adobe block, cement stablzn	4.2	160	Lumber, softwood, airdry	6.0	499
Adobe block, straw stablzn	4.2	202	Lumber, softwood, kilndry	6.0	1,269
Brick, common	4.2	1,075–	Lumber, ¾″ext. plywood	6.1	4,472
		4,085	Lumber, glue-lam beams	6.1	5,531
Concrete block	4.2	370–964	Lumber, plywood	6.1	4,522
Concrete, aerated	4.2	1,548	Lumber: Roughsawn	6.1	163
Glass	4.2	5,934	Plastics, ABS	6.5	47,715
Glass block	4.2	6,200	Plastics, general	6.5	35,389
Straw, baled	4.2	103	Plastics, HDPE	6.5	42,226
Tile, quarry & paving	4.2	9,017–	Plastics, LDPE	6.5	30,560
		22,886	Plastics, PET	6.5	45,800
Tile, struct facing, 6 × 12 × 4″	4.2	8,385	Plastics, polycarb glazing	6.5	68,200
Stone	4.4	446	Plastics, polyester	6.5	23,091
Stone, granite, cut	4.4	2,537	Plastics, polypropylene	6.5	34,260
Aluminum	5.1	67,368	Plastics, polystyrene	6.5	49,607
Aluminum, anodized	5.1	87,294	Plastics, polyurethane	6.5	31,410
Aluminum, extruded	5.1	71,380	Plastics, polybutylene	6.5	25,000
Aluminum, plate & sheet	5.1	93,153	Plastics, PVC	6.5	35,130
Aluminum, struct shapes	5.1	92,200	Rubber, natural latex	6.5	29,013
Aluminum: Recycled	5.1	3,348	Rubber, synthetic	6.5	39,063
Aluminum: Recycled, anodized	5.1	18,447	Rubber, synthetic	6.5	39,063
Aluminum: Recycled, extruded	5.1	7,439	Waterproofing, asphalt	7.1	1,221
Aluminum: Recycled, plate & sheet	5.1	6,364	Waterproofing, paper	7.1	10,500
Brass	5.1	26,660	Insulation, rigid polystyrene	7.2	63,355
Copper	5.1	32,158	Shingles, cedar	7.3	3,870
Copper, pipe	5.1	73,100	Adhesives, epoxy & resins	9.2	35,000
Copper, sheet	5.1	69,700	Adhesive, concrete	9.9	3,010
Copper, struct shapes	5.1	46,800	Adhesive, phenol formaldehyde	9.9	37,410
Iron, cast	5.1	14,891	Adhesive, urea formaldehyde	9.9	33,626
Steel, alloy, struct shapes	5.1	26,900	Paint, exter oilbased	9.9	42,962
Steel, carbon, galv sheets	5.1	27,800	Paint, exter waterbased	9.9	35,672
Steel, carbon, pipe	5.1	25,800	Fabric, cotton	12.0	61,580
Steel, carbon, sheets	5.1	16,800	Fabric, polyester	12.0	23,096
Steel, carbon, struct shapes	5.1	22,700	Pipe, steel	15.1	25,800
Steel, mild	5.1	12,214			

Table 7.13
Average densities of selected landscape materials.

Matl Type	CSI	lb/CY	lb/CF	Kg/m3	equiv.	
soil cement 5%	2.3	2,885	107	1,710		
aggregate	3.0	2,700	100	1,602		
cinder or ash	3.0	1,350	50	801		
clay, dry	3.0	1,701	63	1,009		
cement powder	3.0	2,538	94	1,506		
concrete	3.0	3,967	147	2,354		
earth, loose dry	3.0	2,052	76	1,218		
earth, packed dry	3.0	2,565	95	1,522		
sand	3.0	3,305	122	1,961		
mortar	4.0	2,797	104	1,659		
adobe	4.2	2,628	97	1,559		
bricks	4.2	2,939	109	1,744		
concrete, aerated	4.2	1,312	49	779		
glass	4.2	4,247	157	2,520		
straw, baled	4.2	214	8	127		
tile	4.2	3,646	135	2,163		
stone (nonspecific)	4.4	4,149	154	2,462		
stone, granite	4.4	4,455	165	2,643		
stone, limestone	4.4	3,645	135	2,163		
stone, marble	4.4	4,671	173	2,771		
stone, sandstone	4.4	3,888	144	2,307		
stone, slate	4.4	4,644	172	2,755		
aluminum	5.1	4,503	167	2,672		
copper	5.1	15,041	557	8,924		
steel	5.1	13,230	490	7,850		
zinc	5.1	11,964	443	7,098		
lumber (nonspecific)	6.0	1,669	62	990	5.2	lb/bdft
lumber, hardwood	6.0	1,433	53	850	4.4	lb/bdft
lumber, particleboard	6.0	1,062	39	630	3.3	lb/bdft
lumber, plywood	6.0	1,011	37	600	3.1	lb/bdft
lumber, softwood	6.0	927	34	550	2.9	lb/bdft
polyester	6.5	243	9	144		
polyethylene sheet	6.5	1,635	61	970		
polypropylene	6.5	1,517	56	900		
polyurethane	6.5	244	9	145		
PVC	6.5	2,255	84	1,338		
rubber, natural latex	6.5	1,551	57	920		
rubber, synthetic	6.5	2,136	79	1,267		
bitumen	7.1	1,736	64	1,030	8.6	lb/gal
adhesive, concrete	9.9	1,686	62	1,000		
paint (all types, US)	9.9	2,186	81	n/a	10.8	lb/gal
paint (all types, metric)	9.9	n/a	n/a	1,300	1.3	Kg/l

Table 7.14
Embodied energy of selected landscape materials by volume.

Materials by Volume	CSI	AvgEst Btu/Cu Ft
Concrete, ready CF	3.1	96,100
Concrete, ready CY	3.1	2,590,000
Lumber, hardwood	6.0	9,820
Lumber, softwood	6.0	8,555
Lumber, glue-lam beams	6.1	15,611
Lumber, plywood	6.1	14,883
Lumber: Roughsawn	6.1	495
Waterproofing, asphalt	7.1	8,639
Insulation, rigid polystyrene	7.2	15,300
Paint, exter oilbased	9.9	488,264
Paint, exter waterbased	9.9	489,032
Stains & Varnishes	9.9	503,668

Table 7.15
Embodied energy of selected landscape materials by area.

Materials by Area	CSI	AvgEst Btu/SF
Paving brick 2.25″thick	2.7	133,000
Paving, 4″concr, wire reinf	2.7	44,000
Paving, 6″concr, wire reinf	2.7	60,000
Paving, bitum, 1.5″ (wearing surf only)	2.7	54,600
Reinf wire, welded 4 × 4 10/10	3.2	7,500
Reinf wire, welded 6 × 6 10/10	3.2	5,080
Brick, common:		
wall 2 bricks thick, incl mortar	4.2	281,000
Metal expanded lath	5.7	52,100
Lumber, 1/2″ext. plywood	6.1	2,450–7,710
Lumber, 3/4″ext. plywood	6.1	11,600
Lumber, 3/8″ext. plywood	6.1	5,790
Shingles, asphalt	7.3	26,787
Shingles, cedar	7.3	7,320
Roofing, aluminum .032″	7.4	720,000
Roofing, copper 20-oz.	7.4	97,700
Roofing, plastic corrug'd	7.4	50,000
Roofing, steel 20 gauge	7.4	54,750
Roofing, stnls steel 32-ga.	7.4	46,900
Paint, exter oilbased	9.9	1,390
Paint, exter waterbased	9.9	1,400

Table 7.16
Embodied energy of selected landscape materials by length.

Materials by Linear Measure	CSI	AvgEst Btu/SF
Re-bar #2	3.2	2,620
Re-bar #3	3.2	5,900
Re-bar #4	3.2	10,500
Re-bar #5	3.2	16,400
Re-bar #6	3.2	23,600
Masonry reinf, 4″(truss or ladder)	4.0	3,670
Pipe, ABS 2-inch	15.1	20,459
Pipe, cast iron 2-inch	15.1	86,368
Pipe, copper 2-inch	15.1	32,107
Pipe, PVC 2-inch	15.1	22,984
Wire, copper insulated #10	16.1	1,740
Wire, copper insulated #12	16.1	1,090
Wire, copper insulated #14	16.1	688
Wire, copper insulated #16	16.1	427

Table 7.17
Embodied energy of selected landscape materials by each.

Materials by Each	CSI	AvgEst
Btu/Each		
Brick, common	4.2	14,300
Brick, paving	4.2	25,600
Concrete block 12 × 8 × 16″	4.2	49,400
Concrete block 4 × 4 × 16″	4.2	9,330
Concrete block 8 × 8 × 16″	4.2	27,401
Tile, struct facing, 6 × 12 × 4″	4.2	117,000

evolving. For this reason, we feel it is worth mentioning here.

Architects use LCC routinely; a rather complex explanation of the process is included in *Architectural Graphic Standards*.[47] Landscape professionals who use LCC will certainly reduce long-term costs, both in dollars and in energy, passed on to their clients, a necessary step toward sustainability.

Use LCC for Better Comparative Costing

Life-cycle costing is particularly useful when comparing two or more proposed options, for example, two trucks for a landscape firm. Suppose one model costs $10,000, needs $750 maintenance every year, and gets 20 mpg, while the other costs $12,000, requires an average of $500 service every other year, and gets 30 mpg. Driving each truck 10,000 miles annually,[48] by the end of five years the first truck costs $16,250, and the second $14,915. Shortening the life-cycle to two years before trade-in, the first model only costs $12,500, the second $13,166. The short life-cycle, however, dramatically increases the cost *per year:* keeping either truck five years costs about $3,000 a year, while keeping it only two years raises the annual price to at least $6,250.

This example shows clearly how "sticker price" alone gives misleading comparisons. The person or firm who bought the first truck, or who traded in either truck early, would have to work a lot harder to make a profit. *Including operating costs and specifying duration* is simple life-cycle costing, which gives much more accurate and useful information about the two trucks. Life-cycle costs change with length of service and amount of use.

Conventionally, many design and construction professionals have only concerned themselves with "sticker price" of projects. After all, it is this up-front cost that professionals must convince the client to pay; profits or fees are based directly on this price. Sustainability requires broadening this perspective. If cheap to build means expensive to maintain, up-front profits are ultimately at the expense of society and the environment. The "cheap" truck burns more fuel and causes more pollution the longer it is on the road; trading it in after two years makes it appear cheaper, but actually doubles its annual cost. Whether looking at vehicles, buildings, or landscapes, simple sticker-price estimates encourage waste and short-sightedness. LCC is a tool for designing more sustainably and responsibly.

Learn Basic LCC

Over a project's useful life, costs occur in five major forms.[49] For LCC, these are referred to as Capital, Maintenance, Fuel, Replacement, and Salvage. Using the first letter as an abbreviation for each, the life-cycle cost of a project, system, or piece of equipment can be written as: $LCC = C + M + F + R - S$.

These costs can be in terms of money, or of energy, but not mixed in the same computation. Capital costs in dollars and maintenance costs in energy would not produce a useful total, for example.

Capital costs include materials and construction work, as well as design and engineering services. Most designers and contractors are highly experienced in estimating capital costs. Conventional bid estimates include *only* capital costs, and lack the other four factors.

Maintenance costs include all anticipated *annual* operating expenses, such as routine inspection, seasonal start-up and shutdown, etc. Maintenance, however, does *not* include fuel or replacement—minor parts replaced routinely each year. (Replacement refers to major items occurring only a few times over the life-cycle.)

Although *fuel* costs could be included in maintenance, it is better listed separately. In monetary analysis, the rate of inflation is often greater for fuel prices than for other goods. In energy analysis, it can be valuable to know how much goes directly to fuel.

Replacement represents overhauls that are not annual—for example, new photovoltaic-system storage batteries every eighth year of a thirty-year lifespan.

Salvage (or resale) is subtracted from money costs, usually allowing 20 percent of the original cost of materials. For environmental purposes, salvage can be either a reduced cost (when materials are recycled) or an additional cost (when disposal is required).

Besides these cost amounts, it is necessary to know the predicted *useful life* of the project or equipment being evaluated. The *frequency* of maintenance and replacement tasks must be known, as well as fuel-consumption rates. These figures are usually obtained from manufacturers, or estimated based on professional experience.

When comparing several options, use the *longest* life cycle. For example, alternative power sources for a remote site might be a generator (rebuild or replace every seven years), a windmill (fifteen years between rebuilds), and photovoltaic panels (thirty years before replacement). All three should be analyzed over the thirty-year period, including costs of rebuilding the generator four times and the windmill once.

Try Energy LCC Analysis

For an *energy* LCC analysis, all that is necessary is to add up energy costs for C, M, F, and R, and allow for S. Unlike the simpler forms of embodied energy study, which stop once the project is built and do not consider long-term energy costs, LCC energy analysis reveals differences in durability, operating energy, and maintenance.

From an environmental perspective, the "salvage" factor is especially important. The costs of waste disposal and/or environmental cleanup are poorly accounted for in conventional financial analysis. LCC using energy units has potential to show real costs to society that are otherwise obscured.

Estimate with Monetary LCC

Economic analysis also has value for sustainable construction. Financial cost data are readily available, which cannot yet be said for energy data. Even very environmentally aware landowners and professionals must know the financial costs of proposed work; sometimes cost is the deciding factor in approving sustainable proposals. Money savings can reflect environmental savings, although usually with considerable distortion. LCC using dollar amounts is far preferable to simple capital cost or "sticker-price" analysis, as explained above.

The essential formula (LCC = C + M + F + R − S) is the same, whether plugging in dollars or Btu. You must know dollar costs of capital, maintenance, and so on. There is one major difference, however, called "present value," which applies only to money.

Present value is a conventional financial concept based on the idea that money in hand today is worth more than money promised later, because it can be invested. That is, if you have $100 today, in one year you will have $105 if interest is at 5 percent. If someone promises to pay you $100 in a year, you will only have $100. The promised money is thus considered to be worth 5 percent less; its "present value" would be about $95.

Unless you don't care about interest, all figures used in monetary LCC must be adjusted to present value. The standard formulas, called "present-worth factors," are briefly summarized here. Detailed explanations and tables are found in economics texts, on financial-planning Web sites, and built into computer spreadsheets.[50]

To establish present value, it is necessary to know two things. One is *when* the cost will be paid—at the beginning; annually; or in a specific year of the life-cycle, for example, the ninth year of twenty.

The second item necessary to determine present value is a percentage called the "discount factor." The discount rate is the *expected interest rate* paid on investments, minus the predicted inflation rate. For example, if money invested today would earn an annual 7 percent, with annual inflation predicted at 4 percent, the discount rate would be 3 percent. For some products, especially fuel, price inflation is more rapid than average. Thus, general inflation might be 4 percent, while fuel-price inflation could be 6 percent. If investments were still paying 7 percent, the discount rate for fuel costs would be 1 percent instead of 3 percent. The federal government and many banks publish projections of interest and inflation.

Given the dollar amounts for each cost, its timing, and a guess at the discount rate, you are ready to prepare a monetary LCC estimate.

The capital cost C is always treated as a single expense, paid all at once in the first year of the life-cycle. Because it is paid in the first year, it is already at present value. Even if capital costs will be financed by an interest-bearing loan, no finance charges or interest is included as capital.

All other costs are converted to present value, using one of two formulas (or looking them up in tables based on those formulas).

Costs that *occur regularly every year* (usually maintenance and fuel) are given a present value as follows. If the discount rate is D, and the number of years in the life cycle is L, then $[1 - (1 + D)^{-L}]/D$ multiplied times the *annual* cost gives the present value. For example, to give present value of annual payments over fifteen years at a discount rate of 2 percent, compute $[1 - (1 + .02)^{-15}]/.02$, equaling 12.849. This is called a "uniform present-worth factor," referring to uniform payments over the whole life-cycle. The UPW factor is multiplied times the dollar amount of the payment. In this example, if the annual payment is $400, the present value of payments over the whole period is 12.849 × 400, or $5,139.60.

Table 7.18
Lamp efficacy and "spectral downrating."

LCC Analysis of (project or equipment) _____

Expected life-cycle of project or equipment _____ years "**L**"

For *energy* LCC analysis, ignore investment, inflation, discount, and PW factors

        Projected return on investment during life-cycle ____% "**R**"

        Projected inflation during life-cycle ____% "**I**"

        Projected fuel inflation during life-cycle ____% "**I**$_F$"

Discount rate "**D**" for non-fuel items = R-I = _____

Fuel discount rate "**D**$_F$" = R-I$_F$ = _____

Type of cost	Amount	Year occurring	PW factor	Present Value
CAPITAL	Enter full amount under present value	Full pmt. year I; do not include finance charges	NONE	
Annual Maint	Enter amount ↓	(each year)	$[I-(I+D)^{-L}]/D$	
	_____	_____	_____	_____
	_____	_____	_____	_____
	_____	_____	_____	_____
	_____	_____	_____	_____
	_____	_____	_____	_____
Annual Fuel	Enter amount ↓	(each year)	$[I-(I+D_F)^{-L}]/D_F$	
	_____	_____	_____	_____
	_____	_____	_____	_____
	_____	_____	_____	_____
	_____	_____	_____	_____
	_____	_____	_____	_____
Replacements	Enter amount ↓	Fill in year ↓ "Y"	$I/(I+D)^Y$	
	_____	_____	_____	_____
	_____	_____	_____	_____
	_____	_____	_____	_____
	_____	_____	_____	_____
	_____	_____	_____	_____
Salvage	Enter positive or negative amount ↓	Last year of use ↓ "Y"	$I/(I+D)^Y$	
	_____	_____	_____	_____
	_____	_____	_____	_____
	_____	_____	_____	_____
	_____	_____	_____	_____
	_____	_____	_____	_____
	TOTAL			

Costs that *occur only a few times during the life-cycle* (such as replacement and salvage) are computed by a different formula, called "single present worth." If the discount rate is represented again by D, and Y stands for the year when the cost occurs (counted from today), then the "single present-worth factor" is $1/(1 + D)^Y$. Thus, the factor for a single expense paid 8 years from now, assuming a discount rate of 2 percent, would be $1/(1+.02)^8$, or 0.853. If the actual payment in year eight would be $400, its present value would be 400 times .853, or $341.20. If a cost occurs every 8 years, it would be treated as single costs occurring in years 8, 16, 24, and so on. Thus, the present value of the same $400 replacement in year 16 is less than the present value of the payment in year 8 (SPW factor 0.728, present value $291.38).

A simplified worksheet for LCC is shown in Table 7.18. It can be used for LCC *energy* analysis by ignoring the present-worth factors altogether, making sure to convert all energy costs into the same system of units. It is also easily convertible to a spreadsheet.

Apply Guidelines for Landscape Energy Conservation

- Transportation energy is where landscape professionals can probably make the most difference.
- Cut shipping energy costs by specifying local materials as first preference, then regional products. Use products from distant suppliers sparingly—much like nonnative plants, for special accents rather than the whole landscape.
- Cut worker-transportation energy costs however possible. Make car-pooling a company policy, with incentives. Track worker distances from home to each project; assign workers to short-commute projects where possible and make flexible arrangements for workers when their home is near their current job-site.
- Choose the right machine, tool, or labor for each task with energy consumption in mind. See detailed suggestions on p. 278.
- Improve your ability to analyze energy as part of materials selection and design, using embodied-energy analysis, life-cycle costing, life-cycle analysis, or other big-picture methods.

- Remember that saving energy is an ethical choice, not just a financial one. It will sometimes pay off in immediate dollars, but sometimes will not.

Resources

Know the Costs of Energy over Time

Energy

Search Terms: energy OR power OR fuel || renewable energy || electricity || energy efficiency || energy conservation

Center for Maximum Potential Building Systems 512-928-4786, www.cmpbs.org/: Energy, materials, and economics information concerning sustainability.

US Department of Energy, Energy Information Clearinghouse www.eere.energy.gov/: Wide variety of info on all aspects of energy; the "Buildings" page is the most focused on construction issues. The "Femp" page focuses on contractor issues.

Energy and Environmental Profiles and "Technology Roadmaps" for Steel, Glass, Aluminum US Department of Energy, 1996–98 (seven reports) Office of Industrial Technology, Washington DC

American Institute of Architects. Environmental Resource Guide Joseph A. Demkin, 1994–98 (loose-leaf) Wiley, New York: Loose-leaf, with annual supplements.

Energies: An Illustrated Guide to the Biosphere and Civilization Vaclav Smil, 1999 MIT Press, Cambridge MA

Energy and Habitat: Town Planning and Design for Energy Conservation Vinod Gupta, 1984 HalstedWiley, New York

Energy Basis for Man and Nature Howard Odum, 1981 McGraw-Hill, New York

Environmental Costs of Electricity Richard L. Ottinger, 1991 Oceana Publications, New York

Handbook of Energy Use for Building Construction R. G. Stein, C. Stein, M. Buckley, and M. Green, 1980 US Department of Energy (DOE/CS/20220-1), Washington DC

Timber Reduced Energy Efficient Homes Ed Paschich and Paula Hendricks, 1994 Sunstone Press, Santa Fe NM

Embodied Energy Coefficients of Building Materials Andrew Alcorn, 1995 Building Research Association of New Zealand, Wellington NZ

Office of Scientific and Technical Information www.osti.gov/: Information on all sorts of technology, including energy.

Renewable Energy Policy Project/Center for Renewable Energy and Sustainable Technology 202-293-2898, www.crest.org/: Long-established site for energy and sustainability information.

Master Converter software www.savardsoftware.com/: Shareware converts any measurement from one type of unit to another; invaluable for LCC, estimating quantities.

Energy: site design

Search Terms: energy + (site OR landscape) + design

Energy Conserving Site Design E. G. McPherson, 1984 ASLA, Washington DC, 202-898-2444, www.asla.org

Energy-efficient and Environmental Landscaping Ann S. Moffat and Marc Schiler, 1993 Appropriate Solutions Press, Dover Rd. Box 39, South Newfane VT 05351

Earth-sheltered Landscapes: Site Considerations for Earth-sheltered Environments David Douglas DeBord and Thomas R. Dunbar, 1985 Van Nostrand Reinhold, New York

Landscape Planning for Energy Conservation Gary O. Robinette and Charles McClenon, 1983 Van Nostrand Reinhold, New York

Landscaping That Saves Energy and Dollars Ruth S. Foster, 1994 Globe Pequot Press, Old Saybrook CT

Microclimatic Landscape Design: Creating Thermal Comfort and Energy Efficiency Robert D. Brown and Terry J. Gillespie, 1995 Wiley, New York

Landscaping for Energy Efficiency US EPA, www.epa.qld.gov.au/publications/p00406aa.pdf/Land scaping_for_energy_efficiency.pdf: On landscape elements that can affect operating efficiency of adjacent buildings.

Machinery

Search Terms: (machinery OR tools) + (lightweight OR efficient OR low-impact OR "low ground pressure" OR "non polluting")

Outdoor Power Equipment Institute (OPEI) 703-549-7600, http://opei.mow.org/: Industry group, largely about lawnmowers; rather defensive on environmental issues.

Mini equipment Bobcat, Fargo ND, 701-241-8700, www.bobcat.com/: Division of Ingersoll-Rand.

Mini equipment Northstar/Northern Tool and Equipment, Burnsville MN, 800-221-0516, www.northerntool.com/: Manufacturers/distributors of Trencherman towed backhoes; wide range of grounds maintenance and other tools.

Mini equipment Ramrod, Yorkton SK, Canada, 800-667-1581, tkw@leonsmfg.com: Manufacturers of Ramrod mini skid steer, illustrated.

Mini equipment Wacker Corp., 800-770-0957, www.wacker group.com/webapp/ecomm/Conductor: Manufacturers of small site dumpers, rollers, etc.

Mini equipment and small engines Komatsu and Komatsu-Zenoah/Redmax, 770-381-5147, www.zenoah.net/: Komatsu has many divisions; the Utility division (Vernon Hills IL) makes mini excavators; the Zenoah division (Norcross GA) makes power tools marketed as Redmax.

Small engines Tanaka Engines, 253-333-1300, www.tanaka powerequipment.com/: Manufacturer of PureFire two-stroke engines, an example of new fuel-efficient and less-polluting small engines.

Fuel-cost estimating and other energy data California Energy Commission, www.energy.ca.gov/html/directory.html: Huge directory of energy information; one page gives fuel cost and inflation statistics for LCC and other estimating, with inflation factors.

Electric Ox/Electric Tractor Corp. 877-533-4333, http://www.electrictractor.com/: Battery-powered tractors.

Electric machinery listings www.coate.org/jim/ev/tractors/TNF_article.html, http://www.econogics.com/ev/evtools.htm: List and descriptions of many types of electric outdoor machines and tools.

Tree Toad transplanters 800-479-3099, www.treetoad.com/: Hand-powered, mechanically assisted tree spade carts.

Operating energy

Energy Conservation News Business Communications Co., www.bccresearch.com/: Monthly; articles available at www.accessmylibrary.com/coms2/browse_JJ_E057.

Home Energy Energy Auditor and Retrofitter Inc., 510-524-5405, http://www.homeenergy.org/archive/hem.dis.anl.gov/eehem/95/950109.html: One of many useful articles from this bimonthly magazine; see their home page.

EnergyStar program US EPA and DOE, www.energystar.gov/: Efficiency ratings for products and homes.

Embodied energy

Search Terms: embodied energy || embedded energy || process energy

Athena Sustainable Materials Institute www.athenasmi.ca/: Lists reports on embodied energy research (not available to public through Athena, but may be in libraries).

Building Research Association of New Zealand www.branz.org.nz/: Cutting-edge research on embodied energy of building materials.

Embodied Energy of Building Materials Canada Mortgage and Housing Corp (CMHC), Ottawa ON, 613-748-2000, www.cmhc-schl.gc.ca/en/index.html

Building Materials Energy and the Environment Bill Lawson, 1996 Royal Australian Institute of Architects, www.architecture.com.au/i-cms?page=1: Concise tables on many basic building materials, plus assemblies.

CSIRO: Built Environment Sector www.austehc.unimelb.edu.au/asaw/biogs/A000621b.htm: Pages on embodied energy, sustainable construction; embodied-energy software.

Embodied Energy in Products www.oikos.com/

GeoNetwork—Resources for the Green Design Community www.geonetwork.org/

GOTWH: Building Materials www.eng.mcmaster.ca/civil/sustain/building/Building%20Materials.pdf

Low Embodied Energy Materials Faculty of Architecture, University of Manitoba and Canada Mortgage and Housing Corporation, www.arch.umanitoba.ca/vanvliet/sustainable/design/arch/arch005.htm: A page of the Sustainable Community Design site; other pages include a good bibliography, case studies, and links.

3D-Cad Embodied Energy Software CSIRO Building Construction and Engineering, Australia, www.dbce.csiro.au/brochures/, www.cmmt.csiro.au/brochures/tech/lichee/index.cfm: Information on software under development that will calculate embodied energy directly from Cad quantity takeoffs.

Solar energy

Search Terms: solar energy || solar power || solar electricity || solar OR photovoltaic

Solar Energy Industries Association. SEIA 202-682-0556, www.seia.org/

Stand-alone Photovoltaic Systems: A Handbook of Recommended Design Practices Hal Post and Vernon Risser, 1991 Photovoltaic

Design Assistance Center, Albuquerque NM, 505-844-2154: The Photovoltaic Design Assistance Center is a national research lab. Data and help on all solar-electric questions. The *Handbook* is systematic and realistic. It also includes a good primer on life-cycle costing.

Solar Living Sourcebook, 12th ed., Real Goods, Hopland CA, 877-989-6321, www.gaiam.com/realgoods/: Annual textbook and product catalog.

Ridgway Alternative Power Enterprises 970-626-9842: Seller of pickup-portable camping PV generators.

Soltek (Fleet PV Power) 800-635-7497, www.spsenergy.com/pages/fleet.htm

Solar One 877-527-6461, www.alternative-power.com/systems.htm#harvester: "Harvester" cart- or vehicle-mounted PV generators; also Dark-Sky-compliant, solar-powered, LED outdoor lighting.

Principle 8:
Celebrate Light, Respect Darkness

At night make me one with the darkness; in the morning make me one with the light.
—Wendell Berry, 1980

Landscape lighting is a source of great pleasure, extending use of outdoor space into nighttime hours. Outdoor lighting, however, can be either well designed, or excessive and inappropriate. Extravagant lighting can be wonderful for temporary effects, but as a permanent landscape feature it wastes resources and causes direct damage to living things.

Lighting is one of the largest single uses of electricity in the United States, consuming about 20 percent of all electricity used nationally.[1] Saving energy by more-efficient lighting has been a major priority of most environmental groups. By re-lamping older lighting with energy-efficient bulbs available today, enough energy could be saved to equal all the oil imported by the United States.[2] This immense energy savings could be accomplished without sacrificing existing levels of lighting at all. Further savings can appropriately be achieved by toning down or eliminating excessive lighting. Some progress has been made, but much improvement is still needed.

Since the first edition of this book, the lighting industry has changed significantly, and many of these changes affect landscape lighting directly. Dark-sky initiatives have become a major force in shaping outdoor lighting products and practices. Detailed, though still preliminary, information has been released about effects of artificial lighting on ecosystems and species. LED lighting, which had made its expensive and faintly illuminating US debut in 1999, has advanced so far that the first LED streetlamps are now coming to market. Solar power has become slightly more efficient, and new ways of storing it are being tried.

Landscape lighting, although a fairly small portion of the total, remains one of the fastest-*growing* sectors of the lighting industry. Because the landscape lighting industry is still developing, designers, contractors, and manufacturers have a real opportunity to ensure that efficiency and appropriate design become standard. Without such a standard, rapid growth of landscape lighting will contribute unnecessarily to national energy consumption.

Discussed in This Chapter

Lighting terms.
When to respect darkness and limit or
    eliminate lighting.
Efficiency in design of lighting fixtures.
Controllers and timers.
Low-voltage lighting.
Fiber-optic lighting.
Solar landscape lighting.
Performance evaluation.

Respect the Need for Darkness

The impulse to fight back the night is an ancient, almost unconscious human urge, as old as the discovery of fire. Yet although night held primitive dangers and still holds modern ones, it also offers mystery, and is in fact biologically necessary to most species. It is important not to forget the *value* of darkness when current lighting technology makes it so easy to exorcise ancient fears.

Talk Lighting—a Brief Glossary

Designing sustainably with light is much easier if basic terms are clear.

Lighting products:
Lamp—an artificial light source; laypeople call these "bulbs."
Luminaire—what laypeople call a fixture, holding a lamp/bulb.
Standard—a pole for a luminaire.

Measuring light:
Wattage—describes energy use. When all bulbs were incandescent, "60-watt" was used to mean a specific brightness. New lamp types vary in efficiency, so watts no longer simply parallel brightness.
Light—strange and wonderful stuff, wave-like one minute, separate energy packets (quanta) the next. Not surprisingly, even practical measurements for lighting design require special terms. Asking the following questions may help sort out the terminology.

Light is energy, but do you want to measure its total energy, or only what is visible? Ultraviolet light, for instance, isn't visible to humans, but its energy heats solar houses, sunburns people, is visible to other species, and affects some light pollution studies.

- Light's total energy is referred to as **radiation**, **radiance**, **radiant flux**, and so on. Measuring it is called **radiometry**; units used are **watts** (English) or **joules** (metric)—the same units used to measure electrical energy that powers a light source.
- Visible light includes only those wavelengths to which the human eye can respond. Such measurements are called **photometric**, or sometimes **photoptic**. Photometric measurements involve a second question:

*When dealing with visible light, are you measuring light **production**; light **moving through air**, or light **striking an object**?*

- Light production is called **luminance**. (**Luminosity** is glow-in-the-dark light from phosphorous.) Light production is measured in **candelas**, a rather arbitrary unit based on a standard candle.[3]
- Light moving or flowing through air is called **luminous flux**. It is measured in **lumens**—one lumen is one candela's worth of light in motion. You can't actually see this until it strikes an object. Directional light flow is called **luminous intensity**.
- Light striking an object becomes visible; it is then called **illuminance** or **illumination**. To measure this "lighting level," ask another question:

How big an area is receiving the light, and how far is it from the light source? There are two standard measures of illumination, one English, one metric/scientific. They work the same way, but with different units.

Start with a one-candela light source. Place a one-foot-square surface one foot from the light, and the resulting light level is one **foot-candle**. Place a one-meter-square surface one meter from the light, and the light level there is one **lux**.[4] The one-candela source in both systems produces one lumen. A foot-candle is one lumen per square foot. A lux is one lumen per square meter. Thus, they convert by simple math: one foot-candle is 10.764 lux; one lux is 0.093 foot-candles—ten-to-one for quick conversions.

Talk Lighting—a Brief Glossary *(continued)*

How much lighting bang is available for the energy buck? There are two measures for this, as well.
- **Efficacy** is how well electrical energy is converted to light by a particular technology. It is measured in **lumens per watt**, sometimes expressed as a percentage (a certain lamp has 20 percent efficacy).
- **Efficiency**, to lighting professionals, means how much light comes out of a luminaire, available for illuminating things. Efficiency is affected by the initial lamp efficacy, by reflectors, lenses, diffusers, beam spread, and distance from the fixture to the object being lit.

Color temperature and "spectral de-rating":
Color temperature—a precise color measurement of light. Daylight at noon has a color temperature of 5500K; a 40-watt incandescent bulb, about 2680K. The K stands for degrees Kelvin, the temperature scale starting at absolute zero. A theoretical "black body" heated to a Kelvin temperature glows a specific color; to describe that color, that temperature is used.

Spectral de-rating—lamp efficacy (energy-efficiency) *discounted* for strongly colored light, which does not produce as good visibility as near-white light. Low-pressure sodium lamps, for example, produce a monochrome yellow light that makes the eye work 38 percent harder than light from a daylight-color lamp. Some experts therefore "de-rate" LP sodium lamps by 38 percent. A 90 lumens-per-watt lamp, de-rated 38 percent, would be equivalent to only 55 lumens per watt.

Light Pollution:
Astronomical light pollution—light obstructing night visibility or telescopes.
Ecological light pollution—light that confuses, disrupts, or harms biological and ecosystem functions.
Light trespass—light that violates property boundaries and irritates neighbors.

When we first wrote this book, excessive lighting was still viewed as an offbeat concept, of concern only to hard-core environmentalists. Today, that has changed. As the president of Lumec, a major lighting manufacturer based in Quebec, wrote in the company's newsletter, "What started as a concern among a select group of specialists is now regarded as one of the most fundamental forces changing this industry. The goal of preserving darker skies calls for a redefinition of what 'quality lighting' is. The days of 'more is better' are behind us."[5]

Excessive lighting causes problems in two related ways: when it obscures the heavens and washes out the stars; and when it disrupts the day/night rhythms of plant, animal, or human life. In our first edition, we treated these subjects as one. Because of recent research, in this edition we discuss concerns about visibility separately from species effects. Current thinking classifies the two as "astronomical light pollution" and "ecological light pollution," respectively. It is important to remember that both can result from overuse or misuse of landscape lighting. Other light sources contribute, but outdoor lighting plays an unusually significant role.

As David Crawford, founder and executive director of the Tucson-based International Dark-Sky Association (IDA), has said in thousands of lectures around the country, light that spills over where it is unwanted is *absolute* waste. "We waste $2 billion a year to light the sky, to light the bottoms of airplanes and birds," as he puts it. "Dark sky design is simply good lighting design." In fact, he notes that energy savings are high enough to pay off design, fixtures, and installation of many dark-sky refits in 6 to 24 months.

Celebrate Night-sky Visibility

As recently as 2000, when the first edition of this book came out, concern about excess lighting was primarily astronomical and aesthetic. Researchers found that city lights dimmed their telescopes; laypeople lamented the inability to see the Milky Way, or in some locations, any stars at all. Areas like the American Southwest, where spectacular skies are major attractions, were concerned about lighting's impact on their tourist economies.

A related issue is the limitation of visibility by pollutant haze, something that affects many national parks and scenic areas. Most of this haze comes from factories and coal-fired utility plants, often several states distant from the parks they affect. All the techniques that reduce energy consumption and pollutant output, mentioned throughout this book, thus have potential effects on restoring visibility. Landscape professionals should be actively pursuing such reductions, even though it bucks political trends.

In 2001, the first worldwide atlas of the sky at night was published.[6] It includes graphics of night lighting on each continent as seen from space, and some telling statistics. Night skies are so constantly lit that more than 40 percent of Americans never use the part of the eye adapted for night vision (rod vision). Two-thirds of the country is too bright for the Milky Way to be seen; half the country's youth have never seen that awe-inspiring sight at all.[7]

Photographic studies, carried out by the National Park Service's Dark Sky Team in some of the world's most remote parks and wilderness areas, show that artificial light from over a hundred miles away is prominently visible even in these protected areas. This not only mars the wilderness experience for humans, but in many cases is bright enough to alter ecological dynamics (see below).[8]

"Astronomical light pollution" is caused by lights directed upward, or light that bounces upward from reflective or light-colored surfaces, including sidewalks and roofs. Serious though it is, "up-lighting" is relatively easy to correct. "Cutoff" lighting fixtures that block light above the horizontal are the primary tools (see below). Eliminating this light is relatively painless, because most of it is truly waste.

"Ecological light pollution" is quite a different matter. It can be caused by lights completely shielded skyward, and its effects depend on subtle variations in light color, timing, and intensity. While dark-sky issues are well enough understood that IDA is publishing a model ordinance (see below), research on ecological impacts of lighting is still quite new.

Protect Health and Ecosystems from Excess Light

Most animals and plants have seasonal or daily "circadian" rhythms, regulated by patterns of darkness and light. Natural light's effects on plants, animals, and humans have been extensively studied for a century or more. Although it has long been suspected that excessive lighting could disrupt these patterns and cause serious harm, hard research has only recently begun to emerge.

It is becoming increasingly clear that many species of animals and plants are strongly affected by artificial lighting. Because landscape professionals are in a position to do something very directly about lighting levels outdoors, it is important to have a basic understanding of these issues—and to know when to hire a specialist.

As far as effects on the human animal, artificial night lighting has escaped serious concern for too long. Recent studies indicate that exposure to night light—or to put it the other way, lack of sufficient hours of real darkness—is strongly implicated in extreme increases of breast cancer in the industrialized world.[9] Overly bright nights are also suspect in other human cancers.[10] Other effects were established earlier: children who sleep with constant night-lights are nearly 30 percent more likely to develop nearsightedness; the brighter the light, the greater the chances of myopia.[11] All-night lighting exposure can cause sleeplessness and may contribute to well-known stresses affecting night-shift workers. It has also been shown to play a major role in insomnia, which affects at least 32 million Americans.[12]

Many doctors are researching health and lighting; one is R. G. Stevens of the University of Connecticut Health Center. Stevens makes a critically important distinction between task lighting and light for the "biological clock": "Electric lighting in the built environment is generally more than sufficient for visual performance, but may be inappropriate for normal neuroendocrine rhythms in humans; e.g., insufficient during the day and too much at night. Lighting standards and engineering stress visual performance, whereas circadian function is not currently emphasized."[13] Such findings will likely change lighting design radically, both outdoors and in.

Day length at least partly controls when plants bloom or leaf out. Growing under constant street-lamps, trees could be "confused" into shedding leaves too late in fall, risking damage from early frost; they might bud too early, making them vulnerable to late-winter storms. Very little research has ever been done on this topic. Some research indicates that over-lighted trees fail to show fall coloration. Saplings have been shown to hold their leaves too long in the fall, but mature trees are less sensitive; the question of early budding never appears to have been addressed.[14] Thus, while little is proven, many observant professionals believe that at least some landscape plants are stressed by artificial lighting. Research to prove this should be an important priority. Any stress on landscape plantings may result directly in loss of plants, and indirectly in wasteful resource use. Documentation is at an early stage, but the effect of lighting on plants—both wild and horticultural—is clearly a sustainability issue, especially given other deforestation concerns related to climate change (see "Landscape Changes Affect Climate," p. 15).

Researching light's effects on large woody plants is not easy, because isolating mature trees in laboratory conditions is very awkward. One possible approach, adopted from a light/cancer study, would be to use GIS and GPS information to relate documented light levels to records of tree health.[15] Many municipalities have street tree surveys that record species, locations, and health. Street lighting is tracked on the same cities' utility maps. Ambient light pollution can be tracked from satellite data. By correlating these data sources on a single map, it should be relatively straightforward to gain some hard data about night lighting and plants.

Neither plants nor humans seem likely to go extinct from over-lighting, but for a significant number of animal species this is a real danger. Sea turtles are the best known. Turtles lay eggs in beach-sand nests, and hatchlings emerge at night. They rely on illumination from the ocean (which always reflects light more brightly at night than the land) to guide them back to the water. Artificial lighting on the land side of the beach will mislead hatchlings, which follow light onto roads and into built-up areas. "A single light left on near a sea turtle nesting beach can misdirect and kill hundreds of hatchlings," according to a Florida Bureau of Protected Species pamphlet. Because sea turtles are already endangered by hunting and egg gathering, many coastal communities restrict beachfront lighting during nesting season. The list of light sources that are deadly to hatchling turtles includes almost every type of landscape light: the same pamphlet cites "porch, pool, street, stairway, walkway, parking lot, security, … commercial signs, … and even bug-zappers," as well as spillover from interior lighting. An increasing numbers of luminaires and lamps are designed specifically to avoid endangering turtles (see below).

Moths are another species known for self-destructive attraction to light. Although not as dramatic as sea turtles, moths are pollinators. Extinction of large and unusual species like the turtle would be a tragedy, but lowly moths may be more important: a pollinator lost causes extinction of pollinated plants and creatures dependent on the plants for food or habitat.

Recent research, collected in an excellent book by Longcore and Rich, shows that many more species are affected by artificial lighting than has been considered, even by ecologists and conservationists. Species now known to be affected (usually negatively) by artificial light include turtles, moths, frogs, salamanders, crows, songbirds, most migratory birds, fish, spiders, seals, many rodents, zooplankton, and a wide range of insects.[16]

How lighting affects species varies widely. Light color matters to some species but not others—for example, red and yellow light affects sea turtles less than white. Timing can be critical—if a light appears just after sundown, when foraging creatures are active but winding down, they may graze longer, exposing them to predators. Rate and degree of *lighting change* may be important—frogs and fish have long been hunted by blinding them with sudden light, from which they take hours to recover.

A few species benefit from extra lighting, such as some bats that can hunt insects attracted to street lights. As Longcore and Rich point out, however, extra light is "beneficial for those species that can exploit it, but not for their prey." Much of the so-called Balance of Nature is maintained by preferences for light or darkness—species that would otherwise compete take "shifts" based on light levels or moon phases. Artificial lighting is more and more recognized as affecting not just individual species, but species *interrelationships* critical to ecosystem health.

Lighting can induce activity—from hunting to mating—and can affect individual animals' judgment about locating nests or selecting mates. Some species are attracted by light; others are repelled. Animals that use light to orient themselves may increase activity; animals that navigate in the dark may become disoriented.

Birds in particular are often trapped by lighting— a famous photo shows hundreds of them circling within the temporary WTC memorial's spotlights.[17] According to Toronto-based FLAP (Fatal Light Awareness Program), hundreds of thousands of birds have been killed in a single night because of unusual lighting (lighthouses and tall buildings are common culprits). FLAP estimates that 100 million birds are killed each year, with low-flying songbirds especially hard hit.

The bottom line for designers is that lighting needs to be integrated with site-specific ecological conditions on every sustainability-driven project. Longcore and Rich advocate including light monitoring in all environmental-impact assessments (which often ignore nocturnal species) and development plans.

Even the way light is measured has effects on other species. The common unit of measure, "lux," expresses how the *human* eye perceives brightness. This is obviously useful for human lighting design. But other species see different wavelengths than humans do and respond differently to intensity and color as well. Insects, for example, respond far more to ultraviolet than to "visible" light. For evaluating potential impact on plants and animals, field records must show the full spectrum, direction, and timing of light. For some species, a very small amount of light pollution disrupts important behaviors. Some reptiles, for example, are affected by *one one-hundredth* of one lux;[18] even subdued path lights put out eight lux. Raising regional ambient light levels by .01 lux takes thousands of lights, but occurs cumulatively even from great distances, as Park Service studies (above) show.

Thus, although "cutoff" fixtures are almost off-the-shelf solutions to *astronomical* light pollution, they may or may not improve *ecological* light pollution. It is increasingly evident that human demands for night visibility must be balanced with the pressing need— for animals, plants, and humans—to maintain dark nights.

A new specialty may be emerging: a hybrid of landscape design, lighting technology, and ecosystem/wildlife management, focused on sustainable lighting design. Such a blend of expertise, by a team or a single specialist, is needed when attempting regional regulation or site-specific solutions, discussed in the next section.

Keep the Night Dark

In October 2006, the International Dark-sky Association (IDA) and IESNA (the Illuminating Engineering Society of North America) announced a model Dark-sky Ordinance, expected to be released in spring 2007. The ordinance, according to IDA's Pete Strasser, will help communities avoid well-intentioned but poorly written regulations, and achieve better and fairer enforcement.

The model ordinance will define terms for clear communication between community and industry, and specify how to measure acceptable light levels. It will establish a standard way of classifying luminaires according to light output, direction, and potential for glare or uplight. Five activity-appropriate lighting levels will define a zoning tool; methods to establish a special performance-review process will also be included. The model will likely accept urban expectations, even where those have ecological implications. Although no code can please everyone, the IDA-IESNA model ordinance should be a long step in the right direction. Well-designed lighting adds value and beauty, but for sustainable landscape making, it is critical to balance these against medical, ecological, and aesthetic reasons for keeping the night dark.[19]

Over two hundred US jurisdictions already have dark-sky laws. These have significantly changed the design of outdoor lighting products and installations. For example, uplighting, a design effect that lights objects from below, is prohibited or limited in many areas today.

Most manufacturers of outdoor lighting now have at least some cutoff models among their luminaires. Definitions of "cutoff" have varied somewhat, but those used by the manufacturer Lumec are clear enough to be generally applicable. A "full cutoff" model emits no light above a horizontal plane passing through the bottom of the fixture. "Cutoff" models allow no more than 2.5 percent of their light output to escape above this horizontal, and "semi-cutoff" luminaires direct no more than 5 percent above that line.

Cutoff models are designed in different ways. Placing the light source in a glass-bottomed box is simplest. If a rounded or "sag" lens is used to direct or focus light, however, some light escapes upward from the rounded sides. Considerable cutoff can be achieved by making the top part of a glass globe reflective. This method is popular, creating cutoff luminaires that look, outwardly, like traditional streetlamps or modernist spheres.

Strong cutoff design tends to produce narrower downward illumination patterns as well. This creates a dilemma: narrower spreads require closer pole spacing; closer spacings may increase upward reflectance off light-colored horizontal surfaces. Streetlight studies by Lumec compared semi-cutoff fixtures, whose broader downward light spread allows wide pole spacing, with full-cutoff fixtures that require closer spacing. Semi-cutoff designs produced nearly 40 percent less upward-*reflected* light (bouncing from the sidewalk), more than offsetting the 5 percent direct uplighting that defines them as semi-cutoff.[20] Overall power consumption and maintenance were reduced using fewer, more widely spaced fixtures. While this research was limited to a few models, it shows that *indirect* uplighting must be factored into dark-sky and light-trespass analysis.

Interactions of product performance with mounting height, spacing, surface reflectivity, and other design factors can be complex. Manufacturers list efficacy (lumens per watt of energy), service life, and beam spread for their products. Even given this information, most landscape professionals will want specialist assistance. The International Dark-sky Association Web site is one good resource. ⊃ It lists lighting products approved for dark-sky purposes, and links to help find experienced lighting designers or illuminating engineers (see organizations in Resources ⊃).

Options for Limiting Outdoor Light Pollution

- Where "dark sky" (astronomical light pollution) is the only concern, use cutoff fixtures, remembering to evaluate reflected uplight, and unit height and spacing, to limit total uplighting.
- Evaluate reflectiveness (albedo) of surfaces that will be lighted. High albedo is often desirable to reduce heat-island effects (see p. 220). At night, the same high-albedo surface may reflect undesirable uplighting. Because high albedo can help achieve night visibility with less lighting, a coordinated design may resolve this apparent conflict quite successfully. Alternatively, a neutral surface color might avoid both heat absorption and uplight reflectance.
- Near observatories, consider monochromatic lamp types, like low-pressure sodium; their single-color output can be filtered by telescopes, but is ugly and fairly ineffective at improving ordinary vision.
- Remember that even lighting that perfectly solves dark-sky problems may still cause serious *ecological* light pollution or light trespass. Solutions to ecological lighting pollution will be compromises, involving priorities among diverse demands: human, animal, and plant health; visibility; and commercial advertising or "curb-appeal" lighting.
- Simple light-trespass problems can often be solved using glare shields, similar to cutoff fixtures, but blocking light in specific horizontal directions. Directional screening is also a tool against wildlife impacts. Louvered fixtures are one effective way to control lighting direction, and are often recommended for wildlife-related design.

Figure 8.1a,b,c   (a) High, non-cutoff lighting is cheap (few fixtures), but wasteful and light polluting. (b) Cutoff lighting still lights dead air, bounced uplight remains an issue. (c) Louvered lighting puts light where it is most effective and least polluting. (*Illust.:* Craig Farnsworth, based on http://www.beach tobay.org/.)

- Consider LED lighting (see below) for its extremely tight beam-width (within 3 degrees) and focus. Tiny beams placed very close to illuminated objects may substitute for larger fixtures that light whole areas wastefully. Effects of multiple nearly invisible light sources may be highly aesthetic, too.

- For people, wildlife, and perhaps plants, timing and duration of night lighting can be critical. Timers, photosensors, and motion detectors correctly used can keep lights off except when truly necessary. For certain species, possibly including humans, a gradual change in illumination is less harmful than a sudden one; dimmers can ease essential lights on and off progressively.

- Lighting color may be critical in ecological impact. In Florida, suppliers ⊃ offer compact fluorescent lamps coated with red filter; turtles will not respond to the light, which still provides visibility for humans. Filtering reduces the lamp's efficacy, however—the same energy is used, but visible output is less. LEDs produce colored light without filtering, and one properly designed fixture could change color seasonally or at different times of night. Fiber-optic lights (see below) can also change color without re-lamping.

As with almost all sustainable design, the above options may enhance or conflict with other considerations, such as strict energy efficiency. It is quite possible to imagine situations where reducing ecological impacts of lighting required increasing energy use. Such conflicts are not just between sustainable and unsustainable demands, but between different aspects of sustainability. A positive approach recognizes that sustainable design requires greater-than-usual creativity.

Use Lighting Efficiently

In addition to issues of light pollution, lighting consumes energy and has implications for material use, recycling, and toxicity. All these concerns should be evaluated in sustainability-driven projects. For each project, varying concerns are likely to be prioritized somewhat site-specifically. This balance, rather than narrow optimization of one factor, such as energy savings, best characterizes sustainable design.

Older lighting installations waste up to 90 percent of the energy they consume.[21] Fortunately, great strides in lighting technology have been made in the past decade, and if new efficient lamps were universally used, almost all that waste would be eliminated. Some newer bulbs are designed to work in existing fittings; in other cases, to save operating energy means replacing old fittings.

From an environmental standpoint, lighting is an entirely artificial choice. Unlike protecting food crops from pests, or obtaining water from natural systems, lighting is not a survival need. Thus it is particularly important to use lighting judiciously and to know exactly what it is intended to accomplish. Only then can technology be matched efficiently to need.

Design for Accurate and Appropriate Light Levels

Lights in the landscape need to put light where it is wanted, as bright as needed, and no more. This is accomplished in several ways.

Appropriate illumination levels must be established first. The Illuminating Engineering Society (IES) establishes recommended levels for various settings and activities, widely published in references like *TimeSaver* or *Graphic Standards*. A more-is-better approach has often prevailed in lighting design; IES illumination levels should be met but not exceeded, and in some cases seem excessive. The ratio of illumination level to energy use is not one for one, but is an important indicator of potential energy savings.

One noticeable feature of IES levels is that light-colored surfaces can cut lighting by as much as two-thirds.[22] Light-surfaced steps require 200 lux; dark surfaced, the same steps would need 500 lux. Contrast with surroundings also makes an object easier to illuminate: bright-surfaced risers against dark treads might be visible with only 50 lux. Dark horizontal surfaces decrease upward reflection.

IDA's David Crawford points out that laypeople equate glare with light. "Take away the glare, you actually improve visibility—but people think there's no light." This fundamental difficulty in preventing wasted lighting can only be overcome by public awareness and by setting rational, situation-specific standards.

The levels set by the IES are based rationally on the human eye's ability to distinguish important objects or actions under given light levels; like so many engineering calculations, they err on the side of excess. Light levels, however, are sometimes set by much less justifiable means. Fast-food and all-night businesses, for instance, use very bright lighting for "curb appeal." Levels well beyond any functional need are used to attract drivers' attention and lure them to the business by giving the appearance of warmth and safety. Light as advertising takes many other forms, none of them candidates for sustainability.

Light levels on a surface are set not only by lamp choice, but by distance and angle from lamp to surface, and overlap with any other light source. Carefully use manufacturers specifications, including photometric charts showing light distribution, for maximum effective lighting from minimum energy. This clearly relates to issues of light pollution (see above), but "light trespass" can be a separate issue. It is increasingly a source of conflict between neighbors as development becomes denser. Because a single light may be visible from many directions, shielding all the neighbors can be quite complicated—more so even than preventing skyward light pollution.

The higher the light source is placed, the wider the area it can illuminate (beam spread being equal). This has been considered "efficient" and has resulted in highway intersections lit from fifty-foot poles or taller. This approach to lighting, however, should be thought of as lighting dead air. Lower, closely spaced, lights often produce better visibility with little light trespass, pollution, glare, or energy waste. "Standard" twenty-foot parking lot poles light about fifteen feet of air before reaching cars or pedestrians. Louvered bollards or wall lights better illuminate the area in which cars and people actually move and are widely recommended for wildlife-friendly lighting.

Question "Safety" as Grounds for Overlighting

Overlighting is also done on the recommendation of lawyers, who treat bright-as-day illumination as a liability defense, or draft regulations as emotional response to a publicized crime. However, IDA's David Crawford bluntly says, "There is no correlation between night lighting and safety." Landscape professionals are often pressured for "safety" to over-illuminate areas. IDA is a good source of strong, professional counterarguments.

Once IES or IDA-IESNA standards are met, extra lighting serves no purpose. Area lighting that allows people to recognize hazards can be quite dim. Proper *aim* is more important than extreme bright-

Figure 8.2 Modern street and road lighting usually incorporates cutoff reflectors to prevent light pollution. Landscape features may have cutoff design and should be located with care to avoid glare and spillover. (*Photo:* Kim Lighting/Kevin Willmorth.)

Figure 8.3 End-emitting fiber-optics in Epcot's sidewalk create a moving, color-shifting bed of stars. Attracting more attention than the floodlights, they use far less energy. (*Photo:* Kim Sorvig.)

ness for security lighting, best designed to reveal suspicious behavior rather than show detail. In fact, excessively bright light can actually blind the "good guys" while the "bad guys" disappear into dense shadow. As a deterrent, a motion-triggered bright light is more effective than a constant one. A lawyerly preference for brilliantly (not just adequately) lit property is no excuse for wasted energy and severe light pollution.

Crawford points out, only half jokingly, that historically the more night lighting is used, the *higher* crime rates become. He notes the year that New York City switched to full-cutoff streetlights, the crime rate fell. His theory relates to research showing that animals are stressed by excess lighting (see above). Humans, too, evolved with regular night/day cycles. "If we turn night into day," says Crawford, "we're stressing the human system. Stress probably increases both crime, and worrying about crime."[23]

Use Sensors and Controllers to Avoid Wasted Light

Like any electrical device, landscape lighting can be controlled by "intelligent" switches, such as timers and sensors. Home path-light systems are typically controlled by photocells or clocks or both. These save energy by limiting the amount of time lighting is on. They can, of course, be abused, turning lights on mindlessly when there is no need, like irrigation in a rainstorm. Carefully used, they contribute to lighting efficiency.

Motion sensors are common in security lighting and can control other types of light. They save significant amounts of energy, because the light comes on only if an intruder or visitor is detected. They decrease annoyance and light pollution from constant lights. Detectors must be carefully located and adjusted when used outdoors, or false alarms result. In landscape settings, vegetation that grows into the sensor's line of sight may require trimming. The sensor does not need to be located on the light fixture. Placing the detector remotely requires a little more wire, but often results in greater effectiveness and more flexible adjustment. Wireless links between sensor and light are theoretically possible.

As noted above, gradual dawn- or dusk-like changes in artificial illumination may be desirable for human health or ecological reasons. Dimmers and programmed controllers can accomplish such sequences, even simulating changes in "warmth" and "coolness" of natural light at different times of day.

Try Low-voltage Lighting for Flexibility

The preceding sections discuss efficiency strategies that can be used with any type of lamp, old or new. Almost all new lamps available today are significantly more efficient in converting electricity to light than a decade ago. Several specific types of lighting may save additional energy by putting small amounts of light exactly where wanted.

In strict theory, low-voltage (12 or 24V) wiring is *less* efficient than 110V "line voltage" supplied by utilities; higher voltage loses less during transmission, which is why power companies transmit electricity over very high-voltage cables. Low-voltage lamps, however, were among the earliest to achieve higher light output per watt; in this they compare favorably with line-voltage lamps. Low-voltage lamps also offer two advantages that *indirectly* affect efficiency: size and safety.

A lighting fixture, or luminaire, consists of three main parts: a lamp, a reflector to focus the light, and a mounting system. In most older luminaires, the reflector was the "shade," part of the mounting system. In newer lamps, especially low-voltage systems, the tiny glass bulb contains both lamp and reflector, built-in. This miniaturization has produced a wide variety of special-purpose "self-reflectorized" lamps, from very narrow spots to very wide floods. Putting the reflector in the lamp has also made it possible to design smaller and simpler mounting systems. These in turn are easily located, aimed, and concealed at the precise spot where light is needed.

From a sustainability perspective, miniaturization has several effects. It has significantly reduced the amount of material required to make either the bulb or the fitting. (It has also made the reflector disposable; unless lamps are recycled effectively, a small amount of reflector material goes to waste with each bulb; fluorescents contain mercury and must be carefully recycled.[24]⊃) Miniaturization has also revolutionized lighting *design*, under the motto of "see the light, not the lamp." Precision lighting has generated much excitement for its subtle and dramatic effects. It can also be used to achieve the sustainability goal of more with less.

The second advantage of low voltage is safety. This may not seem like an environmental issue, but in fact has an important effect on precision lighting. Twelve-volt power's only real danger to humans is a painful but harmless shock. As a result, 12V wire can be run anywhere, even underwater, without conduit or other safety protection. Running small wire instead of rigid conduit considerably reduces material use and allows complete flexibility in placing 12V lighting fixtures. Although 110V lamps and fixtures have also miniaturized in the past decade, the need for conduit works against flexible placement, while 12V wiring enhances the advantages of miniature bulbs.

Flexibility and precision have changed the approach of landscape lighting contractors in another important way: because the lights are so precise, the best way to achieve an effect is to experiment in the field. Trial-and-error placement of different lights gives far better results than just drawing a paper plan, according to Jan Moyer, author of *The Landscape Lighting Book*[25] and former head of the Landscape Lighting Institute.⊃ This in turn encourages site-specific sensitivity, which, as we have noted throughout this book, is one of the keys to sustainable landscapes.

Low-voltage systems usually rely on a transformer, which steps the power down from household current to 12V. At the lower voltage, issues like circuit overload and voltage drop become more critical than with line voltage. The size of the transformer must be matched carefully to total lighting load; the length of wiring runs must also be well planned. Voltage drop at the distant end of a wire can be enough to hurt lamp performance and life noticeably. Since both efficiency and service life are sustainability issues, it is important to pay close attention to system design. Some designers, used to the simple assumptions of line-voltage systems, consider the need to design the whole low-voltage system a drawback. Others find it an interesting and rewarding challenge, with benefits far outweighing the extra planning work.

Don't Overlook Fiber-optic Lighting

Although primarily known for its special effects, fiber-optic landscape lighting may have environmental benefits, too. A single lamp, albeit a fairly strong one, can send its light through dozens of optical fibers spread throughout a landscape. The light may be emitted only from the end of the fiber, or all along it in "side-emitting" types, which resemble neon.⊃ The latter are the most common fiber-optics in landscape, used primarily to line path edges or other features with colored light. End-emitting fibers can be used much like spotlights, or can produce remarkable twinkling dots of light when drilled through any material.

Fiber-optics can be energy efficient because they are in fact a single light with greatly extended "lenses." They are even safer than low-voltage lights, because all the power is at the light source. The fibers themselves carry no current at all, only light. The idea of precision lighting as a sustainability benefit, noted above concerning low-voltage lighting, also applies to fiber-optics.

The magical ability to change color instantly is a fiber-optic feature that designers and artists enjoy. It might also have uses, however, in situations like the sea-turtle dilemma (above). A fiber-optic system could provide human safety by outlining paths, yet during turtle hatching season its color and intensity could be changed without re-lamping to decrease its hypnotic attraction to the animals.

Fiber-optics are a good example, in our opinion, of the choices involved in sustainable design and construction. Originally adopted for the delight it provokes, fiber-optic landscape lighting might seem frivolous in view of environmental worries. With careful evaluation and creativity, it may actually serve sustainable goals in ways that have not yet been considered. While not every new technology can be sustainably used, it is important not to become rigid or dismissive about the possibilities.

Figure 8.4 "City Wing" LED streetlight by Philips (Holland). This ultrathin, award-winning design is part of a wave of design innovations made possible by these tiny light sources. LED's energy-efficiency is soon likely to surpass even compact flourescent lamps. (*Photo:* Image from Royal Philips Electronics).

Use Solar Lighting

Lighting the night with power from the sun has gone from paradox to reality in recent years. Development of solar lights is closely related to advances in LED and low-voltage lamps.

LEDs as light sources are improving rapidly (see below). LEDs are appearing in new landscape lighting products almost daily, some powered by solar, wind, or tiny batteries. LEDs are predicted to achieve unprecedented energy efficiency in the near future. If this is realized, the relatively low power output of PV (photovoltaics) may cease to be a limit for landscape lighting.

For lighting, solar fixtures accentuate the characteristics of low voltage: flexibility, economy, and the need for comprehensive evaluation of the whole system during design. Some package-system solar lights appear to avoid the need for system planning. Package solar lighting, however, varies widely; some types, like solar path-lights, have until very recently been weak performers.

PACKAGE PV SYSTEMS: PROMISE AND PROBLEMS

Custom PV systems, which take site conditions and user needs into very specific account, have a high success rate and can power almost anything (see p. 266–67). In offering a "package" system, whether for lighting, irrigation, or other purposes, PV manufacturers attempt to offer universality and convenience transcending site specifics. Package PV systems may work extremely well in one geographic area or for a particular application, and pose problems in another.

SOLAR STREET LIGHTING

Lighting, especially of an area that must be fully lit all night, is probably the most difficult test of a solar-powered system. Street-light packages are perhaps the best-developed solar lighting application. They combine high-efficiency lamps (increasingly LEDs), an ordinary pole mounting, a PV panel, and a battery system. Insulated battery cases are available with some models to improve battery life. The PV panel often acts as a photocell, automatically turning on the lamp when it ceases to receive sunlight. Controllers to prevent high and low voltage, voltage backflow, and other problems are often built-in. Such products typically cost two or three thousand dollars per light.⊃

The panels are usually mounted above the lamp, and aesthetics of many models could use work. Mounting panels lengthways on the lamp support arm makes them less obtrusive. Angling panels to maximize solar exposure increases wind loading, a design trade-off that affects both performance and appearance.

Professional-quality solar luminaires tend to be rugged. Solar powered street lamps for the Miami community of Sorbet were the only electrical items working for nearly three weeks after Hurricane Andrew. Residents complained that power should have been reconnected to their homes first!

At Cholla Campground (See Fig. 7.1.), integration of site, structure, and technology made solar power viable. Restroom facilities were designed with skylights, which cut artificial lighting needs in half. Solar electricity was used not only to power interior and exterior lights on these facilities, but also to operate motion sensors and timers to conserve energy. Solar power success often demands planning ahead for conservation, designing creatively, and reeducating builders as well as users.

Solar Signage Lighting

Solar lighting specifically designed for billboards is also available. These include PV array, controller, battery bank, and insulated battery box. They will light signs from 200 to 700 square feet for an investment in the three- to five-thousand-dollar range. Each system will operate for three nights without intervening sun and provides six hours light per night. Such systems have proliferated since our first edition, and performance has improved.

One significant change in all types of signage since our first edition, which affects solar-powered installations but is not exclusive to them, is that LED lights have become the "lamp of choice" for traffic signals and many other signage applications. LEDs are intense, narrowly directional, and reasonably energy efficient, as well as being vandal proof and having very long service life.

A growing number of federal and state highways have exit signs, steep-grade warning lights, and other signage powered by solar panels. Reliability and freedom from power lines are primary reasons for using PV systems for such applications.

Solar Garden Lighting

Solar path lights have featured prominently in mail-order catalogs and garden centers since the 1990s. These small lights, available in pagoda, coach-light, or wall-mounted designs, look like low-voltage landscape lights, but contain a solar cell and battery. In theory, each light is totally independent and self-contained and can be placed anywhere without wiring of any sort. Even more than transformer-powered low voltage, solar path lights promise flexible, movable placement, and user safety.

Despite the elegance of the concept, professional landscape architects and lighting designers have avoided these lights—until recently. Older models had extremely low illumination levels (equivalent to 20- to 40-watt incandescents), intended only to mark path edges. Operating time per night was limited and in cloudy weather could be almost nothing; high/low settings on some models allowed a choice between brightness and operating time. Some early, cheaply made models suffered from mismatched battery and PV/cell capacity, nonreplaceable batteries and bulbs, or fragile plastic fittings. Others discharged on suppliers' shelves and failed to recharge when installed. Professionals who wanted solar lighting generally recommended regular PV panels powering standard low-voltage layouts.

Standalone solar path lights, however, have come a long way since then and are likely to improve further. Better thin-film PV efficiency and LEDs have combined to improve performance. Professional metal solar path-lights are available with up to twelve LEDs per unit, costing from $35 to $160 each; cost is comparable to low-voltage and line-voltage path-lights, but there is less variety among solar models. Home-center models in plastic today cost as little as $10 per light in multi-light kits, some having only a single LED per unit. This is about twice the cost of the cheapest comparable low-voltage path-lights.

Although the old performance problems are not completely banished, solar path lights today are realistic, quality alternatives for landscape lighting.

Solar Security Lighting

Motion-sensitive prowler lights, which require a brief blast of intense light, are far easier to power with a small PV system than is all-night lighting. Many manufacturers offer such lights, very similar to line-voltage models in operation, but requiring no household power or wiring. Prices are up to twice the cost of line-voltage models, but there are no operating expenses. The use of a capacitor instead of a battery (see below) appears well-suited to security light design.

Capacitator LED Lights

One very interesting development in solar lighting involves substitution of "ultra-capacitors" for conventional batteries. The only application we have discovered to date is a range of small landscape lights manufactured by the SolarCap company in Korea, which offers path lights and roadway guide/flasher lights cast in solid polycarbonate "bricks." Capacitors (once called "condensers") are battery-like, but with two differences: they cannot *generate* any energy, as chemical reactions in batteries do; and they discharge very quickly, where batteries release power more slowly. The advantages of capacitors for solar storage are that they are solid state, very low maintenance, and made without common battery pollutants like lead, nickel, cadmium, or lithium. They operate well in extreme temperatures and recharge quicker than batteries. Adapted for relatively low-output lighting like path lights, capacitors store PV energy enough to provide light all night. Capacitors for higher-wattage solar lighting have yet to be developed, but could be extremely useful.

Evaluate Lamp Performance

Informed decisions about landscape lighting require some awkward comparisons. Power use and efficacy are critical in deciding which lighting is most appropriate and sustainable for a specific setting—yet comparisons are seldom apples to apples. Before the improvements of the past few years, it was often enough to compare lamp wattage. Today more than ever, different lighting models operate on different voltages, have different service lives, and achieve efficacies that vary dramatically. A 25-watt PAR-36 lamp (one modernized low-voltage type) produces as much light as a 100-watt incandescent; yet it can be operated for one-quarter the energy cost.

"Efficacy" is lamp output in lumens per watt. Incandescent bulbs generally have lowest efficacy (8 to 20 lumens per watt). Halogens produce 12 to 24 lumens per watt, while the best fluorescent lamps wring 80 to 100 lumens from each watt, which LEDs will soon challenge. Although inappropriate for many nonindustrial settings, HID (high-intensity discharge) lamps (sodium, metal halide, and mercury vapor) are the most energy-efficient lamp types, when performing at their peak. Surprisingly, these industrial lamps have efficacy ranges so wide that at the lowest, they are little better than halogens.[26]

Since 2000, compact fluorescent lamps (CFLs) have improved slightly in efficacy and become dramatically smaller. The Westinghouse NanoLux line, for example, is about half the size of a standard incandescent and produces between 200 and 1,000 lumens, replacing up to a 60-watt incandescent. Miniaturization was achieved by incorporating very small ballasts in the lamp screw base. Some CFLs are rated for wet locations and thus usable in landscape applications. As discussed below, however, mercury in CFLs is increasingly a concern.

Monetary costs of lamps and luminaires also vary widely. Common low-voltage lamps, for example, may cost as much as fifty dollars apiece, or as little as fifty cents; fixtures vary from amazingly cheap homeowner kits to professional models with contractor prices of two or three hundred dollars. Ballasts for fluorescents, if not built-in, may be an additional cost and always require careful recycling.[27] California's

Table 8.1 .

Lamp efficacy and "spectral downrating."

Type of lamp	efficacy: lumens/watt	spectral de-rating	color temp	service life (hrs)
incandescent	8–20	n/a	2,700	800 to 3,000
halogen	12–24	n/a	2,800–3,100	2,000 to 5,000
compact fluorescent	40–90	n/a	2,700–5,400	8,000 to 10,000
metal halide (HID)	50–115	can be 40%	3,000–6,000	10,000 to 20,000
LED	24–80 today, predicted >100	not established	available in many colors	50,000 to 100,000

Based on figures given in *Building Green* 11, no. 6, plus updates.

To compare performance, multiply lamp wattage times efficacy for output in lumens. Subtract de-rating, if any. Use service life to compute life-cycle cost.

Title 24 building efficiency standards, effective in 2006, classifies all fluorescent lamps as hazardous waste, which cannot be disposed of in household trash due to mercury.[28] The same law sets mandatory levels of lamp efficacy, a combination that is likely to push LEDs into much wider use, because they offer efficacy similar to CFLs (and are predicted to exceed this soon) without the mercury hazard.

The useful life of common landscape lamps varies from 600 hours to more than 10,000; LEDs can last 50,000 or even more. Luminaires vary even more widely. Some early manufacturers of outdoor lighting simply exported their interior models; corrosion from soil chemistry, temperature extremes, ultraviolet light, and other ground-level hazards soon sent them back to the drawing board. Except for the cheapest plastic fixtures, quality has improved, but service life still varies.

Because so many variables are involved, lighting evaluation is a very good candidate for life-cycle costing (p. 283). LCC makes it much easier to evaluate lighting's complex combination of energy inputs, efficiency, and durability.

Join the LED Lighting Revolution

The first edition of this book predicted that multiple-LED lights would become an important part of the lighting world—for which we are rather proud of ourselves. LEDs (light-emitting diodes) are semiconductors, related to computer circuitry. Often likened to a photovoltaic cell running backward, instead of light in and power out, LEDs take power in and put out light. They were originally used only as signal indicators on control panels and came in any color you wanted as long as it was red or green. But by 1999, amber and white LEDs were beginning to be clustered for light output and were commercially available, if only as expensive flashlights. We wrote, "If experience shows these new bulbs to be as good as they sound, they will make many new designs possible—including, perhaps, the elusive standalone solar path light."

In 2006, LED "emitters" have far exceeded any prediction we could have made. They are available in a wide range of colors (the material in a specific LED determines output color), including yellow, green, blue, amber, orange, and red, and very pure "cold" whites. They currently produce 25 to 40 lumens per watt, better than incandescents and on the edge of competing with fluorescents. Higher efficacy is being developed, and at least one company boasts that their LEDs will produce 130 lumens per watt in the very near future.

Individual LED emitters are tiny—4 millimeters, or a little over an eighth of an inch in diameter. Being solid polycarbonate, they are nearly unbreakable. (Whether they are likely to break down from UV exposure in direct sun is untested.) They can be very tightly focused, with beam-widths of as little as three degrees. This has made them ideal for traffic signals, because they appear very bright straight-on, but are dim from the side.

One major advantage of LEDs is longevity, estimated at 50,000 to 100,000 hours. This has the potential to cut energy and materials use for re-lamping quite significantly. Most LEDs lose efficacy over time. They do not burn out suddenly, but give progressively less light, while still consuming the same amount of energy. In newer LEDs, this loss has been decreased. Service life for LEDs is usually listed in the form "75 percent lumen maintenance after 60,000 hours." This indicates that the light will lose no more than 25 percent of its brightness by the end of that period (also called "lumen depreciation").

LEDs disadvantages are the focus of a great deal of design and technical research.

- Each emitter produces only a small amount of light, although it can be intense due to narrow focusing. For illumination (rather than signals), LEDs are usually clustered in ring or grid arrays of tiny individual lights.
- Most emitters are equipped with heat sinks in their mountings; otherwise, heat from the LED can degrade its performance. LED fixtures may also be affected by the heat of direct sunlight.
- The color range of each emitter is very pure; this can be an advantage for some uses, but means that to simulate daylight or bulb-type lighting, LED sources have to be mixed. As in theatrical lighting, red, green, and blue mix to make almost any color.

- Arrays of LEDs tend to produce multiple shadows, one for each LED. To avoid this, and to mix colors, many fixtures are designed with diffusers and lenses. These, however, reduce efficiency to some degree.

- LEDs are related to printed circuit boards, and some of the same manufacturing and disposal issues may be involved. As LED lamps become common, manufacturers must take responsibility and encourage recycling by users, similar to what many computer manufacturers do today. Given how similar the technologies are, LED light recycling might simply piggyback on computer recycling programs.

One very recent LED "lamp" from Renaissance Lighting of Herndon VA ↺ uses an innovative design: the LEDs are installed "backwards," facing toward a parabolic reflector. Conventionally, bulbs and LEDs have faced outward, away from the reflector, but this produces a dark spot at the back of the LED (or bulb). The reversed design ensures that all the light output hits the reflector and is focused outward, producing much more usable light from the same source.[29]

Design with LEDs

Landscape-specific luminaires with LED light sources are emerging onto the market in ever greater numbers and variety. They are still by no means as common as luminaires using other types of lamps, but most major manufacturers, and many smaller firms, offer some LED models. Kim Lighting, for example, offers a six-inch 6-watt ring array and a nine-inch 18-watt array as options for spotlights and in-grade fixtures. It can be difficult to locate specifically LED-based products in manufacturer catalogs—Kim's Web site can't be searched just for LEDs, and Hydrel, which also offers some, will find LED product numbers, which must still be downloaded with the full line of non-LED items. This probably indicates how new LED products really are.

Until very recently, LEDs have seemed better suited to spotlighting than to illuminating wider areas, because of their tight beam configuration. Several LED streetlights, however, have been recently announced. Among these are "SoLED" dark-sky compliant solar-powered LED lights for streets, bus stops, and custom applications from Solar One (Framingham MA ↺); EnviroLum pole-mounted LED lights powered by a dual solar/wind-rotor system, from MoonCell (Stafford VA ↺); and the Philips (Netherlands) "CityWing" LED streetlight, which won an IfDesign Award in 2006. (See Figure 8.4.)

The Philips product shows one of the striking aspects of LED design: because the LEDs are so small, the "head" of the luminaire is a flat plate that appears to be about a centimeter in thickness (about a half inch); mounted in pairs atop a pole, the lights resemble the gull-wing doors of a race car. The small size of individual LEDs and the potential to mount them in almost any configuration promises product designs quite unlike anything achievable with other lamp types.

LEDs, photovoltaics, and aesthetics also intersected in the winning entry for New York City's 2004 City Lights design competition. Thomas Phifer and Partners Design used an arched tube nearly eight feet long, filled with LEDs, as the light fixture, braced on the top of its pole by a graceful triangular cable support. Photovoltaic film on top of the luminaire would collect power and store it, potentially a very large energy input if this design is used widely throughout the city.[30]

Most LED products are what lighting professionals call "specification-grade" items—available off the shelf to professionals, but not yet sold at do-it-yourself outlets. Most landscape architects and contractors would be able to specify such systems with the help of manufacturer's representatives. Alternatively, a lighting consultant could be part of the team.

According to staff at Clanton and Associates, lighting specialists in Boulder CO who are familiar with LED use, designing with the new products involves some new concepts.

The "color temperature" of LEDs, especially in white light, is quite different than any other light source (see glossary, p. 295). White LEDs tend to be "cool" and the colors are extremely pure (emitting light only in a narrow range of the spectrum). For some design purposes, this is desirable. Without color mixing, however, LEDs don't replicate sunlight, incandescent lighting, or fluorescent lighting—the most familiar types of light—and some people, clients and designers alike, may find the results take getting used to. Color mixing, using trios of red, blue, and green LEDs, can produce any color, and have been used to create huge TV-like outdoor displays. (Images 40 meters tall were produced in this way at the 2006 Asian Games in Doha, Qatar.) Clanton's staff recommends field-testing any LED light at night to get a feel for its illumination and color properties.

The narrow beam of any individual LED means that a small amount of light is focused intensely on a restricted area. Lenses and diffusers are usually required when LED arrays are used for area illumination, to spread, blend, or soften the light. The design of these intermediary optics can greatly affect the visual result, as well as efficiency. The reverse-reflector concept avoids loss of efficiency, mixes light, and removes the multi-shadow effect; it cannot, however, soften or change the color of LED light as filters can.

LEDs actually offer completely new ways of thinking about lighting design, and conventional preconceptions about design of "lights" may be a hindrance. They can fit into standard categories of luminaires—spotlights, streetlights, and so on—but there is great potential for using them in entirely new ways.

In the period of a few months while producing this second edition, we have seen an explosion of LED products in garden catalogs. Many incorporate solar power, and most are far smaller than anyone would expect a lamp to be. The efficacy of LEDs means that sufficient power can be generated by thin-film photovoltaics wrapped around the lamppost or even built into the glass globe. We have seen completely self-contained floating lamps, realistic cattails that light after dark, and even a set of "solar powered gnomes." Although some are beyond the fringe of either sustainability or design aesthetics, LEDs are clearly opening new possibilities beyond limit.

In theory, LEDs can be installed without any "fixtures" at all, a tiny light-generating spot on almost any surface. Since they are solid-state, they are almost completely weather- and vandal-proof. Individual battery-powered LEDs can, with some ingenuity, be wedged into a space as small as a mortar joint or a crack in tree bark, and aimed to illuminate small features throughout a landscape rather than whole areas. The effect could be excellent visibility for way-finding, without any awareness of the space being "lighted." This could be magical or creepy. "Invisible lighting," as this might be called, meshes quite well with concerns about reintroducing the experience of darkness, while still providing enough light to entice people out into the night landscape.

LEDs could be deployed directly on trees, where their accurate aiming capabilities could create dramatic branch-lighting effects. This has potential to solve a lingering problem with conventional lighting: manufacturers still tout uplighting of trees for dramatic effect, despite dark-sky and ecological problems. Manufacturers who continue to push uplighting are likely to find their products outlawed in an increasing number of jurisdictions, and they would be wise to begin developing dramatic alternatives, for which LEDs appear to have great promise.

The "fixtureless" approach to lighting means the designer is dealing with the technical aspects of each light and of wiring (or in some cases, battery-powered stick-on mountings), rather than purchasing off-the-shelf luminaires. This is clearly not a challenge every designer will want to take on. We anticipate a variety of truly new LED products, however. Some of these might be similar to "tube lights" or miniaturized step or railing lights. Others, very likely, will reflect renewed creativity, practical and energy-efficient applications, and adaptation to the need to respect darkness.

Resources

Celebrate Light, Respect Darkness

Lighting

Search Terms: lighting efficiency || lighting technology || energy conservation lighting || landscape lighting

Association of Lighting and Mercury Recyclers Montpelier VT, 707-942-2197, www.almr.org/

Landscape Lighting Institute Rensselaer Polytechnic Institute, 518-687-7100, www.lrc.rpi.edu/: Web site has extensive links.

Fiber-optic lighting Lumenyte, 949-829-5229; Fiberstars, 800-327-7877: Two manufacturers with outdoor fiber-optic experience.

The Landscape Lighting Book Janet Lennox Moyer, 2005, 2nd ed., Wiley: Detailed information on lighting hardware, design, and theory.

"Disposal of Fluorescent Lamps and Ballasts" Alex Wilson, Oct 1997, EBN: Detailed discussion of issues and methods for proper recycling or disposal of lighting materials.

www.ledsmagazine.com Online LED industry magazine, free but must sign up; latest developments, including landscape products and architectural uses.

Luxeon LED manufacturing 888-luxeon2, 888-589-3662, askluxeon@futureelectronics.com: Technical information and supplies of LEDs for landscape and other lighting.

Sandia National Labs lighting research http://lighting.sandia .gov/Xlightingaboutsite.htm: Many useful links, but victim of federal defunding.

Light pollution

Search Terms: astronomical light pollution || ecological light pollution || light pollution || artificial night lighting

International Dark-Sky Association (IDA) Tucson AZ, 520-293-3198, www.darksky.org/: Information and links concerning dark-sky ordinances and related concerns.

There Once Was a Sky Full of Stars B. Crelin and A. Ziner, 2003 Sky Publishing, Cambridge MA

Light Pollution: The Global View Proceedings of the International Conference of Light Pollution, La Serena, Chile March 2002 H. E. Schwarz, 2003 Kluwer Academic Publishers, Boston

Light Pollution: Responses and Remedies B. Mizon, 2002 Springer, New York

Ecological Consequences of Artificial Night Lighting Catherine Rich and Travis Longcore, 2006 Island Press, Washington DC: Only book on this aspect of light pollution.

"The Dark Side of Light" Joe Bower, Mar–Apr 2000, *Audubon*, http://www.magazine.audubon.org/darksideoflight.html: Very good summary article.

Light Pollution: The Global View H. E. Schwarz, ed., 2003 Springer, Berlin: Proceedings, International Conference on Light Pollution, 2002: Includes global atlas images.

Does Night Lighting Harm Trees? William Chaney, online article (FNR-FAQ-17) from Purdue University, Forestry and Natural Resources Cooperative Extension, www.ces .purdue.edu/extmedia: One of the most specific analyses of this problem currently available; lists tree species sensitivity to light, and lamp type and wavelengths likely to cause damage.

Fatal Light Awareness Program www.flap.org/: Detailed info on wildlife mortality from lighting.

NPS Night Sky Team 435-834-4904, 760-786-3221, www2 .nature.nps.gov/air/lightscapes/team.cfm: Quantifying light pollution in national parks since 1999; developed instrumentation to measure light pollution and identify sources.

Turtle Watch www.beachtobay.org/: Turtle protection methods, many applicable to other species.

Starry Night Lights www.starrynightlights.com/: Products and info to prevent ecological light pollution.

Turtle Safe Lighting, LLC www.TurtleSafeLighting.com/: Products and info to prevent ecological light pollution.

Solar lighting

Search Terms: solar lights || solar powered lighting || solar landscape lighting

Solar billboard lighting Zomeworks, 800-279-6342, www.zomeworks.com/

Solar garden lights Sun Beam, 800-325-9324; Rockscapes, 306-221-4499; Intermatic, 815-675-2321. See also http://solarlandscapelighting.com/: Gardener's Supply Co. (www.gardeners.com, 800-427-3363) offers many of the latest consumer LED lights, some gimmicky, some solar.

Solar street lighting Kyocera Solar, 800-223-9580; Solar Outdoor Lighting, 800-959-1329: These suppliers may also offer other solar products.

Selux Corporation 800-735-8927, www.selux.com/usa/: Sonne solar-powered Type III full-cutoff luminaires.

MoonCell Inc. 877-396-3142, www.mooncell.com/: Enviro-Lum LED luminaire combines solar and wind power.

Illinois Solar Products www.illinoissolarproducts.com/: Many outdoor solar lights, including path, step, and roadway markers.

Principle 9:
Quietly Defend Silence

The day will come when man will have to fight merciless noise as the worst enemy of his health.
—Robert Koch, 1880

Gardens have traditionally been retreats where silence could be sought and savored. This feature of traditional landscapes is being eroded by the spread of technology and the increase in human population.

Is noise a sustainability issue? One research group concludes that "the most pervasive pollutant in America is noise."[1] Noise has physiological and psychological effects on living things; constant noise is unhealthy. If human lives are to be sustainable not only in basic physical needs, but psychologically, noise reduction becomes an issue much like energy consumption or toxicity.

Today there is almost nowhere on Earth where mechanical noises are truly absent. One professional "sound tracker," George Hempton, travels the world recording and studying noise; he finds it even in the most remote locations, always on the increase. In the mid 1980s, for example, he knew more than twenty places in Washington state where he could catch at least fifteen minutes of natural sounds with no motors, jets, radios, or foghorns; by 1999, there were only three.[2] Besides mechanized noise, crowd noise is pervasive.

Like the darkness of nighttime skies, silence is something worth respecting. Despite technology, darkness and silence cannot be *created*; light and noise can only be masked or excluded. In landscapes, truly excluding either is difficult, since to wall off the landscape is to make it something else than a landscape.

Discussed in This Chapter

Landscape sound barrier myths and facts.
New and developing outdoor noise control options.
Policy approaches to noise pollution.

Understand Noise Terminology

In order to influence design and planning discussions about noise pollution, landscape professionals need to have a basic vocabulary about sound and how it is measured. Fortunately, terms to describe outdoor noise are fairly straightforward.[3]

Sound has two major qualities: frequency or pitch, and intensity or loudness. *Pitch* is measured in vibrations per second or hertz (1 Hz = 1 vibration, wave, or cycle per second). Musical or tonal sound involves a single frequency; for example, "middle C" is about 260 Hz. Multiplying a frequency by an integer gives its "overtones" or "harmonics"; for example, overtones of C-260 would include 520 (× 2) and 1,040 Hz (× 4). Noise, unlike musical sounds, often involves an annoying mix of mathematically unrelated frequencies.

The human ear can normally respond to frequencies between about 16 and 23,000 Hz. The majority of what humans hear, however, is in the range from 500 to 3,000 Hz. (The lowest note on a piano is about 27 Hz, the highest about 4,200; a piccolo, the highest sounding orchestral instrument, can reach 4,500 Hz.)

Loudness is related to the amount of energy in sound waves. What humans register as loudness, however, is not identical to the level of sound energy measured by technical instruments. Variations in physical sensitivity of the ear as well as psychological factors influence how loud a sound seems to a particular person. It is the *perception* of sound that is most important in dealing with noise problems. Insisting that a noise problem is fixed because technical metering says so is seldom a successful approach.

As a unit of measurement for loudness, the decibel (dB) is the one most used in design, planning, and engineering. Breathing quietly produces about 10 dB; conversation, about 60; yelling, 80. Prolonged exposure to 85 dB or so can cause hearing loss, 120 or above causes pain, while at the upper limit of human tolerance, 150 dB can instantly burst the eardrums. ("Boom-car" stereo systems produce 140 dB or more.[4]) Louder sounds can even cause death.

The decibel scale is logarithmic, meaning that every 10 decibels represents a *doubling* of loudness (20 decibels is twice as loud as 10, but 90 decibels is also twice as loud as 80). For this reason, decibels cannot simply be added together. For example, if one car on a road produces 60 dB, two cars do not produce 120, but only 63.

Because the human ear is more sensitive to some frequencies than others (500–3,000 Hz, as noted above), sound engineers have developed a "weighted" decibel scale that simulates human hearing, called the "A-weighted response." Measurements that use this system are noted as dB(A), still read as "decibels." This weighted system causes two problems for sustainability-oriented landscape professionals.

First, the A-weighted decibel is explicitly tailored to human ears. Thus, dB(A) measurements are a poor indicator of noise responses in non-human species. For example, dogs hear from 65 to 45,000 Hz; noise too high pitched to register on dB(A) scale could still drive dogs crazy. Similarly, "bioacoustic" studies of noise effects on wildlife need more information than provided by the A-weighted system. Among land animals, hearing ranges from 16 Hz (elephants) to 91,000 (mice); most birds have relatively narrow hearing ranges, while aquatic species, like porpoises and whales, have very wide ranges reaching up to 150,000 Hz.[5] Just as light pollution outside the human visible range can disrupt animal and plant lifecycles, noise beyond human hearing can have serious effects on non-human species.

The second problem with the dB(A) system is that it downplays sounds that are pitched *below* 500 Hz. Much of the annoying noise produced by trucks, trains, and planes is low-pitched enough to be missed by dB(A) measurements. Measuring traffic noise on the A-weighted scale may thus be misleading. Low-pitched noise is also the most difficult to screen with physical barriers; when barrier performance is rated with before-and-after dB(A) measurements, reductions in higher pitch may be impressive, but low-pitched noise problems may still exist.

Two other noise-measurement methods can be important when evaluating noise barriers. These are NRC (noise reduction coefficient) and STC (sound transmission class). An NRC value of 0 means that a panel reflects all the noise hitting it; a value of 1 means the panel absorbs all noise that hits it.[6] The STC indicates "transmission loss"—the amount of sound, in decibels, that is lost when passing *through* a panel. The higher the STC number, the better the panel insulates against transmitted sound. Combining NRC with STC is often the best way to gauge performance of sound-walls.

Many other terms are used to discuss acoustics and sound physics. Most apply only to acoustics of indoor spaces or are far more technical than necessary for outdoor noise pollution work.

Be Aware of Damage Caused by Noise

Noise is frequently treated as if it were merely a matter of personal likes and dislikes, but research shows clearly that the detrimental effects of noise are quite real. Many technical volumes have been devoted to effects of noise on health and on communities.⊃

Continual exposure to 85 decibels (the level of a food blender, a noisy factory, or a small plane 1,000 feet overhead) creates a serious threat of hearing loss for most people.[7] Complaints about noise are to be expected when the volume reaches about 30 decibels; by 40 to 45 decibels legal action is common, and in many countries anything above this level is legally unacceptable.[8]

Worldwide, over 120 million people suffer from hearing loss due to noise exposure.[9] In the United States, 100 million people are exposed to significant traffic noise and 30 million workers to hazardous noise levels. Among the most affected are the two labor sectors in which *landscape workers* are categorized: construction and agriculture. More than half of all construction workers have noise-related hearing problems; 75 percent of agricultural workers do.

Because noise exposure is hard to monitor, there is disagreement about what its human health effects are. The United States lags far behind the rest of the world in studying noise pollution, in large part because the Reagan administration "defunded" the EPA's Office of Noise Abatement and Control.[10] Scientific studies, however, have linked excessive noise to the following: high blood pressure and heart rate; labored breathing; general stress and irritability; fatigue; susceptibility to colds; reduced sex drive; changes in brain chemistry; damage to fetus; and decreased learning ability. Borrowing a concept from smoking regulations, "second-hand noise" is becoming a serious topic of discussion among environmental health professionals.

Research about negative effects of noise on endangered species is a slowly emerging field, called "bioacoustics." Migratory birds are a particular concern.[11] Mass beachings of whales have also been linked (controversially) to navy use of very loud, low-frequency sounds for echo-location and other military purposes.[12]

A comprehensive 2004 review of research about noise and wildlife showed widespread but inconclusive evidence; effects varied among and even within species in ways that are not yet understood.[13] Much of the research reviewed had focused on aircraft noise and little on roadway noise. In many cases, noise was reported subjectively, but not measured by instruments. Although it has been relatively easy to prove that many species avoid roads at least during nesting or other specific periods, few studies have clearly distinguished noise effects from other factors, such as light pollution, road-kill mortality, or the physical barrier of the road and adjacent structures. At least

one study played recorded roadway noise in roadless habitat and found that animals abandoned habitat near the noise.[14] This type of study has potential to isolate noise from other aspects of road-caused disturbance (some of which, such as mowed grass or water collecting in ditches, actually attracts wildlife).[15]

Theoretically, noise has potential to interfere with animal life in many ways. Almost all vertebrate animals use hearing to navigate, find prey or avoid predators, and, in many species, communicate. Birds rely on songs to communicate, to distinguish among species and maintain habitat ranges, and to discover and attract mates. Even reptiles and invertebrates avoid some sounds and move toward others. As in humans, there is a strong likelihood that noise causes physiological effects, stress, and hearing loss in animals.

Despite the complexity of documenting environmental noise, it is becoming increasingly clear that beyond certain thresholds, noise can truly be "toxic" to living beings, including humans.

Don't Rely on Noise "Barriers" in Most Landscapes

There is a great deal of mythology about the ability of landscapes to *stop* noise. Various methods often proposed as noise stoppers, such as walls, berms, and plantings, are largely ineffective in that role. In a landscape setting, the only real remedy for noise is distance—a significant factor in the "get away from it all" roots of suburban sprawl and in the failure of suburbs to maintain promised quietude as new development moves closer. Sound levels decrease by about six decibels for every doubling of distance between source and hearer.[16] Although constructed barriers can affect noise, the general inability to screen landscape noise contributes directly to excessive consumption of space for residences—clearly a sustainability issue.

Walls

Noise walls can reflect specific noises, such as highway traffic, away from specific places. To do so, they must be quite large and massive: usually at least eight feet tall and often twenty; twice as long as the distance from the noise source to the spot being protected; and of material thick and/or dense enough to provide about four pounds of material per square foot of wall surface.[17] Walls are most commonly concrete, often brutally minimalist; they are also made of wood or brick, and less commonly of metal, glass, or plastics. Such walls can decrease noise levels by five to ten decibels (rarely fifteen)—barely enough to bring air-conditioning equipment at fifteen feet (sixty decibels) down to the acceptable range. Larger reductions are prohibitively expensive.[18] Even "typical" noise walls cost between one and two million dollars per linear mile.[19] A one-foot thick, twenty-foot-tall wall consumes nearly 8,000 tons of concrete per mile.

Besides costs, walls have many drawbacks. They can make the noise *worse* somewhere else, especially if the noise source is in a reflector-shaped valley. Parallel walls on opposite sides of a road can cancel one another completely unless very widely separated (at least ten lanes).[20] Second or higher stories in houses behind noise walls often derive no benefit at all. Walls often physically separate communities and disrupt cross-traffic routes. These factors can lead to perceptions—often justified—that only one part of a community benefits at the expense of others. In some situations, walls may increase risks for drivers, either by making the road featureless and boring, or by increasing severity of accidents.

Depending on their compass orientation, tall walls can cast permanent shadows over the very landscapes they are intended to protect. Walls also act as windbreaks, which may be desirable, but can exclude cooling breezes and may also cause snowdrifts. Wind turbulence produced by the wall is often a problem on its own, and additionally, turbulence "warps" sound waves, diminishing or obliterating the effectiveness of the noise barrier.[21] Walls, unless carefully coordinated with wildlife crossings, can dramatically increase the barrier effect that highways have on animals.

Noise walls are frequently set on top of earth berms (see below). This increases effectiveness, but requires sufficiently wide property for the berm to be constructed. A six-foot berm topped by a ten-foot wall tends to *appear* less massive than a sixteen-foot wall. This strategy, however, does nothing to decrease the length of shadows thrown by the wall.

All in all, performance of reflective noise barriers, evaluated against their economic, social, and resource costs, is extremely poor. Like many urban features,

they are in demand primarily because they allow high-profit land-use density. Since the first US noise walls were built in California in 1968, over 1,300 linear miles of barrier have been built, at costs exceeding $500 million by 2000. The concrete industry, in particular, considers noise walls a growth industry, and lobbies hard for these structures. Many municipalities have made noise walls a prerequisite for zoning permission—not for roads, which are seldom denied permission, but for developments near roads.

Recent research on noise walls appears to be focusing on potential benefits of randomizing the wall's top edge or surface or both in order to disperse sound more fully. The results have been mixed. For example, a T-shaped wall top one yard wide can substitute for adding a yard in height.

If noise walls are unavoidable, they should at least be designed for visual interest. Probably the most spectacular example of an artistic noise barrier is along Pima Expressway in Scottsdale AZ, where giant southwestern-themed motifs—lizards, cacti, native pottery patterns, and so forth—were designed into cast concrete walls, a collaboration of landscape architect Jeff Engelmann, artist Carolyn Braaksma, and architect Andrea Foreman. Rubber-molded designs and textures were layered onto formwork for the panels, then stripped, re-layered in new combinations, and reused. This not only created almost infinite variations on the cast designs, but also applied the principle of materials reuse to this very large project.

At least one wall manufacturer, Zeller International, has filed patents on a wall system made of recycled scrap or even some forms of toxic waste, bonded with proprietary resins. Zeller's Eco-Wall ⊃ reflects inventive thinking: Eco-Walls are envisioned as solar collectors, storage panels for heat or water, or supports for photovoltaics or telecommunications infrastructure. Although these uses add value to the walls, the basic concept of the noise wall is badly flawed, and the Eco-Wall concept might be better applied to other types of construction.

Berms

Correctly sized and shaped, earth berms and other grading can deflect or redirect some noise, with or without a noise wall on top. Putting a roadway in a

Figure 9.1 If noise walls are unavoidable, at least make them astonishing and creative (Pima Expressway, Scottsdale AZ). (*Photo:* Kim Sorvig.)

cut rather than on fill can prevent part of the road noise from spreading directly outward. Low-pitched noises like truck or train rumblings, however, are actually transmitted through the earth itself. Living in an underground or bermed house, or a basement, people can sometimes hear trains a mile or more away, transmitted at low frequency through the soil, while higher sounds immediately outside are damped.

The main limitation on berms is the amount of space required for their footprint. This in turn is limited by the steepest angle at which soil will hold a slope, the angle of repose. Greenwall techniques (p. 118) are frequently used to produce steep berms for noise protection. Bioengineering techniques of woven willow, geogrid, and soil have been used by Weavewall Ltd ⊃ for steep, shrub-covered berms.

According to the FHWA, berms provide one to three decibels *more* sound reduction than a wall of similar height. This is partly due to the vegetated berm surface, which absorbs and dissipates sound. Improved performance is also due, however, to the extra width of the berm creating a longer distance between noise source and hearers. Thus greenwalls, which are vegetated but thin, should be expected to perform better than ordinary walls because of vegetation, but not as well as much thicker berms.

Vegetation as Sound Barrier

Tree plantings as noise barriers are an article of faith with many landscape professionals and their clients.

In fact, to cut noise significantly in terms of actual decibels, a band of planting at least 100 feet wide is required. These plantings must include both dense shrubs and trees; trees alone are ineffective. Even in these widths and with appropriate species, a tree barrier can reduce sound by only about three to five decibels per hundred feet.[22] Any effect from a smaller planted barrier is primarily an out-of-sight, out-of-mind phenomenon—valuable in its own way, but not actually decreasing physical noise.

Thus except on very large properties where a "noise forest" or extensive grading might be used, neither planting nor ordinary landscape walls or berms offer particularly good possibilities for decreasing the actual noise itself.

There are, however, several viable noise-control options for landscape professionals: noise-absorbing panels; noise-reducing pavement; screening the perception of noise; and lobbying for policies that prevent or decrease noise at its source. Each has its limits and its strengths; none will deal with all forms of noise. These options are discussed in the following sections.

Try Noise-absorbing Barriers

Interior noise control relies heavily on acoustic tile and other materials that absorb or deaden noise. Few of these materials will survive outdoors, nor are they manufactured in sizes or configurations that would be easy to use in the landscape.

Figure 9.2   Noise walls can incorporate more than concrete, avoiding problems of shadowing and monotony. They are still not terribly effective against noise. (*Project:* Oslo, Norway; designer unknown. *Photo:* Kim Sorvig.)

There are at least two brands of sound-absorbing panel, however, that can be used outdoors.

For a number of years, the Canadian government has required barriers that primarily absorb noise, instead of reflecting it. The Canadian requirements are specific: an NRC rating of 0.7 (70 percent absorption, minimum) and STC level of 30 (see definitions above). Durisol ⊃, a Canadian manufacturer, makes wall panels that meet these criteria; part of the wall contains air voids that absorb sound, and the wall core is concrete, which prevents absorbed sound from being transmitted through to the far side of the wall.[23]

A recent entry into the US market is Acoustiblok. ⊃ This originated as a very dense proprietary material, three millimeters thick but capable of noise reductions of 26 decibels, according to the manufacturer. This material has been layered between extremely heavy-duty cloth and mounted in steel frames to produce the company's All Weather Sound Panels. These are standard 4 × 8 foot sheets, 2.5 inches thick, weighing about 85 pounds, or 100 pounds if totally saturated by rainfall. They are resistant to oils, chemicals, and pollutants; washable; and UV resistant. Available in a number of fabric colors, it seems likely that creative printing techniques could be used to expand visual design possibilities. The original Acoustiblok is flexible and can be wrapped around some types of noise-producing equipment if proper allowance for air circulation can be made. This suggests that custom panel shapes could be possible.

Both Durisol and Acoustiblok panels can be installed either permanently or as temporary noise screens (for example, around construction sites). They have been used both to screen point sources of outdoor noise, such as generators or HVAC equipment, and as linear barriers along transportation routes. They can be mounted to existing surfaces, hung on cables, or mounted to posts. Thus, they take far less footprint space than any conventional noise-wall and achieve significantly greater noise reductions (some point-source applications decreased noise by 30 decibels). The main weakness of these panels at this time appears to be their relatively monotonous appearance. As noise-absorbing outdoor panels become more widely known, creative design is likely to evolve.

It is important to recall, however, that the overall goal is less outdoor noise, not more and better barriers. Even noise-absorbing barriers can be socially divisive, block cross-connections, and cause microclimate problems. The availability of outdoor absorptive panels should not be used to excuse vehicle and building designs that "dump" noise into the outdoor commons.

Modify Pavement to Reduce Road Noise

Highway noise results from several distinct sources: engine noise; exhaust noise, especially from truck stacks; aerodynamic whistle; acceleration and braking; and tire whine. Each requires a different approach to noise control or reduction, most of them outside the direct influence of landscape professionals. This section deals with a road-construction material that reduces tire whine: rubberized paving.

Various mixes of rubber with binders have been tried for surfacing roads, often motivated by the need to recycle rubber. In Japan, recycled-rubber chunks as aggregate were bonded with polymers to create a porous and flexible pavement. The mix has been tested on roads by the Public Works Research Institute of Japan. ⊃ At last report, the material was being improved for skid resistance and lower flammability.[24] In the Japanese studies, car-tire noise was reduced by fifteen decibels and truck-tire noise by eight decibels.

The state of Arizona has experimented more widely than any other with rubberized asphalt. This consists of 15–18 percent crumb rubber mixed with hot asphalt and additives such that the rubber reacts chemically with the asphalt. According to the Rubber Paving Association, ⊃ this mix, invented in the 1960s, can produce a 50–85 percent reduction in tire noise (comparable to the Japanese findings expressed in decibels). It also recycles about 500 used tires per lane-mile. Although pound for pound it costs 40–85 percent more than conventional asphalt, it can be applied thinner and lasts longer, so that there are life-cycle cost savings. On some roads, re*surfacing* with rubberized asphalt can be an alternative to reconstructing the road, with major savings in materials and costs.

Make Noise Invisible

Decreasing the psychological perception of noise is usually the main or only realistic course for landscape design and construction. Once noise is present, no amount of outdoor construction at the receiving end can eliminate it. Although few people actually see sounds,[25] "making noise invisible" is one important tactic in landscape control of nuisance sound.

It has been shown repeatedly that a noise whose source is unseen is less annoying than noise from visible sources. Thus, coming back to walls, berms, and plantings, for most situations a visual barrier does nearly as much good for making landscapes *feel* quiet as a massive barrier intended to stop sound. Well-known urban "vest pocket parks," for example New York's Paley Park, rely on this as well as on the masking effects of water noise. Visual barriers generally need to be only as high as the user's eye level. Sometimes a solid wall to about five feet, topped with trellis or open grille, can increase the sense of privacy and calm without blocking sun or breeze.

A related factor in noise perception is that sounds over which people feel some control are less bothersome than sounds to which they are exposed involuntarily. The noise of cars from urban streets is as loud, in decibels, as that of a plane in a flight path overhead[26]—but the plane, over which people feel no possibility of control, is more likely to attract complaints. (Similarly, my boom-box is music, while the neighbor's is noise.) This suggests that noise levels that result from community-based decisions might be less upsetting to people than those imposed on them by the usual approach of building roads or factories first and asking questions later.

Fight Noise with Noise

A related, relatively reliable way of dealing with noise outdoors is to add other noises. These can distract from or mask objectionable noise. Like other psychological methods, masking does little to reduce physical risks like hearing loss from noise exposure. Adding noise can at least make the experience more pleasant.

Harmonious or desirable noises close at hand, like a fountain in an urban garden, can mask louder noises further away. It is possible, though relatively uncommon, to plant or construct landscape features specifically for the sounds they produce—aspens for the shimmering rustle of their leaves, or sculptures that chime or whistle musically. Designing and building such elements could be a specialty for landscape professionals, if not directly related to sustainability, at least as a service to mitigate one of the major effects of the unsustainable environments in which many people live.

A high-tech option with intriguing possibilities has recently become available, though apparently little tested in outdoor use. This is the so-called white-noise generator. White noise is sound containing all audible wavelengths, so named by comparison to white light, which contains all colors.

The simplest white-noise generators emit a constant low hissing or crackling that seems to fade into the background, taking some louder and more annoying noises with it. In this sense, it acts much like a fountain, offering a sound that masks other sounds without calling attention to itself. Straightforward white-noise sources like this have been available for some time.

More recently, *interactive* white-noise generators have been developed. These "listen" to ambient noises and immediately generate sounds exactly "opposite" or "complementary" to each new noise. The result is that ambient noise plus generated noise add up to all wavelengths, that is, they combine to create white noise. This strategy is called "active noise control" (ANC) and has been the subject of research since the 1930s.

ANC is the concept behind noise-canceling headphones. The "canceling" speakers in these headsets are at the point where noise enters the ear, and they completely dominate the space around the ear. Cancelling noise outdoors is much more complicated. To cancel a noise, the "opposite" noise must be carefully aligned with its target in both time and space. Outdoor noise sources are multiple, often moving, and the spaces in which they resonate are complex. Despite several tests of outdoor noise cancellation possibilities (most of them in Japan), it has proven very difficult to apply ANC to complex outdoor noise.

ANC still has potential applications that affect landscapes, however. Some large trucks use noise-canceling equipment on their exhaust stacks, and the concept has been proposed for cars. Engine noise, aerodynamic whine, and even braking and tire noise are produced in fixed locations on a given vehicle and are fairly constant acoustically. Noise-canceling devices specific to each of these could be effective if installed on each vehicle. This seems unlikely unless public pressure against noise increases; even noise-canceling car mufflers have been abandoned because they would increase manufacturing costs.[27]

Like physical barriers, noise machines would not exist in an ideal world. Until and unless policy and technology turn down the volume of civilization's many noise sources, technical fixes may be worth investigating.

Push for Quieter Landscape Tools

Even among construction power tools, many landscape machines are known for noisiness. Gas-powered leaf blowers, once voted the worst invention ever created,[28] put out 110 dB, just below the pain threshold. Two-stroke engines on many other lawn and garden gadgets, from lawnmowers to tillers, can also be disproportionately loud. Targeted for their contribution to air pollution (p. 272), such engines have been redesigned significantly since about the time of the first edition of this book. Landscape professionals should vote with their dollars, creating incentives for manufacturers whose machines cause less pollution, including noise pollution.

Electric power tools are usually quieter than gas-powered ones. Although some types of yard equipment need more power than portable electric motors can offer, electric mowers and other equipment can keep landscape work from disturbing the landscape. Cordless electric yard tools (powered by rechargeable batteries) are becoming more widely available (see Principle 10), and are generally quieter than gas-powered equivalents. Better yet, non-powered hand tools are quietest of all and can become a trademark for quality construction and maintenance firms.

Two of the main US anti-noise groups, Noise Free America and the Noise Pollution Clearing-house ⊃, are actively seeking to silence leaf blowers. The latter has a "Quiet Lawns" campaign that offers acoustic information on a variety of landscape equipment.

Protect "Soundscapes" Through Planning

What does the dearth of effective noise-stopping techniques mean for landscape professionals? Because we cannot wall noise out of our landscapes, we have a stake in quieting it at its source.

Architectural and engineering systems often vent their noise to the outdoors, protecting people inside at the expense of any person or creature in the landscape. This avoids the cost of truly effective sound insulation, but its consequences are not sustainable. This is not merely an abstract wish or theory. Commercial products are available to quiet noise from buildings, factories, chimneys, and exhaust stacks.⊃ Landscape professionals should prod any design team they work with to make full use of at-the-source noise-prevention methods.

Traffic noise increases with speed, at about 10 dB per 30 mph increase.[29] Traffic-calming measures (p. 202) are often aimed at noise reduction as well as safety. In addition to reducing aerodynamic, tire, and engine noise by reducing speed, well-designed traffic-calming can smooth the flow of traffic, resulting in less braking and accelerating noise.

For a decade, the National Park Service (NPS) has been struggling to manage noise in some of the nation's most beloved landscapes. Grand Canyon National Park hears over 140,000 sightseeing flyovers, usually at low altitude, every year. Snowmobiles and Jet-Skis were banned from many parks because of noise (as well as other environmental impacts, especially on wildlife).[30] Park maintenance itself contributes to noise with leaf-blowers, chainsaws, and generators. Natural resource specialist Wes Henry, of the NPS's Washington DC office, wrote one of the first parks "soundscape" management policies in 1999; today many parks have one.[31]

On a day-to-day level, many communities have noise ordinances. These are difficult to enforce against individual moving sources of noise, such as cars, motorcycles, or portable CD players, yet most ordinances are aimed at these kinds of sources. What might make better sense would be to target long-term repeat sources, such as HVAC machinery and other architectural service equipment, as well as industrial plants and public roads.

Noise, until perhaps a decade ago, was legally classified as a "nuisance," not a serious environmental problem. This attitude has slowly begun to change. Recent pro-business, anti-regulatory federal administrations have created a situation where federal noise laws exist but are unfunded for enforcement, yet state and local authorities are forbidden to pass legislation stricter than federal statutes.

With at-the-source noise control products available at reasonable cost, community standards could reasonably require that noises stay under a maximum level, and they might also require that noises cease at certain times, such as nights and weekends. New York City, for example, recently undertook a thorough revision of its noise laws with neighborhood-by-neighborhood crackdowns called Operation Silent Night. Noise, like pollution, is a classic example of the democratic belief that one person's freedom ends where it impacts other people.

The impact of noise, especially highway noise, on communities is well-known, and mostly unsustainable. Noise is the number-one complaint by citizens about their community, and their main reason for leaving if they do;[32] in New York City, it tops the list of calls to a municipal hotline, with 1,000 noise complaints per day.[33] William Morrish, former director of the University of Minnesota's Design Center for the American Urban Landscape, puts the case for road-noise control succinctly. Speaking of a traffic-calmed, truck-free landscaped interstate in St. Paul MN, he says, "It costs more than a standard highway, but it's going to be cheaper than bailing out a failing neighborhood."[34]

Awareness is growing that noise is harmful to human (and probably other species,) health, as well as being a factor in psychological well-being. Blocking noise after it leaves its source, however, has high costs, both monetary and environmental. For these reasons, decreasing noise *by eliminating or quieting its sources* should be an issue for sustainability. Proposing to *require* noise control certainly meets with social and technical challenges. Nonetheless, as a profession, we need to be advocates for silence.

Resources

Quietly Defend Silence

Acoustics

Search Terms: acoustics || outdoor acoustics

The International Institute of Acoustics And Vibration www.iiav.org/: Technical papers on "outdoor acoustics," transportation noise, etc.
Acoustics for the Architect H. G. Burris-Meyer, 1984 Van Nostrand Reinhold, New York: Overview of acoustics; little on landscape specific issues.
Acoustics in the Built Environment Duncan Templeton, David Saunders, and Peter Sacre, 1998 Butterworth-Heinemann, Oxford
Soundscape Newsletter World Forum for Acoustic-Ecology, http://interact.uoregon.edu/medialit/wfae/library/new_newsletter/NSNL08.html: Interdisciplinary professional association studies, "world soundscape as an ecologically balanced entity"; newsletter mainly on artistic aspects of designing with sound.

Noise

Search Terms: noise science || noise definition

Environmental Urban Noise A. Garcia, 2001 WIT Press, Boston
The Effects of Noise on Man Karl D. Kryter, 1985 Academic Press, New York
Sound J. A. Ball, J. Ciovacco, et al., 2003 Gareth Stevens Publishing, Milwaukee WI: Discusses the principles of sound, how animals and humans hear, the speed of sound, noise pollution, and the use of sound waves in medicine.
The Handbook of Hearing and the Effects of Noise: Physiology, Psychology, and Public Health Karl D. Kryter, 1994 Academic Press, New York
Urban Sound Environment J. Kang, 2006 Taylor and Francis, London
Environmental Health Perspectives Online www.ehponline.org/: Several good articles on noise and health.
International Bioacoustics Council (IBAC) and *BioAcoustics*

(journal) www.zi.ku.dk/zi/bioacoustics/homepage.html: Researchers and journal on biological effects of noise.

Noise Free America http://noisefree.org/: Information and advocacy.

Noise Pollution Clearinghouse 888-200-8332, www.nonoise.org/: International news about noise issues of all sorts; library, legal database, links on noise control.

Noise control

Search Terms: noise (control OR mitigation OR suppression) || damping || sound insulation

American National Standards Institute (ANSI) 202-293-8020, www.ansi.org/: Publishes noise-related standards for power and garden tools, land-use noise levels, noise barrier types, and measuring noise.

Institute of Noise Control Engineering 515-294-6142, www.inceusa.org/: Books on noise and acoustics, with links to reviews in newsletter.

Transportation Noise Control Center Directors D. C. Karnopp, 530-752-3606, and N. Sarigul-Klijn, 530-752-0682, TNCC may have been defunded; try contacting its Director at http://mae.ucdavis.edu/faculty/sarigul/sarigul.html: Research center has done work on bioacoustics and threats of noise to endangered species.

Weavewall Ltd Botesdale, Diss, Norfolk UK IP22 1LH, 01379-890209: Greenwall-type noise barriers.

Noise wall of laminated glass Industrial Acoustics Co., Bronx NY, 718-931-8000, www.industrialacoustics.com/: Also offers other noise-control products and consulting.

Acoustics and Noise Control Handbook for Architects and Builders Leland K. Irvine and Roy L. Richards, 1998 Krieger Publishing Company, Melbourne FL

Dictionary of Noise and Noise Control Robert Serre, 1989 Elsevier, St. Louis

Effects on Roadside Noise Levels of Sound Absorptive Materials in Noise Barriers G. R. Watts and N. S. Godfrey, 1999 Applied Acoustics, Montreal

Efficiency of a Noise Barrier with an Acoustically Soft Cylindrical Edge for Practical Use Tomonao Okubo and Kyoji Fujiwara, Jun 1999, *JASA* (Journal of Acoustical Society of America), http://asa.aip.org/jasa.html

Engineering Noise Control: Theory and Practice David A. Bies and Colin H. Hansen, 1996 E and F Spon, London

Noise and Noise Law: A Practical Approach Mel S. Adams and Francis McManus, 1995 Wiley, New York

Noise and Vibration Control Engineering L. L. Beranek and Istvan L. Ver, 1999 Wiley, New York: Graduate level and professional reference on all aspects of noise control.

Noise Control in the Built Environment John Roberts and Diane Fairhall, 2000 Gower Publishing, Brookfield VT

Road and Rail Noise—Effects on Housing 1986 Canada Mortgage and Housing Corporation (CMHC), Ottawa ON, www.cmhc-schl.gc.ca/en/index.html, 613-748-2367

The Audible Landscape: A Manual for Highway, Noise and Land Use Nov 1974, US DOT report

Noise Reduction by a Barrier with a Random Edge Profile Steve S. T. Ho, Ilene J. Busch-Vishniac, and David T. Blackstock, Department of Mechanical Engineering, University of Texas at Austin, www.me.utexas.edu/: Abstract online; contact for paper.

Traffic Noise Attenuation as a Function of Ground and Vegetation Rudoff Hendricks, Jul 1995 Caltrans, Office of Materials Engineering and Testing, www.dot.ca.gov/research/research reports/1989-1996/89-09.pdf: Recent study confirming that vegetation less than one hundred feet wide can provide at most one decibel reduction in noise.

Noise Control Computation and Devices Brunel University, Uxbridge UK, Simon.Chandler-Wilde@brunel.ac.uk: Research: effects of terrain, road surfaces on noise; patented noise barriers, computer software.

Noise-barrier design software "Optima" and "Stamina" FHWA, www.fhwa.dot.gov/environment/noise/16.htm

Noise Control: A Primer A. Behar, M. Chasin, et al., 2000 Singular Publishing Group, San Diego CA

Advanced Air and Noise Pollution Control L. K. Wang, N. C. Pereira, et al., 2005 Humana Press, Totowa NJ

FHWA highway noise site www.fhwa.dot.gov/ENVIRONMENT/noise/effects/intro.htm: Technical information on noise and transportation.

Zeller International www.zeller-int.com/: Makers of Eco-Wall noise-wall system; greenwall-type noise barriers.

Public Works Research Institute, Japan www.pwri.go.jp/eindex.htm (English language site; homepage in Japanese): Environmentally oriented construction research; many innovative road projects.

Rubber Paving Association www.rubberpavements.org/: FAQ page especially useful.

Acoustiblok International 813-980-1400, www.acoustiblok.com/industrial2.html: Sound-absorbing outdoor panels.

Principle 10:
Maintain to Sustain

Ask rice fields and gardens for the truth; learn from hedges and walls.
—Zen Master Dogen, 1250 AD

Landscapes are living things. In one important sense, they are never finished. Growth, natural succession, weathering, change of use or ownership or neighbors—all keep landscapes evolving. Except in successfully restored native landscapes, the best of which maintain themselves, change requires maintenance. Maintenance is the way an evolving landscape keeps pace with evolving human demands.

Most landscape professionals, and many landowners, are well aware that sustainability and careful maintenance go hand in hand. Yet the specialist structure of professional relationships often means that maintenance, construction, and design occur in totally separate compartments. At best, a conscientious maintenance contractor tries to guess the designer's intent or the builder's methods and work accordingly. At worst, maintenance is always *somebody else's problem,* deferred until decay and disrepair take over. The landscape is then ripped up and rebuilt, and the cycle starts over. This is unsatisfying to everyone involved and wastes resources that could be more sustainably used.

Maintaining a landscape consists, basically, of three interlaced goals:

- keeping the living part of the landscape healthy
- keeping the inanimate, constructed parts repaired
- and balancing the first two goals against human uses of the space.

Clearly, these goals are sometimes in conflict. Healthy vegetation can overrun the site, burying hardscape and making human access impossible, let alone use. Repairing constructed elements, painting, re-pointing masonry, or fixing pipes or wiring can cause chemical and physical damage to vegetation and inconvenience to users. Excessive or unplanned use can damage either plants or hardscape in ways that cannot be repaired without stopping those uses. The human factor also includes the financial balancing act between ideals of perfect maintenance (often based on groundskeeping practices of the rich and famous) and expenses that real owners can realistically afford.

Despite this complexity, landscape maintenance gets far less respect from society than it deserves: many people view grounds-maintenance professionals as one step up from unskilled labor. It is true that some basic landscape maintenance tasks are simple and can be done at a basic level by unskilled people. Coordinating tasks and people so that their work favors the environment, however, is by no means simple. Anyone who can successfully juggle the above three goals is the equal of any other professional and should be valued as such.

It has been a theme of this book that sustainable landscapes are most likely to result from coordination among designers, contractors, and clients. This chapter offers an *overview* of how maintenance fits into a coordinated approach, with the focus on practices with the clearest *environmental* costs and benefits. A number of these practices overlap or continue sustainable techniques begun during construction or even design.

This is *not* a complete coverage of all the issues of landscape maintenance, nor of published sources on the topic.⊃ Rather, it concentrates on ways in which maintenance practices can contribute to sustainability (or hinder it), and how better coordination and planning can increase the *sustainability* value of good maintenance.

Discussed (Summarized) in This Chapter

Designing for maintainable spaces.
Maintenance machinery, efficiency, fuel, and pollution.
Reducing pesticide use by good planning.
Sustainable use of fertilizers.
Conserving and using on-site resources.
Establishing and maintaining native plants.
Estimating the long-term costs and benefits of maintenance.
Coordinating design, construction, and maintenance.

Know the Resource Costs of Conventional Landscape Maintenance

Conventional maintenance of landscapes uses many resources, particularly fuel and petroleum-based fertilizers and pesticides. We have not found a comprehensive maintenance-specific figure for landscape costs, but some indicators are worth considering.

Research in 1985 indicated that the average cost for maintaining mowed grass landscapes for large institutions was about $500 per acre.[1] This included parks departments and the interstate highway system; the latter averages eight acres of right-of-way maintenance per linear mile of road. With over eight million lane-miles of interstate (p. 198), mowing the interstates alone costs billions of dollars. This source, unfortunately, does not indicate how much of this cost went for fuel, pesticides, or other specifics; it appears to include salaries.

A 1999 report estimates that *25 million acres* of lawns are maintained in the United States alone. The average US household spent nearly $400, as of 1999, on gardening supplies, driving a do-it-yourself landscape supply industry with total sales of $35 billion.[2] A high percentage goes to maintenance supplies.

Owen Dell, a Santa Barbara CA landscape architect-contractor, estimates comparative maintenance costs for a "conventional" garden and a sustainable one, as of 2004. Dell does not define "sustainable" or "conventional," but clearly includes water conservation, soil-health maintenance, and integrated pest management in the former. The sustainable garden requires one-third the maintenance labor, one-fifth the pesticides, and about one-fourth the water of the conventional design. It also avoids dump fees and removal/replacement of unhealthy plants. Over a twenty-year life span, maintenance costs for the sustainable garden are about 37 percent of those for the conventional one. Maintenance is 86 percent of the design and construction cost of the conventional garden, and only 62 percent for the sustainable design.[3] (In a separate estimate, Dell notes that doing design/construction right the first time ends up costing about 57 percent of doing it cheaply and without professional input.)

Mowing lawn is perhaps the simplest item to estimate for fuel costs, yet even that varies widely. Gas-powered mowing with home equipment averages about 125,000 Btu per acre (Table 7.4). Many of those acres are mowed ten to twenty times per year. Per acre, annual gas mowing consumes 125–250 million Btu; electric mowing, roughly half that.[4]

The same source estimates an annual 16 million Btu per acre for irrigation where water is supplied by municipal mains. About 2 million Btu per acre are used annually for conservatively fertilized turf; up to 7 million for some types. For pesticides, 1 million Btu per acre per application is conservative; 2.5 million is common. These figures include embodied energy of materials, and fuel energy to apply them.

The annual cost in energy for all these basic conventional maintenance tasks can be added up. Conservatively, assume each acre is mowed only ten times per year, and sprayed for weeds only twice. As shown in the table below, average energy to maintain *one acre* conventionally lies between 21 and 30 million Btu per year.

For the nation, the total energy is phenomenal—between 500 and 750 *trillion* Btu each year based on 25 million acres. Even though this is not a particularly accurate estimate, it gives a sense of the huge energy investments involved in conventional landscape maintenance.

Table 10.1
Annual energy to maintain one acre of lawn. See also table 7.8.

	One acre, one time	Frequency per year	Annual total
Mowing	0.125 million Btu	10 to 20	1.25 to 2.5 million Btu
Irrigation	n/a	n/a	16 million Btu
Fertilization	n/a	n/a	2 to 7 million Btu
Pesticides	0.625 to 2.5 million Btu	2 or more	2 to 5 million Btu

Plan for Maintainable Spaces

Horticulturists say the most common ailment of landscape plants is Lawnmower Disease. While this may not be scientifically accurate, maintenance machinery commonly inflicts serious damage on the very plants it is intended to serve. Physical wounds allow bacteria, fungi, viruses, and insects to get past plants' first line of defense, which is bark. It is unclear how much plant disease starts in this way, but the percentage is likely quite high. Snow blowers and leaf blowers join mowers in assaulting the bark of trees. Maintenance equipment, like construction equipment, can also stress plants by compacting soil and contributing to air pollution or soil contamination.

Landscape architects and landowners are quick to blame the maintenance contractor for all forms of Lawnmower Disease, and in some cases, contractor carelessness *is* responsible. But equally often, landscape design or construction is also at fault. Maintenance machinery, and even hand maintenance, requires room to work and access to each task, and these are often forgotten in the design process.

People need room to work; average dimensions for these requirements are well-known. Maintenance also uses many machines and vehicles. Like vehicles for transportation, they need specific amounts of space in which to maneuver. No competent designer would think of laying out an office or kitchen without checking human dimensions, or a street or loading dock without checking turning radii of vehicles. Yet in laying out landscapes, it is common to create spaces that cannot accommodate the machines to maintain them.

As discussed in the next section, we do not assume that all or even most maintenance must be done with machinery. However, when it is reasonable to expect that machinery *will* be used, it is shortsighted not to design for that machinery. Lawns, for example, should not have narrow extensions or acute angles where even a hand mower is awkward to use. Grass immediately under trees should be left un-mowed for several inches out from the trunk; a bed of mulch or plantings may serve this purpose, and keeps grass from competing with tree roots. Structures that require regular painting should have a space around them in which no critically important plants are located. Space should be designed to pile shoveled or plowed snow where meltwater helps plantings. The concept is obvious, the possible examples almost infinite—all the more remarkable that this important issue is so often overlooked or ignored.

Part of the problem may be that detailed information on landscape maintenance machinery is not easily available to designers. Exact dimensions for specific models are provided by manufacturers, but are seldom appropriate for design use. The designer needs rule-of-thumb averages, of the sort presented for cars and trucks in the *Graphic Standards* or *Timesaver Standards* series. These standard design sources typically do not even have an index entry for ordinary maintenance. Dimensions of garden tools are given, but only as storage-planning items, and no commercial maintenance equipment is shown. The landscape volume of *Timesavers* does give one turning radius (36″) for a generic "garden tractor." By comparison, it devotes about a dozen full pages to operating-space requirements for cars and trucks of all sizes, and a quarter-page to the turning radius of the Zamboni ice machine! This reflects the odd priorities and compartmentalization of conventional design training. It is quite likely that there are sources of good informa-

Figure 10.1 Design versus maintenance. To prune and remove trash, this worker had to cross the fence on his ladder; no other access was possible. (*Photo:* Kim Sorvig.)

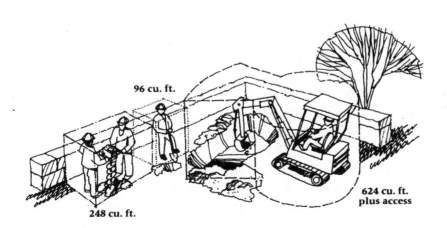

96 cu. ft.

248 cu. ft.

624 cu. ft. plus access

Figure 10.2 Comparative space requirements for machine and hand digging. The more powerful the tool, the greater the required clearance. On wooded sites, these spaces have to be cleared. (*Illust.:* Craig Farnsworth.)

tion on maintenance equipment, used by contractors—but seldom by designers. The authors have not found a single concise reference on this topic (and would welcome titles to list in a future edition).

Besides allowing space for maintenance, other aspects of design can make a difference in sustainability. Grouping plants together by their water requirements not only approximates natural plant associations and saves water, but prevents over- and under-watering, which are major stresses leading to disease. Designing clear transitions between the neatest and the most naturalistic areas encourages users to accept the design, and discourages unwanted mowing and pruning of the naturalistic areas. Proper plant selection, focusing on native plants, can also decrease susceptibility to pests and diseases, resulting in decreased maintenance. The toxic chemical treatments used as a last resort when plants become seriously ill can also be avoided if stress and damage are reduced. Planning for durable materials, rather than the false economy of low purchase price, is another aspect of design with dramatic implications for maintenance.

In many landscapes, such as corporate headquarters, it is appropriate to *interpret the maintenance process* to staff and public. Try botanic-garden–type signage explaining why and how maintenance creates the visible landscape. These and other interpretive devices can raise appreciation for the maintenance staff's work and enhance the company's commitment to sustainability.

Expect Change

Many people think of maintenance as "upkeep," keeping things the same. It is more accurate, especially in landscapes, to think of maintenance as *responding to change.* Plant growth and weathering are powerful forces in all landscapes and cannot be stopped (despite products advertised as "conquering" or "taming" these forces).

People also create change in landscapes, and it is almost as useless to resist these changes as to try to stop the tide from rising. Even well-designed and well-built landscapes change in response to user desires, which change over time or with new ownership. If a design doesn't accommodate user desires, con-

Figure 10.3 Neither wind nor rain . . . but this Sycamore stopped the U.S. mail. Growth and change are inevitable landscape forces that design and maintenance must work with, not against. (*Photo:* Kim Sorvig.)

struction and planting may be trampled as users impose their wishes. To designers, builders, or maintenance workers, this often seems unreasonable, selfish, and uncaring—and in fact it often is. But unless the entire user population can be educated to respect the original design, there is nothing to do but change it.

Use Appropriate Machinery and Fuels

Guidelines for appropriate construction machinery (see pp. 60 and 278) also apply to maintenance equipment. The tendency to use the biggest machine available is even less suitable in maintenance.

Heavy construction equipment causes soil compaction and vegetation loss, but on construction sites major changes are expected, and much damage can be remedied as the job is completed. Maintenance, how-

Figure 10.4 "Desire lines" occur at the point pedestrians see their destination. These lines can be counteracted by visual screening (barriers seldom work)—or they can be opportunities to link design to real-use patterns. (*Photo:* Kim Sorvig.)

ever, takes place in a landscape that people want to *keep as it is*. The difference is like scratching a woodworking project at the rough-cut stage, or scratching it after sanding and oiling. Minor damage to a finished landscape may be worse than major changes made during construction. For this reason, using the lightest possible machinery may be even more important to maintenance work than it is in construction. Maintenance tools in general *are* smaller and lighter than their construction equivalents; for sustainability, use the smallest and lightest tool that can do the job. Pressure to speed up the work by using larger machinery should be evaluated very carefully, using life-cycle costing to reveal whether time savings are worth the trade-offs. Principle 7 offers information on the energy costs of various machines and on life-cycle costing.

Many small machines are powered by two-stroke engines. In general, these produce more pollution per horsepower or per unit of fuel than larger engines. This is because they are less efficient, and their combustion of fuel less complete. Although each individual machine may contribute only a small amount of pollution, small engines are very numerous. For example, home lawnmowers alone number an estimated forty million in the United States, consuming "several hundred million gallons" of gas/oil mix per year.[5] Add the many other consumer lawn and garden machines, plus professional equipment, and it becomes clear that fuel savings can have an important impact on resource use and pollution. As noted on p. 319, small landscape-maintenance machinery includes many egregious noise polluters.

Very recently, significant increases have occurred in two-stroke engine efficiency and cleanness (p. 272). Conscientious (and dollar-conscious) power-tool users will switch to the newer engines sooner rather than later, both because of the 70 percent decrease in pollution, and the 30 percent increase in fuel efficiency. It also appears to the authors that the landscape industry could benefit from sponsoring research into cleaner fuel options for small equipment. For example, natural gas conversion is widespread for warehouse machines (used indoors, where exhaust is lethal) and is becoming more common for transportation. Bio-based fuels (below) are often cleaner than petro-based equivalents. The feasibility of converting small engines may be limited by the size of fuel tank required, but could still be investigated. Creative thinking about tools used in other industries but not widely in landscape work (for example compressed air) might yield insights as well. The design of the tool itself can be a sustainability issue. On one mower that Sorvig had the misfortune of using, the engine required 20 ounces of oil, but had capacity for 56. The oil level could not be seen except on the dipstick because the filler tube was long and bent. There was no way to avoid overfilling, which led to spillage, waste of oil and fuel, fouling of the engine, and finally scrapping the machine. Bad design is clearly a sustainability issue, especially with fuel-consuming machines.[6]

Landscape maintenance tools are increasingly available in electric models, both plug-in and cordless. Corded equipment offers the "unlimited" supply of utility power, but tangled cords and the danger of 115V shock are drawbacks. Cordless equipment solves these problems, but operating times on a single recharge are often short. Operating time and recharge speed are improving, and cordless chainsaws, hedge trimmers, and even cordless electric lawnmowers are now available. It is difficult to rate electricity as a power source, since it is clean at the point of use but often polluting at the generating plant, and suffers up to 60 percent waste in transmission. Solar electricity panels, which avoid these losses, are now portable enough to take anywhere to recharge equipment (p. 268). Solar equipment specifically for fleet vehicles is becoming available (see p. 269).

An innovative solar trash compactor by Seahorse Power ⊃ increases capacity from 40 to 300 pounds (750 percent) by compression; collection trips and fuel use should be reduced 85 percent.

Improving the performance of cordless equipment, and making it easy to recharge from solar power, is a sustainability research goal worthy of industry support. So is investigation of the newest offering in "alternative" energy, the fuel cell (p. 269).

Many landscape maintenance tasks can actually be done better with hand tools. High-quality results, low environmental impact, and the pleasure of quiet, unmotorized work make hand labor an attractive option. Despite social pressures to mechanize every possible task, landscape maintenance remains one of the most appropriate places for craftspeople working with hand tools.

Landscape tools, whether power or hand, can be major vectors for invasive species if not kept clean, from gypsy-moth egg masses on tools left outdoors, to weed seeds on tires. Spreading pest problems on construction equipment is a complicated problem, but keeping tools clean between sites is a simple part of the solution.[7]

Vehicle choice for getting to and from the site also has an impact. For conventional cars and trucks, switching to bio-based fuels and lubricants (see below) is potentially an easy way to cut both emissions and costs. At least one landscape maintenance company (TerraNova, of Santa Cruz CA) sends its twelve employees out on bicycles with equipment trailers. This takes advantage of the fact that maintenance work tends to concentrate in neighborhoods, where distances can be short. Owner Ken Foster credits cost savings from bike transport as a factor in profitability over nearly twenty years in business.

Switch to Bio-based Maintenance Products

Petroleum is ultimately a plant-based material and can in many cases be replaced with products based on renewable plant crops. The idea is not new: Rudolf Diesel, introducing his new engine at the Paris Exhibition in 1909, ran it on vegetable oil.[8]

An exceptionally wide range of commercial bio-based products is available, and a great number of these are relevant to landscape maintenance:

- fuels, including biodiesel, and fuel additives
- engine oils (automotive and two-stroke), as well as hydraulic, brake, power-steering, and transmission oils
- cleaners and solvents, including concrete-surface cleaners, oil- and pesticide-spill cleaners, paint and varnish removers, graffiti removers, and vehicle-washing soaps
- form release agents for concrete and asphalt
- paints, stains, and inks
- dust control sprays
- adhesives and sealers.

Most bio-based products are less toxic in both manufacture and use than conventional petro-based equivalents, or nontoxic. Bio-based paints and solvents (cleaners) in particular are low in polluting and toxic volatile components (VOCs). Most are also biodegradable. Since they are crop based, there can be potential for production at or near the point of use.

Bio-based fuels and oils avoid many of the emissions problems associated with petroleum products. Federal studies of biodiesel, for example, showed that it produced 90 percent fewer toxic emissions than conventional fuel, and 78 percent less CO_2. Similarly, when bio-based oils are burned in two-stroke engines, there are fewer emissions.

Cost and availability of bio-based products varies. In many cases, they are competitive with or less costly than petro-based equivalents; others are more expensive to purchase, but achieve significant total-cost or life-cycle savings. As an example, the Federal Proving Ground at Aberdeen MD changed their paint procurement policies to favor bio-based and other alternatives.[9] The Aberdeen Proving Ground is essentially a small town of 15-18 thousand, with an estimated 40 million square feet of surfaces to be painted. The alternative paints proved to be less expensive than conventional, with direct savings of over $6,300 per year. Because the new paints are not hazardous materials, disposal was $25,000 cheaper, and not tracking inventory saved another $17,000. For many users, the decreased costs of environmental compliance are the most compelling reasons for using bio-based products.

Availability of such products is likely to increase, especially because many federal agencies are including them in Environmentally Preferable Purchasing (EPP) specifications. ⊃ These EPP programs guide an increasing number of government purchases toward greater sustainability in both maintenance and construction. Landscape professionals who contract with government agencies may get incentives or be required to use such products. In many cases, EPP standards are also good sources for help in evaluating sustainable maintenance products, even on nongovernment projects.

Apply Integrated Pest Management

Organic lawn care is a "hot landscaping trend," according to an October 2006 *Wall Street Journal* report.[10] Yet the dangers of pesticides were among the first environmental issues to be documented, notably by Rachel Carson in *Silent Spring*. In 1995, despite forty years of concern and awareness among consumers, government, and industry, Americans still spread 68 million pounds of pesticides on landscapes and gardens yearly.[11] In fact, ten times as much pesticide per acre is applied to the typical landscape as to typical farm fields.[12] The toxicity and persistence of pesticides today has

been reined in since the 1950s; many products are very specifically targeted. Nonetheless, pesticide use remains an automatic, unthinking response to landscape problems for many users, rather than a last resort. It is sobering to recall that, in the San Francisco Bay Area at least, gardening has been shown to be the largest single source of pollutants.[13]

Besides their toxic effects, a large percentage of pesticides are produced from nonrenewable resources, and many have significant embodied energy. Energy use in *applying* pesticides is also a sustainability issue.

There is little need to duplicate in this book the many detailed sources of information on how to reduce volume and toxicity of pesticide use. Most pesticides are (or ought to be) specific to region, species (both the plant to be protected and the species to be killed), and weather conditions at the time of application. Encyclopedic information of that type would be foolish to include in this book. What is important to point out is that these issues are not just homeowner problems, as many books imply. Maintenance professionals are, in many cases, guilty of overusing pesticides and encouraging clients to do likewise. The landscape most likely to be pesticide free is one in which designer, contractor, and owner have worked together to plan for landscape health. Healthy landscapes can fight off a high proportion of pests that would wreak havoc in a landscape under stress.

At the design stage, it can be valuable to "zone" the landscape according to the likelihood of exposure to pesticides, and the hazards posed. For example, on a school playground, any pesticide applied to playing areas is very likely to come in contact with children, who are especially susceptible. In such an area, only low-hazard products should ever be used. Islands in the school's parking lot, which are tough to maintain and where children can be kept from playing, might be acceptable zones for stronger pesticides under some circumstances.[14] Skimpy planters or sidewalk "graves," inadequate irrigation (where it is needed), and other unfriendly hardscape all lead to unhealthy plants that must be coddled along using pesticides (see p. 133). Similarly, during construction, avoid mishandling plant stock, amend soil appropriately, and never bury waste in planting pits.

The maintenance contractor, or the owner who gardens, is the third link in this chain. Ideally, this person needs to be part of early design reviews to spot maintenance issues that require redesign. The American tendency to build (and landscape) on speculation, before a real owner is in the picture, complicates this and many other forms of planning for sustainability. Especially where owner involvement is not possible, the designer should prepare a maintenance calendar as part of contract documents (see p. 335 and Figure 10.7). Maintenance plans, in fact, should be part of every professionally created landscape. For lawns, mowing height, timing, and even reel-versus-power mowers must fit the grass species and coordinate with water availability and fertilizer use, or the lawn will be need higher maintenance.

Use Integrated Pest Management (IPM) ⊃ to control pests that preventive health care doesn't avoid. IPM relies on biological controls (such as predator insects or scent traps) and nontoxic chemicals like diatomaceous earth[15], plus carefully targeted pesticides as a last resort. Chemicals are usually applied with ultra-low-volume sprayers or other methods that minimize waste and drift.

Some pesticides are marketed as "reduced toxicity." In general, this means less toxicity *to humans*, but some of these products are still broad-spectrum poisons, highly toxic to nontarget species. Wherever possible, use pesticides *targeted to the problem species only,* and always evaluate toxicity to other species, not just to humans and pets.

Accurate timing is important in IPM. A nontoxic soap spray may kill larval insects, while the same species at maturity shrugs off the same or stronger chemicals. Rather than using high-strength or high-tech solutions to bring ailing plants back from near death, IPM treats problems when they are small. This requires more field knowledge and observation by maintenance workers and better ability to schedule treatments precisely. These are skills that sustainability-minded maintenance contractors must be willing to learn.

Some of these skills can be aided by the computer. In particular, up-to-the-minute weather information is widely published on the Web. Bob Boufford, author of *The Gardener's Computer Companion*, suggests programming your computer to use weather data for decision making. Certain combinations of temperature, humidity, day length, and precipitation trigger predictable responses from either plants, insects, or diseases: germination, blooming, insect attacks, or spreading fungi. Computers can certainly be programmed to "watch" for these combinations, using information that can be downloaded almost hourly. Once the convergence of conditions is identified, optimum times for specific maintenance tasks can in theory be scheduled automatically.

For greater accuracy, it is becoming possible to track site-specific weather as a basis for maintenance. Sensors for irrigation systems (p. 181) are more and more common and provide information that can be relayed to any computer. Sensors in the gardens of each of a contractor's clients could set off alerts about timely maintenance, not just irrigation. "Smart" irrigation systems already adjust to rainfall variations this way, using radio links. Although futuristic at the time of our first edition, today computer-aided maintenance is only a few steps ahead of common technology. Sensor-and-computer-based scheduling may make it easier to do more with less.

Use Fertilizers Sustainably

Highly refined artificial fertilizers are sometimes likened to addictive drugs, as opposed to foods. In the chapters on construction, we have raised several concerns: that fertilizers are overused, encouraging weak and weedy species to replace hardy natives (p. 90); that artificial fertilizers involve hazardous chemicals and nonrenewable resources in production (Principle 6); and that artificial fertilizers have considerable energy costs (Principle 7). Clearly, these concerns also apply during maintenance. In addition, high fertilizer use (artificial or organic) can promote extra growth of immature vegetative material. This not only increases leaf litter or grass-clipping volume, but can make fast-growing plants more susceptible to stress from drought.[16] Immature growth is also less likely to produce flowers.

Except for overfertilization, these problems can be avoided by using organic fertilizers, manures, and composts. Many organic products are available commercially (p. 92). Their use helps solve problems that occur when these materials are considered as "waste." Using compost decreases the need for additional fertilizer, both because the compost contains nutrients and because it helps the soil structure retain nutrients and make them available to plants.

Transportation to the site is a potential energy concern with any fertilizer, although sources of organic fertilizer are often more or less local. Artificial fertilizers are often transported huge distances. For example, superphosphate fertilizer used in the American Midwest most likely originates in mines at least as far away as Wyoming or Tennessee, and possibly as distant as Morocco or the Pacific Islands.[17]

As with pest management, fertilization requirements are site and species specific. Soil and/or foliar analysis (showing what nutrients have actually been taken up by a specific plant) are essential tools, as is knowledge of local conditions.

Don't Waste On-site Resources

Organic fertilizers with *no* transportation cost are frequently available on-site, and often wasted. Yard waste is raw material for compost. Decomposition of dead vegetation (composting) is how plant communities recycle nutrients. In fact, natural communities survive almost entirely by using and reusing on-site nutrients, plus water and sunshine. Out of horticultural habit these materials are *removed*, breaking this cycle and depriving the site of nutrients. This loss of available nutrients is one main reason why imported fertilizers are ever required. The energy costs alone for removing and replacing on-site nutrients make this practice unsustainable. In addition it takes up landfill space unnecessarily. Simply as an attitude, it devalues resources into "waste."

Compost is one of the most valuable assets for maintaining healthy landscapes. Its ability to improve soil structure, water-holding capacity, and nutrient content has made it worth mentioning in almost every chapter of this book. Any compostable mate-

rial can also be used to produce bio-gas for energy generation. The value of compost for landscape maintenance is so high, however, that the authors are reluctant to recommend using it to produce power.

Lawn clippings can be left on the lawn to compost by using a "mulching mower" that shreds grass finely and spread it while mowing. This is also known as "grasscycling." For clients who find this objectionable, or if using a push mower to save fuel, clippings can be gathered and composted in a bin or pile for reapplication. Leaves can also be composted, with or without pre-shredding. Amounts can be significant: lawns in California have been found to produce 300–400 pounds of clippings per thousand square feet, or eight tons per acre, annually.[18] Clippings with many weed seeds should be pile composted; clippings from pesticide-heavy lawns should be avoided (preferably by avoiding pesticides). In arid climates, use a rotating drum composter to retain as much moisture as possible.

Pruned branches are another overlooked resource. They decompose very slowly if left whole, but can be chipped to make mulch or compost. Some diseased wood, especially from fungal infections, should not be composted and spread near living trees, because fungal spores may persist. The regional Extension Service or university horticulture department can usually offer local advice on which diseases survive composting, and which plants those diseases affect. They can also advise whether termites may be an issue in recycling logs and branches.

Chippers are available in a wide range of sizes. They consume energy, but certainly less than hauling away wood and importing nutrients to replace it. Home shredders cannot handle large branches and logs; maintenance pros and arborists have larger equipment. Many communities also collect yard waste, chip it, and offer it as mulch; this reintroduces transportation energy into the equation. Logs can simply be stacked to provide habitat for many types of wildlife, including butterflies. After rotting a few years, logs can be broken up by hand for composting and replaced with a new habitat stack.

Composting done in piles or bins requires space that landscape designers should include in site plans.

Keeping compost accessible to the kitchen is not always easy to reconcile with people's desire to hide this utilitarian function. John Lyle's attitude on the subject—that seeing such processes is part of environmental education—is worth reminding clients about.

Septic tanks and municipal sewage systems that do not produce composted biosolids (p. 94) also waste valuable organic resources. An alternative is the composting toilet, which produces sterile compost on-site. This compost is less likely than municipal biosolids to contain heavy metals and pollutants. Although a composting toilet is not strictly part of the landscape, it produces an on-site resource valuable enough to be considered for sustainable maintenance planning.

It is still uncommon for Americans to think of sewage as a resource, preferring to put it out of sight and mind—with high environmental and financial costs. Conventional sewage systems require infrastructure, maintenance, energy, and up to 30 percent of a community's residential water supply.[19] Septic tanks return flush water to the site through the leach field, but solids accumulated in the tank are simply pumped and trucked to sewage treatment plants. In either case, the compostable resource is wasted, and a large energy and resource cost is paid for the privilege of wasting it.

Composting toilets were used in traditional communities in Japan and Europe long before they were produced commercially. Half a dozen manufacturers offer various models in the United States today. Modern composting toilets are normally odorless and clean when properly maintained; small solar fans and pumps may be used to keep the composting process active. Compost is easily removed every few months for use.

Composting has been linked in modern people's minds to rural outhouses and brush piles. As energy costs and plant health have become better understood, on-site composting has come to figure prominently in sustainability strategies. Landscape professionals interested in sustainability need to work with on-site composting systems.

One form of on-site waste is real: excess building or repair materials, like concrete. Avoid contaminating water bodies or large volumes of soil with concrete, paint, or other products. Every firm or individual doing landscape work must take responsibility for appropriate site cleanup.

Consider Alternatives to Mowing

One emerging practice, on scattered landscapes in the United States, Canada, Australia, New Zealand, and Europe, is the use of grazing animals to keep vegetation trimmed. Grazing controls grasses and non-woody plants and has been used around residential communities such as Sea Ranch in California. This is actually a very old landscape practice; Olmsted and other nineteenth-century park designers used sheep to "mow" Central Park and around the White House. The practice is reemerging with awareness of the contribution of air-polluting mowers to global warming.

Browsing is a similar concept, using goats that prefer young *woody* plants. Because they will not eat most herbaceous plants, browsers can keep meadows from being overtaken by successional shrubs and trees. They can also be important for fire management (see p. 106), removing small trees and leaving larger ones, producing an open forest less susceptible to intense fires. Both grazing and browsing should be applied more broadly.[20]

Adapt to Using Native Plants

Using native plants has maintenance implications, too. Many people believe native plants can produce that modern fantasy, the No-maintenance Garden. Sometimes they have been told as much by overzealous advocates. Often, it is merely wishful thinking from people tired of maintenance-*intensive* landscapes, the same impulse that leads to Astroturf.

Overall, regionally adapted and native plants *do* require *less* maintenance than exotics. They need as much care, however, as any other planting while getting established, usually the first 1–2 years. Watering is almost always required at first, as well as physical protection against browsing native animals, who are of course well adapted to eat them. Once established, natives need a *different kind* of maintenance, requiring adjustments from the people who care for them.

Because many natives will be completely weaned from irrigation after establishment, it is wasteful to

Figure 10.5 Sheep and goats are a nonpolluting alternative to lawnmowers at Sea Ranch on the California coast. (*Project:* Lawrence Halprin. *Photo:* Russ Beatty.)

install permanent sprinklers in native landscapes. This means that watering during the initial period is done with temporary systems or by hand. To those used to fully automated irrigation, hand watering a few natives for a couple of years may well *seem* like more maintenance than a conventional garden. Hand watering may also be required in periods of extreme drought.

Pruning, another major maintenance job, is also different for native plants. Far fewer natives are as forgiving as their horticultural cousins of shearing or pollarding (also called lopping, see Figure 10.6). In fact, being tolerant of abuse is one criterion for a commercially successful horticultural plant: consider the species that survive being sold through large home-store chains. Even when a native species is tolerant of hard clipping, the style of most native-plant landscapes makes geometric topiary trimming look out of place. Natives are usually pruned naturalistically, which requires the eye and patience of a Japanese garden master. Properly done, such pruning is almost unnoticeable. This can disappoint people used to the showy results of European-style pruning. They may feel that they have spent hours (or paid someone to spend hours) of cautious snipping with little to show for it.

Landscape architect Jon Coe often specifies that his plantings should "prune themselves": only dead wood is to be removed, and only if really necessary. "How did magnolias," this son of a horticulturist muses, "survive 200 million years without us to prune out all that 'disease-attracting' dead wood? Do our planted trees live longer?" Especially with native plants, Coe's words are worth pondering.

These are problems of client education. The resource-conservation and habitat value of native plantings is clear, and although their beauty may be subtle, open minds learn to appreciate it. For the maintenance contractor, knowing how to take care of natives can be a profitable and fulfilling specialty. People who have seen their native landscapes butchered by careless conventional techniques are very loyal to the professional who can do the job right.

Manage Large Public Landscapes Holistically, Too

Environmentally minded gardeners have practiced organic maintenance for years. But can a large commercial property in the heart of a major city pull the plug on manufactured chemicals for fertilizer and pest control? Yes—if property managers support green maintenance and a skilled team makes it happen.

Battery Park City (BPC) in Manhattan—36 acres used intensely every day—is entirely maintained without pesticides or synthetic fertilizers. Organic

Figure 10.6 Lopping is an example of maintenance that damages vegetation and disfigures designed landscapes. Originally a rural woodlot technique for growing poles ("pollarding"), it is unfortunately considered stylish in a few places. (*Photo:* K. Sorvig.)

maintenance on this scale in such a dense urban location required new tools and approaches, according to landscape architect James Urban.[21]

Maintaining a healthy "soil food web" in an urban landscape is not as simple as doing a few tests and adding something to the soil. Organic maintenance must be started with design and construction. Healthy soil requires good drainage as well as suitable organic levels; soil mixes, amendments, and drainage systems must be correctly designed. BPC, like many urban facilities, used manufactured soil, giving the designers control of the entire soil profile from subgrade to mulch level. At BPC, soil that is almost entirely sand is favored for even drainage and stability. Sand accepts organic material well, as part of the initial mix or added during maintenance.

A principal organic tool in keeping soil biology balanced is compost to feed the soil food web. In nature, organic matter is self-replacing; in the urban environment, much of this organic matter is removed. Purchasing specialty compost only when necessary, BPC makes most of its compost in a 2,000-square-foot facility, processing all greenwaste from the site (including park restaurants) plus manure from nearby police-horse stables.[22] The compost is tested for biological activity: the crew looks for active bacteria less than 15 percent of the inactive bacteria count. Finished compost is spread one to two inches deep on plant beds once a year.

To further refine the balance of soil organisms, BPC maintains a bank of compost tea brewers (p. 93). This material gives excellent results in balancing soil microbiology, but is no silver bullet of organic maintenance. Compost tea "is the cream on top of an organic program," says BPC's director of horticulture, but does not work as well without good soils and a composting program.[23] Especially for large-scale urban organic maintenance, coordinated care on a site designed for such practices is essential.

Evaluate Life-cycle Costs of Maintenance Options

The same cost-cutting pressures that made the 1990s the Downsizing Decade have spread deferred maintenance throughout the land. Those who think that maintenance is expensive, however, should consider the cost of neglect.

Landscapes built and then neglected waste resources and have little place in a sustainable future. To understand how wasteful lack of maintenance is, or to convey the idea to a client, use life-cycle costing (LCC, p. 283). This technique takes into account the costs of maintenance work, but also shows the savings that result. Reasonable maintenance is almost always cheaper in energy costs than replacement; frequently (though not always) it costs less money, too. LCC will also reveal when a landscape is so dilapidated that its maintenance is truly too expensive to justify. Maintenance work cannot be evaluated accurately by upfront costs alone. Using LCC, long-term costs and benefits are clearly seen and options easily compared. LCC is an essential tool for profitability and marketing, and takes on even more importance in pursuing resource efficiency and sustainability.

Coordinate Design, Construction, and Maintenance

Perhaps the most important idea of all, going beyond specifics that vary from site to site, is coordination. This has been a theme throughout the book and bears repeating.

The most forward-thinking landscape designers prepare site-specific maintenance plans for their clients.[24] Increasingly, firms have experience in this aspect of landscape work; pioneers include Andropogon Associates (Philadelphia), Carol R. Johnson Associates (CRJA, Cambridge MA), Louise Schiller Associates (Princeton NJ), OLM Inc. (Atlanta), and Site Design and Management Systems (SDMS, Lansing MI).

These firms unanimously emphasize two key elements of such plans. One is making maintenance an issue in the very first design stages, not as an afterthought. The other is building relationships with and educating the owner and any maintenance staff or contractors. Start talking maintenance with the owner while the plan is still on paper. With maintenance craftspeople, walking the site provides "field education" that is usually well received. Because job turnover is high in the maintenance industry, this education is an ongoing process. Frequent site inspections by the designer are essential and need to be negotiated upfront as a retainer or hourly payment.

The plan schedules landscape tasks: pruning some species in spring and others in fall, replacing pond filters every five years, re-pointing brickwork every twenty. But it goes beyond just scheduling. Some issues a good plan needs to address and document include:

- Establish standards for maintenance—how much, what kind, and with what results, including the expected "look."
- Quantify the amount of work required—square feet of lawn or mulch, numbers of lights or sprinklers, linear feet of paths or hedges or fence. These help in-house staff plan or keep contractor bids equivalent.

- Prioritize tasks so that shortages (staff, budget, or resources like water) can be dealt with.
- Set procedures for bidding out maintenance or set staffing levels for in-house work.
- Reward performance, especially for contracted maintenance. Set about 25 percent of the contractor's monthly payment as performance bonus dependent on meeting quality standards. This requires extremely clear performance specifications, but is very effective in rewarding conscientious work and avoiding carelessness.
- Provide for plan review every few years to adapt to changes in site use.

Some large clients, such as parks departments, may have their own standard plan, keyed to public events or financial deadlines as much as to seasonal changes. Maintenance plans may cover staff training, recommend specific products and machinery, or simply act as a reminder when to do specific tasks.

The designer may write the plan, or may hire a horticulturist or maintenance contractor to write it based on as-built drawings. The owner can do all or part of the maintenance, pass the plan to a contractor, or, in some cases, hire a branch of the designer's firm to do the work. The plan is a valuable asset if the property is sold, because it can be passed on to the next owner to ensure continuity. Such a system not only improves long-term landscape health, but increases the likelihood of realizing the designer's vision as the landscape matures.

Not every designer is competent to produce a maintenance plan. This can encourage teamwork. Having a maintenance contractor on retainer as a consultant to a design firm is unusual, but is an excellent way of producing maintainable designs. Despite conventional separation of trades, the ideal team for producing long-term sustainable landscapes includes an ecologist, a designer, a construction contractor, and a maintenance expert. Some design-build firms actually have such a team in-house; a consulting arrangement suits other firms better.

Two new tools can lend accuracy to maintenance plans. These are the similarly named GPS and GIS systems—Global Positioning and Geographic Information, respectively (see p. 43). Their value to main-

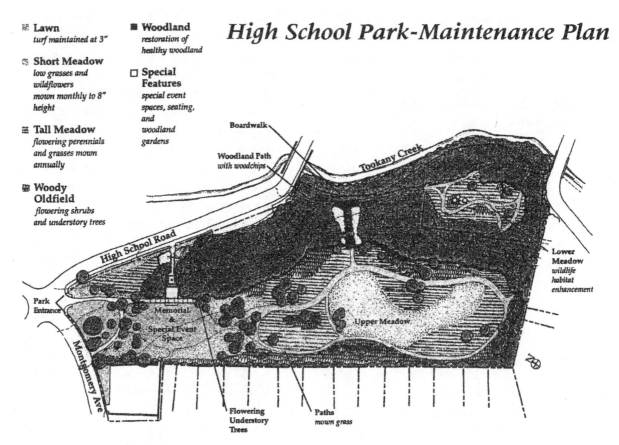

Lawn
turf maintained at 3"

Short Meadow
low grasses and wildflowers mown monthly to 8" height

Tall Meadow
flowering perennials and grasses mown annually

Woody Oldfield
flowering shrubs and understory trees

Woodland
restoration of healthy woodland

Special Features
special event spaces, seating, and woodland gardens

High School Park-Maintenance Plan

Boardwalk

Woodland Path with woodchips

Tookany Creek

High School Road

Park Entrance

Montgomery Ave

Memorial & Special Event Space

Lower Meadow wildlife habitat enhancement

Upper Meadow

Flowering Understory Trees

Paths mown grass

Figure 10.7   Maintenance plans must be specific to the site and adapted to the landowner's way of working and using the place. This example graphically links tasks to specific areas of the landscape. (*Project:* Cheltenham Township PA with Friends of High School Park. Graphic: Andropogon Associates.)

tenance lies in producing and storing detailed yet cost-effective real-world plans. The GPS unit can easily locate construction or repairs as they occur—a must for irrigation, for example, which once buried becomes invisible. GIS can convert GPS or other field measurements into clear diagrams and maps showing actual conditions, not just idealized intentions. If data entry is done with foresight, GIS can also produce task-specific maps from a master file—accurate location maps, for example, of all shrubs of one species, all trees for January pruning, or streetlights due for re-lamping.

Landscapes that do not age gracefully fall short of sustainability, no matter how environmentally sound their original design or construction. Landscapes, more than any other human construction, are about growth, change, and time. There is only one irreplace-

able maintenance tool—an experienced person devoted to the place and the work. Maintenance is the task of adapting to time and change, and it cannot be neglected in the sustainable landscape.

Resources

Maintain to Sustain

Maintenance

Search Terms: maintenance || landscape maintenance || outdoor maintenance

Landscape Maintenance Association (FL) 941-714-0459, www.floridalma.org/: Specific to Florida, but good information; similar groups may exist in other regions.

Database of Landscape Maintenance National Agricultural Safety Database, www.cdc.gov/nasd/

Grounds Maintenance Handbook Herbert S. Conover, 1977, 3rd ed., McGraw-Hill

Landscape Management and Maintenance: A Guide to Its Costing and Organization John Parker and Peter Bryan, 1989 Ashgate Publishing, Aldershot UK

Professional Landscape Management David L. Hensley, 1994 Stipes Publishing, Champaign IL

Landscape Operations: Management, Methods, and Material Leroy G. Hannebaum , 1999, 3rd ed., Prentice Hall, New York: Conventional, but thorough.

Low Maintenance Gardening 1995 Time-Life Books, New York: The Time Life complete gardener.

Owen Dell sustainable landscape show www.owendell.com/, www.citytv18.com/: *Garden Wise Guys* TV show and videos; "Sustainable landscaping with attitude."

Maintenance: energy use

Search Terms: maintenance + energy (use OR efficiency)

"Landscape Maintenance Takes Energy: Use It Efficiently" Helen Whiffen, Feb 1993, *Energy Efficiency and Environmental News* (Florida Energy Extension Service) Gainesville FL, http:// edis.ifas.ufl.edu, 352-392-1761: One of the only landscape-specific studies of energy use; full text at www.p2pays.org/ ref/13/12127.pdf.

Seahorse Power Company 888-820-0300, http://www.seahorse power.com/press.php: "Big Belly" solar trash compactor.

Neuton cordless electric mowers 888-213-2023, www.neuton.com/: Mows one hour per charge; about $375, spare battery $80.

TerraNova Ecological Landscaping 831-425-3514, www.terra novalandscaping.com/: Santa Cruz firm, crews commute with bike trailers.

Bio-based products

Biobased Manufacturers Association (BMA) **800-331-7022, www.biobased.org/: Alternatives to petro-based products.**

Maintenance: organic and IPM

Search Terms: maintenance + (organic OR IPM) || "integrated pest management" || pesticide-free

IPM Research Unit University of CA at Davis, www.ipm.ucdavis .edu/

IPM Research Center Iowa State University, www.ipm.iastate .edu/ipm/

An Illustrated Guide to Organic Gardening 1991 Sunset Books, Menlo Park CA

Gardening for a Greener Planet: A Chemical-free Approach Jonathan S. Erickson, 1992 Tab Books, Ridge Summit PA

Rodale's All-new Encyclopedia of Organic Gardening Marshall Bradley, Barbara W. Ellis, and Fern M. Bradley, 1993 Rodale Press, Emmaus PA

The Organic Gardener's Handbook of Natural Insect and Disease Control Barbara W. Ellis, Fern Marshall Bradley, and Helen Atthowe, 1996 Rodale Press, Emmaus PA

Pests of the West Whitney Cranshaw, 1998, 2nd ed., Fulcrum Publishing, Golden CO: Many pest books cover only Eastern United States.

Maintenance: on-site waste

Search Terms: composting || "on-site materials"

Composting toilets See *The Resource Guide to Sustainable Landscapes* by Groesbeck, cited in Principle 6, section 2-15.1, for supplier listings.

The Humanure Handbook J. C. Jenkins, 2005, 3rd ed., Jenkins Publishing, Traverse City MI, 866-641-7141

Maintenance: plants

Search Terms: horticulture maintenance || plant care || arboriculture || tree surgery

Arboriculture, Integrated Management of Landscape Trees, Shrubs and Vines Richard W. Harris, 2003, 4th ed., Prentice Hall, New York: Author is an officer of the Council of Tree and Landscape Appraisers.

Modern Arboriculture: A Systems Approach to the Care of Trees and Their Associates Alex L. Shigo, 1991 Shigo and Trees Associates, Durham NH, www.shigoandtrees.com: www.chesco.com/ ~treeman/treeinfo.html, 603-868-7459

Tree Pruning, A Worldwide Photographic Guide Alex L. Shigo, 1992 Shigo and Trees Associates, Durham NH: Includes slide set.

Tree Maintenance T. Pirone, 2000, 7th ed., Oxford Press, Oxford OH

Turfgrass Management A. J. Turgeon, 2004, 7th ed., Prentice Hall, New York

Urban Trees, A Guide for Selection, Maintenance, and Master Planning Leonard E. Phillips Jr., 1993 McGraw-Hill, New York

Maintenance: computers and coordination

Search Terms: landscape + maintenance + computers

The Gardener's Computer Companion Bob Boufford, 1998 No Starch Press, San Francisco, www.nostarch.com, 800-420-7240: Landscape graphics software, plant-selection tools, Web sites—any digital item useful in the landscape, some intriguingly wacky.

Computer-aided Facility Management Eric Teicholz, 1992 McGraw-Hill, New York

Conclusions and Beginnings

If you are thinking a year ahead, sow seed. If you are thinking ten years ahead, plant trees. If you are thinking one hundred years ahead, educate the people.
—Chinese proverb

In the landscape, beginnings and endings overlap. Healthy landscapes are ecosystems, and they survive by constant change. In a self-sustaining landscape, marsh becomes meadow becomes forest, then returns to meadow after fires, or even to marsh after floods. Individual plants and animals die, but the community—the landscape—lives on through a constant "recycling" process.

Sustainability is about fitting into this endless cycle. Many conventional landscapes, and an even higher proportion of buildings, are constructed in defiance of the cycle of growth and decay. The cumulative effect of thousands of sites treated this way is what one author has called a "revenge effect"[1]— *too much* success in disrupting the cycle, which spells decline or even death for the land. With current technology, it *is* possible to break the cycle temporarily, but the costs are enormous.

In this book, we have asked which approaches to landscape construction might reverse these destructive trends, or at least help to do so. What we have found is that there are *many* techniques in landscape work that contribute directly to ecosystem health, or decrease damage already done. Taking the hopeful position that humanity still has a chance to live in harmony with the great cycle of life, we have called these techniques sustainable, regenerative, or environmentally responsible.

Sustainable landscape construction is not merely idealistic—it is available and feasible today. Since our first edition, sustainability has been increasingly in demand, and projects far more widespread. This book includes discussion of many real projects, constructed by real people on real budgets, which include sustainable goals and techniques. We have found increasing numbers of professionals doing this work in nearly every region of North America. Other countries are well ahead of the United States in some areas of sustainable construction, and we have included a few examples from abroad. Sustainable landscape construction may be a young profession, but it is no longer an orphan. A growing network of landscape professionals has adopted, tested, and adapted the methods described. A growing number of do-it-yourselfers are also involved.

Although some are experimental and all are evolving, sustainable landscape methods can and do compete successfully with conventional ones on almost any criteria—economic, functional, aesthetic. They are practical (sometimes with a learning curve), durable, and safe. Some are simply conventional methods done with extra craftsmanship, extra care in siting and scaling them to existing conditions, or extra planning and preparation. Others have been resurrected from tradition. Only a few are truly new, and even these have developed enough of a track record that they cannot be called untried.

Not only is landscape making headed toward sustainability, but the landscape itself is gaining theoreticians' and politicians' respect as the measure or unit most appropriate for studying and planning sustainability. As geographer-planner Adrian Phillips states, "In policy terms the appeal of the idea of landscape is that it unifies rather than disaggregates

338

the factors at work in our relationship with the environment."[2] Landscape is the appropriate scale and level of detail for an increasing number of social and environmental initiatives.

Sustainability in general appears to be a trend strengthened by adversity. State and local jurisdictions have pushed harder for sustainable goals because of federal resistance. The 2006 elections threw out the congressional chairs of six major environment-related committees whose environmental records were as low as Defenders of Wildlife could rank them; these law makers were replaced with representatives whose ratings were in the 80–90 percent range.[3] A substantial part of the population, fifty million strong and a prime market for design, the so-called cultural creatives, rates environment and sustainability as a top priority today.[4] Many support the "Not-So-Big House" movement against the lot-line-hugging McMansion. All these trends are positive signs that sustainable design is not a passing fad.

We concluded that sustainable landscape methods were realistic in 2000, and in many ways the profession reached a "tipping point" about sustainability at that time.[5] The ultimate conclusion of this book still depends, in 2007, on further growth in our field. It remains up to committed individuals to apply green principles creatively. Thus, as we end this book a second time, two questions remain, not about what is feasible today, but about influencing the future. These are just as important, if not more so, today as they were just before Y2K.

The first question is this: does present sustainable practice suggest any general themes to guide and expand the landscape professions of the future? Seven key ideas are briefly discussed below, linking together practical principles and techniques from earlier chapters that at first glance might not seem related. These themes or strategies are *not* essential to day-to-day work in sustainable landscape construction, though they may help. Their real value, we believe, will be for those professionals who can step back, even for a moment, and take a longer view, looking to chart a course *beyond* what can be done today.

The second question about the future of sustainable landscape construction is that of education, both professional and public. Unless new students in landscape architecture, construction and construction management, architecture, planning, and engineering are exposed to sustainable methods, they will simply perpetuate the conventional past. This chapter lists a number of specific, and we believe positive, changes for professional schools to consider. It also describes some built landscapes that educate the *public* about sustainability and natural process. In doing so, these projects argue the cause of sustainability and can also become environmental art.

This book describes a changing profession whose focus is also ever-changing. Appropriately enough, the conclusions of this book are beginnings, too.

Learning from the Landscape: Themes and Strategies

Bringing together in one place so many tested and specific methods of landscape work reveals several underlying strategies, from which the specific methods have grown. These themes concern broad ways of dealing with the landscape—in the strict sense where "dealing" means negotiating, exchanging, and interacting. Clearly this is no exhaustive list. Themes or strategies like these, we believe, can guide future creativity and adaptation in our profession. They are also strengths that many landscape professionals already have, and can build on. In these areas, what our professions have learned from the landscape is in short supply—and growing demand—among related professions such as architecture and engineering. These themes offer a direction in which to lead.

Keywords

The themes that emerge from this book can be stated as seven key words, each linked to the others. Although there are certainly others, recalling this abbreviated list may be useful:

• Decentralization
• Coordination
• Resilience
• Synergy

- Community
- Integration
- Vision.

Deal with Landscape Issues near Their Source

As we have researched successful projects and methods of sustaining the land, we have heard this theme expressed time and again: *work close to the source.* Storm water and erosion are best managed with many small structures near the top of the watershed, the "source" of the runoff. Porous paving infiltrates raindrops almost literally *where they fall*—simulating the age-old relationship between healthy soil and precipitation. To keep invasive plants and animals from overrunning native ecosystems, importation and quarantine restrictions *where they enter the country* are far more effective than trying to eradicate a pest that has spread across a whole continent. These examples have one thing in common: acting at the source, where the problem is smallest. This concept resonates with many ancient texts, among them the T'ao T'e Ching.[6]

"Close to the source" rephrases E. F. Schumacher's advice that small is beautiful. Small, in dealing with landscapes, also means decentralized. Any environmental service or problem that requires an infrastructure is likely to be more cost effective if it is decentralized. For example, constructed wastewater wetlands can be built to serve one home, or a small cluster—a significant advantage over large conventional treatment plants and their extensive infrastructure. Reuse is preferable to remanufacturing, in part because centralized recycling requires collection and redistribution.

Similarly, solar electricity and wind generation have increasingly shown potential to *place the source near the use,* eliminating not only miles of infrastructure, but also major losses in long-distance transmission. This principle, however, is widely ignored by people trying to produce solar or wind "farms" to transmit energy across a still-inefficient grid.

Dealing with the "small" problems takes on another meaning in ecosystems. For many types of environmental event—floods, fires, storms, and so forth—it is reasonable to take preventive action against the "ten-year" event, the frequent, low-intensity occurrence. It is impractical, costly, and actually destructive to attempt to prevent the hundred-year event. This is an ethical choice that American society frequently gets backward: while it is ethically essential to devote all possible effort to rescuing a child who *has fallen* down a well, it is impractical and counterproductive to devote the same absolute commitment to making it impossible for any child ever to fall down a well. The insistence on total prevention of risk is one of the most anti-sustainable social forces at work in the landscape today.

This, then, is the first theme that emerges from the many landscape techniques discussed in this book: wherever possible, respond to the land in small, site-specific ways coordinated across a region rather than centralized in a single regional facility.

Coordinate Efforts

Coordination itself is a theme of this book. It applies to the multidisciplinary team doing green design and building. It applies to the well-known slogan of thinking globally while acting locally. It applies to involving a whole community, analyzing a whole watershed, or studying energy flows throughout a system.

Coordination can be lost when no one cooperates or plans ahead, but it can also be lost when all planning is centralized. In modern society, both conditions are obstacles to environmentally sound development. Extreme individualism keeps people from participating in decisions, and fuels single-issue lobbying *against* the common good. At the other extreme, convenience for governmental or corporate decision makers can exclude citizens, while economies of scale (often false) justify centralization. Because it makes such a difference to sustainable projects, coordination and cooperation should be high on the landscape professional's list of guiding values.

Rely on Resilience Rather than Strength

Another theme is that living strength comes from flexibility, not rigidity.[7] This is most clear in bioengineering: roots and branches are individually weaker than steel or concrete, but woven together into the soil, they outperform and outlast most rigid engineering structures. They stabilize soil not by resisting water's attack, but by dissipating the flow of energy. Each small branch may deflect a few drops, each root hair holds a few soil particles—but here small is beautiful *and strong*.

The difference between conventional and sustainable pest control also involves resilience. Biological control of pests and diseases relies on living organisms to neutralize infestations (ladybugs to combat aphids, for instance). Being alive, these controls have a resilience of behavior that no chemical can match. They are often specifically targeted to a single type of pest, a quality that pesticide manufacturers have worked hard to mimic with modern chemistry. In many cases, biological control is resilient over time, too: an introduced ladybug population may regenerate itself next year, or anytime the aphid population explodes. No chemical control can do this.

"Organic" methods of soil fertilization also rely on the resilience and endurance of living organisms, instead of the strength of nonliving chemical inputs. It is not that chemicals are simply bad; the issue is that living organisms respond to their environment in ways more complex and interactive, more resilient, than any nonliving chemical reaction.

Almost by definition, successful landscape *maintenance* is about resilience. No matter how well built (or even overbuilt), un-maintained outdoor structures decay sooner or later. Maintained structures, however, can be sustained almost forever—Taos Pueblo, made of mud but replastered every other year, is arguably the oldest structure still in use in America, inhabited a thousand years. Maintenance is about accepting change and growth, and relying on resilience to accommodate change. Especially in landscapes, with their many living components, rigidly resisting change is not even an option.

Resilience also means knowing when not to resist. In particular, the attempts to completely stop all floods, fires, or storms, no matter what size, is a too-rigid approach. Control can work for smaller events, and these are both the majority and the norm; but real resilience is required to survive and accept the rare and overwhelmingly large events, which simply cannot be controlled.

Build for Synergy

In the landscape, multipurpose solutions *sustain*, while single-purpose solutions usually *consume*. Many of the projects we have highlighted set out to solve a single problem and found that several other functions could be met at the same time.

Natural wetlands are a clear example of diverse functions. Constructed wetlands for wastewater treatment almost automatically serve a second function as habitat. With minimal extra expense, they can also function as public parks. The same wetlands, correctly located, provide stormwater infiltration and flood control. Multiple functions make the facility easier to finance, reflecting increased social and ecological value.

Porous paving is another example of at least dual function: supporting traffic and infiltrating precipitation. By accomplishing two functions in a single space, porous paving preserves land for other purposes. Accomplishing more with less, whether space or resources, is clearly desirable for sustainability.

Synergy also means creatively turning one technique into several by noticing similarities. Structural soil and porous paving, for example, are almost identical in materials and form: crushed aggregate protects space for soil in one, for drainage in the other. Crossover concepts like this are worth exploring, and may yield other regenerative, sustainable innovations.

"Multipurpose" also goes beyond human purposes. Landscape design and construction can and should accommodate species other than humans. Particularly in the case of plants, those species in turn provide environmental services that humans need.

Work from Community

Advocates of sustainability often quote the Iroquois awareness that present decisions affect future generations. Similarly, individual decisions also affect the whole web of *community*. The theme of community-based action has appeared repeatedly in the most successful projects described in this book.

Watershed restoration, in particular, benefits from working with the whole human community (everyone who owns or uses land in the watershed) and with the whole biological community (all the species that use or live in the watershed). Similarly, site restoration is seldom about reinstating one species. Rather, it is about restarting a whole community, giving it time and protection to resume self-maintenance.

The ultimate community—those who have important conditions in common—is the bioregion or eco-region. Landscape-based boundaries for decision making simply work better than the arbitrary political lines—and social communities in fact represent shared eco-regional concerns better than they represent states or counties.

Community-based action takes practical form in projects driven *from the start* by public input. Simultaneously, information is gathered for an understanding of the whole site, seen as a community in a regional context. These community inputs can seldom be replaced successfully either by the wishes of an individual expert, engineer, or owner, or by analyzing only those site features that meet a preconceived development purpose. Truly regenerative, sustainable, or ecological design grows from roots in both human and biological communities.

INTEGRATE NATURAL AND MANMADE

In the landscape, human presence and natural dynamics are best when integrated. Dividing the two puts humans and nature in separate jail cells. Integration is essential even in the "wilderness" preserved for scenic or scientific value—humans must fit in by obeying rules that favor the nonhuman. In the landscapes where humanity dominates, integration is also of great value. Here, it means including at least enough of nature to sustain human well-being.

In a practical sense, integration applies to landscape technology. Bioengineering, for instance, is a pragmatic integration of human technology (the "hard" components and systematic design) with natural dynamics (living plants and soil). Because humans cannot actually create life, a great many landscape technologies actually rely on integration between nonhuman organisms and human construction.

This integration is reflected visually in many of the best-loved landscapes of the world. Japanese gardens frequently mix artificially cut stone with naturally shaped ones, or dry bamboo fencing against a living bamboo grove. Examples of this are less common in European traditions, but they do exist: Luis Barragan's seamless steps in Pedregal's natural rock outcrops, or Richard Haag's formal, hedged reflecting pool amid the Bloedel Reserve woods. This inte-

grative form of design artistry (and the superb craft required to build it) deserve more study and recognition than they have received in recent Western history. Integration is not complete until it satisfies the eye and mind.

ENVISION RICHER FORMS

Many of the techniques described in this book require the ability to envision forms more complex than those of conventional engineering. Although simplicity is a valued goal in design, simplicity in sustainable landscapes comes more appropriately from integration than from geometric minimalism.

Even a slight increase in the complexity of form can result in major improvements in function. The honeycomb structure of porous concrete is slightly more complex than solid cement—yet the increase in function is significant. In wetlands, the convoluted form of the root zone functions far better than a simple mechanical filter, and the variable depths and edges within the basin function better than an engineered, rectangular tank of even depth. The Root-Path Trench is considerably more complex in form than a simple planting pit, but dramatically increases the odds of tree survival.

Envisioning and building these more complex forms places new demands on everyone associated with landscape work. Dreaming up and drawing a complex form, especially a truly nature-like one, is more challenging than designing a simple geometric structure. Reading the plans and building the form challenges the contractor. Understanding why he or she should pay for it is not always simple for the client.

Agent-based modeling and "complexity theory," along with fractal geometry, are important new tools—still underutilized—for envisioning richer yet better-integrated landscapes. The design theorist's prejudice against "nature mimicry" remains a ball and chain that prevents many landscape professionals from taking a serious second look at naturalistic form and function.

In some ways, the will and ability to break free from oversimplified convention and to dream with greater richness is this book's largest theme. Each of our other themes is richer and more complex than its conventional counterpart: integration is richer than overspecialization, community is richer than isolationism, resilience is more complex than rigidity, and so on. Educating ourselves, our students, and the public to understand and appreciate the richness of sustainable landscapes is an immensely important goal.

Green Education in Design and Construction

Education and training are critical to any profession, both for maintaining its standards and enriching its vision. Landscape architecture, landscape contracting, and horticulture are no exceptions. The curriculum of today very directly influences the practices of tomorrow. So do requirements for licensing and for continuing professional education.

To make sustainable and regenerative practice a reality, teaching and training need to be in line with environmental goals. This applies to specialized training in any landscape profession, or in the related professions of architecture, planning, and engineering. Anyone who has had any recent contact with these branches of education knows that sustainability is of growing interest to students—and teachers. In many cases, however, current course content and teaching methods are in conflict with the trends outlined in this book.

James Steele, in his book *Sustainable Architecture*, outlines changes in curriculum to encourage environmental knowledge and attitudes among architecture students.[8] Summarized here, these suggestions apply equally to landscape architecture; most also apply to the training of contractors, engineers, and planners.

- Assign studio problems that involve real sites, real issues, and review by real clients (or realistic role playing).
- Simulate in studio the collaborative team approach students will encounter in their jobs.
- Emphasize holistic context (both ecological and cultural) in lectures and assignments. "Pure-design" assignments should be reserved for specific teaching purposes.
- Broaden perspectives by basing class projects on "appropriate technology" or setting them in Third World situations.

- Require the use of local materials, energy estimates, and recycling as part of solving any design assignment.
- Encourage students to challenge policy limits during design; discuss (but don't grade) how completed projects may conflict with existing policies.
- Foster the ability to think about places from multiple perspectives: diverse cultural meanings of the same place, as well as multiple functionality.
- Expect students to plan for maintenance and constant change, both deliberate and accidental.
- Walk the talk: encourage students and faculty to make their school and their own lives more sustainable.

These goals for education are quite similar to the 1992 Rio Earth Summit recommendations for change in the construction industry.[9] From that list and our own experience, we would add four more educational goals:

- Emphasize site selection (regional) and siting (within the property) in all design assignments.
- Include regional and vernacular traditions of design/building in the main curriculum, not merely as electives.
- Include "constructability" as part of every design review. Offer design-build classes, in which students actually construct what they design, perhaps donating it for public use.
- Insist that students understand the climate-change implications of every design or construction project; use Architecture2030.org as a fundamental course "reading." (Architecture2010 is the parallel effort to change architectural curricula; it is relevant to landscape teaching even while tending to ignore landscapes.)

Many teachers have already arrived at similar ideas, and some schools have made considerable strides toward greener curriculum. (An example is Brian Dunbar, a Colorado State University professor who takes landscape and interior design students to an "eco-tourism" resort in the Virgin Islands as an intensive workshop in sustainable development and technology.[10]) There is a great deal of inertia to overcome, however, and conventional thinking still re-creates itself in each graduating class. Design students still get the message, subtly or blatantly, that the most idiosyncratic and outrageous forms of creativity are the best. Engineering and contracting students are still taught "no-nonsense" and numerical attitudes that dismiss important social and ecological values; they are also indoctrinated with great fear of both regulation and liability. Sadly, accepted wisdom is often perpetuated unthinkingly, by default rather than intent.

Professional registration exams currently place almost no emphasis on sustainability. To some extent this is understandable because the exam sets a *minimum* standard of competence. Changes in practice, education, and the law, however, are eventually reflected in the registration requirements. In time, we hope to see exam questions that focus on greener structures than the tired old joist-sizes-for-decks or retaining-wall-footing problems. Similarly, as building codes become greener, we would expect to see this reflected in professional continuing education. A number of "alternative" courses do exist, but too often they *still* seem like voices crying in a wilderness.

Any change toward professional environmental awareness is, in effect, a step toward equalizing the influence of landscape compared with that of architecture. Professional registration laws today give architects and engineers (and the "hard" methods they represent) great power over site design—in some states, even registered landscape architects cannot seal a drainage plan, for example. This legislated inequality hinders landscape architects from instituting many sustainable site practices. Educating architects and engineers about sustainable alternatives, and lobbying for increased authority to sign drawings for such alternatives, needs to be an expanded part of the ASLA's agenda in particular.

Educators—and students—have a special opportunity to help sustainable landscape making evolve. Many are already taking this initiative, and we hope many more will begin to do so.

The public also needs to learn about sustainable landscapes as a professional activity. Although a landscape architect has finally hit the big time—played by Jude Law as a lead character in the 2006 movie *Break-*

ing and Entering—the character represents the most controversial type of landscape thinker, a deconstructivist who sees naturalistic design as "fraudulent advocacy" and "miniature gestures of appeasement."[11] As this book makes clear, we respect that position's validity, but also its limits. Landscape professionals need to educate their public far more broadly.

Education Means Research, Too

Most institutions of higher education include research in their mission, and education about sustainability needs to do much more of this. Research and documentation about landscapes, however, is not just an abstract and theoretical subject: its subject is largely real-world projects and their real-time effects. This means that research needs serious involvement of landscape practitioners.

One of the most pressing needs in green building is performance documentation. Without documented before-and-after data, no project in the built environment can be evaluated properly, and few well-supported conclusions about the causes of its success or shortcomings can be drawn. Neither baseline nor post-occupancy data are routinely gathered for either conventional or cutting-edge projects; this is unfortunately true both of architecture and landscape work. Even if gathered, these data are seldom cataloged, compared, or compiled.

One of the frustrations that (like most writers on sustainability) we have felt with this book in both its editions is that the work we are reporting feels right and makes sense—but we cannot give more concrete proof than that of its effectiveness. This is common in new fields, but also symptomatic of a build it and forget it approach that is very specific to the design world.

Every "green" project—landscape, infrastructure, or building—for the next decade needs to be treated as a science project as well as a pragmatic job. Much more than a set of points like LEED (valuable in its own right), there needs to be a shared method of documenting baseline conditions and actual performance of everything we construct. Today, for far too many sustainability-driven projects, no one can show what the pre-construction soil erosion rate actually was, nor how much it actually increased or decreased as a result of design or construction techniques. Pre- and post-project erosion is an example of standard data items that should be collected and placed in a national database.

Academic and practicing landscape architects, public and private sector, need to make such data a priority. Research on performance of sustainability techniques doesn't need to go on forever—just until there is clear evidence of what works, under what circumstances. Best Management Practices for sustainable landscapes will never be as cut and dried as current engineering standards (and that is for the better); but they need to be far better grounded in careful observation and measurement of actual performance.

Landscapes as Public Environmental Education

One often-overlooked power of the built landscape is to educate. Landscapes can tell the story—often eloquently—of a place and the people who use or used it. The story might focus on regional ecology, lost or displaced peoples, or industrial archaeology.

Methods of storytelling in landscapes are varied, limited primarily by creativity. Interpretive signs and self-guided tours are simple and effective ways of narrating site history. Educational landscapes can go far beyond these basic methods, however.

This book describes several projects that show visitors something about ecological process. These were termed "eco-revelatory." Places of this sort have also been called "narrative landscapes" or "interpretive landscapes." Whatever they are called, and whatever methods of storytelling they use, such projects are an important tool for sustainability. They raise public awareness of landscape as a vital force in history and in contemporary life. Revealing and interpreting the landscape is a way of working against cultural tendencies that tempt people to ignore the landscape except when they are exploiting it.

Landscapes for schools, libraries, and museums are particularly suited as storytelling spaces. Gilbert AZ's Riparian Preserve (Figure 4.32), located next to the town library, is an example. Like a great number of

constructed or restored wetlands, it has taken on functions traditionally associated with botanic gardens and nature centers.

Los Padillas Elementary School, in Albuquerque NM's South Valley, shows how a sustainable landscape can have double value as an educational facility. When an older sewage-treatment system failed odoriferously, Campbell Okuma Perkins Associates and Southwest Wetlands designed a constructed wetland on school grounds. With pathways, seating, and shelters around the wetland, the site fascinates schoolchildren and serves as an outdoor classroom for biology studies. The children of Los Padillas will grow up with fewer NIMBY and out-of-sight inhibitions

Figure 11.1 Landscapes and education reflect each other perfectly. Students at Los Padillas Elementary (Albuquerque NM) are fascinated by the treatment wetland that serves their building—and learn about biology, ecology, and technology in lessons held outdoors. (*Project:* Campbell Okuma Perkins Associates and Southwest Wetlands. *Photo:* Kim Sorvig.)

Figure 11.2   DPA's Xeriscape Garden eloquently shows that San Diego is at the end of the California water-supply pipe. (*Project and Photo:* Deneen Powell Atelier.)

than most of their peers, a direct result of familiarity with a sustainable landscape

The Jardin Encore (Figure 6.12) performs a similar service for recycling, making it familiar, beautiful, and fun. Every year, King County WA constructs a demonstration garden of recycled materials at the regional flower show. Like the grand prize recycled-products house in the America Recycles Day contest (p. 224), these gardens educate by making recycling real and attractive.

Interpretive landscapes are needed that directly tell the story of sustainable place making. One of the best of these is Deneen Powell Atelier's Xeriscape Garden at Cuyamongue, outside San Diego. The story of how gardens are created, and how they can be more sustainable, gets a comprehensive and entertaining look. Serious information combines with magic and imagination, creating a connection that goes beyond either how-to demonstration gardens or fun-focused playgrounds.

Visiting places where remarkable things happened is a fascination for many people. At memorials, monuments, and historic sites, "being right there" creates a powerful experience that no distant book or museum can match. This same experience can be used to educate people about *natural history*, too, as evidenced by Riverwalk, in Memphis TN.

Riverwalk is a topographic model of the Lower Mississippi—and what a model! Built of concrete at one inch to the mile, it stretches the entire length of a previously deserted island in the great river itself. Riverwalk has transformed Mud Island from waste space into a major attraction. Water flows through the modeled meanders, past street maps of major cities inset into the concrete banks. Visitors, striding thirty "miles" at a step, get a clear and unforgettable sense of how the river works, enhanced by being able to look out onto the real river only yards away.

The redesign of Zion National Park goes one step further: the landscape itself was the focus of the proj-

Figure 11.3 A giant purple pop-up head is a fantastic image for serious information—using non-potable water for irrigation (Xeriscape Garden). (*Project and Photo:* Deneen Powell Atelier.)

Figure 11.4 Landscapes can tell their own story eloquently. Riverwalk (Memphis TN) is a one inch to one mile topographic model of the entire Lower Mississippi, located on a sandbar in the river itself. (*Project:* Roy P. Farrover, FAIA. *Photo:* Kim Sorvig.)

ect, around which even building design was organized. In fact, many functions of the visitor center were deliberately moved outdoors to immerse visitors in the landscape—and also save costs. Shuttle buses replaced private cars, again because of the impact on the landscape and on people's experience of this awesome landscape. Interpretive signage, which in most such parks focuses exclusively on nature, points out the environmental responsibility and sustainable features of the park's human structures.

Public environmental knowledge and awareness are key factors in whether sustainability will ever be achieved. In designing and constructing sustainable landscapes, look for opportunities to tell site visitors what is going on. Whether it is a serious interpretive project or a whimsical use of recycled materials, the *story told* may be as important as the functions fulfilled.

Thinking One Hundred Years Ahead

In the last half of the twentieth century, Americans along with much of the world's population went from complacency about the environment to concern. Despite the usual tendency to shoot the messenger, the bad news was eventually turned into action: public outcry and changes in social expectations about how to treat the land. Landscape professionals played a significant role in that cycle of change, from speaking at the first Earth Day to getting environmental impact assessment into standard practice.

Today, a new or renewed cycle of change is under way. Many people feel alarm and despair over the state of planet Earth. As with any process of change, there is resistance and denial from entrenched interests, and understandable burnout among those who have lived with worry for too long. Yet simultaneously

Figure 11.5 Zion National Park's majestic landscape drove the design of buildings, transportation, and interpretation—which includes information about how sustainable structures fit in. (*Project:* National Park Service, Denver Design Assistance Center. *Photo:* Kim Sorvig.)

and in parallel, more and more people are taking action, if only because inaction is unbearable. Regulatory progress, despite attempts to roll it back, has reined in many sources of major pollution and brought conservation and restoration into common practice. In the next cycle, the action is in bringing change home, down to the details and difficult choices that affect the built environments where we live. In these actions, landscape professionals once again have important roles to play, and we are happy to report that students and young professionals are taking up this challenge in increasing numbers, along with many of their more established colleagues.

Documentable destruction has been so widespread that people have seriously questioned whether nature is dead or was merely a "construct," a nostalgic cultural superstition. But nature is not a thing; it is a dynamic process. If humans ignore it, nature will simply outlive us, bloodied but unbowed. Remembering that we are part of nature, and that it deserves care, respect, and in some places even privacy, is probably our last best hope for survival as a species. May the techniques and attitudes described in this book be part of realizing that fragile and essential hope.

Notes

Introduction: Sustainability in Context

1. Robert France, "The Promise and the Reality of Landscape Architecture in Sustaining Nature," Harvard Graduate School of Design newsletter (Spring–Summer 2003).

2. The latest instance of this persistent theme is Heidi Hohmann and Joern Langhorst, "Landscape Architecture: and Apocalyptic Manifesto," PDF downloadable from www.public.iastate.edu/~isitdead.

3. Meg Calkins, "Green Building Practice Survey," *Landscape and Urban Planning* 73 (Oct 2005): 29.

4. Sonja Bisbee Wulff and Colorado Public Interest Research Group, "Vast Open Spaces Vanishing," *Coloradoan*, 28 Dec 1998, 1.

5. This definition is so widespread that its original author is hard to determine. It was used in the widely circulated World Commission on Environment and Development, Brundtland, Gro H., ed., *Our Common Future* (Oxford: Oxford University Press, 1987). A similar but expanded definition is given in a review of sustainability concepts in John D. Peine, ed., *Ecosystem Management for Sustainability* (Boca Raton FL: Lewis, 1999). 3: "Sustainable development integrates economic, environmental and social values during planning; distributes benefits equitably across socioeconomic strata and gender upon implementation; and ensures that opportunities for continuing development remain undiminished to future generations." The ten published sets of sustainability principles reviewed (Tables 1–10) stress the dynamic, boundary-crossing, and semipredictable qualities of living systems; the need for coordination and teamwork; and the value of open public involvement in sustainability decisions.

6. Robert L. Thayer Jr., "The Experience of Sustainable Design," *Landscape Journal* 8 (1989): 101. Quoted in Robert France's very useful article (above), "The Promise and the Reality of Landscape Architecture in Sustaining Nature." The part of the CELA definition that may be questionable is the idea of increasing species diversity—valid for damaged sites, but potentially damaging if applied to healthy ones.

7. "There is no doubt … that sustainability has been taken up as a rallying cry by two completely different factions and has entirely opposite meanings for each," according to James Steele, *Sustainable Architecture: Principles, Paradigms and Case Studies* (New York: McGraw-Hill, 1997), 22. Steele calls the concept a contradiction in terms; his two factions are, loosely, green capitalists (the Earth as resources to manage) and green socialists (the Earth as the focus of social reform).

8. BASMAA, *Grow It! The Less-Toxic Garden* (San Francisco: Bay Area Stormwater Management Agencies Association, 1997).

9. For thoughtful critique of the potential for authoritarianism in pursuit of ecological goals, see Randolph Hester, *Design for Ecological Democracy* (Cambridge MA: MIT Press, 2006). At the far extreme, an attempt to equate all ecologists with Nazism is analyzed in Kim Sorvig, "Natives and Nazis: An Imaginary Conspiracy in Ecological Design," *Landscape Journal* 13, no. 1 (1994): 58–61.

10. To put things in perspective, recall that the Second Law of Thermodynamics guarantees that over the long term nothing is sustainable!

11. Our evaluations are not intended to be equivalent to instrumented scientific measurement (such as energy inputs and outputs, for example), although they may be based on such studies.

12. Though legitimate programs are of great value, there have been problems with other "green building" schemes. Some programs are, in effect, merely fronts for utility companies who wish to appear green and to promote their brand of fuel or power as greener than others; others have been revamped when it was found that the criteria were "allowing one strong category [of environmental performance] to make up for others." See Alex Wilson, "Green Builder Programs Proliferating," EBN 4, no. 1 (1995): 6–7.

13. Studies of constructability (on video as well as in print) are available from the Construction Industry Institute, Austin TX, 512-232-2000 or http://construction-institute.org/.

14. LEED 1.0, essentially a pilot, was released in 1998. An "expert charrette" (in which Sorvig took part) significantly revised the system for release as LEED 2.0 in March 2000. A further update, LEED 2.1, is primarily about streamlining the documentation process to overcome criticism that the bureaucratic effort was too ponderous. The USGBC planned to revise the system every three years. LEED 3.0, however, has been expected since 2003, but was still accepting ideas and input as late as August 2006.

15. The LEED program's goal and point system is described in section L.1 of *The HOK Guidebook to Sustainable Design*, ed. Sandra Mendler and Wm. Odell (New York: Wiley, 2000). This title is also an excellent general reference on green architecture.

16. A standard set by the American Society of Heating, Refrigeration, and Air-conditioning Engineers.

17. See www.usgbc.org/, Web site of the US Green Building Council, which certifies both projects and designers.

18. Nadav Malin, "Green Globes Emerges to Challenge LEED," *IEBN* 14 no. 3 (Mar 2005): online at www.buildinggreen.com/.

19. Unless otherwise noted, statistics and quotes in this section are from Meg Calkins, "LEEDing the Way: A Look at the Way Landscape Architects Are Using the LEED Green Building Rating System," LAM, May 2001, 36.

20. In fact, if they subscribe to Newt Gingrich's theories, any environmental limits on their right to develop constitutes a

"takings" and gives them the right to sue whoever established that limit as a legal requirement.

21. The terms "Permaculture" and "Xeriscape" have both been trademarked to ensure that they are not abused. Like all other trademarks referenced in this book, they remain the property of their respective owners. The success of trademarking landscape design approaches as a defensive strategy has been mixed, because most theories overlap with others.

22. HOK Architects, *Sustainable Design Guide*, ed. Sandra Mendler (Washington DC: HOK Architects, 1998), iv–vi.

23. Ibid., iv.

24. In this regard, many architecture firms are either ahead of landscape ones, or simply more vocal about it. ARUP, SOM, Gehry (whose focus is on complex structural coordination as much as or more than sustainability), and many others recognize that if the built environment must change, the methods of envisioning and realizing require new teamwork.

25. One of the best sites for detailed information and research supporting these allegations is www.ejrc.cau.edu/, the Environmental Justice Resource Center (EJRC). It offers extensive links (though some are nonfunctional or dated) to hundreds of other sources. The information in this section is primarily compiled from EJRC and a few of its main links.

26. Environmental justice applies to transportation facilities, many of which are risky and polluting. There is some evidence that these considerations have helped shape the Federal Highway Administration's recent shift toward "context sensitive design" of roads, discussed on p. 202.

27. Kim Sorvig, "The Wilds of South Central," LAM (Apr 2002) reports on one of Hester and Edmiston's successful projects, and on demographic research into cultural support for nature conservation.

28. Randolph T. Hester, *Design for Ecological Democracy* (Cambridge MA: MIT Press, 2006), 6–7. The bibliography of this book lists extensive, landscape-specific resources on community participatory methods and environmental justice, including many important articles by Hester himself.

29. Jared Diamond, *Guns, Germs, and Steel: The Fates of Human Societies* (New York: Norton, 1997). Diamond's follow-up volume, *Collapse: How Societies Choose to Fail or Succeed* (New York: Viking, 2005), details how societies that fail to adapt to local ecological assets have collapsed. Both are required readings in Sorvig's University of New Mexico seminar on sustainable landscapes.

30. Rob Thayer made a particularly convincing presentation of these contextual threats at the Sustainable Landscapes Conference, Sacramento CA, Feb 2004.

31. For specifics, see the nonpartisan Natural Resources Defense Council's magazine *OnEarth*, Spring 2003, esp. 10 and 34, and www.nrdc.org/bushrecord/.

32. Vinee Tong, "Buying into Green Building," *Santa Fe New Mexican*, 8 Mar 2007, C-7. Cites "extra" cost for green features as up to 15 percent. This figure is more than double the more common figures (see next note) and appears to originate with building-industry conservatives.

33. Earthtalk, "Do Buildings with Green Features Cost More?" *Santa Fe New Mexican*, 8 Mar 2007, C-7. Unlike industry reports, this one analyzes life-cycle savings, not just capital costs.

34. Brad Knickerbocker, "The Changing Face of America," *Christian Science Monitor*, 15 Oct 2006.

35. Gillian Flaccus, "Hispanics Take Strong Stands on Environment," Associated Press syndicated report, 13 Oct 2006. See related information in Sorvig, "Wilds of South Central."

36. See http://vertical-visions.com/nps.php, which discusses a fatal October 1999 protest against a National Parks prohibition of "base jumping" (parachuting off cliffs).

37. This matches well with other researchers, particularly from Canada, who have found that in developed countries, construction, maintenance, and decommissioning of buildings uses over 40 percent of all annual energy. (The DOE statistics group energy by economic segment—residential, commercial, industrial, and transportation. Mazria's analysis recognizes that all segments use buildings, and regroups the statistics accordingly.)

38. Very similar goals, released in 1997 and targeted for achievement by 2003, were the National Building Goals, from the National Institute of Standards and Technology and the National Science and Technology Council. They aimed for 50 percent reduction in operation and energy costs and in waste and pollution, along with a 50 percent increase in durability, across the construction industry. Reported in Steve Cardamore, "The National Construction Goals," *Southern Building*, Jan–Feb 1997, a magazine apparently no longer published; these goals do not appear in any Web search.

39. The first edition's source was "Study: Land Use Affects Weather," Associated Press syndicated report, 9 Dec 1998. The study's author, Roger Pielke, has a research group with many valuable publications related to land-use and climate change. See www.climatesci.colorado.edu/.

40. Climate effects of land clearance (or landscape transformation, or land-use change) has been estimated by several expert groups. The estimates are listed in the citations that follow, in order from low to high. Some estimate CO_2 (or all greenhouse gases) released when land is cleared; others include direct warming and drying effects, such as exposure of soil to sunlight; and some summarize their findings in terms of the relative importance of fuel burning versus land clearing. The slow but extensive land changes wrought by prehistoric and early historic agriculture are also considered to have raised CO_2 levels, but these figure only in one discussion of the issue. Obviously, these estimates are not completely comparable, but all indicate that the relationship is significant.

15–20 percent: The lowest estimate comes from a 1997 World Meteorological Organization paper called "Common Questions About Climate Change," by K. E. Trenberth et al., "Land Use Changes Are Responsible for 15 to 20% of Current Carbon Dioxide Emissions."

23 percent: "Potential Impacts of Climate Change on Agriculture and Food Supply" by Cynthia Rosenzweig and Daniel Hillel, US Global Change Research Information Office, in their newsletter *Consequences* 1, no. 2 (Summer 1995); agricultural emissions, 15 percent, plus land-use changes, 8 percent.

24 percent: Columbia University's CIESIN (Center for International Earth Science Information Network) and NASA's SEDAC (Socioeconomic Data Application Center) ascribe 24 percent of total greenhouse gas emissions to forestry practices

and land-use change, including soil disturbance. See www
.ciesin.columbia.edu/.

32 percent: The IPCC (Intergovernmental Panel on Climate Change) states that 2.5 Gt (million tons) of CO_2 are generated by landscape transformation, and 5.2 Gt by fuel combustion. This translates to 32 percent from land clearing and related changes. See www.ipcc.ch/.

50 percent or more: In an interview with Rebecca Lindsey of NASA's Earth observatory (http://earthobservatory .nasa.gov/Study/DeepFreeze/, 17 May 2005), Gordon Bonan, a climate modeler for the National Center for Atmospheric Research in Boulder CO, stated, "Land cover change is as big an influence on regional and local climate and weather as doubled atmospheric carbon dioxide—perhaps even bigger." Bonan's findings agree with Pielke's, whom he credits for "bringing people around to the importance" of landscape change as a factor in global climate change.

Tim Flannery, in *The Weather Makers* (New York: Atlantic Monthly Press, 2005), esp. 28 and 66, notes the likelihood that very early agriculture, from about 8,000 years ago to 1800 CE when the Industrial Revolution took hold, increased global CO_2 levels from 160 parts per million (ppm) to 280. By comparison, the rise caused by industrialization is from 280 to 380 ppm, today's level. Clearing, burning, rice-paddy flooding, and other farming activities are thus believed to have created "The Long Summer," the unusually warm and stable period in which all agricultural humanity has lived for the past many millennia. If this is accurate, land clearance produced a 120 ppm increase prior to industrialization, and 15 to 32 percent of the 100 ppm increase *since* industrialization. This would mean that land use is responsible for **61 to 69 percent** of human-caused greenhouse gas increases.

41. The report is available from www.ucsusa.org/news/press _release/ExxonMobil-GlobalWarming-tobacco.html. It particularly links ExxonMobil money to "bought" science from the George C. Marshall Institute, Annapolis Center for Science-based Public Policy, and the Committee for a Constructive Tomorrow, and climate-change-deniers Frederick Singer, John Christy, Willie Soon, Patrick Michaels, and Sallie Baliunas. This public disinformation campaign was in addition to over $60 million spent on lobbying politicians directly; one "expert" associated with it, Phil Cooney, went from an oil trade association, to the President's Council on Environmental Quality, to ExxonMobil! Similar undermining tactics have been aimed against many specific sustainable technologies that threaten oil interests.

42. For details, see www.grida.no/climate/ipcc/land_use/ index.htm, the "IPCC Special Report on Land Use, Land-use Change And Forestry." The mechanisms by which land clearance or deforestation affects climate are common knowledge; what is new is putting these effects together.

43. See Tim Flannery, *Weather Makers*. Other CO_2-exchange mechanisms involve the oceans, oceanic plankton, and carbon-based rocks, such as limestone. These hold far larger *volumes* of carbon than do plants and soil, but it is the relative *speed* of the cycles of uptake and release that makes vegetation and soil the most important site of atmospheric CO_2 exchange. Fossil-fuel combustion is, of course, plant based.

44. Two identically titled books make a compelling case for the belief that soil management is the key to understanding any society's rise or fall. Edward Hyams, *Soil and Civilization* (New York: HarperCollins, 1976); Milton Whitney, *Soil and Civilization* (New York: D. Van Nostrand Company, 1925). A third book by this title, by Elyne Mitchell, is an Australian work; out of print; it can be obtained electronically through www .soilandhealth.org/copyform.aspx?bookcode=010163.

45. "Clearance" does not need to be total to cause most of the warming effects noted. To be truly accurate, clearance should be discussed in percentage terms. One hundred percent clearance would mean bare soil. The baseline (0 percent clearance) is biomass that is equivalent to the region's most mature successional vegetation. Deliberate removal of 20 percent of this mass would be "20 percent clearance." If 100 percent clearance causes x amount of warming, 20 percent clearance probably causes similar effects at something like 20 percent intensity. To our knowledge, the exact relationship cannot be quantified without further research, and it is probably variable by region.

46. Excerpt from Alex de Sherbinin, "Land-use and Land-cover Change," http://sedac.ciesin.columbia.edu/tg/guide _frame.jsp?rd=LU&ds=1, joint project of CIESIN and the Land-Use and Land-Cover Change International Project Office, Louvain-la-Neuve, Belgium; see Web site for further details.

47. Paul Hawken, *The Ecology of Commerce* (New York: HarperCollins, 1993), 21.

48. Associated Press, "Housing Construction Booms; Industrial Output Flat in January," *New Mexican*, 18 Feb 1999.

49. For the full visual impact of forest clearance in the United States, see comparative maps in *Smithsonian*, Sep 1999, 22. For a global deforestation map, see www.greenpeace.org/ international/campaigns/forests/our-disappearing-forests/.

50. Lost to agriculture is the United States Department of Agriculture (USDA) estimate; it is not specifically about clearing land that previously supported native vegetation communities. The 1.5 million acre estimate is based on the US NRCS National Resource Inventory, which shows that in 1997, 98 million acres of US land had been developed, a 34 percent increase since 1982. Assuming the same rate each year (the rate is actually increasing), this would mean 1.6 million acres developed each year. The 500,000-acre estimate is based on new housing starts, commercial construction, and new roads statistics from various US agencies. These tend not to include accurate areas for landscape around the facilities.

51. Statistics cited in Charles Lockwood, "Save the Shade," *Hemispheres Magazine*, Sep 2006, 60–63.

52. Earthtalk, "Which Trees Best Combat Global Warming?" *Environment*, 12 Feb 2007. See the research center's Web site, www.fs.fed.us/ne/syracuse/.

53. Chris J. Hanley, "Carbon Trading Creates Questionable Deals," AP syndicated report, 22 Oct 2006. For US state emissions totals and per-capita rankings, see www.tonto.eia .doe.gov/state/. To calculate your own CO_2 footprint, go to www.safeclimate.net/calculator/. The IPCC recently estimated that increasing the cost of gasoline one dollar per gallon would fund stabilization of greenhouse gases by 2030;

this cost has also been compared to about 3 percent of economic growth worldwide (Marc Kaufman, "Scientists Put Price Tag on Strategies to Combat Global Warming," *Washington Post*, 3 May 2007).

54. "First Look," *Consumer Reports*, Jan 2007, 7.

55. Lewis Ziska, weed ecologist, USDA Crop Systems and Global Change Laboratory, quoted in *Life* (author unknown), 25 Aug 2006.

56. Rachel Kaplan and Stephen Kaplan have explored this concept in several books, including *The Experience of Nature: A Psychological Perspective* (Cambridge: Cambridge University Press, 1989).

57. E. O. Wilson, *Biophilia* (Cambridge MA: Harvard University, 1986).

58. Alex Wilson, "Biophilia in Practice: Buildings That Connect People with Nature," EBN, Jul 2006, www.buildinggreen .com/.

59. Robert L. Thayer Jr., "The Experience of Sustainable Landscapes," *Landscape Journal* (Fall 1989): 101–9.

60. Joan Nassauer, "Messy Ecosystems, Orderly Frames," *Landscape Journal*, 14, no. 2, 1995: 161–170.

61. William MacElroy and Daniel Winterbottom, "Toward a New Garden," *Critiques of Built Works of Landscape Architecture*, LSU School of Landscape Architecture (Fall 1997): 10–14.

62. William Thompson, "Cleansing Art," LAM, Jan 1997, 70.

63. Participants in the eco-revelatory committee were Brenda Brown, Terry Harkness, Douglas Johnston, Beth Randall, and Robert Riley.

64. Peter Whoriskey, "Louisiana Erosion Project Calls for River Diversion," *Washington Post*, 2 May 2007, 5.

65. Benoit Mandelbrot, *The Fractal Geometry of Nature*, updated ed. (New York: W. H. Freeman, 1983). Although many other books (and movies!) have built on Mandelbrot's work, this remains a classic explanation of a truly revolutionary new discipline. See esp. chapter 1, "Theme"; for a straightforward graphic that explains the concept of fractals, see the Koch snowflake illustrations on pages 42–44.

66. J. W. Baish, Y. Gazit, N. Safabakhsh, M. Leunig, L. T. Baxter, and R. K. Jain, "Fractal Characteristics of Tumor Vascular Architecture: Significance and Implications," *Microcirculation* 4 (1997): 395–402.

67. For an overview of this research, see John P. Wiley Jr., "Help Is on the Way," *Smithsonian*, Jul 1999, 22–24.

68. "Wild" is another difficult term. Most places on earth are in some way influenced by human management, politics, pollution, or preservation. In this sense, no place is pristine. This fact is not, in our view, an excuse for failing to preserve those places that are closest to being wild, those that are most nearly self-sustaining. It is not the romance of being untouched that makes these places important, but rather what they show about the dynamics of biodiversity and how they preserve diversity lost elsewhere. Further discussion in Kim Sorvig, "Nature/Culture/Words/Landscapes," *Landscape Journal* 21, no. 2 (2002): 1–14.

69. George Hazelrigg, "Peeling Back the Surface," LAM, Apr 2006, 112.

70. For details, see Michael Leccese, "No Shirking Columbine," LAM, Nov 2003, 84.

71. Exhibit catalog, by the same title, available from Princeton Architectural Press.

72. Mary Beth Breckenridge, "Green and Gorgeous: Designers Help Environmentalism Go Upscale," *Akron OH Beacon*, 27 Nov 2005.

73. Meg Calkins, "Assignment: Eco-friendly Campuses," LAM, Jul 2002, 38.

74. Gary W. Cramer, "Naturally Secluded," LAM, Jan 2006, 46.

75. Mary Padua, "Touching the Good Earth," LAM, Jan 2006, 100.

76. Andre Viljoen et al., eds., *Continuous Productive Urban Landscapes: Designing Urban Agriculture for Sustainable Cities* (London: Architectural Press, 2005).

77. Calkins, "Assignment," 40.

78. Peggy Bartlett and Geoffrey Chase, eds., *Sustainability on Campus: Stories and Strategies for Change* (Cambridge MA: MIT Press, 2004), Introduction, p. 5. The book contains one chapter on a native-plant experiment; the other chapters range from integrating environmental lessons throughout the curriculum to organizing faculty and staff initiatives.

79. "A New Option for Afterlife," EBN, Mar 1999.

80. Edvard Munch, *Kunskabens Træ på godt og ondt* , page T 2547-A41. This work is an unpublished scrapbook that Munch made himself; parts of it were published in "Edvard Munch: Symbols and Images," an exhibition catalog from the National Gallery, Washington DC, 1978. Thanks to Gerd Woll and Tor Edvin Dahl, of Oslo, for tracking down this quotation's real source.

81. Memorial Ecosystems, www.memorialecosystems.com/.

82. Although in theory land preservation could be accomplished while retaining conventional sealed-casket burials, the degree of land disturbance caused by this approach reduces the "fit" considerably. It would, however, reduce the pesticide and energy inputs currently required to maintain the barren monocultural landscapes found in most conventional cemeteries.

83. Information on greening the slopes comes from two sources: a syndicated article by the editors of *E* magazine, "Ski Resorts Try to Cut Damage They Do," 10 Dec 2001; and from the Web site of the National Ski Area Association, www.nsaa.org/.

84. K. Sorvig, "Renewing Zion," LAM, Nov 2001, 62.

85. Brian Skoloff, "Remodeling of Yosemite Pits Preservation Against Access," Associated Press, 14 Dec 2003. The criticisms, from a group called Friends of Yosemite Valley, are disputed by (among others) the National Parks Conservation Association.

86. See www.hawaii.gov/jud/23080.htm. The case was dismissed on December 6, 2002, by the Hawaii Supreme Court, to the immense relief of tourism promotion boards everywhere. The court ruled that the Sierra Club lacked standing (legal right to sue) because the club itself had no concrete interests that would be damaged by the tourism advertising—only the environment would be damaged! This argument has repeatedly been abused to make it impossible to sue to defend public lands.

87. L.A.G. Moss, *The Amenity Migrants: Seeking and Sustaining Mountains and Their Cultures* (Cambridge MA: CABI, 2006), 5.

88. Among them, the Centers for Disease Control and the Robert Wood Johnson Foundation. An overview report on the rela-

tionship between urban landscapes and obesity appeared in *USA Today*. Martha T. Moore, "Walk, Can't Walk," 23 Apr 2003.

Principle I: Keep Healthy Sites Healthy

1. Conversely, Ian McHarg often compared humans to a planetary disease, noting how sprawling modern cities seen from on high look like mold growths.

2. Paul R. Ehrlich, Gretchen C. Daily, Scott C. Daily, Norman Myers, and James Salzman, "No Middle Way on the Environment," *Atlantic Monthly*, Dec 1997, 98–104. See esp. p. 101, which lists environmental services and states, "These services operate on such a grand scale, and in such intricate and little-explored ways, that most of them could not be replaced by technology—even if no expense were spared, as Biosphere 2 showed."

3. Hard figures on this perennial subject are surprisingly rare. Federal courts have ruled that loss of a single mature tree reduced property value by 9 percent. "The Value of Landscaping," Texas A&M Horticultural Sciences, 1999, http://aggie-horticulture.tamu.edu/syllabi/432/article1.html. The Urban Land Institute, in a study cosponsored by the ASLA (but involving only architects and development experts in actual research), considers the perception that landscape adds to property value as believable but unproven due to lack of quantification. Developers interviewed for the study indicated 5 percent increase in value for individual gardens and 20 percent increase for public landscape amenities affecting the whole development (this increase equals six times the extra construction cost for the amenities). Presumably these figures relate to *newly installed* landscaping. Lloyd W. Bookout, Michael Beyard, and Steven W. Fader, *Value by Design* (Washington DC: Urban Land Institute and American Society of Landscape Architects, 1994). Other anecdotal evidence tends to be in this range, though the authors have heard realtors state that *mature* landscapes can add 75 percent to the sale price of a home. *Appraisers* are more likely than developers to know values for mature landscapes, and a study of appraising formulas would probably be revealing. Some wonderfully varied estimates of the value of specific trees are shown in Table 3.2, p. 134.

4. See chapter 1 of John D. Peine, *Ecosystem Management for Sustainability* (Boca Raton FL: CRC Press, 1998).

5. For overview and links, see www.friam.org/ and www.santafe.edu/.

6. Associated Press, "UNM Builds Terrain-survey Computer," *Santa Fe New Mexican*, 16 Sep 2003. The lead researcher is Louis Scuderi, tree@unm.edu.

7. Samira Jafari, "Google Earth Used to Show Effects of Mining," AP syndicated report, 5 Nov 2006.

8. Herb Schaal, FASLA, is a master of such methods; see K. Sorvig, "Drawing the Experience of Place," LAM, Oct 2005, 170–78.

9. James S. Russell, "Wetlands Dilemma," *Architectural Record*, Jan 1993, 36–39. The architect was Elide Albert.

10. Thanks to Eric Evans, GPS specialist at Holman's surveying supply in Albuquerque (www.holmans.com/), for up-to-the-minute information and pricing on GPS. Because we have not found a good lay-professional's book on surveying (as op-

posed to hiking) with GPS, such expert information is especially valuable.

11. GPS satellites also "rise and set" in the sky; at some times of day, this may prevent surveying.

12. Concerns about the aging grid work toward better records; fear of terrorism works against it.

13. For some utilities, it is desirable to have a wide *legal* easement to keep trespassers away, but the full width does not need to be clear-cut.

14. Stuart H. McDonald, "Prospect," LAM, Sep 1993, 120.

15. Ben Campanelli, "Planning for Cellular Towers," *Planning Commissioners Journal* 28 (1997): 4.

16. An example is the cell-and-clock tower at Arroyo del Oso golf course in Albuquerque, where city council members attempted to require that cell towers be concealed.

17. Robert Thayer, *Grey World, Green Heart* (New York: Wiley, 1994), 46.

18. Jon Frandsen, "System Uses Cable Instead of Towers," *Gannet News Service*, 22 Mar 1998.

19. Real Goods, John Schaeffer, ed., *Solar Living Sourcebook*, 9th ed. (Ukiah CA: Real Goods, 1996), 374–76 and 546.

20. Knight Ridder News, "Devices Will Let Households Generate Power, Experts Say," *New Mexican*, 7 Jul 1999, A4.

21. Center for Watershed Protection, *Model Development Principles to Protect Our Streams, Lakes, and Wetlands* (Ellicott City, MD: Center for Watershed Protection, 1998). The specific guideline, Principle 19, p. 15: allowable clearing distance. It is based on 1991 standards from the Maryland Department of Natural Resources.

22. Phillip J. Craul, *Urban Soil in Landscape Design* (New York: Wiley, 1992), 135–37.

23. Ibid., 109.

24. Ibid., 45. The original gives figures per gram of soil; converted by authors.

25. William Thompson, "A Long Road to Freedom," LAM, Feb 1998, 50–55.

26. See note 3, above.

27. Ann Brenoff, "Locution, Locution, Locution," *Los Angeles Times*, 14 Jan 2007, discusses various effects of wording in real-estate listings.

28. R. J. Hauer, R. W. Miller, and D. M. Ouimet, "Street Tree Decline and Construction Damage," *Journal of Arboriculture* 20, no. 2 (1994): 94–97.

29. See I. R. Jones et al., "Detection of Large Woody Debris Accumulations in Old-growth Forests Using Sonic-wave Collection," *Transactions of Important Tree Scientists* 120, no. 2 (Mar 2002): 201–9.

30. Craul, *Urban Soil*, 137.

31. Robert Adams Ivy Jr., *Fay Jones* (Washington DC: AIA Press, 1992), 35.

32. Donald Hoffmann, *Frank Lloyd Wright's Fallingwater: The House and Its History* (New York: Dover, 1985).

33. Information from a photocopied graph attributed to AASHTO; title and date unknown.

34. Lisa Cowan and David Cowan, "Review of Methods for Low Impact Restoration," paper presented at the ASLA 1997 Annual Meeting.

35. Kathleen Corish, "Clearing and Grading: Strategies for Urban

Watersheds," Washington DC: Metropolitan Washington Council of Governments, 1995. European laws protecting trees, forests, and special land types are also worth studying.

36. Alex Wilson, "Dewees Island: More Than Just a Green Development," EBN, Feb 1997, 5–7. Descriptions that follow are from this article.

Principle 2: Heal Injured Sites

1. The EPA defines brownfields as "abandoned, idled or underused industrial/commercial facilities where expansion or redevelopment is complicated by *real or perceived* environmental contamination," an typically politic definition. Quoted by Alex Wilson, editor of EBN; personal correspondence.

2. Definition from www.nahbrc.org/greenguidelines/user guide_site_select.html. For other sources, see Resource list. ⊃

3. Sam Roberts, "Bloomberg Administration Is Developing Land Use Plan to Accommodate Future Populations," *New York Times*, 26 Nov 2006.

4. Historic restoration is primarily a concept from architectural preservation, and even for buildings, picking the date to re-create is not always simple. See Kim Sorvig, "Relocating History," 2004 proceedings of ALHFAM annual conference (Association of Living History and Farm Museums), from www.alhfam.org/.

5. Rural decline can create similar conditions and may benefit from similar efforts.

6. Linn's vision, never implemented in Newark, was expressed in *From Rubble to Restoration*, published by Earth Island Institute, www.earthisland.org/. This brief, out-of-print title is still relevant if a used copy can be found.

7. For one US example of this approach, as part of the UN's Man and the Biosphere program, see John D. Peine, ed., *Ecosystem Management for Sustainability* (Boca Raton FL: Lewis, 1999).

8. www.greenworks.tv/rough_terrain/urbangardening/index .htm.

9. O. L. Gilbert *The Ecology of Urban Habitats* (London: Chapman and Hall, 1989), 40.

10. "Activists Rescue New York's Community Gardens," *Washington Post*, 13 May 1999.

11. Peter Bareham, "A Brief History," *Landscape Design*, Apr 1986.

12. Michael Lancaster and Tom Turner, "The Sun Rises over Liverpool," *Landscape Design*, Apr 1984, 36.

13. Rodney Beaumont, "Focus on the Festivals," *Landscape Design*, Jul–Aug 1992, 18.

14. Jon E. Lewis, "How Green Is My Valley," *Landscape Design*, Jul–Aug 1992, 11.

15. Andrew Grant, "Life on Earth," *Landscape Design*, May 1993, 33.

16. Jane Porter, "The Earth Center," *Landscape Design*, Feb 1996, 12.

17. Grant, "Life on Earth," 33.

18. This was Massachusetts's first effluent reuse project, according to CDM, and important because of Cape Cod's limited freshwater resources. Strict monitoring protects the aquifer.

19. A. D. Bradshaw, "Landfill Sites—Outstanding Opportunities for Amenity and Wildlife," paper presented at the *Design Now for the Future: End-use of Landfills*, Nov 1992. Bradshaw is a researcher at the University of Liverpool. Similar findings by M. C. Dobson and A. J. Moffat, in "The Potential for Woodland Establishment on Landfill Sites" (publisher and date unknown) resulted in rescinding a British directive against trees on capped landfills. Further supporting these findings, no problems have been reported from closed landfill festival gardens that include trees.

20. William Young, "Creation of Coastal Scrubforest on Landfill," date and publication unknown.

21. *Fresh Kills Park: Lifescape* (draft master plan), Staten Island NY Parks Department, Mar 2006.

22. See Mira Engler, *Designing America's Waste Landscapes* (Baltimore: Johns Hopkins University Press, 2004). Although greatly overstated, this book raises many points about US attitudes toward waste.

23. Kathleen Spain, "Get It Right at the Start," *Waste Age*, Feb 1993, 57.

24. For an interesting look at the lives of reforestation workers, see *Handmade Forests: The Treeplanter's Experience* by Helene Cyr (Stoney Creek CT: New Society Publishers, 1999).

25. See www.habitatnow.com/index.htm for information. Financial return on restoration often involves enrolling in the federal agricultural Conservation Reserve Program or similar programs. Revegetation against global warming may produce parallel opportunities for nonagricultural restoration.

26. Both quotes from Horst Schor, "Landform Grading: Building Nature's Slopes," *Pacific Coast Builder*, Jun 1980, 80–83.

27. Gullying is "damage" from a conventional perspective and can literally undermine vegetation trying to reestablish a foothold. In the longer view, however, gullying is nature's first step in restoring the landform to its proper, irregular shape. The flatter and steeper a slope, the more destructively gullying attacks, until erosion and deposition begin to come back into dynamic equilibrium—something that can take far too long for human purposes. See note 29 below on the diffusion model.

28. Horst Schor, "Landform Grading and Slope Evolution," *Journal of Geotechnical Engineering* 121, no. 10 (Oct 1995): 729–34. Full text now available online at www.pubs.asce.org/ WWWdisplay.cgi?9505325.

29. See D. B. Nash, "The Evolution of Abandoned, Wave-cut Bluffs in Emmet County, Michigan," Ph.D. dissertation, University of Michigan, 1977. This research supports the "diffusion model" of slope formation, which states that natural processes optimize slope forms so that materials removed upslope balance downslope deposition. The resulting slope cross-section is an S-curve; top and toe of slope are both rounded. As Schor points out, this model strongly indicates that "a planar slope with constant inclination, typical of conventional grading practice, is not a stable, long-term equilibrium slope" (732).

30. Schor, "Landform Grading and Slope Evolution," 732.

31. John Haynes, "Stepped Slopes: An Effective Answer to Roadside Erosion," *Landscape Architect and Specifier News*, Feb 1990, 31.

32. Joseph A. Todd, *Some Experiences in Stepping Slopes* (Gatlinburg TN: FHWA Bureau of Public Roads, 1967).

33. William Comella (FHWA Regional Engineer, Arlington VA), interview, 28 July 1971.

34. Phillip J. Craul, *Urban Soil in Landscape Design* (New York: Wiley, 1992), 237.

35. Ibid., 237.

36. Ibid., 239.

37. See, for example, P. Newman and J. Kenworthy, *Sustainability and Cities: Overcoming Automobile Dependence* (Washington DC: Island Press, 1998).

38. William Thompson, "Banking on a River," LAM, Sep 1998, 50–55.

39. See www.cbf.org/.

40. Examples of this in the mega-ditches of Albuquerque have been documented by Paul Lusk, former city planner and professor of architecture and planning, University of New Mexico.

41. J. G. Bockheim, quoted in Craul, *Urban Soil*, 86.

42. For example, Leslie Sauer, *The Once and Future Forest* (Washington DC: Island Press, 1998), 154–57, discuss soil protection and restoration. This is an excellent source for details on forest protection and restoration.

43. Based primarily on Craul, *Urban Soil*, 290–91.

44. V. P. Claassen and R. J. Zaoski, *The Effect of Topsoil Reapplications on Vegetation Reestablishment* (Sacramento: California Department of Transportation, 1994).

45. Orus L. Bennet, "Land Reclamation," in *McGraw-Hill Encyclopedia of Environmental Science and Engineering*, ed. Sybil Parker and Robert Corbitt (New York: McGraw-Hill, 1993), 329.

46. For a complete description of this project see Sauer, *The Once and Future Forest*.

47. Richard Wolkomir, "Unearthing Secrets Locked Deep Inside Each Fistful of Soil," *Smithsonian*, Mar 1997, 74–84. Wolkomir interviews scientists at the Soil Tilth Laboratory, Iowa State University. One of the interviewees comments about the ripping out of native vegetative communities that "agriculture is a violent activity."

48. Simon Leake, "Reuse of Site Soils," *Landscape Australia*, Aug 1995.

49. O. L. Gilbert, *The Ecology of Urban Habitats* (London: Chapman and Hall, 1989), 47–51.

50. Sauer, *The Once and Future Forest*, 156.

51. Robert Nold, *Penstemons* (Portland OR: Timber Press, 1999), 24. Elsewhere he notes that penstemons occur in severe soils considered so useless for agriculture or development that they are often the locations of reservoirs "built to satisfy the unquenchable thirst of endless expanses of compulsively planted lush green lawns" (52).

52. Whitney Cranshaw, *Pests of the West* (Golden CO: Fulcrum Publishing, 1992), chapter 1. See also Sauer, *The Once and Future Forest*, chapters 17 and 22.

53. Donna Mitchell, *Compost Utilization by Departments of Transportation in the United States* (Gainesville FL: University of Florida Department of Environmental Horticulture, 1997), 8.

54. Mitchell, *Compost*, 9.

55. Wesley A. Groesbeck and Jan Striefel, *Sustainable Landscapes and Gardens: The Resource Guide*, 3rd ed. (Salt Lake City UT: Environmental Resources Inc., 1996), 59.

56. Ohio State University, *Composting Factsheet* (Columbus OH: Ohio State University Extension, n.d.).

57. "Breakthroughs," *Discover*, Jul 1994, 18.

58. Mitchell, *Compost*, 16.

59. Mitchell, *Compost*, 14.

60. For information go to www.compostingcouncil.org/index .cfm and look for the tab labeled "STA" (the full name of the testing program is not spelled out on the homepage).

61. This title is associated with health foods for people and may be trademarked for that use.

62. This was developed at Battery Park City, discussed in more detail in Principle 10.

63. Terry Logan, *Lead Contamination in the Garden Factsheet* (Columbus: Ohio State University Extension, n.d.). This source also recommends peat moss; local organic material is far preferable, and usually plentiful.

64. Bill Thompson, personal communication.

65. Associated Press, "Report: Toxic Chemicals Recycled into Fertilizers," *New Mexican*, 7 Jul 1997.

66. US EPA, *Biosolids Recycling: Beneficial Technology for a Better Environment* (Washington DC: National Center for Environmental Publications and Information, n.d.), ref: EPA 832-R-94-009. Legal standards are in part 503, Code of Federal Regulations.

67. Craul, *Urban Soil*, 197.

68. Anita Bahe, "Science and Policy: The Biological, Environmental, and Policy Implications of Organic Waste Reutilization in Urban Landscape Management," Ph.D. dissertation, North Carolina State University, 1995.

69. Michael Leccese, "Fresh Fields," LAM, Dec 1996, 44.

70. Mitchell, *Compost*, 18.

71. Ibid., 17.

72. Phillip Craul, "Designing Sustainable Soil," in *Opportunities in Sustainable Development: Strategies for the Chesapeake Bay Region*, ed. Margarita Hill (Washington DC: American Society of Landscape Architects, 1997), 49.

73. Ibid.

74. George Hazelrigg, "The Ultimate Spectacle," LAM, Dec 2006, 56–63.

75. Joe Alper, "Wicked Weed of the West," *Smithsonian*, Dec 2004, 33–36.

76. Federal Interagency Invasive Species Council, *Draft National Invasive Plant Management Strategy* (Washington DC: US departments of Interior and Commerce, 1996). For a clear discussion of horticultural introductions that have caused ecological havoc, see Francis M. Harty, "Exotics and Their Ecological Ramifications," *Natural Areas Journal* 6, no. 4 (1986): 20–26.

77. For a pragmatic and thorough way to define and assess a species' invasiveness, see the criteria developed by the California Invasive Plant Council (http://cal-ipc.org/). Critics of the very idea of invasiveness are mostly postmodern theorists who insist that any plant that can adapt to a region is good and that "native" is an elitist term. They base this on analogy rather than science: by comparison to the racism that can be implicit in classifying people as native or not; and by the analogy between ecosystems and economic markets, in which (they seem to believe) pure competition is the only legitimate approach.

78. This information is from a presentation on invasives and landscape practice at the ASLA annual meeting in San Jose CA, 2002.

79. Seth Hettena, "Officials Work to Eradicate Water-grubbing Shrub," AP syndicated report, 15 June 2003.

80. Benjamin Everitt, "Chronology of the Spread of Tamarisk in the Central Rio Grande," *Wetlands*, Dec 1998, 658–68. Everitt's finding that Tamarisk invaded only after water-level

disruptions has been used by some activists as proof that the plant is harmless and should be left alone.

81. Statistics from Alper, "Wicked Weed of the West." Cal-IPC's newsletter, *Noxious Times*, Fall 2004, 6–9, notes that "many studies have shown that exotic plants transpire more water than California's indigenous plants," and sets a financial benefit of eradicating invasives, for California's economy alone, at up to $11 billion.

82. All information on knapweed from Alper, "Wicked Weed of the West."

83. An ASLA presentation at the San Jose annual meeting, 2002, showed a wide range of species for which these effects have been studied in detail. Because the same plant's effect may differ between regions, the best sources of such information are usually state and local invasive plant agencies.

84. Paul Gobster and Bruce Hull, *Restoring Nature: Perspectives from the Social Sciences and Humanities* (Washington DC: Island Press, 2000). The Chicago Restoration Controversy, as it is widely known, is reported in Gobster's introduction; he was a participant in the events. While Gobster's perspective is thoughtful and broad, some of the articles in this collection, notably coeditor Hull's, border on deconstructivist polemics. In his contribution, for example, Hull asserts that there is no real difference between the "different natures" found in parks or parking lots. Clearly, natural processes occur even in the most constructed environment; arguments like Hull's, however, tend to deny any *qualitative* value for the diverse, coevolved, self-sustaining systems that "nature" usually refers to. Although less strident, the Chicago public was also convinced that there was no qualitative difference between their planted forests and the native vegetative communities of the region.

85. Some titles, cited by Gobster, included "Prairie People Compile Tree Hit-List!" and "Guru's Restoration Plans Read More like Destruction."

86. A voluntary code of conduct for landscape architects was first proposed at a 2001 workshop organized by the botanic gardens in Missouri, Chicago, and Kew (London). "Linking Ecology and Horticulture to Prevent Plant Invasions," authors unknown. The code urged self-education, elimination of regionally invasive plants from designs, and lobbying suppliers not to sell invasives. As noted earlier, ornamental horticulture bears a large responsibility for the historical introduction of many invasives; some in that industry still actively and aggressively resist attempts to stop spreading these plants.

87. From DR Trimmer/Country Home Products (800-446-8746). Like many equipment manufacturers, DR portrays its clients as beating back unruly nature, an attitude that itself is problematic.

88. For a discussion of the ways in which patterns change over time, known as the shifting mosaic steady state, see *Sustainable Development in Forestry: An Ecological Perspective* by Bryant N. Richards, viewable at www.forestry.ubc.ca/schaffer/richards .html.

89. Sauer, *The Once and Future Forest*. See especially pages 165–193 and 298–300.

90. J. Zickefoose, *Enjoying Bluebirds More* (Marietta OH: Bird Watcher's Digest Press, 1993); like many birder's books, this contains extensive lists of trees, shrubs, and vines that attract birds.

91. Presciently foreseen as early as 1984 by Edward Theurkauf, MLA, at University of Pennsylvania.

92. Amy Adams, "Heavy Metal Garden," *Utne Reader*, May–Jun 1998, 86.

93. Len Hopper, *Landscape Architectural Graphic Standards* (New York, Wiley, 2007). Figures given in table, page 803. Conversion from hectare to acre, and phytomethods as percentage of other methods, by Sorvig.

94. "Tumbleweed Could Be Low-tech Tool for Uranium Contamination Cleanup," syndicated AP report, no author, 10 Nov 2004; John Fialka, "Salute the Jimson," *Wall Street Journal*, 18 Jun 1992, A5; Elizabeth Weise, "Watercress Engineered to Detect Land Mines," *USA Today*, 3 Feb 2004, 4D. Experiments with salt-tolerant plants have been widespread since the "Green Revolution" of the 1970s.

95. Steven Rock, "Possibilities and Limitations of Phytoremediation," in *The Standard Handbook of Hazardous Waste Treatment and Disposal*, ed. Harry Freeman (New York: McGraw-Hill, 1997), 6.

96. We are indebted to Tawny Allen, who produced an exceptionally clear summary of technical differences among phytoremediation methods for Sorvig's University of New Mexico sustainable landscapes seminar, 2005.

97. Philip Rea, "Plants May Clean Out Poisons at Toxic Sites," *Philadelphia Inquirer*, 12 Jun 1999. Rea is the primary researcher on this University of Pennsylvania project.

98. Brian Kamnikar, "Biomounds Pass Tests in Minnesota," *Soil and Groundwater Cleanup*, May 1996, 34–43.

99. "Munching Microbes Make a Meal Out of Toxic Substances," *Purdue News*, Apr 1997.

100. "Bioremediation of Environmental Contaminants," originally at http://gw2.cciw.ca/internet/bioremediation/whatis.html appears to have been removed from the web.

101. Paul Bradley, title unknown, *Environmental Science and Technology*, Jun 1999, reported by wire services, 19 Jun 1999. For list of this author's titles on similar subjects see http://toxics.usgs.gov/bib/bib-Solvents-on-line.html.

102. UWI is the term preferred by Firefighters and "Firewise" activists, occasionally flipped as "WUI"; the latter phrase is from Tom Wolf's excellent *In Fire's Way: A Practical Guide to Life in the Wildfire Danger Zone* (Albuquerque: University of New Mexico Press, 2003).

103. This phrase is the subtitle of *The Wildfire Reader* (Washington DC: Island Press, 2006), which Wuerthner edited. The many contributors to this volume focus on fire as an ecological necessity, and on the deep-seated problems of conventional forest management regarding fire. (It contains relatively little about managing *development* in forests, but is essential reading for the background facts required to make sense of UWI issues.)

104. John MacDonald, "Researchers Say Fire Becomes Political Tool," AP syndicated report, 20 Apr 2003. The timber industry has used fear of fire as a lever to allow more tree removal in national forests under the guise of "thinning." Timber money probably explains the heavy federal funding of thinning programs. These political concerns are detailed in both Wolf, *In Fire's Way*, and Wuerthner, *The Wildfire Reader*. Wolf also notes that the current system rewards fire depart-

ments more for fighting fires than for any prevention work (22–23).

105. Ted Williams, "Burning Money," *Audubon*, Jan 2001, 34. President Bush called the San Diego fires "nature at her worst," but in fact, conditions for most recent wildfires are as much man-made as natural.

106. Kim Sorvig, "Will Wildfire Ravage Our Profession?" LAM, Dec 2001, 32; "Crying Fire in a Crowded Landscape," LAM, Mar 2004, 26.

107. Ventura County CA, which enforces harsh regulations and still suffers repeated destructive fires, was the basis for estimating clearance area and percentage. Since UWI clearing, by definition, occurs in the wilder parts of the county, it represents far more than 3 percent annually of the little uncleared land that remains in most regions. In many counties, 90 percent or more of the forested or wooded areas that existed prior to about 1800 have long been cleared. Thus, a single year's UWI clearance could theoretically represent destruction of *30 percent* of the *remaining* woods.

108. Sorvig, "Crying Fire."

109. Quoted in Wolf, *In Fire's Way*, 36. The USFS has ostracized Cohen for statements like this and is especially displeased that environmental groups have used Cohen's sensible and honest findings to combat timber-industry pressure politics. (See MacDonald, "Researchers Say Fire Becomes Political Tool.")

110. Jonathan Thompson, Thomas Spies, and Lisa Ganio, "Salvage Logging, Replanting Increased Biscuit Fire Severity," *Proceedings of the National Academy of Sciences*, 12 June 2007. This study found fire intensity was 16 to 61 percent higher in areas salvage logged and replanted that suffered a second burn, compared to areas that were allowed to revegetate by themselves after one fire, and then suffered a second. The authors note that "the hypothesis that salvage logging, then replanting, reduces re-burn severity is not supported by these data."

111. Restoration goals must be based on sound ecological understanding of specific ecosystems. (The Bush administration's so-called healthy-forest initiative is purely bogus.) Interviewees for Sorvig's articles (cited above) note that some environmental groups fear timber industry meddling so much that they insist that no management of any sort be allowed in burned public forests (reflecting the belief that nature must be untouched by human hands). This makes it impossible to undo the damage caused by a century of fire suppression, and actually leads some of these groups to support clearance around every structure.

112. This paraphrases the title of S. Arno and C Fiedler's useful book *Mimicking Nature's Fire: Restoring Fire-prone Forests in the West* (Washington DC: Island Press, 2005).

113. He made this point in his book-signing talk in Santa Fe NM, 27 Nov 2006.

Chapter 3: Principle 3: Favor Living, Flexible Materials

1. Donald Gray and Robbin Sotir, *Biotechnical and Soil Bioengineering Slope Stabilization* (New York: Wiley, 1996), 3.

2. Ann Riley, *Restoring Streams in Cities* (Washington DC: Island Press, 1998) discusses the history of these methods, including the Works Progress Administration and Civilian Conservation Corps.

3. These points were culled from USDA Natural Resource Conservation Service, *Soil Bioengineering for Upland Slope Protection and Erosion Reduction* (Washington DC: Natural Resource Conservation Service, 1992), 18-1 through 18-8.

4. USDA, *Soil Bioengineering*, 18-5.

5. Coe now lives and practices in Australia.

6. Gray and Sotir, *Biotechnical and Soil Bioengineering*, 149.

7. Ibid., 148.

8. USDA, *Soil Bioengineering*, 18-31 and 18-32.

9. It is almost impossible to resist making jokes about the anti-environmental president of the same name—but we won't go there.

10. Theodore Eisenman, "Raising the Bar on Greenroof Design," LAM, Nov 2006, 22.

11. Michael Hough, *City Form and Natural Process* (New York: Van Nostrand Reinhold, 1984).

12. Tom Liptan et al., *Integrating Stormwater into the Urban Fabric* (Portland, OR: American Society of Landscape Architects, 1997), 89.

13. Eisenman, "Raising the Bar."

14. Ibid.

15. Ibid.

16. Underground or earth-bermed houses (such as Sorvig's) may have several feet of soil over the roof, maintaining a year-round baseline temperature of 54°F, easily solar heated in winter, and cool in summer.

17. Christopher Hawthorne, "Building Designers Add Pizazz to Views from Above," *Los Angeles Times*, 10 Nov 2006.

18. Alex Wilson and Mary Rickel Pelletier, "Using Roofs for More Than Keeping Dry," EBN, Nov 2001.

19. Questions about both hydro-gels and wind erosion were raised in Wilson and Pelletier, "Using Roofs."

20. Jacklyn Johnson and John Newton, *Building Green: A Guide to Using Plants on Roofs, Walls, and Pavements* (London: London Ecology Unit, n.d.), 64.

21. See Linda McIntyre, "Greenroof Guru," LAM, Jan 2007, 64, which reviews Snodgrass's work.

22. Theodore Eisenman, "Chicago's Green Crown," LAM, Nov 2004, 106.

23. Intensive greenroofs fall between thin-soiled extensive greenroofs and roof gardens, but are closer kin to the former in intent, structure, and plant choices. Their deeper soil can retain more stormwater, but is not suitable for trees.

24. Lisa Owens Viani, "Prairie from Ground to Sky," LAM, Dec 2006, 28.

25. Lorraine Johnson, "The Green Fields of Ford," LAM, Jan 2004, 16.

26. Under section 319(h), Clean Water Act.

27. Theodore Eisenman, "Sedums over Baltimore," LAM, Aug 2004, 52.

28. In her contribution to *Landscape Architectural Graphic Standards* (New York: Wiley, 2007), "Living Green Roofs and Landscapes over Structures," p. 713, Susan Weiler of Olin Partnership prefers the term "landscape over structure" for roof gardens with soil deeper than 8 inches. She states that greenroofs and landscape over structure should not be compared. We agree that comparison should not be adversarial, but all sustainability-oriented landscapes benefit from deliberate evaluation.

29. Jacklyn Johnson and John Newton, *Building Green: A Guide to Using Plants on Roofs, Walls, and Pavements* (London: London Ecology Unit, n.d.), 48. Over ten million square feet of German greenroof are older than 1989, for example.

30. Ecover, *The Ecover Manual* (Oostmalle, Belgium: Ecover Publishing, 1992), 24.

31. For information on waste-treatment greenroofs, see www.epsrc.ac.uk/pressreleases/growingthenextgenerationofwaterrecyclingplants.htm.

32. Trying to encourage sustainability by skimping on other compliance is risky even with good intentions. "Streamlining regulation" has disguised Reaganite bad intentions against environmental and social laws.

33. Cutler is cited in an in-flight magazine, possibly itself a first for any landscape architect! Quote and statistics on urban forests from: Charles Lockwood, "Save the Shade," *Hemispheres Magazine* (United Airlines), Sep 2006, 60–63. Article available on-line at www.hemispheresmagazine.com/sept06/shade.html.

34. R. J. Hauer, R. W. Miller, and D. M. Ouimet, "Street Tree Decline and Construction Damage," *Journal of Arboriculture* 20, no. 2 (1994): 94–97.

35. The author and date of this study are not known.

36. Pimentel's study was published in *Bioscience*; reported in John Yaukey, "Environment's Output Placed at $2.9 Trillion," *Ft. Collins Coloradoan*, 14 Dec 1997.

37. The study, cited on www.treelink.org/, is credited to Dr. Rowan Rowntree, n.d.

38. Statistics from Lockwood, "Save the Shade." USFS study by the Center for Urban Forest Research.

39. Blanc's excellent lectures were compiled in Alan Blanc, *Landscape Construction and Detailing* (New York: McGraw-Hill, 1996).

40. Phillip J. Craul, *Urban Soil in Landscape Design* (New York: Wiley, 1992), 1.

41. Craul, *Urban Soil*, 122.

42. This quote is from Urban's contribution to Ramsey, Sleeper, and Hoke, *Architectural Graphic Standards*, 9th ed, rev. (New York: Wiley, 1998). Note that even the 1994 edition showed planting standards that Urban states to be actively harmful to trees.

43. This section is an updated version of Kim Sorvig, "Soil Under Pressure," LAM, June 2001, 36.

44. CU-Soil is a registered trademark. Like all other trademarks referred to in this book, it remains property of its developers. "Structural soil" is a generic term.

45. H. F. Arnold, "The Down and Dirty on Structural Soil," LAM, Aug 2001, Letters, pp. 9–11. This letter responded to Sorvig's "Soil Under Pressure." The article, focused on the CU-Soil patent and enforcement controversy, did not discuss Arnold's system. This gave the mistaken impression that neither the historical nor horticultural aspects of Arnold's work were appreciated. Hopefully, that misapprehension can be laid to rest here. Arnold gives general concepts for site-adjusted soil mixes in his book *Trees in Urban Design* (New York: Van Nostrand Reinhold, 1992).

46. "Gap-graded soil," based on sieved angular sand, provides golf greens' smooth, consistent surfaces. Porous paving (aka "open-graded friction course") uses asphalt or cement to bond "no-fines" aggregate as pavement with voids through which water drains easily. Structural soil is unbonded, and soil fills the voids.

47. Interestingly, soil mixes are essentially recipes, and recipes cannot be copyrighted because they are simply lists of common ingredients and known procedures. To patent a recipe, the ingredients, processes, or outcome must be *significantly* different than common practice. UHI's strategy, called a "defensive patent," is not uncommon; Xeriscape was trademarked in a similarly unsuccessful attempt to enforce consistency. Given the near-infinite site-specific variations possible and necessary with almost any horticultural process, enforcing such patents is nearly impossible.

48. Nina Bassuk and Peter Trowbridge, "Soils, Urban and Disturbed," in *Landscape Architectural Graphic Standards*, ed. L. Hopper (New York: Wiley, 2007), 646–61.

49. Bruce Ferguson, personal communication. Ferguson is probably the greatest US expert on land-focused stormwater management and one of the few landscape architects to pursue "hard" research on such subjects.

50. Sorvig's article (see note 43 above) apparently made UHI defensive. The text of that article, edited *without permission* to express Nina Bassuk's objections to Sorvig's conclusions, was reprinted *under Sorvig's name* (!), in *City Trees*, journal of the Society of Municipal Arborists, Nov 2003. The *City Trees* version is extremely misleading, contradictory to Sorvig's researched findings, semi-incoherent, and intellectually dishonest. Anyone concerned with evaluating structural soils fairly will avoid the *City Trees* article.

51. So far as we can determine, none of these installations have been dug up or monitored with instrumented methods, but they do provide strong observational evidence.

52. A consummate gentleman, Craul names no names, to avoid embarrassing the designers.

53. The guidelines are summarized from James Urban's contribution to Ramsey et al., *Architectural Graphic Standards*, 81–82.

54. We have seen recommendations for an establishment period as long as seven years for some regional species. Always get local expertise and aim to wean plants off human assistance gradually.

55. Wild accusations have been made that defining plants as natives and aliens is comparable to racism against "alien" humans; see Kim Sorvig, "Natives and Nazis: An Imaginary Conspiracy in Ecological Design," *Landscape Journal* 13, no. 1 (1994): 58–61.

56. See entries for *Abies magnifica* in Elbert Little, *Audubon Society Field Guide to North American Trees, Western Region* (New York: Knopf, 1980); and John Kricher, *Ecology of Western Forests* (Peterson Field Guides, New York: Houghton Mifflin, 1993).

57. Contact Western Polyacrylamide or the Colorado Forestry Department for studies on polymer use.

58. From the 1999 seed catalog of Wildseed Farms, www.wildseedfarms.com.

59. Ted Steinberg, *American Green: The Obsessive Quest for the Perfect Lawn* (New York: Norton, 2006), 7. Steinberg is also the author of the wonderful *Slide Mountain, or, the Folly of Owning Nature*, and several other books tracing our often comical social and legal attempts to corral the natural world.

60. The cause of drought, along with other extreme weather, is probably the greenhouse effect and global climate change. Water-use restrictions such as those that have made artificial turf popular are being passed both by legislators who deny global warming, and by those who recognize it. Evaluating the sustainability of local drought measures requires looking at their larger-scale and longer-term implications.

61. Jessica Boehland, "Which Grass Is Greener? Comparing Natural and Artificial Turf," EBN, Apr 2004. Unless otherwise noted, statistics in this section are from Boehland's article. We agree with her conclusion that neither conventional nor artificial turf is particularly sustainable.

62. www.airfieldturf.com/.

63. The speaker is Chris Reuther, a botanist and science writer at Philadelphia's Academy of Natural Sciences. The original source appears to be a 1999 article, title and publication unknown; Reuther was quoted in both EBN and LAM discussing artificial turf issues.

64. Washington Post, "1 Out of 8 Plant Species Faces Extinction, Survey Says," *New Mexican*, 8 Apr 1998, B-1.

Principle 4: Respect the Waters of Life

1. Russell Ash, *Incredible Comparisons* (London: Dorling Kindersley, 1996), 23.

2. Ambrose Bierce, *The Devil's Dictionary* (Cleveland: World Publishing Co., 1941). Bierce's definition of "lexicographer" is also worth noting in regard to footnotes generally: "A pestilent fellow who, under the pretense of recording some particular stage in the development of [an idea], does what he can to arrest its growth, stiffen its flexibility, and mechanize its methods."

3. Michael Jameson, *Xeric Landscaping with Florida Native Plants* (Miami: Association of Florida Native Nurseries, 1991).

4. Paul Simon, *Tapped Out: The Coming World Crisis in Water and What We Can Do About It* (New York: Welcome Rain Publishers, 1998).

5. L. D. Rotstayn and U. Lohmann, "Tropical Rainfall Trends and the Indirect Aerosol Effect," *J. Climate* 14 (Aug 2002): 2103–16. Rotstayn is a research scientist at Australia's Commonwealth Scientific and Industrial Research Organization. His research shows that pollutants from industrial countries, especially sulfur dioxide from power plants, affect cloud and precipitation patterns thousands of miles away in the Sahel desert in Africa, and that the start of emissions controls in industrial countries correlates with the return of rains to the Sahel. Abstract (and full text by subscription) available through the American Meteorological Society Web page, www.ametsoc.org/, "Journals" section.

6. John Fleck, "Hotter & Drier," *Albuquerque Journal*, 24 Jun 2006, A1, gives a regional example of increased rainfall offset by decreased availability.

7. Harvey M. Rubenstein, *A Guide to Site Planning and Landscape Construction*, 4th ed. (New York: Wiley, 1996), 189.

8. Dawn Thimany et al., "The Economic Contribution of Colorado's Green Industry," Apr. 2004, economic development report, Colorado State University Coop. Extension EDR-04-01, http://dare.agsci.colostate.edu/extension/pubs.html.

9. Stuart Echols and Eliza Pennypacker, "Art for Rain's Sake," LAM, Sep 2006, 24.

10. BASMAA, *Start at the Source* (San Francisco: Bay Area Stormwater Management Agencies Association, 1997), 7, italics added.

11. In 1998 dollars; certainly more today. Rocky Mountain Institute, Studio for Creative Inquiry, and Bruce Ferguson, *Nine Mile Run Briefing Book (draft)* (Snowmass CO: Rocky Mountain Institute, 1998), 20. ⊃

12. This is a much more readable paraphrase of the EPA's legal definition. See www.epa.gov/owow/wetlands/what/definitions.html.

13. Donald A. Hammer, *Creating Freshwater Wetlands*, 2nd ed. (Boca Raton FL: Lewis Publishers, 1997), 16.

14. John Berger, *Restoring the Earth: How Americans Are Working to Renew Our Damaged Environment* (New York: Knopf, 1985), 61. Constructing the marsh requires a wider strip of land than the revetment; cost of land may or may not be an issue in such projects, and is not included in Berger's figures. In 1982 dollars, revetments cost $150/linear foot, marsh $15–$25.

15. Hammer, *Creating Freshwater Wetlands*, 115.

16. Ibid., 12.

17. This list is based on Hammer, 139.

18. Ibid., 171. Further comments throughout, notably pp. 137, 258, and 311.

19. As noted below, it is unclear whether this can ever be accomplished fully.

20. Hammer, *Creating Freshwater Wetlands*, 23, 337.

21. Ibid., 337.

22. Required under the EPA's 2003 National Pollutant Discharge Elimination System (NPDES) Construction General Permit (CGP), *Federal Register* 68, no. 126 (1 Jul 2003): 39087, http://cfpub.epa.gov/npdes/stormwater/cgp.cfm. This law has teeth, making it an important site-protection tool, especially on local road and public-works projects, where conventional engineers have often felt revegetation was decorative and optional.

23. Procedural "streamlining" is a legitimate need, but has also been used as a smokescreen for removing regulations.

24. Mary Kentula, Robert Brooks, Stephanie Gwin, Cindy Holland, Arthur Sherman, and Jean Sifneos, *An Approach to Improving Decision Making in Wetland Restoration and Creation* (Boca Raton FL: CRC Press, 1993), 17–19.

25. Lisa Owens Viani, "A Question of Mitigation," LAM, Aug 2006, 24.

26. Susan Galatowitsch and Arnold van der Valk, *Restoring Prairie Wetlands: An Ecological Approach* (Ames, IA: Iowa State University Press, 1994), 150; see also chart on p. 49 of the same work.

27. Hammer is a strong advocate of this approach, for example.

28. Kentula et al., *An Approach to Improving Decision Making*, see particularly pp. 17–19 and 111–12. See also Galatowitsch and van der Valk, *Restoring Prairie Wetlands*, esp. chapters 1 and 3.

29. Hammer, *Creating Freshwater Wetlands*, 39.

30. Hammer 194, is one of many who have reported this concern.

31. Polly El Aidi, "Innovations in Wetlands Trail Construction," LAM, Jul 1993, 120–22.

32. Design recommendations from Hammer, *Creating Freshwater Wetlands*, 201, 215.

33. Ibid., 299.

34. Another list of invasive plants, not specific to wetlands, is found in appendix B of Leslie Sauer, *The Once and Future Forest* (Washington DC: Island Press, 1998); it pertains to deciduous forests of the Eastern United States.

35. Hammer, *Creating Freshwater Wetlands*, 264, 318–23.

36. "Sligo Creek: Holistic Stream Restoration," *Watershed Protection Techniques* 1, no. 4 (1995): 192.

37. This is a major theme of Ann Riley, *Restoring Streams in Cities* (Washington DC: Island Press, 1998), esp. 30–31.

38. Bruce Ferguson, "The Failure of Detention and the Future of Stormwater Design," LAM, Dec 1991, 76–79. See also *Introduction to Stormwater* (New York: Wiley, 1998), 162–64.

39. Erich Smith, "Trees for Streams," syndicated AP report, 10 Jan 1997.

40. Riley, *Restoring Streams in Cities*, 362.

41. Ibid., 31.

42. These included the Metropolitan Washington Council of Governments, the Maryland-National Capital Park and Planning Commission, and Maryland Department of Environmental Protection.

43. A useful published (but unbuilt) example is Rocky Mountain Institute, Studio for Creative Inquiry, and Ferguson, *Nine Mile Run Briefing Book (draft)*.

44. Alex Wilson, "Rainwater Harvesting," EBN, May 1997, 1.

45. Bill Mollison, *Permaculture: A Designers' Manual* (Tyalgum, NSW, Australia: Tagari Publications, 1988), esp. chapter 7.

46. Bruce Ferguson, *Introduction to Stormwater* (New York: Wiley, 1998); see chap. 10. Example projects are University of Arizona's *Casa del Agua* in Tucson, and Arizona Public Service's *Environmental Showcase Home* in Phoenix

47. Kenneth Brooks et al., *Hydrology and the Management of Watersheds* (Ames IA: Iowa State University Press, 1997).

48. For example, the all-rainwater Santa Fe Railyard Park design: Kim Sorvig, "Railyard Remake in Santa Fe: Supplanting the Usual with the Unusual?" *Competitions* 12, no. 3 (Fall 2002): 13.

49. Echols and Pennypacker, "Art for Rain's Sake," 26.

50. Olwen C. Marlowe, *Outdoor Design: A Handbook for the Architect and Planner* (New York: Watson-Guptil, 1977), 102–4.

51. Ibid., 104.

52. Bousselot et al, "Sustainable Landscaping," Colorado State University Extension, publication 7.243, www.ext.colostate.edu/Pubs/Garden/07243.html.

53. See Virginia Scott Jenkins's book, *The Lawn: History of an American Obsession* (Washington DC: Smithsonian Press, 1994). The British, of course, share responsibility for this cultural fixation; see Tom Fort, *The Grass Is Greener: Our Love Affair with the Lawn* (London: HarperCollins, 2000).

54. Estimated at between seven and eleven billion acre-feet. See Amy Vickers, *Handbook of Water Use and Conservation* (Amherst MA: Waterplow Press, 2002).

55. Maude Barlow, "The Commodification of the World's Water," *Earth Island Journal*, 22 Mar 2002, page unknown. See also www.ci.norman.ok.us/finance/trivia.htm for revealing water factoids.

56. From the Federal Energy Management Program (FEMP) water-management Web pages, www1.eere.energy.gov/femp/pdfs/strategic_plan.pdf. These cost increases were computed for federal facilities, but probably represent changes for other types of users.

57. Wesley Groesbeck and Jan Striefel, *The Resource Guide to Sustainable Landscapes and Gardens*, 2nd ed. (Salt Lake City UT: Environmental Resources, 1995), 39.

58. Quote from Tony Whelan, "Irrigation for a Growing World," May 10 2006; a white paper available on www.rainbird.com/. Rainbird might be accused of bias in this matter, but the observation that water-conservation ordinances harshly and exclusively target the horticultural industry have been made by many others. Sorvig, for example, has noted that in Santa Fe NM, the only industry other than landscape horticulture that faces any restrictions is commercial car washes, and only after virtually all landscape use has been completely banned.

59. Ibid.

60. Joshua Siskin, "The Next Generation in Automatic Sprinklers," *Los Angeles Daily News*, 1 Oct 2005, online at www.dailynews.com/search/ci_3075423.

61. Elizabeth Brabec, Jim Urban, Andropogon Associates, and Oehme van Sweden Associates, *Save Water, Save Maintenance, Save Money* (Washington DC: Anne Arundel County Department of Utilities, 1989), 5.

62. The Xeriscape council ceased to function some time ago, and the trademark reportedly passed to the University of Texas Extension.

63. Janet Reilly, "Drip Irrigation—A Tool for the Future," May 2005, online publication at www.johndeerelandscapes.com/_Products/Irrg_index.asp. The author is the landscape drip marketing manager at Rain Bird Corporation.

64. Robert Kourik, "Drip Irrigation Hardware: Selection and Use," LAM, Mar 1993, 74–78.

65. From www.owue.water.ca.gov/landscape/faq/faq.cfm, a useful site with answers to a variety of common irrigation questions, maintained by the California Department of Water Resources, Office of Water Use Efficiency.

66. Denny Schrock, "Water-efficient Gardening and Landscaping," 7 Jun 2006, Department of Horticulture, University of Missouri, Columbia, online at https://muextension.missouri.edu/explore/agguides/hort/g06912.htm. Automatic overwatering by 30 to 40 percent, and 10 percent by hand, is reported by Phillip Meeks, "Finding Solutions to Landscape Irrigation Runoff," *Stormwater*, Sep–Oct 2002, 12, based on research by Brent Mecham, Northern Colorado Water Conservancy District, "Responsible Lawn Watering," available online at www.ncwcd.org/ims/ims_info/responsi.pdf.

67. Undated information flyer. BECC's Web site is www.conservationcenter.org/.

68. From Sacramento-based Water Education Foundation booklet "California Water Facts," n.d., watededfdn@aol.com, 916-444-6240.

69. These statistics are from Weathertrak, an ET controller that in 2003 was licensed for use in Toro products. Other controllers claim similar or greater reductions in waste.

70. Originally based on Kourik, "Drip Irrigation Hardware" and "Drip Irrigation for Lawns," LAM, Mar 1994, this list has been slightly updated with information from current manufacturers' catalogs.

71. Kourik, " Drip Irrigation Hardware," 78.

72. Kourik, "Drip Irrigation for Lawns," 40.

73. Dr. Rao presented this prototype to the California Urban Water Conservation Council, Sep 2004. See www.cuwcc.org/Uploads/committee/Plenary/Plenary_Circular_Sprinkler_04-09-08.ppt to download slides from this presentation. We hope this patent-pending concept can find a manufacturer. Dr. Rao is with the Civil and Environmental Engineering Department, Cal. State Fullerton, and can be reached at 714-278-3525 or mprasadarao@fullerton.edu.

74. The name seems slightly absurd, since virtually all water uptake occurs through the roots except in a few rare plant species. These devices are sometimes called "deep watering" systems, which is perhaps more accurate.

75. Kourik, "Drip Irrigation for Lawns," 41. This is in stark contrast to perceptions of drip as complicated.

76. From embodied energy tables, now posted at www.SustainableLandscapeOnline.com/.

77. Richard V. Sole and David Alonso, "Random Walks, Fractals and the Origins of Rainforest Diversity," Santa Fe Institute, 1998, Ref: 98-08-60, working paper; and Wim Hordijk, "A Measure of Landscapes," Santa Fe Institute, 1995, Ref: 95-05-049, working paper, are examples of such math research, primarily in ecology and molecular biology. A number of working papers are available on related topics at www.santafe.edu/. Use of the term "landscape" for such widely varying and nonphysical concepts as a "fitness landscape" (evolutionary theory) or "the political landscape" (journalism) make electronic information searches in our profession both difficult and entertaining.

78. These are available at www.irrigation.org/. The BMPs are extremely general; for more tangible recommendations, see the practice guidelines that flesh out the BMPs.

79. Robert Kourik, "Graywater for Residential Irrigation," LAM, Jan 1995, 30–33.

80. Barry Jeppesen and David Solley, *Domestic Greywater Reuse: Overseas Practice and Its Applicability to Australia* (Melbourne: Urban Water Research Association of Australia, 1994).

81. See Kourik, "Graywater," and Groesbeck and Streifel, *Resource Guide*, 41–43.

82. Alex Wilson, "Rainwater Harvesting," EBN, May 1997, 12.

83. Alex Wilson, "On-site Wastewater Treatment," EBN, Mar–Apr 1994, 18.

84. Estimate from Professor Brad Finney, Humboldt University Constructed Treatment Wetland System Performance database, personal correspondence.

85. The project won an ASLA award and was published in LAM, but never built.

86. Hammer, *Creating Freshwater Wetlands*, 312.

87. Rich Patterson, "From Wasteland to Wetland," *Public Risk*, Jan 1998, 29.

88. Mary Padua, "Teaching the River," LAM, Mar 2004, 100.

Principle 5: Pave Less

1. From www.bts.gov/publications/national_transportation_statistics/2003/html/table_01_06.html. Up 117,348 lane miles since 1996.

2. From www.earth-policy.org/Alerts/Alert12_data2.htm. If the standard space is 10 × 18 feet, this represents about 1.15 billion spaces. The International Parking Institute's Web site, www.parking.org/, listed 105.2 million in 1999, clearly a different method of estimating.

3. Bruce Ferguson (University of Georgia) estimates US paving, based on volumes of asphalt and concrete sold, at a quarter-million to half-million acres each year. This is a growth rate of 1.5 to 3 percent of our estimated total area—higher than the population growth rate!

4. Russell Ash, *Incredible Comparisons* (London: Dorling Kindersley, 1996), 26.

5. Ben Kelley, *The Pavers and the Paved* (New York: Donald Brown, 1971).

6. Mark Childs, *Parking Spaces* (New York: McGraw-Hill, 1999), 195.

7. Ibid., 197.

8. Tom Schueler, *Site Planning for Urban Stream Protection* (Ellicott City MD: Center for Watershed Protection, 1995), 148.

9. Ibid.

10. This was known as SAFE-TEA, a broad transportation act that includes clarification of accountability for "flexible" but well-reasoned designs. It was signed by President George W. Bush in 2005. The CSD resource information Web site, www.contextsensitivesolutions.org/, confirms that "most legal experts agree that context-sensitive solutions will not cause the engineer [liability] problems as long as they are well reasoned and comprehensively documented." For the authoritative source on this subject, see Richard O. Jones (Federal Highway Administration Regional Counsel, Region 8), Transportation Research Board 2004 Distinguished Lectureship, "Context Sensitive Design: Will the Vision Overcome Liability Concerns?" available from the above Web site.

11. Erik Sherman, "Tales of Commuter Terror," *Computerworld*, 30 Oct 2000. Statistics from Texas Transportation Institute study of 1999, www.tti.tamu.edu/. ("We were waiting for the 2000 study, but the researchers got stuck in traffic," notes the writer wryly.)

12. The transit part of these cities was deliberately killed by auto interests, as fictionally depicted in the 1988 film *Who Framed Roger Rabbit?*

13. Cited by David Gram, "Paving Costs Skyrocket with Rising Oil Prices," syndicated AP report, 16 Jun 2005. The article notes that the financial costs are due almost entirely to the high energy costs of paving.

14. FHWA Pavement Preventive Maintenance Guidelines, update of 27 Mar 27 2001, no author, 5. FHWA-HI-00-007, online at www.fhwa.dot.gov/pavement/pub_details.cfm?id=463.

15. These policy suggestions are based on University of Georgia School of Environmental Design, *Land Development Provisions to Protect Georgia Water Quality*, ed. David Nichols (Athens: Georgia Department of Natural Resources, 1997).

16. *Impervious Surface Reduction Study* (Olympia WA: City of Olympia Public Works Department, 1995), ref: final report, 84–85.

17. Center for Watershed Protection, *Model Development Principles to Protect Our Streams, Lakes, and Wetlands* (Ellicott City MD: Center for Watershed Protection, 1998), 76.

18. Richard S. Wilson, "Suburban Parking Requirements and the Shaping of Suburbia," *Journal of the American Planning Association* 61, no. 1 (1995): 29–42.

19. Center for Watershed Protection, *Model Development Principles*, 73.
20. Ibid., 75.
21. Richard Unterman, "Office Park Paradise," LAM, Aug 1998.
22. Linda McIntyre, "Blue Nuns Go Green," LAM, Nov 2006.
23. Like any other useful policy, it can be used as a smokescreen, where speedway standards are still the outcome and "public input" simply means "you had your say, now shut up."
24. K. Sorvig, "Paving of County Road 42 Without Storm-water Measures Gouges 8 Foot Deep by 100 Yard Gullies in Private Property," publication pending.
25. EPA regulations (NPDES Phase Two) require permanent soil stabilization for all projects larger than one acre; state and federal road projects in the same county routinely comply.
26. Technically, the "Green Bible" is titled "A Policy on Geometric Design of Highways and Streets," 5th ed., AASHTO. The problem of engineers insisting on *inflexible interpretations* of this document is so great that AASHTO also publishes "Flexibility in Highway Design," a precursor to CSD. From https://bookstore.transportation.org/, or www.contextsensitivesolutions.org/, also the source for R. O. Jones, "Context Sensitive Design" (above). Jones explains the engineering community's overblown fear of liability and attempt to avoid it through rigid "standards" as a response to the historical loss of "sovereign immunity" for state officials in the 1950s, with no more-specific limitations on design liability until the 1980s. Any engineer schooled in that period is likely to verge on paranoia about liability.
27. This and following quote from R. A. White were found on his office's Web site (www.tlcnetwork.org/bobwhite.html), which has since been removed
28. From the Web site www.Drivers.com/. While many motorists associations treat traffic calming as a government conspiracy against their "rights," Drivers.com takes a very balanced view of the issues.
29. On traffic calming and scenic roads, see www.bts.gov/ntl/DOCS/vsb.html: "Design and Information Requirements for Travel and Tourism Needs on Scenic Byways—Final Report," by Christiana M. Briganti and Lester A. Hoel.
30. These acts, renewed periodically, have names like IS-TEA and TEA-21.
31. Paper presented at 2001 annual meeting of US Transportation Research Board; online at www.cts.cv.ic.ac.uk/documents/publications/iccts00203.pdf, from Imperial College, London UK, where Noland is on the faculty.
32. Italics added. The study differentiates between controlled-access freeways, where some widening and straightening can improve safety, and other road types. On non-freeway roads, lanes wider than eleven feet encourage speeding and inattentiveness, and result in more accidents and a higher percentage of accidents resulting in serious injury or death.
33. FHWA's research center Web site: www.tfhrc.gov/.
34. Alex Wilson, "Traffic Calming Ahead!" EBN, Mar 2003.
35. Daniel B Wood, "American Cities Clearing Streets to Lure Residents Out of Their Cars," *Christian Science Monitor*, 25 May 2007.
36. This paranoiac view appears in T. Peter Ruane, "Zealots Would Stop Road Work," ENR (*Engineering News-Record*), 14 June 1999, 11. Ruane, president of ARTB, even considered urban sprawl to be "in the public interest," for obvious self-serving reasons.
37. Center for Watershed Protection, *Model Development Principles*, 33.
38. Crystal Atkins and Michael Coleman, "Influence of Traffic Calming on Emergency Response Times," *ITE Journal* (Aug 1997): 42–47.
39. A. Ann Sorensen and J. Dixon Esseks, "Living on the Edge: The Costs and Risks of Scatter Development," *American Farmland Trust Newsletter*, Mar 1998.
40. Wilson, "Traffic Calming Ahead!"
41. See the Drivers.com Web site.
42. General information on road ecology is primarily from the Web site of the UC Davis Center for Road Ecology, http://roadecology.ucdavis.edu/.
43. See James T. Carlton and Gregory M. Ruiz, "Vector Science and Integrated Vector Management in Bioinvasion Ecology," in *Invasive Alien Species: A New Synthesis*, ed. H. A. Mooney et al. (Washington DC: Island Press, 2005). It is well established that road construction, with soil disturbance and heavy equipment movements, is a major vector for invasive plant seeds.
44. Beginning with the 1997 transportation policy TEA-21, wildlife protection has been eligible for federal "intermodal" and context-sensitive funding.
45. From STPP's report "Second Nature—Executive Summary," 22 Apr 2003, posted at www.transact.org/report.asp?id=207.
46. The same concept, using attacking forces to protect oneself, distinguishes "soft" martial arts like aikido or tai chi from "hard" ones like karate or tae kwon do.
47. *Impervious Surface Reduction Study*, executive summary, 20.
48. Gary Cramer, "Naturally Secluded," LAM, Jan 2006.
49. BASMAA, *Start at the Source* (San Francisco: Bay Area Stormwater Management Agencies Association, 1997), 15; Bruce Ferguson was one of the consultants for this book.
50. John E. Paine, *Pervious Pavement Manual* (Orlando: Florida Concrete and Products Association, n.d.).
51. Porosity figures are from B. Ferguson, personal communication to Sorvig.
52. Grasspave² brochure from Invisible Structures.
53. *Impervious Surface Reduction Study*, 79–80.
54. James Sipes and Mack Roberts, "Grass Paving Systems," LAM, Jun 1994, 33.
55. *Henderson Field Demonstration Project Summary* (Olympia WA: City of Olympia, 1996), 13.
56. Sipes and Roberts, "Grass Paving Systems," 33.
57. "Henderson Field," 7–13.
58. Matthew Evans, Nina Bassuk, and Peter Trowbridge, "Sidewalk Design for Tree Survival," LAM, Mar 1990, 103.
59. Adam Arvidson, "A Green Demonstration," LAM, Sep 2006, 50.
60. Meg Calkins, "Cooling the Blacktop," LAM, Feb 2007, 54–61.
61. Hashem Akbari, US EPA, Climate Change Division, Lawrence Berkeley Laboratory, and US Department of Energy, *Cooling Our Communities: A Guidebook on Tree Planting and Light-colored Surfacing* (Washington DC: Government Printing Office, 1992), US Lawrence Berkeley Laboratory report, LBL-31587.
62. Childs, *Parking Spaces*, 196.

63. Information on these coatings comes from interviews with DecoAsphalt in California, and Integrated Paving Concepts, in Canada. Information on integral asphalt color from interviews with Asphacolor (Madera CA). See resources for more information.

Principle 6: Consider Origin and Fate of Materials

1. Quoted in William Thompson, "Is It Sustainable? Is It Art?" LAM, May 1992, 56–57.
2. Kathleen Baughman, "The Use of Recycled Materials in the Landscape," unpublished, Washington State University, 1995, 16.
3. Reported in K. David Pijawka, "Dozens of Activities Mark Second Annual 'Arizona Recycles Day,'" *AZ Recycling Review*, Spring 1999, 16.
4. Maurice Nelischer, quoted in Thompson, "Is It Sustainable? Is It Art?"
5. See Table 7.9, p. 277 for these and other transportation energy rates.
6. Kevin Killough, "The Recycling Crisis," 17 Apr 2003, *Crosswinds Weekly* (Santa Fe NM), 10–13. Statistics cited are from Killough's interviews with solid-waste management specialists throughout the United States.
7. Robert Weller, "Copper Snatchers Moving On to Aluminum," syndicated AP report, 6 Jun 2006. The article notes that such thefts have been common on the East Coast for years, but have spread, partly driven by demand from China.
8. Even the formidable AIA *Environmental Resource Guide* (Joseph Demikin, ed. [New York: Wiley 1997]) misuses the term "renewable," making it a synonym for recyclable (p. 06118:2).
9. HOK Architects, *Sustainable Design Guide*, ed. Sandra Mendler (Washington DC: HOK Architects, 1998), iii. (This was the in-house edition; see above for Wiley publication of this title.)
10. Rainer Stange, "Bjørnsons hage i Vika, Oslo," also published in German as "Garten in Oslo," *Garten und Landschaft*, Nov 1997.
11. "Adobe" derives from Egyptian *al-tub*, showing how ancient this material is.
12. A large population building expansive adobe homes could threaten its own farmland, as appears to have happened in some areas of Egypt. Whether this should be blamed on adobe, overpopulation, or McMansion consumerism is debatable.
13. Baughmann, "Recycled Materials," 19.
14. These projects were featured in an article in *Dwell* magazine, Apr 2002. The supplier/designer was The Glass Garden, of Los Angeles, www.landscape2go.com/.
15. Baughmann, "Recycled Materials," 29.
16. Barbara Ryder, "Glass: Landscape Applications," LAM, Jun 1995, 28.
17. Baughmann, "Recycled Materials," 29.
18. Ibid., 39.
19. "Waste Tire Problem Becomes Opportunity for Erosion Control," *Land and Water*, Mar 1998, 36.
20. "Recycled Tires Turn a Problem into a Solution," *Erosion Control*, Sep 1998, 18–21.
21. According to Pliny Fisk, tire surfaces pick up some pollutants from road contact, but these are removed by simple washing. Fisk notes that the EPA has tested the chemical content of tires because they are so common in playgrounds and found them inert.
22. "Recycled Tires."
23. Kim Sorvig, "Brave New Landscape," LAM, Jul 1992, 75–77.
24. The most recent edition is from 1996. Despite this, many of the listings are still valid.
25. Alex Wilson, "Test Methods Approved for Plastic Lumber," EBN, Oct 1997, 4. (Includes contacts for further information.)
26. Daniel Winterbottom, "Plastic Lumber," LAM, Jan 1995, 34.
27. New Mexico designer Buck Dant refers to it as "woodworking with pasta." It occasionally gums up power tool bits and blades.
28. "Where the Rubber Meets the Trail," *Rails to Trails*, Winter 1999, 5.
29. San Jose Mercury News, "Old-growth Forests Get a Break from Home Depot," *New Mexican*, 29 Aug 1999, D-1. We have been unable to get a response from Home Depot about the effect of this policy, possibly because (according to rumor) the company is undergoing a shakeup as we complete second-edition revisions.
30. Daniel D. Chiras, *Environmental Science: Action for a Sustainable Future*, 4th ed. (Redwood City CA: Benjamin/Cummings, 1994), 203–9.
31. This insistence that all environmental standards be voluntary and self-policing typifies American policy, from certified lumber to LEED to refusal to ratify the Kyoto protocols.
32. Information from *EPP Update* newsletter, a US EPA publication, issue 8, Feb 2001, 6, www.epa.gov/oppt/epp/. "EPP" stands for environmentally preferable purchasing, which is governmentese for sustainable products.
33. Pliny Fisk, *Comparison of Available Wastes and Production of Wood Products* (Austin TX: Center for Maximum Potential Building Systems, 1993). This information is graphed from data by the US Department of Commerce, Natural Resources Research Institute, US EPA, and the Institute for Local Self-Reliance.
34. Information on AERT thanks to Pliny Fisk.
35. The EPA's recommendation for maximum indoor concentration of radon, four picocuries, was set at the average amount of radon found naturally in outdoor air.
36. This concept is formally called "the precautionary principle."
37. Phillip J. Craul, *Urban Soil in Landscape Design* (New York: Wiley, 1992). Based on Craul's Table 6.1, p. 186.
38. Indoor air/environmental quality is IAQ or IEQ to specialists.
39. Paula Baker, Erica Elliott, and John Banta, *Prescriptions for a Healthy House* (Santa Fe NM: InWord Publishers, 1998), xv–xvi.
40. Ibid., 55–59.
41. Kingsley Hammett, "When Building 'Green' Isn't Green Enough," *Designer/Builder*, Nov–Dec 2006, 27–28.
42. Mark Matrusek with Bill McKibben, "Live Better with Less: Our High-powered Economy Is Based on Growth, So Why Is All Our Stuff Making Us Less and Less Happy?" *AARP* magazine, May–June 2007, 54–57.
43. Real Goods, *Solar Living Sourcebook*, ed. John Schaeffer, 9th ed. (Ukiah CA: Real Goods, 1996), cites Lovins on 374–76 and presents related information on 546.
44. This figure, and the following ones for logging and construction, originates with the US EPA, cited in Frits van der Leeden, *The Water Encyclopedia* (Boca Raton FL: Lewis Publishers, 1990). Other experts have claimed increases up to 40,000 times the baseline.

45. Nadav Malin and Alex Wilson, "Material Selection: Tools, Resources, and Techniques for Choosing Green," EBN, Jan 1997, 1, 10–14; American Institute of Architects, *Environmental Resource Guide*, ed. Joseph A. Demkin (loose-leaf, current through 1998; supplement ed., New York: Wiley, 1998); Tracy Mumma and CRBT staff, *Guide to Resource Efficient Building Elements* (Missoula MT: Center for Resourceful Building Technology, 1995).

46. Fisk's work is reported in many publications, but is not as well-known or widely used as it should be. In the following citations, ASES refers to the American Solar Energy Society, www.ases.org/. Pliny Fisk III and Richard MacMath, "Carbon Dioxide Intensity Ratios: A Method of Evaluating the Up- stream Global Warming Impact of Long-Life Building Materi- als," *ASES National Conference Proceedings*, 2000. Pliny Fisk III, Gail Vittori, and Roldolfo Ramina, "BaseLine Green and GreenBal- ance: A Step Beyond Sustainability in Building Performance," *ASES National Conference Proceedings*, 2000. Much of this literature is available at www.cmpbs.org/flash/download.htm.

47. EPA/625/R-94/006, Sep 1994, "Guide to Cleaner Tech- nologies: Organic Coating Replacements." Viewable at http://es.epa.gov/program/epaorgs/ord/org-coat.html.

48. Meg Calkins has added to this list via her publications.

49. On PVC, see AIA, *Environmental Resource Guide*, Mat-09652: 35–37. On wood preservatives, see Alex Wilson, "A Call for CCA Phase-Out," EBN, Mar 1997, 2, and other articles in EBN.

50. Meg Calkins, "To PVC or Not to PVC," LAM, Mar 2006.

51. John Motloch, quoted in Calkins, "To PVC or Not to PVC."

52. www.greenpeace.org/international/campaigns/toxics/ polyvinyl-chloride/pvc-products/.

53. AIA *Environmental Resource Guide*, Mat-09652: 36. Additional information for the revised edition on PVC comes from Calkins, "To PVC or Not to PVC," and from the Greenpeace Web site, cited above.

54. The quoted example, from the Greenpeace Web site, empha- sizes how downcycling uses the landscape as a "sink" for ma- terials that are not acceptable in other uses.

55. These findings are summarized from Calkins, "To PVC or Not to PVC."

56. Tristan Roberts, "Treated Wood in Transition: Less Toxic Options in Preserved and Protected Wood," EBN, Aug 2006. Roberts provides an excellent historical perspective on changes in the industry and EBN's involvement in calls for improve- ment. This section summarizes information from the EBN ar- ticle, plus earlier sources as specifically noted.

57. Alex Wilson, "Using Wood Outdoors," LAM, Sep 1999, quoted from manuscript.

58. Alex Wilson, "CCA Phase-Out," EBN, Jan–Feb 1993, 10; earlier research backing up the phase-out proposal.

59. The AAPFCO's rules on metals are found on their Web site, www.aapfco.org/. The Washington levels are noted in a re- port, *Holding the Bag*, by Washington Toxics, an activist group, available at www.watoxics.org/. The latter table shows levels found in fertilizers in the state.

60. Associated Press, "Report: Toxic Chemicals Recycled into Fertilizers," *New Mexican*, 7 Jul 1997, and other reports subse- quently.

Principle 7: Know the Costs of Energy over Time

1. See Landscapes Against Climate Change, p. 14, for further in- formation on Architecture 2030. Statistics for other countries are similar, from 40 to nearly 50 percent. In the first edition, we noted that the American Institute of Architects estimated more than 30 percent of US energy went to buildings (Amer- ican Institute of Architects, *Environmental Resource Guide*, ed. Joseph A. Demkin (loose-leaf, current through 1998; supple- ment ed., New York: Wiley, 1998) (AIA-ERG). The differ- ence probably represents greater sophistication in Mazria's more recent statistical methods; the AIA has endorsed Archi- tecture 2030.

2. R. G. Stein, C. Stein, M. Buckley, and M. Green, *Handbook of Energy Use for Building Construction*, Vol. DOE/CS/20220-1, *Energy Conservation* (Washington DC: US Department of En- ergy, 1980), 9–10. These statistics are based on conditions in the 1970s and are probably not exactly comparable to the AIA figures.

3. Tracy Mumma, "Reducing the Embodied Energy of Build- ings," *Home Energy*, Jan 1995, 19–22.

4. Kenneth M. Swezey, *Formulas Methods Tips and Data* (New York: Harper and Row, 1969), 595, 620; based on a average density for different species of pine of 37.5 lbs/cf, and an average of 12.5 million Btu per cord (128 cf).

5. Both statistics from AIA-ERG, closely comparable to Stein.

6. This use of the term is scattered throughout the several in- formative publications of the DOE's Office of Industrial Technology.

7. HOK Architects, *Sustainable Design Guide*, ed. Sandra Mendler (Washington DC: HOK Architects, 1998), 2.21, for example.

8. Mumma, "Reducing Embodied Energy," 19.

9. Ibid., 20. Costs are in energy terms, not in dollars paid for energy.

10. Work and time comparison from Erik Bruun and Buzzy Keith, *Heavy Equipment* (New York: Black Dog and Leventhal, 1997), 10 (assume a full work day means eight hours in this context). Horsepower of scraper from pp. 22–23 (a bulldozer or second scraper is often required to push the working scraper in hard soils; this doubles the energy consumption, but is not included here). Horsepower to gallons per hour from Herbert L. Nichols Jr. and David A. Day, *Moving the Earth: The Workbook of Excavation*, 4th ed. (New York: McGraw- Hill, 1998), 12.111. Gallons to Btu based on Table 7.1. Hu- man energy expenditure per workday based on Richard C. Dorf, *The Energy Factbook* (New York: McGraw-Hill, 1981), 10, ca. 0.7 kw per worker per day, converted to 2,500 Btu; some sources give much higher energy use for human labor, which is very variable and, in a mechanical sense, inefficient.

11. The concept of ERoEI (energy return on energy invested, aka net energy) is useful for understanding both fuels and foods in terms of the energy used to produce them. Specifics, how- ever, are hotly debated, and often distorted by pro-oil/anti-oil partisanship. Only the briefest overview is appropriate here. Petroleum products' ERoEI varies widely: difficulty of discov- ery, depth of well, distance to refinery, and so on all affect it. Historically, however, the rate of return has fallen drastically: as recently as the 1940s, one barrel of crude invested in pro- ducing more crude returned 100 to 200 barrels. Today, even

oil-industry estimates admit a 1:30 ratio, and many sources indicate that 1 barrel invested now produces only 5 to 7 barrels. For some offshore or otherwise difficult wells, ERoEI can actually be negative. Transporting the crude to refinery, and the refined products to consumers, is apparently not included consistently. The best "alternative" energy sources have ERoEI in single digits, but despite oil-industry disinformation, these ratios are positive, and renewability makes a serious difference. As for food, "primitive" societies, because they grow food where it is used and recycle local organic wastes to do so, manage to squeeze just slightly more calories from their harvests than are used to grow those crops (ERoEI about 1.1). "Advanced" agribusiness, using petro-based fuels, fertilizers, and pesticides, and distributing food thousands of miles from where it is produced, gets less energy (ten times less, by some estimates) out of food than is embodied in its production. Even using ERoEI, comparing human and animal energy to machine energy is seldom precise. It is clear, however, that human labor generally uses energy more sustainably: renewably, and without pollution. For more information, try www.eroei.com/ (look for the Net Energy List). Howard Odum's many works are also a good source; he terms this issue "eMergy."

12. Kim Sorvig, "Sun on the Water," *LAM*, Sep 1994.

13. See www.solarexpert.com/pvbasics2.html, and also Vaclav Smil, *Energies: An Illustrated Guide to the Biosphere and Civilization* (Cambridge MA: MIT Press, 1999), xvi, Table 7.

14. The standard is 1000 watts/m² insolation at a cell temperature of 25°C (77°F).

15. Professionals should also vote with their dollars for more efficiently designed machines.

16. Nadav Malin, "Battery Fanatic," EBN, Mar 1993, 4.

17. It is possible that the extra drag from the generator decreases fuel efficiency so much that it negates the value of the electricity produced, making the concept unmarketable.

18. Associated Press, "General Motors Unveils New Stationary Generator," syndicated article, 8 Aug 2001.

19. See http://auto.ihs.com/news/2006/, "European Fuel Cell Bus Project Extended One Year" (search this site for "fuel cell"), and Joel Makower and Ron Pernick, "Clean Energy Markets," *Solar Today*, Sep 2002, 30.

20. The National Fuel Cell Research Center, University of California, Irvine, has a Web site that explains fuel cells from both technical and market perspectives, in clear language and diagrams. Start at www.nfcrc.uci.edu/fcresources/FCexplained/FC_Types.htm.

21. These are the 1997 record holders for largest truck and largest hydraulic excavator in the world, both built by Komatsu. Even these, picked because they resemble familiar equipment types, are far from the world's largest or heaviest equipment, since bucket-wheel excavators range up to nearly 15,000 tons, moving 10,000 or more cubic yards of soil per hour. Bruun and Keith, *Heavy Equipment*.

22. These are rough figures within what is actually a range of energy, influenced especially by temperature and elevation at the site. Diesel, for example, can produce between 132,000 and 152,000 Btu per gallon. For extremely detailed information on this topic, see John B. Haywood, *Internal Combustion Engine Fundamentals* (New York: McGraw-Hill, 1988). Eventually, evaluation will have to include biodiesel, ethanol, and other bio-fuels.

23. Nichols and Day, *Moving the Earth*, 12.111. Figures for two stroke are from Haywood, *Fundamentals*, 887.

24. Properly speaking, the horsepower figure should be actual, tested horsepower. For *rough* estimating and comparison of different machine *types*, using the rated or theoretical horsepower is probably accurate enough; it is often the only figure available.

25. Machinery engineers seem to rate fuel usages in pounds. Nichols and Day, *Moving the Earth*, 12.110–12.111, gives the basic figures; conversion to Btu and to light/heavy percentages by authors.

26. In the first edition, Sorvig made a dumb math error, giving diesel an unwarranted efficiency boost of over 30 percent! This in turn affected Table 7.3 and a few examples given in that edition. *Diesel Btu/hp-hr should be 8,400*, as corrected in this edition. To correct the former edition's tables, multiply any diesel listing in old Table 7.3 by a factor of 1.5. We thank the sharp-eyed Australian who brought this to our attention.

27. Tanaka was one small-engine manufacturer that met stringent CARB emission standards from *before* the 2000 deadline. Others include Komatsu-Zenoah and Redmax.⊃

28. The two engines on which these comparisons are based are Tanaka's conventional TBC-3010, at 29cc or 1.6 hp, and the new "Pure-Fire" TBC-270PF at 26cc or 1.4 hp.

29. Felicity Barringer, "Greener Way to Cut Grass Runs Afoul of Powerful Lobby," *New York Times*, 24 Apr 2006, A1. Information on the political machinations against the CARB effort are from this article. OPEI's statement of support for the regulations is posted on its Web site.

30. The senator who controlled the EPA's budget during this period was Kit Bond, a Republican from Missouri, where Briggs and Stratton has two lawnmower plants. Fire safety was used, unsuccessfully, as a Detroit argument against catalytic converters on cars in the 1970s. A 2005 study by the EPA found that converters on mowers posed little increased fire risk (see http://epa.gov/). For a conservative Republican, Bond was remarkably willing to use taxpayer money to force the EPA and National Research Council to beat this dead horse, and he is reportedly (in the *New York Times*, cited above) considering even further studies, one of them with a $650,000 price tag, to get the desired results.

31. Irwin Post, "Horsepower: Is Bigger Really Better?" *Independent Sawmill and Woodlot Management*, Apr 1999, 15–17.

32. John P. Rollins and Compressed Air and Gas Institute, *Compressed Air and Gas Handbook*, 5th ed. (Englewood Cliffs NJ: Prentice Hall, 1989), 846, Table 13.31.

33. Helen H. Whiffen, "Landscape Maintenance Takes Energy: Use It Wisely," *Energy Efficiency and Environmental News* (University of Florida Extension), Feb 1993. This newsletter is viewable at http://edis.ifas.ufl.edu/.

34. Based on Dorf, *Energy Factbook*, 11. Human metabolism and energy output are notoriously variable. Other experts consider 300 Btu per hour an average for light labor, like desk jobs or driving a truck, and rate very heavy labor up to 1,500 Btu per hour.

35. Tree Toad products are available directly from http://tree toad.com/.

36. Vaclav Smil, *Energies: An Illustrated Guide to the Biosphere and Civilization* (Cambridge, MA: MIT Press, 1999), 90.

37. The calculation is based on the tonnage hauled by an 18-wheeler, but similar ton-mile efficiency is achieved by some large construction trucks. From a very interesting and unusually objective Web site on all matters truck related: www.yondar.com/yondar/faq.htm. The Web site has been removed; contact for Yondar International: Ray Gompf, President and General Manager, 2889 Haughton Street, Ottawa, ON K2B 6Z4 Canada, 613-596-5173.

38. Figures in table based on Bill Lawson, *Building Materials Energy and the Environment* (Red Hill, Australia: Royal Australian Institute of Architects, 1996), 12, and Dorf, *Energy Factbook*, 79.

39. Howard T. Odum and Elizabeth C. Odum, *Energy Basis for Man and Nature* (New York: McGraw-Hill, 1976), 34, figure 2-5.

40. Based on Lawson, *Building Materials*, Tables 1.2 (road transport) and 1.3 (brick embodied energy).

41. This section's heading is borrowed from one of the first articles on embodied energy in construction: Nadav Malin, "Embodied Energy—Just What Is It and Why Do We Care?" EBN, May–Jun 1993, 8–9.

42. Lawson, *Building Materials*, 12, Table 1.1.

43. Baird, G., R. Jacques, A. Alcorn, P. Wood, and J.B. Storey. "Progress toward the specification of embodied energy performance criteria for New Zealand buildings." Ponrua NZ: Building Research Association of New Zealand, 1998.

44. ASMI website, www.athenasmi.ca/; click heading "The Challenge."

45. Malin, "Embodied Energy," 9.

46. Mumma, "Reducing Embodied Energy," 22.

47. 1994 edition (Wiley), 122–23.

48. Gas, observant reader, is exactly $1 per gallon; prehistoric.

49. Based on Hal Post and Vernon Risser, *Stand-alone Photovoltaic Systems: A Handbook of Recommended Design Practices* (Albuquerque, NM: Sandia National Laboratory, 1991), Ref: SAND87-7023, revised, 59–64 and worksheet on B-57.

50. Although the two terms are used interchangeably, present *worth* seems to refer to the formulas or factors used to compute present *value*.

Principle 8: Celebrate Light, Respect Darkness

1. John Schaeffer and Real Goods staff, *The Book of Light* (Ukiah CA: Real Goods, 1996), 4–11, discusses energy use and lighting. Since publishing the first edition, we have heard claims that fans for heating and cooling are the single largest use of electricity. We have been unable to confirm whether this is accurate and, if so, whether our earlier source was wrong, or the distribution has changed since 2000. It appears that lighting may be the largest single use for commercial buildings. In any case, energy use for lighting is a significant part of the total.

2. Real Goods *Book of Light*; the original source of this information appears to be Amory Lovins and the Rocky Mountain Institute.

3. If you really care, one candela is the light production of a standard whale-wax candle, $7/8$ of an inch in diameter and weighing $1/6$ of a pound; this determines the candle's density and how fast and bright it burns. Once whale-wax fell out of favor, candelas were redefined in terms of the electromagnetic spectrum (monochromatic radiation at 540 terahertz with an intensity of $1/683$ watt per steradian)—but all that was a mathematical way of describing the output of the same old candle. Aren't you glad you asked?

4. The one unit square, one unit from the source point, also defines the steradian, or "solid angle," used for measuring directional intensity. The steradian is a cone or pyramid with its tip at the source point; its base is the one-by-one surface. The point is considered to be the center of a sphere with a one-unit radius, and the steradian is a wedge taken out of that sphere.

5. J. F. Simard, *Lumec Chronicles*, Spring 2001, 1 (editor's comments in manufacturer's newsletter).

6. P. Cinzano et al., *The First World Atlas of the Artificial Night Sky Brightness*, 13 Aug 2001, Royal Astronomical Society, available in high resolution from www.lightpollution.it/dmsp/.

7. Deborah Schoch, "Fading Glory," *Los Angeles Times*, 20 Oct 2003, D-1.

8. www2.nature.nps.gov/air/lightscapes/team.cfm.

9. R. G. Stevens and M. S. Rea, "Light in the Built Environment: Potential Role of Circadian Disruption in Endocrine Disruption and Breast Cancer," *Cancer Causes and Control* 12, no. 3 (Apr 2001): 279–87, www.ncbi.nlm.nih.gov/.

10. S. Davis and D. K. Mirick, "Circadian Disruption, Shift Work and the Risk of Cancer: A Summary of the Evidence and Studies in Seattle," *Cancer Causes and Control* 17, no. 4 (May 2006): 539–45.

11. Richard A. Stone, "Infant Myopia and Night Lighting," *Nature*, 13 May 1999.

12. www.cureresearch.com/i/insomnia/stats.htm; 2003 figures.

13. Stevens and Rea, "Light in the Built Environment."

14. Nina Bassuk, personal communication.

15. I. Kloog, B. Portnov, and A. Haim, "Light Pollution as a Risk Factor for Breast Cancer: A GIS-assisted Case Study," 21 June 2005, conference paper, available at www.israelrsa.org.il/meeting/Cancer%20incidence.ppt.

16. Catherine Rich and Travis Longcore, *Ecological Consequences of Artificial Night Lighting* (Washington DC: Island Press, 2005).

17. WTC photo at www.flap.org/

18. Study reported in Ben Harder, "Light All Night: New Images Quantify a Nocturnal Pollutant," *Science News* 169, no. 11 (18 Mar 2006): 170.

19. Karen Peterson, "Night-sky Law Needs to Be Tougher, Researchers Say," *New Mexican*, 8 Apr 1999, B-4. Exemptions, from prisons to ordinary billboards, are commonly pushed through by lobbyists.

20. J. F. Simard, *Lumec Chronicles* (manufacturer's newsletter), Spring 2001, 9. Lumec's report did not claim that semi-cut-off designs were always better at reducing reflection.

21. Based on the fact that new lamps *save* up to 90 percent; see multi-LED bulb description in this chapter.

22. Charles W. Harris and Nicholas T. Dines, *Timesaver Standards for Landscape Architecture* (New York: McGraw-Hill, 1988), 540-11–540-13.

23. All D. Crawford information is from his videotaped lecture at University of New Mexico, Albuquerque, n.d., Santa Fe Public Library collection.

24. Alex Wilson, "Disposal of Fluorescent Lamps and Ballasts," EBN, Oct 1997, 1, 9–14.

25. Janet Lennox Moyer, *The Landscape Lighting Book* (New York: Wiley, 1992). This has a truly remarkable amount of detail on materials, operation, and design.

26. Harris and Dines, *Timesaver*.

27. Wilson, "Disposal of Fluorescent."

28. Full Line of Residential LED Lighting Arrives (Product Review), EBN, July 2006.

29. This is a good example of the difference between efficacy and efficiency, as used in lighting. The efficacy of the LEDs (how much light they put out per watt of energy) remains the same, but the efficiency of the whole fixture (how much light comes out where it is useful) is increased by the reversed-reflector design. This design is also used in high-performance flashlights for emergency rescue personnel (Pelican Products, Torrance CA).

30. Described in an article posted at www.archlighting.com/.

Principle 9: Quietly Defend Silence

1. Eric Rosenberg and Ilene J. Busch-Vishniac, "Continued Investigation of Noise Reduction by a Random-edge Noise Barrier," paper presented at the 133rd Acoustical Society of America Meeting, State College PA, 17 June 1997.

2. Associated Press, "Population Boom Makes for a Noisy Planet," *New Mexican*, 27 Jun 1999, A-1, A-3. Ironically, the next item on the page with this article was a small ad headed, "Hearing Loss? 24-hour recorded message."

3. Information on the description and measurement of noise is compiled from the following sources: Peter Yost, "Building Green, Quietly," Jan 2001, EBN, 1; www.lsu.edu/deafness/ HearingRange.html (hearing ranges for humans and other species); http://hypertextbook.com/; and http://encarta .msn.com/. There is some variation in the range-of-hearing estimates, and varying conventions on exactly what pitch a musical instrument is tuned to.

4. Ron Chepesiuk, "Decibel Hell: The Effects of Living in a Noisy World," *Environmental Health Perspectives*, Jan 2005, www .ehponline.org/docs/2005/113-1/focus-abs.html. The author quotes Les Blomberg of Noise Pollution Clearinghouse ⟳ as noting that even ordinary cars today have far bigger speakers than those used in concerts by the Beatles!

5. www.lsu.edu/deafness/HearingRange.html.

6. A "panel" refers here to a noise barrier of a specific material and a specific thickness. In some cases, the shape or design of the panel also influences NRC and STC ratings, for example, if the surface is rough or if there are openings through the panel.

7. Sleeper Ramsey and John Ray Hoke Jr., *Architectural Graphic Standards*, 9th ed. (New York: Wiley, 1994), 59, tables.

8. Charles W. Harris and Nicholas T. Dines, *Timesaver Standards for Landscape Architecture* (New York: McGraw-Hill, 1988), 660–65, tables.

9. Information on noise and health is from several articles appearing in the January 2005 issue of *Environmental Health Perspectives*, online at www.ehponline.org/. This is a peer-reviewed publication of the National Institute of Environmental Health Sciences. Chepesiuk, "Decibel Hell"; John Manuel, "Clamoring for Quiet: New Ways to Mitigate Noise," www .ehponline.org/members/2005/113-1/innovations.html;

Charles W. Schmidt, "Noise that Annoys: Regulating Unwanted Sound," www.ehponline.org/docs/2005/113-1/ spheres-abs.html.

10. The second Bush administration took the same attitude toward global warming: "If we don't study it maybe it will go away." This denial-based policy has prevented even *current* knowledge from being applied to sustainability issues, especially those that might cost industry money.

11. Some research on the subject of bioacoustics, related to endangered birds and legislation to protect them from excessive noise, has been done at the Transportation Noise Control Center, a research institute at University of California, Davis.⟳

12. For those interested in this topic, search the web for LFAS (Low-Frequency Active Sonar).

13. Paul A. Kaseloo and Katherine O. Tyson, *Synthesis of Noise Effects on Wildlife Populations* (Washington DC: Federal Highway Administration, 2004), report HEP-06-016, www.fhwa.dot .gov/ENVIRONMENT/noise/effects/intro.htm. Information on suspected effects on animals are from this review and from Yost, "Building Green, Quietly."

14. Ronald P. Larkin, "Human Noise and Wildlife," 1995, Illinois Natural History Survey, download from www.inhs.uiuc .edu/inhsreports/sr05-index.html.

15. Note that recording equipment and speakers are designed with human hearing in mind and in this sense may "filter" the original sounds. A recording might sound lifelike to humans and still be very different in the ranges perceived by animals.

16. Yost, "Building Green, Quietly." Remember that a ten-decibel reduction would indicate noise levels cut in half, and six decibels represents much more than 60 percent of that.

17. Harris and Dines, *Timesaver*, 660–3, and FHWA online information (see www.fhwa.dot.gov/, and click to the "environment/noise" section). Weight per surface area can be increased either by using denser materials, or by using a thicker wall, or both. Some older sources indicate that as little as 1.3 pounds per square foot is sufficient for sound barriers, but this appears to be inaccurate according to current publications. The FHWA indicates that a wall that blocks line of sight to the road (usually about six to eight feet tall) offers 5 dB reduction; that for each additional meter (or yard) in height, about 1.5 dB additional reduction can be achieved; and that the maximum feasible reduction is 10 dB. This strongly suggests that a twenty-foot-tall wall is the maximum useful height, because by the height criteria just noted, it will achieve 10 dB reduction.

18. Harris and Dines, *Timesaver*, 660–63.

19. Rosenberg and Buesch-Vishniac, "Continued Investigation of Noise Reduction."

20. FHWA online information (see www.fhwa.dot.gov/ and click to "environment/noise" section). The FHWA considers parallel walls to degrade each other's performance unless they are ten times as far apart as either wall's height. Noise walls are typically at least twelve feet tall, which is the equivalent of one traffic lane.

21. Some of the best research on this subject is by K. R. Fyfe of the University of Alberta, Canada. Check www.mece.ual-berta.ca/staff/fyfe/RoadNoise/BarrierModeling.html

(1997) and other articles. Most design-engineering methods still ignore atmospheric decreases when estimating noise barrier effects. The FHWA's approach acknowledges the effects, but merely recommends that measurements of noise not be made when the wind is blowing!

22. Harris and Dines, *Timesaver*, 660–66.6

23. Yost, "Building Green, Quietly."

24. S. Meiarashi, "Porous Elastic Road Surface as an Ultimate Highway Noise Measure," the 22nd World Road Congress, Oct 2003. Download from the Public Works Research Institute, www.pwri.go.jp/eindex.htm/.

25. There is, however, a rare psychological gift called synesthesia in which people see specific colors simultaneously with hearing certain sounds. Does noise torment them like an allergy?

26. Ramsey and Hoke Jr., *Architectural Graphic Standards*, 59, table.

27. This information is from an excellent introduction to active noise control, http://users.erols.com/ruckman/General.htm. It was last updated in 2001, so it is not completely current with emerging research, but readably explains the concept and its history.

28. Reported by Noise Free America on their Web site, www.noisefree.org/, this distinction was the result of a national poll.

29. This statistic is from the Web site of Industrial Acoustics Co., www.industrialacoustics.com/.

30. The Bush administration, predictably, pushed to rescind the ban.

31. Associated Press, "Park Service Officials Want to Get a Word In: 'Quiet,'" *New Mexican*, 3 Jul 1999, A-1, A-2.

32. Information from Noise Free America's home page, www.noisefree.org/.

33. John Fecht, "New York Mayor in Fight Against Noise Pollution," *City Mayors*, 10 Jun 2004.

34. Quoted in Phillip Langdon, "Noisy Highways," *Atlantic Monthly*, Aug 1997. Full text online at www.theatlantic.com/issues/97aug/langdon.htm.

Principle 10: Maintain to Sustain

1. Research by University of Wisconsin landscape architecture professor Darrel Morrison, reported in John Berger, *Restoring the Earth: How Americans Are Working to Renew Our Damaged Environment* (New York: Knopf, 1985), 124.

2. Gwendolyn Bounds, "Organic Lawn Care: It's Not for Wimps," 7 Oct 2006, *Wall Street Journal*, P5. Bounds's estimate of the total horticulture-care industry is $9 billion greater than the $26.6 billion we cited in the first edition, based on 1999 sources.

3. Owen Dell and Melanie Yanke, *Recent Writings* brochure published by Dell's County Landscape & Design, 2004, www.owendell.com/. Dell has been active in promoting a sustainability pledge among southern California landscape professionals; see http://groups.google.com/group/Fossil-Free-Landscaping.

4. Helen H. Whiffen, "Landscape Maintenance Takes Energy: Use It Wisely," *Energy Efficiency and Environmental News* (University of Florida Extension), Feb 1993. Still one of the best attempts to summarize landscape maintenance energy con-

sumption—there should be more studies like this for each bioregion.

5. Wesley Groesbeck and Jan Striefel, *The Resource Guide to Sustainable Landscapes and Gardens*, 2nd ed. (Salt Lake City UT: Environmental Resources, 1995), 39.

6. Briggs & Stratton 6.5 OHV Intek. Its design also made it impossible to change the sparkplug without interference from an air-filter cover, a throttle cable, and the engine housing. Design flaws like these afflict most manufacturers occasionally; sustainability makes quality engineering imperative. B&S (as noted in Principle 7) has actively opposed pollution and efficiency regulations for two-stroke machines.

7. USDA Animal and Plant Health Inspection Service, publication 1329, n.d. For spreading gypsy moth, and potentially for other major pests, the USDA has the authority to level significant civil penalties.

8. Information in this section is primarily from the United Soybean Board, a major bio-based product marketing and research fund (www.unitedsoybean.org/). Other agricultural crops can also be used for bio-based products. The United Soybean Web site and publications cite a large number of federal studies (DOE and USDA, primarily) for statistics quoted here. For details, see the board's Web site, and their pamphlet *The Soy Products Guide: A Listing of Soy Industrial Products*.

9. Information on the Aberdeen paint standards, and on Environmentally Preferable Purchasing programs, is from US EPA publication EPA742-R-99-005, *Painting the Town Green: Aberdeen Proving Ground's Paint Pilot Project*. See http://www.epa.gov/opptintr/epp/. The estimate of painted square footage is a rough one, based on fourteen million square feet of building floor space, and assuming an average ten-foot-wall height, painted inside and out. It is intended only to give a sense of scale to the overall savings quoted.

10. Gwendolyn Bounds, "Organic Lawn Care: It's Not For Wimps," *Wall Street Journal*, 7 Oct 2006, P5.

11. Groesbeck and Striefel, *Resource Guide*, 39

12. City of Boulder (CO) Environmental Affairs office pamphlet *Take Control with Integrated Pest Management*, Aug 2001. Pamphlet cites "Natural and Environmental Resources Report, Jan/Feb 1995" as the source of the statistics quoted—author and publisher unknown.

13. BASMAA (Bay Area Stormwater Management Agencies Association), from its executive director, Geoff Brosseau. Similar results have been found for many other regions.

14. This concept, similar to Xeriscape zoning, was developed by Phil Boise, Ag Ecology Consulting, Gaviota CA, and published as a working paper by the National Foundation for IPM Education. Boise calls his system "PHAER Zones," for Pesticide Hazard and Exposure Reduction. More details may be available by googling this phrase.

15. Diatoms are tiny algae, whose beautiful silica-based skeletons are minutely sharp. These nonpoisonous shells, in what is called diatomaceous earth, are applied as pest deterrent around plants.

16. See, for example, Janet Hartin et al., *Best Management Practices to Reduce Production of Organic Materials in Landscape Plantings*, Jun 2001, California Integrated Waste Management Board publication 443-01-022, http://www.ciwmb.ca.gov/.

17. Gessner G. Hawley, *The Condensed Chemical Dictionary*, 10th ed. (New York: Van Nostrand Reinhold, 1981), entry for Phosphate Rock, 809.
18. Janet Hartin and Ali Harivandi, *Reusing Turfgrass Clippings to Improve Turfgrass Health and Performance in Central and Northern California*, Jun 2001, California Integrated Waste Management Board, publication 443-01-021.
19. Groesbeck & Streifel, *Resource Guide*, 39.
20. Russell Beatty, "Prescribed Grazing," LAM, Mar 2005, 50.
21. James Urban, "Battery Park City's Invisible Landscape," LAM, Feb 2004.
22. The stables are reportedly to be moved, an example of the extra complexity involved in on-site or near-site sourcing of materials.
23. James Urban, "Organic Maintenance: Mainstream at Last?" LAM, Mar 2004.
24. Information on current practice with maintenance plans is from interviews with Leslie Sauer of Andropogon or summarized from Jo Kellum, "The Legacy of Design," LAM, Sep 1999, 108. Jo Kellum refers to the difficulty of maintenance coordination as being similar to herding cats.

Conclusions and Beginnings

1. Edward Tenner, *Why Things Bite Back: Technology and the Revenge of Unintended Consequences* (New York: Vintage, 1996). Tenner is former science and history editor at Princeton University Press. His lively account of technology proves you should be careful about what you wish for.
2. A. Phillips, "International Policies and Landscape Protection," in *Landscape and Sustainability*, ed. J. F. Benson and M. H. Roe (London: Spon Press, 2000). Other chapters in this book reinforce the concept that landscapes (often viewed bioregionally) are unifying constructs within which a variety of sustainable policies has the greatest chance at success.
3. Rodger Schlickeisen, "Finally, A Happy New Year for the Environment," *Defenders of Wildlife* magazine, Winter 2007, 5. Schlickeisen is the president of the Defenders of Wildlife.
4. P. H. Ray and S. R. Anderson, *The Cultural Creatives: How 50 Million People Are Changing the World* (New York: Three Rivers Press, 2000). See also James Richards, "Placemaking for the Creative Class," LAM, Feb 2007, 32.
5. Malcolm Gladwell, *The Tipping Point: How Little Things Can Make a Big Difference* (New York: Back Bay Books, 2000).
6. Lao Tzu. *Tao Te Ching*, translated by gia-fu Feng and Jane English. (New York: Vintage, 1997). "Deal with problems when they are small" is a central tenet of this Taoist classic.
7. This concept can be studied in detail through the "soft" martial arts, such as aikido; Sorvig has been teaching this discipline for many years, and applies it to ecological concepts as well.
8. James Steele, *Sustainable Architecture: Principles, Paradigms and Case Studies* (New York: McGraw-Hill, 1997), 244.
9. For a summary, see Steele, *Sustainable Architecture*, chapter 1. Construction-specific recommendations were section 4 of the original report.
10. Sonja Bisbee Wulff, "CSU Students Learn Sustainable Landscape Design at Tropical Resort," *Coloradoan*, 12 Jul 1999, A5.
11. For those deeply interested in the difficulties of defining or communicating about the nature/culture "split," see K. Sorvig, "Nature/Culture/Words/Landscapes," *Landscape Journal* 21, no. 2 (2002): 1–14. Clearer communication about these issues is ever more essential, even in the most pragmatic landscape or planning practice.

Index

Names of individuals and firms are in **boldface**; projects and place-names are *italicized*.